Afro-Atlantic Dialogues

The School of American Research thanks the Wenner-Gren
Foundation for Anthropological Research for supporting
the seminar from which this book springs.

Publication of the Advanced Seminar Series
is made possible by generous support from
The Brown Foundation, Inc., of Houston, Texas.

D1568343

**School of American Research
Advanced Seminar Series**

James F. Brooks
General Editor

Afro-Atlantic Dialogues

Contributors

Faye V. Harrison
Department of Anthropology and African American Studies Program
University of Florida

J. Lorand Matory
Departments of Anthropology and African and African American Studies
Harvard University

Richard Price
Departments of Anthropology, History, and American Studies
College of William and Mary

Sally Price
Departments of Anthropology and American Studies
College of William and Mary

Sabiyha Robin Prince
Department of Anthropology, American University

John W. Pulis
Department of Anthropology, Hofstra University

Joko Sengova
Department of Child and Family Studies, University of South Florida

Theresa A. Singleton
Department of Anthropology, Syracuse University

Arlene Torres
Department of Anthropology and Latina/Latino Studies Program
University of Illinois

Peter Wade
Social Anthropology, School of Social Sciences, University of Manchester

Kevin A. Yelvington
Department of Anthropology, University of South Florida

Afro-Atlantic Dialogues

Anthropology in the Diaspora

Edited by Kevin A. Yelvington

School of American Research Press

Santa Fe

School of American Research Press

Post Office Box 2188
Santa Fe, New Mexico 87504-2188
www.sarpress.sarweb.org

Acting Director: Catherine Cocks
Manuscript Editor: Margaret J. Goldstein
Design and Production: Cynthia Dyer
Proofreader: Kate Talbot
Indexer: Joyce Goldenstern

Library of Congress Cataloging-in-Publication Data:

Afro-Atlantic dialogues : anthropology in the diaspora / edited by Kevin A. Yelvington;
contributors, Faye V. Harrison ... [et al.].
    p. cm.— (School of American Research advanced seminar series)
   Includes bibliographical references and index.
   ISBN 1-930618-45-x (cl : alk. paper) – ISBN 1-930618-46-8 (pa : alk. paper)
   1. Ethnology—Africa. 2. Ethnology—America. 3. African diaspora. 4. Africans—Research.
5. Africans—America—History. 6. African Americans—Migrations. 7. African Americans—
Antiquities. I. Title: Afro-Atlantic dialogs. II. Yelvington, Kevin A., 1960–
III. Harrison, Faye Venetia. IV. Series.

GN645.A342 2005
305.8'00954–dc22

                  2005018107

Cover illustration: Man's shoulder cape, collected by Melville Herskovits in 1928 or by
Melville and Frances Herskovits in 1929 in the Saramaka village of Munyenyenkiiki,
Suriname. Patchwork in trade cotton with embroidery. Sammlung Herskovits 1930,
copyright © Museum für Völkerkunde Hamburg—30.51.66 (96 cm).

Contents

Plates

The color section appears after page 114

Figures

Tables

Acknowledgments

The essays presented here were first written for a School of American Research (SAR) advanced seminar titled "From Africa to the Americas: New Directions in Afro-American Anthropology," held April 11–15, 1999.

From my position as convener, I thank the seminar participants for their essays and spirited discussions and for their patience through the editorial, rewriting, and publishing process. I think we all came away with a sense of intellectual community, of a diverse group of scholars striving to answer a similar set of anthropological riddles, and with a renewed sense of purpose. The exchanges—and debates—were invigorating, and several years after the seminar, it is still clear that we all learned a lot. The participants and I made new friends and reacquainted ourselves with old friends.

For their generous support of the advanced seminar, I thank the School of American Research and the Wenner-Gren Foundation for Anthropological Research. On behalf of the participants, I would like to thank Douglas W. Schwartz, then president of SAR, for his wonderful hospitality and good humor; Sarah Wimett, Jennifer Alvarado, Linda Arguello, Genevieve Gonzales, and Kim Warner for taking care of our living needs during our wonderful week at SAR in Santa Fe; Nancy Owen Lewis, Cecile Stein, and Joan K. O'Donnell for their assistance with and support of this project; Peg Goldstein for her editing skills; and Catherine Cocks and James Brooks of SAR Press for their patience and encouragement. I especially thank Catherine Cocks and Peg Goldstein for all their efforts in shepherding the book through the various stages leading to publication.

The publication of this book has benefited from a grant from the Publications Council at the University of South Florida. I thank Michael V. Angrosino, Valerie Janesick, Janna Merrick, Muhammad M. Rahman, and the other members of the committee for their generous support. I would also like to thank the following artists for permission to use their works: Emma Amos, Jonathan Green, and Faith Ringgold. I thank, as well, Lori Collins for drawing the maps. And I am grateful to the following people, who facilitated the publication of the illustrations in this book: Christine Campbell, Irene M. Castagliola, Nancy Conine, Mary Kay Davis, Lara De Meo, Jaclyn Donovan, Maureen Feldman, Queen Quet Marquetta L. Goodwine, Chieftess of the Gullah/Geechee Nation, Annette Gordon, Leslie Green, Parker Hathcock, Jean Herskovits, Andrew Hill, Adam Hirschberg, Ronald L. Jagger, Anne L. Lyons, Becky Malinsky, Grace Matthews, Paula Mazzotta, Renee Miscione, Vincent P. Nesi, Daisy Njoku, Nicole Nowatzki, Janet C. Olson, Marvette Pérez, Rachel Quinn, Jenny Ramkalawon, Noelle Rice, Fath Davis Ruffins, Stephan Saks, Monique Singletary, Amy J. Staples, Jamie Sterns, Vyrtis Thomas, Steve Velasquez, and Anine Wagenhoffer.

And, finally, a special thanks to Bárbara C. Cruz for all her help and support.

Kevin A. Yelvington

Dedication

para mis caribeñas, Cristina y Amanda

Afro-Atlantic Dialogues

1

Introduction

Kevin A. Yelvington

One prominent trend in the history of the serious study of the African diaspora in the New World has been a *diachronic* orientation. The central focus of anthropological approaches to this subject—in one way or another, explicitly or implicitly, despite and in some ways because of national and historical variations in anthropological paradigms and practices—has revolved around the question, "What has Africa given America?"—to take the title of a 1935 article by that foremost practitioner Melville J. Herskovits. The answers to this question had to be made with reference to history—what was "inherited" from Africa, what had changed, and why?—and answering it involved not only evoking the culture concept in the search for the origins of practices and ways of being in the world that were termed "cultural," but also invoking not always unproblematic anthropological notions of time and "history."

Another trend has seen the search for the exact mix of Old World cultural origins and New World cultural inventions sidestepped by those who focus instead upon the cultural construction of identity occurring in a *dialectical* relationship with class, nation, region, and language. Here, there are degrees of emphasis between, on the one hand, the forms and mechanisms of oppression and, on the other, the development of identity under the rubric of "race," "ethnicity," or, more recently, "blackness," which oftentimes is conceived of as an agglomeration of "race" and "ethnicity." In disciplines related to anthropology, one thinks of the classic mid-twentieth-century work of Oliver C. Cox (1948) on "caste, class, and race" and John Dollard's (1937) *Caste and Class in a Southern Town.* Or of the earlier, wide-ranging work of W. E. B. Du Bois, struggling to come to terms with the "race and class" dynamic, beginning with his 1899 *The Philadelphia Negro* and his 1903 *The Souls of Black Folk* up through the mid-twentieth century with his further contributions. Or, within anthropology per se and in the mid-twentieth century still, Davis, Gardner, and Gardner's (1941) *Deep South: A Social Anthropological Study of Caste and Class,* or Hortense Powdermaker's (1939) *After Freedom.* Similarly, a dialectical approach can be identified where the dialectical relationship is transposed in and through the concept of diaspora and pitched at the level of "The Dialectic between Diasporas and Homelands," as in the title of an influential chapter by anthropologist Elliot P. Skinner (1982). Diachrony enters in this dialectical orientation, too, when social structure and identity are conceived of as occurring in "moments," according to dialectical language. An element of the dialectical approach informs the diachronic, too, in so far as oppression and the agency underlying identity are seen to constitute cultural and historical change.

The present book heralds a new approach, or series of approaches, that might be called *dialogic.* These encompass but do not efface the insights of the diachronic and dialectical research traditions. However, the approaches that might conceivably be termed dialogic represent a departure when applied to the African diaspora in the New World: These approaches entail a critical concern with the historical fashioning of anthropology's categories simultaneous with an insistence on viewing processes of multiparty interaction in the creation and transformation through history of determined material social relationships and myriad symbolic media—that is, an interrogation of the anthropological self as much as the nature of the Other, as well as an acknowledgment of the already-givenness of the anthropological encounter in terms of prior interpretations on everyone's part. Furthermore, in this approach, subjects—be they conceived of as "behavior," "culture," or

"structure," or as individuals enacting some aspect of culture or structure—are seen through the lenses of power inequities, and this vision
is combined with an intense attention to the dynamic qualities and the
processural emergence of never-finished, open-ended behavioral forms
and repertoires via contested interactions over rights and reason.

The contributors to this volume trace the substance of these
modalities, both historically and in the present. Suggestions for a dialogical anthropology emerged with the rise of postmodernist perspectives in the 1980s. Tedlock (1979, 1987; Tedlock and Mannheim 1995)
was one of the first anthropologists to utilize the work of Russian literary critic M. M. Bakhtin, who developed a distinction between analo-
gism and dialogism, between meaning as fixed and meaning as the
expression of heteroglossia, contestation, negotiation, and multiple,
diverse contexts and voices. Bakhtin himself was concerned with language and consciousness as evidenced in literary works. He maintained
that language had two fundamental aspects, an active creative capacity
and the contested and evaluative struggle over meaning, in which
knowledge of context and the social hierarchies it involves is central
for speakers and outsider analysts alike. Discourse and consciousness
are dialogic, that is, inherently interactive, responding to prior context
but constantly generating new meanings. This process occurs on a synchronic axis, in a specific historical instantiation, but also on a diachronic axis, as a response to previous utterances and the meanings
and significance they contained, but simultaneously providing the
basis for future transformations. But "dialogue" does not mean free
exchange. Rather, for Bakhtin, it involves socially determined ideological conflicts and social power struggles involving community and class
normative dictates.

As a "concept-metaphor" (see Moore 2004), dialogue has much to
recommend itself, but the challenge remains how to bring dialogue to
bear on African diaspora anthropology. In some hands, dialogue could
refer to the interplay of historical forces and more concretely, given
the subject at hand, the multilayered interaction and self-
fashioning of communities throughout the Afro-Atlantic. While not
necessarily conceived or named as such, there is a pedigree for this
approach across disciplines (e.g., Sarracino 1988; L. D. Turner 1942;
Verger [1968] 1976). More recently, the deep historical reciprocal

relationships that give the concept-metaphor substance have been extensively documented by historians and others (e.g., Blyden 2000; Curto and Lovejoy 2004; Gilroy 1993; Mann and Bay 2001; Otero 2002; cf. Lazarus 1995; Piot 2001). Scholars of African American literary theory (e.g., D. Hale 1994; Peterson 1993) and African diaspora cultural studies (e.g., Gilroy 1987; Mercer 1988) and history (e.g., Smolenski 2003) have found dialogic approaches useful, and these seem to have been picked up by contemporary anthropological theorists of the African diaspora (e.g., E. Gordon 1998; Gordon and Anderson 1999; Matory 1999a, 1999b, 1999c; Palmié 2002; Wirtz 2004; cf. Yelvington 1999, 2001a, 2003a, 2004). The dialogic approaches taken by the individual authors in this volume cannot be reduced to Bakhtin's propositions—he is hardly cited here, and my own position, for example, is one of "materializing" and "dialectizing" Bakhtin (Brandist and Tihanov 2000; Roberts 2004; cf. Yelvington 2005), which entails an understanding of the limitations of his theories for understanding social action as much as an understanding of how we might positively apply them—nor certainly can these dialogic approaches be confined to matters of text, language, and communication. I do want to invoke a dialogic principle, however, in order not to present the usual authoritative and defining "Introduction to the Edited Volume." This would be a "monologic" discourse act in Bakhtin's sense, authoritarian and pretending to be the "last word" on the subject. The contributors can certainly speak for themselves, and if you listen, you can hear them in dialogue with one another. The best thing I can do is get out of the way and historicize the project that leads to this collection.

In conceiving of this School of American Research advanced seminar, "From Africa to the Americas: New Directions in Afro-American Anthropology," I was placed in the wonderful (but, ultimately, extremely difficult) position of choosing from an excellent crop of scholars working on various aspects of the African diaspora in the Americas. I wanted established scholars, as well as emerging voices who would renew and hopefully renovate the forms of inquiry, from theory building to theory- and politics-informed rules of ethnographic engagement. Several general considerations emerged. I felt it most important to preclude neither particular avenues of inquiry nor theoretical approaches out of hand, but at the same time I sought some broad common ground among participants in order to facilitate a productive seminar. At some level, I wanted the participants to engage in a critique of mechanical and essentialized notions of culture—and even question whether we should go on using that concept—where culture is seen as a reified, thing-like entity that may be "possessed," "maintained," or "lost"; may "decay"; or is "resistant" in the face of "cultural contact." Adopting this general critical perspective would force us to reconsider the whole question of cultural origins. This approach meant donning an outlook in which culture is conceived of as a process, a historical process, where culture—again, if that is going to be a useful frame of reference (see Abu-Lughod 1991; Brightman 1995; Trouillot 2003; S. Wright 1998)—is made and remade (and occasionally transformed) under certain conditions characterized by structures of domination, power relations, and inequality.

I also hoped for a consideration of the differential insertion of communities of blacks into the global political economy and transnational cultural flows, including constructions of diaspora, but at the same time an awareness of the extreme diversity therein. In other words, I hoped for a careful consideration of the varied historical contexts in which New World Africans and their descendants have found themselves, from slavery to the present. This process would include a consideration of ideologies of "race," ethnicity, and nationalism in the construction of blackness, both from within black communities and from without. To do so, I thought, we must analyze not only the importance of these cultural constructions for the people who are the subjects of our studies but also the role of notions of "race," ethnicity, and nationalism in the shaping of the discipline of anthropology itself. This analysis also includes all aspects of cultures, from material cultures to religious and communicative practices, and how they are identified as "black" and might be seen to be appropriated by others.

Relatedly, I thought we should make a distinction between the phenomena that some anthropologists have called African cultural "survivals" and the *discourses*—anthropological, political, and popular—about such survivals, and the efficacy of "survivals," if that is what the behaviors this term denotes are, and discourses about them as ideological forces. What is more, I felt that we should be in a position to take account of the "politics of reception" of academic theories and understand when, where, and why certain perspectives would be positively or negatively evaluated by the academy and by the informed public. In this holistic view, black cultures will be conceived of as dynamic and interactive, and blacks conceived of as knowing subjects who are active agents in the construction of their own cultural worlds—within limits, of course, to be specified by historical and social science scholarship. They are not, in other words, to be conceived of as passive receptacles of "culture."

If we decided, I thought, to focus on "syncretism" and "creolization"—two dominant concept-metaphors in the history of African diaspora anthropology—we needed to be cautious, because these ideas-cum-theories arose when anthropological theory was dominated by notions of integrated social systems and/or of holistic and bounded cultural units. These positions had been severely questioned for some time by theorists of anthropology's cutting edge. Syncretism and creolization, as the hybridization or amalgamation of two or more cultural traditions or a set of what was referred to as cultural "traits," were (and are) conceived of as occurring under certain conditions of change. The product, called culture, trait, tradition, or whatever, was seen to some degree as novel and, variously, depending on the theorist, to some degree as traditional, retaining essential features that transcended the process of historical change.

I thought that we ought to be aware, too, if we wanted to continue to talk about syncretism and creolization, that creolization and cultural syncretism and synthesis are often camouflaged as such, depicted by participants and outsider analysts as "pure" or "native." Further, we should remember that creolization and syncretism occur not only between colonizer and colonized but also between ex-colonized peoples. This approach would leave room for a consideration of "anti-syncretism" too (Palmié 1995a). A final point on my wish list was the hope that, at whatever level possible, a reconsideration of West and Central African societies could be incorporated, not as simply points of origin but as active in the formation of the African diaspora in the New World.

While my own ethnographic and archival research had focused on the Caribbean and on African American communities and ethnic politics in the US South, by the time of the seminar my interests had turned with those of many others to the history of anthropology—in this case, the history of Afro-American anthropology in an attempt to understand the social history behind received anthropological "ways of seeing." I asked for papers that would implicitly or explicitly incorporate history into their frameworks, that would either explore the development of anthropological perspectives or inform ethnographies with particular historical processes—or both. As a devotee of solid ethnography, I also wanted papers representing historical contexts from an "up-close" perspective. Finally, in terms of geographic and substantive diversity, I wanted papers on North and South America, the Caribbean, and a variety of subjects, including not only sociocultural anthropology but archaeology and linguistic anthropology as well.

This wish list of scholars who would address "New Directions in Afro-American Anthropology" entailed a further prerequisite of understanding something about the past of Afro-American anthropology. The conventional framing of this history is the debate between Euro-American Boasian anthropologist Melville J. Herskovits (1895–1963) and African American Chicago School sociologist and antiracist activist E. Franklin Frazier (1894–1962). Herskovits developed a culture area, culture traits, and diffusionist approach for his 1923 library Ph.D. dissertation on the "cattle complex" in East Africa under Franz Boas at Columbia University and then moved to physical anthropology with a project on "race-crossing" among African Americans. After briefly taking up an assimilationist perspective on African Americans in the United States by arguing that they had fully acculturated to mainstream "American culture" (e.g., M. Herskovits 1925a, 1925b), starting in the late 1920s (see his early statement in M. Herskovits 1930a), he spent the rest of his career charting what he saw as "Africanisms," African cultural "survivals" in the New World in the context of acculturation (see Redfield, Linton, and Herskovits 1936) in various cultural forms such as speech, family organization, cooperative labor, and, paradigmatically, religion (e.g., M. Herskovits 1937a, 1937b; Herskovits and Herskovits 1947).

For Herskovits, these Africanisms (see Holloway 1990) endured des-pite the enslavement process, albeit in transfigured forms existing below the surface of the cultural styles that characterized New World blacks, and they could be traced to particular ethnic points of origin on the African continent (M. Herskovits 1933a, 1936a). He deployed a number of concept-metaphors—such as "retentions," "reinterpretations," "syncretisms," "cultural focus," and "cultural tenacity," resulting here in "mosaics" and there in "amalgams" of cultures (see Baron

2003)—to describe the existence of Africanisms under acculturative conditions. Even these adaptations, he argued, could be seen as originating in Africa: "On the most comprehensive level, the manner in which New World Negroes have syncretized African and European custom into a functioning culture different from either of its ancestral types points to *psychological resilience as a deep-rooted African tradition of adaptation*" (M. Herskovits 1948a:10).

A champion of cultural relativism and a positivist-scientistic approach to anthropology, Herskovits may be conveniently classified as a "culture and personality school" adherent and one who has earned praise for his courage in daring to study African Americans seriously and attack racism in the context of a palpable upsurge in white racism and nativism in the United States of the 1920s and 1930s. He sought to make a political point with the publication of *The Myth of the Negro Past* (1941), in which he aimed to combat anti-black prejudice by showing that rather than a deficit (of) culture, African Americans had a past in the ancestral cultures of Africa, extending back beyond slavery sand manifested in Africanisms, of which they could be proud. Furthermore, African culture—and therefore African Americans—could be shown to have contributed to contemporary American culture. He felt that once this fact was made known to the general public, racism would diminish. Through institution building and gatekeeping, Herskovits became an important figure in American anthropology (see Baron 1994; Bourguignon 2000; Gershenhorn 2004; Hatch 1997; W. Jackson 1986; Rossbach de Olmos 1998; Simpson 1973; cf. Dillard 1964; Mintz 1964; Szwed 1972; Whitten and Szwed 1970a).

Frazier, following his mentor, Robert Park, emphasized the traumatic effects of slavery and racism on Afro-American culture (see Figueiredo 2002; Platt 1991). Positioning himself in opposition to Herskovits, Frazier argued that this structural situation in the United States made the maintenance of Africanisms impossible. In oft-cited lines from his book *The Negro Family in the United States*, Frazier (1939:12) wrote that "as regards the Negro family, there is no reliable evidence that African culture has had any influence on its development." For Frazier, "probably never before in history has a people been so nearly completely stripped of its social heritage as the Negroes who were brought to America." They had "through force of circumstances" to "acquire a new language, adopt new habits of labor, and take over, however imperfectly, the folkways of the American environment." Therefore, "of the habits and customs as well as the hopes and fears that characterized the life of their forebears in Africa, nothing remains" (21–22). But disorganization gave way to reorganization, and there was a positive result in that African Americans had "gradually taken over the more sophisticated American culture" (479).

There are at least five caveats to this framing. One is the still largely untold history of the intellectual workers who preceded Herskovits or were his contemporaries, many of whom were African American and focused on the African diaspora but were marginalized from the anthropological canon (see L. Baker 1998; Drake 1980; Fluehr-Lobban 2000; I. Harrison and F. Harrison 1999; D. Lewis 2000; Liss 1998; Willis 1972) or were women, such as Ruth Landes (see Cole 1994, 1995, 2003; Corrêa 2000, 2003; Healey 1998; Matory 2003; Park and Park 1989; Landes 1970) or Hortense Powdermaker (Fraser 1991; Williams and Woodson 1993; cf. Adams and Gorton 2004), and were also elided from consideration as leading theorists of the anthropology of the African diaspora.

Second, this narrative is US-centered; there is an equally long if not longer tradition of Afro-American ethnology in several countries in Latin America and the Caribbean, especially in Brazil (see, e.g., Azeredo 1986; Birman 1997; Corrêa 1987a 1988, 2003; Fernandes 1958; Grimson et al. 2004; Massi (Peixoto) 1989; Motta 1978; Peirano 1991; Peixoto 2000; Peixoto, Pontes, and Schwarcz 2004; Pontes 1995; Ribeiro 2000; Rubino 1995), Cuba (e.g., Bronfman 2002a, 2002b, 2004; Civil 1999; Dianteill 1995, 2000, 2002a; Díaz 2003; Font and Quiroz 2005; Ortiz García 2001; Palmié 2002; Puig-Samper and Naranjo Orovio 1999; Rodríguez-Mangual 2004), and Haiti (e.g., Antoine 1981; Célius 2005; Fluehr-Lobban 2000; Magloire 2005; Magloire and Yelvington 2005; Price-Mars 1978; Ramsey 2002, 2005, n.d.; Shannon 1996).

Relatedly, the third caveat is that Herskovits and other North American anthropologists interacted with and were influenced by Latin American and Caribbean anthropologists (see my chapter in this volume and some of the references therein). Fourth, the differences between Herskovits and Frazier have been overdrawn. Frazier and Herskovits sparred in print, for example, in a debate over the form of the family in Bahia, Brazil, where both did fieldwork in the early 1940s

(Frazier 1942, 1943; M. Herskovits 1943; cf. M. Herskovits 1948a:4). Also, Frazier is reported to have made a speech before the Harlem Council of Social Agencies, chiding Herskovits by saying, "[I]f whites came to believe that the Negro's social behavior was rooted in African culture, they would lose whatever sense of guilt they had for keeping the Negro down. Negro crime, for example, could be explained away as an 'Africanism' rather than as due to inadequate police and court protection" (Myrdal 1944:1242, quoted in L. Baker 1998:179).

But these apparent oppositions obscured areas of convergence. Frazier accepted the Herskovitsian view of acculturation (Frazier 1957:243–246), and he cited Herskovits favorably to the effect that African survivals existed in the Caribbean and Latin America especially in religion (1939:5–6), arguing that the differing experiences of enslavement had enabled Africanisms to survive outside the United States, where as they could not in the United States (Frazier 1939:7–8, 1957:336). For his part, Herskovits never dismissed the effects of the enslavement process on Afro-Americans, writing in Frazierian language about the "stripping from the aboriginal African culture" their "larger institutions, leaving the more intimate elements in the organization of living" (Herskovits and Herskovits 1947:7).

The fifth and final caveat is that this convenient framing cannot account for the plethora of research traditions and substantive scholarship on the Afro-Americas that makes no reference to these debates, nor feels a need to. For many scholars (including contributors to this volume), these questions were (and are) not the relevant or interesting ones, and many others sought (and seek) to go beyond them (see D. Scott 2004, especially 105–112, for anthropology; for anthropology and black studies, see Cerroni-Long 1987; cf. R. Kelley 1999).

The anthropologist R. T. Smith (1992:279–280) is impatient with the implications of this framing, writing that "the day is long past when scholars could seriously assert that African slaves were stripped of their culture in the passage to the New World, and the repeated invocation of the opposition between Frazier and Herskovits on this question merely gets in the way of serious study." Yet this framing is perhaps understandable in that it comes out of mid-twentieth-century American cultural anthropology, with its emphasis on tracing cultural traits driven by a kind of "culturalism." Here I mean *culturalism* not necessarily in the sense that Appadurai (1996:15) uses the term when he defines it as "the conscious mobilization of cultural differences in the service of a larger national or transnational politics," although the kind of culturalism I mean, in which culture is viewed as a bounded whole and made to be both the explanandum and the explanans, can become the basis of this kind of mobilization. Thus, it came to be that mutually exclusive camps were formed, as complex and nuanced positions were reduced to a simple bifurcation: Herskovits/Africanisms versus Frazier/cultural stripping. And scholars often found themselves other-identified and boxed in by implication or association. There was, of course, a politics of reception. As Orlando Patterson (1971) shows, there were and are both radical and conservative manifestations of "survivalism" and "catastrophism," and the reception of each scholar's work since the 1920s has changed with historical currents.

In anthropological circles, Herskovits's thought has been and continues to be the subject of positive evaluations, as well as critical appraisals. The challenge to the Herskovitsian program now comes from those who self-consciously identify as creolization theorists and define the subject of their inquiry as creolization (Buisseret and Reinhardt 2000). The word *creole* comes from the Latin root meaning "to raise" or "give birth to" and "of local origin" (*crioulo* in Portuguese, *criollo* in Spanish) and was apparently first applied, depending on the time and place, to people born in the New World of varying social statuses and ethnic identities; since then it has been applied to any number of things, from language to food to domesticated animals. According to Fleischmann (2003:xv–xvi), the first known use of *creole* was recorded in a letter of April 2, 1567, from the Batchelor García de Castro in the vice-kingdom of Peru, referring to those of Spanish origin though born locally. The term became expanded to encompass other groupings and began to structure identity politics. An ideology of "creolism," of extolling the creole, combined with notions of *mestizaje* ("race" and culture mixing), is traceable to the early colonial period and continues to be part of nationalist imagining throughout the Americas (for recent discussions, see Bennett 2003; C. Hale 1996; L. Lewis 2003; Miller 2004; Wade 2001, 2004; Yelvington 2001b).

The notion of creolization comes to anthropology from linguistics, where it is not unproblematic (see, e.g., Jourdan 1991; cf. Drummond

1980). The most acclaimed and widely cited work on African diaspora anthropology is that of Mintz and Price (1992), influential since its first publication in 1976 (Mintz and Price 1976). They begin with the premise of ethnic and cultural heterogeneity among the enslaved Africans, but that this heterogeneity was what made inter-African cre-olization, as well as African-European creolization, vitally necessary. They deny that such encounters—and they varied fairly widely, depending on historical period, world and local economic context, local demographics, national tradition of the enslavers, and other fac-tors—can be adequately captured by a view of culture as some sort of undifferentiated whole: "Given the social setting of early New World colonies, the encounters between Africans from a score or more dif-ferent societies with each other, and with their European overlords, cannot be interpreted in terms of two (or even many different) 'bod-ies' of belief and value, each coherent, functioning, and intact. The Africans who reached the New World did not compose, at the outset, *groups*. In fact, in most cases, it might even be more accurate to view them as *crowds*, and very heterogeneous crowds at that" (Mintz and Price 1992:18). The enslaved could become communities only "by processes of cultural change": "What the slaves undeniably shared at the outset was their enslavement; all—or nearly all—else had to be *cre-ated by them*" (1992:18).

In taking up the questions posed by Herskovits, who again drew on the work of others before him, Mintz and Price (1992:9–10) argue that "it is less the *unity* of West (and Central) Africa as a broad culture area," a position associated with survivalism, than "the *levels* at which one would have to seek confirmation of this postulated unity," adding that "an African cultural heritage, widely shared by the people imported into any new colony, will have to be defined in less concrete terms, by focusing more on values, and less on sociocultural forms, and even by attempting to identify unconscious 'grammatical' principles, which may underlie and shape behavioral response." Here, "grammatical principles" refer to "basic assumptions about social relations" and "basic assumptions and expectations about the way the world functions phenomenologically." Taking the point of focus to another level, Mintz and Price (1992:10)propose that "certain common orientations to reality may tend to focus the attention of individuals from West and Central African cultures upon similar kinds of events, even though the ways for handling these events may seen quite diverse in formal terms," and if this is so, then "the comparative study of people's attitudes and expectations about sociocultural change...might reveal interesting underlying consistencies." Acknowledging that the "underlying principles will prove difficult to uncover," Mintz and Price affirm attempts to "define the perceived similarities in African (and African-American) song style, graphic art, motor habits, and so forth," reasoning that "if the perceived similarities are real, there must exist underlying principles (which will often be unconscious) that are amenable to identification, description, and confirmation." In the end, "in considering African-American cultural continuities, it may well be that the more formal elements stressed by Herskovits exerted less influence on the nascent institutions of newly enslaved and transported Africans than did their common basic assumptions about social relations or the workings of the universe" (1992:11). They take up a Herskovitsian position when they say that they "recognize that many aspects of African-American adaptiveness may themselves be in some important sense African in origin" (1992:95; cf. Apter 2002).

It is hard to underestimate the number of anthropologists and historians who work on the Afro-Americas based in and outside North America that orient themselves toward some aspect of the above-mentioned scholarly traditions (and against others). This situation is evident in historical inquiry (see R. Price's chapter in this volume), archaeology (see Singleton's chapter in this volume), ethnohistory (e.g., Bilby 2005), bioarchaeology (e.g., Blakey 2001), medical anthropology (e.g., Benoît 2000), and linguistics and linguistic anthropology in which the creolization of languages has been a prominent preoccupation (for a recent review, see Mufwene 2004 and Sengova's chapter in this volume; cf. M. Morgan 1994a, 1994b, 2002). In cultural studies, "diaspora" as a kind of identity is defined quite closely with notions of "hybridity, fluidity, creolization and syncretism" (Brubaker 2005:6). Leading cultural studies theorist Stuart Hall (1990:235) famously writes that the "diaspora experience...is defined, not by essence or purity, but by the recognition of a necessary heterogeneity and diversity; by a conception of 'identity' which lives with and through, not despite, difference; by *hybridity*" (cf. Bennett et al. 2003; Mercer 1994; Puri 2004).

It is not possible to begin citing even a fraction of this work in a meaningful way, even when restricted to anthropology, and particularly in the space marked out as "religion" or "performance" or music or dance; these have been some of the predominant spaces of investigation in African diaspora anthropology, a fact that is, itself, revealing of anthropological motivations but cannot be pursued here. Indeed, it is really not possible to offer the sometimes expected comprehensive "review of the literature" anywhere in this introduction. This literature includes recent work within anthropology and archaeology on the "genealogies of religion" (pace Asad 1993) in the diaspora, emphasizing dynamism and invention (e.g., Ayorinde 2004; Bilby and Handler 2004; D. Brown 2003; Burdick 1998; Clarke 2004; Fennell 2000; Ferretti 2002; cf. Goldschmidt and McAlister 2004; Greenfield and Droogers 2001; Handler and Bilby 2001; Hess 1991; McAlister 2002; Motta 1994, 2002; C. Price 2003; Selka 2005; Zane 1999; for overviews and typologies, see Glazier 2001; Murphy 1994; and Pollak-Eltz 1994).

Newer work includes religious idioms studied linguistically (e.g., Álvarez López 2004), how diasporic religion interacts with commercial (e.g., Hearn 2004; Long 2001; Motta 1988; Romberg 2003), intellectual (e.g., Hess 1991; Palmié 2002; Ramsey 2002, 2005; Román 2002; Sansone 2002; Seeber-Tegethoff 1998; Wirtz 2004), and state (Edmunds 2003; Henry 2003) spheres, where "Africa" becomes a contested sign in symbolic politics (Chude-Sokei 1997; Sansone 2002; Segato 1998), and that demonstrates an awareness of the constructedness of religious traditions in Africa itself (e.g., Doortmont 1990; Farias 1990; Peel 2000; cf. Barnes 1997; Murphy and Sanford 2001). This work also includes anthropological studies of dance that place dance within larger frames (Browning 1995; Daniel 1995; Gottschild 1996; cf. Browning 1998), as well as grapple with history (e.g., Gerstin 2004) and the history of the anthropology of dance (Daniel 2004).

Some anthropologists, some archaeologists, and those in allied pursuits conceptualize and define the African diaspora in and through the history of the "race" concept (Blakey 1999; Brace 2005; Gregory and Sanjek 1994; Orser 2004; Smedley 1993; cf. Brace 1995; Brodwin 2002; MacEachern 2000; Santos and Maio 2004) and in histories of interactions with other peoples in crossings of the "color line" (e.g., Bourgois 1989; Brooks 2002a, 2002b; Duany 1999; Forbes 1993). This work is usually located within nationalism, and anthropologies of myriad kinds of identity politics, such as "racial democracy" in Brazil (e.g., Goldstein 2003; McCallum 2005; Sansone 2003; Sheriff 2001; Twine 1998), gender and blackness (J. Brown 1998; Phillips 2003; Sunderland 1997), ethnogenesis (Bilby 1996; Whitten 1996; B. F. Williams 1992), or representations of slavery in museum settings (e.g., Handler and Gable 1997; A. Jackson 2003; Silpa 2003; Yelvington, Goslin, and Arriaga 2002).

Newer work on the generation of diasporic spaces (J. Brown 2000; cf. Byfield 2000; Lemelle and R. Kelley 1994) is tied to political movements, such as the identification of pan-Africanism within those spaces (Carnegie 1999), including anthropological and archaeological takes on Afrocentricity (Haslip-Viera, Ortiz de Montellano, and Barbour 1997; cf. D. Kelley 1995). Anthropologists and other scholars of the diaspora using anthropological theory are renewing their examination of the role of the state (Crichlow 2005; Guss 2000; Martínez 1995, 1999, 2003; Maurer 1997; cf. Derby 1994; Turtis 2003), and newer urban anthropology is reworking the "culture of poverty" critique (Leacock 1971; Stack 1974; Valentine 1968) in new, multiclass, neoliberal contexts (Goode and Maskovsky 2001; Gregory 1998; J. Jackson 2001; R. Kelley 1997; Prince 2004; B. Williams 1999). In terms of methodology, and to general questions having to do with the politics of how anthropology constructs its object (Keane 2003), anthropologists and others are interested in how diasporic spaces are generated in cyberspace (Ebeling 2003; Eshun 2003; Everett 2002; Nelson 2002; Petty 2004; Ronkin and Karn 1999; cf. Axel 2004) and are taking up debates on "native anthropology" (Bolles 1985; Carnegie 1996; Haniff 1985; Jacobs-Huey 2002; Rodríguez 2001; Ulysse 2002; Whitehead 1986; cf. McClaurin 2001; Trouillot 1991), not to mention debates on globalization versus area studies (Guyer 2004; Maurer 2004; Slocum and Thomas 2003) and the production of "diaspora" as an academic object of study (Anthias 1998; Axel 1996) and political pursuit, to name only a few important topics and to cite even fewer important authors.

Let me relay a personal anecdote in this regard. In 1999 I was commissioned to write an article for the *Annual Review of Anthropology* on the anthropology of Afro-Latin America and the Caribbean (Yelvington 2001a). The geographical field had been narrowed for me to exclude North America (although I did review some works on Afro-Caribbean migration to the United States), and I narrowed the focus

thematically myself to those works that explicitly spoke to questions of
defining diaspora. Furthermore, I thought it most useful to concen-
trate on more recent work. The target I was given by the editors at the
Annual Review of Anthropology was an article of 7,000 words and no more
than 150 references. For a year I reviewed books and articles in
English, Spanish, French, and Portuguese; developed an outline; and
started writing. When I was about what I thought was halfway through,
I decided to do a word check to see how I was doing. It turned out that
I had more than 8,500 words and more than 450 citations. Needless to
say, I had to cut text and references even as I continued to write and
cover what I saw as necessary ground (and I ended up exceeding the
limits on both counts anyway). The point is that, for a number of reasons, attempting to discuss rather than just document the literature *en
toto* would not necessarily be useful, even if it were possible. And a full
discussion would take much more space than allotted here and would
further divert us from the following original works, which, in any
event, see to the appropriate contextualization in the literature.

Criticisms of creolization models tend to come from neo-
Herskovitsian positions (for only some of the latest, see Chambers
2001; Eltis 2000; Falola and Childs 2004; Gomez 1998, 1999; G. Hall
1992; Heywood 2002; Lovejoy 2000, 2003; Lovejoy and Trotman 2003;
Palmer 1995; Sweet 2003; Thornton 1998a; Walker 2001; Walsh 1997;
Warner-Lewis 2003; cf. Chambers 1997, 2002; Fennell 2003; Lohse
2002; Northrup 2000), and so in a sense the creolization theorists have
come to take the place of the Frazierian catastrophistic model in the
eyes of many (although theorists such as Mintz and Price are hardly
identifiable with Chicago School sociology). These historian critics
who emphasize the relative endurance of African ethnicities outside
the continent are inspired by new work on the Atlantic slave trade. The
remarkable resource *The Trans-Atlantic Slave Trade: A Database on CD-
ROM* (Eltis et al. 1999) charts 27,233 transatlantic slave ship voyages
made between 1595 and 1866. This work augmented Curtin's (1969)
standard-setting census (see table 1.1), and historical documentation
in this vein not only revises Curtin's numbers (see Eltis 2001; cf.
Geggus 1990) but also permits a finer-grained understanding of where
enslaved Africans came from and where they arrived in the New World
(see tables 1.2 and 1.3). These critics are also given impetus and institutional support by UNESCO's international slave route project, initi-

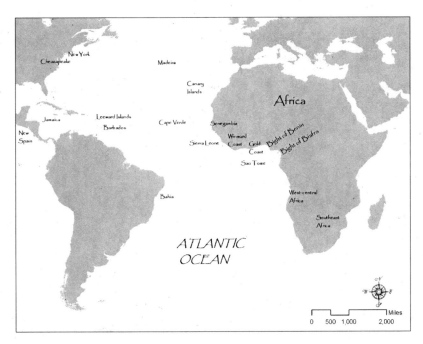

FIGURE 1.1

Some principal points in the early Atlantic African slave trade. Map by Lori Collins.

ated in 1994 (see Diène 2001; cf. Teye and Timothy 2004). They join
with anthropologists and others and tend to argue that specific African
ethnic identities and ethnic cultures remained identifiable, stable, and
salient through the enslavement process, resisting in important ways
the tendencies toward creolization. Yet, anthropologists might further
interrogate this history writing in the present "condition of postmodernity" (Harvey 1989), where multiculturalism is in intellectual
and political fashion (see C. Hale 2002; cf. Laurie and Bonnett 2002;
D. Thomas 2004), and points to a tradition in the historiography,
exemplified by the politically conscious Walter Rodney (1969), where
colonial power was emphasized in the construction of African ethnicities, and question to what extent in this model an uncritical notion of
"culture" is (ironically) made to trump "history" (Dirks, Eley, and
Ortner 1996; cf. Fabian 1983; Thomas 1989). Other anthropologists,
working in the present, focus their gaze on the politics of identity representation and how ethnic designations are produced, such as the
transformations from "Negro" to "black" to "African American" in the

TABLE 1.1

Estimated Slave Imports into the Americas, by Importing Region, 1451–1870

Importing Region	1451–1600	1601–1700	1701–1810	1811–1870	Total per region
British North America			348,000	51,000	399,000
Spanish America	75,000	292,000	578,600	606,000	1,552,100
British Caribbean	-	263,700	1,401,300	-	1,665,000
Jamaica	-	85,100	662,400	-	747,500
Barbados	-	134,500	252,500	-	387,000
Leeward Is.	-	44,100	301,900	-	346,000
St. Vincent, St. Lucia, Tobago, Dominica	-	-	70,100	-	70,100
Trinidad	-	-	22,400	-	22,400
Grenada	-	-	67,000	-	67,000
Other BWI	-	-	25,000	-	25,000
French Caribbean	-	155,800	1,348,400	96,000	1,600,200
St. Domingue	-	74,600	789,700	-	864,300
Martinique	-	66,500	258,300	41,000	365,800
Guadeloupe	-	12,700	237,100	41,000	290,800
Louisiana	-	-	28,300	-	28,300
French Guiana	-	2,000	35,000	14,000	51,000
Dutch Caribbean	-	40,000	460,000	-	500,000
Danish Caribbean	-	4,000	24,000	-	28,000
Brazil	50,000	560,000	1,891,400	1,145,400	3,646,800
Old World	149,900	25,100	-	-	175,000
Europe	48,000	1,200	-	-	50,000
São Tomé	76,100	23,900	-	-	100,000
Atlantic Is.	25,000	-	-	-	25,000
Total	274,900	1,341,100	6,051,700	1,898,400	9,566,100
Annual Average	1,800	13,400	55,000	31,600	22,800

Source: Curtin (1969:268, Table 77). Reprinted by permission of The University of Wisconsin Press.

TABLE 1.2

Estimates of Regional Distribution of Slave Exports to America from Africa, 1662–1867

Decade	Senegambia	Sierra Leone	Gold Coast	Bight of Benin	Bight of Biafra	West Central Africa	Southeast Africa	Total	Annual Exports
1662–1670	3,232		12,174	23,021	34,471	9,695	91	82,684	9,187
1671–1680	5,842		20,597	22,753	24,021	15,794	309	89,316	8,932
1681–1690	10,834		15,333	71,733	21,625	32,760	5,392	157,677	15,768
1691–1700	13,376		17,407	103,313	12,115	30,072	190	176,473	17,647
1700–1709	22,230		31,650	138,590	23,130	109,780	0	359,940	35,994
1710–1719	36,260	34,560	37,540	138,690	51,410	132,590	0	402,870	40,287
1720–1729	52,530	6,380	65,110	150,280	59,990	179,620	0	516,650	51,665
1730–1739	57,210	9,120	74,460	135,220	62,260	240,890	0	599,510	59,951
1740–1749	35,000	29,470	83,620	97,830	76,790	214,470	0	551,060	55,106
1750–1759	30,100	43,350	52,780	86,620	106,100	222,430	0	581,890	58,189
1760–1769	27,590	83,860	69,650	98,390	142,640	266,570	0	783,200	78,320
1770–1779	24,400	178,360	54,370	111,550	160,400	234,880	0	717,820	71,782
1780–1789	15,240	132,220	57,650	121,080	225,360	300,340	0	793,860	79,386
1790–1799	18,320	74,190	73,960	74,600	181,740	340,110	0	759,240	75,924
1800–1809	18,000	70,510	44,150	75,750	123,000	280,900	0	605,770	60,577
1811–1815	19,300	63,970		34,600	33,100	111,800	8,700	203,000	40,600
1816–1820	48,400	4,200		59,200	60,600	151,100	59,600	328,300	65,660
1821–1825	22,700	9,000		44,200	60,600	128,400	43,200	259,900	51,980
1826–1830	26,700	4,000		70,500	66,700	164,400	58,100	333,200	66,640
1831–1835	27,400	4,900		37,700	71,900	102,800	3,000	240,900	48,180
1836–1840	35,300	1,100		50,400	40,800	193,500	99,400	325,700	65,140
1841–1845	19,100	5,700		45,300	4,400	112,900	20,300	181,900	36,380
1846–1850	14,700	200		53,400	7,700	197,000	66,700	273,500	54,700
1851–1855	10,300	700		8,900	2,900	22,600	12,800	45,000	9,000
1856–1860	3,100	300		14,000	4,400	88,200	11,300	110,000	22,000
1861–1865	2,700	300		2,600	0	41,200	2,700	46,500	9,300
1866–1867	0	0		400	0	3,000	0	3,400	1,700
Total	599,864	756,390	710,451	1,870,620	1,658,152	3,927,801	391,782	9,529,260	46,035

Source: Klein (1999:208–9). Reprinted with the permission of Cambridge University Press.

TABLE 1.3

Percentage Distribution of the African Regional Origins of Slaves Arriving in Major British Colonies, 1658–1713

	Chesapeake	Barbados	Jamaica	Antigua	Montserrat	Nevis
Senegambia	34.2	5.3	5.4	2.5	21.8	8.9
Sierra. Leone	0	0.8	0.5	3.0	0	5.0
Windward Coast	0	0.2	0.4	0	0	2.9
Gold Coast	16.5	39.6	36.0	44.8	37.8	32.1
Bight of Benin	4.0	25.7	26.0	13.9	8.1	12.0
Bight of Biafra	44.0	13.4	11.5	32.3	12.6	24.7
West Central Africa	1.2	10.2	20.1	3.6	0	13.1
Southeast Africa	0	4.8	0.2	0	19.7	1.4
Number of Slaves	7,795	85,995	72,998	8,926	2,037	14,040

Source: Eltis (2000:245). Reprinted with the permission of Cambridge University Press.

United States (e.g., Houk 1993; cf. Philogene 1994; T. W. Smith 1992).

Some sympathetic critics of the creolization positions point out the still existing danger of biogenetic analogies tied to creolization, such as "hybridity" (Brah and Coombes 2000; Hutnyk 2005; Maurer 1997; Palmié n.d.; cf. Werbner and Modood 1997), while others (Khan 2001, 2004a, 2004b; M. Trouillot 1998) correctly insist on seeing creolization as the product of power relations. But the idea is flexible enough to accommodate scholars tracing the origins of cultural, as well as linguistic, creolization back to the coast of Africa (McWhorter 1997, 2000b; Thornton 1998a), while others temporalize creolization stages (Abrahams 2003; Berlin 1996; Burton 1997; Duany 1985; Olwig 1985, 1993) or spatialize creolization processes (Berlin 1980). Some see creolization as an apt concept-metaphor for other regions (Hannerz 1992; cf. Khan 2001), while scholars such as Mintz (1996, 1998) argue that concepts such as creolization are found to be useful to scholars of globalization but the Caribbean modernity it referred to was historically unique. Further, the emphasis is on the struggle to build culture despite contexts not conducive to the success of such projects: "What typified creolization was not the fragmentation of culture and the destruction of the very concept, but the creation and construction of culture out of fragmented, violent and disjunct pasts" (Mintz 1996:302).

With the terms of the weight of the historical debate in the present outlined, the task came to identify seminar participants. Because I would be writing about an aspect of the history of Afro-American anthropology from the point of view of a practicing, ethnographic anthropologist, as opposed to a specialist historian of anthropology (see Yelvington 2003b), but nevertheless at somewhat of a distance, I also wanted theorists-ethnographers who were close to the ethnographic material, as well as the history and politics of theory. Therefore, I invited Richard Price to reconsider the career of the Mintz and Price (1992) creolization model while writing on the subject of creolization itself, and Sally Price to explore the various interpretations of Afro-American visual arts and the anthropological interpretations made of them. The chapters by Richard Price and Sally Price derive from their thirty-plus years of ethnographic engagement with the Saramaka Maroons of the Suriname and French Guiana rain forests and towns (e.g., R. Price 1975a, 1983a, 1990; R. Price and S. Price 2001; S. Price 1984; S. Price and R. Price 1980, 1999), arise out of one of their latest books on the place of art in Maroon life, and use artistic creations to show what they conceive of as more general, deep-level creative processes (S. Price and R. Price 1999).

Dialogical interaction could be conceived of and shown in different ways—of this I was aware. But instead of esoteric reflections or attempts to apply, say, Bakhtinian theory to a particular ethnographic situation, I wanted papers that would illustrate dialogue in action. With this in mind, I invited J. Lorand Matory, who had done fieldwork in both Nigeria and Brazil and had invoked the dialogue metaphor in various recent publications (1999a, 1999b, 1999c), to consider "dialogue" in contrast to other metaphors. I also asked John W. Pulis, whose work on Afro-Caribbean religion and diaspora (1999a, 1999b, 1999c, n.d.) is complemented by his archival research on Afro-American loyalists who dispersed to the Atlantic world with the withdrawal of the British from North America (1999a, 1999c), to use his archival research to show one episode of dialogue: the enduring legacy of African American religious leaders in Jamaica in the late eighteenth century. The linguist Joko Sengova is a scholar whose range of interests was relevant to the theme of the seminar. He had written on national language policy in post-colonial Africa with respect to Sierra Leone (1987), as well as a reevaluation of pioneering African American linguist Lorenzo Dow Turner's research on the Gullah/Geechee language from the perspective of a native Mende speaker (1994). I asked him to reflect on the history of his involvement with the Gullah/Geechee-Sierra Leone connection. I invited Theresa A. Singleton, an archaeologist of plantation America, to discuss how archaeology might dialogue with sociocultural anthropology and history, and vice versa, and also to show how an awareness of this archaeology's place and history might affect the work of getting on with archaeological research.

Because the anthropology of the African diaspora has always been historical in orientation, and given Herskovits's concern to use history for the purposes of social betterment, preceded as it was by the praxis of luminaries such as W. E. B. Du Bois and Carter G. Woodson, I invited Sabiyha Robin Prince, who had conducted cross-class fieldwork in Harlem (2004), to present her work on public anthropology and history's potential role in presenting histories of Africans and their descendants in Manhattan. Thinking of contrasting constructions of blackness, I invited Arlene Torres to present her new work on museum representations of Afro–Puerto Ricans in the venerable Smithsonian Institution. She had researched depictions of blackness in Puerto Rico itself (1995, 1998a) and how these depictions arose in and through nationalist projects. Here was a chance to see what happens when these nationalist projects become part of traveling culture (Clifford 1997; cf. Hansing 2001). If blackness is a floating signifier, it is not constructed out of thin air. Manifestations of blackness in performance had been a prominent theme in the literature, but I often found that works devoted to them dislocated "culture" from the rough-and-tumble of ethnic politics. Peter Wade was invited to share from his work on how black music and representations of Africa in Colombia (e.g., 2000) are neither politics-free nor bereft of ideological import.

To assess what our efforts would mean, I invited Faye V. Harrison to be a discussant. Here was a scholar whose work had straddled all our concerns. An ethnographer of the Caribbean, she was the editor of a special issue of *Urban Anthropology* titled "Black Folks Here and There: Changing Patterns of Domination and Response," in which she set out a programmatic statement (1988). Her edited book *Decolonizing Anthropology* (1991) called for an "anthropology of liberation"—liberating anthropology from racism, sexism, and classism and using anthropology itself to address these social ills. She had written on "race" as an ideological construct and material relationship (1995), guest-edited a contemporary issues forum on "Race and Racism" in *American Anthropologist* (1998), and was about to be involved in issues of "race" and human rights with the UN's World Conference against Racism, Racial Discrimination, Xenophobia, and Related Intolerance in South Africa in 2001 (2000). At the same time, she was deeply aware of the history of Afro-American anthropology, having researched the role of W. E. B. Du Bois's anthropology (1992) and coedited *African-American Pioneers in Anthropology* (I. Harrison and F. Harrison 1999). Her role was to place the participants' efforts in the context of that history.

As a whole, then, the book unites in dialogue somewhat diverse traditions in scholarship and, not to be forgotten, the perspectives of diverse scholars. To the extent that there is a "there" there, I can imagine that there will be no easy agreement as to the status of what or where "it" is. I hope that the reader will see the unity in the diversity, however. To the end of placing the arguments herein, the book is divided into four sections: Part I: Critical Histories of Afro-Americanist Anthropologies; Part II: Dialogues in Practice; Part III: The Place of Blackness; and Part IV: Critical Histories/Critical Theories. My own chapter begins Part I by questioning the formation of Afro-American anthropology by delving into the sources of Herskovits's thought. I trace his connections to ethnographers/ethnologists based in Latin America and the Caribbean, such as Jean Price-Mars in Haiti, Fernando Ortiz in Cuba, and Arthur Ramos in Brazil. I suggest that their own work was reflective of differing modes of modernity as they— similarly, but with differing effect and purpose—sought to document the black presence as part of nationalist projects. They were, in turn, responding to and involved in local developments to promote blackness. I also show how these relationships went into what I call an "intellectual social formation" of diverse and dispersed scholars, who nevertheless were able to define anthropological paradigms.

In chapter 3, Sally Price begins by tracing contextual changes in the reception and valuation of art across the world and how aesthetic evaluation—once operating in predictable fashion, assigning variable high and low, art and craft, modern and primitive status to various works—is becoming transformed as critics and evaluators begin engaging in reflexive strategies and revaluations of their own. In the midst of collapsing borders, arts of the African diaspora are traveling as they never have before. And with their proliferation comes increasing theoretical attention to particular media, including quilts and stitched cloth textiles. These readings have a politics, Price shows us, and she does not call for endless interpretation and esoterica but admonishes these theorists—and us—to do archival homework in the first instance.

Richard Price is the coauthor with Sidney Mintz of an acclaimed book (Mintz and Price 1992, first published in 1976) that represents a major rethinking of the Herskovitsian African cultural retentions and survivals paradigm. As outlined above, their emphasis is on culture building and cultural creation. Yet, they suggest that enslaved Africans shared basic cultural "grammatical principles" beneath the surface of behavioral response, and it is at this level that similarities through the African diaspora in the New World may exist. In chapter 4, Price reflects not only on the model but also on the politics of the model's reception in anthropology and in other disciplines, such as history and linguistics.

Part II begins with J. Lorand Matory's chapter, which elaborates a notion of dialogue as a multiplex set of relationships through time, discursive styles, ideologies, and religious traditions that are mutually constitutive between peoples of African descent on both sides of the Atlantic. He surveys what he calls the "analytic metaphors" employed in the anthropology of the African diaspora and shows how many of them, or parts of many of them, can be seriously misleading in how they regulate our anthropological vision. "Africa" is not merely a symbol, nor a point of origin that fades in importance once we awake from the nightmare of the Middle Passage, but it is active in creating its own diaspora, and the diaspora is active in creating Africa.

John W. Pulis is also concerned with intra-diaspora movement and especially how such movement affects local religious idioms. In chapter 6, he employs archival research with anthropological interpretive skill to illuminate the careers of African American preachers who went to Jamaica when, as loyalists, they evacuated the North American colonies with the British in the era of the American Revolution. Some of these preachers, such as Moses Baker and George Liele, are well-known to African diaspora scholars, and Pulis shows something of how their religious life and influence on Afro-Christianity in Jamaica were intertwined with local politics and economics.

What happens when the researcher is part of the subject he or she studies? Or better, can we go on pretending that all of us are not part of what we study? In chapter 7, Joko Sengova reflects in an experimental way on multiple levels of understanding derived from his experience doing fieldwork in the Sea Islands of South Carolina and Georgia—predefined as "black" and "African" spaces. He provides us with an account of his involvement with a research team from Sierra Leone that set out to investigate linguistic and human connections from the period of the slave trade between that African country and the Sea Islands. He narrates attempts to make communion from both sides in a fascinating example of dialogue in action.

In chapter 8, Theresa A. Singleton shows how the sociocultural anthropology and archaeology of the African diaspora, at least in the United States, developed with similar concerns and methodological preoccupations (and limitations). Her mode of dialogue is layered and multi-directional. She demands that US four-field anthropology live up to its billing as encompassing all subfields. In a slice of her latest fieldwork in Cuba, she demonstrates ways in which questions become posed—or how they remain unthinkable—in particular disciplinary regimes and how the archaeology of the African diaspora in the Americas is uniquely positioned to provide the answers for historians, anthropologists, and others.

Sabiyha Robin Prince begins Part III with a long discussion (chapter 9) of some aspects of the history of blacks in colonial Manhattan, from the time of the Dutch settlement in the early seventeenth century until emancipation in 1827. She relies on the burgeoning secondary sources for the still little-known history of slavery in New York to tell the stories of largely anonymous enslaved toilers and their contributions. This discussion is framed anthropologically in two ways. On one side, Prince ploughs through the history to offer up evidence of cultural practices of significance to anthropologists: religious ritual, the vicissitudes of everyday life, and resistance to power, among others. On the other, she suggests a role for public anthropology and history in presenting these stories—and takes the African Burial Ground as an exemplary case—in present-day identity politics.

Arlene Torres follows (chapter 10) with a consideration of the ways in which identity, culture, and citizenship are presented in official institutions such as museums. Once identity and culture are "fixed" with their exhibition, what becomes of the dialogue that is known to constitute and reconstitute such phenomena? she asks. Her substantive focus is on an exhibit titled "A Collector's Vision of Puerto Rico" at the National Museum of American History at the Smithsonian Institution. From her position as a participant observer, paid consultant, and Puerto Rican anthropologist, she goes about documenting the myriad ways "race," class, and ideology and signification styles are enacted in this space.

In chapter 11, Peter Wade's substantive focus is on the representations of blackness, and more recently Africanness, in Colombian popular music. He shows how "Africa" as a sign is now utilized in Colombia, in multiple and often contradictory ways by the state, anthropologists, black activists, and non-blacks. This is a historical development. Images of Africa were not used the same way in the past; indeed, blacks were in many ways rendered "invisible" in nationalist discourse and practice. But at the same time, their difference and distance from whiteness under the "whitening" ethos conjoined with *mestizaje* meant that their existence and visibility were always assured. Wade traces these changes through the effects of the globalization of images and commodities in international commerce, as well as through national legislation. Bringing us in some ways full circle, Wade argues that anthropologists cannot easily separate out so-called Africanisms as such from the way people perceive and talk about blackness and Africa, and he calls into question an arbitrary anthropological focus on *either* what people say *or* what they do.

Part IV consists of Faye V. Harrison's commentary (chapter 12). In her remarks, she employs a mode of "rehistoricization" that involves reclaiming the discipline's exposed and unexposed past and highlighting the struggles over the politics of knowledge. She places the contributors' efforts in a conceptual framework that underscores the development of concept-metaphors and how these are responsive to politics at many levels; the ways in which the anthropology of the African diaspora can engage intra- and interdisciplinarily, asking what concrete historical moments call for methodological innovation and the stretching of disciplinary boundaries; a concern for structured inequalities that must be integral to anthropological consideration and awareness and cannot be simply bracketed off; and, finally, the nature of the presentation of self—both from the perspective of the anthropologist and from the people who teach us much of what we know, our consultants and, in some cases, collaborators, who have conventionally been designated as "subjects" or anthropological "informants."

At around the same time as the appearance of the massive *Africana* encyclopedia (Appiah and Gates 1999) and specialist overviews of African Americans in North America (R. Kelley and Lewis 2000) and Latin America (Andrews 2004; cf. Martínez Montiel 1995a, 1995b, 1995c; from earlier, see Pollak-Eltz 1972 and T. Price 1954), it seems that there are endless edited books on the Afro-Americas (see Manning 2003 for a long review of two). A number include chapters on North America, South America, and the Caribbean, all in the same volume. Some recent ones are Jalloh and Maizlish's *The African Diaspora* (1996), Okpewho, Davies, and Mazrui's *The African Diaspora: African Origins and New World Identities* (1999), and Hine and McLeod's *Crossing Boundaries: Comparative History of Black People in Diaspora* (1999). There is a special issue of the journal *African Studies Review* (vol. 43, no. 1, 2000) titled "Africa's Diaspora," a special issue of *Mamatu: Journal for African Culture and Society* (nos. 27–28, 2003) titled "A Pepper-Pot of Cultures: Aspects of Creolization in the Caribbean," and a special issue of *Historical Archaeology* (vol. 38, no. 1, 2004) titled "African Diaspora Archaeologies: Present Insights and Expanding Discourses," among many others. Anthropologists are prominent as contributors, and the landmark *Afro-American Anthropology: Contemporary Perspectives* (Whitten and Szwed 1970b) was for many years (and still is) the standard against which others in this genre are judged.

More recently, there are also fine examples whose titles indicate that they are unified around particular themes, such as Rahier's *Representations of Blackness and the Performance of Identities* (1999), which links performativity with identity; Palmié's *Slave Cultures and the Cultures of Slavery* (1995b), which uses ethnohistory to investigate the past of the

KEVIN A. YELVINGTON

creolization dynamic; and Whitten and Torres's two-volume set, *Blackness in Latin America and the Caribbean: Social Dynamics and Cultural Transformations* (Torres and Whitten 1998; Whitten and Torres 1998), which, in presenting mostly well-known republished articles, is comprehensive in its coverage of Latin America and the Caribbean, regionally and topically (on the region, cf. García 2002; Weik 2004; Whitten 1976).

Afro-Atlantic Dialogues does not necessarily cohere along topical lines but instead represents the diversity of the contemporary anthropology of the African diaspora in the Americas. The perspectival unity despite topical and regional diversity comes from a shared awareness of the profound historicity of situated knowledges, as well as a common orientation in these chapters toward movement, interaction, contestation, emergence, and innovation, in both large and small frames. This approach means that the book is of broad importance to anthropology in general for at least three reasons. First, many of the staple theoretical concepts in cultural anthropology in the past, such as acculturation, assimilation, and syncretism, in part emerged from the concerns of Afro-Americanists, even though this was often not acknowledged. In this regard, many contributors synthesize a vast amount of anthropological literature and offer an evaluation of the history of anthropological theory. Second, some of the new perspectives found herein address central issues in contemporary anthropological theory. Besides the interest in the history of anthropology, examples include the globalization of cultures, creolization, hybridity, transnationalism, colonialism, postcolonialism, and political economy, as well as the argument that anthropologists, no less than the people we learn from, are political "positioned subjects." The contributors to this volume critically address and assess these concerns, providing a valuable evaluative function for contemporary theory.

Finally, this book is important to anthropology because the discipline needs to lend its expertise to ongoing societal issues and social movements related to the topics of the seminar, including the politics of the "culture wars" in the United States, Brazil, the Caribbean, and elsewhere, such as multiculturalism and the movement for "racial" and cultural rights, for example, as these movements affect the populations of African descent across the Americas (see table 1.4). Oftentimes, these debates turn on anthropological theory, even if parties to the

TABLE 1.4
Populations of African Descent in the Americas, c. 1990

Country	Population (thousands)		Percent of Total	
	Minimum	Maximum	Minimum	Maximum
Brazil	9,477	53,097	5.9	33.0
United States	29,986	29,986	12.1	12.1
Colombia	4,886	7,329	14.0	21.0
Haiti	6,500	6,900	94.0	100.0
Cuba	3,559	6,510	33.9	62.0
Dominican Republic	847	6,468	11.0	84.0
Jamaica	1,976	2,376	76.0	91.4
Peru	1,356	2,192	6.0	9.7
Venezuela	1,935	2,150	9.0	10.0
Panama	35	1,837	14.0	73.5
Ecuador	573	1,147	5.0	10.0
Nicaragua	387	559	9.0	13.0
Trinidad and Tobago	480	516	40.0	43.0
Mexico	474	474	0.5	0.5
Guyana	222	321	29.4	42.6
Guadeloupe	292	292	87.0	87.0
Honduras	112	280	0	5.0
Canada	260	260	1.0	1.0
Barbados	205	245	80.0	95.8
Bahamas	194	223	72.0	85.0
Bolivia	158	158	2.0	2.0
Paraguay	156	156	3.5	3.5
Suriname	146	151	39.8	41.0
St. Lucia	121	121	90.3	90.3
Belize	92	112	46.9	57.0
St. Vincent and the Grenadines	94	105	84.5	95.0
Antigua and Barbuda	85	85	97.9	97.9
Grenada	72	81	75.0	84.0
Costa Rica	66	66	2.0	2.0
French Guiana	37	58	42.4	66.0
Bermuda	38	39	61.0	61.3
Uruguay	38	38	1.2	1.2
Guatemala	*	*	*	*
Chile	*	*	*	*
El Salvador	**	**	**	**
Argentina	0	**	0	**
Total	64,859	124,332	9.0	17.2

* presence of people of African descent acknowledged but no official figures given
** no figures available

Source: Monge Oviedo (1992:19).

debate are unaware of the origins of these ideas. These debates will
continue without anthropologists, and it is our responsibility to engage
in them.

Notes

I would like to thank Catherine Cocks, Sidney W. Mintz, and the two anonymous reviewers for SAR Press for their helpful comments on this introduction.

1. Some criticisms of Herskovits are that he was unable to wholly escape the
"racial" thought he ostensibly combated and that he uncritically accepted colonial
historiography and ignored the ways "Africa" was constructed in the diaspora.
More generally, to these criticisms could be added a view of culture as a reified,
bounded, thing-like entity, a static conception of acculturation and culture
change, a related inadequate reading of African ethnic group traditions as fixed
and enduring rather than fluid and porous, a lack of serious interest and attention to politics and power differentials affecting change on both sides of the
Atlantic, and, like Boas before him, suffering from an incomplete critique of evolutionism. Cultural "survivals," it must be recalled, constituted a central element
in the evolutionism of E. B. Tylor. I refer to some criticisms of Herskovits in
chapter 2.

2. Creolization models can fall into the same trap as static culturalism by
wielding a "strong" culture concept, in which culture trumps time. The concept
could also be teleological, as when a particular period is studied and then projected into the present, where continued creolization is assumed to be inevitable.
Also, the converse problem: when the present is projected into the past and contemporary forms are labeled "creole" by virtue of political processes and might
lead to new trait analysis, conceptualizing a "creolism" on a par with an
"Africanism."

Part I. Critical Histories
of Afro-Americanist Anthropologies

2

The Invention of Africa in Latin America and the Caribbean

Political Discourse and Anthropological Praxis, 1920–1940

Kevin A. Yelvington

Historicism contents itself with establishing a causal connection between various moments in history. But no fact that is a cause is for that very reason historical. It became historical posthumously, as it were, through events that may be separated from it by thousands of years. A historian who takes this as his point of departure stops telling the sequence of events like the beads of a rosary. Instead, he grasps the constellation which his own era has formed with a definite earlier one.

—*Walter Benjamin*, "Theses on the Philosophy of History"

In his book *The Invention of Africa* (1988), V. Y. Mudimbe dissects the ways in which the concept of "Africa" was invented and used in the European colonial project—perhaps by now mundane to those initiated into this expanding literature on imperial policy, public opinion, scholarship, and beyond (e.g., Apter 1999; Coombes 1994; Curtin 1964, 1972, 2000; Falola and Jennings 2002; Vail 1989, among many others), but frightful nonetheless. He also shows how the *discourse* of "Africa" pervades and invades even African liberation projects, the result being that "Western interpreters as well as African analysts have been using categories and conceptual systems which depend on a Western epistemological order" (Mudimbe 1988:x). Certainly, colonial and Western discourse on Africa is the most visible and tangible, but it is not the only discourse on Africa. In certain places in Latin America and the Caribbean, Africa has been invented, not only on the part of colonial authority—with its attendant religious, educational, and military components—but also on the part of colonialism's subjects (understood in the multiple senses of this word) that is, from "below," among peoples of African descent. The image of Africa and things African as "primitive" and in need of European tutelage was, of course, one way in which Europe defined itself and rationalized colonial plunder and subjugation. In resistance to hegemonic colonial authority and culture, many Latin American and Caribbean people of African descent avowedly sought, and seek, to "Africanize" religious practices and personal identity, investing "Africa" with positive connotations. A tension has existed and still exists among these multiple and multivalent discourses, complicated by the fact that images of Africa can be constructed and invented only within cultural spaces inhabited by power.

Mudimbe identifies three levels of discourse: a "sort of zero degree discourse," a "primary, popular interpretation of founding events of the culture and its historical becoming"; a second-level discourse actualized as intellectual disciplines, "as disciplinary knowledge transcending the first-level discourse and, by their critical power, domesticating the domain of popular knowledge and inscribing it in a rational field"; and a third-level discourse, one that "should be critical of the other discourses (interrogating their modalities, significance, and objectives) and, at the same time, by vocation, one which should be autocritical." It is at this third level where a "meta-discourse" could "bring about a history of histories of a given culture": "From this perspective, it is obvious that to approach the questions 'What is Africa?' or 'How do we define African cultures?' one cannot neglect a body of knowledge in which Africa has been subsumed by Western disciplines such as anthropology, history, theology, or whatever other scientific discourse" (Mudimbe 1994:xiii, xiv; cf. Apter 1999). Seen in this light, the discourse of "Africa" in the New World becomes more than an index to the way the place of "Africa" within the nation is imagined in Latin America and the Caribbean (e.g., Agier 2000; Chude-Sokei 1997; Davies and Fardon 1991; Motta 1994; Palmié 2002; Sansone 1997,

2002, 2003; Segato 1998; Wade, this volume). "Africa" indeed becomes a "multivocal" symbol (V. Turner 1969, 1974), but not in a hermetic system autonomous from other structural and cultural forces. Rather, "Africa" obtains the status of a leitmotif, an organizing principle embedded in social and cultural relations in general. Under certain circumstances, it forms the subject of ideological interpolation, with ideology understood as discursive representations of political positionings, located within discourse and discursive fields; a practical, elaborated political doctrine. So to stretch Mudimbe, we have to see how these levels of discourse are interrelated and mutually constitutive. We have to understand how each kind of discourse presupposes the other(s) and, moreover, how they are all structured in and constituted by political practice.

While Mudimbe can provide us with hints on how to analyze this problematic, there are two qualifications to this beginning—one being a qualification on the use of the rhetoric of "invention" and the other a critical look at Mudimbe's Foucaultian approach to discourse (Diawara 1990). On the first, a recuperation of the idea of cultural invention is in order. Critics of the "Invention of Tradition" literature (Hobsbawm and Ranger 1983; cf. Babadzan 2000; Handler and Linnekin 1984) have sought to equate the use of "invention" with a perspective that disparages local knowledges and subordinate identities as somehow "inauthentic" (e.g., Briggs 1996; cf. J. Jackson 1989; Phillips and Schochet 2004). Desai's engaging article "The Invention of Invention" (1993) raises the question about the status of "invention" itself as a concept. However, my use of the term here is meant to signal agency and intentionality, consciousness and ideology, implying a perspective on the historical and political "work" of culture, including the cultures of scholarship and the agency of intellectual workers and their placement within not only their own societies but also international scientific circuits and networks.

The second qualification is this: the notion of discourse is so often tied up with the idea of *authoritative* discourse, a set of higher-order linguistic practices that emphasizes "rationality" and "legitimacy," simultaneously claiming for itself the rational and legitimate high ground, obscuring in the process the social basis of its claims to knowledge and what it claims as a subject for/of its academic and political knowledge.

This positioning is achieved by discourses operating in the "elaborated-formal" mode (Grillo 1989; cf. Spivak 1988), acquiring an authority in the practices of science, technology, and the political and industrial orders, providing a language for "ideas." But here a break with Foucault is in order. As one critic finds, in Foucault's work "[t]here is no general theory of causality. He emphasizes the political, which would seem to abstract agency from geography and history" (Fiehrer 1997:441; cf. Sangren 1995). In his deficient "historical" method, Foucault could not properly account for the causation of the positionality of discourse. The result was a view of discourse as rather disembodied from the social groups that originate a particular discourse and those whose ends are served by it. A revised concept of discourse would locate ideology—with its political and economic concomitants—within discursive fields, themselves multivalent and diverse, and show how the wielding of a particular discourse is tied to the production of and resistance to hegemony.

A study of the anthropological discourse on Africa in the New World must be centered, though not exclusively, on the work of the North American anthropologist Melville Jean Herskovits (1895–1963). Herskovits, who did ethnographic fieldwork in Suriname in 1928 and 1929, Dahomey in 1931, Haiti in 1934, Trinidad in 1939, and Brazil in 1941–1942, was a key actor because his theoretical positioning came to occupy a central place in the anthropological investigations of the African diaspora in the Americas, as I point out in the introduction to this volume. In this chapter, I want to trace some aspects of Herskovits's *social* positioning within scientific social networks and to suggest how this positioning was related to his theoretical positioning. Here I mean not only Herskovits's social relationships with other scientists but also some aspects of the social conditions out of which those networks arose.

A critical analysis of Herskovits's work is in order as part of a reflexive inquiry within the discipline of anthropology, but also into the discursive fields where anthropology has been diffused. As David Scott (1991:262) wrote,

> what is noteworthy is that even in nonanthropological discourse, anthropology, taken as the (self-described) "science

of culture," is often seen as crucial in providing the authoritative vocabulary in terms of which the claims of difference are established. Anthropology—and for quite definite historical reasons, American cultural anthropology more specifically—has often been taken as providing what we might call the foundation discourse for the cultural politics of identity among peoples of African descent in the New World.

Herskovits's thought has been subject to positive evaluations and critical appraisals, from assessments of his sincere, liberal social conscience, as exhibited in his strict adherence to and promotion of cultural relativism (Baron 1994; Bourguignon 2000; Fernández 1990; Gershenhorn 2004; Hatch 1997; Mudimbe 1990), to praise for his courage in daring to study African Americans seriously and attack racism in the context of a palpable upsurge in white racism and nativism in the United States of the 1920s and 1930s (Mintz 1990; Simpson 1973), to critiques claiming that he was unable to wholly escape the "racial" thought he ostensibly combated (Apter 1991; Michaels 1995:123–127), that he uncritically accepted colonial historiography and ignored the ways "Africa" was constructed in the diaspora (Matory 1999b and this volume), that his perspective on culture lent itself to nationalistic claims (Coundouriotis 2001), that his view of social change was static and neglected an analysis of consciousness (Palmié 1995a), and that his fieldwork practices were inadequate conceptually and practically (Blier 1989; R. Price and S. Price 2003b). The origins of his thought have been traced to that of his mentor Franz Boas (1858–1942) (Baron 1994; Gershenhorn 2004; W. Jackson 1986; Stocking 1974; cf. Murray 1990)—at the same time, Boas's own ideas on "race" have been reevaluated (Allen 1989; L. Baker 1998; Beardsley 1973; Hyatt 1985; Liss 1998; W. Willis 1972). Estimations of Herskovits's influence on the field of Afro-American studies began immediately upon his death (Dillard 1964; Mintz 1964; Szwed 1972).[1]

However, a fuller archaeology of his thought will reveal that he was influenced more than had heretofore been realized by African American scholars, such as the linguist Lorenzo Dow Turner (1895–1972) (see Wade-Lewis 1992, 2001), and even somewhat indirectly by a

Caribbean intellectual abroad, Puerto Rican–born Arthur A. Schomburg (1874–1938). Such an archaeology will also reveal the defining influence on Herskovits's thought by ethnographers of Afro-America situated outside North America, in Brazil, Cuba, and Haiti.[2]

What follows is an attempt at a "rehistoricization" of the anthropology of Afro-America by placing ethnography and theory building within a historical and political context. In the "observers observed" (Stocking 1983) mode that follows, I suggest how these ethnologists, namely, Fernando Ortiz Fernández (1881–1969) in Cuba, Jean Price-Mars (1876–1969) in Haiti, and Arthur Ramos (1903–1949) in Brazil, among others, through decades of correspondence, personal relationships, and institution building with Herskovits, played a crucial role in defining the field of Afro-American anthropology in North America, given their involvement in international scientific organizations and given Herskovits's own well-placed positioning within North American anthropology. Therefore, I am not directing our attention to Herskovits to claim for him pioneering status (nor, conversely, to deny his significant contributions). I am also not doing so out of a kind of North America–centered anthropological chauvinism. I am doing so to explicate the kinds of international social relationships and institutional arrangements that have been implicated in the history of the anthropology of the African diaspora. To this end, I hope that this discussion lives up to the goals highlighted by F. Harrison and I. Harrison (1999:6–7), who wrote that "the delineation of the 'triangular trade' in the various knowledges of the black or pan-African world is clearly a worthy project, especially in light of anthropologists' growing interest in diasporas and transnational social fields and identities." My hope is to contribute to a process that problematizes, for those of us working in the present, the anthropological ways of seeing that we have inadvertently or purposively inherited. As David Scott (1990:108) said, "a critical anthropology of the Africa diaspora has to be constituted through a close attention to the history of its own categories and to the extent to which it assumes their transparency."[3]

THE EARLY FORMATION OF HERSKOVITS'S ANTHROPOLOGICAL THOUGHT

Herskovits was born in Ohio to Jewish European immigrants to the United States, and for a while he considered becoming a rabbi, attending Hebrew Union College in 1915. But he came not to identify with an immigrant ethos or seek to consciously maintain a "Jewish culture" through practice, seeing himself with what might be regarded as an assimilationist perspective (see Frank 2001; Yelvington 2000; cf. D. Lewis 1984). He left Hebrew Union, rejecting a possible military deferment based on his status there, joined the US Army in 1917, and served in the Medical Corps in France in World War I. After the war ended, he was unable to return home right away, so he briefly attended the University of Poitiers, where he studied history with a royalist professor (interview with Jean Herskovits [b. 1935], daughter, September 30, 2000). In 1919 he returned to the United States and immediately enrolled for a degree in history at the University of Chicago. After receiving his degree there in 1920, he moved to New York, where he became a student of Elsie Clews Parsons (1875–1941), Alexander Goldenweiser (1880–1940), and Thorstein Veblen (1857–1929) at the New School for Social Research and of Franz Boas at Columbia University. Turning fully to anthropology, he began graduate work at Columbia University receiving his A.M. in political science in 1921 and completing his Ph.D. work in 1923 with a library dissertation—utilizing the resources of W. E. B. Du Bois's (1868–1963) personal library (Baron 1994:114)—titled "The Cattle Complex in East Africa." In his dissertation, he drew on Boas's (somewhat estranged) student Clark Wissler's (1870–1947) elaboration of the "culture area" concept, tracing the diffusion and distribution of cultural traits (cf. Woods 1934). The work was later serialized in the *American Anthropologist* (M. Herskovits 1926a, 1926b, 1926c, 1926d; cf. M. Herskovits 1924).

In New York he met his future wife and partner in anthropological endeavors. Frances Herskovits (née Shapiro) (1897–1972) was born in Russia and immigrated to New York with her family when she was eight. They were married in Paris on July 12, 1924. In New York, where they lived in a bohemian apartment near Columbia, their anthropological companions associated with Columbia and the New School included Margaret Mead (1901–1978) and her first husband, Luther S. Cressman (1897–1994), Ruth Benedict (1887–1948), A. I. Hallowell (1892–1974), and the sociologist Malcolm M. Willey (1897–1974) (see Cressman 1988:98, 194).

In 1923 Boas succeeded in having Herskovits named to a three-year fellowship to the Board of Biological Sciences of the National

Research Council (NRC)—formed in 1916, ostensibly for research in the war effort but in the context of anti-immigrant and antilabor politics. Until the early 1920s, the NRC had been the site of struggles within anthropology between "scientists," including eugenicists, and the Boasians. Along with fellowships for Herskovits, there were those for Mead for her work on Samoan adolescence and for psychologist Otto Kleinberg (1899–1992) for his work on the question of "race" and intellectual differences. These developments served to further the Boasian program (Barkan 1992:111–114; T. Patterson 2001:55–64; Stocking 1968:270–307). Boas saw these three projects "as part of a coordinated attack on the problem of the cultural factor in racial differences" (Stocking 1979:42). In the case of Herskovits, the research problem was directly related to Boas's earlier work on the plasticity of physical features in the presence of acculturative forces in the US context (e.g., Boas 1911a, 1911b; cf. Barkan 1992:76–95; Stocking 1968:161–194).

It has been argued that Boas's anthropological perspective on "race" was paradoxical, especially as it related to supposed "racial" differences between whites and African Americans, but his views were mitigated by his liberal humanitarianism. Boas criticized the racial typology of his day but operated as if "races" existed and could be distinguished even if their distinguishing features overlapped (e.g. V. Williams 1996:1–36; cf. Liss 1998). The NRC fellowship enabled Herskovits to engage in a physical anthropological research project on the effects of "race crossing" on the bodily form of African Americans (W. Jackson 1986:98–99; T. Patterson 2001:75–77; Stocking 1979: 42–43). When the NRC fellowship concluded, Boas secured Herskovits funding from the Columbia University Council for another year. Herskovits's research was conducted in three places: in Harlem, in rural West Virginia, and at Howard University in Washington, DC. In Harlem his field assistants were two African Americans studying anthropology, Zora Neale Hurston (1903–1960) and Louis E. King (1898–1981), and these assistants took anthropometric data from African American residents. King also took physical anthropological measurements for Herskovits in rural West Virginia. Herskovits taught at Howard University in 1925, and there he engaged in intellectual exchanges with philosopher Alain Locke (1886–1954), whom he had met in Harlem earlier, biologist Ernest E. Just (1883–1941), sociologist E. Franklin Frazier (1894–1962), and economist Abram L. Harris (1899–1963), who assisted him in measuring Howard students.

Herskovits produced two books (1928, 1930b) and a number of research articles from these investigations. In these publications, he argued that the "American Negro" was a racially mixed "amalgam" that was "distinctive among human beings," was in the process of forming its own "definite physical type," and was a "homogeneous" population of "low variability" that, because of North American racism, was becoming more "Negroid." Thus he argued, as Boas had done before him, that it was ultimately American cultural forces that affected "race." At the same time, he used culture to dispel other popular racist misconceptions. He argued, based on his work with Howard students, that contrary to studies that showed a supposed link between intelligence and the amount of "white blood" in African Americans (the more intelligent the more "white," and vice versa, the argument went), there was no correlation between physical type and academic performance (M. Herskovits 1926e). Herskovits's physical anthropological results surprised Boas, who described them as pointing to the "darkening of the whole colored population" (Boas 1928:177).

The combination of the effects of the war on American liberals (Kaplan 1956), returning to the United States during the "Red Summer" of 1919, so called because of the amount of blood spilled in anti-black riots in US cities such as Chicago (Tuttle 1970), and the conflict-ridden and contradictory social forces of the 1920s—the "tribal twenties" of the eugenics movement and a resurgence of anti-immigrant nativism (e.g., Higham 1955), the height of anti-Semitism and a crucial time of black-Jewish engagement (e.g., Diner 1977), alongside a cultural permissiveness and a reevaluation of received moral wisdom in many areas of life, and living and working in proximity to the happenings of the Harlem Renaissance (e.g., Favor 1999; Helbling 1999; Hutchinson 1995; D. Lewis 1981)—no doubt inspired and influenced Herskovits's anthropology in various ways. Through his ethnicity, immediate environment, and social networks, not to mention personal proclivity, Herskovits stood (pre)disposed to be part of Boasian anthropology. He early on joined the intellectual fight against racism by writing a number of book reviews criticizing eugenics and anti-immigrant nativism in such publications as the *New Republic*, the *Nation*, the book review section of the *New York Herald-Tribune*, and the *Literary Review* of the *New York Evening Post*. He also took up many assumptions of the "culture and personality" school made ascendant by Benedict and Mead. As Stocking (1986:7) argues, throughout the nineteenth century, "the dominant ideological impulse of the anthropological tradition has been 'progressivist' rather than 'primitivist.'" However, after World War I, "the 1920s saw a resurgence of the motif of romantic cultural exoticism in the work of younger anthropologists, and their thinking about problems of culture and personality was motivated at least in part by their participation in the more general 'revolt against civilization.'...Although they were by no means all cultural radicals, they tended to be set apart by ethnic background, or gender consciousness, and political conviction from the culture of *Middletown*" (Stocking 1986:7).

In 1924 Locke, with whom Herskovits had had conversations about Boasian anthropological concepts, asked Herskovits to contribute an article titled "Harlem: Mecca of the New Negro" to a special issue of *Survey Graphic* magazine devoted to Harlem. Locke wanted Herskovits to provide "an analysis of the Negro's peculiar social pattern, and an estimate of its capacity in social survival and culture building" (Locke to Herskovits, April 24, 1924, quoted in W. Jackson 1986:101). Yet Herskovits's perspective was quite the contrary (Herskovits 1925a). He ended up taking an assimilationist line, downplaying if not disparaging the notion of a "peculiar social pattern" and instead looking at how the culture of Harlem blacks was converging with that of the white mainstream.

What kind of community was Harlem? Herskovits wondered. "Should I not find there, if anywhere, the distinctiveness of the Negro, of which I had heard so much? Should I not be able to discover there his ability, of which we are so often told, to produce unique cultural traits, which might be added to the prevailing white culture, and, as well, to note his equally well-advertised inability to grasp the complex civilization of which he constitutes a part?" He wrote (1925a):

> And so I went, and what I found was churches and schools,
> club-houses and lodge meeting-places, the library and the
> newspaper offices and the Y.M.C.A. and busy 135th Street

and the hospitals and the social service agencies. I met persons who were lawyers and doctors and editors and writers, who were chauffeurs and peddlers and longshoremen and real estate brokers and capitalists, teachers and nurses and students and waiters and cooks. And all Negroes. Cabarets and theaters, drugstores and restaurants just like those everywhere else. And finally, after a time, it occurred to me that what I was seeing was a community just like any other American community. The same pattern, only a different shade!

Historically, after emancipation blacks strove "to maintain, as nearly as possible, the standards set up by those whom they had been taught to look up to as arbiters—the white group." Business people "tried to make money as their white fellows did." Schools taught "not the language and technique of their African ancestors, but that of this country, where they lived." As a result, "in Harlem we have today, essentially, a typical American community. You may look at the Negroes on the street. As to dress and deportment, do you find any vast difference between them and the whites among whom they carry on their lives? Notice them as they go about their work—they do almost all of the things the whites do, and in much the same way." There were Greek-letter fraternities and sororities and the Business Men's Association. "The difference between this gathering and that of my own Rotary Club is imperceptible." There was "complete acculturation" in that "sexual rigidity" was "the ultimate idea of relations between men and women," and "certainly there was no more indication of a leaning toward the customs to be found in ancestral Africa than would be found among a group of whites." Intellectuals? Their universalistic humanism was "another striking example of the process of acculturation." (M. Herskovits 1925a)

Herskovits homed in on the central question, "Does the Negro have a mode of life that is essentially similar to that of the general community of which he is a part?" upon which he deployed the culture concept. "The Negro came to America endowed, as all people are endowed, with a culture, which had been developed by him through long ages in Africa. Was it innate? Or has it been sloughed off, forgotten, in the generations since he was brought into our culture?" He invoked the Boasian separation of "race" from "culture" and asked, "If ability to successfully live in one culture were restricted to persons of one race, how could we account for the fact that we see persons of the most diverse races living together, for example, in this country...?" Acculturation meant that something discernibly "black" or "African" could not exist, but what was distinctive were only regional cultural carryovers from the recent migrants' southern backgrounds: "What there is today in Harlem distinct from the white culture which surrounds it, is, as far as I am able to see, merely a remnant from the peasant days of the South. Of the African culture, not a trace. Even the spirituals are an expression of the emotion of the Negro playing through the typical religious pattern of white America." Exhibiting a belief in the power of the acculturative process and identifying blacks with other ethnic groups, he showed little patience for claims of black distinctiveness:

> That they have absorbed the culture of America is too obvious, almost, to be mentioned. They have absorbed it as all great racial and social groups in this country have absorbed it. And they face much the same problems as these groups face....All racial and social elements in our population who live here long enough become acculturated, Americanized in the truest sense of the word, eventually. They learn our culture and react according to its patterns, against which all the protestations of the possession of, or of a hot desire for, a peculiar culture mean nothing. (M. Herskovits 1925a)

To this, Locke felt compelled to add an editorial note to Herskovits's contribution. He wrote:

> Looked at in its externals, Negro life, as reflected in Harlem, reveals a ready—almost a feverishly rapid—assimilation of American patterns, what Mr. Herskovits calls "complete acculturation." It speaks well for both the Negro and for American standards of living that this is so. Internally, perhaps it is another matter. Does democracy require uniformity? If so, it threatens to be safe, but dull. Social standards must be more or less uniform, but social expressions may be different. Old folkways may not persist, but they may leave a mental trace, subtly recorded in emotional temper and coloring social reactions. (Locke 1925a:676)

"Harlem: Mecca of the New Negro" was expanded and became the book *The New Negro*, edited by Locke (1925b). Herskovits was one of the few non-black contributors to this book, which became a definitive statement of and for the Harlem Renaissance and modernism (e.g., H. Baker 1987). Herskovits's contribution was published as "The Negro's Americanism" (M. Herskovits 1925b). He was virtually alone among the contributors in his perspective. One contributor, Afro–Puerto Rican cultural and political activist Arthur Schomburg (see James 1998:ch. 7; Sinnette 1989), wrote that a "racial motive" is "legitimately compatible with scientific method and aim" in the writing of history:

> The work our race students now regard as important, they undertake very naturally to overcome in part certain handicaps of disparagement and omission too well-known to particularize. But they do so not merely that we may not wrongfully be deprived of the spiritual nourishment of our cultural past, but also that the full story of human collaboration and interdependence may be told and realized. Especially this is likely to be the effect of the latest and most fascinating of all of the attempts to open up the closed Negro past, namely the important study of African cultural origins and sources. The bigotry of civilization which is the taproot of intellectual prejudice begins far back and must be corrected at its source. Fundamentally it has come about from the depreciation of Africa which has sprung up from ignorance of her true rôle and position in human history and the early development of culture. The Negro has been a man without history because he has been a man without a worthy culture. But a new notion of the cultural attainment and potentialities of the African stocks has recently come about....Already the Negro sees himself against a reclaimed background, in a perspective that will give pride and self-respect ample scope, and will make history yield for him the same values that the treasured past of any people affords. (Schomburg 1925:237)

While we cannot be sure what effect the words of Locke and Schomburg had on Herskovits, it is clear that Herskovits for the rest of his life devoted himself to their implications. In what was perhaps his major and most influential work, *The Myth of the Negro Past* (1941), Herskovits gave almost the exact same justification for the study of the "Negro past"—without citing Schomburg—saying that "though it has often been pointed out that the skin-color of the Negro makes him an all too visible mark for prejudice, it is not so well realized that the accepted opinion of the nature of the Negro's cultural heritage is what makes him the only element in the peopling of the United States that has no operative past except in bondage." Further,

> there is still another point of practical importance that should not be overlooked in appraising the implications of proper study of Negro backgrounds and of the retention of Africanisms. And this is the effect of the present-day representatives of this race without a past, of the deprivation they suffer in bearing no pride of tradition. For no group in the population of this country has been more completely convinced of the inferior nature of the African background than have the Negroes.

Herskovits's task would be to provide blacks with that past through the scientific documentation and systematic presentation of "Africanisms" in New World Negro culture:

> To give the Negro an appreciation of his past is to endow him with the confidence in his own position in this country and in the world which he must have, and which he can best attain when he has available a foundation of scientific fact concerning the ancestral cultures of Africa and the survivals of Africanisms in the New World. And it must again be emphasized that when such a body of fact, solidly grounded, is established, a ferment must follow which, when this information is diffused over the population as a whole, will influence opinion in general concerning Negro abilities and potentialities, and thus contribute to a lessening of interracial tensions. (1941:30–31, 32)

Almost immediately upon the publication of *The New Negro*, Herskovits was discussing African cultural "remnants" in his private correspondence, but he moved somewhat slower in his publications.

For at least two more years, he maintained in most of his published work that blacks in the United States were characterized by their acceptance of white culture and that they had, for the most part, failed to exhibit any influences of their ancestral cultures (e.g., M. Herskovits 1927). At the same time, he seemed to see African cultural "survivals" in other settings, such as among the Maroons (descendants of escaped slaves) in the Dutch colony of Suriname (e.g., M. Herskovits 1926f). He wrote to the Austrian ethnomusicologist Erich Moritz von Hornbostel (1877–1935) about Hurston, his research assistant. Although she was "more White than Negro in her ancestry," Herskovits said, her "manner of speech, her expressions—in short, her motor behavior" were "what would be termed typically Negro," and he suggested that these movements, observed when Hurston was singing spirituals, had been "carried over as a behavior pattern handed down thru imitation and example from the original African slaves who were brought here" (Herskovits to von Hornbostel, June 10, 1927, quoted in W. Jackson 1986:107).

In January 1926, Herskovits wrote a grant application titled "Plan for Research on the Problem of the Negro," in which, whether or not he knew it, he basically laid out much of his career to come. In the application, he proposed to study the provenance of New World Negroes, to chart the changes in their bodily form, to determine whether there were any temperamental similarities between them and Africans, and to track African cultural survivals among blacks. To these ends, he proposed to do fieldwork in Liberia, take anthropometric measurements of various peoples in the Ivory Coast and Gold Coast, conduct more fieldwork on the physical and cultural natures of blacks in the Carolina Sea Islands and other isolated parts of the US South, and then do more fieldwork in the Caribbean, Brazil, and Suriname, all the while employing a Boasian perspective to locate the historical diffusion of cultural traits. In late 1926, he wrote a review of the travel book *"Tom-Tom"* by American author John W. Vandercook (1902–1963). This book (Vandercook 1926) was on the "Bush Negroes" of the interior of the Dutch South American colony of Suriname. These Maroons were the descendants of escaped slaves who fought Dutch colonial troops to maintain their freedom. For Herskovits, Vandercook presented much evidence of the existence of "an African culture—one of West Africa." He was now talking about the survival of cultural traits that Vandercook had revealed, even though the pity for Herskovits was that Vandercook was not a trained ethnologist: "Mr. Vandercook has done a service to students who are interested in the roots of the American Negro peoples. For it is only through the consideration of survivals, in this hemisphere, of cultural traits which were brought from Africa that the problem can be approached with any hope of solution" (M. Herskovits 1926f:10). Herskovits was obviously taken by the book, and by the images of the descendants of escaped slaves in Suriname. This was to be a turning point for Herskovits, and Suriname and its Maroons would play a crucial role in the development of his thought (see R. Price and S. Price 2003b).

HERSKOVITS IN DIALOGUE

I start my delineation of the "triangle trade" (pace F. Harrison and I. Harrison 1999)—or my attempt at third-level discourse (pace Mudimbe 1988)—with reference to some aspects of the multiple discourses of "Africa" at work in Latin America and the Caribbean between 1920 and 1940, an Africa *of* Latin America and the Caribbean (pace Mintz 1984). At least four ideologically laden types of discourses might be discerned in these postcolonial societies (and in the case of some Caribbean territories, *colonial* societies). One was that of the ruling elements and state representatives, who presumed the existence of "races" that were determinative of "culture" and thus explained the relative economic and political development of nations. Another discourse was that of somewhat more educated and middle-class black mobilizers, often with pan-African aims and sentiments, such as Marcus Garvey (1887–1940), or the middle-class blacks of Cuba and Brazil (among others, see Butler 1998; de la Fuente 2001; Devés Valdés 2000; Figueiredo 2002; Guimarães 2004a; Kraay 1998; Morrison 1999; Schwartz 1977). A third discourse of Africa was found in manifestations of popular consciousness, often in a religious idiom, such as in the Brazilian Candomblé, Haitian Vodou, Santería in Cuba, and Rastafari and Myalism in Jamaica, although the ways in which "Africa" was realized in practice and in discourse, or on the other hand was erased, varied widely. And finally, there was an interpretive-scientific discourse by elite scholar-politicians asserting a privileged status for their views by virtue of training and institutional location. Many of these modernist and modernizing scholar-politicians utilized ethnographic and ethnological data to extend, but sometimes challenge, notions of the racialized nation that were tied to notions of progress. They were positivists and were looking to use scholarship to provide social solutions to societal ills often expressed in racialist idioms with reference to physical disease, degeneration, and pathology (e.g., see Birman 1997; Borges 1993, 1995; Bremer 1993; Bronfman 2002a, 2002b, 2004; Corrêa 1998; Dávila 2003; de la Fuente 2001; Dianteill 1995, 2000, 2002a; Font and Quiroz 2005; Guerra 1998; Helg 1995; R. Moore 1994, 1997; Motta 1978; Nunes 1994; Palmié 2002; Peard 1999; Puig-Samper and Naranjo Orovio 1999; Rodríguez-Mangual 2004; Román 2000; Schwarcz 1999).

In Cuba, for example, the campaign against *brujería* (sorcery) (see Bronfman 2002a, 2002b; Chávez Álvarez 1991; Helg 1995) was joined by Ortiz, a white lawyer-politician who had represented newly independent Cuba abroad. Ortiz's (1906) first foray was "un estudio de etnología criminal" of "los negros brujos," the blight on the body politic (Guerra 2003; Mullen 1987; Wirtz 2004). It was a positivist and racialist approach, reflecting the stamp of Italian criminologist Cesare Lombroso (1835–1909) (who wrote a preface) (Bremer 1993; cf. D'Agostino 2002; M. Gibson 2002; Horn 2003), as well as the influence of the pioneering Brazilian Afro-Americanist Raymundo Nina Rodrigues (1862–1906).

Ortiz was in many ways co-opted by Afrocubanismo, a literary and artistic movement beginning in the 1920s, and in a remarkable turnaround he became the movement's patron and source of legitimacy (see Kapcia 1992; R. Moore 1994, 1997; Santí 2002; W. Santiago-Valles 1997). He never lost his nationalist bent (Le Riverend 1973), however, and his concept of *transculturación* (F. Ortiz 1940) to denote a kind of mutual cultural fashioning can be seen as a way of coming to grips with a new dispensation brought about by politically active blacks by now imagining Cuba as a *mestizo* (racially and culturally mixed) nation (see Coronil 1995; Díaz Quiñones 1998, 2000; Iznaga 1989). He became a central international figure in the study of the African diaspora in the New World. Like Ramos in Brazil and others elsewhere in the region, through the 1930s and 1940s, Ortiz emphasized "culture," not "race," to account for behavior and sought to define and lead the "nationalization of culture" (Löfgren 1989) and assimilation under that rubric (Ortiz 1945; Ramos 1943, 1944; cf. Bolland 1992; Borges 1993, 1995; D. Davis 1998, 1999, 2000; D. Williams 2001; Wirtz 2004).

The discourse of Africa was affected by the political, military, and cultural dominance of the United States. Cuba was formally occupied twice and was under US political and economic control. US Marines occupied Haiti from 1915 until 1934. In Haiti, Price-Mars (1919) chided the Eurocentric elite for their weaknesses in allowing the US Marines to occupy the country, and in his work of ethnohistory and ethnography titled *Ainsi parla l'Oncle (So Spoke the Uncle)* (1928), he gave inspiration to a literary flowering that had "Africa" as a central theme (Dash 1981). This work was conjoined with actual resistance on the part of peasants to US military excesses. Price-Mars, the son of a successful agriculturalist from the north of Haiti who was elected to the House of Representatives, studied medicine in Paris and in his spare time attended lectures on anthropology and sociology. While studying in Paris, Price-Mars read with great anticipation Gustave Le Bon's *Les lois psychologiques de l'évolution des peuples* (1894) and discovered, to his bitter disappointment, its racist message. Years later he met Le Bon, who admitted that his judgment might have been hasty and urged Price-Mars to write a book about Haiti. For the rest of his life, he tilted against the likes of Le Bon. Like Ortiz, he represented his country abroad, in several postings throughout his long career. Politically connected, he held government jobs, was elected a representative and senator, and ran for president. Yet he was a black member of the upper middle class, itself *mulâtre* in identification and comprador bourgeoisie in avocation. He railed against middle-class *"bovaryisme collectiff,"* "collective Bovaryism," or being what one is not, in this case referring to what he saw as the denial of African origins, and called for Haitians to valorize what he outlined as the African heritage of what he liked to refer to as four-fifths of their population. He urged Haitian blacks to follow the lead of the Harlem Renaissance. He saw anthropology (broadly conceived) as a means of achieving a patriotic education. He founded the Institut d'Ethnologie, where he taught "Africology" (Antoine 1981; Magloire 2005; Magloire and Yelvington 2005; Shannon 1996; H. Trouillot 1956; cf. Dash 1992).

These upper-middle-class scholar-politicians used anthropology—

ethnology and the study of folklore specifically—to construct and renovate the nation by prescribing the place of "Africa" within the nation (e.g., Borges 1993, 1995; Ortiz García 2003; Ramsey 2002). Anthropology and politics were mutually constitutive in many respects. Nationalist politics could bolster its claims by recourse to the science of anthropology, but anthropology could not do the reverse: it assumed the mantle of scientific objectivity. These scholars, despite their important differences, had many commonalities in their orientation to the question of Afro-American cultures. They all thought that particular cultural practices they were observing had their origins in the specific ethnic culture of named African ethnic groups, with one group dominating in one cultural institution in a particular New World locale because of diverging historical circumstances. Yet despite "Dahomean" cultural traits dominating in religion here and "Yoruba" or "Bantu" traits dominating there, it remained the case that these apparently differing African-derived forms of worship exhibited basic commonalities, usually conceived of as a kind of common psychology. Given these connections, it followed that research in the Americas could reveal something about African religious forms and, reciprocally, research in Africa could be made to inform the student of New World African-derived religions. These scholars felt that identifiably African cultural practices could persevere—"survive"—through generations behind the mask of acculturation. These would typically include cultural practices conceived of as cultural traits (see Lyman and O'Brien 2003) associated with religion, but they were also evinced in folklore and language. Depending on the context, not to mention the politics of the ethnologist, these survivals could be a good or a bad force. In the work of Nina Rodrigues and the early Ortiz, these survivals could be seen behind "atavistic" and criminal behavior. For Price-Mars in occupied Haiti, African cultural survivals were to be embraced as the true cultural heritage of the masses.

By 1927 Herskovits had taken a position as the only anthropologist in the Sociology Department at Northwestern University, and he would stay at that institution until his death in 1963. In February 1928, as a thirty-two-year-old assistant professor, he wrote to Jean Price-Mars in Haiti, saying he had been told "of some of the interesting publications and studies you have made on the subject of Voodoo in Haiti":

> I am exceedingly interested in cultural connections between
> the African and American Negroes and I am planning to
> spend next summer among the Bush Negroes of Surinam. I
> should really be grateful were you to send me copies of your
> publications or references as to where I might find them.
> (MHP, Box 19, Folder 1)

Thus began years of correspondence, the exchange of views and
publications, the sharing of personal news, and attempts to forge institutional ties with Caribbean and Latin American ethnologists.[4]
Herskovits's revelation that he was, as he wrote to Price-Mars, "exceed-
ingly interested in cultural connections between the African and
American Negroes" seemed to indicate a significant revision of his
position of just a few years previous. While the relationships he entered
into with these ethnologists were crucial to the formation of his
thought, Herskovits himself needed to bring in ethnographic data of
his own if he was going to be a legitimate player in the scene he was
setting for himself. That came early on with his two field trips to
Suriname.

It was Parsons who suggested to Herskovits that he look for African
cultural survivals in Suriname, where they were sure to be strongest
(see MHP, Box 18, Folder 3). Parsons had worked on folklore in the
southwestern United States and among blacks in the United States and
the Caribbean. She traced folktales in quest of their points of origin,
which she thought could be discerned. For example, about her work
on Andros Island in the Bahamas, she said, "Whatever may have been
the provenience of the tales in Africa, Portuguese or other, I have no
doubt that by far the greater number of the Bahama tales were learned
there—learned, not in America, but in Africa" (Parsons 1918:xii, cited
in Zumwalt 1992:198). Between 1917 and 1937, she was a guest editor
of and contributor to fourteen special issues of the *Journal of American
Folk-Lore* on African and African American folk traditions, then under
the general editorship of Boas, also underwriting the cost of their
publication (L. Baker 2000:43, 71–76; cf. Deacon 1997; Willis 1975;
Zumwalt 1992). The result was that Parsons's work on the African diaspora was held up by the New Negroes of the Harlem Renaissance,
including folklorist Arthur Huff Fauset (1899–1983), in what Baker

(2000:71) calls their heritage project "to demonstrate that the New Negro was unique and had a distinct culture with a proud history and heritage. In this emergent discourse, scientists and artists identified African cultural continuities within African American culture as a source of empowerment, beauty, inspiration, and authenticity." Parsons paid for the Herskovitses' fieldwork in Suriname in the summers of 1928 and 1929, as well as their field trip to Dahomey and other parts of West Africa in 1931. She also provided publishing subventions for the books coming out of the Suriname trips (Herskovits and Herskovits 1934a, 1936) and for their other book manuscripts (see MHP, Box 18, Folder 3).

The trip to Suriname was arduous fieldwork for Herskovits. Richard Price and Sally Price (2003b) show through reading his field diaries that it was wrought with physical maladies, emotional frailties, professional doubt, and not a little culture shock and culturally inappropriate behavior—as first fieldwork trips often are. They were guided by the experiences of Willem Frederik van Lier (1877–1957), an amateur ethnographer and colonial official with a special interest in the Maroons. But while Herskovits (1941:6) retrospectively represented this experience as a kind of scientific discovery, it is clear that his experience was framed by his emerging theoretical orientation going into the field, by Parsons and her influences, by the work of the Latin American and Caribbean ethnologists he was starting to read, and even by Vandercook, whose book he took with him during the first field trip in 1928.

Early the next year, Herskovits wrote an introductory letter to Fernando Ortiz in Cuba, referring to a discussion of Ortiz's work in the *Journal of American Folk-Lore* that interested him "very deeply":

> I myself am primarily concerned with the African origins of the New World-Negroes and to this end I spent last summer with the Bush-Negroes of Dutch Guiana, to whom I shall return next summer.
>
> If it would be possible for you to send me reprints of your publications on Afrocuban folk lore and other papers of this type, I should be most grateful to you. I have not as yet published any results of my research among the Bush-Negroes, but I should be most happy to send you papers on

the subject which should appear from time to time in the future. (MHP, Box 17, Folder 15)

At the same time, resuming his correspondence with Price-Mars, Herskovits then asked whether he could meet with Price-Mars, as the ships he and Frances were taking to and from Suriname were stopping at Haiti: "I should be deeply grateful for an opportunity to meet you and discuss some of the problems of Haiti and Ethnology and Anthropology with you, as I hope some day to be able to extend my studies to the West Indian Islands." The Herskovitses did meet with Price-Mars, albeit briefly, when their Suriname boat docked at Port-au-Prince. Price-Mars had given Herskovits a pamphlet he authored. Herskovits wrote:

> We found that the little pamphlet you gave us was exceed-
> ingly valuable and that there are many more correspon-
> dences than I thought possible between Haiti and
> Suriname. Since my return I have started once more the
> attempt to study the provenience of these Negro cultures in
> the New World and I am sure that the numerous resem-
> blances I find to Dahomey will strengthen your hypothesis
> of the importance of that point for a knowledge of the ori-
> gin of the Negro cultures of the New World. (MHP, Box 19,
> Folder 1)

Shortly thereafter, Price-Mars sent Herskovits a copy of *Ainsi parla l'Oncle* (Price-Mars 1928), which had just been published. Herskovits confirmed upon receiving it that "there are already many interesting and important correspondences with what we found in Suriname, which begin to appear." Price-Mars replied with a certain humility regarding *Ainsi*: "I ask you to give me your impressions when you have finished the reading. Your appreciation has such a great scientific authority that I would receive with pleasure any observations you may have" (MHP, Box 19, Folder 1). The two exchanged letters and opinions—on, for example, W. B. Seabrook's *The Magic Island* (1929), a book on Haitian Vodou that Herskovits reviewed in the *Nation*, calling it "a work of injustice," another "sensational exploitation of the lives and customs of the Caribbean Negro peoples" (M. Herskovits 1929:

198; cf. Gregory 1992), and which Price-Mars criticized strongly in *Le Temps*, a Port-au-Prince newspaper.

Herskovits continued to send Price-Mars his papers and books, and Price-Mars continued to be approving and encouraging. When he returned from his 1931 Parsons-sponsored fieldwork in Dahomey, Herskovits wrote to Price-Mars, sending along his article "Some Aspects of Dahomean Ethnology" (1932), saying, "I am sure that many of the aspects of the culture described...will be familiar to you from knowing the customs of the people of the interior of Haiti" (MHP, Box 19, Folder 1). In early 1933, Price-Mars wrote an extremely flattering review of Herskovits's oeuvre up to that point in the Haitian journal *La Relève*, commenting in a letter with characteristic understatement that "obviously my remarks only give a weak idea as to the grandeur of the work. I hope, however, that the article will have people's curiosity alerted enough to go to the original source themselves" (MHP, Box 19, Folder 1). Of Herskovits, Price-Mars (1933:11) wrote in his review, "It is with great reserve that I attempt to analyze generally the works of Professor Melville J. Herskovits in a simple article in the review," because "[t]hey embrace so many relevant subjects in anthropology and sociology, that the young scientist brought up so many new points of view in his research that most of his study would each merit to be discussed at length and under a special genre." He called Herskovits's *The Anthropometry of the American Negro* (1930b) a "monumental work with no equal in scientific annals" because it shows

> that a new race has been born in the United States that, from a physical point of view is just as distinct from the original stock imported from Africa as from the Caucasian factor or the aboriginal Indian factor with which they mixed also. It is a curious and baffling thing, this race has already acquired a biological homogeneity which protected it from variation or more exactly that the variations were so slow that we find the same behavior from the old historical races stabilized for thousands of years. From lightest to darkest, the American Negro type is a new product which borrows its characteristics right from the diverse factors where it was derived, the absolutely curious conclusion where Professor Herskovits arrives. (Price-Mars 1933:13–14)

He hoped that the "psychological result of this interesting phenomenon of cross-breeding" could be analyzed with the "same scientific rigor" through "the procedures of psychometry and the method of tests which the fanatics of the Davenport school abuse," referring to American eugenicist Charles Benedict Davenport (1866–1944), who had railed on against "miscegenation" in the United States and had also published on "race crossing" in Jamaica (Davenport and Steggerda 1929). Noting Herskovits's fieldwork in Dahomey, Price-Mars publicly invited him to undertake fieldwork in Haiti: "As I wish that the young scientist could fulfill his generous promise he made me to come investigate the Haitian race and how I would be happy if, we as the initiators of this project, he could find here participants to figure out the complexity of races [about] which politics and literature have already made such foolish and disconcerting assumptions" (Price-Mars 1933:14). But in the meantime, "I am happy to give my tribute of admiration to this valiant pioneer in science where the concern is to study human races without being preoccupied with repercussion, to provoke his steps in a muddied world in the pus of prejudice, of injustice and of foolishness" (14–15).

Upon receiving the review from Price-Mars, Herskovits immediately wrote back with gratitude:

> I hasten to write you to tell you how deeply moved I was at reading your extremely complimentary remarks on my work. I was the more appreciative since I realize how honest you are in your comments on works that come to your attention as is particularly illustrated by your reviews of Seabrook's book. I like especially the invitation contained in your article for me to continue work in Haiti. I assure you that since having been in Dahomey I am most eager to follow up my findings among those fascinating people by carrying on investigations among the equally fascinating folk of your country. And, while the present economic condition renders it difficult to arrange these matters, I am far from giving up hope that eventually this will be possible. (MHP, Box 19, Folder 1)

Around this time, Price-Mars translated the Herskovitses' article "A

Footnote to the History of Negro Slaving" (1933) into French when it was published in *La Relève* for a Haitian audience (1934b). By now, Melville Herskovits was feeling competent enough to contribute an article on Haitian ethnology to an Italian social science encyclopedia (M. Herskovits 1933b). Price-Mars wrote: "I approve everything that you said about the content and I congratulate you for having so well penetrated the ancestral beliefs of the Haitian people."

Meanwhile, Ortiz wrote back almost two years after Herskovits's first letter, at the suggestion of Herminio Portell Vilá (1901–1992), a Cuban historian working in the United States and known to both men. Ortiz said it gave him great pleasure to write to Herskovits, and he included a recent conference paper that contained a list of his publications. He said he would gladly supply any works that might be of interest to Herskovits. When Herskovits replied, saying that he was ordering two of Ortiz's books from his publisher and that he was sending along a paper of his own that he hoped would be of interest, Ortiz responded that Herskovits should ask him for the books he needed and that they would be sent without cost. Herskovits, still in a formal mode, requested Ortiz's *Hampa afro-cubana: los negros brujos* (1906) (*Afro-Cuban Underworld: The Black Sorcerers*), *Hampa afro-cubana: los negros esclavos* (1916) (*Afro-Cuban Underworld: The Black Slaves*), and *Glosario de afronegrismos* (1924) (*Glossary of Black African Sayings*) and asked that he be sent the publisher's bill. Shortly thereafter, the three volumes arrived in Evanston, and Herskovits wrote back with gratitude, with a sense of intellectual confraternity and admiration for what he regarded as pioneering work by the older scholar, and no doubt bolstered by what he saw as independent confirmation of some of his emerging ideas:

> Permit me to thank you most deeply for the three magnificent volumes which reached me yesterday. I have been spending most of my time since their arrival in going through them and I cannot express to you how deeply I am impressed by their value for the study of the Negro nor how delighted I am that I have finally been privileged to go through them. I am particularly impressed with the material in your volume "Los Negros Brujos," and I agree with you

completely that the material you found in Cuba stems
directly from Yoruban in West Africa. You may be interested
in knowing that some of the personal charms which you figure in that work are almost the exact duplicates of those
which were found by myself among the Dutch Negroes of
the interior of Dutch Guiana. Your work also demonstrates
how closely the religion of the Cuban Negroes ties up with
that of the Brazilian ones for, according to an article in
"Anthropos" for 1908, the same pantheon you found in
Cuba is also found in Brazil. I might say that I, too, found
many of the same spirits in Dutch Guiana as you mention for
Cuba. (MHP, Box 17, Folder 15)

Herskovits closed by mentioning that he and Frances were headed
to West Africa for fieldwork and added, "I should be most happy to
receive from you any questions which have raised themselves in your
mind and which I might be helpful in answering" (MHP, Box 17,
Folder 15). The *Anthropos* article Herskovits referred to was by the *abbé*
Etienne Ignace (1908) and was known by Ortiz, as were the works of
other members of the Afro-Brazilianist school.

As he was about to go off to Dahomey to investigate what he saw as
a cultural baseline for Afro-America, he replied to something Ortiz had
written by saying,

I quite agree with you in what you say as to the unity of
Negro culture in Brazil and Cuba. My impression is that
both of these stem from the Yoruba of Nigeria. I also agree
that the Haitian religious practices come from Dahomey
and I hope to have interesting correspondences as the result
of my approaching field trip (MHP, Box 17, Folder 15).

Herskovits then, without having yet been to Dahomey and having
touched down in Haiti for only a short period, was convinced of the
Dahomey-Haiti cultural connection. There seems little question that
this connection was confirmed for him upon reading Price-Mars's
book *Ainsi*, received at the end of 1928 (figure 2.1).

Herskovits emerged from these exchanges by making an early,
definitive statement in "The Negro in the New World: The Statement

FIGURE 2.1

Melville J. Herskovits, circa 1935, at Northwestern University. Photo by John D. Jones, courtesy of Northwestern University Archives. *

of a Problem" (1930a). Here, the "New World Negro" became a scientific object of study, a research "problem" amenable to a kind of experimentation. The history of slavery was known, according to Herskovits, so that provided a time horizon, acting as a kind of historic control. For him, it was possible to chart the scope and intensity of Africanisms both spatially and across cultural institutions (for example, religion versus child rearing or language). And it was possible, too, to identify the sources for the cultural influences in a particular New World territory—for example, "Yoruba" for Cuba and Brazil, "Dahomey" for Haiti.

FIGURE 2.2

Frances S. Herskovits doing fieldwork in Paramaribo, Suriname, 1928. Photo by Melville J. Herskovits. Eliot Elisofon Photographic Archives, National Museum of African Art, Smithsonian Institution. Used with permission of Jean Herskovits.

FIGURE 2.3

Jean Price-Mars. Photo courtesy of Lyle W. Shannon.

These connections paid off for Herskovits. In the summer of 1934, Price-Mars aided the Herskovitses in doing fieldwork in Haiti. Upon hearing the news, Price-Mars wrote, "For a long time, you know, I have wished with all my soul for this mission." He offered to help locate a fieldwork site; met the Herskovitses when their ship docked and, as a senator, helped them through customs with the film equipment for their fieldwork; suggested a field site; smoothed over relations with local notables so that fieldwork could proceed unhindered; and even arranged a meeting with the president (Magloire and Yelvington 2005). The resulting book, *Life in a Haitian Valley* (M. Herskovits 1937b)—focused mainly on acculturation and the Vodou religion, maintaining that Vodou was a legitimate and authentic religion—was praised by Price-Mars, and this praise resulted in Herskovits's being

FIGURE 2.4
Fernando Ortiz, circa 1916. From his Hampa afro-cubana: los negros esclavos *(1916).*

given the Officer of the Haitian Order of Honor and Merit award. The book justified Price-Mars's call for Haitians to be proud of their cultural traditions and embrace the African aspects of Haitian culture.

Herskovits was pleased with what he found in Haiti and what his fieldwork there taught him about the New World Negro. As he wrote to Ortiz of Haiti,

I found it fascinating there, both because of the great number of Africanisms which I encountered, and because of the manner in which the Haitians, like your Cuban Negroes, have interlarded their aboriginal African tradition with beliefs and ceremonies drawn from Catholicism. The matter goes so far as to be fantastic, as for example, when Vodun drums or Vodun spirits must be baptized, or when a Saturday night Vodun dance breaks up at dawn so that people can prepare to go to Mass. (MHP, Box 17, Folder 15)

Arthur Ramos was Herskovits's contemporary of the Afro-Brazilianist school (e.g., Ramos 1934, 1935, 1937, 1942) who used psychology to refashion and update the concerns of Nina Rodrigues (Barros 2000; Borges 1993, 1995; Carneiro 1951; Sapucaia 2003). It was the Brazilian writer and champion of the idea of "racial democracy" and the study of black culture and history Gilberto Freyre (1900–1987), who knew Herskovits, who suggested that Ramos contact Herskovits (see MHP, Box 7, Folder 40). Ramos contacted Herskovits, and they exchanged letters and publications (Guilmarães 2004b). Again, there were mutual influences in each other's work, especially vis-à-vis the concept of "acculturation." In 1937 Herskovits sent an already published contribution (M. Herskovits 1937a) to the second Afro-Brazilian Congress. In it, he utilized Ramos's idea of religious "syncretism," although Herskovits did not acknowledge it as such at the time. He helped Ramos obtain a grant to travel to the United States and lecture at Louisiana State University and to provide guest lectures at various other institutions. They finally met when Ramos came to Northwestern University to spend a term working with Herskovits and giving public talks, such as a joint talk with Herskovits on "The Race Problem in Brazil and the United States" (see *Daily Northwestern*, February 11, 1941, p. 1, and *Daily Northwestern*, February 18, 1941, pp. 1, 5). Herskovits conducted fieldwork in Bahia and elsewhere in 1941–1942, making numerous anthropological connections at various conferences in Brazil. He went on to train three Brazilian anthropologists at Northwestern: Octávio da Costa Eduardo (b. 1919) earned his master's degree in 1943 and his Ph.D. in 1945, René Ribeiro (1914–1990) earned his master's in 1949, and Ruy Galvão de Andrade Coelho (1920–1990) earned his Ph.D. in 1955.

In what way did this intellectual interaction challenge Herskovits's own theoretical grounding in Boasian anthropology? Stocking (1974:17) suggests "as a hypothesis deserving further study" that "Boas' students did tend to share...underlying assumptions" and "to a very great extent their anthropology developed along lines implicit in these assumptions." For Stocking (17), "one can distinguish temporal phases of development; and one can distinguish what might be called 'strict' Boasians," which included Herskovits (17). Herskovits did take on rather completely Boas's historical-cultural particularism (pace Marvin Harris 1968), his diffusionism, the emphasis on tracing the geographical distribution of culture traits, and the interest in culture areas (Zwernemann 1983), as well as Boas's explicit interest, articulated in the 1920s (e.g., Boas 1920, 1924), on acculturation (cf. Murray 1990).

It could be added that Herskovits also inherited Boas's incomplete critique of E. B. Tylor's (1832–1917) evolutionism (e.g., Boas 1896), in that while Boas devoted much energy to this critique (see Stocking 1968:195–233), the Tylorian idea of cultural survivals (see Hodgen 1936) was not completely dismissed. According to Boas (1924:342), Tylor wrongly assumed that "the antiquity of one particular type is essentially due to a classification in which the form that appears as the simplest from any one point of view is considered at the same time as historically the oldest." Tylor felt the "weakness of this assumption" when he tried to support his thesis by "the study of survivals which indicate the character of earlier developmental stages" (Boas 1924:342). The problem was that "it cannot be claimed that a systematic attempt has ever been made to substantiate the theory of a definite evolutionary sequence on the basis of the study of survivals. All that can be said is that fragments of earlier historical stages are bound to exist and are found" (1924:342). Boas (343) illustrated the existence of these "fragments" with a discussion of the survival of matrilineal forms of kinship in patrilineal society: "this, however, does not by any means provide that everywhere matrilineal society must have been the earlier form."

What united Tylor and Boas was the idea of the "cultural trait" (Lyman and O'Brien 2003), which was instrumental in the thought of Herskovits (even though he claimed that he was critical of the idea at certain points), as well as implicated in the orientation of Ortiz, Price-Mars, and Ramos. So the way was left open for Herskovits to pursue the

idea of survivals in the context of historical-cultural particularism with
a focus on acculturation (Redfield, Linton, and Herskovits 1936).
Later, he refined this idea with the notion of "Africanisms" (see Baron
2003). After all, for Boas as well as Herskovits, under acculturation it
was still the *geist*, or "genius of a people," that molded borrowed elements to a traditional pattern—and Herskovits viewed this pattern as
"African." And in this he was consistent with the positions taken by
Ortiz, Price-Mars, and Ramos.

AN INTELLECTUAL SOCIAL FORMATION

Herskovits, Ortiz, Price-Mars, and Ramos, along with other social
scientists in various locations throughout the Americas, formed what
might be called an "intellectual social formation," one inhering in
"intellectual practices" (pace Mato 2002) and one that was international in membership. These were researchers who, from Brazil to
Puerto Rico, from Mexico to Haiti, from Cuba to the United States,
were interested in some aspect of the "Negro problem" and who
sought, with broadly similar theoretical lenses, to understand it vis-à-vis
an orientation to African survivals and a search for the cultural origins
of blacks in African preplantation-slavery "tribal" cultures. Not only did
this formation represent congruent perspectives within varying local
discourses of nationalism—by this I mean that the same argument on
African survivals could be put to different uses in the nationalist discourse of, say, Brazil as opposed to the United States, Haiti as opposed
to Cuba—but also these intellectual bonds were cemented by bonds of
a more personal nature: each of these scholars existed within a dense
social network of like-minded others, and they supported one another
(and one another's students and colleagues) in various ways.

Herskovits's activities not only consisted of writing but also no less
than an attempt to organize and define a subfield within anthropology. Here, a subfield means the definite development of a specialization
within an academic discipline, with specialized knowledge and training
being specified, core texts being identified, authorized histories being
written, and bodies of specialists being identified, all of which implies
boundary maintenance (see, e.g., Collier 1997). And, what is more, he
attempted to institutionalize a whole interdisciplinary research effort
under the rubric the "New World Negro." In the 1920s and 1930s, he

wrote a number of unsuccessful grant applications to fund large fieldwork projects and program development. In 1938 he founded the
Anthropology Department at Northwestern, becoming its chair and
recruiting graduate students who worked on the Afro-Americas and in
Africa.

In 1936 Herskovits applied to Frederick P. Keppel (1875–1943),
president of the Carnegie Corporation, for a large grant for funding a
substantial research project on Africa, the Caribbean, and the United
States. Herskovits did not know that, at that time, Keppel was trying to
choose someone to head a major study of the American Negro.
Herskovits was considered to direct the study but was then rejected
when Keppel heard a rumor that he was hard to work with. Keppel
wanted a foreign researcher in the mold of an Alexis de Tocqueville
(1805–1859), and he asked Herskovits for suggestions. Herskovits said
that if a foreign scholar were appointed to direct the project, it was
important for that scholar to be from a country without a history of
colonialism, and he suggested his friend the Swiss anthropologist
Alfred Métraux (1902–1963). Herskovits conspired with another
friend, sociologist Donald Young (1898–1977), to become part of the
project and direct a team of social scientists from the United States;
they also advocated the inclusion of African Americans such as Abram
Harris on the research team (W. Jackson 1990:26–31). Métraux wrote
for a specialized academic audience, and Keppel eventually decided
that he needed someone familiar with policy implementation. And so
it was Swedish economist Gunnar Myrdal (1898–1987) who was named
to direct the project that resulted in the classic book *An American
Dilemma* (Myrdal 1944). Herskovits was angry that he was not named to
head the study. As his former student Alvin W. Wolfe (b. 1928) recalled,
Herskovits felt that Myrdal was appointed "on the principle that ignorance is equivalent to objectivity" (author interview with Alvin Wolfe,
March 10, 1999). Ultimately, Myrdal did not care for Herskovits's
approach to African cultural survivals, and Herskovits himself disap-
proved of a policy orientation to scholarship. Myrdal hired thirty-one
researchers, including E. Franklin Frazier, who went on to do fieldwork
in Brazil, and Ruth Landes (1908–1991), who had just returned, to
write memoranda. A number of African American scholars were
included. Myrdal decided to include Herskovits for reasons of acade-

mic politics. Herskovits's memorandum turned out to be his classic work *The Myth of the Negro Past* (1941), completed in less than one year with the significant assistance of his wife and collaborator, Frances.

While basically excluded from the Carnegie project, Herskovits was approached by Waldo G. Leland (1879–1966), the secretary of the American Council of Learned Societies (ACLS), to establish a conference on Negro studies, intended to counter the Social Science Research Council (SSRC), which had been advising the Carnegie Corporation on the Myrdal Negro project. The conference, held at Howard University in 1940, and the ACLS's Committee on Negro Studies were designed to promote the ACLS's view of the humanities (O. Cunha n.d.; R. Harris 1982). Herskovits was named the chair of a committee of eight scholars, including Young, Klineberg, and the historian Richard Pattee (1906–1989) of the US State Department, an associate of Ramos's and the translator of Ramos's *O negro brasileiro* (Ramos 1934, 1939), as well as an associate of Ortiz and Price-Mars and a promoter of an appreciation of the contribution of blacks in Latin American and Caribbean national life (e.g., Pattee 1943). Three committee members, including the linguist Turner, who did fieldwork in Brazil in the 1940s, were black. Most of these scholars' theoretical views accorded with those of Herskovits. Herskovits tried to expand his empire by trying to create a joint committee on African and Negro studies with the ACLS, the SSRC, and the NRC. But the attempt failed when the SSRC refused to join, and therefore the ACLS limited the committee's purview to the history, literature, and culture of black people in the Americas.

During the decade the committee was in existence, it added and lost some members. Some black members pushed for a more activist approach to research and tried to organize a conference on discrimination against black scholars. When this happened, in 1950, Herskovits had the committee disbanded. (This situation was somewhat understandable, given Herskovits's views of applying anthropology. He held a dim view of applied anthropology when it was undertaken on behalf of an organization or group. This process, he felt, would challenge the anthropologist's scientific objectivity.[5] But ironically, the whole point of his *The Myth of the Negro Past* was to provide documentation that would give blacks pride in their past and inform whites of this past, thereby lessening racism.) During the 1940s, Herskovits was involved with Pattee, Ortiz, Price-Mars, and others to establish the short-lived Institute of Afroamerican Studies in Mexico City and the journal *Afroamérica*, of which only two issues appeared (O. Cunha n.d.). During this time, he was able to consolidate his position within the discipline, for example, becoming president of the American Folklore Society (1945), editor of the *Journal of American Folklore*, and, from 1948 to 1952, editor of the *American Anthropologist*. In 1948 he established the Program of African Studies at Northwestern.

There were academic challenges to be met. Perhaps best known is Herskovits's debate with E. Franklin Frazier (Frazier 1942, 1943; M. Herskovits 1943; see Whitten and Szwed 1970a). After publication of *The Myth*, Locke criticized Herskovits from the opposite direction from which he had criticized him in the *Survey Graphic* issue. In the era of assimilationist aims by black leadership, not all blacks would have welcomed Herskovits's arguments. Locke called *The Myth* "inevitably an important book," one in the vindicationist-revisionist genre that attempted to negate negative stereotypes of blacks. However, he took sharp issue with Herskovits's ameliorative reasoning in presenting evidence of cultural development: "It is argued that knowledge of this cultural background will lessen prejudice and rehabilitate the Negro considerably in American public opinion—a strangely moralistic corollary, arguing well for the author's humanity but scarcely realistic enough to justify this moralistic departure from scientific objectivity" (Locke 1942:87).

The charge against his scientific objectivity would have been a blow because Herskovits saw himself as upholding objective scientific standards. For example, Du Bois had proposed to edit an *Encyclopedia of the Negro* as early as 1931, but Herskovits, worried that activists would be involved and would be less than scientific, engaged in a letter-writing campaign behind the scenes to undermine the project, even though he was on good personal terms with Du Bois, had used his personal library when researching his Ph.D. dissertation, and later interceded on Du Bois's behalf in his dispute with Atlanta University (see MHP, Box 7, Folder 19; cf. Gershenhorn 2004; D. Lewis 2000). Louis E. King, his assistant in his NRC study, applied for a position under Du Bois at Atlanta University, but Herskovits wrote a letter very critical of King's abilities, effectively ending King's chance for an academic career (on King, see I. Harrison 1999). And Herskovits was initially supportive of Katherine Dunham (b. 1909) and directed her fieldwork in the Caribbean but was less enthusiastic once she became an initiate in the Vodou religion; Hurston, who had applied for the grant that Dunham received, seemed to feel that Herskovits did not do all that was possible to help her cause (Aschenbrenner 2002; Helbling 1999; Hemenway 1977; Ramsey 2000). Some have charged that Herskovits tended to exclude black students, seeing them as not objective enough to study Africa or Afro-America (e.g., Skinner 1999:57). At least one former student, Johnnetta Betsch Cole (b. 1936), seemed to agree (see Yelvington 2003d; but see Gershenhorn 2004). The number of black students who were recruited during his career and received their doctorates in anthropology was substantial for the time (Bledsoe, personal communication, 2005).

But there were also signs of heterodoxy from within this social formation. In 1936 Robert Redfield, Ralph Linton, and Herskovits published their "Memorandum on Acculturation" in various journals (e.g., Redfield, Linton, and Herskovits 1936), and in 1938 Herskovits published his book *Acculturation*, reflecting his major orientation to the study of cultures in contact. However, in his *Contrapunteo cubano* (1940), Ortiz jettisoned the term *acculturation* and invented the term *transculturación*:

> I am of the opinion that the word *transculturation* better expresses the different phases of the process of transition from one culture to another because this does not consist merely in acquiring another culture, which is what the English word *acculturation* really implies, but the process also necessarily involves the loss or uprooting of a previous culture, which could be defined as a deculturation. In addition it carries the idea of the consequent creation of new cultural phenomena, which could be called neoculturation. ([1947] 1995:102–103)

In his introduction, Bronislaw Malinowski (1884–1942), who had become Ortiz's associate, went even further. *Acculturation*, he claimed, was an ethnocentric word with a moral connotation. The immigrant has to *acculturate* himself; so do the natives, pagan or heathen, barbarian or savage, who enjoy the benefits of being under the sway of our great Western culture....The "uncultured" is to receive the benefits of "our culture"; it is he who must change and become converted into "one of us."

Transculturation, on the other hand,

> provides us with a term that does not contain the implication of one certain culture toward which the other must tend, but an exchange between two cultures, both of them active, both contributing their share, and both co-operating to bring about a new reality of civilization (Malinowski [1947] 1995:lviii, lix).

Of course, this critique occurred in the context of academic politics (Coronil 1995). Even though Herskovits had brought Malinowski to Northwestern for a series of lectures in 1933 (W. Jackson 1986: 110–111), Malinowski had in 1939 published a lengthy review article that was critical of Herskovits's book *Acculturation* (M. Herskovits 1938; cf. Malinowski 1939). When Herskovits received his copy of *Contrapunteo cubano* and read the remarks in the introduction by Malinowski, he wrote to Ortiz, strenuously objecting to what he felt was a misunderstanding of his use of the term *acculturation* (MHP, Box 17, Folder 15).

Despite these events, there were also crucial moments of closing ranks and boundary maintenance. This maintenance occurred in Herskovits and his associates' dealings with American anthropologist Ruth Landes, a student of Boas and Benedict at Columbia who received her Ph.D. there in 1935 (see Cole 2003; Corrêa 2000; Healey 1998; Matory 2003). Landes did fieldwork in Bahia, Brazil, for eight months in 1938–1939, after a year of apprenticeship doing teaching and research at Fisk University, suggested by sociologist Robert E. Park (1864–1944). At Fisk, she was assisted by Park's student Donald Pierson (1900–1995), who shared Brazilian materials with her. Pierson had worked in Bahia in 1935–1937 (Pierson 1942). Upon Landes's arrival, she paid her due respects to Ramos, by now the gatekeeper of Afro-Brazilian studies. She also met up with Édison Carneiro (1912–1972), a mulatto journalist and amateur ethnographer of Afro-Brazilian religions who was known to Ramos (see Oliveira and Lima 1987). Landes and Carneiro immediately formed a fieldwork partnership and ultimately a love affair. For whatever reason—sexual jealousy, racism, shock over a perceived lack of propriety or a perceived lack of deference—this turn of events apparently riled Ramos. Landes's writings on Afro-Brazilian cults (Landes 1940a, 1940b, 1947) and the attention she paid to the homosexuality of many male cult leaders prompted Ramos to malign Landes publicly and privately. He began to spread rumors about Landes's supposed unethical fieldwork conduct and her supposed many sexual adventures. Sally Cole, Landes's biographer (1994, 1995, 2003), describes her project and how it ran counter to anthropological paradigms:

> Landes chose as her ethnographic focus the woman-centered Afro-Brazilian spirit-possession religion, *candomblé*, and began participant-observation that contextualized candomblé in local history and politics. This theoretical and methodological approach ran counter to peer efforts within American anthropology that employed the concept of culture as static, internally consistent, and outside history and that interpreted Afro-American culture in terms of African survivals. Landes's theorizing of gender and sexuality, particularly as it yielded descriptions of women ritual leaders and male homosexuality, intensified the controversies surrounding her work. (Cole 1995:168)

Landes left Brazil not necessarily of her own volition and next tried to take up a position in the Myrdal "Negro in America" project. Myrdal sought to incorporate, or at least not alienate, established scholars of Afro-America (W. Jackson 1990). According to sociologist Guy Benton Johnson (1901–1989), who worked closely with Myrdal on the project, Landes showed up one day in 1939 at the project offices in New York, saying that Benedict had said that she had been offered a job. Johnson went to see Ralph Linton (1893–1953), the chair of the Anthropology Department at Columbia. Linton said that he had heard of Landes's troubles in Brazil. He said, according to Johnson, "she was getting involved with too many men in her studies of some of these Brazilian cults and what-not and was getting to be a little too much of a participant, and the government just frankly got worried about her safety and told her that they preferred that she give up and go home." Linton said, "I know this, and this is why she came home, and she and Benedict are just trying to pressure Myrdal for a job" (Grossner 1967:29–32).

Linton obviously had already heard the rumors, and his reaction could also have been based on his known and intense hostility toward Benedict, Landes's sponsor (Mintz 1981:161). It is likely that Linton and others heard rumors about Landes from a well-placed American anthropologist in contact with Ramos. The circumstantial evidence points to Herskovits, even though he had not met Ramos personally yet. In fact, Herskovits had seen Landes as competition before she had gone to Brazil. As early as August 1937, Benedict was writing to Boas, wondering whether "Papa Franz" could take occasion to "mollify Mel about Ruth Landes going to make the negro study in Bahia." Landes was applying for a Rosenwald Fund grant, and, given Herskovits's connections with foundations, Benedict said, "I wish Mel could be won over to saying a good word for her. I don't know his objections to her work in Bahia," and she presumed that Herskovits's objections were for reasons of theoretical orthodoxy, that "he feels no one should go until he has been in Nigeria. Of course Ruth would love to go to Nigeria first!" (Franz Boas Papers, Benedict to Boas, August 24, 1937, p. 2). In addition, Herskovits had heard rumors of Landes's having an affair with an older, married, black colleague at Fisk from his associate Rüdiger Bilden (1893–1980), who had trained at Columbia in history and political science, had written on Brazil as a racially democratic "laboratory of civilization" (1929), and was training Landes informally in New York and later at Fisk for her Brazil study (MHP, Box 3, Folder 26).

When Landes showed up at the Carnegie study offices, Myrdal felt that he could not afford to alienate Benedict, so Myrdal and Johnson employed Landes to write what became a research memo titled "The Ethos of the Negro in the New World" (Landes 1940c). The manuscript was completed in late 1939. In January 1940, the project sent the memorandum to several scholars, including Herskovits and Ramos, for comment. Landes had begun corresponding with Herskovits upon her return from Brazil, asking for advice and sharing her observations on Brazil. She also told him that upon her suggestion, the Carnegie project would be sending him her manuscript for comments, which it did (MHP, Box 12, Folder 13). Herskovits replied to Johnson's request for comments that he had been "so terribly busy" with the memo he was writing for the project (which became *The Myth of the Negro Past*) that he was returning the manuscript "without having done more than to page through it." He did aver to comment, however, that "[w]hat I cannot understand is how the concept of ethos helps in such a study, or how in her approach she has done anything other than the most conventional student of culture traits would have done in running them down" (MHP, Box 14, Folder 2). Ramos, on the other hand, replied to the Myrdal team with a scathing appraisal of Landes's memorandum, a copy of which he promptly sent to Herskovits (MHP, Box 19, Folder 14). He followed up with a chapter in a subsequent book devoted to tearing apart the research and person of Landes (Ramos 1942:181–195).

Meanwhile, Landes was dropped from the project. A Carnegie internal staff list shows her salary as two hundred dollars a month from July 10 until November 10, 1939, but it notes her performance as "unsatisfactory" (Carnegie Corporation Archives, Series 1, Box 260, 1943). The project did not expect to hire her. She was taken on short term, mainly for political reasons, because she was Benedict's student, and given the task of "covering" the project on "culture" and "cultural history." As Johnson said, "It was a difficult subject, almost an impossible subject; and of course she did about as well with it as anybody could be expected to do" (Grossner 1967:32), but it did not fit in well with what Myrdal had in mind. Her fate on the project was sealed before Herskovits's reaction and Ramos's review of her memo, but perhaps not before the rumors reported by Linton had affected the project staff's opinion. A staff meeting memo of January 23, 1940, declared that "Dr. Ruth Landes is a finished chapter" (Guy B. Johnson Papers). In this climate, Landes could not find an academic publisher for her book, *The City of Women*. When Macmillan did publish it in 1947, it marketed it as a trade book. It was reviewed, however, in academic journals. Herskovits reviewed it in the flagship journal *American Anthropologist*, providing a harsh and dismissive evaluation (M. Herskovits 1948b). Landes became an academic nomad and did not obtain a full-time

FIGURE 2.5

Arthur Ramos. From the Daily Northwestern *(February 19, 1941), p. 1. Courtesy of Northwestern University Archives.*

academic appointment until she was hired at McMaster University in 1965—at age fifty-seven, thirty years after her Ph.D.—and that was on the strength of her later work among the Ojibwa (e.g., Landes 1937, 1938).[6]

CONCLUSION

By way of conclusion, I want to make three points briefly. The first is that the history of anthropology might be studied anthropologically, wherein the social groupings of intellectual workers, as well as the institutional matrices and regimes of rewards governing their practice, serve as the starting point for understanding the shape of knowledge production. In the history of Afro-American anthropology, these groupings were transnational in nature, and such a realization might require a rethinking of the development of the discipline as a whole to

FIGURE 2.6

Ruth Landes in 1939 (Golde 1970:117). Reprinted by permission of Aldine Transaction, a division of Transaction Publishers.

emphasize how anthropologies cross borders. These border crossings have their own history. In the late 1920s and early 1930s, given Herskovits's new, wider interest in the diaspora, not only within but also beyond the United States, later enshrined in his concept the "New World Negro," it is natural that Herskovits would have sought out ethnographic work on the subject. The question becomes, What work was Herskovits aware of and when, and how was this work reflected in his own thought? Ortiz and Price-Mars did not convert the younger scholar, but their work informed his, confirming for him many of his propositions and providing evidence for his programmatic statements on the New World Negro. At the same time, Herskovits's influence on them, as well as the legitimacy conferred by his leadership of an international intellectual social formation dedicated to the study of "Africa" in the nations of the Americas, can be discerned. Later, in

FIGURE 2.7

Édison Carneiro in Bahia in 1939. Photo by Ruth Landes. Ruth Landes Papers, National Anthropological Archives, Smithsonian Institution.

tandem with Ramos, Herskovits was becoming more established, more able to control fonts of academic cultural capital, and his energies were devoted to gatekeeping strategies of inclusion and exclusion.

Following on from this, the second point is that the claim that social scientific theories are the result purely of conceptual systems within the science can no longer be sustained. Despite how knowledge claims are represented to dilute the salience of political forces and contexts, anthropologists such as Herskovits and his interlocutors had an interest in maintaining the appearance that "the data" were straight-forwardly "out there" to be collected and made sense of. Herskovits never seems to have acknowledged their influence on his emerging *theoretical* perspective but rather seems to have seen them as self-taught ethnologists who were simply documenting what was before their eyes. And third, the goal of making the history of anthropology relevant for contemporary ethnographic practice requires working backward from the present in order to interrogate how received theoretical appara-tuses came to be, and under what conditions they are evaluated—in other words, seeing the relationship underlying historical phenomena such as anthropological theories as one of preconditions and results.

The foregoing rehistoricization of key moments in the making of Afro-American anthropology was not done out of some adherence to Santayana's oft-quoted warning: "Those who cannot remember the past are condemned to repeat it." Nor was it, on the other hand, a call to return to that past, to uncritically (re)appropriate what we define at this point as useful or expedient. It is rather to be seen as a first step in an active re-engagement with Afro-American peoples and cultures through an understanding of the historical-contextual and political basis of anthropological endeavors. As David Scott (1991:262–263) writes: "[I]f anthropology, in its capacity as the science of culture, has been able to claim for itself, or have claimed for it, the role of a high-er or more foundational authority in the matter of cultural difference, then there is an initial labor of internal, disciplinary interrogation to be carried out, a prior critical accounting for the kind of theoretical object this anthropology establishes and circulates in its authoritative texts on the cultural practices of peoples of African descent in the New World." The challenge remains for us to fashion a critical anthropolo-gy in dialogue with the past of the discipline, more fully aware of the conditions of the production of anthropological knowledge.

Notes

Some of the research for this chapter was funded by grants from the Mellon Foundation and the Latin American and Caribbean Center, Florida International University, by a University of Florida Library Travel Grant from the Center for Latin American Studies, by a Presidential Young Faculty Award from the University of South Florida (USF), and by grants from the Latin American and

Caribbean Studies Program and the Humanities Institute, USF. I also appreciate the support of Jane I. Guyer, then director of the Program of African Studies, Northwestern University.

A number of archivists and librarians have been extremely kind and helpful in assisting with my research. I would like to thank Stellan Andersson and Klaus Misgeld of the Arbetarrörelsens Arkiv och Bibliotek, Stockholm, Sweden; Katheryn Beam, Special Collections Librarian, Hatcher Library, University of Michigan; Andrea Beauchamp, Program Assistant, Hopwood Awards Program, University of Michigan; Suzanne Calpestri, John Rowe Librarian at the George and Mary Foster Library of Anthropology, University of California-Berkeley; Rachel Canada, Departmental Assistant, Manuscripts Department, Southern Historical Collection, University of North Carolina–Chapel Hill; Lori Cavagnaro and Mary Marshall Clark, Columbia University Oral History Office; David L. Easterbrook, George and Mary LeCron Foster Curator at the Melville J. Herskovits Library of African Studies, Northwestern University; André Elizée, Diana Lachatañeré, and the staff at the Schomburg Center for Research in Black Culture of the New York Public Library; Joellen El Bashir of the Moorland-Spingarn Research Center, Howard University; Christraud M. Geary and Carol Maryan-George of the Eliot Elisofon Photographic Archives, Smithsonian Institution, National Museum of African Art; Brenda Hearing, Curator, Carnegie Corporation Archives, Columbia University; John P. Homiak, Daisy Njoku, and Jeannie Sklar of the National Anthropological Archives, Smithsonian Institution; James Lambert of the Université Laval Archives; Janet C. Olson, Allen J. Streicker, Kevin B. Leonard, and Patrick M. Quinn at the Northwestern University Archives; Richard Phillips, Head, and the staff of the Latin American Collection at the University of Florida libraries; William Roberts, University Archivist, Bancroft Library, University of California-Berkeley; Naomi Schultz of the University of California-Berkeley Archives; William John Shepherd Sr., Assistant Archivist, Catholic University of America; and the interlibrary loan department at USF for their considerable assistance, as well as the officials at the National Library of Jamaica, the Jamaica Archives, the libraries of the University of the West Indies in Jamaica and Trinidad, the British Library Newspaper Library, the British Library, and the Public Record Office.

I would like to thank all the advanced seminar participants for their insightful comments on the first draft of this chapter. Their criticisms and suggestions have been taken seriously and with much appreciation, and I hope that I have competently incorporated their constructive advice. I also acknowledge that advanced seminar participants Faye V. Harrison, J. Lorand Matory, Arlene Torres, and Peter Wade helped in important ways in the conceptual stage of writing this chapter, as did Lillian Guerra. Alejandro de la Fuente generously shared rare research material and offered his guidance. The following people have provided important advice, information, sources, and other kinds of support, and I thank them all very much: Amina Alio, Patricia Alio, Laura Álvarez López, Andrew Apter, Lance Arney, A. James Arnold, Anete Arslanian, Lee D. Baker, Robert Baron, the late Berta Bascom, Greg Beckett, Bernadete Beserra, Kevin K. Birth, Caroline H. Bledsoe, A. Lynn Bolles, Yarimar Bonilla, Erika Bourguignon, Bridget Brereton, Vincent Brown, Lambros Comitas, Johnnetta B. Cole, Sally Cole, Justine Cordwell, Mariza Corrêa, Lauren R. Derby, Ellie Duplass, Mary Ebeling, Amos Esty, James W. Fernández, Thomas Fiehrer, Kesha Fikes, Carolyn Fluehr-Lobban, Katherine Fouché, Gelya Frank, John D. French, Christraud M. Geary, Jerry Gershenhorn, Jorge L. Giovanetti, Olívia Maria Gomes da Cunha, Neill G. Goslin, Andrew Green, Jane I. Guyer, Peter Hammond, Richard Handler, Jack Harris, Faye V. Harrison, Ira E. Harrison, Mark Alan Healey, Jean Herskovits, Rosemarijn Hoefte, Max Hunter, Antoinette T. Jackson, Walter A. Jackson, Francisco Jarque Andrés, Thomas LePere, Herbert S. Lewis, Angela Lühning, Gérarde Magloire, Marcos Chor Maio, the late Louis Mars, Bill Maurer, Kate Mazurek, Amy McGhee, Keith McNeal, Kym Morrison, Roberto Motta, Sidney W. Mintz, Viranjini Munasinghe, Annie Ngana Mundeke, John V. Murra, Janelle M. Novak, Sylvester Okwunodu Ogbechie, Simon Ottenberg, Richard Pattee Jr., Stephan Palmié, Fernanda Arêas Peixoto, David H. Price, Richard Price, Sally Price, Isabel Pruna Lamadrid, Kate Ramsey, João José Reis, Carole Rennick, Leah Rosenberg, Lioba Rossbach de Olmos, Livio Sansone, David Scott, Lyle W. Shannon, the late Magdaline W. Shannon, Leni M. Silverstein, Arnold A. Sio, Melford E. Spiro, George W. Stocking Jr., Verena Stolke, Hans F. Vermeulen, Estella Walsh, Gene Walsh, Patricia Waterman, Andrew Hunter Whiteford, Lois Turner Williams, Drexel G. Woodson, Alvin W. Wolfe, and especially Bárbara C. Cruz. And to anyone I've forgotten to mention, a heartfelt thanks.

1. For intellectual biographies of Herskovits, see W. Jackson (1986) and Simpson (1973) and, more comprehensively, Baron (1994) and Gershenhorn (2004). Another important source is Merriam's (1964) obituary published in *American Anthropologist*. Accompanying the obituary is a complete list of Herskovits's publications.

2. Historians of anthropology outside the United States have not failed to see the transnational connections in the development of Afro-American anthropology. Some works that may be consulted fruitfully include Bronfman (2004); Corrêa (1987b, 1988, 1998, 2003); Dianteill (1995, 2000); Fernandes (1958);

Figueiredo (2002); Massi (Peixoto) (1989); Palmié (2002); Peixoto (2000); and Rodríguez-Mangual (2004).

3. Those readers steeped in the controversies in the historiography of anthropology will recognize this as a statement on the "historicism" versus "presentism" debate. Stocking (1965) laid down the terms of the debate four decades ago. See Yelvington (2003b) for a position on what I see as an inevitable presentism.

4. Herskovits wrote in English, and these scholars wrote in their own languages (Ortiz in Spanish, Price-Mars in French, and Ramos in Portuguese). Their words have been translated here.

5. On Herskovits's views of applied anthropology, see Herskovits (1936b). See the remarks by his student Alvin Wolfe in Yelvington (2003c).

6. Landes came to write about her experiences, relying as well on Carneiro's (1964) defense of her in print. She said that "late in 1939" Ramos and "an American ally," meaning Herskovits, "wrote a voluminous letter about me to Gunnar Myrdal, for whom I was working in New York on his American Negro study, and he showed me the letter while ridiculing its fixation on my alleged eroticism and incompetent scholarship" (Landes 1970:128; see also Park and Park 1989). I have not been able to locate this letter in the Ramos papers in Rio de Janeiro, in the Landes papers in Washington, in the Carnegie Corporation Negro Study Archives in New York, in the Myrdal papers in Stockholm, or in the Herskovits papers in Evanston.

---

*The caption (see figure 2.1) to this photo in W. Jackson (1986:96) describes it as "Melville Herskovits holding a West African religious artefact." Mintz and Price (1992:ix–x) comment: "In fact, however, the sacred object that Herskovits holds (as well as the stool, the firefan, the wooden implements on the table before him, and the stool directly above his head) were made not in West Africa, but by Saramaka Maroons in Suriname (where he collected them with Frances Herskovits in 1928 and 1929), more than two centuries after the ancestors of the Saramaka were forcibly transported from their West and Central African homelands. Herskovits, much of whose life was spent trying to plumb the cultural relationships between Africa and the Americas, would probably approve of having this Old World/New World clarification placed on record here."

3

Seaming Connections

Artworlds of the African Diaspora

Sally Price

This chapter considers interpretations of visual art in societies of
the African diaspora, setting them within the context of recent theoretical shifts in the disciplines of anthropology and art history/criti-
cism. I will be arguing for the relevance to Afro-American studies of
these broader disciplinary changes, which have fundamentally reori-
ented scholarship on arts that, for the most part, fall outside what
Joseph Alsop (1982) has dubbed "The Great Traditions." Toward that
end, I begin with a general assessment of these theoretical shifts
("Anthropology and Art History Shake Hands"), before moving into an
exploration of their impact on Afro-American studies ("Mapping the
Afro-American Artworld"). I then adopt a still narrower focus ("Seaming
African American Connections"), looking at historical interpretations of
what we might (or might not) consider a single medium—the stitched-
together fabrics on clothing (among Maroons), quilts (in the southern
United States), and gallery art (in work by such artists as Faith
Ringgold, Emma Amos [plate 1], and Joyce Scott)—in order to assess
scholars' readings of the relationship between these forms and the
edge-sewn textile traditions of Africa, and the uses scholars have made

of those readings in drawing broader conclusions about the culture history of the African diaspora. Finally, I offer some thoughts on the conceptual and methodological approaches that might be most promising for future studies of artworlds in the African diaspora as a whole ("Zooming in, Zooming Out").

ANTHROPOLOGY AND ART HISTORY SHAKE HANDS

Looking first at shifts in the field of "fine arts" over the past two decades or so, I would argue that the increased attention to art *worlds* (or, in the writing of Arthur C. Danto [1964] and others, "artworlds") ranks at the very top of the list. The complex workings—social, cultural, economic, political—that give structure, texture, and (contested or uncontested) meaning to the more traditional matters of objects and their collective history have been moving steadily into greater prominence. Both scholarly and popular writing on art have been engaging in energetic scrutiny of museum ethics, curatorial strategies, auction politics, market dynamics, collecting agendas, and the complex hierarchy of connoisseurship and authority. Artworks once viewed as visual entities set into more or less elaborate wooden borders are now being framed in a completely different sense, as contextualized productions undergoing contextualized readings. Setting art objects, artists' biographies, and the evolution of stylistic sequences more forcefully in the context of perceptions conditioned by social and cultural factors brings them closer to long-standing anthropological concerns and interests and acts to erode the lingering temptation (stronger for some commentators than others) to view art history as the pristine, apolitical study of aesthetic forms. And sacred territories of art historical scholarship, where original works authenticated by erudite connoisseurship once held pride of place, are being quietly invaded by a growing interest in copies, fakes, appropriations, and derivative forms.

Approaches to "ethnographic" art have also undergone what we might consider sea changes over the same period. Especially pivotal has been a diminished focus on cultural isolates; just as art history/criticism has been widening its aperture on works of art, the study of societies and cultures is being set in broader fields of vision, with important repercussions for the anthropological study of art. While scholars once strained to discern the stylistic essences of particular arts in particular cultures, they are now directing their gaze more frequently toward the doorways where artistic and aesthetic ideas jostle one another in their passage from one cultural setting to the next. While the emphasis was once on abstracting back from an overlay of modernity to discover uncorrupted artistic traditions (Franz Boas holding up a blanket to block out the two-story houses behind the Kwakiutl natives he was filming for the anthropological record [PBS 1988]), modernization now lies at the heart of the enterprise, providing a springboard for explorations of cultural creativity and self-affirmation. While the site of artistic production was once located in lineages of convention within bounded communities, it now spreads into the global arena, pulling in players from every corner of the world, from every kind of society, and from every chamber of the artworld's vast honeycomb.

Not surprisingly, these shifts are being accompanied by a marked, if gradual, rapprochement among the various sectors of the popular and scholarly artworlds. In museums, the most visible evidence has been an explosion, over the past decade or two, of exhibitions integrating anthropological and art historical issues and scholarship, juxtaposing arts from previously segregated categories, and calling attention to the defining (and redefining) power of display context. Concern with the ethics of cultural ownership is also moving center stage, thanks largely to the rising volume of voices coming from third and fourth world populations, cultural studies programs, and spectators of the postmodern scene from the fields of literature, history, philosophy, economics, and political science. Rights of interpretation are under lively discussion; cultural authority is being renegotiated; the privileged status of long-established canons is under attack; and museum acquisition policies designed to maximize the preservation of data and the growth of scientific knowledge are being contested by more ethically focused debates aimed at responsible de-accessioning and repatriation.

We are also witnessing, across the board, a growing tendency for the hierarchies that assigned distinct roles (and value) to fine and folk, art and craft, primitive and modern, high and low, to give way to investigations of these categories' interpenetrations and an insistent deconstruction of the categories themselves. This change is especially important for the debates before us in this volume, simply because writing on African diaspora arts has spread over these categories more (that is, has privileged one particular category less) than, say, writing on European or African or Far Eastern arts. While it would not be grossly off the mark to depict European art history as devoting its primary attention to the "fine" arts, African art history to "tribal" (or "primitive" or whatever label people use for the "not-so-fine") arts, and Central American art history to "folk" arts, people writing on arts of the African diaspora have shown a greater tendency to become as comfortable in one such category as another.

Although these changes are multifaceted in the extreme, they all operate in the direction of breaking down barriers—barriers between disciplinary perspectives, between geographical focuses, between hierarchized settings, between elite and popular media, and more. The signposts and contributing agents are too myriad to enumerate exhaustively here, but a few key markers will serve to evoke the general trend over the past decade or two. In 1984 prestigious art museums of New York City, from the Museum of Modern Art to the Metropolitan, hosted simultaneous celebrations of "tribal and modern affinities" in art, Maori art (organized by Maori curators and inaugurated with ceremonies that included nose-rubbing greetings between Mayor Koch and Maori elders flown in from New Zealand), Ashanti artifacts crafted from gold (for which the mayor returned as ceremonial host, this time in a massive parade through Central Park), Indian art from the Pacific Northwest, and arts of African adornment (see S. Price 1988). The Center for African Art opened its doors for the first time, and both Sotheby's and Christie's held large, mediatized auctions of "primitive" art. The next year, the College Art Association added sessions on anthropological themes to its annual meeting for the first time. In 1988 and 1989, the Smithsonian sponsored major symposia exploring the role of museums in a rapidly evolving social and cultural environment (Karp, Kreamer, and Lavine 1992; Karp and Lavine 1991). In 1990 National Public Radio, in collaboration with the Mexican Museum of San Francisco, formed the impeccably multicultural Working Group on a New American Sensibility to discuss the same range of issues for radio.[1]

Meanwhile, Paris's global-art extravaganza, Magiciens de la Terre, had been propelled into the center of a heated debate over its not totally successful realization of an uncategorized embrace of "the arts of the world" (Centre Georges Pompidou 1989). Since then, the city has hosted several large-scale, international conferences designed to explore ethical and legal issues concerning cultural property, repatriation, and the like (see, e.g., Galard 2001; Taffin 2000; Vaillant and Viatte 1999). In the Netherlands, museum scholars have been asking hard questions about the political and ethical dimensions of museum displays (see, e.g., Bouquet 1999; Leyton 1995; Leyton and Damen 1993). In England, Routledge has been bringing out one after another volume devoted to the same series of issues (see, e.g., Barringer and Flynn 1998; Greenberg, Ferguson, and Nairne 1996). In Switzerland, nineteen contributors to an exhibit-cum-book titled *L'art c'est l'art (Art Is Art)* reflected on this whole bundle of issues, including contact zones, cultural strategies behind today's art critical discourse, the international traffic in art, the classificatory transfer of objects from "ethnography" to "art," and the overlaps in categories of art such as "*contemporain, appliqué, populaire, classique, pompier, pauvre, transgressif, convenu*" (Gonseth, Hainard, and Kaehr 1999). And on literally every continent, community museums, with vigorous local participation, have sprung up in unprecedented numbers, providing active loci for grassroots cultural creativity and self-representation.

The metaphor that many recent commentators have adopted to reflect this gaze on the artworlds of a planetwide network evokes a jet-age scenario of travel, with or without cultural baggage: titles refer to art "in transit" (Steiner 1994), the "traffic" in culture (Marcus and Myers 1995), "unpacking" culture (Phillips and Steiner 1999), "destination" culture (Kirshenblatt-Gimblett 1998), and the like. Performance artist Guillermo Gómez-Peña (1996:6) captured the flavor of this trend when he painted himself as migrant/smuggler: "Home is always somewhere else. Home is both 'here' and 'there' or somewhere in between. Sometimes it's nowhere....Here/there, homelessness, border culture, and deterritorialization are the dominant experience." In short, Jim Clifford (1997) was not acting alone when, with a flick of the pen and a wink of the eye, he shifted the gaze from roots to routes.

In the mid-1980s, when all these developments were just getting off to a roaring start, there was a real danger that even as new kinds of art were being graciously admitted to elite establishment settings, the conceptual perspectives and aesthetic frameworks of the artists and critics responsible for providing them were being kept out. When the sculpture was from Oceania, the interpretive text was still, more often than not, from a mainstream Northern Hemisphere tradition of discourse. Although this discrepancy has not disappeared, it is beginning to come under more explicit attack, and there seems to be some promise of change. Commentators across the board have noted, quite poignantly, that a central sticking point of every artworld, mainstream or otherwise, is the question of artists' control over meaning—or lack thereof (see, e.g., Belting 1987; Lippard 1990; Marcus 1995; Sullivan 1995). Supplying the product is one thing; having a say over what it represents (aesthetically, iconographically, referentially, historically) is quite another. As we will see below, the struggle over this issue is becoming an active part of new directions in the study of art in the African diaspora.

MAPPING THE AFRO-AMERICAN ARTWORLD

None of the developments outlined above were even distant rumblings when Melville J. Herskovits pioneered the study of African diaspora cultures in the 1930s. A quick mini-flashback to the environment that nurtured his vision and the ways that he applied and refashioned it will serve as backdrop for a consideration of interpretations that both refined and modified that vision in the very different political, social, and intellectual climate of our own recent fin de siècle.

Herskovits's teacher Franz Boas, even while stressing the conservatism of "primitive art" and the heavy weight of tradition on its makers, radically rephrased the task of understanding such art by placing the artist, rather than the object, at center stage. Boas insisted on thorough, firsthand field research, on the elicitation of native explanations, on attention to the "play of the imagination" ([1908] 1940:589) and the role of virtuosity, and on consideration of the artistic process as well as the finished form. In this context, the development over time of cultural expression (such as verbal, musical, or visual arts) was not, as previous generations of scholars had often assumed or argued, a reflection of unilinear human evolution but rather a more complex mixture of diffusion, borrowing, independent invention, and a host of other processes effected by individuals both following the guidelines of their respectively inherited traditions and gently adapting them under the influence of their creative impulses and their lived experiences, which included modest amounts of intercultural contact. In the regnant anthropological models of Herskovits's training, individuals were beginning to be recognized as something more than passive executors of an inevitable march from savagery to barbarism to civilization, but they remained firmly anchored in the cultural heritages of their birth, despite the leeway of individual difference and variable amounts of stimulation from "outside."[2]

In the context of this volume, it is hardly necessary to spell out the ways that Herskovits built on this general foundation, developing ideas such as "retention," "syncretism," and "reinterpretation." Suffice it to say that such concepts served to bring a comprehensible sense of order, helping him deal with the history of a social and cultural universe unlike any of those confronted by his anthropological predecessors (or even his peers)—one built by vast numbers of people wrenched from the settings of their birth, transported far away in death-drenched hordes, and forced to mold a viable way of life in cooperation with others from different settings who had undergone the same recent trauma. Unlike the work of American Indianists of his generation, which involved the analytical reconstruction of decimated cultural wholes (Boas's goal of abstracting back past modernity to reach a vision of what had once been a viable "authentic" culture), Herskovits's task centered on both loss and creativity, both rupture and continuity. Interpreting the world of Africans in the Americas was a new challenge, requiring the invention of new analytical tools, and those that Herskovits fashioned on the basis of his training and his multiple field experiences allowed him to propose models for cultural transitions of a rapidity unprecedented and unparalleled in the anthropological record.

Within this vision, history often took the form of continent-to-continent processes, involving peoples more than people and discernible largely through culture-to-culture comparisons. The historical study of art, which constituted part of the enterprise, followed suit. Artistic specificities in the New World tended to be explained in terms of more or less direct linkages to particular or generalized African origins more than to cultural developments in particular or generalized environments in the Americas, though the latter came into play as well.

Still fast-forwarding through developments that need no elaboration in the present volume, we zip past Herskovits's debate with E. Franklin Frazier (see Yelvington's and Singleton's chapters in this volume for contextualization) and pause at the Mintz and Price (1992) position just long enough to note its attempt to sharpen our vision of early cultural processes. Not eschewing Herskovits's claims for the importance of African input (as some commentators have imagined) but rather applying new standards for tracing the nature of intercontinental connections, Mintz and Price endorsed a position more firmly anchored in nonspeculative history and more concerned with the actual mechanics of cultural process (in specific places, at specific historical periods, under specific conditions of colonial rule). They benefited, of course, from a wealth of ethnographic information that had not been available to Herskovits, but they were also writing at a time when many of their arguments had to be presented in programmatic terms. What they offered were suggestive leads that, when submitted to the test of further historical and ethnographic research, held the chance of producing a closer, more verifiable vision of the ways that real people, both individually and as groups, worked out cultural solutions to the challenges posed by their remarkable collective ordeal.

One linchpin of their argument came straight from Herskovits. "To trace Africanisms in the behavior of [US] American Negroes," he wrote, "comparison with the Negroes of the Caribbean must be made before we can think of correlation with the complexities of West African civilizations" ([1935] 1966:169). The range of ethnographic sites he incorporated into his research reflected his firm commitment to the importance of thinking in broad comparative terms; his gaze on the arts was no exception. But in many subsequent studies of art, following through on the kind of all-encompassing spread that Herskovits attempted to include in his ethnographic field (spanning, on this side of the Atlantic, Brazil, Haiti, coastal and interior Suriname, Trinidad, the United States, Cuba, and more) has frequently provided the icing more than the cake.[3] The widespread tendency to conceptualize "Afro- or African America" as "Afro- or African USA" has been responsible for limiting the scope of any number of comprehensive art surveys when more robust attention to regional comparison could have significantly enhanced the country-based insights. Widely read books such as

Samella Lewis's *African American Art and Artists* (1990) and Sharon Patton's *African-American Art* (1998), which fail to mention even the most influential of Caribbean artists, such as Wifredo Lam, show how persistent this tendency is, even among experienced scholars writing authoritative texts for today's market.[4]

Herskovits's call for a broad geographical definition of our responsibilities needs to be complemented by a parallel call for breadth in our disciplinary and "typological" vision of the field. Partly because of all the "traffic" that recent scholars have underscored and partly because of the new prominence of crossover influences (folk/fine, and so on), scholars have begun to reflect increased awareness of the extent to which the study of art in this or that setting leaves important factors out of the picture.[5] The "affinities" between Picasso's art and African masks or the surrealists' love affair with the Pacific Northwest and Oceania in the early part of the twentieth century could be analyzed in terms of a "here" (homes, galleries, museums, and studios in Europe and the United States) and a "there" (remote settlements far away), with selected objects being transported along a one-way route. But artworld traffic now runs along a much busier thoroughfare—in terms of cultural geography, in terms of the hierarchy of traditional art scholarship, in terms of the division between producers and commentators, and in terms of media. It is no longer a one-way route, it is no longer just the objects that are traveling, and participants from the African diaspora are among the most frequent flyers.

Picasso's exploitation of African masks as inspiration for the prostitutes in *Les Demoiselles d'Avignon* may have caused European art history to turn a corner in the early years of the twentieth century, but today's appropriative possibilities are being defined in more multilayered terms. The *Demoiselles* themselves have been reappropriated by African American artists—see, for example, Faith Ringgold's *Picasso's Studio* (plate 2) and Robert Colescott's *Les Demoiselles d'Alabama* (plate 3) discussed and illustrated in A. Gibson 1998 and Patton 1998:236–38, respectively. Or again, Ringgold's *The Picnic at Giverny* (plate 4) depicts Picasso as the (nude) model in a gender reversal of Manet's *Le Déjeuner sur l'Herbe*, set in the garden of Monet's *Nymphéas*, with Ringgold and ten other (fully clothed) American women artists and writers having a picnic and discussing the role of women in art.[6] Margo Humphrey's

SALLY PRICE

The Last Bar-B-Que gives a twist, at once self-critical and celebratory, to one of Western art history's most venerated scenes (Powell 1997: 160). In the hands of Jean-Michel Basquiat, who took from Pollock, de Kooning, and Rauschenberg on the one end and "the guys painting on the trains" on the other, a depiction of "him and Andy Warhol duking it out in boxing attire is not as innocent and playful as it appears to be" (hooks 1995:36, 42).

Diverse back-and-forths of cultural expression have nurtured developments in the diaspora ever since its transport-initiated beginnings, with significant contacts marking every period. The specifics of those contacts—the history of the late-nineteenth-century slave trade to Cuba and Brazil; the migrations and return migrations linking Caribbean islands with Amsterdam, New York, London, Miami, Paris, and Toronto; the aesthetic notions carried by Haitian higglers, Saramaka loggers, southern US day laborers, and the like, as they traveled away from home; the pilgrimages of early-twenty-first-century US African Americans to West African sites determined by genealogical research; and so forth—are essential to respect in any attempt to map the arts of the African diaspora.

The border-crossing complexity of today's international artworld is apparent in any number of contexts. I cite a few random examples. Maroons from the rain forest of the Guianas now appear frequently on the stages of France, Germany, Holland, and the United States, and their arts back home incorporate elements of Western culture such as satellite-launching rockets (in woodcarving motifs) and Coca-Cola bottling machines (in "traditional" genres of dance). Bob Marley's music is global. Martiniquan plasticians trained at Paris's School of Fine Arts devote much of their artistic energy to capturing the spiritual essence of Carib Indian culture. Romare Bearden worked into his collages the "obeah" ceremonies of Haitian immigrants in Saint Martin, which he knew about thanks to his friendship with an American graduate student in anthropology. Carnival art throughout the diaspora—from Toronto to Bahia and from Brooklyn to Notting Hill Gate—takes its inspiration from globewide offerings (Pocahontas as the mascot in Martinique after the Disney movie came out, Monica "A-Boca-de-Ouro" Lewinsky being "honored" in Bahia's 1998 carnival, and so on).

The aspect of this global network that remains underdeveloped, relative to actual artistic production, is, as bell hooks has pointed out, art criticism. Citing a *Time* magazine cover story called "Black Renaissance: African American Artists Are Truly Free at Last" (October 1994), she lamented that it

> assessed the development and public reception of works by black artists without engaging, in any way, the ideas and perspectives of African American scholars who write about the visual arts. The blatant absence of this critical perspective serves to highlight the extent to which black scholars who write about art, specifically about work created by African American artists, are ignored by the mainstream. Ironically, the insistence in this essay that the "freedom" of black artists can be measured solely by the degree to which the work of individual artists receives attention in the established white-dominated art world exposes the absence of such freedom. (hooks 1995:110–111)

Although minor progress has been made toward an African American presence in the art history programs of mainstream universities (I had one African American graduate student when I taught in the Princeton Art Department, the chair of Duke's Art History Department is African American, and so on), most of the work remains to be done, even in contexts that should by any reckoning be well ahead of *Time* magazine: *African Arts* is still a largely white-run enterprise; Grove's new $8,800 dictionary of art (J. Turner 1996) consists of thirty-four hefty volumes but has no entry on Romare Bearden; and the texts for many colleges' introductory art history courses follow suit, despite their 800- to 1,200-page comprehensiveness. But it's useful to remember that traditional entrées into a field are not the only ones, and it seems to me that, even without passing through academic departments or glossy magazines, African American voices are beginning to contribute to the arena of interpretation and gatekeeping in other ways.

Unlike some African societies, where it is said that particular individuals are identifiable as "critics" (see, e.g., R. Thompson 1973:22–23), communities in the diaspora tend not to assign artistic criticism to designated specialists. Among Maroons in Suriname, for example, there is no notion of designated "connoisseurs," whose pronouncements about particular works of art might hold particular authority, and there is no conceptual dividing line between artist and critic.[7] And in the United States, Bearden took time out from his prolific artistic production to write both an analytical study of composition and a comprehensive history of (US) African American art (Bearden and Henderson 1993; Bearden and Holty 1969).[8]

Indeed, African American (like other nontraditionally mainstream) artists have begun exploiting, with increasing frequency and impressive vigor, direct textual means of getting their perspectives through. The effect is to force their intended focus onto the canvas (broadly defined) itself and cut off at the pass irrelevant art-historical readings, or at least underscore their status as outside opinions. Conceptual artist Adrian Piper represents a particularly stunning example, saturating her visual art with direct speech from artist to viewer—via cartoon bubbles, calling card texts, loudspeakers, headphones, and any other means she can harness. Much photographic art by African Americans also draws viewers in through text: Lorna Simpson combines body language and printed plaques; Clarissa Sligh's art "always includes words ...as an attempt to correct what is written about black people as 'criminals and on welfare'" (Lippard 1990:52, 21); Pat Ward Williams covers photographic works such as *Accused/Blowtorch/Padlock* with scrawled writing to create scathing political statement (Patton 1998:fig. 130); and Floyd Newsum uses densely written script as a frame (S. Lewis 1990:182). Similar expressive strategies are central to the "image-text" art of Keith Piper (Mercer 1997:56) and others in the "Black British" artworld (D. Willis 1997). A long autobiographical poem by "NuYorican" Miguel Piñero holds pride of place in an oil painting by his friend Martin Wong, who fills marginal plaques with additional texts, one of which he further inscribes as part of the painting itself in the form of hands signing for the deaf (Lippard 1990:184). And for US artist Aminah Robinson, the narrative is embedded "deep inside the quilt," but just to make sure that it gets across, she supplements her simultaneously "traditional" and dazzlingly innovative patchwork pieces with handwritten stories that "snake and twist around" in a style critics have compared to the indirection of black rap (Grudin 1990:36–37).

Not necessarily emerging from these artists' ethnic identity as such, the insertion of a verbal component into a visual work of art reflects, I would argue, their response to a system in which creative individuals marginalized by the mainstream artworld insist on having their say—and in expressive modes of their own choosing. Examples from the work of Chicanos, Asian Americans, Native Americans, and others support this interpretation; the text/image merger has been carried to its logical extreme in the *imagenes apalabradas* ("verbalized images") of Puerto Rican graphic artist Antonio Martorell, in which the very density of his cursive script becomes a powerful visual statement, and the composition of his imagery constitutes its own interpretive text.[9] Even when such texts do not offer anything that could be construed as art critical "interpretation," they perform the very important task of calling attention to artistic agency. Behind this work, they say, stands an articulate individual, someone with a specific point to communicate, who demands that as you, the viewer, commune with the visual form, you also listen for the (cultural, political, or social) message that it's trying to get across.

Let's turn now to the specific realm of African American textile arts.

SEAMING AFRICAN AMERICAN CONNECTIONS

Acknowledging that textile arts were severely underrepresented in studies of African American art until very recently, I begin with the most notable exception to the rule. Robert Farris Thompson has pioneered art historical connections across the entire "Black Atlantic" with stunning ambitiousness and personal gusto. In what is certainly the boldest attempt on record to pin down the seam that joins the textile arts of two continents, he has argued that the aesthetics of "the creolized cloths of Bahia, the over-one-shoulder capes of the Djuka and Saramaka maroons in Suriname, and the string-quilts of the black South in the United States...are unthinkable except in terms of partial descent from Mande cloth" (1983:208). It is just this sort of connection-drawing that has inspired so many others interested in uncovering the foundations of African American expressive culture to follow his lead. His enthusiasm, and the compatibility of his stance with an ideological climate thirsty for connectedness to the African continent, has prompted many to read such assertions as uncontestable truths. What begins as an art historian's marveling at visual similarities of color and composition becomes, in its recycling, historical fact. Michael A.

Gomez (1998:86), for example, writes: "The research of Thompson... has revealed that, at least in the area of quiltmaking, African Americans exhibit what are clearly Mande influences."

The joy that Thompson finds in similarities between cultural forms in African and African American societies has shown itself to be both contagious and ideologically empowering, and one might argue that pushing too hard on its foundation is an act of gross curmudgeonliness. And yet, if the story of Africa's legacy to the Americas is to be told with the respect it deserves, it ultimately needs to fit with everything we know. In that spirit, let's take a dispassionate look at the basis of claims such as that which makes textile arts in Brazil, Suriname, and the United States "unthinkable" except in terms of Mande origins. Close examination of the endnotes to *Flash of the Spirit* (R. Thompson 1983) reveals that numerous pivotal assertions cannot be traced by readers because the sources are listed as unpublished work in progress by Thompson and others (e.g., 282, 284, 292, 298, 300) or because they rely on phone conversations (e.g., 286, 287, 297), notes he made on a "family scrapbook" (289), or "personal communications" (throughout). Furthermore, Thompson "modifies, elides, or adds to" some quotations (300) and has "slightly retranslated" or "expanded" others (276, 277, 279, 281, 302). He has also "corrected" attributions (215–217, 279, 296), misreported statistics (215, 296), and given dates that are, at best, "informed guesses" (275). A particularly striking feature of the scholarly apparatus is the tendency to document important claims by reference to studies that turn out to have been papers written for him by undergraduate students at Yale (293–296).

Perhaps the ultimate indication that Thompson has successfully imbibed the essence of Anansi, the mischievous trickster spider of West African and African American folktales, is provided on page 221 of *Flash of the Spirit*. There, an assertion of the power of patchwork dress to afford protection against *jumbie* spirits in the British West Indies bears an endnote that reads simply "*Yale Course Critique*, 1973, p. 60" (fig. 3.1). Although few readers will go back to the original document, those who do will find the image of a handsome young man attired in a fashionable sports jacket for sale at the Yale University branch of Saks Fifth Avenue. The text (based on statements provided by a local enthusiast of Caribbean patchwork?) explains:

FIGURE 3.1
Yale University Course Critique *illustration (1973, p. 60).*

In the Antilles, patchwork means good luck.

Every true West Indian wears patchwork so the jumbie has no resting place. The continentals who visit there will be joyfully received, when wearing our evil spirit-defying patchwork madras sport coat. Predominantly red or blue for 36 to 44 sizes, $70.

I am in no way suggesting that informal interviews, phone conversations, personal communications, course critiques, and the like, should be off-limits for responsible research; no scholar fails to use such resources occasionally to confirm, reinforce, or add rhetorical flavor to less elusive documentation. But the discovery of silent misrepresentations in sources that *are* traceable (through dogged, doubt-driven detective work—submitting interlibrary loan requests, consulting colleagues at work in various parts of the diaspora, conducting complex Internet searches, e-mailing middle-aged Yale graduates at their law offices and consulting firms) tends to unsettle the credibility of the myriad personal conversations, on or off the phone, on which Thompson hangs so much of his narrative. I offer just one more example from the realm of textile arts (for others, see S. Price 1999): Thompson (1983:215) presents an early-nineteenth-century illustration of a garment labeled "Indian loincloth" (declaring on grounds of an alleged color preference that it had, in fact, been a Maroon loincloth, but see below) and speculatively links it to Ashanti weavers "working under Mande influences radiating from Kong and from Bonduku, northwest of the Akan and north of Cap Lahou, whence sailed to Suriname 50 percent of a sample of Dutch slaving ships." The source in his note could scarcely be more impeccable: Richard Price's *The Guiana Maroons* (1976:14–15). The glitch becomes evident only when we look back at that source and discover that the 50 percent figure does not refer simply to a random "sample of Dutch slaving ships" but rather to a (fifty-six-ship) sample of *those Dutch slaving ships that transported Africans from the Windward Coast*—an area that, as Price's pages 14 and 15 make clear, supplied between 0 and 49 percent of Suriname slaves (depending on the particular moment) during the course of the eighteenth century (see S. Price 1999 for a demonstration that both the "corrected" attribution and the alleged color preference also crumble when tested against primary sources).

Similarly mischievous tactics have been found to lie behind Thompson's claims for unbroken historical continuities in Brazilian *capoeira*. Luiz Renato Vieira and Mattias Röhring Assunção (1998: 85–86) examine a set of widespread myths that surround this dance/ martial art form, including the idea that the *berimbau* (now considered "the soul of the *capoeira* orchestra") can be traced directly to Africa, and label Thompson's support for this popular misconception "a manipulation of sources and facts." They cite his commentary on an 1835 engraving (*Jogar Capoëra ou danse de la guerre* by Johann Moritz Rugendas) in which the only musical instrument is a small drum, different from the *atabaque* used today, and in which "none of the traditional instruments of modern capoeira appear," and quote Thompson as follows:

> No later than 1835 berimbau...was being used to fuel the capoeira martial art. This we know because Rugendas in an illustration shows two men in a roda, one doing the basic step, the ginga, at left, and the other, at right, apparently executing a step called queixada. They are in combat. Handclapping and a drum accompany their battle. But close examination of a man standing next to the drummer shows that he has a musical bow and is pulling open his shirt, probably to place the calabash-resonator of his instrument against his naked stomach in Kongo-Angola manner. (85–86).

Vieira and Assunção argue that if the painter had seen this supremely "exotic" instrument (depicted by other artists of his time, but never in the context of capoeira), he would have had every motivation to show it as part of the scene he was representing. Ultimately, they invite their readers to view the engraving and confirm for themselves that no berimbau lurks within its shadows.

These can easily be seen as picky, esoteric, and potentially irritating arguments—not the sort of sleuthing that historical and anthropological researchers normally like to conduct, especially because of the danger that it could be interpreted in personal terms. To my knowledge, the only other writer who has called Thompson to task in anything like this fashion is bell hooks, who goes to some lengths to reiterate the non-ad-hominem nature of her position. "Although I am critical of his theory and practice, this did not mean that I did not like him," she writes, quoting herself speaking to a conference organizer who had assumed the contrary.[10] "The fear of being perceived as personally attacking colleagues, or of making personal enemies, effectively censors meaningful critique and closes off the possibility that there will be meaningful, dialectical, and critical conversation and debate among colleagues," she continues, insisting nonetheless that "the theory and practice that inform Thompson's work should be rigorously and critically interrogated" (hooks 1995:114).

Sprinkling a few grains of salt on Thompson's monumental contribution does not, fortunately, desiccate African and African American textile research. On the contrary, there has been an explosion of attention to both sides of the Atlantic (with special weight given to the southern United States), a certain amount of it directly due to the inspiring lectures and writing of Thompson himself (for starters, see Adler and Barnard 1992; Ferris 1982, 1983; Fry 1986, 1990; Grudin 1990; Idiens and Ponting 1980; Leon 1987, 1992; Tobin and Dobard 1999; Vlach 1990; Wahlman 1993).

Three central contributions to the African diaspora portion of this literature—Gladys-Marie Fry's *Stitched from the Soul* (1990), Eli Leon's *Models in the Mind* (1992), and Maude Wahlman's *Signs and Symbols* (1993)—may serve to exemplify key aspects of current scholarship on the subject. I begin with Walhman and Leon. We note, first, that both pay respectful homage to the quilters whose work is featured, in the form of individual photographic and narrative portraits. Also, both represent attempts to identify the African components in US African American quilts, taking care to raise the question of alternative influences from Euro-American traditions before, for the most part, dismissing them in favor of an African-based interpretation.[11]

The forty-four women and one man featured in these two books are all twentieth-century (US) African American quilters—most of the illustrated pieces postdate 1970. Their work is compared with numerous twentieth-century (or in a few cases undated) African pieces, plus a light smattering of examples from other points in the diaspora (Caribbean islands, Suriname, Brazil).[12] The illustrations thus create a corpus of several hundred contemporaneous elements, which serve as the visual foundation for the authors' arguments. In both cases, the thesis is that, in Wahlman's (1993:vii) words, "most African-American quiltmaking derives its aesthetic from various African traditions, both technological and ideological." As Leon (1992:3) puts it, "carried in memory—transmitted from generation to generation without printed instructions—patchwork esthetics and technology had the potential, even under the extreme adversity of the African-American experience, to survive the Atlantic crossing and thrive on this continent."

In both cases then, a historical argument is illustrated with an ahistorical corpus of objects. This situation leaves several (complementary, not competing) options for supplying the historical connection. Among the many possibilities, one could, for example,

1. Delineate the features most responsible for the visual similarity in the late twentieth century (compositional principles, use of colors, and so on) and reason that they are most likely to have occurred via a generation-to-generation transmission in the specific realm of textiles.

2. Scour museums, archives, and other primary sources for early African American objects that display aesthetic or technological similarities with African pieces from a comparable period, thus pushing the visual match closer to a time when Africans were being transported to the Americas, reasoning that this increases the plausibility of asserting a direct, medium-specific continuity.

3. Probe the recollections of African American quilters (some of whom were quite elderly when they were interviewed by Leon, Wahlman, and others) for specific fragments of the collective memory that Leon evokes, working back toward a clearer vision of the technological, ideological, and aesthetic considerations that would have guided quilters in the middle and late nineteenth century.

4. Explore regional constants across the various textile arts of Afro-America through elicitation (from the producers and users of the textiles) of technological, ideological, aesthetic, or social associations in an attempt to bolster and/or correct Western-authored speculation about what it is that constitutes a conceptual link between the African and African American examples.

5. Expand the playing field to include aspects of life that have nothing to do with cloth, looking for evidence that particular features common to both corpora of illustrations were kept alive in some form even when they were not being transmitted through textile arts.

Of these, option 1 enters the picture to some degree in virtually any exploration of the subject; it does not, however, pass (art) historical muster on its own because of the extent to which it represents undocumented conjecture. For this reason, every scholar addressing the subject has attempted to supplement it with more specific, concrete arguments.

Option 2 is the strategy that Thompson tried to implement by reading an early nineteenth-century loincloth illustration as the depiction of an African American artifact. The transmission he proposes is far from direct: the patchwork construction of the loincloth is attributed to a "radiation" of influence that occurred in an area to the northwest of the Akan and to the north of a port (Cap Lahou) that supplied a particular portion (more in Thompson's view than in my reading of the sources) of slaves to Suriname. There the loincloth was made by a Maroon and then traded to an Indian, whose preference for solid red (Thompson asserts) was strong enough that he wouldn't have made it, but weak enough that he might well have bought it from the Maroon.[13] Like Gomez (1998), Wahlman has recycled Thompson's Mande/Akan/Cap Lahou/Suriname slave/Suriname Maroon/Suriname Indian scenario as fact, deleting two of the principal players (the Indian and Thompson) and, under the heading "African Textiles in the New World," declaring that "an 1823 illustration shows a Mande-like loincloth made from three strips of cotton, two patterned and the center one plain, as in nineteenth-century Asante cloth from Ghana" (Wahlman 1993:25).

Option 3 has been endorsed in principle by much of the recent scholarship on the subject, and the inclusion of biographical sketches signals a welcome respect for the individual artists behind the textiles.[14] To date, however, the interviews on which these sketches are based have dealt mainly with anecdotal childhood memories instead of the stylistic specifics that would produce art historical depth. The artists tend to make mention of family relations, daily life, technical details of sewing, and the personal joy of creating a beautiful pattern, without devoting attention in any sustained fashion to the relationship between their late-twentieth-century art and that of their grandmothers (that is, specific similarities *and differences* over time in materials, compositional principles, social uses, symbolic meanings, and so on).

The literature on African American textile arts has also utilized option 4, though I would characterize its attention to other parts of the diaspora as scattered and relatively token, compared with what it could be. In general, the comparative material in US-focused studies is selected on the basis of its power to support unifying connections, often through purely visual similarity, and it thus constitutes an unrepresentative sample of the larger corpus.[15]

It is useful to note that the debut of this literature on transatlantic connections in art came at a time when interest in African roots was exploding in the United States.[16] From the flowering of black studies programs to the TV serialization of Alex Haley's *Roots*, a tidal wave of interest in the African contribution to American culture was sweeping the country. It was in this particular climate that outsiders defined the recognized range of Maroon textile arts (which included at least five aesthetically and technically distinct styles, from appliqué to cross-stitch), focusing attention virtually exclusively on the narrow-strip art in vogue during the half century ending around 1970. This focus continues to be true, even though the very different techniques that preceded and followed (or coincided with) that style have now been amply documented for about two decades. The choice, though unacknowledged as such, made strategic sense for scholars bent on establishing medium-specific links with Africa—narrow-strip textiles bore a striking visual resemblance to numerous African textile traditions and hence played well in the reconstruction of transatlantic tie-ins. Other forms of decorative sewing practiced by the Maroons receded into the background, and narrow-strip patchwork was offered up as *the* Maroon textile art as surely as men's woodcarving had been presented as *the* art of the Maroons by earlier generations, who thus overlooked artistic forms produced by women. In photographs that set African textiles side-by-side with Maroon textiles (see, e.g., R. Thompson 1983:216), there is no visual indication that one is composed of strips that are locally woven, selvaged, and edge-sewn and the other consists of pieces of imported trade cotton with raw edges that are seamed and then turned under on the wrong side to form a meticulously hemmed finish. Nor is it usual to call attention to this distinction in the accompanying text. Rather, the photographic similarity is assumed to speak for itself, testifying to the power of African sensibilities to survive the Middle Passage, slavery, and three centuries of life in the Americas.

This brings us to option 5. Leon's notion of "models in the mind"

flirts with this approach, interpreting the "uncanny similarities" visible
between African and American textiles partly through an emphasis on
spontaneous improvisation that plays out aesthetic principles and
motifs from other media (designs painted on walls, chalked on walls,
incised on calabashes, and hammered on brass containers), calling on
them to "inform spontaneous esthetic decisions" in the medium of textiles as well (Leon 1992:21, 17, 4). This image of innovation in a particular domain drawing on models experienced outside that domain is
not far from the "underlying principles" that lie at the heart of Mintz
and Price's (1992) program for an understanding of early African
American culture history. The argument for attention to this option in
interpretations of the developmental history of Maroon textile arts
has been presented in detail elsewhere,[17] but a nutshell summary will
be helpful here because it ultimately represents the most concrete
demonstration of the "Mintz and Price approach" to transatlantic connections that I know of in the realm of art.

It begins with a dilemma. Despite the visual closeness of Maroon
narrow-strip patchwork to countless African textiles, we know from
ethnographic, archival, and museological evidence that the Maroon
version did not exist before to the second half of the nineteenth century. If this realization forces us to abandon the idea that it was
handed down from generation to generation (by which process it
would have passed from one continent to another), how can we then
account for the undeniable aesthetic similarities? The answer most
compatible with the full range of evidence currently available hinges
on a convergence, triggered by events in coastal Suriname, of continuities in separate domains of Maroon life. On the one hand, Maroon
rhythmic aesthetics have always favored interruptive patterns in everything from informal speech, song, and folktales to dancing and
drumming. On the other, Maroon visual aesthetics favor sharp color
contrasts over close color blending. Both of these preferences have
been documented through time, beginning in the eighteenth century
with the remarks of resident German missionaries who complained, for
example, that sermons were being punctuated with interjections from
the congregation (see R. Price 1990:254) or Dutch observations that
Maroons liked to dress in combinations of "jumping-at-the-eye" colors
(see, e.g., Coster 1866:26–28; van Coll 1903:538). Finally, we must factor in the sewing practice by which Maroon women have, for as far

back as we have evidence, joined pieces of cloth with meticulously finished seams to create garments of the proper dimensions (see, e.g., S. Price and R. Price 1999:figs. 4.1, 4.32, 4.33, 4.34, 4.35).

Stylized interruptions not only are crucial to every form of speech, narrative, music, and dance but also enter into the conceptualization of personal feuds, creating an *hors-de-l'art* parallel to the disjunctive structure of patchwork; this is a culture in which the pan-Afro-American pattern of "call and response" informs literally every aspect of social and cultural activity. In terms of the aesthetics of color contrast, twenty-first-century dress continues to reflect an explicit preference for contrasts rather than blends (for example, a red waist kerchief with a yellow and green wrap skirt). And long-term ethnography among contemporary Maroons has not only documented a continuation of the color preferences picked up by early observers but also suggests the influence of those preferences in contexts undiscoverable through visual observation. Maroon women talk about their gardens as being intentionally laid out in patchwork-like alternations of rice varieties that they classify as "red" and "white," even though the different kinds look and taste virtually the same once they get to the cooking pot. As for sewing techniques, garments from every documented period of Maroon textile history include seams joining pieces of same-color cloth.

The most plausible reading of the nature of the connective tissue between African models and twentieth-century Maroon patchwork thus relies on the uninterrupted presence of such aesthetic and technical aspects of life in the interior of the Guianas in combination with specific events in Suriname's economic and labor history. My own long-term ethnographic fieldwork, extensive museum research, consultation of archives, and reading of the literature strongly suggest the following scenario. With cultural preferences that were deeply embedded in a variety of verbal, visual, and conceptual realms other than textiles, and with an equally strong but completely separate textile tradition of patching cloth through meticulous seams, the scene was set for Maroon seamstresses to create an art, executed with seams, that combined interruptive patterning and sharp color contrasts. There are compelling reasons to believe that both the aesthetic framework and the material technique were firmly in place and that the only thing lacking prior to the twentieth century were the appropriate raw materials.

When Maroon men began earning enough money during their

periodic wage-labor trips to bring back large amounts of cloth and coastal stores began stocking bolts of colorfully striped trade cotton in addition to their earlier offerings of monochrome cloth, Maroon women, never hesitant to carry artistic ideas from one medium to another when material resources permit, would quite naturally have begun to play with the new materials. Narrow-strip patchwork would then have begun with an external spark (new cloth supplies) igniting an amalgam between long-standing elements embedded in the cultural life of the Maroons. Representing both a continuity and an innovation, these textiles can be viewed as reflecting the heritage of the earliest Africans in the Suriname interior, the creative spirit of their descendants, and the material dependence of Maroons on worlds well beyond the villages of the rain forest.

This approach to Maroon textile history is based on a profoundly pre-postmodern genre of anthropological research. Because the players in the story it reconstructs began to form a cohesive community three centuries ago, upon their arrival in the South American rain forest, our principal focus has been on New World developments, with the ethnographic and art critical contribution of Africanists supplying a historical base that recedes progressively as the Maroon story unfolds in time. The resulting model (developed more fully in S. Price and R. Price 1980, 1999) has depended, in innumerable, very specific ways, on consideration of ethnographic detail through time, including attention to

- Cloth, thread, and yarn supplies

- Names given to particular designs and embroidery stitches

- Cross-media design transfers and structural similarities (between different visual media, visual and musical or narrative genres, and the like)

- Changes in fashion (as conveyed through interviews, song lyrics, travelers' accounts, linguistic play, and other sources)

- Cultural principles of kinship and conjugal relations

- Labor patterns

- Trends in the consumption of coastal imports

- Understandings about gender-specific aesthetic preferences and aptitudes

- Techniques of sewing, storing, and laundering clothes (and even recycling them after they are torn)

- The nature and frequency of aesthetic discourse

- The social environment of art-making

- The tools and sequences of steps involved in each medium

- Many more details—all very decisively followed through time as much as oral history, archival records, museum collections, and reading of the literature allow

At this point, the pleas being made by African scholars such as Kwame Anthony Appiah to recognize "Africa" as a Euro-American invention (condensing "enough cultural diversity to satisfy the wildest multiculturalist" into a slave-era construct viewing it as "the home of the Negro" [Appiah 1997:47]) deserve to be brought into the picture. As Appiah (47) has put it, "only recently has the idea of Africa come to figure importantly in the thinking of many Africans; and those that took up this idea got it, by and large, from European culture...the central cultural fact of African life, in my judgment, remains not the sameness of Africa's cultures, but their enormous diversity." Despite art historical maps, routes of influence traced from Mande to Akan, invocation of the specifics of Kuba barkcloth, and the like, the bottom line of much recent writing on African American textiles constitutes an effort to identify (and celebrate) their origins in a schematic, quasi-essentialized "Africa."

Whether we phrase the problem of origins in terms of continents, countries, ethnicities, or personal contacts, no art springs nakedly from a particular source. People conduct their lives in social, economic, ideological, and physical environments, producing art on the same days that they cultivate gardens, hunt or fish, discipline children, perform rituals, discuss politics, worry about money, gossip with one another, sing, flirt, and daydream. Despite their brevity, mini-biographies like those presented by Leon and Wahlman make it clear that for the quilters who were interviewed, all these kinds of activities rubbed elbows in a single memory frame. Even the physical forms that bear witness to

SALLY PRICE

the aesthetic sensibilities of their makers and inspire the aesthetic admiration of their viewers carry quiet evidence of this embeddedness of art in non-art aspects of life. Discussing Akan goldweights in a recent exhibit, Appiah (1997:46) comments:

> Anyone who has handled a decent number of the weights...will have noticed quite often among these elegant objects, so obviously crafted with great skill and care, one that has a lump of unworked metal stuffed into a crevice, in a way that seems completely to destroy its aesthetic unity; or, sometimes, a well-made figure has a limb crudely hacked off. These amputations and excrescences are there because, after all, a weight is a weight: and if it doesn't weigh the right amount, it can't serve its function. If a goldweight, however finely crafted, has the wrong mass, then something needs to be added (or chopped off) to bring it to its proper size.

The visible form of works of art can depend, in ways that are invisible to the most discerning critic's eye, on considerations anchored in decidedly non-art areas of their maker's life. This is why we must exercise such care in characterizing, for example, an apparent staggering of design elements as "deliberate" (Wahlman 1993:47) or asserting that a medieval cloth's blue and white colors represent a "deliberate clashing of 'high affect' colors...in willful, percussively contrastive, bold arrangements" (R. Thompson 1983:209). Aesthetic "deliberation" surely constitutes a fundamental prerogative of the artists themselves, and their increasing participation over recent decades in clarifying what is or is not the intent behind their art cannot help but introduce a salutary breath of fresh air into future art critical (and culture-historical) discourse.

Attentive readers will note that after singling out three key contributions to the literature on African American quilts, I've gone on to discuss only two of them. No, I have not forgotten Gladys-Marie Fry.

Stitched from the Soul (Fry 1990) documents the world of slave seamstresses in the antebellum US South. It describes the quilts in terms of their finished form but also (and more important for the issues raised in this chapter) explores the world in which they were conceptualized, sewn, slept under, laundered, torn into wartime bandages, used to decorate graves or hide children escaping to the North, and more. In the process, we get precious glimpses of slave women expressing their individuality and humanity in an anonymizing, dehumanizing environment, and we are able to see quilts as part of a specific social and historical setting. Focusing on a well-defined time period and documenting her claims not by phone calls, personal communications, or undergraduate term papers but rather by ample doses of citations taken from books, articles, Ph.D. dissertations, and archival documents, Fry offers a textured portrait of a cultural environment that has often been slighted in traditional histories because of the dual blinders of sexism and racism. Historically and ethnographically specific descriptions of this sort are what we need more of in order to trace links across regions and periods in the African diaspora with real confidence, building, somewhere down the line, a less speculative basis than we have today for assertions about the role of Mother Africa and the expressive ways her children defined their new lives in the Americas.

ZOOMING IN, ZOOMING OUT

I end with two suggestions that point in opposing but, I would hope, compatible directions.

As the "traffic in culture" continues to erode the distinctions once segregating first and third or fourth (art)worlds, "high" and "low" genres, producers and critics, and even anthropologists and art historians, lanes are being opened up in many exciting directions. With anthropologists reading art historical literature, and vice versa, with artists increasingly demanding an interpretive role, and with the influx of voices from previously underrepresented groups gaining momentum, students of African American art are becoming increasingly well equipped to complement research questions raised by the historical and cultural results of the Middle Passage with exploration of issues born of more contemporary geographical, ideological, disciplinary, and identitarian passages. We are intellectually enriched by being able to read the interpretive texts of Faith Ringgold's acrylic and strip-cloth story quilts, talk to Saramakas about the meaning of the dances they are performing on the Washington Mall, visit an exhibition of "Black British" art conceptualized by Caribbean-born curators based in New York, and study Romare Bearden's analysis of compositional principles, in which paintings of the Italian Renaissance are seen through the eyes of an artist equally familiar with the one in Harlem.

At the same time, the suggestive leads that such a multiplicity of resources can produce need to be reined in by the most rigorous scholarly standards, somewhat the way a Saramaka possession god (powerful, inspirational, and untamed when it makes its first appearance) needs to be ritually "domesticated" before it can provide useful service to the community. In my own Maroon research, for example, probing details of the most nitty-gritty sort has turned out to be essential for an understanding of textile art history: Where do Maroons get their thread, what do they use to tuck under the raw edges in preparation for hemming, and how close are their stitches? What words do they use to label these cloths as they pass from men's coastal purchases to conjugal presents to women's skirts to sacks of edge trimmings to unsewn patterns on the ground and then back to conjugal presents, men's formal wear, pieces of laundry, and finally threadbare rags? What roles do textiles play in marriages, in worship, in political investitures, in popular songs, in legal disputes, in funerals? Do people talk among themselves about aesthetic principles? What, if anything, do they have to say about symbolism? Why do they always fold clothes, wrong side out, into little wallet-size packets? Why do seamstresses sometimes lather up a newly sewn textile with bar soap and leave it in the sun before rinsing out the suds? Why, after carefully concealing the tiny stitches used to make a seam, do they lead the thread onto a part of the cloth where it shows clearly before cutting it off? How do they deal with slips, errors, and botched designs? What features of a textile inspire praise (from men, from women), and what features are disparaged? Are clothes mended when they tear, and if so, how? What tone do people adopt when they critique a six-year-old's first attempt to sew a patchwork apron? How do they talk about the obsolete arts of their grandmothers? What parts of a garment do women use to test out new ideas, and how do their experiments affect fashion trends? Do they cut the cloth with scissors, knife, or razor? Or is it ripped?

Giving more consistent attention to these kinds of ostensibly "peripheral" questions (pushing them back in time with the help of every resource available, whether published, archival, museological, or oral historical), as a complement to the broader strokes that reflect visual images of African and African American art forms, could save us from many enticing but ultimately untenable readings of Old World/New World connections. And if the Maroon case is any indication, a recognition that cultural continuities do not always respect boundaries between one context and another (that is, that they travel freely from textiles to songs, from drum rhythms to naming practices, from oracles to body language, and more) may often help fill the breach. By simultaneously zooming in on the ethnographic "trivia" (at the scissor/knife/razor or seam/edge-sewn level) and zooming out to a gaze that places particular arts in their full cultural context and cultural systems in their full regionwide context, the complex and often very subtle ways that threads of African origin weave in and out of the diaspora's cultural fabric may come into clearer view. And as the discussion continues to shift from art things to artworlds, the growing participation of commentators from one or another segment of the African diaspora, including the artists themselves, cannot but help lead to newly enlightening visions.

Notes

1. The group met a number of times over two or three years. In addition to the organizers, it included Henry Louis Gates Jr., Suzan Harjo, Steven D. Lavine, Lawrence Levine, Mari Matsuda, Raymund Paredes, Richard Price, Bernice Johnson Reagon, John Kuo Wei Tchen, Trinh Minh-Ha, Marta Moreno Vega, Jim West, Tomás Ybarra-Frausto, and me.

2. Others trained by Boas were assessing the contribution of individuality to cultural patterns in the context of American Indian ethnography; see, for example, Ruth Bunzel's ([1929] 1972) careful exploration of the creative imagination in Pueblo pottery. Across the Atlantic, Herskovits's contemporary Raymond Firth ([1936] 1979:28) responded to the British variant of this approach by stressing the freedom of individuals within the normative systems that served to circumscribe acceptable behavior and by focusing attention on "the position of the creative faculty of the native artist in relation to his conformity to the local style."

3. There are, of course, many exceptions. To name just a few, Sandra Barnes's (1989) excellent collection of studies on Ogun explores variants of this West African god in the Americas in terms of religion, body arts, dance, and more. Her introduction to the volume offers an insightful reading of the balance

between specificities and common ground. Contributions by art historian Henry Drewal, performance theorist Margaret Thompson Drewal, anthropologist Karen McCarthy Brown, and others bring material from Brazil, Haiti, and other parts of the Americas into focus with ethnographic research on West African societies. John Nunley and Judith Bettelheim (1988) integrate New Orleans, Brooklyn, Toronto, and London in their overview of Caribbean festival arts. Richard Powell's (1997) excellent overview of contemporary US African American art and culture in the Thames and Hudson World of Art series shows a healthy willingness to stray beyond the country's borders when artists' lives and patterns of influence demand a wider purview.

4. Regional scope inevitably raises the question of whether (and how) we can talk about "black" culture or art (see, e.g., Powell 1997). In a series of lectures presented in 1997 at the College of William and Mary, novelist David Bradley argued against the notion of a "black" anything. Recounting the story of a student who once presented him with what she called a "black sonnet," he defended his position that she had produced nothing of the sort. To convince him that her poem was a "black sonnet," he told her, she would have to show that its metric structure was characteristic of poems by other black poets, and uncommon else-where. The fact that she had written a poem and that she was black, he insisted, was irrelevant to the definition of a genre of sonnet. My own position is that the common thread running through plastic and graphic arts in the (entire) African diaspora is not purely (or even necessarily) a matter of the artist's phenotype or the object's formal properties (though one could argue the case) but that it also emerges from more broadly defined cultural orientations that nurture the form, meaning, context, and uses of art objects, as well as the nature of the creative process that produces them.

5. Another (absolutely defining) contribution to the workings of today's art-worlds that Herskovits had no need to consider in his vision of diaspora art (and that had remained virtually negligible when I began writing about Maroon art) is that of legislators, lawyers, and judges. The whole thorny bundle of questions con-cerning cultural property and the legal definition of artistic originality in an age of sampling and Photoshop is deeply entangled in multicultural ideologies and rapidly inflating economic stakes.

6. The women include Emma Amos, Michele Wallace, Johnnetta Cole, and seven others—all identified; the text running between the acrylic-on-canvas scene and the patchwork fabric border, about nine hundred words, spells out the thoughts Ringgold wanted to communicate (about Paris, nature, painting, sexism

and feminism, racism, artistic freedom) and preempts the critics' role by, for example, explaining why the artist at the easel is wearing a white dress. For the full text, see Cameron et al. (1998:131–132).

7. The generalization of art criticism within a given population means that studying its criteria often requires an openness to modes of expression that do not fit the researcher's expectations. As Clifford Geertz (1983:94–120) has put it, "art talk" has been reported as rarely as it has for non-Western societies, not because people in such societies don't engage in it but because it frequently assumes forms that are different from those of Western art criticism. This important point has an exact parallel in discourse about history (see R. Price 1983a:6–8).

8. It should be noted that this approach contrasts sharply with the European tradition, in which, as Dominique de Menil put it,

> Matisse's "Those who want to give themselves to painting should begin by cutting out their tongues" and Braque's remark that "in art, there's only one thing that matters: that which cannot be explained" are brutal reminders that, as Malraux said it, "the only language of painting is painting." And even Baudelaire spoke of "the dreadful uselessness of explaining no matter what to no matter who." (Menil Foundation 1984:11)

(Or, as Picasso is said to have said, "Don't talk to the driver.") For more on the separation (and even countercurrent agendas) of art production and art commentary, see Belting (1987).

9. See Martorell (1991, 1995), Tió (1995), and, for further examples of the use of text in the imagery of a "multicultural" range of US American artists, Lippard (1990).

10. The line she draws between personal affect and critical thinking applies just as emphatically to my own critique. During the five years Richard Price and I spent in New Haven in the 1970s, dinners with the Thompsons ranked among our most enjoyable and stimulating social evenings. Conversely, I would argue, it is perfectly possible to admire the work of a scholar for whom one does not have a great deal of admiration in personal terms.

11. It bears noting that *patchwork* and *quilt* are frequently paired but definitely not synonymous terms. This distinction becomes relevant when we consider the nature of African textile traditions (barkcloth or woven strips edge-sewn along their selvages), because, as Leon points out from the start, it introduces different technical considerations in planning the composition. In contrast to the very

great majority of both African and US textiles, Maroon patchwork is neither quilted nor edge-sewn, another technical distinction that demands to be taken into account when examples from tropical Afro-America are added to the comparison.

12. Wahlman also includes one illustration of a cloth fragment from the eleventh or twelfth century. Leon dates one illustrated cloth as "c. 1870–1900."

13. The demonstration that this scenario doesn't hold, which depends on a number of ethnographic details and historical sources, has been spelled out in S. Price (1999). In addition to the data presented there, the illustrations of patterned Indian garments in Stedman's eighteenth-century *Narrative* ([1790] 1988:319, 467) provide further proof against Thompson's claim that Indians wore only solid-color clothing, as does, in fact, the woman's pubic apron shown right next to the loincloth on which Thompson builds his claim of Mande influence.

14. Photo portraits, biographical information, and interviews on/with artists are becoming, if not standard, at least increasingly common in the literature on art of the African diaspora; see, e.g., Beauchamp-Byrd and Sirmans (1997); Chopin and Chopin (1998); Ferris (1982); Fortune (1994); and SECCA (1990); Wardlaw and Rozelle (1989). This development constitutes a crucial enrichment to the field, allowing "folk" artists to emerge from the anonymity that much writing from an earlier era had consigned them to.

15. In other fields as well, succumbing to the temptation to select data according to how well it supports a pet theory carries significant, if imperceptible, costs. For an exploration of the consequences of this risk in feminist interpretations of menstrual customs, see S. Price (1994).

16. As Eva Grudin (1990:7) notes, "quilt texts published before 1970 hardly ever mentioned the existence of black-made quilts. Before 1970 the African-American quilting tradition was largely ignored, even in the black community."

17. The argument was proposed in S. Price and R. Price (1980) and has most recently been laid out in S. Price and R. Price (1999).

1. Emma Amos, Malcolm X, Morley, Matisse & Me *(1993). Art © Emma Amos/Licensed by VAGA, New York, NY.*

2. *Above. Faith Ringgold,* Picasso's Studio *(The French Collection Part 1: #7) (1991). Faith Ringgold © 1991.*

3. *Facing page, top. Robert Colescott,* Les Demoiselles d'Alabama (des Nudas)*, 1985. Courtesy Phyllis Kind Gallery, New York.*
4. *Facing page, bottom. Faith Ringgold,* The Picnic at Giverny *(The French Collection Part 1: #3) (1991). Faith Ringgold © 1991.*

5. Broom Grass, *1995, by Jonathan Green, oil on canvas, 48 by 60 inches. Collection of Allison Powe. Photograph by Tim Stamm. Jonathan Green © 1995.*

Esclava de Puerto-rico   Esclavo de Puerto-rico

6. Luis Paret y Alcázar, A Slave Woman of Puerto Rico. *Smithsonian Institution Collections, National Museum of American History, Behring Center, Division of Home and Community Life.*

7. José Campeche, Isabel O'Daly *(circa 1808). Smithsonian American Art Museum, Teodoro Vidal Collection.*

8. Pío Casimiro Bacener, Autoretrato *(1894). Smithsonian American Art Museum, Teodoro Vidal Collection.*

9. José Campeche, San Juan Nepomuceno *(circa 1798). Smithsonian American Art Museum, Teodoro Vidal Collection.*

4

On the Miracle of Creolization

Richard Price

Some twenty years ago, when we were colleagues at Johns Hopkins, Sid Mintz used to tell me that when he opened his mouth to say something in a seminar, he was often afraid that moths might fly out. Getting up to the age he was then, I'm beginning to know whereof he spoke. In Kevin Yelvington's proposal for this School of American Research advanced seminar, my specific assignment was to expand upon certain ideas in the essay I wrote with Sid in 1972—which we presented publicly in 1973, brought out in offset in 1976, and published commercially, with a new preface, as *The Birth of African-American Culture* in 1992. The preface went over some history of the work's reception, noting that the original publication

> was greeted in some quarters by a—for us—surprising hos-
> tility, accompanied by the charge that it denied the exis-
> tence of an African heritage in the Americas. It seemed that
> many such reactions originated in a desire to polarize Afro-
> Americanist scholarship into a flatly "for" or "against" posi-
> tion in regard to African cultural retentions. For instance,
> Mervyn Alleyne dubbed us "creation theorists," charging us

with exaggerated attention to the cultural creativity of
enslaved Africans in the New World; yet his own book
reaches conclusions close to our own (1988). Daniel
Crowley castigated Sally and Richard Price's *Afro-American
Arts of the Suriname Rain Forest*, which develops the conceptual
approach in a particular historical context, as "badly over-
stating a good case" (1981). Joey Dillard found the authors
"not completely on the side of the angels," their arguments
"controversial if not positively heretical" (1976). (Mintz and
Price 1992:viii)

During the past few years, since that essay has reached a wider
audience, these controversies have intensified. Indeed, I now find
myself (and my work, including but hardly limited to the Mintz and
Price essay) caught up as never before in a series of sometimes acri-
monious debates. My intent in this chapter is to try to define some of
the issues, clarify what is theoretically and methodologically at stake,
and suggest ways that aspects of the "M&P model" might usefully be
employed in the continuing exploration of African American pasts.[1]

It is among historians of North American slavery that these issues
have come under fiercest debate of late (perhaps because American
historians of slavery have come to the study of "process" so recently).
As has now become clear, many of the canonical works on US slavery
and slave communities—for example, Blassingame (1972), Genovese
([1974] 1976), and Rawick (1972)—treated the "peculiar institution"
largely synchronically, basing their interpretations almost exclusively
on the seductively rich nineteenth-century antebellum record. During
the past several years, however, a virtual flood of historical works has
been devoted to the uneven and regionally variable *development* of
North American slavery, and much of that debate has turned on changing aspects of the slaves' cultural life. With increasing frequency,
American historians are now asking the following sorts of (formerly
anthropological) questions: How "ethnically" homogeneous (or heterogeneous) were the enslaved Africans arriving in particular localities,
and what were the cultural consequences? What were the processes by
which these Africans became African *Americans*? How quickly and in
what ways did Africans transported to the Americas as slaves, and their
African American offspring, begin thinking and acting as members of

new communities—that is, how rapid was creolization? In what ways did the African arrivants choose to—and were they able to—continue particular ways of thinking and doing things that came from the Old World? How did the various demographic profiles and social conditions of New World plantations in particular places and times encourage or inhibit these processes? Even a cursory glance at much discussed works such as Ira Berlin's *Many Thousands Gone*, Michael Gomez's *Exchanging Our Country Marks*, Philip Morgan's *Slave Counterpoint*, or John Thornton's *Africa and Africans in the Making of the Atlantic World, 1400–1800*—all published within the past several years—shows how important, and contentious, these questions have suddenly become for practitioners of American history.

A second set of issues—arguably of less interest to historians proper—has surfaced most forcefully in an essay by Jamaican anthropologist David Scott (1991), who suggests that anthropologists studying Afro-America ought to turn their attention away from the futile and perhaps even morally suspect effort to represent, verify, or corroborate "authentic Afro-American pasts" ("what really happened") and focus instead on how African Americans in various parts of the hemisphere envision, talk about, and act in terms of their pasts.[2] Our focus, he argues, should be on "tradition"—the ways that African Americans employ, for example, "Africa," "slavery," or "the Middle Passage" "in the narrative construction of relations among pasts, presents, and futures" (278). "What space," he says we should be asking, "do Africa and slavery occupy in the political economy of local discourse?" (279). In short, we should focus on "discourse" and the realities it creates rather than engage in futile attempts to reconstruct "event." Throughout his essay, Scott uses the work of Melville Herskovits and my own *First-Time* (R. Price 1983a) as exemplars of two stages in what he views as a unitary anthropological quest. "Not surprisingly," he argues, Afro-American anthropology "manifests a deep, humanist inclination toward a story about continuities and embraces the earnest task of demonstrating the integrity and the intactness of the old in the new, and of the past in the present" (262). And in this narrative, "Africa" and "slavery" form the points of reference. "In the discursive or narrative economy of this anthropological problematic, *slavery* and '*Africa*' function as virtually interchangeable terms, or, to put it in another way, slavery in the work of Price comes to perform the same rhetorical-conceptual labor as

Africa in the work of Herskovits" (263). "Both," he continues, "turn on a distinctive attempt to place the 'cultures' of the ex-African/ex-slave in relation to what we might call an authentic past, that is, an anthropologically identifiable, ethnologically recoverable, and textually representable past" (263).[3]

Whatever Scott's discomforts about this master narrative of continuity and the ideology he believes underlies it, there seems little doubt that historians of slavery, like Afro-Americanist anthropologists, have generally endorsed it. (Indeed, I would argue that it is a quintessentially *American* [US] narrative, arising in part from the specificities of North American racism, instead of a strictly anthropological one. Europeans, Africans, and South Americans—scholars and laymen alike—have, with a few notable exceptions, been uninterested in the particular polemics under discussion here.)

I would like to distinguish and explore two competing versions of what Scott sees as a single master narrative, for I believe that a considerable and significant chasm remains between the Herskovitses' account of Saramaka pasts and that of the Prices, or between John Thornton's or Michael Gomez's account of the development of slave life in colonial North America and that of Ira Berlin or Philip Morgan. I would also insist, for present purposes, that these competing versions of this master narrative of continuity differ significantly—ideologically, methodologically, and theoretically. Later on, I will try to suggest how Scott's focus on discourse might be combined with an interest in more traditional history to generate an anthropological approach to Afro-American pasts that is at once robust, rigorous, and ideologically defensible.

The contemporary version 1 of the master narrative of continuity is militantly Africa-centric, stressing the continuing role of African ethnicities in the Americas, and is often explicitly mounted against the arguments of the M&P essay. I take two recent works to be exemplary: Gomez (1998) and Thornton (1998a). But I would first set the stage with some snippets from a more programmatic piece by Paul Lovejoy (1997:1, 2, 4, 6, 7, 16), which captures the flavor of the discourse:

> An "African-centric" perspective overcomes a fundamental
> flaw in the history of Africans in the Americas as analyzed by
> many historians of slavery, particularly those identifying with

the "creolization" model articulated by Sidney Mintz and Richard Price....The focus from Africa implies that not all of the enslaved who went to the Americas were thoroughly deracinated[,] as the "creolization" model assumes.... The implications of these Africanist assumptions are in sharp contrast to those of the "creolization school," which implicitly denies the possibility of significant ongoing links, even if intermittent, between Africa and the diaspora....The creole model assumes that African history did not cross the Atlantic because the enslaved population was too diverse in origins to sustain the continuities of history. Disjuncture is the key concept.... Because of this depersonalized background, only "deep-level cultural principles" survived the Atlantic crossing.... [According to the creolization model,] [c]reolization resulted in the rapid assimilation of enslaved Africans to a "new" hybrid culture evolving in the Americas.... In rejecting Herskovits's preoccupation with "survivals,"...Mintz and Price and their protégés in effect subscribe to E. Franklin Frazier's view that the culture of the Americas was "new".... For creolists..."creole" inevitably meant the "Europeanization" of the oppressed slaves....I would argue that the concept of creolization as usually applied is Eurocentric, emphasizing how African culture becomes subsumed and amalgamated under slavery into an "American" mold that reenforced the domination of people of European descent.... The Mintz-Price process of adaptation and invention in the Americas assumes the destruction of African cultures....The focus on the Americas, which is explicit in theories of creolization, effectively neutralizes African history....The perspective of the Americas as conceived by the creolization school often misrepresents Africa and indeed is ahistorical.

In my view, this currently popular[4] "African-centric" rhetoric unfortunately serves to polarize and inflame—by the creation of "schools," by the insistence on the superior perspective of Africanists, and by egregious distortions of the M&P model—distracting scholars and students from the properly historical challenges that confront us.

The story that Michael Gomez (1998) tells in *Exchanging Our Country Marks: The Transformation of African Identities in the Colonial and Antebellum South* follows in the cultural nationalist tradition of Sterling Stuckey's *Slave Culture* (1987) but is inflected by a far more detailed knowledge of Africa. The book's overarching claim is that "from the colonial to the antebellum periods, Africans gradually underwent a process whereby the basis of their self-concept changed from ethnicity to race" (Gomez 1998:242). But this anodyne assertion is complemented by countless anecdotes and examples intended to bolster the hypothesis that particular African ethnicities played a more determinant role—and for a much longer period—in the lives of American slaves than was previously thought. To cite a typical example, Gomez (174) writes that

> Anna Miller of Frogtown and Currytown, on the western limits of Savannah, also testified in the 1930s that several of the older workers on the Butler Island plantation spoke a "funny language." Tony William Delegal, more than one hundred years old at the time, could even sing an African song.... The fact that Delegal (a form of Senegal?) could remember these words is itself testimony that African languages were kept alive by the African-born and passed on to descendants in certain instances.[5]

Such anecdotes and examples are bolstered by what seem to me quite groundless (and usually unhistoricized and unregionalized) assertions. For example,

> there exists sufficient evidence to demonstrate that many, if not most, Africans continued to speak their native language in North America.... There is no hard evidence to support the popular notion that newly arrived Africans of the same ethnicity or area of origin were separated. Rather, there is every reason to believe that they were kept together.... In the absence of information that would support intraethnic divisions as a general phenomenon, one can only posit the likelihood that captives from the same area were purchased and housed together.... At any one time prior to 1830, it is possible that from two-thirds to three-fourths of all African-born

slaves either could not or did not speak recognizable
English or French. This means that they were either speaking their native languages to one another or a version of
English/French so Africanized as to be unintelligible to
whites, or both.... The removal to the Maroon was an
attempt to re-create Africa in the swamps and inner recesses
of America, and as such would have entailed to some degree
a reaffirmation of ethnicity.... In 1720, then, the slave community [in North America] was for all practical purposes
African.... Throughout the colonial period, the vast majority
of African-born slaves and their progeny continued to practice various African religions.... The development of African
American society through 1830 was very much the product
of contributions made by specific [African] ethnic groups.
(172, 173, 180, 184, 194, 246, 291)

It is worth noting that the challenges faced by the slaves, as
Gomez depicts them, sound very much like those evoked by M&P—for
example,

in the course of African-African American interaction, there
were many items to be negotiated. Day-to-day concerns provided the framework for a great deal of the exchange.
Women and men from both sides of the Atlantic would have
necessarily discussed what were the best ways to nurse children and instill discipline, the proper care of the aged and
infirm, the best fishing methods, and what constituted
respectable behavior in the company of elders.... That is,
black folk had to re-create their society, their collective
inner life, drawing from any number of ethnic paradigms
and informed by the present crisis. (14–15)

But Gomez's understanding of how the slaves met these challenges
differs radically from the M&P model, consistently emphasizing the
persistence of (quasi-essentialized) African ethnicities. His detailed
maps of West and Central Africa, with the putative destinations of various African ethnicities in North America, beg exactly those questions
I think historians should be exploring with as open a mind as possible.
For me, the organization of Gomez's book—with central chapters

devoted to the fate in the Americas, first of people from Senegambia and the Bight of Benin, then of Islamicized Africans, next of Sierra Leoneans and the Akan, and finally of Igbos and West Central Africans—constitutes a hypothesis that remains both unproven and, in many cases (some of which should be clear from the citations above), entirely counterfactual. In my view, Gomez is at his best in maintaining an emphasis on the importance of hegemony and subjugation—and resistance—as he explores the development of African American culture, and in reminding us that African Americans often "engaged in polycultural rather than syncretic life-styles" (10).

John Thornton, in *Africa and Africans in the Making of the Atlantic World, 1400–1800* (1998a), reiterates the plea for a specifically Africanist perspective on the playing out of ethnicity in particular places and periods in the Americas. Nevertheless, his materials seem to me to be far more convincing regarding Africa—particularly West Central Africa—than the Americas. (Indeed, the first edition of his book broke new ground in demonstrating the pervasiveness and significance of movements of people and ideas, of exchanges between cultures, and of various kinds of syncretisms and creolizations—sometimes involving European invaders and traders and sometimes not—within Africa itself.) When he turns to the Americas, however, Thornton begins to write explicitly against the M&P model, claiming that it depicts "the resulting mixture" as "distinctly European and European-oriented, with the African elements giving it flavor rather than substance" (184).

On the crucial question of the cultural heterogeneity of Africans imported into the New World, while Thornton notes that "on the whole, modern research has tended to side with Mintz and Price, who argue that there were major differences among the cultures of the Atlantic coast of Africa" (184), he tries to show that this argument represents an exaggeration and that Africans were "not nearly so diverse as to create the kind of cultural confusion posited by those who see African diversity as a barrier to the development of an African-based American culture" (187). (Needless to say, neither Mintz nor Price has ever imagined that there was "cultural confusion," nor has either ever seen diversity as a "barrier." Rather—and here I speak explicitly for myself—I have consistently presented African cultural diversity *as an encouragement to inter-African syncretism and creolization.*) Thornton further claims that on large plantations in the Americas, "slaves would typically have no trouble finding members of their own nation with whom to communicate" (199) and that "the slave trade and subsequent transfer to New World plantations was not, therefore, quite as randomizing a process as posited by those who argue that Africans had to start from scratch culturally upon their arrival in the New World" (204). I would note that the idea of Afro-Americans "starting from scratch" is not a position anyone has endorsed for decades, despite Lovejoy's claim (cited above) that "Mintz and Price and their protégés in effect subscribe to E. Franklin Frazier's view that the culture of the Americas was 'new.'"

In Thornton's version of the Big Picture, Africa consistently reigns triumphant. For example, he writes that

> on the eve of the revolution in Saint-Domingue, Kikongo was also, in all likelihood, the most commonly spoken first language, or was a close runner-up to French. In fact, the creole leaders of the revolution in 1791 complained that most of their followers could "scarcely make out two words of French." (321)

But from an Americanist perspective, it might be useful to signal that these people's speech options were not simply limited to an African mother tongue or French. Indeed, these Haitians would in great majority have been speaking to one another in *their own shared language*—neither Kikongo nor French but a new language that they (and the generations of enslaved Africans and their descendants who preceded them) had created in Saint-Domingue: Haitian Creole.[6]

I would note the tendency for proponents of the Africa-centric position to systematically ignore the mass of contrary data that continues to accumulate across the Americas (including work by Sally and me on rapid creolization in Suriname). It was with great eagerness that I awaited the publication of the revised edition of Thornton's *Africa and Africans*, the first edition of which ended in 1680—that is, just before the founding of Suriname's Maroon communities. Because the second edition promised to bring things up to 1800, I had it "FedExed" from the US to Brazil, where I was teaching for the semester. But as the

French say, *Quelle déception!* Not a word (not even a typo) was changed
or revised in the first ten chapters. And the new, final, eighteenth-
century chapter devotes but a single paragraph to the Suriname
Maroons (whose early history and cultural development is now as carefully documented as perhaps any society in Afro-America and who by
themselves constitute such a powerful counterexample to Thornton's
generalizations), and that paragraph is based on a single source—a
brief article by a Dutch lecturer in anthropology who has never done
fieldwork among Maroons.

Surely this sort of motivated erasure of countervailing scholarship
is as unfortunate as it is unnecessary.[7] The two camps purport to share
the same intellectual goals. We would seem to be in the presence of a
(pseudo)debate based to some extent on careerism (a rivalry between
Africanists and Americanists and sometimes between historians and
anthropologists) but more importantly on underlying ideologies or
partis-pris (which have barely been acknowledged and certainly not yet
analyzed in print). As Trouillot (1998:8–9) remarks dryly,

> theories of creolization or of creole societies, assessments of
> what it means to be "creole" in turn, are still very much
> affected by the ideological and political sensibilities of the
> observers....All seize creolization as a totality, thus one level
> too removed from the concrete circumstances faced by the
> individuals engaged in the process. All these models invoke
> history....Yet the historical conditions of cultural production
> rarely become a fundamental and necessary part of the
> description or analyses that these models generate. Calls for
> a more refined look at historical particulars [and here he
> points to a footnote to the M&P essay] remain unheeded. [8]

The M&P essay tried first and foremost to propose an *approach* for
studying the African American past (indeed, this effort was explicit in
its original title: *An Anthropological Approach to the Afro-American Past*).
For the study of slavery across the Americas, it tried to lay out the kinds
of constants (for example, the realities of power differences) and the
kinds of variables (for example, demographic, cultural, geographic)
that merited scholars' attention. It assumed that, despite certain commonalities based on relations of power, slavery in nineteenth-century

Virginia, for example, was in significant ways a different institution from slavery in seventeenth-century Mexico or slavery in eighteenth-century Saint-Domingue, and it tried to point to the kinds of processes that brought about these differences. The clarion call of the M&P essay was historicization and contextualization—the same careful exploration of sociohistorical particulars that Mintz (1971) had first called for in the study of creole languages in the 1960s. Yet in arguing its brief, the M&P essay seems to have given the impression to some readers that processes of creolization that were relatively smooth and rapid and irreversible were necessarily the norm throughout the Americas. That is, it may at times have gone further in suggesting a model of "what really happened" (as opposed to a *methodological* model) than its authors intended. And here, I would suggest, my own then recent Saramaka experience may be partly to blame.

David Scott (1991:269) has suggested that both Herskovits and I "found" our models for Afro-American anthropology among the Saramaka (who he says have thus become "a sort of anthropological metonym...providing the exemplary arena in which to argue out certain anthropological claims about a discursive domain called Afro-America"). A recent reading of Herskovits's Saramaka field diaries (R. Price and S. Price 2003b) supports Scott's implication that Herskovits largely found that which he set out to demonstrate (see also F. Herskovits 1966). But in my own case, I believe that I was genuinely surprised by (and unprepared for) the importance of "first-time" (resistance-to-slavery) discourse in present-day Saramaka life. In any case, to the extent that Scott is underlining that the anthropologist is a product of his time and place and (dare I say?) subject position and that Africa was very much in the air in 1920s Harlem-Renaissanced New York City, just as resistance (to slavery and other more current oppressions) was very much in the air (as was tear gas) in 1960s Cambridge and New Haven (Bobby Seale and the Panthers were on trial a few blocks away on my first day of teaching at Yale), he's undoubtedly on to something. While collaborating on the M&P essay, I had my recent Saramaka experiences very much in mind, and much of my contribution to that work must have been shaped by them. And the fact that the ancestors of modern Saramakas—because of the specificities of their historical situation—forged their society via more rapid, smoother creolization processes than did African arrivants in some parts of the Americas may well have influenced the summary sketch we gave. Which is why it remains crucial to separate out the methodological model, which I believe still has quite general relevance, from the particular examples we presented (which today could be very much expanded on the basis of all that scholars have learned in the intervening thirty years).[9]

As Trouillot suggests, we must continue to insist on historical particulars.[10] And when Thornton and other Africa-centric historians move from the Big Picture (where "ideological preferences" drive their narrative) to "the concrete circumstances faced by the individuals engaged in the process" of creolization, they often provide provocative insights and raise important problems for further study.[11] For example, Thornton's explorations of the role of Kongo-born slaves among participants in the 1739 Stono Rebellion (1991) and the Haitian Revolution (1993) open intriguing new perspectives.[12] It would appear that the more specific (limited in time and space) the Africa-centric study of American phenomena, the better its chances of being historically persuasive. An article by historian of the Gold Coast Ray Kea (1996) about an eighteenth-century slave rebellion in the Danish West Indies is a case in point: he is able to tease out the consequences of the "Amina" backgrounds of the slaves involved with considerable subtlety, helping us imagine something of the mindset (ideologies, notions about authority, ideas about death) held by people being shipped out of a particular port at a particular time because of particular local circumstances in Africa, and to describe how some of these features played themselves out in a specific event in the New World. In short, there is little doubt that such an Africanist perspective has its place in our tool kit for understanding the ways enslaved Africans and their descendants created communities and institutions in their new homes. If used in the service of greater contextualization and historicization, rather than to promote a generalizing, creolization-bashing parti-pris, such perspectives, informed by rich knowledge of African history, cannot but add to our understandings of events on this side of the Atlantic.

Returning to the Big Picture—the master narrative of continuity—we might sum up version 1 as a militantly Africa-centric contemporary successor to the narrative of African survivals crafted by Herskovits in the 1920s and 1930s and embellished by Robert Farris Thompson in the 1970s and 1980s. Compatible with African American cultural nationalist positions, it stresses the staying power of African ethnicities and plays down processes of creolization or blending.

Version 2, as expressed by contemporary American historians, grows out of scholars' deep knowledge of New World as opposed to African realities and is therefore richer in its historical texture regarding slavery. It is fully compatible with the project of the M&P essay, as well as with other roughly contemporaneous writings that stressed New World creativity, blending, and creolization, such as Bastide ([1960] 1978), C. Joyner (1984), or Levine (1977). For present purposes, we may take recent works by Ira Berlin and by Philip Morgan as exemplary.[13] In each, the starting point is systematic comparison (among regions and through time), and the complexity of cultural development is highlighted.

Berlin (1998:3) opens his book with the credo that "understanding that a person was a slave is not the end of the story but the beginning, for the slaves' history was derived from experiences that differed from place to place and time to time and not from some unchanging transhistorical verity." And he generalizes shortly thereafter that "rather than proceed from African to creole or from slavery to freedom, people of African descent in mainland North America crossed the lines between African and creole and between slavery and freedom many times, and not always in the same direction" (5).

Berlin's developmental model of North American slavery begins with the charter generation—the first slaves off the ships, who in no way fit the time-worn stereotypes of saltwater Africans. In the Chesapeake region, for example, "although some of the new arrivals hailed directly from Africa, most had already spent some time in the New World, understood the languages of the Atlantic, bore Hispanic and occasionally English names, and were familiar with Christianity and other aspects of European culture" (29). In Florida, the equivalent charter generation of "Atlantic creoles" managed to survive into the late eighteenth century, whereas in the South Carolina Lowcountry, the charter generation was much more quickly swamped by new Africans imported to labor on the great rice plantations that sprang up at the end of the seventeenth century. Meanwhile, Berlin argues, Louisiana witnessed a different (more Caribbean-like) progression, a smoother and more unidirectional passage from African to creole but also a passage from being a "slave society" to becoming "a society with slaves" (77).[14] Overall, in Berlin's North America, slavery and race were being constantly constructed and reconstructed according to changing historical circumstance.

Berlin's description of the dramatic re-Africanization (and subsequent recreolization) of the Chesapeake contrasts with the picture drawn by Gomez or Thornton. In describing how, under the new harsh tobacco regime, "African slaves and their descendants, sometimes in league with remnants of the charter generations, began to reshape black life," Berlin insists that "through the entire period [of re-Africanization], the majority came from ports as distant from one another as Senegambia and Angola" (114). And after discussing where slaves came from, how they arrived and were sold, and where they ended up during this period of intense re-Africanization, he summarizes: "Thus the slave trade in the Chesapeake operated to scatter men and women of various nations and diminish the importance of African nationality" (115). The "African moment" ended in the fourth decade of the eighteenth century, when Chesapeake life was once again transformed "as a new generation of African Americans eclipsed the African majority, ending the era of African domination....The Chesapeake once again became a creole society.... The African moment in Chesapeake history was passing, as the African population aged and the rising generation of African Americans came into its own" (126–128).

In short, for this one region—and Berlin takes us through similar changes for other parts of North America—we get a picture of immense variation in which African ethnicity plays a role only selectively, in both time and space, and in which creolization—though rarely discussed explicitly in this book, which focuses more on results than process—is an ever-present motor of development and change.

Berlin's book makes clear how foolhardy it would be to base a general model of the development of slave culture on Lowcountry South Carolina in the early eighteenth century (where, in Thornton's [1998a:320] fine phrase, "African culture was not surviving—it was arriving"), on the Chesapeake during the Revolutionary era, or on

early-nineteenth-century Louisiana (or, for that matter, on seventeenth-
and eighteenth-century Saramaka). The historical particulars *matter*,
and the pace and rhythm and nature of creolization differed. But
the methodological and theoretical assumptions matter too. Berlin's
understanding of ethnicity (like Morgan's [see below]) strikes me as
sensitive and theoretically informed and comes much closer to that
shared by most anthropologists than does that of Gomez, Thornton, or
the other Africa-centrists. Berlin points to the absence of an idea of
"Africa," and the ultimate flexibility of ethnicities, in the minds of the
recently enslaved:

> Africa houses hundreds, perhaps thousands, of different
> "nations"....The language, religion, domestic organization,
> aesthetics, political sensibilities, and military traditions that
> Africans carried from the interior to the plantations cannot
> be understood in their generality but only in their particu-
> lars, for the enslaved peoples were not Africans but Akan,
> Bambara, Fon, Igbo, or Mande....New identities [in the
> Americas] took a variety of forms....Competition, as well as
> cooperation, within the quarter compounded the remnants
> of ancient enmities, giving nationality or ethnicity an ever-
> changing reality and with it new meanings to Akan,
> Bambara, and Fon identity. In this changing world, national-
> ity or ethnicity did not rest upon some primordial commu-
> nal solidarity, cultural attribute, or common experience, for
> these qualities could be adopted or discarded at will. In the
> Americas, men and women identified as Angolans, Ibos, or
> Males frequently gained such identities not from their
> actual birthplace or the place from which they disembarked
> but because they spoke, gestured, and behaved like—
> or associated with—Angolans, Ibos, or Males....For most
> Africans, as for their white counterparts, identity was a gar-
> ment which might be worn or discarded....Choice, as well as
> imposition or birthright, determined who the new arrivals
> would be....In short, identity formation for African slaves
> was neither automatic nor unreflective, neither uniform nor
> unilinear.[15] (103–105)

If Berlin's book paints the Big Comparative Picture for North America, Philip Morgan's equally ambitious *Slave Counterpoint* (1998) focuses more single-mindedly on the development of slave culture itself.[16] Unlike Berlin's book, which is organized by a regional and chronological grid, Morgan's is organized by institutions (viewed through time), examining material life, work in the fields, skilled labor, exchanges between whites and blacks, family life, and so forth. Morgan synthesizes a remarkable amount of data in comparing cultural developments in the Chesapeake and the Lowcountry, beginning with the demographic givens: creoles formed a majority in Virginia by 1720 (and by 1780, 95 percent of Virginia slaves were creoles), whereas in South Carolina the African-born held a majority till mid-century, with creoles making up a two-thirds majority by 1780 (Morgan 1998:95). Morgan treats African ethnicity as important at certain moments but as a variable that faded relatively quickly in terms of the slaves' identity politics, both because of rapid creolization and because of the growth of widespread race consciousness in the later eighteenth century. "In the Chesapeake, creoles were a majority on most plantations and neighborhoods by the early eighteenth century; they set the tone and tenor of slave life in the region remarkably early. Africans learned the ropes from them.... The lessons largely flowed from creoles to Africans" (460–461). Though Lowcountry developments were different in detail—"In Charleston, even the most sophisticated creole slaves lived cheek by jowl with Africans" (461)—"in the long run, however, Africans, even in the Lowcountry, were aliens in a strange land" (456). Indeed, Morgan ultimately views ethnicity, as well as other aspects of African culture, mainly as "a resource on which...slaves could draw" in forging a new African American culture (457). And his detailed discussion of the development of slave religion in North America likewise draws on M&P-like assumptions:

> The religion of slaves in eighteenth-century British America
> highlights how blacks, laboring under extreme hardships
> and in radically different settings, managed to preserve
> some deep-level principles drawn from their African heritage. Much was lost: few priests and almost no collective rituals survived the passage.... [But] at the fundamental level

of epistemological beliefs, interpersonal relations, and expressive behavior, slaves kept alive a measure of their African "character." They engaged in a process of selective appropriation or structured improvisation in which values and practices were reinterpreted as they were incorporated.[17] (657–658)

That Morgan (and Berlin) draws on many of the same sources (and often the same quotations) as Gomez only serves to highlight the extent to which their interpretations of "what really happened" contrast. Morgan has Africans "learning the ropes" from creoles; Gomez has second- and even third-generation African Americans being "dominated" by first-generation and "native" Africans. In one of the more bizarre twists to this debate, a recent book by Lorena Walsh, *From Calabar to Carter's Grove: The History of a Virginia Slave Community* (1997), seems to be read almost like a Rorschach test by the various players. A review in the *William and Mary Quarterly* (Sidbury 1998) states that

the most important issue that Walsh discusses involves the ways enslaved Africans became Afro-Virginians, processes outlined in the pioneering work of anthropologists Sidney W. Mintz and Richard Price. Walsh's portrayal fits their creolization model, as new Africans and creole slaves forged a syncretic culture during the eighteenth century.... Historians of early American slave communities have been reevaluating the Mintz-Price model for understanding the emergence of African-American communities under slavery. Some insist that, contrary to the model, early slave communities retained ethnically specific African cultures....Walsh's work suggests that even in conditions that were, by Virginia's standards, ideal for testing this revisionist position—Carter's Grove contained many slaves who shared a regional African heritage—creolization proceeded rapidly. (631–633)

Berlin draws similar conclusions from Walsh's book: "A close analysis of the holding of a single planter family over more than a century [Walsh 1997] reveals how, even when slaves derived from a single catchment area, changes in the slave trade over time, the entry of small groups from other parts of Africa, and the internal sale and movement of slaves prevented the direct transfer of any single African nation or culture to the Americas" (Berlin 1998:410). Nonetheless, Walsh herself appears to resist these conclusions at any cost. In a recent overview of the role of African ethnicity in North America, drawing heavily on the data from her book, she criticizes Morgan (for such statements as "The homogenizing tendency of stressing cultural unity in Africa, of emphasizing the non-random character of the slave trade, and of seeing the dominance of particular African coastal regions or ethnicities in most American settings, is at variance with the central forces shaping the early modern Atlantic world" [Morgan 1997:142]) and lauds Gomez (for such statements as "A more informed discussion of the role of ethnicity can only further elucidate an examination of acculturation" [Gomez 1998:9]). It is hard to escape the conclusion that ideology and politics—the specificities of North American identity politics—continue to direct the master narratives, as well as influence how they are read (see Mintz and Price 1992:xiii–xiv; H. Gates 1998).

Perhaps, as Trouillot (1998:20) suggests, it is simply too early to generalize about creolization—"we have not thought enough about what went on in specific places and times to produce a framework sensitive enough to time, place, and power." But the North American cases we have examined here suggest that we may need more than increased knowledge about sociohistorical particulars. In anthropology, the classic cases of rival interpretations involve restudies (from Redfield versus Lewis on Tepoztlán to Mead versus Freeman on Samoa), in which changes resulting from the lapse of several decades of change on the ground are not always easy to separate out from paradigm shifts in the discipline or differences due to the ethnographers' skills and personalities. What is striking in the current North American slavery debates is that we have scholars writing simultaneously, using much the same data—and often citing the exact same primary sources—coming to opposing conclusions. Perhaps in the present case, the players simply need to continue to duke it out in public and in their publications, in the hope that Truth and Reason will emerge victorious.

As one who, in the wake of Herskovits and Mintz, has always argued for a pan-Afro-American perspective (see, e.g., R. Price 1996), I would advocate here also the need for broader comparison, both across Afro-America and across disciplines, as a way of nudging these debates beyond particular ideological battlegrounds. (American historians seem even more parochial in these respects than their colleagues abroad.) For surely, similar general processes of culture-building were at work everywhere. To cite but two examples of the kind of work that might help bring peace to the protean wars of North American historians: In an erudite book that crossed my desk shortly before I was writing this chapter, *"Chi ma nkongo": Lengua y rito ancestrales en El Palenque de San Basilio (Colombia)*, Armin Schwegler (1996) demonstrates first that songs sung at the most apparently African of all Palenquero rites, the *lumbalú*, are (in the words of one reviewer) "not the partially decreolized outcome of original African songs, but rather are essentially modern [that is, eighteenth-century or nineteenth-century] creations, based on a combination of regional Spanish and Palenquero [the local creole language], to which African and pseudo-African words and onomatopoeic elements have been added," and, second, "that the active use of spoken African languages in Palenque disappeared very early, if in fact the population ever used an African language as the primary means of communication" (Lipski 1998:357). (This second point, about the early development and predominance of a creole language, is especially interesting in that Schwegler is able to show that the Africans who founded Palenque were characterized by a relative linguistic homogeneity, with Bantu languages, particularly ki-Kongo, providing the main substratum for the new creole.) In his review, Lipski (1998:359–360) calls this book "at once a masterful analysis of the elusive *lumbalú* language and a major breakthrough in Afro-creole studies...a benchmark against which future studies of creole languages and cultures will be measured."

More generally, how can we best encourage our students, and one another, to read and react to such work—in this case, an expensive two-volume work published in Germany, written in Spanish, about a black community in the hinterlands of Colombia, but one that has crucial lessons to teach every one of us interested in questions of "Africanisms" and African ethnicity in the Americas, whether in tidewater Virginia or Bahia? Or again, I had the privilege of reading in manuscript J. Lorand Matory's historical study (Matory 2005), which brilliantly analyzes the ideological role of African ethnicity, and the ongoing creation and redefinition of African ethnicities in Bahia. My own strong feeling is that we must follow such leads and get on with the work of historical interpretation, leaving the posturing to others. In my view—which, on this issue, has not budged since the M&P essay—African ethnicity remains *one* (among many) of the ways enslaved peoples brought to the New World thought about (and in some parts of the Americas continue to think about) themselves, and it played varied roles in different aspects of life for varying periods in different places in the New World.

Perhaps the most thoughtful and up-to-date summary of this position may be found in an article by Philip Morgan (1997), in which he draws on the latest data about the Atlantic slave trade to consider the overall cultural implications for New World societies. Also, for some very important recent materials from the African side, which afford detailed support to this position, see the work of David Northrup (2000, 2002).

As noted earlier, David Scott has suggested a reorientation of Afro-American anthropology away from "this sustained preoccupation [which he finds in the work of Herskovits and Price] with the corroboration or verification of authentic pasts" and toward "discourse." "Between that event (Africa or slavery) and this memory," he writes, "there spreads a complex discursive field we may usefully call 'tradition'" (D. Scott 1991:278). As I read it, Scott's radical critique would deny the primary object of historical study—pasts that exist independent of a cultural imagining of them. But I am not enough of a postmodernist—or so afraid of essentializing—to be willing to discard, say, the facts of eighteenth-century demography or colonial statutes or accounts of tortures meted out to recaptured Maroons. For all these I believe have *effects*, and not just on discourse or tradition, in the present. I submit that we should embrace the written, oral, and artifactual traces left us by the past in all their epistemological complications (and fully accept their constructedness) and then do our level best to represent them honestly. Saramakas are more than an "anthropological metonym...providing the exemplary arena in which to argue out certain anthropological claims" (D. Scott 1991:269). They are at once socially and politically marginalized African Americans who have heroic Maroon traditions, who have against all odds created a vibrant culture, and whose lives (and way of life) are as threatened today as they have been at any moment since the end of the colonial wars two and a half centuries ago. Sally and I feel a deep responsibility, as anthropologists and friends, to help Saramakas tell their story, in part as a means of self-defense against severe ongoing repression (see R. Price 1995, 1998a; R. Price and S. Price 2001, 2003a).

The agenda of *First-Time* was multiple, and not all of its aims fit together smoothly. Like any ambitious work, it tried to address several quite different concerns that were in the air at the time of its composition. One of its targets was skeptical historians, those powerful traditionalists in every university who continued to deny the possibility that "primitive peoples"—particularly those without writing—could have a sense of their own past that transcended "myth." My book, like that of my undergraduate- and graduate-school buddy Renato Rosaldo on the Ilongots of the Philippines (1980), was, in part, intended to give historians (and some anthropologists, including Sahlins and Lévi-Strauss) a wake-up call on this hoary issue. A related concern, more resolutely Herskovitsian in nature, was to demonstrate that these particular African Americans did have a past—the project that Scott is more directly concerned about. (Here the aim was double—showing not only that there were, among Saramakas, historians who behaved, despite cultural differences, rather like our own but also that their collective vision of the Saramaka past could be fruitfully compared with more traditional records constructed by non-Saramakas.) A third goal of *First-Time* was purely documentary—to present, and thus preserve for posterity, "the historical vision" of the Saramaka Maroons (generalized in the book's subtitle to "an Afro-American people" in order, if memory serves, to try to appeal to a wider-than-anthropological audience).[18]

In addition to these concerns, *First-Time* tried to focus attention on the dialectic between event and memory, in the belief that Afro-Americanist anthropologists must ultimately figure out how to analyze and represent both. Scott suggests that *First-Time's* "bold and innovative ethnographic strategy" is plausible "only...insofar as we accept the conceptual premise that pasts are preservable and representable," and he chooses to "differ with what appears to be Price's view, namely that both the oral testimony of his Saramaka informants and the written texts of the Dutch colonizers are culturally different, yet conceptually uncomplicated ways of re-presenting the past in the present" (D. Scott

1991:267–268). Perhaps because it is not my style to wear my theoretical assumptions on my authorial sleeve, I am probably partly responsible for Scott's misunderstanding of my views here. So I would like to put on record that *First-Time* takes off from the credo that both ethnographic truths and historical truths are always *partial* truths—as Jim Clifford (1986) quickly understood.[19] And I begin (again *pace* Scott) with the assumption that both oral testimony and archival documents are enormously complicated conceptually. From this perspective, my aim in *First-Time* was not to corroborate contemporary Saramaka memories by using eighteenth-century archives but to show how (and in many cases why) modern Saramaka discourse on the one hand and colonial Dutch documents on the other each constitute partial truths—that is, I tried always to keep in mind the relevant political, ideological, and other influences on the selection, transmission, and silencing of the past—the production of history—in each case. Such a strategy poses severe representational challenges, which is why *First-Time* assumes its unusual organization and page layout. It is also why I did not discuss at greater length the political, ideological, and other considerations that shape the Saramaka discourse I presented in the book (though I did offer examples of how these work themselves out)—that is, I explicitly chose not to overwhelm the reader with local clan and personal names and the detailed history of internal political disputes. Nor did I rehearse at length the complicated issues of the making of the Dutch archives and other written sources, which I covered more extensively in another book published the same year (R. Price 1983b). In any case, my concerns about problematizing oral, written, and ethnographic sources are, I believe, ever-present in *First-Time*, but I chose not to dwell overly on them in order to achieve even that level of representational clarity I managed in presenting quite foreign and complex cultural realities to an English-speaking audience.

I believe that rather than privileging discourse, which runs grave dangers, Afro-Americanists must embrace both discourse and event, figuring out imaginative representational strategies to handle them together. (Trouillot [1998:15] notes that "as social theory becomes more discourse-oriented, the distance between data and claims in debates about creolization…increases. Historical circumstances fall further into a hazy background of ideological preferences.") One strategy, which I used extensively in *First-Time*, is to hold both in mind but to treat them, alternatively, as figure and ground. Several of the essays in Trouillot's *Silencing the Past* (1995) constitute admirable attempts to achieve similar ends for Haiti in the revolutionary period. *Alabi's World* (R. Price 1990) and particularly *The Convict and the Colonel* (R. Price 1998b) constitute other attempts of my own, adopting different representational strategies, toward the same ends. At the simplest level, I am arguing that to fully understand "discourse" (collective memory and the ways meaning is attributed to such figures as slavery, resistance, or Africa in the present), we must simultaneously consider "event" (demography—including ethnicity—through time, the sociology and economics of particular plantation regimes, and so on), and that in order to understand "event" or "history," we must also consider "discourse" and ideology. For example, how can one begin to comprehend the significance (the enormity) of current erasures and silencings of the slave past among peasants and fishermen in Martinique without knowing that Martinique was, in some sense, the slave society par excellence—one-fourth the size of Long Island but receiving roughly the same number of enslaved Africans as the whole of the United States (R. Price 1998a)? In sum, I believe that our understanding of the African American past must embrace both memory and event if we are to understand either, which is why (in my writing and teaching) novels and poetry rub shoulders so closely with historical and anthropological monographs. History depends, in part, on the imagination, just as collective memory depends, in part, on past events.

Undoubtedly, generational differences underlie some of the gap between Scott's critique and my response.[20] In a sense, to consider the M&P essay or *First-Time* as canonical is to convert them into artifacts of a status quo ripe to be surpassed. Given the new and often competing (even contradictory) agendas that relate to their respective *problématiques*—and all the attached anxieties—in the modern academy, it is hardly surprising that critiques as divergent as Lovejoy's and Scott's have now been voiced. Despite continuities in the brute realities of North American racism through time, the academy has undergone a sea change in the past three decades. Identity politics, issues of race and postcolonialism, postmodernism, and much else situate the young fin- de-siècle scholar very differently from the anthropologist trained at the end of what George Stocking (1992) called the "classical period" of the discipline (circa 1925 to circa 1965). But that doesn't prevent the old anthropologist from playing new tricks. If *First-Time* was marked by a tension between event and discourse—between trying to corroborate authentic Afro-American pasts and trying to deconstruct the production of history—*Enigma Variations*, a recent novel written with Sally (R. Price and S. Price 1995), is marked by the tension between its protagonists' trying to appraise the authenticity of pieces of "primitive art" and the authors' trying to deconstruct the idea of authenticity. *The Convict and the Colonel*, about a rather different postcolonial African American society, takes on event (slavery, the *bagne*), memory (mine, theirs), and discourse (academic, literary, and "folk"), as well as nostalgia, to consider more generally where we've been and where we might be going. As Stocking found, it is far more difficult to historicize the extended present—the period since the 1960s, now almost as long as the "classical period"—than the more distant past. Many of the concerns in the academy and society at large when the M&P essay and *First-Time* were written have faded, and a very different set has taken their place. The passions remain, whether about ethnicity or discourse, but they have been radically displaced.

At last, perhaps anticlimactically, we arrive at the "unconscious principles" that Kevin Yelvington asked me to elucidate. As Trouillot (1998:21) now frames the project:

> Sidney Mintz and Richard Price suggest that the West African cultural heritage is to be found mainly in unconscious, underlying "grammatical principles": cognitive orientations, attitudes, expectations common to the diverse communities whence most of the enslaved came. They argue that these underlying principles ordered the process of creolization by making certain choices more appealing or more significant than other possible ones. This argument needs to be refined in light of more sustained research on the institutional impact of African ethnicity on slave practices in specific territories. In other words, the underlying principles that Mintz and Price highlight had to work through tensions among Africans in order to produce

138

meaningful practices and we need to know how and when they did so. More important, however a modus vivendi on cultural grammar was obtained among slaves, shared principles—old and new—had to survive the European exercise of power. How did they do so? When and how were they given space and time to breathe and to breed? How did they survive and reproduce themselves enough to generate new institutions?

The idea of deep-level, unconscious principles as a key to unraveling the African American past is an old one (for Herskovits's "grammar of culture" statement, see Mintz and Price 1992:11). One could read much of Sally's and my work as an attempt to demonstrate its power in specific domains—from an overview of Afro-American naming patterns written three decades ago (R. Price and S. Price 1972) to a more recent book that deals in detail with a range of aesthetic domains (S. Price and R. Price 1999). From postures to costume, from embroidery to narrow-strip sewing, from woodcarving to calabash carving, and from music and dance to tale telling, we try to show how widely shared African aesthetic principles have played themselves out through three centuries of Saramaka history, beginning with the demographics of the slave trade and working our way through event and memory up to present-day production techniques. Because that lengthy work is now available for critical consideration and the argument about "unconscious principles" is laid out in some detail (see also Sally's chapter in this book), neither our descriptions and analyses of "creolization Saramaka-style" nor our accounts of the intricate fieldwork involved in teasing out these "unconscious principles" require rehash or re-presentation here. The proof, as far as we are concerned, should not be in our claims but in the pudding.

It is worth noting, however, what that 1999 book—the fruit of more than three decades of thinking about the development of Saramaka culture—does *not* (indeed cannot) say about creolization. Miracles ultimately depend on faith, and the miracle of creolization has not yet proved to be an exception. Berlin and Morgan for North America, or Matory and the Prices for South America, provide extensive contextualization for the processes of culture change among the recently enslaved and their descendants in the New World. When such works are at their best, we feel almost as if we are witnesses to the particular conflicts and acts of solidarity and imagination involved in the shift from one kind of identity to another, or from an Old World tradition to a new one. But however far we are able to push back in time the documented beginnings of such cultural developments, we find ourselves stuck in the paradoxical position, like Achilles in Zeno's paradox, of never quite being able to catch the tortoise. Like physicists with their big bang birth of the universe, we can theorize the event (or the process), but we seem ever unable to observe it effectively. So the ultimate miracle of creolization remains, at least for now, impenetrable. We can imagine (or theorize) how the women and men on Plantation X worked out the procedures—the rites, the music, the beliefs—appropriate to the birth of twins, beginning when that first hypothetical mother brought her babies into the New World, but we can never be present at the blessed event itself. We know that it must have happened and that it happened over time in tens of thousands of often-independent cases throughout the Americas. A miracle that repeated itself endlessly.

For Saramaka, we can now reliably push its date back before the mid-eighteenth century—three decades of archival research since the M&P essay permits unequivocal demonstration that, in general, African ethnicities were not by that time salient for Saramakas culturally, in terms of identifying individuals or as markers for groups. In other words, we can demonstrate that Saramaka society at the time of the Peace Treaty of 1762 was far closer to Saramaka today, in terms of cultural development, than it was to Africa. Yet, though we have been able to push the major creolization processes ever earlier in time, we are still unable to examine them directly.

Because our anthropological model of creolization derives from linguistics, it may be worth a final detour to consider briefly the state of the art among our linguist cousins. Even in a discipline that prides itself on relative systematics and scientific method, ideology and parti-pris (and subject position) seem to dominate at least as much (and for similar reasons) as they do in other disciplines related to Afro-American studies. Exclusivistic and monocausal theories of creole genesis—whether based on Portuguese-pidgin monogenesis, African substrata, European superstrata, or the putative bioprogram—seem as prevalent today as in the past. One example may suffice. In a recent review article on historical creolistics, Derek Bickerton (1999:98) casually but pointedly notes that "like many (most?) Francophone creolists, and unlike most, if not all non-Francophone creolists, Guy Hazaël-Massieux sees creoles as modified continuations of their superstrates." Is it not remarkable—however understandable, given the way the French think about their language—that Francophone creolists still insist on—despite all the evidence brought by non-Francophone creolists—the primacy of French in the creation of Haitian, for example?[21] Or again, consider the vitriol Bickerton summons up to characterize John McWhorter's (1997) account of creolization on the west coast of Africa, which Bickerton (1999) claims is filled with "half-truths, non-sequiturs, and mistakes [and] also plain falsifications," adding that "to support such a sociolinguistically unlikely scenario, McWhorter can produce not a single citation, not one iota of historical evidence." Even a glance at the *Journal of Pidgin and Creole Languages* would show that such inflated (and self-serving) rhetoric is almost par for the course on all sides of the debate. To the extent that creolist linguists depend ultimately on historians for their sociocultural context and must infer the actual process of creolization from post-facto linguistic features, they are really little better off than the rest of us. Whether it's Bickerton's Saramaka Adams and Eves in the Suriname rain forest or McWhorter's ancestors of the Saramakas hanging out at Coromantee, we can still only imagine, using all the data at our disposal, something of what it might have been like.

This leaves us, I suppose, considerably humbled, with our task to once again put our collective noses to the grindstone. In the end, it is only when the competing narratives are confronted, and weighed carefully against one another, that we can begin to develop reasons for giving greater credibility to one or the other. We have little choice but to keep on tilling the fields. At the beginning of the twenty-first century, "creolization"—even if resistant to direct observation—still remains, in Trouillot's apt characterization (1998:8), "a miracle begging for analysis."

Notes

I wish to thank Phil Morgan, Peter Redfield, David Scott, and Rolph Trouillot, as well as the members of the SAR advanced seminar, for their generous and helpful comments on a draft of this chapter. I would also like to thank the College of William and Mary for a faculty summer research grant that, in part, supported this project. I would also like to acknowledge that the title phrase is shamelessly borrowed from Michel-Rolph Trouillot's (1998) recent excursion into the wondrous phenomenon of creolization.

1. I wish to make clear at the outset that I speak here only for myself. I have not discussed any aspect of this chapter with Mintz.

2. Writing against "the ideological assumptions that serve to secure the seeming authority of such anthropological arguments regarding [Afro-American pasts]," Scott (1991:268) says:

> These ideological assumptions have to do with the kind of anthropological object that the Afro-American or the Afro-Caribbean (or anyway the New World Negro) has historically been constructed as. I would argue that at least one of the pervasive ideological assumptions through which this theoretical object has been constructed is that peoples of African descent in the New World require something like anthropology, a science of culture, to provide them with the foundational guarantee of an authentic past."

3. It may be worth noting that in contrast to the recent attention given by card-carrying historians and anthropologists to the history of such debates in Afro-American studies, Afro-Americanist scholars in the discipline of cultural studies have tended to ignore the debates of the past fifty years, thus leaving the field rhetorically free for their own "discoveries." Brackette Williams makes the point in her trenchant critique of Paul Gilroy's *The Black Atlantic* (1993) when she urges attention to its silences. In this much discussed book, she argues that

> we lack an intellectual connection with past efforts to understand processes of cultural production which are products and producers of trans-cultural, pre-national, or extra-national conceptual and grounded unities....Silenced are several generations of scholars from and students of the Caribbean and Latin America whose work speaks to the issues Gilroy raises throughout the Black Atlantic. With differing degrees of success, these scholars of varied hues have tried to understand processes of cultural production and identity formation in conceptual units spanning geographical spaces and overlapping economic regimes (Brackette Williams 1995:181, 188).

In a note, she makes clear that she is referring to, among other works, the M&P essay. In a separate comment, Mintz (1998:128) opined similarly that "the recent fuss about Caribbean modernity and the Black Atlantic is just the wheel being rediscovered—C. L. R. James, among others, knew it long ago."

4. Lorena Walsh (1998:2) goes so far as to point—I think, with considerable exaggeration—to "an emerging orthodoxy that sees slaves as forming identifiable communities based on their ethnic or national pasts."

5. If such anecdotes prove anything, we might add that one of my Russian-born grandmothers taught me a song and Sally's Swedish grandfather taught her a single phrase—"Do you like to fish?"—each of which constitute the only words of their mother tongues they passed on directly, or via their children, to their American grandchildren.

6. Thornton's consistent use of the phrase *the colonial language* (that is, the European colonizer's language, which he opposes to various African languages) throughout his new, eighteenth-century chapter exposes his parti-pris. In his account, creole languages—which in most territories at most times were the most widely used means of communication among slaves—scarcely exist.

7. I should add that none of this is, to my knowledge, in any way personal. The opposing scholars hardly know one another and have no private grudges known to me—which makes it all the more interesting intellectually.

8. Stephan Palmié (1997) makes similar observations about the misuse or misreading of the M&P essay:

> Despite its theoretical sophistication and methodological soundness, the "rapid early synthesis" model suggested by Mintz and Price fell short of stimulating a thorough historicization of African-American anthropology. Instead, and quite contrary to these authors' intentions, it sometimes seems to have encouraged hypostatizing the concept of creolization to a degree where it allows glossing over history.

9. By trying to heed the Saramaka proverb "Lizard says: 'Speed is good, but so is caution'" and thus achieve some balance, I may protest too much in this paragraph. Two readers of this paper—Phil Morgan and Rolph Trouillot—while agreeing that the thrust of M&P is surely methodological (an "approach to"), urged me (in Trouillot's words) "not to give up the central point of the speed issue," though of course "to leave room for decreolization, recreolization, or other processes, which is another matter," and (in Morgan's words) "to hold on to the early creolization model and not give too much ground on that score....I would guess early creolization applies in most places."

This may be the place to acknowledge explicitly the influence of the late Dutch missionary-linguist Jan Voorhoeve on the notion of early creolization used in the M&P essay. A major reassessment of his work is Meel 1997.

10. This is very much the tenor of the most recent visit by Sally and me to this general issue, in a footnote to *Maroon Arts* (S. Price and R. Price 1999:329–330), where we note that

> Monica Schuler has taken R. P. to task for (over)emphasizing the rapidity of creolization and has, in contrast, stressed what she sees as the continuing importance of African ethnic solidarity (Schuler 1970, 1979, 1980; see also Karasch 1979). Some scholars have claimed that planters in some colonies at some moments encouraged the maintenance of African ethnic solidarity as a means of control, while others have pointed to widely-attested planters' practices of separating slaves of a particular ethnic origin for the same purpose (see, for references, R. Price 1979:142). R. P. has cautioned that "such statements, which originate in data from particular societies at particular historical moments, can be converted into generalizations only at the risk of obscuring the very variation that is crucial to understanding the nature of New World slavery" (R. Price 1979:143).

We go on to suggest that Roger Bastide, working with Brazilian materials, espoused a perspective that dissolves many of these difficulties. "We know little about Afro-Brazilian religions in those distant times," wrote Bastide ([1960] 1978:47–48),

> but we should certainly give up the notion of [African] cult centers surviving through centuries down to the present day...and think rather of a chaotic proliferation of cults or cult fragments arising only to die out and give way to others with every new wave of [African] arrivals. The candomblés, xangôs and batuques of today are not survivals of ancient sects reaching back into the Brazilian past but relatively recent organizations.... We should therefore think of the religious life of Africans in Brazil as a series of events lacking any organic links—traditions that were broken and resumed but that nevertheless retained from one century to the next...the same fidelity to the African mystique or mystiques.

And J. Lorand Matory's recent research on Bahian Candomblé and on Yorùbá religion lends considerable muscle to Bastide's assertions (Matory 2005).

Finally, we express our sympathy with Edward Kamau Brathwaite's poetic and imaginative critique of Monica Schuler's attempt to specify Jamaican myal as a solar, "Kongo" retention. "It may have been so in Central Africa," writes

Brathwaite (1979:152), "but in Jamaica it was (and is) a fragment or aspect of a larger creolised form which includes obiah, jonkonnu, and kumina/pukumina, 'convince,' congo and ettu."

11. There exists a substantial bibliography of works emphasizing the cultural contributions of specific African ethnicities to one or another New World colony. Among the more interesting, I would cite Chambers (1996); G. Hall (1992); Karasch (1987); Littlefield (1981); Palmer (1995); Reis (1993); Schuler (1980); and Walsh (1997).

12. More recently, Thornton (1998b) has suggested an Africanist perspective as a more general research strategy, though the two case studies he presents in support—one from early-eighteenth-century Kongo and the other from nearly contemporaneous Dahomey—however rich in their African texture, in fact, tell us little about the consequences of the specific African events for the New World communities in which the expelled slaves landed. Years ago, I wrote an extended critique of (it so happens) a Kongo-centric approach to the study of Saramaccan lexicon (R. Price 1975a), trying to suggest some of the dangers within—dangers I believe are not entirely absent even from the more sophisticated recent Africa-centric works.

13. At the time of the SAR advanced seminar, these two books had only recently been published. By the time of the first-draft chapter submission for this collection (six months later, in October 1999), they had already garnered, between them, more than a dozen major book prizes.

14. In another context, I might argue with some of the particular trajectories Berlin posits for his various regions, for example, the Lower Mississippi Valley. But his general stress on variation and uneven development nevertheless seems cardinal.

15. Paralleling this position from an African perspective, Kwame Anthony Appiah has written eloquently on the historically contingent nature of ethnic identities—part of the reason why the idea of establishing an African "baseline" for New World studies has been so fraught with problems. He cites Chinua Achebe's remarks about the relative recency of the "Igbo" identity in Nigeria: "For instance, take the Igbo people. In my area, historically, they did not see themselves as Igbo. They saw themselves as people from this village or that village.... And yet, after the experience of the Biafran War, during a period of two years, it became a very powerful consciousness" (Appiah 1992:177) Then he cautions that

recognizing Igbo identity as a new thing is not a way of privileging other Nigerian identities: each of the three central ethnic identities of

modern political life—Hausa-Fulani, Yoruba, Igbo—is a product of the
rough-and-tumble of the transition through colonial to postcolonial status. David Laitin has pointed out that "the idea that there was a single
Hausa-Fulani tribe...was largely a political claim of the NPC [Northern
People's Congress] in their battle against the South," while "many
elders intimately involved in rural Yoruba society today recall that, as
late as the 1930s, 'Yoruba' was not a common form of political identification.".... Modern Ghana witnesses the development of an Akan identity, as speakers of the three major regional dialects of Twi—Asante,
Fante, Akuapem—organize themselves into a corporation against an
(equally novel) Ewe unity....Identities are complex and multiple and
grow out of a history of changing responses to economic, political, and
cultural forces, almost always in opposition to other identities. (Appiah
1992:177–178)

16. Growing, in part, out of the same intellectual milieu as the M&P essay—
the Johns Hopkins Program in Atlantic History and Culture of the 1970s and
1980s—Morgan's book could be read as the most detailed implementation of the
general M&P project yet attempted for North America (though, of course, it is
much more than this). Indeed, it uses language of a strikingly similar kind in discussing a range of cultural issues throughout its more than seven hundred pages
(see, e.g., xxii, 257, 261, 442, 559, 580).

17. Contrast these passages with the following ones from Gomez's book
(parts already quoted above): "In 1720, then, the slave community [in North
America] was for all practical purposes African. The American-born constituent
was present, and continued to grow from 1740 to 1760....However, many of these
were first-generation Americans, so that they would have fallen under the encul-
turative provenance of African parentage. The combination of these first-
generation blacks and a native African population resulted in their domination
of second- and third-generation African Americans" (194).

18. In a reading very much of its time and place, Scott seems to suggest that
the fact that Saramaka Maroons represent, particularly from a North American
perspective, a relatively noble response to slavery makes them (and their ethnographers) somehow suspect. Such reasoning meshes with the "demotion" of the
figure of the once heroic (literary) Maroon by the contemporary Martiniquan
créolité movement (see R. Price and S. Price 1997) and would seem to be part of
a more general postcolonial Caribbean intellectual move.

19. *First-Time*, Clifford (1986:7) writes, "offers a good example of self-
conscious serious partiality...evidence of the fact that acute political and episte-

mological self-consciousness need not lead to ethnographic self-absorption, or to the conclusion that it is impossible to know anything certain about other people. Rather, it leads to a concrete sense of why a Saramaka folktale, featured by Price, teaches that 'knowledge is power, and that one must never reveal all of what one knows.'"

20. For more on Scott's project of retheorizing the horizons of postcolonial politics, see his 1999 book. His chapter on the poetry of Kamau Brathwaite (106–127), in which he attempts to "disarticulate Brathwaite's vision from the anthropological epistemology through which he seeks to guarantee it" (127), is particularly relevant to the issues in this chapter.

21. See R. Price and S. Price (1997) for a discussion of the anti-African (pro-French) extremes to which Martiniquan créolistes have carried such arguments about the development of their native tongue.

PART II. Dialogues in Practice

5

The "New World" Surrounds an Ocean

Theorizing the Live Dialogue between
African and African American Cultures

J. Lorand Matory

My best friend in Brazil is a priest of Candomblé, a stunningly beautiful religion of divination, healing, spirit possession, and celebration that is often taken as proof that African culture has "survived" in the Americas. Indeed, my friend Roberto knows a fantastic array of songs in languages called Jeje and Nagô, which he and his priestly colleagues agree are African. They largely agree on the moments in any serious Candomblé ceremony (the likes of which they also tend to consider African) when any given song is to be sung. Roberto's command of the ritual standards, songs, and aesthetic values of the Jeje nation, or denomination, have won him not only acclaim but also a wide following.

Yet Roberto fears that the substance of his power is draining away as the number of people who know how to respond to the songs in the Jeje language—and thereby know how to celebrate and activate the gods of the nation—declines every year. The Yorùbá-affiliated Nagô, or Quêto, nation so dominates the religious landscape (including the attention of the Brazilian mass media and the sponsors who fund the most lavish ceremonies) that the Jeje nation is in danger of a progressive form of extinction that Roberto and his friends call *anagonization*.

For example, because audiences at the great public festivals know few Jeje songs, Roberto must compromise the purity of his nation by singing Nagô songs in honor of his gods.

On the day we met in August 1987, Roberto thought that I was from Africa, which is at least one reason he immediately invited me into the shrine of the messenger god Exú to witness the annual sacrifice. I am certain, however, that some measure of spontaneous affection was also among his motives. We've been friends ever since. To most people in Brazil—not to mention West and West Central Africa—I look African, but Roberto was none too disappointed to discover that I had simply spent a great deal of time in Africa, mostly in Nigeria, where I had studied the gods of the Nagô-affiliated Yorùbá people.

Roberto has always been disinterestedly kind toward me, but soon after we met, he asked me to teach him some Yorùbá. Some of it rang a bell for him and some didn't, though he had spent much time in the great Nagô temples of Bahia (such as Casa Branca and Aizinho's Pilão de Prata), where the priests are reputed to speak, and, above all, sing in "perfect Yorùbá." Roberto soon tired of these lessons and set his goals higher. He wanted to go to Savalou, the African capital of the Savalú—his Jeje subnation—which I had told him was located in the People's Republic of Benin. He was anxious to visit there and to recover all that his Brazilian Jeje-Savalú forebears had forgotten or—out of spite, selfishness, and stupidity—refused to divulge to their successors before they died.

I could not imagine the immediate means of getting my friend to Savalou, but I promised to visit the place on his behalf and to find out as much as I could. I also agreed to bring him some African wild buffalo horns and instructions on how to make African black soap, which simply cost too much in Brazil. I quietly strategized on how I would get him plenty of some other ritual items, which I knew mainly by their Yorùbá names—ẹfun (white river lime), osùn (camwood powder), and atare (alligator pepper). A priestess friend—or actually the lively caboclo Indian spirit who spoke to me through her body at the priestess's fortnightly Candomblé "sessions"—sent me off with an order for a whole suit of pano da costa, the costly handwoven Yorùbá cloth worn around the waist, typically in more affordable quantities, by female Candomblé elites. Other priests and priestesses simply sent me off with so much love and generosity that I was anxious to bring them whatever ritual items, photographs, and bits of information I could find. Indeed, their demands, curiosities, concerns, and preoccupations profoundly shaped my questions and activities during the month I then spent in Savalou and the twelve additional months I then spent in Ìgbòho, Nigeria, in 1988 and 1989.

From one travel fellowship to the next—with more or less extended stopovers in London, Paris, Chicago, Washington, Cambridge, and Williamstown in between—I continually squirreled away ritual items, photocopies, books, song texts, praise poetry, newspapers, sculptures, vocabulary lists, and other information whose value would multiply when I took it to friends in places where it was less easily available. I have not yet been able to get Roberto to Savalou, but his several university-sponsored trips to the United States have, besides adding much joy and depth to our friendship, added some small height to his already enormous stature within the Candomblé. Such visits have also enabled him to compare his own beliefs and practices with those of my *santero* friends, practitioners of the Cuban and US Latino counterpart to Candomblé.

I am not the only friend to have sponsored Roberto's travels abroad. His itinerant spiritual godchildren have hosted him in Switzerland, France, Italy, and Spain. Nor is Roberto the only person who has benefited in some minor way from my transnational gratitude. Nor am I the only traveler to maintain such a network of friends who have some material, intellectual, or religious investment in the traveler; I am the successor and the predecessor to tens of thousands of such travelers. Indeed, there have been times in Brazilian and West African history when such investments were the basis of many livelihoods and furnished the foundational principles of major religious trends.

My friendship with Roberto is but a minor illustration of a major dialogue shaping the cultures and politics of the Afro-Atlantic world. Far from being the scattered and fading (or, in a few cases, heroically preserved) remains of "African culture," the cultures of the Afro-Atlantic have continually been refashioned through the voluntary exchange of people, objects, and ideas. The modes of musical creativity, the religious practices, the motor habits, and the linguistic dispositions cited as evidence of African Americans' collective "memory" or the "survival" of the African past have continually been reinscribed, not simply with meanings specific to their local American or African contexts but also with meanings generated specifically by *dialogue* among Afro-Atlantic locales.

ANALYTIC METAPHORS

This scholarly project employs the insight of Lakoff and Johnson that all perception and thought are mediated by metaphors, which involve the comparison of one domain of experience (the metaphoric "target") with another (the metaphoric "source"). Because of its experiential concreteness and clarity, the source helps illuminate the nature or structure of a target that is less concrete and less clear to those who wish to understand it. Any given metaphor, continue Lakoff and Johnson, tends to highlight particular aspects of the target in ways that another metaphor would not, while hiding other aspects of the target that another metaphor would not. For example, representing an argument as a battle (as in the expressions "Your claims are indefensible" and "He shot down all my arguments") highlights the competitive and mutually destructive aspects of debate while hiding its cooperative aspects (such as the shared effort toward mutual understanding) (Lakoff and Johnson 1980:4,10).

While Lakoff and Johnson are concerned chiefly with the metaphors that structure daily language and experience, I am keen to address the specialized set of metaphors that structure our *scholarly* language about and perception of reality. These we will call "analytic metaphors." Like theories, they should be judged not as true or false but as more or less useful in highlighting important dimensions of the realities we seek to explain and as more or less parsimonious in the explanations they allow.

The phenomenon that my colleagues and I wish to reconsider in this volume is the cultural history of the African diaspora. We are heirs to a family of well-established and productive analytic metaphors in our area of study. While they usefully highlight much about that cultural history that had previously been ignored, they also hide many dimensions of that cultural history that are long overdue for recognition. At times, I will argue, certain well-established metaphors even patently distort the phenomena they are intended to explain.

Thus I wish to propose here a new analytic metaphor in the discussion of the cultural history of Africa and its diaspora—dialogue. Though it arises from my research on African diaspora religion in Brazil, Cuba, Nigeria, and the United States, I think it helps us understand the similar historical dynamics of music, dance, politics, education, and so forth, around the Atlantic perimeter and other heavily traveled transgeographical complexes, such as the Silk Road and the circum-Mediterranean, circum–Indian Ocean, circum-Saharan, and medieval Islamic worlds.

ANTHROPOLOGY'S FOUNDATIONAL METAPHORS

The student of human culture always faces the quandary of how to explain what is far too complex to reduce to an article, a book, or even a lifelong scholarly opus. Analytic metaphors have helped us discern structural or otherwise salient aspects of social reality in such a way that makes summary sense of the details. For example, the term *culture* itself represents intergenerationally learned aspects of collective lifeways as something like *cultivation*—the agricultural selection, training, and reshaping of nature for the fulfillment of human bio-social needs. Even diasporas are compared, in the Greek etymology of the term, to *sowing*, or the dispersal of seeds.[1] Anthropologists have also represented human lifeways metaphorically as organisms (as in A. R. Radcliffe-Brown's organic metaphor) and as symbolic systems akin to languages or texts (as in Claude Lévi-Strauss's structuralism and Clifford Geertz's interpretive anthropology).

Such analytic metaphors have been convenient tools in highlighting the *synchronic* functioning of any given society or culture, and they emerge from an early-twentieth-century anthropology that was generally averse to the speculative histories of armchair ethnologists, evolutionists, and diffusionists. These metaphors sustained the image of the self-contained, isolated, bounded, and internally integrated society or culture. Yet sustaining that image in an era of worldwide colonialism required the erasure of history and the fiction of the "ethnographic present." Whereas British social anthropology typically endeavored to capture precolonial sociopolitical orders (often complementing the colonialist objective of resurrecting them as administrative units), the German American Franz Boas and the Frenchman Claude Lévi-Strauss shared the somewhat different aim of archiving precolonial lifeways before they were swept away by Western influence and expansion.

Yet the proximity of Columbia's Boas and his students to the black intellectuals and political leaders in New York City—including W. E. B. Du Bois, Marcus Garvey, and the literati of the Harlem Renaissance—made it inevitable that American cultural anthropology would turn its analytical eye toward the politically central theme of black difference. Yet Afro-Americanist anthropology remained marginal to the broader discipline. Two reasons stand out. First, from the standpoint of Boas's antiracist anthropology, it was not obvious that African Americans were culturally different from white Americans. Boas's influence lent itself equally both to Melville J. Herskovits's pursuit of what was historically (and had therefore remained) subtly distinctive about African American lifeways and to the argument of Howard University's influential sociologists and jurists that any difference of conduct or values among the races in the United States was but circumstantial, quantitative, and largely the result of unequal structures of opportunity (see L. Baker 1998 and Yelvington's chapter in this volume). Neither model, however, suited African Americans to the image of absolute otherness that had long dominated anthropologists' choice of their objects of study. Second, both the cultures and the very presence of people of African descent in the Americas were so obviously the consequences of a highly transformative, ongoing, and documentable history that an analysis devoid of history seemed not only fictional but also false. African Americans are collectively the product and agent of one of the oldest, largest, and most revolutionary colonizations in the world. Indeed, the triangular trade on which these colonizations depended belies the fashionable conviction that transnationalism is new (Matory 1999a, 2005).

Before it was obvious about any other group that anthropologists had studied, it was obvious about African Americans that they could not be studied in isolation from global political, economic, and cultural forces. Thus, notwithstanding the apparent marginality of Afro-Americanist anthropology, scholarship on African Americans has arguably been the sand in the oyster of the discipline, foreshadowing late-twentieth-century/early-twenty-first-century efforts to restore global political, economic, and cultural forces to the portraits of local societies. Early Afro-Americanists articulated, under these and other names, theoretical themes—such as cultural resistance, alterity and the subaltern, hybridity, reflexivity, collective memory, embodiment and habitus, diaspora and transnationalism, and the more general rethinking of continent-based area studies divisions—that have become standards across the discipline.[2]

Afro-Americanist anthropology stands to make a greater contribution still to the discipline, in a way anticipated by Herskovits's "work of comparing cultures in a single historic stream" (e.g., [1956] 1966: especially 76; [1930] 1966; [1945] 1966). That is, the African regions that supplied the slave trade are culturally varied but not infinitely so, and the peoples of African descent in the Americas are culturally varied but not infinitely so. Moreover, many of the political and economic forces that have shaped the differences between African and African American cultures, as well as those that have shaped the differences among African American cultures, are well documented. Therefore, it is difficult to imagine a finer terrain for the comparative study of how geography and history shape culture and how a translocal culture might shape local imaginations of geography and history. The dividends of comparativist Afro-Americanist anthropology are potentially both empirical and methodological. Indeed, on the basis of a comparison of African and African American cases, the present study is intended to revise the range of analytic metaphors devoted to the anthropological study of all dispersed populations.

A HISTORY OF AFRO-AMERICANIST METAPHORS

When Africa is regarded as part of the cultural and political history of the African diaspora, it is usually recognized only as an origin— as a "past" to the African American "present," as a "source" of cultural "survivals" and "retentions" in the Americas, as an essence "preserved" in collective "memory," or as the "roots" of African American branches and leaves. Neither Herskovits nor his numerous followers have ignored the transformative adaptations, "syncretisms," or "creolizations" that have reshaped what remains of African culture in the Americas, but most have focused on the one-way transmission of culture from a past Africa to a present America. Yet this representation of the cultural history of the Afro-Atlantic world is itself culturally, politically, and historically conditioned in ways worthy of study in themselves (see the chapters by Yelvington, Sally Price, and Richard Price in this volume). What that representation highlights is valuable, but what it hides is often equally important.

From the time of Herskovits, the central analytic metaphors of Afro-Americanist anthropology could not but invoke history and imply the need for its reconstruction and preservation. The tropes in which that history was represented—not only the recently popular trope of "diaspora" but the older "survival" metaphor as well—seem to bear the signs of a uniquely black-Jewish dialogue. In an age and in a nation where collective political identity was increasingly associated with territory and with the new, republican principles defining the role of all citizens, it seems no surprise that an intellectual project involving chiefly Jews and blacks in New York City would generate models of corporate "survival" that rely on continuities of ritual, musical, and sartorial form. European and immigrant American Jewish identities had had an ambivalent and more often contrary relationship to territory, defined alternately by the group's distance from its ancestral home territory, its alienness within the land of residence, and its exclusion in many places from the right of land ownership. Rituals commemorating the past became much of the substance of Jewish collective identity and corporate survival. African Americans, too, could be imagined as a landless people, defined alternately by their distance from an ancestral home territory, their alienness within the land of residence, and their exclusion from numerous rights of citizenship within the American territorial nation-state. To an even greater than usual extent, the blacks of New York City from the 1910s onward were refugees from places where they had worked the land and where there were more recent memories of being owned, like the land, than of being landowners. For similar reasons, neither group had reasons for full confidence in the nation-state's much-vaunted promises of "modernity," as Gilroy (1993) summarizes the fundamental dilemma of the African diasporic experience. Yet for both groups, the option of abandoning one's past, renouncing pre-American identities, and melting in seemed to require more struggle, reflection, and debate than it did for other non-indigenous ethnic groups in the United States.

Thus, in dialogue with the black intellectuals of the Harlem Renaissance, Herskovits generated a series of metaphors highlighting continuity against the odds and implicitly acknowledging subaltern agency in the transmission of culture over time—through "survivals," "retentions," and "preservations" of not only practices but also "deep-seated cultural orientations" that guided the selection and "reinterpretation" of cultural precedents in the American context. Herskovits later borrowed the term *syncretism* from Afro-Brazilianist Arthur Ramos to describe the processes of selection and reinterpretation that allowed African practices and creative principles to "survive" in apparently Western milieus. For Herskovits ([1945] 1966:57), syncretism was "the tendency to identify those elements in the new culture with similar elements in the old one, enabling the persons experiencing the contact to move from one to the other, and back again, with psychological ease." In the classic example, Herskovits employed the term to describe Haitians, Brazilians, and Cubans' use of the images of Roman Catholic saints in the worship of iconographically similar African gods.[3]

In their day, Herskovits's "survival" and "reinterpretation" metaphors helped highlight what had been overlooked—the reality of cultural continuity and transformation in African American history. However, one might justly be dissatisfied with Herskovits and the Herskovitsians' relative inattention to diverse contextual meanings of apparently similar signifiers. For example, highlighting the formal similarities among possession by the Holy Spirit in North America, the river goddess Yemoja in Nigeria, and the eponymous sea goddess Iemanjá in Brazil might lead the analyst to overlook the radically different theologies and ritual complexes that buoy them.

Herskovits was far more attentive to psychological and unconscious "dispositions" than to agency and strategy in the reproduction of cultural forms. What, for example, might be any given actor's *motive* (beyond inertia) to reproduce an African cultural form or to identify such a form as "African"? Such an actor is likely to have alternatives to the African-looking form and might risk reprisal or disapproval for adopting even the most camouflaged of non-Western forms. And he or she might choose to interpret that form as non-African in origin. Are antecedent and intergenerational "dispositions" or the desire to hold on to the past (now trendily called "cultural resistance") sufficient explanations for the genealogy of African American cultural choices?

Herskovits's methods have invited the same criticism that diffusionism generally has attracted—that it renders culture as a "thing of shred and patches," to invoke Robert Lowie's (1920:441) memorable phrase (although Lowie referred here to "civilization"), rather than as an integrated, synchronic whole. Indeed, Herskovits deserves more credit for his contributions to the study of cultural *process* than to the study of synchronic issues of meaning, function, and structure. Moreover, as later generations of anthropologists have come to doubt the integrity of any given culture and to recognize the diversity and contradictory relationship among local discourses, it is not clear that Herskovits's critics are more correct than he.

Afro-Americanist anthropology is indebted to Sidney W. Mintz and Richard Price (1976, 1992) for their creolization model. Extending Roger Bastide's work on Afro-Brazilian religions, Mintz and Price focus on the New World social institutions, organizations, and sanctioned spaces that made the practice of African creative models possible in the Americas, as well as the situational constraints that transformed them into distinctly *African American* logics of creative production. Mintz and Price argue that such newly African American logics took shape quickly and enduringly—on slave ships and in the early years of any given American slave society. "The rapidity with which a complex, integrated and unique Afro-American religious system [or presumably other cultural systems] developed" and stabilized in a particular American locale is shown to be analogous to the rapidity with which the local creole language variety developed and stabilized (Mintz and Price 1992:22–26, especially 25). Mintz and Price are ultimately less concerned with arguing that all African American cultures formed rapidly or remained fixed than with recommending a search for the precise local *institutional history* by which each culture took shape and changed over time (R. Price, personal communication, April 12, 1999; see also Richard Price's chapter in this volume).

I will argue that the political and demographic contexts shaping African American cultures are *seldom* produced through a once-and-for-all departure from Africa and are seldom isolated from a broader, circum-Atlantic context. I submit that, unlike languages (as they are conventionally understood), African American cultures should not be considered integrated, internally systematic, and bounded in discrete units; they are crosscut (à la Bakhtin, for example, 1981) by multiple transnational languages, discourses, and dialogues.

The most recent analytic metaphor to take anthropology (including its Afro-Americanist varieties) and Afro-American literature by storm is the conception of "collective memory" and "forgetting" as the model and core features of sociocultural reproduction and (in the cases that most concern us here) the model and core features of diasporas' relationships to their homelands. The rhetorical effect of the "memory" metaphor in African diaspora scholarship is to highlight the implicit expectation that African Americans have (amid the ravages of enslavement, oppression, and poverty) lost contact with their past but retain at least mnemonic traces of that past.

Following Maurice Halbwachs, Bastide and others have argued that the recollection of myths, for example, can occur only when the social relationships or places to which they refer, or the institutions to which they are relevant, remain intact. For example, Bastide argues that the Yorùbá goddess Yemǫja continues to be thought of as a mother in Brazil because (according to Bastide) lower-class Afro-Brazilian families tend to be "matriarchal." In general, asserts Bastide, the preservation of ancestral images and practices depends on the social relationships and landmarks in which they are "preserved" (Bastide [1960] 1978:243, 247–248).

As evidenced in his apparent influence upon Mintz and Price, Bastide has contributed much more to the study of social structural issues in the practice of Afro-Brazilian religions than to the study of "memory" per se. Yet the failings of his "collective memory" metaphor are instructive. Bastide equates the collective preservation of ancestral images and practices with "memory" because he understands personal memory as a paradigmatic manner of preserving information and technical competency. Yet there are ways in which the reproduction of images or the teaching of techniques in society are *not* self-evidently forms of "preservation"; they are as likely to be forms of appropriation, quoting, mockery, propagandistic nostalgia, and so forth. The selective and strategic interpretation and invocation of the past are not the same as the "preservation," "retention," or "memory" thereof.

Bastide's conception of "collective memory" focuses on what "memories" are structurally possible or conditioned by the circumstances, rather than on social actors' *choice* of possible practices and images to reproduce or the purposes and motives behind those specific reproductions. Indeed, the "memory" metaphor seems semantically inconsistent with such agency.

In fact, Connerton (1989) identifies bodily practices as a privileged form of collective memory because, in his view, they are exempt from controversy and therefore from the influence of ongoing reinterpretations of the past. On the contrary, I argue that bodily practices—such as ways of walking, dancing, or hand gesturing—become the subject of controversy *as soon as* they are recognized as signs of a collective past or of a legitimate present. Cross-culturally, styles of sacred dance and postures of prayer, for example, often become signs of rival factions and charters for new cult groups. Even *scholars* who declare the historical significance of a bodily practice are moved by particular socially conditioned motives and purposes when they choose which bodily practice to highlight and declare it part of one historical narrative or another. Furthermore, these scholarly pronouncements often enter into the public debate over which versions of history are right. For example, Herskovits's argument in *The Myth of the Negro Past* (1941) that religious "shouting" demonstrates black North Americans' African cultural roots is neither politically disinterested nor uncontroversial. The debate over this matter between Herskovits and E. Franklin Frazier is significant less for the *scholarly* correctness of one or the other argument than for how it framed a debate that would continue in the general African American population throughout the century and continue to articulate diverse programs for the uplift of African Americans. In other words, such scholarly debates also ultimately affect the object of study. In fact, the involvement of multiple parties, multiple classes, and multiple interest groups makes the intergenerational reproduction of culture a dialogue and a "struggle for the possession of the sign" (Hebdige 1979) instead of a form of "preservation." If it is obvious that the intergenerational transmission of culture resembles and entails a dialogue, it should be almost as obvious that personal memory, too, is shaped by dialogue and controversy.

However, the contributions of the literature on "collective memory" are not to be overlooked. In this genealogy of thought appear Dayan (1995), K. Brown (1989), and Gilroy (1993), who have shown that present-day ritual and verbal forms *indirectly* reveal past cultural dispositions, events, and conditions that have otherwise been overlooked (see also D. Scott 1991). Brown argues that the prominence of warrior gods in Haitian Vodou reveals the Haitian experience of military dictatorship, and Dayan shows that the coquettish goddesses of Haitian Vodou reveal the experience of mulatto mistresses under the regime of slavery.[4] Gilroy argues that memories of slavery are manifest—through their metaphorical displacement by lyrics of lost love—in current black music. To Gilroy, lost love itself is the key metaphor in black popular culture's commentary on the failed promises of "modernity." That the oppressed possess the intelligence and the means to think or act about their past—even when those means are indirect—is worth pointing out.

The "collective memory"–based literature on the African diaspora thus contains several rich discussions of ways in which changing social conditions and political needs shape the selective reproduction, meaningful transformation, and meaningful reinterpretation of past cultural forms. Diaspora scholars would do equally well to recognize that *commemoration* is always *strategic* in its selections, exclusions, and interpretations.[5]

So why call such cultural reproduction *memory*—a term that hides rather than highlights the unending struggle over the meaning and usage of gestures, monuments, words, and memories? It implies the organic unity of the collective "rememberer," anthropomorphizing society rather than highlighting the heterogeneity, strategic conflicts, and unequal resources of the rival agents that make up social life. Of course, experts on the psychology of personal memory know how complex, variable, and socially conditioned it is. For example, personal memories are reshaped by conversations and conflicting collective interests. However, if we are seeking a metaphoric *source* that makes the process of cultural reproduction *easier* to understand, isn't it unwise to choose an analytic metaphor whose implications and entailments are so unsettled and so unclear? Metaphors are usually chosen for the concreteness and clarity of the *source*, which enables it to clarify what is otherwise unclear or *inchoate* about the *target* (Fernández 1985). As the scholarly literature indicates, the source itself (that is, personal memory) needs just as much clarifying as the target (that is, the collective interpretation and reenactment of the past).

Invoked casually, the comparison of collective cultural practices to the recording system of an individual mind suggests a certain passivity, involuntariness, absence of strategy, and political guilelessness and neutrality that seem quite foreign to the processes that have, in fact, shaped African and African American cultures over time. In general, the "memory" metaphor complements the nationalist personification of the nation and the fiction of innocent, pristine, and primordial folkways that give proof that the nation has always been one and is rooted in God and Nature rather than in human strategy or history.

Among the unavoidable failings of the "memory" metaphor is that by making a figurative *person* of the collective rememberer, this analytic metaphor risks concealing the fundamental pluralness of the agents of this "collective memory." Any memory that might be called collective is ready ground for sharp disagreements and interested rivalries, and any form of *personal* memory describable in terms of "sharp disagreement" and "interested rivalries" would be considered nonnormative—or sick. In fact, as richly suggestive as all of them have been, the "survival," "reinterpretation," and "creolization" metaphors share the potential for similar underestimations of heterogeneity and conflicting strategy. They lend themselves to the premise that, like the survivor of a disaster, like the interpreter of a text, or like a creole language, any given Afro-Atlantic culture is self-existent, internally integrated, bounded, and possessed of its own agency and autonomous authorship; that it is not rent by multiple and contradictory discourses, languages, perspectives, and interests; and that each such Afro-Atlantic culture has evolved in organic isolation or discreteness from the others.

An alternative metaphor might represent these cultures not as self-existent but as organically part of a *dialogue*—less as evolving *langues* or as isolated readers of self-contained national pasts than as interacting and changing sets of participants in a conversation. The metaphor of dialogue places traditions—or strategically constructed genealogies of cultural reproduction—into a context beyond nation and region, a context from which they are rarely extricable.

SOME PRECEDENTS OF THE "DIALOGUE" METAPHOR

In the same year, art historians Michael D. Harris (1999) and Moyọ Okediji (1999) and I (Matory 1999c) simultaneously but independently published essays likening the transformative exchange of people and ideas between Africa and the Americas to a "dialogue." There must have been something in the air that year, knitting together a range of conceptual and empirical precursors to our concerted move.[6]

The empirical fact that people of the African diaspora have traveled, carrying goods and ideas among various locales on the Atlantic perimeter, has long been known. The intercontinental movement of corn, cassava, cowpeas, peanuts, tobacco, palm oil, and cowries has, over the past five hundred years, wrought incalculable demographic and political changes everywhere on the Afro-Atlantic—changes dwarfing the oft-cited consequences of Europe's importation of the potato. Afro-Atlantic peoples were not only victims but also major agents of these seismic shifts, during and long after the transatlantic slave trade. Focusing on the migration and commerce between Bahia (Brazil) and West Africa, Pierre Verger ([1968] 1976)described this phenomenon as "*flux et reflux*" ("flow and counterflow"). Yet this ongoing transatlantic exchange of people and goods also shaped the well-documented political and cultural histories of Liberia, Sierra Leone, Angola, and South Africa. Such transatlantic exchange is also the foundation of Zairean/Congolese Soukous music, of Senegalese president Léopold Senghor and Fort-de-France mayor Aimé Césaire's widely cited Négritude poetry, and of Ghanaian president Kwame Nkrumah's pan-Africanism—all of which have origins and reciprocal outcomes in the African diaspora. The Afro-Atlantic dialogue is economic, political, literary, and musical.

Just as Africa and its diaspora are linked, diverse African diaspora locales are linked to one another by migration, commerce, and the mutual gaze among them, which are the subjects of Gilroy's *The Black Atlantic* (1993). Focusing on the English-speaking peoples of the Afro-Atlantic diaspora, Gilroy retheorizes the scope and mechanisms of cultural reproduction that he sees posited in the nationalist and racist cultural histories of blacks in the West. For him, cultural exchanges *among diasporic locales* undermine and falsify the boundaries that nationalists imagine around the races, nations, and cultures of the Atlantic perimeter. Thus, for Gilroy, the ships that carry ideas and cultural artifacts between locales are more emblematic of black Atlantic culture than are the national boundaries and watery divides that separate one locale from another. In the place of continuous forms of "memory" constituting geographically bounded cultural units, Gilroy prioritizes the "discontinuous" forms of cultural reproduction by which ideas and images from one place constantly amplify and modify the cultural genealogies of other places (see also Roach 1996).

Gilroy charts recent developments in black Atlantic culture in real historical time, documenting how the Anglophone blacks of England, the United States, and the West Indies have—through travel and commerce in, for example, phonograph records—influenced one anothers' cultural and political responses to their common exclusion from the promises of the French Enlightenment and from full citizenship in the ideally democratic polities inspired by it. Thus, Gilroy prioritizes cultural exchange across territorial boundaries over the divergent but uninterrupted "memory" of Africa posited by Bastide and many Herskovitsians in the genesis of the Anglophone black Atlantic culture.

Yet Gilroy remains curiously comfortable with the metaphor of the African diaspora's apparently continuous "memory" of slavery. For example, Gilroy believes that black Atlantic ballads about lost love symbolically commemorate slavery. But when genres inaugurated by one ethnic group, nationality, or race are adopted by another, whose collective past is being "remembered," and who is the rememberer? Weren't the regimes of slavery in the different "remembering" communities, nations, and regions different? Wouldn't the diversity of musical genres suggest that the rememberers are diverse and at least partially constituted and distinguished by nationality? Yet Gilroy, like Appadurai (1990), represents the territorial nation and the local identities it generates as contradictions to (rather than constituents of) these ship-borne cultural crossings.

And if for Gilroy "collective memory" usefully highlights something about Afro-Atlantic people's relationship to their past, why is the "memory" of *Africa* selected for denial in Gilroy's analytic model? Perhaps Gilroy is simply much more interested in the cultural exchange between blacks and whites, as well as among English-speaking black diaspora locales, than in Africa. Gilroy's representation of "black Atlantic" culture essentially as a black response to exclusion from the promises of the European Enlightenment renders Africa irrelevant. Yet the credibility of this representation in Gilroy's account relies less on a critique of the existing contrary positions than on a silence about them.

Although Gilroy borrows the term *black Atlantic* from Herskovits's leading successor, art historian Robert Farris Thompson, Gilroy fails to cite not only Thompson but also the entire descriptive literature on the apparently "continuous" forms of cultural reproduction that have invited designation as memory, retention, survival, syncretism, and so forth. The main fields of African diaspora culture that Herskovitsians and Bastideans have represented as the products of "continuous" reproductions of African culture have been structurally and texturally African-looking forms—"Africanisms"—in American religion and music. Yet Gilroy (1993:28) studiously ignores the forms and aspects of African diaspora music that have been cited as proof of "continuity," while inexplicably dismissing African American religion as "the central sign for the folk-cultural, narrowly ethnic definition of racial authenticity." In fact, Gilroy's anthropological and art historical predecessors have usually enlisted African diaspora music and religion as evidence of transethnic and transnational cultural commonalities (*not* national closure) among peoples of African descent. Moreover, *whites'* adoption of African-inspired folk culture and religion from their African diaspora neighbors is a frequent theme in the writings of Herskovits, Bastide, and their successors (e.g., Bastide [1960] 1978; Herskovits [1935] 1966; Philips 1990; P. Wood 1974, 1975).

Hence, my criticism of Gilroy does not result from any belief on my part that cultural reproduction is "continuous" or nationally bounded. In fact, I believe that Gilroy is correct in emphasizing "discontinuity" and the cross-territorial nature of cultural reproduction. Rather, I disagree with Gilroy's ironic exclusion of Africans' participation in this cross-territorial phenomenon and his premise that the changing experiences, cultural conventions, and cultural vocabularies that make up African diaspora cultural history *began*—temporally and conceptually —at the moment blacks encountered the ideas of the European Enlightenment. Such a premise smacks of the same anticosmopolitan boundary making that Gilroy's entire oeuvre is arrayed against.

Perhaps, however, a single oversight at once shapes Gilroy's historical periodizations and his citation practices. At first sight, the type of "culture" documented in the ethnohistorical literature appears distinct from the type treated in the cultural studies literature. On the one hand, Herskovits, his avowed successors, and his critics focus on the *anthropological* stuff of culture—the everyday practices and beliefs of the everyman, including the religions and musical genres of what appear to be common people. On the other hand, Gilroy and other cultural studies specialists tend to focus on the writings and political gestures of the highly educated, the efforts of cultural reform move-ments, and the sort of art forms diffused by professional publishers, recording industries, and museums. To my mind, this division of intel-lectual labor results less from the empirical accuracy of the low cul-ture/high culture distinction in the Afro-Atlantic cultures than from many of these authors' *trained inattention to the intimate dialogue that unites these cultural spheres.*

I intend to illustrate the empirical and theoretical utility of attend-ing to this dialogue. For example, the literary activities of artists, schol-ars, and travelers—including those with transatlantic social connections, commercial interests, and political aspirations—have played a signifi-cant but under-recognized role in shaping the local *religious* cultures of the Afro-Atlantic. I wish to show that both Africa and non-English-speaking parts of the Americas were deeply involved in this dialogue, that not only political but also cultural transformations were in the offing, and that various African and African-inspired "folk" cultures (of the sort Herskovits and his successors privilege) are among the prod-ucts of this dialogue.

Joseph Roach has given a further treatment to the cross-cultural exchanges shaping Afro-Atlantic culture, highlighting their symbolic mediation and the rhetorical uses of these exchanges. Through his notion of "circum-Atlantic performance," Roach (1996) observes that diverse peoples on that ocean perimeter have mimicked one another for five hundred years as a fundamental condition of each such peo-ple's formation of its own cultural identity. However, Roach largely ignores (without denying) the active role of Africans in Africa in this dialogue. Unlike Gilroy, Roach calls attention to the frequently ironic and fictional quality of one people's mimicry of another—as in African American and European theatrical performances of "Africanness" and "Native Americanness." Such mimicry—itself often secondary to liter-ary and celluloid caricatures of the black Other—is a further important element of the Afro-Atlantic dialogue.[7] Nigerians, Jamaicans, Brazilians, and US African Americans often perceive one another through books and films, many of which are produced or distributed by whites. For example, some Jamaicans in the United States and in Jamaica imitate black US hip-hop fashion as an assertion of toughness, modernity, and cosmopolitanness, whereas others accentuate the aspects of Jamaican style that *distinguish* them from African Americans in order to defy American and African American cultural imperialism or to exempt themselves from the forms of white American discrimination that target African Americans.

Much inspired by Verger, Gilroy, and Roach, this chapter focuses on the metaphor of "dialogue" as an alternative to the ethnohistorical metaphors of "collective *memory*" and historical *sequence* in order to highlight some major processes in the selective reproduction of culture across time and space—and, more important in the continually changing inscription of meaning—that have produced some of the best-known "traditions" and most pervasive trends on the black Atlantic. That is, when cultural forms are selected, inherited, borrowed, and imitated, their new users invariably inscribe them with new meanings and enlist them for new purposes. Bakhtin employs a similar analytic metaphor—the "dialogic"—in his explanation of the novel, which embodies the speech of such diverse social classes that Bakhtin doubts the authorship, or agency, of the novelist (Bakhtin 1981). Applied to cultural reproduction generally, Bakhtin's analytic metaphor might rightly suggest that multiple agents are powerfully involved in the production of any given culture and that multiple cultures are "quoted" in the production of any one culture. However, Bakhtin's analytic metaphor might incorrectly imply that all of these agents and quoted cultures are equally powerful in the production of local or regional culture. My dialogue metaphor is not, however, intended to suggest political and economic equality among the interlocutors, however.

A major service of Gilroy's *The Black Atlantic* (1993) is that it demonstrates that blacks in the United States are not the lone creators of black Atlantic cultures. Gilroy usefully illustrates the role of Anglophone West Indians and black Britons in the process. However, this insurgent and democratizing move also recapitulates a form of Afro-Atlantic inequality that becomes more obvious when one broadens the scope of the analysis. The Afro-Atlantic dialogue encompasses the speakers of not only English but also a half dozen other European languages, a dozen creole languages, and hundreds of African languages. The members of these Afro-Atlantic language communities far

ᅟ

outnumber the approximately forty million black or mulatto native speakers of English in the United States, the West Indies, and the United Kingdom. However, Anglophone blacks have exercised a disproportionate influence on the contemporary making of all Afro-Atlantic cultures. It is no less true—notwithstanding Gilroy's effort to question the centrality of black North Americans—that the blacks of the United States have been more influential than any other group in the twentieth-century reproduction and reshaping of Afro-Atlantic culture. In general, literacy, economic power, commercial contacts, and command over the English or French language have made certain Afro-Atlantic voices louder than others.

Unlike Gilroy (1993) and Appadurai (1990), I do not believe that international cultural exchange and migration undermine or negate the reality of territorial boundaries and national identities. Rather, the phenomena I describe as dialogue are shaped directly, though not entirely, by the territorial boundaries and political priorities of empires and nation-states. In fact, the transatlantic dialogue has allowed the *creation* of such territorial nation-states as Liberia and Sierra Leone. Two decades ago, Elliot Skinner (1982), too, theorized a "dialectic between diasporas and homelands," showing that the African, Jewish, Irish, Indian, and Chinese diasporas have often aided in the formation of independent nations in their homelands and that such independent homelands often enhance the political stature of their diasporic kin despite the ambivalence that homelanders and diasporans often feel toward each other. Thus, the dialogue metaphor does not posit that every interlocutor is an atom. Relative wealth, linguistic proficiency, nationality, and access to the means of communication distinguish *groups* of actors from one another.

On the other hand, the dialogue metaphor does posit one type of equality: temporal equality. It posits the radical "coevalness" (Fabian 1983) of Africa, Latin America, and the United States in a dialogue that, even following the conclusion of the slave trade, has continually shaped them all. In other words, Africa is not, as Herskovits's "social laboratory" would suggest, the past of Afro-Latin America. Nor does either set of cultures represent the past of black North American culture, as Herskovits also suggested (Herskovits 1941, 1956).

The fiction that they do represent the past of black North American culture reproduces the ethnocentric teleology whereby

Europeans classified the Americas as the "New World." The sense in which that world was new to Native Americans would require some explanation. Perhaps the "New World" represents the culmination—the true "Jewel in the Crown"—of European imperialist expansionism, but it might just as easily represent a decline or retrogression for the teleologically oriented historians of, say, the Aztec Empire. Rather than emphasize the newness of any given territory or the advanced temporal stage of any given nation or ethnic group, I prefer to emphasize the newness of the *dialogue* that has united Africans, Europeans, and Native Americans so intimately over the past five hundred years and the newness of the political identities and cultural formations that have resulted on both the eastern and the western shores of the Atlantic. Thus, in my view, the "New World" surrounds an ocean.

If my suggestion is taken seriously, African Americanist cultural historians will no longer begin books with the conventional chapter about Africa (usually based on colonial-era accounts of African culture and history) and then demonstrate the stages by which an African American culture evolved over time out of that "original" African one. The dialogue metaphor instead highlights ways in which the mutual gaze between Africans and African Americans, multidirectional travel and migration between the two hemispheres, the movement of publications, commerce, and so forth, have shaped African and African American cultures in tandem, over time, and at the same time. It highlights the ways in which cultural artifacts, images, and practices do not simply "survive" or endure through "memory"; rather, they are interpreted and reproduced for diverse contemporary purposes by actors with culturally diverse repertoires, diverse interests, and diverse degrees of power to assert them. As in a literal dialogue, such interpretations and reproductions can also be silenced, articulated obliquely, paraphrased, exaggerated, or quoted mockingly.

THE LIVE DIALOGUE

Here I wish to detail just one of the many phenomena that would be difficult to understand if "highlighted and hidden" merely through the standard analytic metaphors of African diaspora studies—"survival," "reinterpretation," "creolization," and "collective memory" (for numerous other cases, see Matory 1999c).

The case study derives from my own study of religion in Nigeria

and Brazil. Much American religious culture that is thought most effectively to have "survived" Africans' enslavement was, in fact, introduced,
sustained, and deeply modified by free migrants circulating between
Africa and the Americas. The Brazilian Candomblé religion, for example, is often identified as an exemplary, if not *the most* exemplary, survival of African culture in the Americas.

Yet the oral history identifies many founders of its leading institutions as voluntary immigrants from Africa. For example, Otampê
Ojarô, founder of Bahia's Alakêtu Temple; Marcos Pimentel, a nineteenth-century chief priest of the Mocambo Temple on the island of
Itaparica; and, most important, Iyá Nasô, founder of the ancient Casa
Branca Temple in Bahia, are all identified as free immigrants from
Africa. Iyá Nasô's mother is said to have secured her own manumission
in Bahia and returned to Africa but voluntarily moved to Bahia to
found this first of the three most famous Candomblé temples in Brazil.
Her successor, Marcelina, is said to have gone voluntarily from Africa
to Bahia and returned to Africa for an extended sojourn before returning finally to Bahia, where she assumed leadership of the Casa Branca
Temple. Verger reports that it was Marcelina who first brought to Bahia
the famous Manoel Rodolfo Baṁgboṣe—a *babaláwo* diviner from
Ọ̀yọ́ or Abẹ́òkutà and founder of Brazil's most illustrious line of male
priests (Abimbọla 2000; Aizinho de Oxaguiã, personal communication,
1999; Matory 1999a; Verger 1980).[8] Though buried in Bahia, this international priest and traveler appears to have given his name to the main
street in the "Brazilian Quarter" in Lagos.

Similarly, in Cuba, the famous African-born Adechina is said to
have been enslaved in Cuba but returned to Africa for initiation as a
babaláwo diviner, later returning to Cuba. The oral history also identifies a freeborn African woman named Efunche (also Ẹfunṣetan or La
Funche) who traveled as a free person to Cuba and there reformed
Afro-Cuban religion in the nineteenth century. In the twentieth century, Cuban and Cuban American priests continued to rely on handwritten notebooks, or *libretas*, inherited from such free travelers as
sources of authoritative religious and linguistic knowledge.

Two of the most influential of these libretas were written by free
persons who had freely emigrated from British colonial West Africa.
The *santero* Sixto Samá came from Sierra Leone (Cabrera 1980:2), and

Andrés Monzón "learned to read and write in an English mission in
Nigeria" (Cabrera 1986:16). His libreta included a version of the
Lord's Prayer in a Hispanicized version of the Yorùbá orthography generated by Anglo-Yorùbá missionaries in Freetown, Sierra Leone—a
British colony founded as a home for freed slaves (see Cabrera
1986:17; Matory 1999b). Another of Cabrera's priestly informants in
the mid-twentieth century, Miguel Allaí, had lived in Sierra Leone and,
according to Cabrera, had learned to speak Yorùbá fluently (Cabrera
1986:17). Also among the most influential writers of *libretas* was Nicolás
Angarica. In the mid-twentieth century, he employed a West African
Yorùbá dictionary and the Yorùbá translation of the Bible (also written
by Anglo-Yorùbá missionaries in British colonial West Africa) to verify
the orthography of his multiple primers of Afro-Cuban religious language and ritual practice (see Angarica 1955:4).

In the 1930s, Afro-Bahian high school students also had access
to imported books with which to study Yorùbá language and culture (Pierson 1942:314). Even after World War II, Bastide (1973:263)
reported that Opô Afonjá, reputedly the most "purely African" of
Brazil's temples, based its ritual calendar upon a lunar calendar found
in its copy of the Yorùbá-language Bible.

These reports concerning the ongoing movement of people, texts,
and ideas between Africa and the Americas are made credible by
archives documenting the return of thousands of Afro-Brazilians and
hundreds of Afro-Cubans to the West African coast. Moreover, in the
lamentably incomplete Bahian archives of return voyages from Lagos,
I have counted dozens of ships and hundreds of free Africans traveling
from Lagos *to* Bahia or *through* Bahia to Rio de Janeiro or the state of
Pernambuco, Brazil, between 1855 and 1898. Journalistic, epistolary,
and ethnographic evidence from that period reveals repeated journeys
of another score of African Brazilian travelers up to the 1930s.[9] Many
of them carried British passports, and most appear to have engaged in
commerce. The Brazilian travelers sold ethnically marked Brazilian
merchandise (such as salted meat and Afro-Brazilian religious paraphernalia) to returnees in West Africa and "authentically African" merchandise (such as the kola nuts and woven cloth [*pano da costa*] used
in the Candomblé) to their black customers in Brazil. Thus, under
British protection and motivated by their own commercial interests, a

generation of back-and-forth travelers consolidated a set of novel, religiously coded, and transnational identities unprecedented before the slave trade and as yet fragmentary before the nineteenth-century return of Afro-Brazilians and Afro-Cubans to Africa. These were the "Jeje" and even the "Yorùbá" identities in West Africa (Matory 1999a, 1999b, 2005).

Thus, as these identities blossomed in early-twentieth-century Brazil, they displayed not only the "memory" or "survival" of religious icons, myths, and practices from the Africa that preceded the slave trade but also the effects of the radical ideological transformations of late-nineteenth-century Yorùbá ethnogenesis, which occurred primarily *after* the end of the slave trade.

The interaction of Westernized African recaptives and returnees in Sierra Leone and Lagos in the nineteenth century had produced, for the first time, a self-ascribed "Yorùbá" identity that embraced the diverse peoples of Òyó, Èkìtì, Ìjèbú, Ègbá, Ègbádò, Iléṣa, and so forth. Their Western education gave the returnee advocates of this identity privileged access to international markets and to the emergent colonial administrations of British and French West Africa. Moreover, their literacy allowed them an unparalleled opportunity to articulate their own vision of their culture and history.

Therefore, at the British-dominated crossroads of African/African American interaction, the Yorùbá acquired a highly publicized reputation for superiority to other Africans. This reputation for superiority was useful in the 1880s and 1890s, as the bourgeois black Lagosians faced new forms of economic disadvantage and racial discrimination. Their reaction was the Lagosian Cultural Renaissance, whose literary champions extensively documented Yorùbá "traditional" religion, advocated racial and cultural purity, and popularized the adoption of African names in lieu of the European ones with which many returnees and recaptives had grown up.

These nineteenth-century developments in colonial West Africa have reverberated in the Americas, not only persuading Candomblé Nagô and Santería/Lucumí priests to describe their religion as "Yorùbá" but also convincing American governments, elite sponsors, and the general public that these "Yorùbá"-affiliated religions deserve more respect and tolerance than other African-inspired religions, such as Candomblé Angola in Brazil and Cuba's Palo Mayombe and Abakuá

(Matory 2005). Thus, certain traditions have been privileged over others in the production of "traditional religion."

Equally surprising in light of the conventional analytic metaphors of "survival," "memory," "creolization," and "syncretism" (with its "African god/Catholic saint" paradigm case) is the centrality of British cultural imagery in the performance of "African tradition" and in the literal dialogue among geographically separated subtraditions. We have, in passing, referred to the British-inspired orthography of Yorùbá established by Sierra Leone–trained Anglo-Yorùbá missionaries such as Samuel Ajayi Crowther. It has now come to be regarded as the correct and African way of writing words that Brazilians and Cubans had long written in their respective Romance-language orthographies. In 1987, while receiving Nigerian priestly visitors Wande Abimbọla and Ọmọtọsọ Eluyẹmi, I heard the prominent Bahian priestess Stella de Azevedo lament in Portuguese to one of her subordinates, "I have *got* to learn English so that I can understand what they are saying!" English is as much a lingua franca in the Afro-Atlantic religious world as it is in the business world. The Afro-Atlantic dialogue is indeed a *circum-*Atlantic dialogue, shaped by the history of European imperialism and mediated by the economic, linguistic, and religious consequences of that imperialism.

It is for this reason that British Freemasonry has also deeply penetrated Afro-Atlantic iconographies of divinity and priesthood. As a secret society, Freemasonry possessed attractive similarities to a range of West African religious sentiments and organizations—including the Yorùbá òrìṣà priesthoods and Ogbóni Society and the Ekpe Society of Calabar (now in Nigeria), as well as the Ekpe-inspired Abakuá Society of Cuba, oricha/orixá worship in Cuba and Brazil, and the Vodou religion of Haiti. As we shall see, the influence of Freemasonry is evident in the present-day West African Ṣàngó priesthood and in the various male-dominated African American priesthoods. In Cuba, Abakuá and Palo Mayombe priests, like Freemasons, use special handshakes to distinguish members from nonmembers. One informant tells me that Abakuá members and Freemasons also change their handshakes periodically in order to exclude lapsed or inactive members (Tata Àngel, personal communication, 1996). Haitian Vodou is also full of the iconography, handshakes, and personnel of Freemasonry (see, e.g., Cosentino 1995:33, 44–55).[10]

Beyond its resonance with the secrecy and initiatic character of West African priesthoods, Freemasonry acquires an additional resonance for African-inspired priests in Roman Catholic countries. Freemasons and African-inspired priests share a defiance of Roman Catholic ecclesiastical disapproval and of Christian chauvinism generally. Often referring directly to Masonic symbols and terms for the high god—such as the compass representing the "Great Engineer"—the African-inspired religions of the Americas stress their belief in the high god and thus appeal for ecumenical understanding just as Freemasons do (Tata Àngel, personal communication, 1996, and see Cosentino 1995:44).

Freemasonry has empowered African religious resistance in still further ways. In both Africa and the Americas, Freemasonry bears an association with wealth and temporal power, and the secret cooperation among Freemasons is widely understood to facilitate the endeavors of all members. Also apposite to this story are Freemasonry's origins in early-eighteenth-century England. It is part of a projection of British symbolic power appropriated strategically and with special enthusiasm by Afro-Latins under the domination of Roman Catholic elites. Equally available for the subversion of white power generally is the Freemasons' avowed debt to the esoteric knowledge of Egypt and their denial of the exclusively Greek origins of "civilization" professed since the 1840s by the Aryanist European racial chauvinists (Bernal 1996:94). Numerous literati and religious figures—including German Yorubanist Leo Frobenius ([1913] 1968), Nigerian J. O. Lucas (1970: especially 272), and Bahian Mãe Aninha (see Pierson 1942:293)—have articulated similarly Egypt-centered defenses of African cultural dignity or have asserted the ancient Egyptian origins of Yorùbá culture. Simultaneous references to both Freemasonry and ancient Egypt have been a repeated theme in the twentieth-century work of canonizing Yorùbá culture (see also Akintola 1992; Anyebe 1989: especially 53, 57, 79, 102, 106).

Thus it is no surprise that in the 1930s, the side of babaláwo diviner Felisberto Sowzer's house in Bahia bore a seal featuring an Ifá divining board, the Masonic compass, the Yorùbá proverb *Suru ni oogun aiye* ("Patience is the medicine of life"), and two biblical inscriptions in English, "The Lord is my Helper" and "Wait on the Lord and keep his way." Pierson's drawing of this seal is reproduced in figure 5.1

FIGURE 5.1

Reproduction of the seal on the side of the home of Bahian diviner Felisberto Sowzer. From Donald Pierson's (1942) Negroes in Brazil: A Study of Race Conflict in Bahia. *Used with permission of the University of Chicago Press.*

(see Pierson 1942:259).[11] Indeed, Sowzer is part of an impressive dynasty of Brazilian-Lagosian travelers and priests, beginning with his diviner grandfather, the aforementioned Manoel Rodolfo Baṁgboṣe, and ending with numerous priestly grandchildren in Lagos, Bahia, and Rio.

Perhaps the only transatlantic dynasty more famous than the line of Baṁgboṣe is the Alakija family.[12] Though they are not noted for any particular connection to the Candomblé, they are a central feature of latter-day memories about the relation between Bahia and the "Africa" from which Candomblé originated. Thus it is telling that numerous Alakijas in Nigeria and Bahia are Freemasons. Appearing in figure 5.2, Plasido Alakija (aka Sir Adeyẹmọ Alakija) was a district grand master of the Freemasons in Nigeria. His nephew and my main informant in the family, psychiatrist Dr. George Alakija, is also a Freemason.

It is further noteworthy that the Alakijas were involved in local Nigerian secret societies. One of the oldest and most widespread secret societies in Nigeria is called *Ogbóni*. Devoted to the worship of the Earth divinity (Onílẹ̀), it encompasses family heads, chiefs, and priests

FIGURE 5.2

Plasido Alakija (aka Sir Adeyẹmọ Alakija) of Nigeria, wearing his Masonic attire (probably 1930s or 1940s). Original photograph owned by Dr. George Alakija of Salvador, Bahia.

of various òrìṣà, and in many kingdoms it counterbalances the authority of the king. In 1914 Westernized Christians, attracted by Ogbóni ritual and undoubtedly motivated by a nativist response to mounting

British racism, founded the Reformed Ogbóni Fraternity. Paralleling the syncretic activities of nationalist bourgeoisies elsewhere, these bourgeois Lagosians aimed to systematize and "refine" the practices of their Ogbóni forebears. This process appears consciously to have entailed assimilating Ogbóni to Freemasonry in its beliefs and iconography. Sir Adeyẹmọ Alakija was the first "overall political head," or Olórí Olúwo, of the Reformed Ogbóni Fraternity, an office he occupied until his death in 1953.[13]

Equally important in positioning this transatlantic family in the formation of Yorùbá identity is the fact that Sir Adeyẹmọ served as the first president general of the Yorùbá nationalist organization Ẹgbẹ́ Ọmọ Odùduà (Association of Odùduà's Children). Founded by Ọbafẹmi Awolọwọ in 1945, the Ẹgbẹ́ seemed at least partly intent on resisting Igbo ethnic preeminence in the emerging independence movement (Akintọla 1992, especially 7; Anyebe 1989:108; Paul Lọla Bangbose-Martins, personal communication, 1995; Comhaire 1949:43; Fadipẹ [1939] 1970:248).[14] Collectively, the Alakija family linked extraordinary success in West African British colonial society and culture, including Freemasonry, with the will to reshape indigenous religious institutions in the service of African nationalism. Yet as the North American case reveals, Freemasonry could also empower assertions of *independence* from the British overlords. Figure 5.3 depicts George Washington in his Masonic regalia.

In Bahia, too, the Western-style accomplishments of the Alakijas are extraordinary. The Bahian branch of the family includes a lawyer, an otolaryngologist, a psychiatrist, and a civil engineer (see Rotilu 1932). During his research in the Bahia of the mid-1930s, Donald Pierson was shown a feature article in the *Nigerian Daily Times* (on whose board of directors Sir Adeyẹmọ was the only African member) that documented the family's transatlantic success (see Rotilu 1932). Moreover, as in the case of Felisberto Sowzer, their membership in the Freemasons appears to have remained something of a support to their African-inspired religious commitments, although other peculiarly American ideological dynamics have shaped their participation in African-inspired religion.[15] For example, my Bahian informant Dr. George Alakija, a Freemason and prominent psychiatrist, respects the Candomblé much as other highly educated Bahians do—that is, as a

FIGURE 5.3

George Washington in Masonic regalia. Courtesy American Antiquarian Society.

beautiful aspect of the national legacy. He is not a member of any temple, but as a Brazilian government representative at the 1977 World
Black and African Festival of Arts and Culture in Lagos, Dr. Alakija presented his writing on a theme that Brazilians recognize as typically
African and that the psychiatrists of northeastern Brazil, ever since psychiatrist Raimundo Nina Rodrigues founded Afro-Brazilian studies as
we know it, have made a major object of investigation: "The Trance
State in the Candomblé" (Alakija 1977).[16]

The character of such families' cultural commitments in Bahia is
distinctive in other ways as well. Whereas adopting "African" names
became a focus of these transatlantic families' "culture-building"

(Caulfield 1969) in colonial Nigeria, Nigerian-associated English names and Anglicized Portuguese names became their trademark in Bahia. Throughout the generations of their twentieth-century residence in Bahia, the Brazilian branch of the family has borne English names such as *George* and *Maxwell* (see also Pierson 1942:243). Ironically, while the Anglo-Africanness of the Bahian family members facilitated their assimilation into the Euro-Bahian elite, their persons and activities lent to Yorùbánness an enduring symbolic power, even as the male-dominated Ifá priesthood died out and the female-dominated possession priesthood of Candomblé became the preeminent manifestation of that transatlantic nation in Bahia.

Memories of Africa in the Bahia from the late 1930s onward were not only shaped by the complex cultural hybridity of their bearers but also reinforced by the haughty defensiveness of elite Afro-Bahians in a racist time and place. Pierson (1942:272) recorded the remark of one Afro-Bahian as follows:

> These people here in Bahia think Africans are all barbarous and uncivilized. They won't believe we write our language and that books are printed in it....They don't know that in Lagos there are good schools, better than they've got in Bahia. Look at this [photograph of a school in Lagos]! Is there anything in Bahia as fine as that?

This is a genre of recollection of Africa prominent in Bahia during the first half of the twentieth century. These memories are not of the pristine African, or Yorùbá, culture that the victims of New World slavery *remembered* well enough to *retain* and *preserve*. No, they are based upon the experiences, souvenirs, and photographs of a class of literate and well-traveled Africans who helped bring "Yorùbá culture" as such into existence, established its prestige around the Atlantic basin, and canonized it as the preeminent classical standard of African culture in the New World, notwithstanding the North American attraction of black nationalists to Islam and ancient Egypt.[17] What many Bahians remembered was a nineteenth- and twentieth-century West African coast in which English language, Roman script, Masonic temples, and a lively press were among the stuff of daily life.

"Traditional religion" (*ẹsìn ìbílẹ̀*) in the twentieth-century Yorùbá

FIGURE 5.4

Nigerian Ṣàngó possession priest from Ọ̀yọ́, in the attire of the Aborigine Ogbóni Fraternity of Nigeria, chanting before a Ṣàngó shrine in the city of Ìbàdàn. Photograph by J. Lorand Matory, 1986.

hinterland—often represented as the primordial origin of Candomblé's and Santería's "survivals" and "memories" of Africa—is deeply inscribed with evidence of this ongoing Afro-Atlantic dialogue. The Freemasonry-inspired iconography of the Reformed Ogbóni Fraternity has penetrated the òrìṣà priesthoods of even the "Yorùbá proper," the Ọ̀yọ́-Yorùbá. The shrine room door of my friend from the town of

Ìgbòho, the Ṣàngó priest Adeniran, bears various insignia of his membership in a local chapter of the Reformed Ogbóni-style fraternity—three unblinking eyes on an inverted V and three vertical shapes within it. In 1986 I met another Ṣàngó priest in Ìbàdàn, who chose to pose for a photograph in a Masonic-inspired apron bearing again the inverted V and three vertical shapes within it. In figure 5.4, he poses before the Ṣàngó shrine in Ìdí Arere, Ìbàdàn. Despite his wifely coiffure and wrap skirt (marking his relationship to the god who possesses him), this priest thus bears an unmistakable resemblance to his African Brazilian Masonic antecedent, Sir Adeyẹmọ Alakija (known to my informant Dr. Alakija as "Uncle Plasido"), shown with an apron and inverted Vs in figure 5.2. The number *3* has long been a shibboleth in the unreformed Ogbóni Society. But, of course, syncretic reformulations are evident in this "ancestral" garb. The 1986 priest is no Freemason, nor a member of the Reformed Ogbóni Fraternity. Rather, the Masonic signs authenticate his membership in a later, explicitly nativist organization. His hand-painted membership certificate (figure 5.5) comes from the "Aborigine Ogbóni Franternity [sic] of Nigeria," with its secretariat at Ilé-Ifẹ̀.

CONCLUSION

The study of the African diaspora has generated a series of productive analytic metaphors, highlighting the cultural, historical, economic, and political dimensions of diaspora with increasing refinement over time. Yet, much that the existing analytic metaphors in Afro-Atlantic studies have led us to overlook is productively highlighted in a new metaphor—one that represents homelands not as the past but as the contemporaries of their diasporas, and diverse diasporic locales not as divergent streams but as interlocutors in supraregional conversations. Africa and its American diaspora reflect the effects of an enduring dialogue and a dialectic of mutual transformation over time.

The dialogue metaphor is not intended to posit equality of influence or power among the interlocutors, just their continuous and meaningful *presence* in one another's cultural history and self-construction. Indeed, the two English-speaking imperial powers have furnished the means for certain black "interlocutors" to "speak" far louder than others.

FIGURE 5.5

Close-up of the Ṣàngó priest's membership certificate from the Aborigine Ogbóni Fraternity of Nigeria. Photograph by J. Lorand Matory, 1986.

Though I question the likeness of Afro-Atlantic creole lifeways to quick-forming, bounded, and internally integrated "languages," the analytic metaphor I propose builds on the legacy of the linguistic analogy. I must emphasize that "dialogue" is a metaphor and is not intended to suggest that all or even most aspects of Afro-Atlantic cultural exchange and reproduction are linguistic. Not all aspects of this exchange and reproduction are *like* language, but even the paradigmatic aesthetic forms of the Afro-Atlantic world—dance and music—bear traces of it and bear comparison to it. For example, Afro-Atlantic music regularly includes lyrics, imitates the tones and patterns of speakers' mutual responsiveness, or is emically understood to "speak to" people and to "call" gods. But, of course, music involves techniques and produces feelings beyond the range normally associated with speech.

Nonetheless, I am arguing that the cultural reproduction of dispersed ethnic groups, neighboring ones, and ones surrounding ocean perimeters regularly shares in the coeval and interactive qualities of dialogue and that those who dominate the imposition of *verbal* meaning on the gestures and artifacts of social life enjoy a *disproportionate* influence on the social consequences of those gestures and artifacts.

The image of oceans and seas as the foci and paradigmatic venues of intercultural dialogues is an opportune metaphor for a further revision of the anthropological model. Like other bodies of water, these circum-oceanic units have shores, but these shores shift. They are impermanent. And just as important as the shores, where a certain boundedness appears relatively enduring, every body of water flows from and into others and maintains a constant osmotic exchange with the surrounding air and land. Thus, flows, overflows, seepage, evaporation, wind, and precipitation continuously unite one body of water in exchange with others. Amid increasingly worrisome publicity, ocean-going vessels accidentally transport life forms previously common in one body of water into bodies of water where they had previously been unknown, radically altering not only the contents but also the ecosystem of the new habitat. Using dikes, dams, and canals, human beings have long engineered these processes, with intended and unintended consequences.

So for natural and human-made reasons, the "Seven Seas" seem more like one, the boundaries between them as imaginary, provisional, and contingent as the boundaries between cultures. Perhaps *culture* is better spoken of in the singular and regarded as a *process* than in the plural and as a discretely countable set of *things*.[18] As countable and discrete things, cultures are but the provisional, debated, and evanescent assertions of political leaders, marketing experts, and unreformed anthropologists.

The Afro-Atlantic is one of the most important transnational cultural fields of the past five hundred years. Yet it has long engaged in a mighty dialogue with the Middle East and the Indian Ocean as well. Various Afro-Atlantic interlocutors have embraced and transformed

Islam (see, e.g., I. M. Lewis 1989; Lincoln 1973) and even Hinduism (see Rush 1999) for their own purposes. Cuban santeros employ Chinese porcelain vessels and "syncretize" the *orichas* with various avatars of the Buddha and the Chinese fertility goddess Kwan Yin. Moreover, this model of mutually transformative interregional communication in the genesis of culture is applicable to non-black subcultures of the Atlantic perimeter as well. Indeed, there is no natural reason to isolate the "black Atlantic" from the Atlantic world as a whole, any more than there is a reason to isolate the Atlantic perimeter from the Mediterranean, Indian Ocean, and Far Eastern regions with which it has long interacted. The field of Atlantic history has similarly examined the politics, economics, and ideas that have united the Americas with Europe, not the least of which constituted the slave trade (see Bailyn 1996). Like it, the "Afro-Atlantic" construct targets the politics, the economics, the ideas, and above all the *will* of a specific group of people to communicate and shape one anothers' lives. Hence, by the efforts of people who reason strategically about their sameness and their diversity—and therefore about the pasts that unite and divide them—the Afro-Atlantic world has always been *focused* instead of *bounded*.

Like Gilroy's "black Atlantic," the logic of the "Afro-Atlantic dialogue" highlights the underexamined mobility and agency of black people in creating this world and the specific role of black *consciousness* in the creative and historical making of black *distinctiveness*. Like Robert Farris Thompson's "black Atlantic," "Afro-Atlantic dialogue" restores Africa, Africans, African cultures, and Americans' vision of Africa to a central role in the making of the black Atlantic world. Borrowing Fabian's parlance, this model posits the "coevalness" of Africa and the Americas, rather than imagine present-day Africa as the past of the black Americas.

Closer to home, for example, the dialogue model requires us to reassess the *locus classicus* of African "survivals" in the United States, embodied, as it were, in the Gullah/Geechee people of the Georgia-South Carolina Lowcountry and Sea Islands. These people have long been the focus of scholarly investigation into what remains culturally African about black North Americans, despite what all agree is their generally high degree of acculturation to Western ways. Relative geographical isolation long kept the speech and lifeways of the Sea Coast Islanders distinctive. Various scholars have sought to explain that distinctiveness as a debt to the cultures of what are now the settler colonies of Sierra Leone and Liberia.

In the second half of the eighteenth century, the rice farmers of the Sea Coast Islands drew many of their enslaved workers from the rice-growing regions of Sierra Leone and Liberia. On one hand, the term *Gullah* might derive from the ethnonym of Sierra Leone's Gola people. On the other hand, African captives came to these islands from many other regions as well, and students of the local creole language, known as "Gullah" or "Geechee," have identified an extremely diverse set of African origins in its lexicon and in its justly famous basket-making tradition. Indeed, some identify the term *Angola* as the more likely source of the term *Gullah* (Rosengarten 1997; L. D. Turner 1949).

As African Americans have grown more willing to embrace Africa as a cultural model and emblem of collective identity, the decline of Gullah language and crafts has been reversed. Indeed, the "Africanness" of Gullah basketry has become its major selling point and a means of livelihood for many craftswomen in coastal South Carolina. However, it was Joseph Opala, a Euro-American anthropologist and former member of the Peace Corps in Sierra Leone, who recently established the local conviction that Sierra Leone, in particular, was the source of the islanders' Africanness and the appropriate target of their "return" to the motherland (see the chapter by Sengova in this volume).

Indeed, the interest in this ahistorically specific tie was reciprocal. President Joseph Momo of Sierra Leone paid a highly public visit to the Sea Coast Islands in 1986 and encouraged the islanders to visit their "ancestral homeland," which a party of them did in 1989. President Momo continued the American tradition of attributing the islanders' linguistic distinctiveness to their African roots and identified the similarity of Gullah/Geechee language to Sierra Leonean Krio, or Creole, as proof (see the 1990 film *Family across the Sea* and the 1998 film *The Language You Cry In*).

In fact, both language varieties are predominantly English in their lexicons. Krio initially came about because of the interaction of African American returnees, diverse British-educated recaptives, British administrators, and Anglophone missionaries in Freetown. Thus the

Sierra Leonean and South Carolinian creole language varieties share features primarily on account of *the parallel circumstances of their genesis*, not on account of some shared, primordially African roots or of Gullah's having originated in Krio. In sum, the shared features of Gullah and Krio are highly ambiguous evidence of the Gullah people's Sierra Leonean or African "roots."

Nonetheless—and this is what makes the dialogue metaphor useful—a complex, politically, economically, and academically shaped dialogue has made the highly creolized Gullah dialect into emically persuasive grounds for a powerful new kinship—a web of living, albeit recent, social connections between Sierra Leoneans and South Carolina Gullah/Geechees.

The implications of this model should not be missed for regions other than the Atlantic perimeter, such as the Indian Ocean region (see also Chaudhuri 1990), the circum-Saharan world, and increasingly the Pacific Rim. And the analytic metaphor I propose also stands to highlight important but underexamined dimensions of smaller communities that have conventionally been called diasporas and transnational communities—such as the Jewish, Chinese, Irish, South Asian, and Lebanese diasporas, not to mention the countless transnational communities that have taken shape since World War II. Their future is likely to reflect much that the past and present of the African diaspora is already available to teach us. Diasporas and homelands continue to make each other over time, and they are shaped by a dialogue among numerous other coeval interlocutors of unequal power and unequal access to the means of communication.

Notes

1. See, for example, Otero 2000.

2. Consider Herskovits and his successors' study of "syncretism" and "creolization," both forms of cultural hybridity, as well as Eugene Genovese's seminal reflections on economic, cultural, and what James C. Scott would later call "everyday" forms of resistance (Genovese [1974] 1976; cf. J. Scott 1985). See Sally Cole (1994) on Ruth Landes's reflexive ethnography. Consider Roger Bastide's ([1960] 1978) early study of collective memory. Like Pierre Bourdieu (1977) and Paul Connerton (1989), Herskovits and his followers have sought in learned motor

habits a central mode of sociocultural reproduction. See Matory (1999a, 1999b) for an examination of the nineteenth-century transnationalism documented early on by the likes of Pierre Verger ([1968] 1976). From the 1920s onward, Afro-Americanist anthropology has studied interregional and intercontinental links that defy the norms of area studies as conventionally constituted.

3. Note that the use of the syncretism trope links Herskovits and his followers to a rather different figuration of Africa's "ethnohistorical" links to the Americas. Herskovits's elder, Raimundo Nina Rodrigues, in Brazil; his contemporary, Fernando Ortiz in Cuba; his junior colleague, the French sociologist Roger Bastide; and their followers emphasized the consequences of "transculturation" (Ortiz), the "interpenetration of civilizations" (Bastide), and similar forms of Afro-European cultural hybridity in shaping whole national cultures rather than being merely the effects of an ironic African continuity on the black minority and its neighbors.

4. In an essay intended to challenge the positivist narration of "history," Trouillot presents, in passing, a similar challenge to the memory metaphor. Trouillot problematizes the assumptions that "memory" is like a storage-and-retrieval system of knowledge from the past and that history is merely the collective version thereof. Both memory and history, he argues, are produced and continually reshaped by the positionality of the present-day rememberer or historian (1995: especially 14–16). His notion of "silencing," whereby the political motives of present-day historians motivate their choices of which events to exclude from narrations of the past, is equally relevant to my doubts about the "memory" metaphor.

5. Of course, the literature addressing sociocultural reproduction *beyond* the African diaspora in terms of such tropes as cultural memory, social memory, and collective memory is also broad and deep, addressing agency and strategy to variable degrees. That literature addresses, among other themes, the political and technical conditions under which history is narrated and debated (e.g., Appadurai 1981; Malkki 1995); the rituals, bodily practices, and modes of dress that retain traces of past events (e.g., Comaroff and Comaroff 1987; Connerton 1989; Stoller 1995); the marks that past crises have left upon our current vocabulary and legal procedures (Schudson 1997); the use of monuments in the selective commemoration of past heroes and the concomitantly selective authorization of present-day leaders (e.g., Werbner 1998); and the role of literal dialogue—that is, conversation among particular people—in shaping those people's recollection and articulation of past events (Middleton and Edwards 1990).

6. In my 1999 essay (Matory 1999c), I attempted to catalog the contexts and themes of the nineteenth- and twentieth-century Afro-Atlantic dialogue with more of an eye toward empirical exhaustiveness than toward theory. I was concerned that a more selective manner of illustrating my point would allow some readers to believe that the phenomena highlighted by the dialogue metaphor are unrepresentative of and exceptional in Afro-Atlantic history. Readers of the present chapter are encouraged to review that essay for further illustrations of the Afro-Atlantic dialogue, which I *briefly* illustrate in this chapter.

7. Roach (1996) employs "dialogue" as an analytic metaphor in a sense quite different from my own. He briefly analogizes culture to a *scripted* dialogue, which is reproduced or "remembered" as each new actor replaces a deceased one in the same dramatic role. Though the performance is necessarily somewhat modified, the endurance of the role or space left by the dead or by the apparently forgotten constitutes a collective cultural memory. In contrast, the feature of "dialogue" I wish to highlight in my analytic metaphor is the fact of the interlocutors' coevalness and diversity of interests in the interpretation and reproduction of the past.

8. By most reports, Bam̃gbose came from Ọ̀yọ́. However, Aizinho himself identifies his grandfather's origin as Abẹ́òkutà.

9. Arquivo Público do Estado da Bahia (hereafter APEB), Registro de Entrada de Estrangeiros, 1855–56, Seção Colonial e Provincial (hereafter SCP), livro 5667 (January 9, 1855; March 21, 1855; November 20–21, 1855; January 11, 1866; January 28, 1856); APEB, Presidência da Província (hereafter Pres Prov), Polícia do Porto (hereafter Pol Por), Mapas de Saída e Entrada de Embarcações (hereafter Mapas) 1886–93, SCP, Maço 3194-5, file for 1889, June 12, 1869 (note, this 1869 item is out of place but was indeed found in the 1889 file); APEB, Pres Prov, Pol Port, Mapas, 1873–78, Maço 3194-3, see January 31, 1876. See also APEB, Pres Prov, Pol Port, Mapas 1878–85, Maço 3194-49, file for 1879, July 15, 1879; APEB, Pres Prov, Pol Port, Mapas, 1878–85, Seção Colonial e Provincial, Maço 3194-4, December 20, 1878; APEB, Pres Prov, Pol Port, Mapas, 1878–85, SCP, Maço 3194-5, file for 1889, June 4, 1889; APEB, Pol Port, Registro de Entrada de Embarcações, 1886-1890, Maço 5975, e.g., May 27, 1885 [sic]; October 22, 1885 [sic] and 1889–92, Maço 5976, e.g., p. 7, SCP; APEB, Livros da Inspetoria da Polícia do Porto, Entradas de Passageiros, vol. 6, Anos December 4, 1891, to March 21, 1895, August 27, 1892, p. 80; APEB, Livros da Inspetoria da Polícia do Porto, Entradas de Passageiros, vol. 8, Anos: January 2, 1896, to December 31, 1898, March 7, 1898; APEB, Polícia, Registros de Passaportes, 1881–85, Book

5909, and 1885–1890, Book 5910, SCP. Also see M. Cunha (1985:123, 125); Lindsay (1994:43–44); Moloney (1889:255–76); Olinto (1964:266–67); Pierson (1942:239); L. D. Turner (1942:65); and Verger ([1968] 1976:464). This theme was prominent in interviews I conducted in 1995 in Lagos, Rio de Janeiro, and Bahia with Paul Lola Bam̄gboṣe-Martins of Lagos and Rio, Regina Souza of Salvador, Beatriz da Rocha of Salvador, Aïr José Sowzer de Jesús of Salvador, Albérico Paiva Ferreira of Salvador, George Alakija of Salvador, and Yinka Alli-Balogun of Lagos—all descendants of turn-of-the-century African Brazilian travelers and many of them travelers in their own right. For a complete list of sources, see Matory (2005).

10. The "compass" and "Great Engineer" iconography of Freemasonry also appears in the ground drawings of the Trinidad Shouters (see Simpson 1966:540, 543, 544, 547). See also Simpson's sketch of a Freemasonry-influenced "Trinidad ground-drawing" in R. Thompson (1983:112).

11. Sowzer's daughter Irene confirms that Pierson's depiction of the seal, which has now been painted over, was accurate (Irene Souza, personal communication, 1996).

12. Apparently of Ẹgbá origins, this dynasty of doctors, lawyers, and chiefs, some of whom conducted their professional studies in England, has appeared in newspapers, magazines, and books published in Brazil, Nigeria, and the United States.

13. Of lesser longevity, Dr. Abayọmi Cole's West African Psychical Institute-Yorùbá Branch, founded in 1901, appears to represent another neotraditional, nationalist religious development by coastal and culturally creole Africans (see *The Lagos Standard*, April 17, 1901, p. 3).

14. Mr. Bam̄gboṣe-Martins normally resides in Lagos, but I met him first on one of his many extended sojourns in Rio. He identifies Adeyẹmọ Alakija as the last president of the Reformed Ogboni Fraternity. On the contrary, Anyebe (1989:108–113) identifies Sir Adeyẹmọ Alakija as the first president, and his nephew, Nigerian chief justice Sir Adetokunbọ Adegboyega Ademọla, as the second.

15. On the other hand, existing studies of Brazilian returnees to West Africa emphasize their tendency to avoid African-inspired religious practices and to emphasize their Catholicism (M. Cunha 1985; J. M. Turner 1974).

16. The community linking Cuba to Lagos in this cycle of African American return also boasted some extraordinary Anglophone figures. For example, the Cuban-born Hilario Campos "returned" to Lagos, where he reportedly became

the "mayor." Despite the denials of Campos, Fernando Ortiz reported that Campos had been a babaláwo, or diviner. Andrés Muñiz was born to freeborn parents in Cuba in 1894, and the whole family "returned" to Lagos at the turn of the century. After earning his bachelor's degree in England, Muñiz returned to Cuba in 1919 as an employee of a British firm. He continually corresponded with his family in Lagos, as did his children after his death in 1944. His family denies that he professed Yorùbá religion but admits that he believed "in the power of the eyes." According to some friends, "when his opponent in a dispute over the job at the sugar mill appealed to 'witchcraft' in order to intimidate Andrés…Andrés reacted by dissecting the majá (a large snake) and the owl that appeared in his quarters on the plantation" (Sarracino 1988:70).

17. In the nineteenth and twentieth centuries, with similar creativity, black North American Protestants also identified strongly with Ethiopia as their biblical counterpart and exemplar.

18. Consider also the useful suggestion by Appadurai (1996:12–13) that we emphasize the adjective *cultural* over the noun *culture*. He argues that culture is too often regarded as a substance rather than as the aspect of social conduct and self-representation intended to distinguish one's own group from other classes, genders, roles, nations, and so forth. Indeed, this Barthian *differentiating function* of culture is also what unites apparently diverse peoples in what I have called "superregional dialogues."

6

"Important Truths" and "Pernicious Follies"

Texts, Covenants, and the Anabaptist Church of Jamaica

John W. Pulis

In his retrospective history of Jamaica, the Baptist missionary James M. Phillippo (1843:270) commented on what he referred to as the "irreligion" of the recently emancipated black majority:

> Absurd, monstrous, and discordant as were the elements which composed their religious system, there is yet to be united with it another ingredient which, if less revolting in its aspect and character, was not only equally unproductive of rational piety and consistent morality, but far more injurious in its consequence. Many of them acquired a knowledge of the formularies of the English Church and at the conclusion of the war with America some, who had been imported from that continent, mysteriously blending together important truths and extravagant puerilities, assumed the office of teachers and preachers, disseminating far and wide their pernicious follies.

Phillippo's diatribe was directed at a small but influential group of African Americans, the most notable of whom was the folk preacher

George Liele. Liele was one of several African Americans caught up in the religious fervor known as the Great Awakening, that swept North America before the Revolution (Gallay 1989:ch. 2, ch. 3; Lambert 1994:ch. 5, ch. 6). He underwent an epiphany while attending one such meeting and went on to establish one of the first black congregations in Savannah, Georgia, during the British occupation (1778–1782). Like many enslaved blacks, Liele opted to serve "King and Crown" rather than the "patriots," and he was transported to Jamaica in a loyalist diaspora when hostilities ceased (see B. Brown 1975; J. Davis 1918; J. P. Gates 1943; Holmes 1964; Little 1995; Pulis 1999a).[1] Similar to African Americans, such as Boston King, Thomas Peters, and David George in Sierra Leone, Liele became a voice in the black community. He organized a series of congregations, trained a cadre of preachers, and drafted a document detailing the provenance of what he called the "Anabaptist Church of Jamaica."

This chapter discusses Liele's "Covenant of the Anabaptist Church of Jamaica."[2] Although not a narrative in the traditional sense of the term, it is a rare and unique document in which Liele drafted twenty-one "articles" that codified the practice of what European missionaries to Jamaica termed "Native Baptism" (Anabaptism). Whereas Peters and George petitioned the British for land claims in Africa, Liele did so concerning religious practice in Jamaica. A "close reading" of this document will tell us not only about the black loyalist diaspora but also about the relation between rituals, beliefs, and everyday life in a colonial polity. The proper way to begin a close reading is with a discussion of context, and this chapter opens with an overview that situates Liele and his fellow covenantors in the rhythms and events that brought them to the island of Jamaica.

THE AFRICAN AMERICAN DIASPORA TO JAMAICA

The American Revolution set in motion one of the largest diasporas in the Atlantic world. As scholars such as Quarles ([1961] 1996: ch. 6), Frey (1991:173, ch. 4), and P. Morgan (1983:110–111) have suggested, upward of 500,000 "black loyalists" were removed from the American colonies and transported to Canada, England, and various islands in the West Indies.[3] Black loyalists were African Americans (some free, most enslaved) who served the British rather than the "patriots." Courted by proclamations that offered manumission in return for service, they migrated to cities such as Savannah, Charleston, and New York, where they toiled in various capacities and were evacuated with their white counterparts when peace was declared. In the West Indies, the largest number of loyalists (black and white) went to the island of Jamaica. Absolute numbers are difficult to ascertain, but a survey of evacuation returns and shipping registers indicates that 5,000 white loyalists, 15,000 to 20,000 slaves, and approximately 1,000 black loyalists were transported to the island.[4]

Reconstructing the history of this diaspora exceeds the scope of this chapter, but a biographical survey is necessary to frame a profile of the black community and provide social and historical details concerning Liele and those who became "Elders and Rulers" in his church. Unlike their white counterparts, the black loyalists were required to register their names and means of manumission with local vestries or parishes.[5] In Jamaica, as in other plantation societies (for example, Barbados, Saint Kitts, and Antigua), the House of Assembly enacted local statutes or "slave codes" to control the black population, and free blacks were required to register in each parish. Among the 150 Americans registered in the parishes of Kingston and Saint Catherine, 28 were members of a military formation known as the "Black Pioneers," one of several all-black units raised by the British during the Revolution. They served "King and Crown" as auxiliaries and were manumitted for the services they rendered to various regiments and commanders. The nineteen male and nine female Black Pioneers who settled in Jamaica enlisted in 1778 and served with generals Campbell, Clarke, Coote, and Balcarres (future governors of Jamaica) during the British invasion of Georgia and South Carolina. The unit was transported in 1781 at the behest of Governor Campbell, and all twenty eight were awarded "Certificates of Freedom" and pensions when the unit disbanded in 1784 (JA-LGR 2/6/277, p. 97, March 17, 1791).[6]

The Pioneers were not the only military attachés sent to the island. At least ten blacks and two Native Americans served as aides-de-camp. James Walden served with the Loyal Irish Volunteers of New York. He was awarded a Certificate of Freedom in 1778 when the unit left North America for Jamaica. Three blacks—Mary Miles, Hector Lloyd, and Cuffee—and two Native Americans—Mary Bowen and Sarah Willis—

were aides to Campbell, and they received their certificates when Campbell departed for India in 1784. Three black men—Tom, Dublin, and John Waters—and three black women—Nancy, her daughter Mary, and Christobal—arrived from Charleston bearing certificates issued by Sir Henry Clinton for services rendered (see JA-LGR, 2/2/277, p. 43).[7]

Military commanders were not the only officials who manumitted black Americans. Kate, Phoebe, and Windsor arrived in Jamaica bearing certificates issued by Patrick Tonyn, the British governor of East Florida. Although William Bull, the governor of South Carolina, never became a resident of Jamaica, he owned several plantations in the parishes of Trelawny and Saint Ann, and he awarded certificates to Susan Towers, Rosetta Douglass, Susan Burrows, and Dublin Waldren and to three black families, Solas and Amelia Duberdue, John and Frances Lampert, and George and Elizabeth Vinyard of Charleston. Of those mentioned, George Vinyard is of special importance. He became a folk preacher associated with Liele in Kingston and later established his own congregation near the hamlet of Delve in the parish of Westmoreland. He and William Kitt became associates of Moses Baker in Saint James and an elder in Saint John's Chapel, the second Native Baptist congregation to form in Jamaica. Saint Johns was organized by Thomas Nicholas Swigle, a "free brown man." Vinyard preached for eighteen years in Kingston before Baker called him to Saint James. A planter in Westmoreland named Hilton gave him a residence, a small salary, a plot for provisions, and a chapel, and he amassed a following of 1,400 worshippers (M. Baker 1803; Brathwaite 1971:254–255; Curtin 1955:32; Mullin 1992:ch. 8; Rippon 1802:1144–1156; Stewart 1992: ch. 4; M. Turner 1982:57–58, 81–87).

Although the largest number of blacks arrived from Georgia and South Carolina, a small but by no means insignificant number arrived from New York. Frank Lope registered in Kingston in March 1783, bearing a certificate issued by Peter Dubois, magistrate of police in New York. He was followed by Ishmael York, Oly Adams, William Kenty, and a woman named Silva, all of whom carried certificates issued by Edward Williams, Major of Brigade. Fellow New Yorkers William Kitt, Henry York, Cesar Moncrieff, Prince George, and Augustus Ryall, while laying claim to the status of "free people of color," did not possess certificates of their own and had their status substantiated by the testimony of fellow New Yorker Moses Baker. Like George Vinyard, Baker became a folk preacher affiliated with Liele. Unlike Liele and Vinyard, Baker was a free person of color who underwent a spiritual conversion, or "rebirth," while in Jamaica. Liele located his church in Kingston. Baker traveled to Saint James, where he drafted his own covenant, established a chapel congregation known as Crooked Spring, and "labored" until his death in the 1820s (JA-LGR 2/6/277, pp. 44, 45, 46, 49, 54, 57, 66, 110).[8]

Although nominally free, the black loyalists were, in fact, disenfranchised in that they were not allowed to participate in local politics or transfer personal estates worth more than £2,000. They had to petition the House of Assembly for "the rights and privileges of an English subject." The Free Negro Law required all free people of color to register the means by which their manumission was achieved with each and every parish of residence (Assembly of Jamaica:vol. V, 311; vol. VI, 537; vol. VII, 448, 537). The free community of color expanded rapidly from the mid- to the late eighteenth century, and its members occupied a social, racial, and political position between enslaved blacks and a minority of whites. They were expanding in power and numbered about four thousand when the black loyalists arrived.

The colonial state was receptive to the plight of white loyalists and provided assistance in the form of tax relief and land grants, but the black loyalists were perceived as threats. None were relieved from taxes or given land grants, and the planter-dominated House of Assembly enacted increasingly repressive legislation in an attempt to control all facets of black life.[9] Nonetheless, armed as they were with mandates, proclamations, and Certificates of Freedom, the black loyalists were by no means minor actors in local and global affairs. Similar to Thomas Peters, Boston King, and David George in Africa, George Liele waged a "war of words" in Jamaica and left a legacy in the form of deeds, wills, correspondence, and covenants. These documents were, by inception, political. Whereas Thomas Peters and David George petitioned the Colonial Office in London to honor claims for land in Sierra Leone, Liele wrote to evangelicals concerning those most cherished of republican ideals—free speech and free religious practice. He had been arrested in Kingston for preaching in a public venue (a typical North

American practice), and he sought the aid of evangelicals in an attempt to circumvent a series of "anti-preaching laws" enacted by the assembly to curtail his "work." The presence of black Christians in Jamaica came as a surprise to evangelicals in England, and Baptists like John Rippon pursued a correspondence with Liele in Jamaica.[10]

Liele was born into slavery in Virginia around 1730. In the 1760s, Henry Sharpe took him to Georgia, where he was caught up in the Great Awakening. He apparently experienced a religious event or epiphany while attending a meeting, and the local congregation applauded him for his oratorial skills. He received a license to preach and was one of several black itinerants (including Amos Scriven, David George, Joseph Paul, George Vinyard, and Jesse Peters) who plied the Southern Provinces preaching to whites and blacks. Along with his brother-in-law Andrew Bryan, he established one of the first black churches in North America (cf. T. Hall 1994; Hodges 1993). Henry Sharpe was a loyalist, and Liele worked for or assisted the British during the invasion of Georgia and was transported to Kingston in 1782 (see R. Davis 1980; W. Harris 1978; Huddlestun and Walker 1976).

Phillippo (1843:271) refers to Liele only once in his *Jamaica: Its Past and Present State*, but there can be little doubt that Liele was a key personage in the practice of Afro-Jamaican Christianity. Along with carrying on a lengthy correspondence, he trained a cadre of preachers, established a network of congregations, and drafted a covenant in which he detailed the biblical basis of what he referred to as the Anabaptist Church of Jamaica. Liele's covenant is a rare and unique document (one of the few surviving from these early and in many ways formative years of black authorship), and a close reading will tell us about rituals, beliefs, and exegesis during a critical era in the formation of black interpretive tradition.[11] Unlike his letters, published to support abolition, this all-important document was not distributed until 1804, and the proper way to frame a close reading is with a discussion of provenance.

TEXTS, CONTEXTS, AND AFRO-CHRISTIANITY

Liele became a spokesperson for the black community, and he sent a copy of his covenant to Rippon, along with his correspondence. The Baptist Missionary Society printed a copy of this copy (with modifications) in 1796, and it was republished in Baptist-sponsored periodicals such as the *General Baptist Repository* as debate over slavery and the struggle to end the slave trade intensified in the early nineteenth century. According to a Baptist historian, this copy was "lost" for a century, only to be "rediscovered" in the 1960s, when it was reprinted again in a Baptist periodical (Rusling 1968) and later by Mechal Sobel ([1979] 1988:152) in *Trabelin' On: The Slave Journey to an Afro-Baptist Faith.* The edition of 1796 is on deposit and available at the Angus Library at Regent's Park, London, England. In what could only have been an act of foresight, Liele entered a handwritten copy of the original into a local record group ("Deeds & Conveyances") in the Colonial Record Office (now the Island Record Office) in Spanish Town, Jamaica. I ran across an entry for this copy in the "alphabets" (index) to the nine hundred volumes that constitute this record group while searching for documents relating to the black loyalist community. The Liele family was heavily engaged in the local provision trade, and they recorded more than one hundred deeds, conveyances, and contracts in their operation of a family-owned business (see Pulis 1999a:201–202, 219–220, n. 50).

Unlike deeds, which recorded the transfer of property, covenants were "spiritual contracts" that bound a group of people into an association based on a set of religious principles. They were, by inception, exclusionary and were drafted as much to distance and separate as to unite. They constituted the basis of a community, in this case a church society, in which biblical injunction superseded secular law. The copy published in Rusling (1968) and later in Sobel ([1979] 1988) is different in several respects from both originals. Omitted from both of these published versions are all of what Liele and his covenantors called "proofs"—that is, the statements, clauses, and interpretations that accompanied the twenty-one articles included in the handwritten and printed edition of 1796—in addition to the names of the Elders and Rulers of the church. Among the signatories to this spiritual contract— the names inscribed (half of them with an encircled X, indicating a lack of writing skills) on a copy of the original, registered and filed on October 14, 1796—were twenty-four individuals referred to as "Elders and Rulers." Along with Liele, who was cited as "Pastor," the Elders and Rulers were James Pascall, James Cargill, Ann Lindsay, Eliza Gordon,

William Wilson, John Liele, George Liele Jr., Amos Stiles, Charles
Price, John McIntire, John Harris, John Baptiste, George Good,
William Good, Hannah Liele, Frances Swigle, Diana Price, Jane
Williams, Silvia Stiles, Sarah Savage, Eliza Good, Mary Brown, Eleanor
Bonner, and Sabina Johnson.[12]

If Moses climbed the mountain and returned with the Ten
Commandments, then Liele went to Jamaica and inscribed twenty-one
articles on a sheet of parchment. Exactly what were these articles, and
why are they unique? Unlike the Ten Commandments, Liele's articles
were compound statements composed of three interrelated clauses. A
one- or two-sentence declarative statement stipulating the basic principles of the church was accompanied by a "proof," a lengthy explanatory paragraph in which the meaning of the declaration was clarified.
Both were followed and supported by references to chapters and vers-
es of scripture. Spatial considerations preclude a full text presentation
of all twenty-one articles, but the first and in many ways key article
reads as such:

> I. We are of the Anabaptist persuasion because we believe it
> agreeable to the Scriptures. Proof. In those days came John
> the Baptist preaching in the Wilderness of Judea, and saying
> repent ye, for the kingdom of heaven is at hand; for this is
> he that was spoken of by the Prophet Elias, saying; the voice
> of one crying in the wilderness; prepare ye the way of the
> lord, make his paths straight. Be ye not unequally yoked
> together, with unbelievers, for what fellowship hath right-
> eousness with unrighteousness, and what communication
> has light with darkness, and what concord hath Christ with
> Belial, or what part hath he that believeth with an infidel,
> and what agreement hath the Temple of god with Idols? for
> ye are the Temple of the Living God; as God hath said, I will
> dwell in them, and walk in them; and I will be their God, and
> they shall be my people, wherefore come out from among
> them, and be ye separate saith the Lord, and touch not the
> unclean thing; and I will receive you, and will be a father
> unto you, and ye shall be my sons and daughters, saith the
> Lord Almighty. Matthew, Chapt. III, verse 1,2,3; 2nd
> Corinthians, Chapt.VI, Ver. 4,15,16,17,18.

While the articles are identical in form and the three-part format (declarative statement, explanatory proof, biblical citation) is maintained throughout the document, the content of each article shifts topically and thematically, from defining the church and describing rituals to stipulating "laws" and appointing "saints" or officiating boards. For example, articles III ("We hold to be baptized in a river"), IV ("We hold to receiving the Lord's Supper"), V ("We hold to the ordinance of washing one another's feet"), VI ("We hold to receive and admit young children"), and VII ("We hold to anointing oil and praying over the sick") are essentially descriptive in that Liele delineated the rituals he and his covenantors associated with their practice of Christianity. As Isaac (1982), Lambert (1994), and Frey and Wood (1998) have detailed, rituals such as washing feet, open-water baptism, and the admittance of children occupied center stage in the Great Awakening. Such practices constituted what anthropologists call "rituals of inversion" in that they functioned to shift the focus of piety and subservience from the colonial elite and clergy to an alternative or higher authority. Like the sugar planters Liele confronted, the Anglican Church was one of the largest slave owners in Jamaica, and inclusion of the above in his covenant brought the ritual armamentarium of the Awakening to bear on contesting, challenging, and subverting the hegemony of Jamaican elites, as well as state-sanctioned institutions such as the Church of England.[13]

Covenants were exclusionary and served to differentiate one group from another. Whereas washing feet and immersion were instrumental in transforming a disparate group into a community of believers, articles I (above), XII ("We are forbidden to swear not at all"), XIV ("We are forbidden to wear costly raiments, such as superfluity"), XVI ("To avoid fornication, we permit none to keep each other, except they be married, according to the word of God"), X ("We are forbidden to shed blood"), and XIII ("We are forbidden to eat blood, for it is the life of a creature, and from things strangled, and from meats offered to idols") served to erect barriers and demarcate boundaries through the delineation of dietary prohibitions, social decorum, and affinity. Liele's use of the term *Anabaptist* is instructive. The term carried multiple meanings and was associated with a group of European sects that advocated a clear and distinct separation between church and state, the former understood as the body of Christ and the latter as that of Satan. A central Anabaptist tenet clearly articulated by Liele was that of the "elect" (the belief proposed by Calvin that only certain people were destined for salvation), and Liele's linking of salvation with prohibitions and injunctions served several purposes. On the one hand, it served to situate his newly founded church within a recognized tradition and, in so doing, legitimated his practice of Anabaptism to dissenters and nonconformists in the metropole. On the other hand, it served to distinguish the rituals and beliefs promoted by Liele from those associated with "Belial" in article I. Several Afro-Christianities were practiced in Jamaica, and monogamy and dietary restrictions linked with notions of the "elect," the "unclean," and the "Temple of the Living God" served to differentiate Liele and his Anabaptists from the Christianity practiced by fellow black Americans such as George Lewis and Afro-Jamaicans such as Cudjoe.

By contrast, articles II ("We hold to keep the Lord's day throughout the year in a place appointed for Public Worship"), XV ("We permit no slaves to join the Church without having a few lines from their owners of their good behavior"), and VIII ("We hold to laboring, one with the other, according to the word of God") express Liele's ability to negotiate the cracks and fissures of plantation society. Suffice it to restate that Jamaica was a slave society and Liele and others were placed in a color-caste hierarchy between the enslaved black majority and the all-powerful or hegemonic white minority. Hegemony, as Williams suggests (1977:108), is never monolithic. Black Americans were disenfranchised, but they were not without influence, and they learned early on to wield a power out of proportion to their numbers. As I mentioned earlier, Liele was arrested in Kingston for preaching in public, and the above cited articles express his ability to organize a black congregation in a slave society. Unlike in North America, where itinerant preachers (Baptist, Wesleyan, and Moravian) traversed the colonies, mobility was restricted in Jamaica, and the open-air "revivals" characteristic of the Awakening violated local legislation. Purchasing property and building chapels for "public worship" expressed the means and ability to transform itinerancies modeled after those in America into a religious institution protected not by local but by metropolitan legislation (the Act of Toleration), and it is not unwarranted to suggest that the monies needed to purchase land and construct chapels were produced collectively via article VIII ("We hold to laboring one with the other"). Along with public worship, evidence suggests that freedom in the form of manumission constituted an equally important goal of collective labor. Few individuals possessed the ability (materially or politically) to manumit family, friends, or fellow brethren from bondage. A survey of manumission records indicates that Liele purchased the manumission of "Cesar." Cesar was the slave name of James Pascall, one of the twenty-four Elders and Rulers of the Anabaptist Church who signed the original covenant.[14]

Like the Mayflower Compact of the Puritans, Liele's covenant constituted the basis of a society within a society, and a number of articles are jural or legal in theme and express the way biblical law superseded civil or secular authority. For example, articles XVIII ("If any of this religion should transgress and walk disorderly, and not according to the Commands which we have received in this covenant, he will be censured according to the word of God"), XIX ("We hold, if a brother or sister should transgress any of these articles written in this covenant, he or she shall be put away from us, not to keep company, nor eat with him"), and XX ("We hold if a Brother or Sister should transgress, and abideth not in the doctrine of Christ, and he, or she, after justly dealt with according to the 8th article, they shall be received into the Church again and have all privileges as before") defined the parameters of "sin" or transgression. Despite claiming to be the "elect," members were known to "lose their way." Whereas collective labor enabled Liele to manumit brethren, the power to censure or exclude was an effective means of maintaining control, and the above articles express the way in which members could achieve restitution for violating the codes and norms of acceptable behavior. In addition to codifying laws, articles IX ("We hold to appoint judges and such other Officers among us, to settle any matter according to the word of God"), XVII ("If a slave or servant misbehave to their owners they are to be dealt with according to the word of God"), and XI ("We are forbidden to go to law with another before the unjust, but to settle any matter we have before the Saints") established the structure and organization of a theocracy, the black counterpart of the planter-dominated House of Assembly. Like the "slave courts" that formed on plantations, the brethren appointed as saints became arbiters and mediators in a legal system that was repressive. The church's laws and officiating bodies served as an alternative means of justice for those who were denied what little benefits a judicial system based on slavery had to offer people of color (cf. Hodges 1993; Pitts 1993; Raboteau 1978).

Whereas the content of each article in Liele's covenant told us about the relation between rituals and everyday life, deconstructing the form (declarative statement, explanatory proof, biblical citation) will open a window on the emergence of a black exegesis. Liele's use of biblical citation as a "proof" for his interpretation involved the employment of "cant-phrases." Cant-phrases were biblical citations (for example, Psalm 68) accompanied by one or two lines of scripture that characterized the passage ("Ethiopia shall stretch forth her hands unto God"). Initially, missionaries used them as a shorthand approach to teaching "scholars" and "communicants" in mission schools how to read the Bible. Unlike Catholic missionaries, Protestant missionaries promoted the tenet that individuals should learn how to read, but in a manner consistent with Protestant doctrine. They stressed a way of reading known as "figuralism" or "typology." As Frei (1974) and others (e.g., Theophus Smith 1994) have documented, biblical figuralism is a type/antitype method in which text-based stories, characters, and figures (Adam, Exodus, Noah) are linked to internal or intertextual references (Genesis, Isaac, Psalms) and to external references in the form of people, places, and contemporary events. It differs from other forms in that each figure or type in a type/antitype dyad "shadows," or prefigures, the other and rather than one type or figure replacing or superseding another, the latter complements and fulfills the former.[15] Along with the grammar and intonation of biblical prose, scholars and communicants were introduced to cant-phrases, and it did not take long for them to reject traditional frames (the type/antitype dyad) and replace them with their own interpretations or "constructions." According to the lead article in the *South-Carolina Gazette* (April 24, 1742), Anglican catechists were chastised for "filling their [blacks'] Heads with a Parcel of Cant-Phrases, Trances, Dreams, Visions, and Revelations." One such catechist, Francis Lejau, wrote in his correspondence that "the best Scholar of all the Negroes in my Parish put his own construction on one such phrase," and these constructions aroused fear among the planters that the enslaved would rebel.

If we can read the preceding as a "tradition in emergence," then with Liele's covenant we get the first clear example of a distinctly Afro-Jamaican exegesis. In addition to detailing the structure and function of a church, the three-part format (declarative statement, explanatory proof, biblical citation) exemplifies the way Liele co-opted the type/antitype method and subverted accepted or formulaic frames, and it is not unwarranted to suggest that what we are reading is the creolization of European, African, and African American rituals and beliefs. While all the articles are identical in form, Liele linked his declarative statement to a citation or set of citations that were clarified and explained not by reference to text-centered types and figures but to black life in plantation society. It does not take a long stretch of the imagination to probe beneath the surface of articles I, IX, and XI and suggest that if Liele equated his church with Christ and its members with saints, then the planter elite personified or "shadowed" the unjust, and the House of Assembly represented the workings of Satan or evil.

Along with laying the foundation for a black theology, Liele's use of his covenant tells us about the relation between exegetical practice, discursive activities, and the formation of an oral narrative, or "living testament." Although the articles were inscribed on paper, the covenant functioned less as an icon venerating the printed word and more as an instrument that legitimated and supported an oral or mixed aural-printed tradition. According to his correspondence, Liele read each article out loud so that members of his congregation could hear and see them performed, and the ability to read or cite cant-phrases became part of Afro-Jamaican folk preaching, along with performative genres such as call-response, testifying, and narrative sequencing.

Suffice it to say, in conclusion, that what Phillippo dismissed as folly was an alternative and oppositional religious practice that drew upon an encyclopedia of biblical types, figures, and characters. Along with chapels, Liele constructed schools, and the scholars and communicants in his Anabaptist schools were beginning to assemble a black concordia replete with characters, figures, and cant-phrases, the meanings of which would be subject to reinterpretation as they were passed from one generation to the next. Although phrases such as "No man can serve two masters" and "Ethiopia shall stretch forth her hands unto God" did not find their way into Liele's covenant (he was arrested for preaching on the former), their importance to the formation of Afro-Jamaican Christianity was to be crucial. The first phrase was deployed by a Native Baptist, "Daddy" Sam Sharpe, and it became the rallying cry of the Baptist, or Christmas, Rebellion of 1831–32. The second became the clarion call for Rastafarians, who saw in the 1930 coronation of the Ethiopian emperor Haile Selassie the complement or fulfillment of the messiah "shadowed" in Psalm 68.[16]

Acknowledgments

The research on which this paper is based was supported in part by a National Endowment for the Humanities Travel Grant, an American Philosophical Society Grant, a Fulbright-Hays American Republics Research Award, a Library Company of Philadelphia Grant, and an NEH Summer Seminar. I would like to thank the following individuals: Barry.W. Higman, then of the Department of History, University of the West Indies, Mona, Jamaica, for affiliation while I was a Fulbright scholar; Elizabeth Williams and the staff of the Jamaica Archives; Mr. Rhone and the staff of the Island Record Office; Mr. Simpson, Ms. Johnson, and the staff of the National Library of Jamaica; John Van Horne, Phil Lapansky, and the staff of the Library Company of Philadelphia; and Richard Price, Faye V. Harrison, Kevin A. Yelvington, and the rest of the participants at the 1999 SAR advanced seminar for the opportunity to debate many of the ideas presented here.

1. The literature concerning loyalists is voluminous, and no attempt at a bibliographic compilation is made here. The exodus of North Americans, referred to as "Tories," "good Americans," "American loyalists," "black loyalists," and/or "refugees," has attracted the attention of various scholars who have documented loyalist communities in Canada, England, and Africa. See, for example, W. Brown (1965, 1969, 1985, 1992); Callahan (1967); M. Clarke (1981); Craton and Saunders (1992); K. G. Davies (1976); Dodge (1979); Kozy (1991); C. Moore (1994); Norton (1972); Quarles ([1961] 1996); Riley (1983); Robinson (1992); Saunders (1983); Siebert ([1913] 1972); Tyson (1975–76); J. Walker (1976); E. Wilson (1976); Winks (1971); E. Wright (1976); and the contributors to Pulis (1999c). See Hodges (1996) for overviews and estimates. In addition, see the pioneering work of William C. Nell (1855).

2. See IRO (Old Series, liber 432, folio 288) for an original copy of this document.

3. For the Revolution in the South, see, for example, Coleman (1958), Crow and Tise (1978), Higgins (1979), and Pancake (1985).

4. For Georgia, see BHQ-CP 5,268 (3); for Charleston, see BHQ-CP 10,026, p. 4; 10,277, p. 6; 10,316, p. 1. Seven convoys and 120 ships (35,000 tons) removed ten thousand people from Charleston between December 14 and December 17, 1782. The largest convoy (15,406 tons) removed the military, related personnel, and stores to New York. The second largest, a fleet of twenty ships (8,131 tons), transported 3,873 people (591 white men, 291 white women, 378 white children, and 2,613 blacks) to Jamaica. They arrived on January 13, 1783. See BHQ-CP 10,316, p. 1, for Florida. Some 11,716 people were removed from Saint Augustine: 1,748 white men, 2,482 white women and children, and 7,163 blacks. See BHQ-CP 8,066 (2), p. 161, for June (1,783 departures); BHQ-CP 9,728 (5) for October departures to Abaco in the Bahamas; and BHQ-CP 9,730 for other West Indian departures. See BHQ-CP 10,427, "Book of Negroes," Book I, pp. 98 and 100, for Abaco departures of August 21 and August 22, 1782; see BHQ-CP 10,427, "Book of Negroes," Book II, p. 111, for the Cat Island departure of November 3, 1783; and BHQ-CP 10,427, "Recapitulation," p. 157, for aggregate totals. There are several copies of this document, and these figures are taken from a copy in the National Archives (microcopy 332, roll 7). This important document has been reprinted with notes in Hodges (1996). See H. Davies (1976:vol. XIX, 452; vol. XXI, 223–224) for aggregate numbers from New York. There are two departure dates listed, October 12 and November 24, 1783, with separate totals of 29,278 and 35,010. It is unclear whether these numbers are running returns or aggregate totals for two separate departures. See also Troxler (1981:21, 27–28). As noted above, precise numbers are always suspect. Siebert's ([1913] 1972) contention that five thousand African American and four hundred white families arrived from Savannah is a gross overinflation taken from the Reverend George Bridges.

5. Although the British colonial bureaucracy posted various and numerous returns, they do not always contain information suitable to life history, and the sketch that follows is based on a compilation of biographical/life history materials mined from and linked to both primary and secondary sources. Where possible, I have relied upon sources such as the British Headquarter Papers and manuscript materials in Jamaica, linking them to edited compilations such as that of Davies (1976). The profile of African Americans was compiled from two registers and various returns. Like all free people of color, black loyalists were required to register with local vestries, and the following is based on two such registers (JA-CGR 2/6/277, "Register of Free People in Kingston"; JA-CGR 2/2/vol. 2BA, "Register

of Free People in St. Catherine"). Names from these records were linked to primary sources, such as returns, registers, and tax lists in Jamaica and the British Headquarter Papers and to secondary sources as per the notes below. I have been able to construct a working profile of the African and European communities as they existed in Kingston and Saint Catherine circa 1783–1800. See Stone (1977) and Watson and Watson-Franke (1985:46–70) for collective biography and life history.

6. The Black Pioneers were one of several black military and auxiliary units raised by the British. See a letter dated February 16, 1782, in which Campbell discusses a suspicious fire that destroyed eighty-three houses in Kingston; one of March 25, 1782, in which he argues that the loyalty of local militiamen was suspect and that they were incapable of defending the island from the French and Spanish; and one of June 5, 1782, in which he calls for the use of black troops (BHQ-CO 137/82). See also BHQ-CO 137/82, p. 12 (Charles Montagu to Lord George Germain, on raising troops in the South Carolina backcountry for use in and Jamaica); BHQ-CP 4798 for a listing of regiments sent to Jamaica; and BHQ-CP 6492 for a salary scale of the Black Pioneers at the rate of four-eights for lieutenants, three-eights for ensigns, 1 shilling for sergeants, and 8 and 6 pence for corporals and privates.

7. See Library of Congress, Broadsides, January 4 and January 11, 1779, for Campbell's proclamation, and March 4, 1779, for Prevost, Parker, and Campbell's joint proclamation. See BHQ-CO 5/181, pp. 122–159, for Clinton's proclamation. Also see Quarles ([1961] 1996:ch. 7) and Frey (1991:ch. 5) for British activities in South Carolina.

8. Moses Baker carried a certificate issued by Edward Williams under orders from General Birch on June 4, 1783, and his wife and children bore certificates issued by William Walton, Magistrate of Police, June 18, 1783. William Kitt was a signatory and trustee to three acres of property, on which Liele constructed his Windward Road Chapel (IRO:Old Series, liber 384, folio 161, February 13, 1790).

9. See Brathwaite (1971:338–342) for a partial listing of Jamaican slave laws. Few facets of black life, including procreation, festivities, and social relationships, were left unregulated by whites.

10. It must be stated that these letters were edited by Rippon, and I use them with caution, knowing full well that despite empathy for Liele, anything not in keeping with Baptist religious practice would most certainly have been removed. There is nonetheless a wealth of ethnographic or descriptive material, and for a historically informed anthropologist such as myself, it opens windows on

the signs and symbols, rituals and practices, and values and norms of conversion. Liele's preoccupation with death, misread by Rippon, resonates not with European but with an African tradition that venerates deceased family members who remain part of everyday or lived experience.

11. My understanding of tropes, subtexts, hidden transcripts, and black narrative tradition is based on Bell (1987), H. Gates (1988), and J. Scott (1990).

12. See IRO (liber 432, folio 288) for an original copy of this document in Jamaica. Although Kitt and Thomas Nicholas Swigle were listed in the deed of trust, they were not elders in the Windward Road Chapel. In his correspondence with Rippon, Swigle stated that he, too, had a covenant for his Saint John's Chapel, and he listed Moses Baker among the elders there. Swigle's chapel was located on James Street in Kingston and was the third such chapel established on the island. See Rippon (1802:vol. III, 212–214) for Swigle's chapel; see Baker (1803:366) for Baker's covenant.

13. It is not my intention to suggest that there were no prior or earlier forms of religion practiced on the island. Quite the contrary. See Pulis (1999a:221, n. 56) for references to "Cudjoe," also known as Joseph Fuller, who in 1745 petitioned the assembly on behalf of the people of Cush, demanding all the rights and privileges accorded to English subjects. Although they were denied, their petition, cast in the name of Cush, and their reference to Egypt, slavery, and bondage expresses a link among an emergent black religion, Jamaican biblical interpretation, and group of free people of color (Assembly of Jamaica:vol. 4, 122–123). See also Brathwaite (1971), Curtin (1955), S. Gordon (1996), Mullin (1992), Stewart (1992), and M. Turner (1982) for histories of missions and missionaries and a general overview of the activities of the Moravian Brethren in Jamaica. See J. Clarke (1869:9–93) and Samuel (1850:23–40) for Native Baptists, native Wesleyans, and a host of African, American, and Jamaican preachers.

14. See IRO (liber 431, folio 37) for the transfer of Cesar from George Kinghorn, a merchant in the slave trade, to George Liele on August 25, 1792. See also JA-CGR 1B/11/6/vol. 22, folio 18, for the manumission of Cesar or James Pascall on June 13, 1794. The process of manumission was a costly affair. Liele paid Kinghorn £150, but this was only the first step. He then had to post a bond or security deposit with the local churchwarden to ensure that Cesar would not become a ward of the parish. This deposit was a fee of anywhere from £100 to £200, and one had to draft a document, pay the necessary filing fees, and have the document and manumission entered into the Island Record Office. The evidence suggests that Liele purchased the freedom of Ann Lindsay as well.

15. Biblical figuralism or typology is a form of interpretation. It differs from other forms and methods, such as allegory, in that each type/antitype dyad complements rather than replaces the other, so one signifies, represents, and fulfills the other. For a more detailed discussion, see Frye (1982). For its application to North America and African American biblical tradition, see Sollors (1986) and Theophus Smith (1994). Compare to Frei (1974) and H. Gates (1988).

16. See Brathwaite (1977) for the "Baptist War," Afro-Christianity, and the role of Native Baptists such as Sam Sharpe and others. On Rastafari, see Chevannes (1994, 1995), Pulis (1999b), and Dijk (1993), among others.

7

"My Mother Dem Nyus to Plan' Reis"

Reflections on Gullah/Geechee Creole
Communication, Connections, and the
Construction of Cultural Identity

Joko Sengova

Gullah/Geechee[1] language and culture in the Georgia-South
Carolina Lowcountry, and the Gullah/Geechee "cunneckshun" linking this African American population—the descendants of enslaved
Africans, held in bondage and forced to work on cotton, rice, and indigo plantations in the Georgia-South Carolina Lowcountry and coastal
islands, whose numbers are now estimated between 200,000 and
500,000 in the Sea Islands of South Carolina, Georgia, North Florida,
and beyond—with its so-called African (and specifically Sierra
Leonean) "roots" became paradigmatic in early African diaspora studies. The unique nature of Gullah/Geechee language and culture—and
cultural practices and artifacts (such as praise houses, "shouting" during religious worship, conjuring, Brer Rabbit stories, and coiled basketry) that have become emblematic of Gullah/Geechee identity,
perhaps stereotypically so—attracted many early anthropologists, sociologists, folklorists, and linguists. Their work includes that of Guion
Griffis Johnson (1930), Guy B. Johnson (1930), and T. J. Woofter Jr.
(1930), as part of a research project of the Institute for Research in
Social Science at the University of North Carolina and funded by the
Social Science Research Council, and Elsie Clews Parsons's *Folk-lore of*

the Sea Islands, South Carolina (1923). Melville J. Herskovits sent at least two of his Africanist students in search of "Africanisms" for summer fieldwork in Georgia and South Carolina.[2] The publication of Lorenzo Dow Turner's *Africanisms in the Gullah Dialect* attracted the most attention (L. D. Turner 1949; cf. Wade-Lewis 1988, 1992, 2001).

Turner successfully drew scholarly attention to the Gullah/Geechee language and its importance (and uniqueness) as a vehicle of communication in predominantly African American communities in the United States. It was Turner who first documented the thousands of words and expressions of African language origin he had found in the Gullah/Geechee language spoken mainly along the southeastern stretch of barrier islands throughout the Carolinas and Georgia. Turner's work helped us understand that people of predominantly African descent in the southeastern United States were speaking a variety of English resembling that of their Caribbean kinsfolk, but at the same time rife with numerous linguistic features of multiple African language backgrounds. Turner was followed by leaders in creole linguistics, some of whom argue that Gullah/Geechee exists as a separate creole language (e.g., Alleyne 1980; Cassidy 1980; Cunningham 1992; Hancock 1971, 1975, 1980, 1988; Jones-Jackson 1987; Mufwene 1986a, 1986b; Mufwene and Gilman 1987; Rickford 1980) and some of whom argue that Gullah/Geechee as a separate language no longer exists or is in the final part of the process of "decreolization"—that is, the process of a creole language becoming less and less different from its lexifier (e.g., Bickerton 1975; Dillard 1972). At another level, the parties to linguistic anthropological debate acknowledge Gullah/Geechee as a unique cultural linguistic system, perhaps an unusual language and mode of communication in the American experience, with visible markings of other distinct languages, including practices and traditions that clearly set it apart from others (see, e.g., Creel 1988; Jones-Jackson 1987; Montgomery 1994; Mufwene and Gilman 1987; Sengova 1994).

As well, the Gullah/Geechee past has been investigated by historians and others who have been interested in their conditions of enslavement and plantation life (e.g., Creel 1988), in the putative African contribution to the production of rice in the Lowcountry (e.g., Carney 2001; Dusinberre 2000; C. Joyner 1984; Littlefield 1981; Opala 1986;

J. Smith 1985; P. Wood 1974; but cf. P. Morgan 2002), and in the creolization process (C. Joyner 1984; P. Morgan 1998) in the context of Lowcountry slavery (e.g., Hudson 1997; C. Joyner 1989; Lockley 2000; P. Morgan 1998). A central question has been to what extent Africans from the "Rice Coast," including what is now Sierra Leone, were sought for their knowledge and skills in rice production and what specific African ethnic traditions were responsible for the generation of planter wealth and power in the colonial and antebellum periods. From a linguistic perspective, Sierra Leone has been often identified as a source, if not the main source, of Gullah/Geechee language. The question has been what precisely Gullah/Geechee language owed and owes to which language in Sierra Leone.

These debates have not been just academic but were part of the intellectual questions of plantation society. There, Gullah/Geechee language, and what it supposedly indicates about Gullah/Geechee cultural origins, was of some concern. Not surprisingly, characterizations tended to be racist and paternalistic. This reference to Gullah speech by Methodist Episcopal clergyman William Pope Harrison, prepared in the 1850s, is a good example: "Thousands of them could only speak English in a broken way; hundreds still jabbered unintelligently in their Gullah and other African dialects." Such characterizations were by no means the first of many that no doubt contributed to the stigmatization of the substantive linguistic structure and content of creole languages and their African relatives (inaccurately labeled "dialects" by Harrison and Turner) *and* the populations who used them as their native vehicles of communication. Even more pejoratively, Stoney and Shelby (1930), referring to Ambrose Gonzales's classic book *Black Border* (1922), attempt a rather crude construction of "Gullah's" etymology: "Their speech was a guttural staccato that made a Dutchman name them the 'Qua-Quas,' because they gabbled like geese. A Gola negro on a plantation was a marked man, his quacking tongue would betray him; and his speech was 'gullah' (uncouth) to the other negroes. With dramatic justice, their general jargon became 'Gullah' to the white man." Among other things to mention is Stoney and Shelby's distinction between *Gullah* and *gullah*, with capitalization of the initial consonant in reference to "the white man," whereas in its "uncouth" African morphology the initial consonant is lowercase.

Stoney and Shelby bring us to the controversial issue of the etymology of the name *Gullah*, which today's linguists still debate (see Sengova 1994:178). Questions as to whether *Gullah* derives from *Gola*, the name of an ethnic group in Sierra Leone and Liberia, or from *Ngola*, an Angolan ethnic group, occupy today's scholars and the Gullah/Geechees themselves. The questions also preoccupied observers in the past, as in the Reverend John G. Williams's article in an 1895 edition of the *Charleston Sunday News* (February 10), in which he gave his own explanation of the name's genesis, with obvious geographic inaccuracies. "Note," he wrote, "'Gullah' is very probably a corruption of Angola, shortened to Gola, a country of West Africa, and a part of lower Guinea, from which a great many negroes were brought to this country in the days of the slave trade." Later on, Turner addressed the issue but did not indicate a clear position on the debate. Similarly, what about *Geechee*? Turner points to *gifi* (1949:90), which suggests Sierra Leone-Liberia, but also *makifi* (1949:127), a reference to a "heathen" tribe in Angolan folklore. The trade relations between Sierra Leone and South Carolina, and an ethnic group called *Kissi*, make this name the likely candidate for *Geechee*. However, some scholars assume that the name derives from the Ogeechee River of Georgia. But even if the Mende language had been predominant in some parts of Sierra Leone in the days of the slave trade, it could be that ethnic groups such as the Gola, Kissi, Krim, Vai, and Shabro spoke Mende (as well as other languages), and this, in turn, could reflect Mende dominance over southern and eastern Sierra Leone. This theory could lend further credence to arguments for a Sierra Leonean source for both *Gullah* and *Geechee* (cf. Matory's chapter in this volume).

In Sierra Leone, too, there is an awareness of historical transatlantic connections, because peoples of African descent from the diaspora have played a key role in the development of Sierra Leonean society. In addition to indigenous groups, Sierra Leone was peopled by hundreds of poor blacks from London as part of the Sierra Leone Settlement Scheme; more than one thousand blacks loyal to the British in the American Revolution; more than five hundred Maroons from Jamaica, via Nova Scotia, at the end of the eighteenth century; and more than fifty thousand "recaptives"—enslaved Africans from a number of cultures and regions liberated from slave ships by Britain's Royal Navy between 1808 and around 1860 and taken to Freetown, the capital of the British crown colony. Krio society, culture, and language developed through the interaction of these and indigenous groups— many of whom moved to Sierra Leone as the result of conflicts elsewhere, so the term *indigenous* is relative. The resulting Westernized Krio ethnic group has dominated Sierra Leonean economic and civic affairs. The Krio language has become a lingua franca in the ethnically and linguistically diverse country, which today has approximately seventeen distinct languages spoken by at least thirteen different ethnic groups (see Sengova 1987). Aspects of this history and these "cunneckshuns" are represented in fiction, such as Yéma Lucilda Hunter's creative *Road to Freedom* (1982), a fine blend of history and fiction surrounding the early settlement of Krio society. Some of the novel's scenes are set in Birchtown, Nova Scotia, which in 1783 was settled by free blacks, many of whom eventually left for Sierra Leone (see Niven and Davis 1999). Also, there is Syl Cheney-Coker's *The Last Harmattan of Alusine Dunbar* (1990), which, like Hunter's *Road to Freedom*, depicts conversational dialogue via the linguistic medium of pidginized and creolized language varieties, African languages, and European languages, and this language serves to symbolize transnational, interethnic interactions and linkages (see Hunt, Sengova, and Sengova 1995).

It is obviously the case that colonial and postcolonial political contexts, and diaspora awareness, along with the various modes of theorizing across disciplines, have all intertwined in the past. And this is certainly the case in the present. These changed and changing forces inform(ed) the intellectual propositions in establishing a theory and practice of what has been called the "Sierra Leone–Gullah/Geechee connection." I therefore think it is important to give a contextual account of the connection, as a researcher-participant who was, himself, involved in its earlier implementation stages, at least in their academic manifestation. The questions for me are, To what degree can a fair equilibrium be struck between my mixed bag of loyalties, first to the Sierra Leone–Gullah/Geechee connection and second to other, much larger transatlantic "cunneckshuns"? In general, is there any such thing as a critical and objective analysis or interpretation of data if the researcher-analyst is both part of that data and subject/object of that study? To what degree does academic research affect identity politics in the African diaspora, and to what extent is it affected by these politics? These are the starting points for what I want to pursue in this chapter, employing a partial autobiographical perspective to explore the making of transatlantic partnerships such as the Sierra Leone–Gullah/Geechee connection and the role of academic discourse in ethnogenesis and nationalist movements.

THE SIERRA LEONE-GULLAH/GEECHEE CONNECTION

As a key participant in the launching mechanisms and implementation of "the connection," I think it is important to review some of its initial outcomes as they may have impacted ordinary folks on both sides of the Atlantic. It is also necessary to assess critically some of the continuing research focused on further illuminating and strengthening the complex historical issues and cultural linguistic strands underpinning the "Sierra Leone–Gullah connection," as this expression became known to many in African diaspora studies. In doing so, I am taking a much closer look at the transatlantic bridge that I believe I partly helped construct.

The connection grew in the early 1980s out of shared intellectual and research interests among a dozen or so African and American scholars from various disciplines at Fourah Bay College (FBC), University of Sierra Leone, Freetown. In 1985 the FBC group launched a project under the rubric "Sierra Leone–Gullah Research Committee," with the primary purpose of studying Gullah/Geechee language, history, and culture. The project agenda focused on parts of the southeastern United States, where the committee became specifically interested in following rich archival and field data on Gullah/Geechee language and history that were unavailable in Sierra Leone at the time. Two faculty members on the committee submitted a research grant proposal for a Senior Fulbright African Scholars' Award to collect archival and field data in the United States in 1987 and 1988. Akintola Wyse (who recently passed away) and I were among the scholars awarded the Fulbright fellowships. Beginning in the fall of 1987, we worked with colleagues at the University of South Carolina and the University of Georgia, as well as other scholars, including Salikoko Mufwene. At the same time, our colleague Joseph Opala, a white American anthropologist and former Peace Corps volunteer in Sierra Leone who was also then teaching at FBC, was doing work on the history of the slave trade from Sierra Leone to the Carolinas. In studying Bunce Island, the British slave castle, and commercial relations among slaving interests, London merchants, and Carolina planters, he discovered that many African captives were sent directly to the Lowcountry, where their rice-growing skills were in demand.[3]

In the United States, we painstakingly tapped institutional resources in search of information on Gullah/Geechee history, language, and culture—especially anything to do with Sierra Leone. We made use of numerous opportunities to record and reproduce any information we felt was vital to establishing "the connection," especially Turner's field notes, which at the time had only recently been donated to Northwestern University's Melville J. Herskovits Africana Library, and his field recordings at Indiana University's Archives of Traditional Music. Wyse and I shipped much of the documentation to Sierra Leone in 1988. Opala, Wyse, and I were also guests at several festivals celebrating Gullah/Geechee heritage in the Lowcountry, notably the 1987 end-of-the-year Saint Helena–Beaufort Sea Island Festival, where we spoke Krio in complement to Gullah/Geechee greetings extended to us by our hosts ("*wi fambul dem*").

We pored over Turner's *Africanisms* as well as his field notes. In *Africanisms*, Gullah/Geechee language is analyzed as displaying thousands of "basilectal" creole features derived from approximately forty distinct African Niger-Congo languages, in addition to "acrolectal" features of its English-language-derived lexicon. Turner (and a number of others after him) looked at Gullah/Geechee language as an important vehicle and a cultural link to several linguistic groups found in West Africa, including those in Sierra Leone and its two closest neighbors, Guinea and Liberia. One such African language is my native or birth language, Mende, which I had also studied for my Ph.D. dissertation at the University of Wisconsin (Sengova 1981). Mende became a lively ingredient in plotting and promoting the connection, essentially because of its own cultural linguistic centrality in Turner's Gullah/Geechee data collected in the 1930s. Mende, in fact, has featured prominently in the presentation of more recent evidence purporting to the "continuity" and "survival" of aspects of Mende language and culture in the Lowcountry.

One of the most interesting topics of diaspora discourse to me has been establishing, through elements of language and material culture, links between the African American diaspora and an African genesis (Sengova 1993, 1994). I was the first native speaker of Mende to attempt research on Mende's role in Gullah/Geechee language (Sengova 1994). In this research, I picked up on Hair's (1965) observations that two Sierra Leonean languages, Mende and Vai, together account for 25 percent of the African personal names and 20 percent of the nearly four thousand lexical items in Turner's data. Put another way, Mende and Vai origins account for around six hundred personal names, sixty words used in everyday conversation, and ninety expressions in folklore and prayers—a total of about seven hundred and fifty words (see also Hancock 1969).[4] In fact, most such passages that Turner collected are in Mende, a language spoken almost solely in Sierra Leone and Liberia. On the other hand, Vai and the Futa-Jallon dialect of Fulbe, evident in the Gullah/Geechee counting system (one to nineteen), are mainly spoken in Sierra Leone's neighboring states, Liberia and Guinea. Following Turner's work, Hair did a good job of drawing scholarly attention to African substrate influences in Gullah/Geechee, though the question over whether such influences constitute African "survivals," elements of "continuity," "retentions," and so forth, continues to be hotly debated (see, e.g., Montgomery 1994; Mufwene 1993).

My procedure was to analyze some of Turner's data, especially songs and stories. Apart from Turner's category of "personal names," no other genre Turner collected displayed so extensively evidenced Mende influence. I endeavored to show how Mende represented what I call "transparent" African language substrate items (items reflecting direct retention in both form and content and requiring no reconstruction) and "opaque" items (Mende elements that were leveled to suit Gullah/Geechee language patterns, contrast sharply with modern Mende, and must be retrieved and reconstructed). While much of Turner's data reflect transparent substrate items, despite his painstaking and extensive research he could not identify what constituted opaque items, probably because of his nonnative linguistic competency in African languages. One song collected by Turner (1949:256) that I analyzed (Sengova 1994:182–187) was a repetitive funeral chant sung by Amelia Dawley, from an isolated fishing village called Harris Neck, Georgia. It was rendered entirely in Mende—although a Mende that was indicative not of an active and competent speaker of the language, but of rote memorization and formulaic expression. But when the language is reconstructed, the song is acceptable to modern-day Mende speakers, as are the other songs and stories I reviewed and reconstructed.

News of our Sierra Leone–Gullah/Geechee research created excitement in official circles back in Sierra Leone. In 1988 Joseph Saidu Momoh, then president of Sierra Leone, visited Gullah/Geechee country. A scene from Tim Carrier's award-winning 1990 documentary film, *Family across the Sea*, shows Momoh in creole interaction with South Carolina Gullah/Geechee native Emory Campbell, director of the Saint Helena Island–based Penn Center, whose mission is to preserve Sea Islands history, culture, and environment. In front of a large audience of transatlantic kinsfolk assembled at the center, Campbell delivered a moving welcoming address in Gullah/Geechee to his Sierra Leone kinsmen and kinswomen. Momoh responded in heavily accented, "decreolized" Krio, stating that Gullah was simply the South Carolinian version of Krio! Campbell said, "How oona do today? We glad oona be with we today for greet we famly from Afrika. We want tell them all 'bout we islan'....We want make them feel like them de home." Then it was Momoh's turn to point to the similarities between Gullah/Geeche and Krio, making no claims (as far as I remember) of one having birthed the other but rather indicating his own naive sense of their cognateness: "*Mi brother ɛn sista dɛm, mi ɛn ɔl mi pipul wey kam tu una hapi tu mɔch fɔ de ya.*" Momoh then invited the audience to a "homecoming" in Sierra Leone the next year.

The Gullah/Geechees arrived in Sierra Leone in November 1989. Amelia Dawley's song became the focus of attention. Turner had recorded her song in July 1931, and for a decade afterward, he played the recording for African students studying in the United States, asking them to help him determine the song's language. The song Dawley sung was apparently handed down through generations in her family, and she was unaware that the song contained a foreign language. One African student, Solomon Caulker from Sierra Leone, recognized that the recorded song was in his own Mende language. He had never heard the song before but felt it had been used to assemble villagers for a funeral.

Weeks before the "homecomers" were to arrive in Sierra Leone, Opala was busy making preparations, including lining up musical performances that would highlight the Sierra Leone–Gullah/Geechee connections. He remembered the Dawley song and thought it might be part of fourteen hours of Turner's tapes housed at Indiana University's archives. He had copies shipped to Sierra Leone by Wyse and Sengova. Time for the visit was drawing near, so Opala asked Cynthia Schmidt, an American ethnomusicologist working that year at FBC, to review the tapes. She did, and a week before the Gullah/Geechees arrived, she came across the Dawley song. Opala and Schmidt then took the song to the Freetown Players, the group performing at homecoming. When they performed the song, it was a cause célèbre in Sierra Leone. The Homecomers attended a daylong traditional Mende festival hosted by paramount chief Eddie Gbappi III of the Taiama village. Most of Chief Gbappi's festivity ceremonies and rituals were primarily conducted in Mende, simultaneously interpreted or translated into Krio and English. Thus, Mende plays a central role in this situational communicative interaction, complemented by two other languages suiting the linguistic competencies of everyone, especially the *hotangaa* (guests) gathered at the staged "national" event in Gbappi's village. Feasting the Gullah/Geechee homecomers with a taste of Mende rice culture, with its assorted vegetable cuisines, including *hakpei* (or *plasas* in Krio, from the English "palava sauce"), was of pivotal significance to the connection saga. Rice forms an important part of the equation, given the "rice and slaves" theory of the Sierra Leone–Gullah/Geechee connection. It was this single element of the home visitation, apart from the homecomers' experiences on Bunce Island, that sparked the strongest feelings about events of the Atlantic slave trade for both the visitors and the hosts (cf. R. Shaw 2002). The visiting party (and, I believe, the hosts again as well) also found significant healing in the traditional crowning of delegation leader Emory Campbell as an honorary paramount chief, adorned with full ceremonial regalia and staff of office of the kingdom.

The Dawley song evoked perhaps equally strong feelings. One homecomer, Lauretta Sams of coastal Georgia, promised to try to locate Dawley's descendants upon her return. Meanwhile, when the homecomers left Sierra Leone, Opala and Schmidt set out to see whether the song was still sung anywhere in the country. Sierra Leonean linguist Tazieff Koroma recognized one word as unique to Waanjama Mende, a Mende dialect spoken only in the southern part of the country, which is also my paternal home. This part of the connection story is the subject of the 1998 film *The Language You Cry In* by Álvaro Toepke and Angel Serrano, which highlights the detective work performed by Opala, Koroma, Schmidt, and Edward Benya. The researchers went from village to village, playing the recording of Dawley's song. On their last day in the area, they played the song in the now devastated Waanjama Mende village of Senehum Ngola, about one hundred miles south of Freetown. A group of women recognized the song and started singing along. They pointed to one woman, Baindu Jabati, who as a young girl had learned the song from her grandmother, who would often sing it as she worked in the rice fields. It is a funeral song, performed during a graveside ceremony called *tei-jami* ("crossing the river"), but it is also a women's song, in that women in Mende culture perform death rituals. The grandmother had urged Jabati to pass the song on to younger women and apparently once told her to expect a return of *nyá bòndá á* (family or kinsfolk) and that she would know them by this song. Jabati changed the words a bit to make it less sentimental and worked to teach it to other women in the village and have them incorporate it into their celebrations. Village elders said that the song had been used to call the village together for funerals but that Mende troops who had been drafted by the British in World War I and exposed to Christianity and Islam had, upon their return to the village, discouraged the song and demanded that the old "pagan" ways be stopped.

In 1990 Opala and Schmidt went to visit Sams in Georgia. She reported that she had indeed located a descendant of Dawley, her daughter, Mary Moran, age sixty-nine, who lived in a rural area near the former site of Harris Neck (the US Army bulldozed the town in 1942 to create an airstrip). Not only did Moran remember the song and sing it in a way almost identical to her mother's version, but she also reported remembering Turner's coming to record the song back in July 1931. She remembered that he had given her mother twenty dollars, a not-too-paltry sum back then and a tremendous boon for a Depression-strapped rural black family. But like her mother, Moran did

FIGURE 7.1

Baindu Jabati and Mary Moran. Photo courtesy of California Newsreel <www.newsreel.org>.

not know the that song was in the Mende language—she thought it was a play song, a nursery rhyme, to which she had danced as a child. Emotions poured out as she heard her own mother's voice in Turner's recordings—Dawley died in 1955—and when she learned that there were women in Sierra Leone who could still sing the song, she broke down and cried.

Opala returned to Senehum Ngola in 1991 to tell Jabati and the other villagers about Moran, and they wondered when she would visit. This historic meeting was delayed by a brutal civil war that left thousands dead and a million homeless, including Jabati herself. Finally, in 1997, Moran and fourteen members of her family accompanied her to Sierra Leone (figure 7.1). After an emotional visit to Bunce Island, they were embraced with ceremony in Senehum Ngola. Nabi Jah, the village's blind, ninety-year-old chief, organized a teijami ceremony for the occasion, thus renewing a tradition fallen into disuse. Opala asked the chief why an enslaved woman would choose this song, and not another one, to pass down to her descendants. The chief regarded the question as foolish. He said, "There was nothing else she could take." He asked rhetorically, "Did they allow her to take any of her possessions, even her clothes?" But the song "would be the most valuable thing she could take, because just by singing it, it would connect her to all her ancestors, all the way back, and to their continued blessings." And he added a Mende proverb: "You know who a person really is by the language they cry in."

In light of the continuing saga of the connection, this exceptional find provides a vital "missing link" connecting the Mende-Gullah/Geechee historical, cultural, and linguistic past and present. It was quite exciting for the researchers, because it at least connected loose strings no one had hitherto been able to find. Though several failed attempts had occurred in the same geographic areas of Mendeland, it is extremely important that the find was made in the village of Senehum Ngola. Whether by a stroke of fortune or other fate, it is significant that this town's name is suffixed by *Ngola*, the Mende word for "forest" and one of the putative sources for the word *Gullah*.

Presented as empirical evidence of a connection, then, Amelia Dawley's song symbolizes an authentic Africanism and linkage between the Lowcountry and Sierra Leone. It seems to be the kind of evidence researchers needed to help strengthen their argument in support of an African language and cultural retention in a New World creole language, Gullah/Geechee. The sharp distinction in overall linguistic structure between Dawley's (and Moran's) recollected formulaic version and that sung by Baindu Jabati should not be missed, however. While the find could be a significant boost for a straightforward retentions theory, for instance, in terms of variable surface renditions in the transcripts, a side-by-side comparative analysis of morphological and syntactic forms of both the Dawley/Moran and Jabati versions would help to explain formally diachronic change—that is, what exactly got transformed, including linguistic features of such change (or reconstruction) from the Old to the New World. In other words, the issue is one of emphasis, on origins or by contrast on development and change—the process of creolization.

My overall position is that Gullah/Geechee is an Atlantic creole with African-language substrata and, of course, at the same time a variety of American English. Mende items do exist in Turner's data, but they might be considered "lost" forms, words, and expressions uttered as formulaic patterns but not necessarily matching today's spoken Mende (how Mende has changed in the past three hundred years is a question I cannot take up here). But these Mende items are amenable to reconstruction, and in this process of reconstruction, particular features of Mende grammar such as contraction, consonant mutation, and determination are revealed. And of course, what is crucial is not only how language is used but also the meanings given to language use for everyday Gullah/Geechee speakers, no less than for culture brokers, players in cultural politics, and academic researchers (sometimes a single person can be all these things).

A more global analysis of African American speech should take into account the multiple African linguistic inputs, as in a "substratum theory" compatible with continental scenarios of multilingualism. Similarly, so-called superstrate input from certain European languages would be complementary to such analysis, as studies of Gullah/Geechee and numerous other creole languages have shown. I also think that in proposing the theory of "Africanisms" in an American speech variety, Turner (1941, 1949) empirically underscored this global analytical perspective by showing that a large group of Niger-Congo languages had provided lexical and morphological input into Gullah/Geechee, historically and realistically reflecting the diverse origins and backgrounds of African captives shipped into the Carolina-Georgia Lowcountry.

Gullah/Geechee language may have emerged through a pidgin-to-creole process—that is, from a blend of African "substrata" such as Mende and other Niger-Congo languages during its early continental African history, and Euro-American "superstrata" such as varieties of English and perhaps, just perhaps, some Native American tongues spoken by those with whom its speakers interacted in the diaspora. Based upon this hypothesis, the position of the Krio language and culture of Sierra Leone is not necessarily that of a missing link but of a cognate, creole linguistic system (see Wyse 1989).

To this extent, it might be helpful to think in terms of parallel development of Gullah/Geechee and other languages, such as Krio spoken in the putative source(s) for Gullah/Geechee. As a fluent Krio speaker, I find it quite an extraordinary and beneficial cultural linguistic experience to listen to speakers of other Anglophone creole languages in the diaspora, such as Gullah/Geechee, Jamaican Creole English, and Trinidad and Tobago Creole English. The senses are sharply drawn toward levels of similarity not only with Sierra Leonean Krio but also with varieties of Liberian Creole English, Cameroon Pidgin English, Gambian Krio, and Nigerian and Ghanaian Pidgin English, with whose speakers I have been privileged to interact, mostly in West Africa. But there are also important differences between Gullah/Geechee and Krio. For example, in terms of intonation and pronunciation, Gullah/Geechee has much more in common with varieties of Liberian Creole English and the Caribbean creoles than with Krio. Varieties of Liberian Creole English evoke this feeling of communicative intelligibility and prosodic familiarity strongly in me, obviously because of the proximity of those speech communities to the area where I was born. In addition, overall it might be argued that Gullah/Geechee and Krio are decreolizing but that Gullah/Geechee is moving toward the (standard English) lexifier whereas Krio is decreolizing away from it (Sengova 1994). The emphasis here is on change, now seeing Gullah/Geechee as a contemporary decreolized form, reflecting significant change not only from Turner's more creolized samples of the 1930s but from data collected during the 1970s, 1980s, and early 1990s as well.

With these sensibilities fired in me, I decided to go headlong into Gullah/Geechee country and check out the degree to which my Krio speech would be understood and spoken by older speakers in the Lowcountry—that is, *if mi fambul dɛm de yɛri Kriyo, ɛn if dɛm de tók Kriyo.* In my research in 1992, I decided to simply infuse into the conversational interaction and dialogue the simultaneous use of the three linguistic systems that were of interest to the project: Gullah/Geechee, Krio, and English. The overriding principle of this method involves the creole element found in both Gullah/Geechee and Krio, which theoretically allows for mutual intelligibility and some degree of shared communicative competence among interlocutors. Presumably, the "shared" intelligibility and competence further imply a high probability of alternating linguistic interaction or "code switching" between the two creole systems. This theory suggests that while English is the principal lexifier source of these two Anglophone creoles, it may actually function as a "neutral" linguistic vehicle that mediates communicative interaction or dialogue based on the needs of the interlocutors. It is similar to Krio's neutrality, a lingua franca that mediates effective communication among speakers of more than a dozen Sierra Leonean languages.

Designed as a research technique to get at the hearts of my Gullah/ Geechee informants, the alternate switch from English to Gullah/ Geechee and then to Krio, and vice versa, back and forth again, seemed plausible as a Gullah/Geechee field data collection method. Theoretically, one could also elicit and obtain data with a great degree of clarity from a Krio speaker, using forms of Gullah/Geechee that appear to be emergent varieties. This strategy is probably similar to what nonnative Krio-speaking researchers would do in Sierra Leone, without the help of an interpreter and with an urge to "try their tongue" at Krio.

As I listened to my Gullah/Geechee *fambul dem* juggle around with details of their experiences, sometimes digressing here and there with no constraints of time linearity, the participants spoke excitedly about their recollections of both Old and New Worlds. In many cases, they had learned of the old ways from older family members, other relatives, and friends, but in quite a significant number of cases, many female participants had, themselves, experienced the specific events they narrated with such command. I suppose that the impact of a specific event on anyone's life can be impetus enough for such detail of narration and style of presentation. Like their older continental African peers, my informants soon turned every conversation into a storytelling event. The narratives I found most interesting were those describing rice production—*how dem nyus to grow reis*—showing how indigenous technology was ingenuously implemented in a New World setting, based essentially upon its everyday fundamental practice as experienced in an Old World setting in West Africa.

The Gullah/Geechee text in table 7.1 is actually part of a larger transcript dealing with rice production that was collected in the Lowcountry in 1992. I provide its transliterated Krio rendition to show the languages' similarities and differences through an interpretive cultural linguistic analysis. I do not provide an English translation but instead invite the reader to come up with his or her own reading(s) of the text. Each text is divided into three paragraphs in order to highlight the three main "communicative acts" involved in the rice production event, as well as the detailed manner in which the narrator portrays her experiences (Saville-Troike 2003). The first act covers a sort of historiography of rice cultivation, including initial stages of land preparation and sowing of the seed grains. The second and third acts focus on rice care strategies, harvest time, and variable utilization of the crop as staple and subsistence. In the first paragraph, we get historical information affirming that families grew rice in the Carolinas for subsistence, in addition to information about its commercialization in the hands of wealthy plantation owners. Our *fambul* oral historian also describes the rice cultivation as specifically swamp- or marshland based, again common in the Lowcountry ecosystem of the time. One of the highlights of this labor-intensive technology, under the physical control of Africans in the rice paddies of the Lowcountry and similar to that practiced in many parts of West Africa, was the construction of extensive dike systems. These dikes were used to dam and harness the tidewaters of the creeks to manage the flooding of the rice fields or to keep the deluge under control when necessary.

A very vivid picture of flocks of birds invading the newly planted rice paddies and the excitement of scaring them away, usually a chore assigned to young children or young adults, also forms part of this narrative experience. I felt especially nostalgic listening to the narrator enact the shrill sound of *minin'* the birds and was reminded of similar childhood experiences I had had driving away birds from our rice farms in southern Sierra Leone: *"My mother used to plan' tha' rice, we used to plan' an' used to min' the bird. We used to run and mama say, 'go yu'all, go, run go, the bird in the rice field.'"* The bird-hunting trips by "white" people are also an interesting part of the narration, because they remind me of similar trips where I grew up, usually by bird-hunting Lebanese. Lebanese poachers hunted the birds for fun but also as a food-gathering practice. Only unintentionally were these hunters rendering assistance to farmers whose crop was being ravaged by the hungry pests. The next stage of production is harvest time, when the rice grains ripen and are ready to be painstakingly harvested, one by one. Here, the elder narrator makes reference to "new rice" of the first harvest, believed in Sierra Leone to be the most delicious, as well as a delicacy of the rice species. Finally, we learn about the preparation of the harvested rice, first by means of the traditional milling process, involving pounding the rice with a pestle in a dugout mortar skillfully carved from a tree. A labor-intensive method of milling, this was the only option available to small farmers before the days of more mechanized farming practices, and it is still used in many parts of Africa where rice is the staple.

What we see here is the skillful art of oral performance or story telling, used to tell a simple story of rice cultivation for home consumption. But in the rich oral narrative content and texture, we also find interesting cultural information, as well as the human experience of the total event. As labor-intensive as this process was, it seemed that people found ways of bringing excitement to rice agriculture—for example, the art of throwing the pestle around in the air from end to end to sort of thwart what would ordinarily become a boring event, not to mention the blistering hands the rice beater had to contend with afterward. The same form of this art can be observed in traditional rice-milling events in Sierra Leone, mostly among women. Beating rice in Sierra Leone usually involves similar fun and entertainment, such as singing along with the rhythm of pounding the rice in the mortar with a pestle, as we see in the texts. Women are sometimes teased about their rice beating songs, which some people believe are often interspersed with laments about a secret lover, an impending tryst or rendezvous, and so forth.

Table 7.1

"Mai Mɔde Dɛm Nyus te Plan Reis"

Gullah/Geechee Text

My mother them used to plan' rice. Rice grow by a pond, all the time na water. Anybody way got reis field e by a pond. Sometime no water, sometime water and tha's what I call a pond, them big pond. My mother used to plan' tha' rice, we used to plan' an' used to mine the bird. We used to run and mama say, "go yu'all, go, run go, the bird in the rice field." That time they 'light down on that rice and here's how we go: "huu-huu-huu-huu-huu; hii-hii-hii-hii-hii..." an' we run through that field and yet they just 'light our faith...they light it right up! An' then those white people now, anytime they want to catch bird. They shoot

down any bird they come by them rice field. Then when the rice done ripe up,
e yalla. They all fiba. Then you take that rice and you cut am got a reef…just cut
am an' pull tha' thing an' put am in pile an' cut am like…an' roung am roung
am and tie am. Tha' time now bunch look beasley.…I have love tha' new rice!
Ain't but one thing with the new rice they don't sell like these other rice you see.
When they done pull am off, they take the rice an' you throw am right down in
there. Then you had a pestle. On both end you could change am. O lord, my
brother them could have beat tha' rice! They put tha' rice and then they…
Bumtode- Bumtode- Bumtode- Bumtode-Bum.…Then sometime they take am
out like this and throw up in they han' and throw in the other han'…Bum- Bum-
Bum- Bum- Bum-.…They beat tha' rice entill when they done, they get the
fanner and they take am out, 'bout a little bit. They fanner and ray am like that,
ray am entill tha' hocks hardline top just get off, and throw away for the
hog…entill you get tha' rice clean pretty. And tha' new rice, I like to for eat am!
E so good and have a different smell. I like the smell, the smelling when you
cook am.

Krio Translation
" Mi Mami/Wi pipul Dem bin de Plant Rɛs"
Mi mami dɛm bin de plant rɛs. Rɛs na swamp I kin gro, ɔl tɛm na wata. ɛnibɔdi
we gɛt rɛs fam i lib nia swamp. Sɔntɛm no wata nɔ ba de, Sentɛm wata kin de, so
na dat a de kɔl swamp, dɛm big swamp. Mi mami dɛm bin de plant rɛs, we kin
plant ɛn drɛb dɛm bɔd. Wi kin rɔn so dɛn mama kin se, "wunu ɔl go, go, rɔn go,
dɛm bɔd de na di rɛs fam." Da tɛm de dɛm kin dɔn kamdɔng insai da rɛs dɛn na
so wi kin de hala: "huu-huu-huu-huu-huu; hii-hii-hii-hii-hii…" dɛn wi rɔnata dɛm
na di fam ɛn' pan ɔl dat na so dɛm kin jɔs mek wi at lait…dɛm kin mek wi at
gladi so! ɛn na so dɛm wetman sɛf nau, ɛnitɛm nɔmɔ dɛm kin wan kech bɔd .
Dɛm de shut ɛni bɔd we kam na dɛm rɛs fam Dɛn we di rɛs dɔn I drai, I kin yala
so. Na so ɔl kin fiba. Dɛn yu tek da rɛs yu kɔt am mek bɔnch lɛk rif…jɔs kɔt am
ɛn pul da tin ɛn put am na lɛk pail so ɛn kɔt am lɛk…dɛn yu tɔn-tɔn am raund ɛn
tai am. Da tɛm de nau na so di bɔnch kin big/lagba so.…Ah mi, I bin lɛk da niu
rɛs de! Bɔt na wan tin dat nɔmɔ pan niu rɛs, dɛm nɔ ba sɛl am so lɛk dɛm ɔda
kain rɛs, yu siWɛn dɛm dɔn pul am dɔn, dɛm tek di rɛs ɛn trowe am rait dɔng
insai de. Dɛn yu bin gɛt di mata-pisul/pɛnsul. Pan ɔl tu sai yu kin cheng am. O
lɔrd, mi brɔtha dɛm, nɔtɔ kɔmɔn bit dɛm kin bit da rɛs! Dɛm kin put da rɛs dɛn
dɛm de…Bumtode- Bumtode- Bumtode- Bumtode-Bum.…Dɛn sɔntɛm de dɛm
kin pul am kɔmɔt lɛk dis dɛm de trowe am ɔp so na dɛm ɔda an dɛn trowe am

bak na di ɔda an…Bum- Bum- Bum- Bum- Bum-….Dɛm kin bit da rɛs de sotee dɛm dɔn. Wɛn dɛm dɔn, dɛm gɛt di fanna ɛn pul am kɔmɔt, smɔl-smɔl/bit-bai-bit. Dɛn dɛm kin fanna am ɛn blo-blo am am lɛk dat, sotee ɔl da ɔks ɛn bɔku ebi dɔti ɔntɔp dɔn kɔmɔt, dɛn dɛm trowe am gi dɛm hɔg…sotee yu ebul mek da rɛs klin gud-gud fashin. Ɛn da niu rɛs de, a lɛk fɔ it am baad!…I swit bad ɛn i gɛt difrɛn smɛl so. A lɛk au I kin smɛl, nɔ lɛk wɛn yu de kuk am.

Linguistic Symbols
Vowels:

/ə/	Mɔdə—"Mother"
/ɛ/	Mɛnde; Rɛs—"Rice"
/ɔ/	Wɔ'ɔ—"Cry"; kɔl—"Call"

Consonants:

/ɓ/	Fulɓe—indigenous name for

Fula/Fulani/Fulfulde
ethnic group

I attempted eliciting information from participants through a sort of decreolized variety of Krio and my approximation of spoken Gullah/Geechee, in addition to standard English. The ensuing inter-language communication was often unstructured, but it yielded rich historical, cultural linguistic information. In addition, it generated a relaxed atmosphere in which *mi fambul dem* and I enjoyed the utmost fun without tension and unease about focal topics of African American history and personal life stories. In table 7.2, I list ten sentences from various Gullah/Geechee conversations I recorded and provide Krio and English equivalents to illustrate them.

TABLE 7.2
Examples of Gullah/Geechee and Krio Speech with English Translation

---

1. Mai ɔda anti we stay ya, mai mɔdə sistə.

   Mi ɔda anti we lib ya, mi mami (im) sista.

   My other aunt who stays here, my mother's sister.

2. Mai mɔda sik sɛvintin deis an sɛvintin naits.

Mi mami sik fɔ sɛvintin deis ɛn sɛvintin naits.
My mother was sick for seventeen days and seventeen nights.

3. ən' bɔt mi wan mai mɔdə hæv.
Na mi wan gren mi mami bɔn/gɛt.
I am my mother's only child.

4. Hi hɔsban bin nem Frɛnchie Bukman.
Im man/ɔsban bin nem Frɛnchie Bukman.
Her husband's name was Frenchy Bookman.

5. Mai anti kɔl mi an tɛl mi se, mai fada dai, dai dɛm bɛri-am.
Mi anti kɔl mi ɛn tɛl mi se, mi papa dai, dai dɛm bɛram.
My auntie called me and told me my father was dead, and they had already buried him.

6. Mi an hi de wɔk on di pɔch, wɔk ɔl nait ɛntil deklin!
Miən im de waka na di pɔch, waka ol nɛt tee doklin!
He/she and I paced back and forth on the porch all night long till daybreak!

7. Hi se hi de kɔm fɔ pik yu up.
I se I de kam fɔ kam pik yu up.
He said he would come and pick you up.

8. Hi se to mi, wan de God de bless yu.
I tɛl mi se, wan de God de/go bless yu.
He/she told me one day I will be blessed.

9. Dat taim sɛf, Ai no notən; mai hart gɛt puld!
Da tɛm de sɛf, A nɔ no natin; mi at kɔt so!
At the time I knew nothing; I felt so uncomfortable!

10. Wɛn mai gran' dai, A krai tu krai!
We mi grani dai, A krai tu tɛm krai!
When I lost my grandmother, I grieved for two reasons (burial expenses and loss)!

No serious gaps of comprehension resulted in most instances of collection. For the most part, my Gullah/Geechee interlocutors and I understood each other with little difficulty. The three-way linguistic code-switching strategy often commenced with an approximation of Gullah/Geechee and then transitioned into English, then into "decreolized" Krio. Our conversations were carried on at a mutually intelligible level, reflecting the participants' communicative will and fervor instead of their education and socioeconomic status. Of equal significance was my nonnative English proficiency, sometimes described as being "correct" English (meaning that I had a distinguishing non-American accent in my pronunciation).

But the origins discourse was compelling. Rather than emphasize the parallel creolization process, at least as far as language goes, what was established was a point of origin in a named place, Sierra Leone, a nation in a world of nations, and in a point of arrival, the Lowcountry. For connection proponents, this origin was preferable to an "Angola"/Bantu or Native American origin for words and practices, and their eyes were focused on Sierra Leone specifically and on the Mano River Union tri-states of Sierra Leone, Liberia, and Guinea generally. Some have even started referring to the "Mende people of South Carolina."[5] The "rice and slaves" background fit nicely into emerging Gullah/Geechee "contributionist" discourses that emphasized the story of Carolina planters seeking enslaved persons from the Rice Coast whose knowledge and technology constituted the main contribution to the planters' wealth and to the development of the society. At the same time the connection became established, Steven Spielberg released his 1997 film *Amistad*, which tells the story of Joseph Cinque, or Singbe Pieh, a Mende from Sierra Leone and leader of a group of captive Africans who seized the Spanish schooner *Amistad* off the Cuban coast in 1839. The group made their way to the United States, where they were eventually freed by a US Supreme Court decision. The tale ends with the group's being returned to Sierra Leone three years after the start of their voyage (for Sierra Leone–US connections here, see Osagie 2000).

It became impossible—if it ever is really possible—to delineate in clear-cut terms an intellectual research agenda as distinct from significant political goals envisaged (or perhaps largely gained) as part of the collaboration. For both transatlantic partners, it was deemed extremely important to build and maintain "better relations" between Sierra Leone and the United States, perhaps with some clairvoyance on the part of the principals about today's reality—that is, the mess of Sierra Leone's recent history of carnage. During the past decade of civil war in Sierra Leone, various Sierra Leone–Gullah/Geechee organizations and alliances have emerged, especially in the United States, and Gullah/Geechee–Sierra Leone connections have been taken up by already established organizations: the National Organization of Sierra Leoneans in North America, the Coalition of Concerned Africans, the National Summit on Africa, the TransAfrica Forum, Friends and Patriots of Sierra Leone, and others. These coalitions lobbied at the state and national congressional level for assistance in freeing Sierra Leone from the grip of Corporal Foday Sankoh and his Revolutionary United Front. For example, on March 20, 1999, the Atlanta-based organization Friends and Patriots of Sierra Leone cosponsored a workshop with the Penn Center to formalize lobbying efforts. The goal of that meeting was to formulate strategies that US organizations and individuals could use to influence public officials to devote more resources and attention to the crisis in Sierra Leone. At the Lomé Peace Accord, signed between the warring factions on July 7, 1999, Sierra Leonean–American organizations, as well as the Reverend Jesse Jackson and former congresswoman Cynthia McKinney, provided both visible and behind-the-scenes advocacy for restoration of a stable democracy in Sierra Leone. More recently, the Saint Helena Island–based Gullah/ Geechee Sea Island Coalition launched its "Save the Sea Islands Tour 2000 Gullah Cunneckshun" fund-raising projects, aimed at assisting Sierra Leone's refugees and its Gullah/Geechee Reclamation Fund.

THE RISE OF THE GULLAH/GEECHEE NATION
Since the 1950s, the Gullah/Geechees have seen their island land acquired by developers, seen gated communities arise and block access to traditional fishing and crabbing grounds, and seen their image commoditized as part of tourist promotion. Perhaps the most famous symbol people have come to associate with the Gullah/Geechee is the Lowcountry coiled fanner basket, sewn with sweetgrass and used in rice

FIGURE 7.2

Geechee man crabbing from a boat, Shrimp Creek, Georgia, 1950. Photograph by Simon Ottenberg. Simon Ottenberg Papers, National Anthropological Archives, Smithsonian Institution.

cultivation since before the 1700s. The baskets are now sold all along Highway 17, the main highway into Charleston, and on the city's streets and are displayed in tourist brochures as a symbol of Charleston and the Lowcountry's "otherness" (Rosengarten 1987, 1997). The Gullah/ Geechees have also seen an exodus of many young people to the "mainland" and urban centers (see Faulkenberry et al. 2000; Jones-Jackson 1987; Slaughter 1985). There are, of course, plenty of "pull" factors inducing out-migration. For example, there were no schools, hospitals, or supermarkets on Sapelo Island when I spent a couple weeks there collecting oral histories in the summer of 1992. Young people, I was told then, simply found the old ways too "boring" and "unprogressive" and tended to move to nearby towns and cities such as Brunswick and Jacksonville, where they would find jobs or get an education. My experience talking with older-generation Gullah/ Geechee (the ones often targeted by scholars and the media) was that they already felt overexploited by outsiders, especially media operatives and tenure-earning researchers gathering information for fruitful scholarship and education or personal gain that hardly benefited *dem fambul*—and then not even sharing their research results with the community. This situation makes for a somewhat ambivalent attitude toward the research in general. It is sometimes seen as a harbinger of trouble on the horizon. "When the anthropologists appear, the developers are never far behind," said Emory Campbell (Rosengarten 1997: 5–6). But the results of academic research are certainly used selectively in promoting claims to cultural and ethnic distinctiveness and authenticity.

The Gullah/Geechee have responded to these processes much like other dispossessed communities worldwide—they have started what might be called an "ethno-nationalist" movement of their own. The Gullah/Geechee movement has achieved much of its current status through the efforts of Marquetta L. Goodwine, a descendant of two Gullah families who grew up on Saint Helena Island and holds degrees in mathematics and computer science from Fordham and Columbia universities. A writer, lecturer, historian, and self-styled "artivist," she began leading small tours in 1986 and now leads De Gullah Root Experience Tours. In 1996 she founded the Gullah/Geechee Sea Island Coalition, which "promotes and participates in the preservation of Gullah and Geechee history, heritage, culture, and language," "works toward Sea Island land re-acquisition and maintenance," and "celebrates Gullah and Geechee cultures through artistic and educational means electronically and via 'grassroots scholarship'" (Gullah/ Geechee Sea Island Coalition 2003). The coalition's website says:

> A direct link to the continent of Africa exists in the Sea Islands of the United States. In the islands that are a part of South Carolina, Georgia, and North Florida, Gullah and Geechee culture began during the enslavement of African people in America. It is directly related to the African traditional cultures of the people of the Windward or Rice Coast of West Africa. Due to isolation on islands off the coast, the

> African people there did not have too much contact with
> people of other races except Native Americans. Thus, they
> were able to maintain their culture, language, and traditions
> unlike African people that were living on the "mainland."
> Gullah and Geechee Sea Islanders transformed these tradi-
> tions into a new and distinct African American culture.

Included is what has become the coalition's motto: "*Mus tek cyear a de root fa heal de tree*" (Gullah/Geechee Sea Island Coalition 2003).

The coalition's genesis might be seen as part of a wider "Gullah revival," as shown through the recent establishment of festivals and other forms of display and organization. The Penn Center's Heritage Days Celebration is held in November. The Gullah Festival is staged each May in Beaufort's Waterfront Park. On Hilton Head Island, the Native Islander Gullah Celebration takes place throughout the month of February. And in February 2003, the Native Island Business and Community Affairs Association hosted its seventh annual Native Islander Gullah Celebration. Yet the coalition's focus is somewhat different. The coalition sponsors a number of activities that unite preservationist, celebratory, and academic concerns. Most recently, for example, in July 2002 the coalition hosted the Ourstory and Heritage Conference under the theme "Gwine Bak: Gullah/Geechee Living Ways." The conference featured interactive sessions titled "How Wi Git Ya: African Diasporic Connections," "They Took the Drums Away: Sound and 'Riddims' of the Sea Islands," "From De Bush Harbor Tuh De Chu'ch: Spirituality and Survival," "Wi Wods: Storytelling, Folklore, and History," "So, You Think You Know? Researching the Gullah/Geechee Story," and "Where De I Go? Tourism, the Government, and Gullah/Geechees."

As with any identitarian movement, the coalition needed significant rituals to consolidate legitimacy and leadership. In July 2000, there was one in the "enstoolment" of Goodwine as Queen Quet, Chieftess of the Gullah/Geechee Nation (figure 7.3). First was the invocation of the organization's history:

> As the sun rose on July 2, 2000, the sounds of the drums that
> had been silent for many generations could be heard again.
> Denmark Vesey's body that had been hung on this very date

Figure 7.3

Queen Quet Marquetta L. Goodwine, Chieftess of the Gullah/Geechee Nation. Courtesy of Queen Quet Marquetta L. Goodwine.

in 1822 had his spirit renewed. Gullah and Geechee people began their practices of getting the babies washed and the families fed and the members off to Sunday school and church as they would any other Sunday, but this Sunday (just like the one in 1822) was going to be one that went down in the annals of history. This is the date of delivery of the Gullah/Geechee Nation.

Goodwine recalled the experience:

> Amidst the drumming and praise of Gullah/Geechee peo-
> ple again gathered together on this island (but this time of
> their own free will and in celebration instead of in chains
> and misery), the media floated from point to point snap-
> ping shots and recording. All were awaiting this person that
> people were here to enstool and ordain as "queen."
>
> Finally, the procession came from the water. The brooms
> swept the yard clean as the incense, drums, libation, and
> Gullah/Geechee flag came forth. The elders proceeded in
> to the beat of the drum carrying the items from the center
> of the circle. Amidst the crowd was St. Helena's own,
> Marquetta L. Goodwine flanked by her family adorned in
> purple, white, and black all trimmed in gold.
>
> As I emerged from the sands with the Atlantic Ocean at
> her back, I came forth in chains just as my ancestors had
> done when they arrived in the New World and these Sea
> Islands. I took the long journey from the shoreline to the
> middle of the circle where everyone was still shoutin'. As I
> kneeled down on top of a perfectly cast net, some people
> shook from the sign of the chains. (Rise of the Gullah/
> Geechee Nation, http://www.coax.net/people/lwf/gg_rise
> .htm).

She emerged from the ceremony as Queen Quet, Chieftess of the
Gullah/Geechee Nation, and later proclaimed: "*Hunnuh mus tek cyare
de root fuh heal de tree!* The healing has begun and our Nation is ONE!"

Goodwine/Queen Quet has lectured about the coalition and the
Gullah/Geechee people and has produced a number of writings,
including the first three volumes of a proposed thirty-book series titled
Gullah/Geechee: The Survival of Africa's Seed in the Winds of the Diaspora
(Goodwine 1997a, 1997b, 1997c), envisaged as "an encyclopedia of Sea
Island history and heritage." Goodwine has also coedited *The Legacy of
Ibo Landing: Gullah Roots of African American Culture* (Goodwine and the
Clarity Press Gullah Project 1998). A main theme of this work is to look
backward into the past in order to move forward:

In the process of evolution we must take the old and build on it to fit the new circumstances and environment. Any old structure needs to be examined and analyzed before it is added to. There may be reinforcements that are necessary before any additions can be made. If the structure is too faulty, then it may have to have parts removed or be completely torn down and rebuilt.

Many have realized or are realizing that there are cultures that are hundreds of years old which can provide guidelines to teaching a number of things including self-sufficiency and respect. Community respect is often the driving force behind those that realize the value of their native languages and traditional practices and they are proud to present them in any setting. These individuals have learned the value of language not as a commodity, but as a mode of survival—survival of culture, traditions, heritage, ancestral ties, education, and community. Thus, they are willing to work to preserve and build up the community.

As mi people dem sey, "empty sak cyan stan upright 'lone." (Goodwine 1998a:13)

Another theme is to affirm the distinctiveness of Gullah/Geechee culture as the most African of African American cultures:

Is it too much to say that what we allow to become of the Gullah in America will speak to what we will have allowed to become of ourselves? For after all, of all African people in America, it is the Gullah who have clung most dearly to what we once were, who have suffered and endured ignominy, deprivation and even death to preserve it. The Gullah have much to teach us still. If we allow what they have preserved to perish from this earth, the loss will also be our own.

Cum toggedda wid we people
fa hold on ta de tings wa wi peopol lef wi
Mus' tek cyear a de root fa' heal de tree.
(Goodwine 1998a:13)

She also warns against "development" that would threaten traditional lifeways (Goodwine 1998b; cf. Faulkenberry et al. 2000; Jones-Jackson 1987; Slaughter 1985) and seeks to establish rules of engagement for researchers on Gullah/Geechee language and culture, as there were complaints that natives had spent much of their time with outside researchers and had received nothing in return, not even a copy of a publication or thesis deposited in local repositories (Goodwine 1998c). These rules include the following admonitions: "Do not attempt to speak Gullah to native speakers as a means of trying to be accepted" and "Do not push people to begin to speak Gullah to you or in your presence" (1998c:203).

Goodwine/Queen Quet has more and more called for Gullah/Geechee political autonomy, although what exactly this means has not been made explicit. An organization called the International Human Rights Association for American Minorities, with consultative status with the United Nations, asked Goodwine to make a presentation to the UN's Conference on the Right to Self-Determination in Geneva, which she did via video in April 1999 (see Kly and Kly 2001). In January 2003, Goodwine/Queen Quet made a visit to the US State Department in Washington, DC, to brief the foreign press on efforts for Gullah/Geechee autonomy (figure 7.4).

At the same time, the coalition backed US representative James E. Clyburn, a Democratic congressman representing South Carolina's District 6, in trying to add Gullah/Geechee culture to the National Park Service (NPS) program. A fiscal year 2000 bill authorized the park system's Low Country Gullah Culture Special Resource Study (SRS), designed to "identify and evaluate the role of the National Park Service (NPS) in preserving and interpreting Gullah/Geechee culture" (National Park Service 2003). The goals of the SRS were announced as analyzing "the multi-faceted components of this living, breathing culture using the established criteria for the study of areas for potential inclusion in the National Park System" and outlining "a set of management options for consideration by Congress." The three-phase NPS study included community input and an inventory of cultural "resources" to determine whether "resources associated with Gullah/Geechee Culture have potential national significance consistent with the criteria for National Historic Landmarks" (National Park Service

FIGURE 7.4

Marquetta L. Goodwine/Queen Quet briefing the press at the Foreign Press Center, US State Department, January 2003. On the right is Paul Denig, director of the Foreign Press Center. Photo courtesy of the US State Department.

2003). The process involved the geographical locating (and bounding) of culture through the use of Global Positioning System technologies, as well as ethnographic and other methodologies. Presumably, these methods would seek to identify the presence of "Africanisms," which is part of official NPS thinking: "The Gullah/ Geechee people possess linguistic traits, artisan skills, and agricultural and cultural practices attributable to African knowledge systems retained by those descendants. This survival is due to the relative isolation of the areas and the concentrated and late influx of Africans from the same cultural zone. Gullah/ Geechee culture is a repository of Africanisms and should be evaluated in light of African culture" (B. Joyner 2003:40).[6] And, finally, in evaluating the feasibility and suitability of NPS involvement in preserving and interpreting Gullah/Geechee culture, the NPS completed a set of "conceptual management alternatives," which were presented to "project stakeholders" in public meetings completed in fall 2002. While such a turn of events would enshrine Gullah/Geechee culture in objective, namable ways—after all, "having" a "culture" is the first step to "having" a "nation" (see R. Handler 1988)—and thus coincide with coalition goals, Goodwine/Queen Quet and the Council of Elders wanted to make sure that Gullah/Geechees had a strong role in any interpretation: "The story is ours and we will no longer allow others to simply buy, sell, and rename us." She urged Gullah/Geechees to write to their members of Congress "to insure that any and all alternatives are done in a way to respect, protect, and properly represent ALL Gullah/Geechee people and not to simply create this as another NPS unit that will be left to the interpretations of whoever is in charge as a superintendent or manager for a time." After all, "the ones that know how to keep that culture alive have proven that we know how. Thus, we should be the ones to teach the National Park Service and all others that want to interpret and present our story. We intend to live into the future" (Urgent from Queen Quet and the Gullah/Geechee Nation, http://www.bjmjr.com/gullah-geechee/letter112202.htm).

Part of this aspect of what might seem like a Gullah/Geechee revival was a spike in the 1990s in literary and cultural production on Gullah/Geechee themes, including academic work from a variety of disciplinary and theoretical perspectives (e.g., Brown and Green 1998; Guthrie 1996; Montgomery 1994; Twining and Baird 1991), including a cultural traits and physical anthropology analysis (Pollitzer 1999). Charles Colcock Jones Jr.'s *Negro Myths from the Georgia Coast Told in the Vernacular* (1888) was republished as *Gullah Folktales from the Georgia Coast* ([1888] 2000). Popularly oriented books on Gullah/Geechee history (Branch 1995), language (Geraty 1997), art (Green 1996, see plate 5), cookery, especially the Africa-rice connection (K. Hess 1992; Polke 1999; Robinson and Smith 2003), "hoodoo" magic (Pinckney 1998), and herbal medicine (Mitchell 1998; Yronwode 2002) were also published. US Supreme Court justice Clarence Thomas, who grew up on the Georgia coast, has said that he would like to write a book about "the culture." The Nickelodeon (Nick Jr.) cable TV channel produced a series called *Gullah Gullah Island*, filmed on and around Saint Helena Island, with Natalie and Ron Daise. And for many Gullah/Geechees, the connection took on added meaning. Cornelia Walker Bailey, a Sapelo Island native who traces her ancestry to Bilali, the most famous and powerful African to inhabit the island, was among the 1989 home-comers. In her memoir she writes of how she saw similarities to Sapelo on her visit: "Everywhere. In the faces of people, in the language, the food, the terrain and some of the old traditions." It was in Sierra Leone, she reports, that she learned that *Geechee* probably did not come from the Ogeechee River but from Kissi, a modern tribal designation of the Sierra Leone–Guinea–Liberia area. The trip is figured as a jour-ney of self-discovery:

> I had stepped foot on the soil my ancestors came from. I knew more of my people's history. The words "African American" had more oomph! behind them now because I had the inner power to back them up. I was determined that nothing or no one would ever defeat me again and I would be totally my own person from then on. I knew how to carry myself. I knew how to portray myself. I knew exactly who I was for the first time. (Bailey and Bledsoe 2000)

CREOLE ROOTS

This ideological and identitarian discourse surely puts an empha-sis on "roots" figured as a "source." This emphasis is evident in the coalition's philosophy, which seems to be of caring first for the root of the Gullah/Geechee tree in order to preserve the entire tree. Stated in Gullah proverbial terms, "*Mus tek cyear a de root fa heal de tree*," which I take to mean, "Healing a tree must start from its roots." Taken out of its literal context, the root seems to be a reference to the totality of the African American essence associated both with a continental African genesis and with a New World transformation as a result of the realities of historical displacement. As African proverbs sometimes tend to do, this Gullah/Geechee version creates an interesting problem of ambi-guity posing a challenge to semantic specificity in terms of matching history, provenance (or locus), and identity. If interpreted to mean "Old World Africa-based roots" and "New World diaspora-based trees," the proverb clearly indicates reference to millions of human "trees" once "uprooted" from the Old World African soil, brought to the New

World, transplanted, and left to wither. Now those surviving trees must be cared for, the coalition seems to say, beginning from their very foundation, the roots (which apparently lie in Africa), to ensure the survival of all the trees and their progeny. Of course, such interpretation only points to one thing, predicating an African past as the origin of the African diaspora. As clear as daylight some would say—but not quite, if we think in terms of a more rounded picture.

If, on the other hand, we could interpret the proverb's singular principal metaphors "root" and "tree" ("*Mus tek cyear a de root fa heal de tree*") within a more universal, global context to mean black people in general, everywhere, then perhaps this interpretation would amount to explaining the possible black contexts first—for example, all the trees and roots of the United States, Jamaica, Suriname, individual African states, the continent as a whole, and so forth. Analyzed this way, the proverb may be, as in a "generative grammar," considered a "transformation" of that above, reflecting the Gullah/Geechee propositions such as "*Mus tek cyear a de African root fa heal de Gullah/Geechee tree*," "*Mus tek cyear a de Gullah/Geechee root fa heal de Gullah/Geechee tree*," and so forth. This way, I believe, one at least brings a more holistic picture to understanding centuries of Africa-diaspora dialogue and interaction.

But there is another procedure in place of searching for "roots," at least in terms of the common connotation of that word. And that is searching for creole origins, if that is not a contradiction in terms. This process was at least partially implied when Goodwine/Queen Quet was the guest of honor in February 2003 at the Virgin Islands National Park's twelfth annual Folklife Festival, held under the theme "Gullah Meets Creole: A Cultural Exchange." There, she endeavored to demonstrate some similarities in diaspora cultures as seen in the Sea Islands and the Virgin Islands, drawing parallels in religion, food, language, and other practices.

I have tried to argue that the Gullah/Geechee experience in the New World is perhaps best interpreted not as a continuity of proscribed African roots (such as culture, language, religion, and the arts) but rather in terms of a more holistic context in which an African genesis and diaspora renaissance are richly blended. Obviously, African American life and communicative and social behavior are rich with innovations or transformations upon well-established African ways that may not always be admonished by the individual psyche.

Interpreted this way, New World experiences will begin to match the fundamental dynamism that is reality in social and communicative behavior everywhere on the African continent (S. Moore 1993). In other words, it is implausible to suggest that African cultures simply birthed diaspora cultures by infusing in them cloned legacies of the Old World that they practiced unchanged forever. As some scholars point out, when we look at cultural linguistic entities with such symbolic New World identities as African American Gullah/Geechee, we ought to be looking at history in both its stability and its dynamism across time spans. On the other hand, it is important to remember that what the African diaspora left behind did not simply remain static, as if void of any dynamism whatsoever. If anything, Africa displays a scenario of constant changes, some startling in their complex demographic realities.

Attempts at constructing associations such as the Sierra Leone–Gullah/Geechee "connection" or other "cunneckshuns" are attempts to legitimize identities where they have been ignored and defamed. Effectively negotiated, such constructs ultimately create transatlantic bonds in kinship, ethnicity, culture, language, and even personal relationships that may be hard to extinguish. From the perspective of language and culture, the real connection is a creole connection, the parallel and seemingly paradoxical development of practices and ideologies "here" and "there" that characterizes the African diaspora.

Notes

Let me pay homage here, as is customary of my Mende upbringing, to all who have helped in the writing of this chapter, by direct association or incidental inclusion. Many thanks to my friend and colleague Kevin Yelvington for inviting me to participate in the School of American Research advanced seminar and to all the seminar participants, an intellectually vibrant and exciting group of scholars, some established and some newcomers in the business. Many thanks go to Mario Hernández for rendering administrative support toward my participation in the seminar. And to all the people them nar the "connection" ya and crus di wata, Ar gi oona all lasting peace from di present woes and worries; hope you like fa read this about youself—and that's only "decreolized" Gullah, it yent raw Gullah!

1. I shall henceforth use a slash to link *Gullah* and *Geechee*, as it is now often

done in the Georgia-South Carolina Lowcountry, even though some scholars tend
to explain the names' distinct etymologies in distinct origins. In the past, *Gullah*
has referred to the language, culture, and group identity of African American
residents of the Sea Islands of the Carolinas, and *Geechee* has referred to those in
Georgia and North Florida. Interestingly, *Gullah/Geechee* has been adopted in
recent proto-nationalist discourse and dialogue by, for example, the
Gullah/Geechee Sea Island Coalition referred to in this chapter.

2. For example, William R. Bascom (1941) conducted fieldwork in Georgia
and South Carolina in the summer of 1939, and Simon Ottenberg (1959) worked
in Georgia in the summer of 1950. Ottenberg recalled: "I started graduate work at
Northwestern in September 1949, and wanted to get some field experience before
going to Africa for my Ph.D. research. Bascom [then on the faculty at
Northwestern] suggested working among the Gullah, and Herskovits (my chair)
approved. The latter gave me $50 for the research out of the African Studies
funds, hardly enough to cover it, but helpful. They were interested in my finding
Africanisms. I chose the location, using a WPA [Works Progress Administration]
guide which detailed many of the communities" (personal communication to
Kevin A. Yelvington, 2003). Here, Ottenberg is referring to *Drums and Shadows:
Survival Studies among the Georgia Coastal Negroes* (1940), a project of the
Savannah Unit, Georgia Writers' Project that included Herskovits, Bascom, and
Guy B. Johnson on its board of advisers.

3. I was coprincipal investigator, with the late Akintola J. G. Wyse, of a grant
proposal titled "Rice and Slaves: The Sierra Leone Gullah Connection," which
received a Senior Fulbright African Scholar's Award in 1987–1988, allowing us to
study field and archival historical linguistic evidence on this subject, both in the
United States and in Sierra Leone. A Sierra Leone–Gullah committee comprising
its founder, notable American anthropologist Joseph Opala, and several Sierra
Leonean scholars, including Abdul Karim Turay, Cecil Magbailay Fyle, Akintola J.
G. Wyse, Cyrus Macfoy, and me, was formed in 1985, becoming the core research
project group. Several scholarly publications by members of the group have
emerged since the late 1980s, with some citations in this chapter. But I think that
the 1989 SCETV documentary *Family across the Sea*, produced by Tim Carrier, and
the more recent video production *The Language You Cry In* best exemplify the collaborative and interdisciplinary efforts that have gone into the research project
and dissemination of its findings. Moreover, they are the principal vehicles
through which language, dialogue, film and graphic media, popular arts, and theater are fully exploited to convey the salient messages of the "connection." For

access to both first- and secondhand information on the present state of the connection, I am thankful to all my friends and colleagues at various transatlantic
points of the diaspora who still celebrate "the connection."

4. Cassidy (1980) believes that these statistics, and especially those in
Hancock (1969), are greatly exaggerated because of an error in calculation.

5. See *Lifestyle of the Mende People of South Carolina* (http://www.angelfire
.com/sc/jhstevens/pictures.html). The Penn Center's (1998) website identifies
Gullah/Geechee origins thus:

> Located just under the hump of West Africa on the Atlantic Ocean, the
> sovereign republic of Sierra Leone is one of the smaller African coun-
> tries, only a bit larger than South Carolina, with a population of approx-
> imately four million people. Sierra Leone is in the center of what is
> called the Mano River region, a tri-state area including Liberia to the
> south and Guinea to the north.
>
> It is from this region that thousands of Africans were stripped from
> their homeland and families to be transported across the sea. Their first
> stop was Bunce Island located on the Sierra Leone River near Freetown.
> This was a holding place for Africans being sold as slaves and special-
> ized in sending slaves to the Sea Islands of South Carolina. Slaves from
> this region had direct experience in agriculture, particularly rice farm-
> ing and were often sold at a higher price. They brought not only their
> labor and knowledge of rice but their culture, a culture that still thrives
> today.

The Beaufort, South Carolina, tourism website, however, mixes ethnonyms
and geography in an interesting way: "The word Gullah itself is thought to be a
derivative of Angola and the Gola tribe. Geechee is a West African ethnic group.
Anthropologists generally classify those people living on the South Carolina coast
as Gullah and those living on the Georgia islands and their mainland relatives as
Geechee—however, the Gullah don't use these designations" (Beaufort, South
Carolina 2003).

6. The NPS also repeats the idea that Gullah/Geechee culture is distinctive
because of its "isolation," where *isolation* is taken to mean isolation from Euro-
American culture:

> Gullah/Geechee people are a distinct group of African Americans who
> are descendants of enslaved Africans from the Rice Coast of West
> Africa. Because of their geographic isolation and strong sense of com-
> munity, the Gullah/Geechee were able to develop a distinct creole lan-
> guage and preserve more of their African cultural tradition than any

other black community in the United States. Although many rural Gullah communities still exist, they are increasingly being threatened by encroaching development, lack of jobs, and diminishing population.

The isolation of Atlantic sea island communities stretching from southern North Carolina to northern Florida was crucial to the survival of the Gullah/Geechee culture. Within their rural communities, Gullah/Geechee people were able to maintain language, arts, crafts, religious beliefs, rituals, and foods that are distinctly connected to their West African roots. More recently, real estate development, changing job markets, and population shifts have forced many to leave their traditional family lands. Along with such change and decreasing isolation comes the threat of losing a unique culture that has survived since colonial times. (National Park Service 2003)

8

African Diaspora Archaeology in Dialogue

Theresa A. Singleton

It is the archaeologist's sadness to have to study people through material remains, chipped flint, burnt clay, but it would be the ethnographer's madness to try to comprehend the complexity of culture through one kind of expression.

—*Henry H. Glassie,* Passing the Time in Ballymenome

Ceremonies befitting royalty—the firing of musketry, the singing of dirges amid traditional drumming and dancing—welcomed the remains of two individuals of African descent in the Americas brought to Ghana for reburial. The reburial formed part of a weeklong event held in 1998 commemorating Emancipation Day, the abolition of chattel slavery in the British colonies on August 1, 1834. This unique Ghanaian celebration, however, was the first of its kind on the African continent. Assin Manso, a former slave market, located in the Central Region of Ghana, was selected as the site for reburial. At Assin Manso, slave traders checked enslaved persons for their overall fitness and bathed them in the Slave River (Ndonkor Nano) before purchasing and sending them to coastal slave dungeons, where they awaited shipment on the Middle Passage to the Americas (*Daily Graphic,* July 30, 31; August 1, 1998).

Archaeologists recovered the two individuals: a male, presumed to be Samuel Carson, from the site of the Brooklyn Naval Yard Cemetery, New York; and a female, designated as Crystal, from a house-yard compound of the Seville Plantation on the north coast of Jamaica.[1]

Carson rose to become an officer in the US Navy, and his presumed living descendant, Sunny Carson, was part of a thirty-member delegation that came to Ghana to participate in the reburial activities. Crystal, on the other hand, was given her name because of a crystal stopper found on top of her coffin. She was obviously an enslaved plantation worker, sixteen to nineteen years old, who suffered from severe chronic anemia, a condition that may have contributed to her early death (Armstrong and Fleischman 1993:44). Reinterment of excavated human remains, often with some form of funerary rites, is a standard archaeological practice today. Crystal had been previously reburied in a ceremony held in Jamaica in 1997 for the four individuals recovered from archaeological investigations of Seville Plantation (*Weekly Gleaner*, North American edition, July 31–August 6, 1997). This first-time repatriation of human remains to Ghana for reburial resulted from the work of the Committee to Honor Our African Ancestors, based in New York.

Additionally, the current leadership of Ghana has actively encouraged exchanges with communities of the African diaspora. In particular, African Americans are being targeted for Ghana's growing tourist industry, in which the slave dungeons in Elmina and Cape Coast castles have become a major focus (Bruner 1996; Singleton 1999c). Owraku Amofa, deputy minister of tourism in 1998, said, "[T]he significance of the [human] remains was to undo all the atrocities meted out to African slaves by the Europeans. Emancipation Day should serve as a unifying bond between Africans on the continent and those in the Diaspora" (*Daily Graphic*, July 31, 1998, p. 12). To further promote Amofa's sentiment, the chiefs and the people of Assin Manso have offered the lands covering the slave market, the burial grounds, and the Slave River for the development of a historical memorial complex to the pan-African world.

That archaeology could play a symbolic role in nurturing a dialogue between Africans and descent communities of the African-Atlantic diaspora is indeed commendable. The episode of exclusionary politics, public protest, reconciliation, and public involvement in the African Burial Ground project in New York City is perhaps the best-known example in the United States (see, e.g., Epperson 1999; La Roche and Blakey 1997). But what is the substantive role of archaeology in scholarly dialogues concerning the African diaspora? I raise this question because in spite of the tremendous popular interest in and growth of the archaeological study of the African diaspora, this research is just beginning to emerge outside the field of archaeology as a useful means to understanding the history and culture of African and African-descended peoples in the Americas. Many non-archaeologists are quite skeptical about the value of archaeology in helping us understand the recent past. Indeed, this skepticism was even expressed at the School of American Research advanced seminar from which this collection of essays on the African diaspora springs. This situation is somewhat ironic insofar as Afro-American archaeology, to the extent it has engaged in theoretical development, has been informed by the same conceptual dilemmas and directions as has the sociocultural and linguistic anthropology of the African diaspora. These diverse subfields, on the one hand, have actually shared preoccupations, while on the other, the sociocultural and linguistic branches have tended to elide archaeology and diminish its potential for solving common research (not to mention political) concerns. Happily, some sociocultural and linguistic anthropologists of the African diaspora are beginning to realize the value of archaeology, but in the main it has tended to be a very one-sided dialogue.

In this chapter, I begin by providing some examples of archaeological investigations in the diaspora—it is not possible here to present a full history or overview of the archaeology of the African diaspora[2]—with a dual purpose: to demonstrate shared concerns and to suggest at the same time that some developments in Afro-American archaeology can play a key role in diaspora scholarship as a whole. My goal here is to address the charges of those who see little value in the archaeological study of the African diaspora. I hope that my response will generate discussion among both archaeologists and non-archaeologists and lead to new efforts to enrich the scholarly value of this research interest. In this chapter, I examine the ways in which some theoretical developments in anthropology have guided the archaeological study of the diaspora. One of these developments—the critique of essentialized notions of culture—frames this discussion. Although this critique is reshaping archaeological approaches to the study of both Africa and the African diaspora, several impediments within archaeology limit the application of dynamic models of culture to archaeological practice. I discuss these issues and offer some avenues for future research directions. I use my ongoing research in Cuba as a case study to illustrate dialogue not only between subfields of anthropology (for example, sociocultural anthropology and archaeology) but also among anthropology and history and other academic disciplines. And I hope that the possibilities for dialogue between anthropology and communities in the African diaspora—and anthropology's usefulness and critical function in this dialogue—will be apparent.

ARCHAEOLOGY, THE AFRICAN DIASPORA, AND THE DEBATES OVER CULTURAL ORIGINS

The archaeological study of the African diaspora began in the late 1960s with the systematic testing of sites once occupied by enslaved Africans or their descendants. Initially inspired by a combination of black activism and historic preservation legislation in the United States, this research has become a well-established area of interest in the archaeological study of the modern world. Although most of the work has been undertaken in the United States (in at least thirty states), investigations have taken place elsewhere, including Canada, several Caribbean islands (for example, the Bahamas, Barbados, Cuba, the Dominican Republic, Jamaica, Montserrat, Puerto Rico, and the US Virgin Islands), South America (Argentina, Brazil, and Suriname), and Central America (Belize and Panama).

Increasingly, the archaeology of the African diaspora is making inroads in both public interpretation of the African diaspora and general scholarship. This development is possibly the consequence of archaeologists' concerted efforts to present their work to general audiences (e.g., Deagan and MacMahon 1995; Deetz 1993, 1996; Ferguson 1992; Singleton 1991; Singleton and Bograd 2000; Yenstch 1994). Archaeologists write primarily for the consumption of archaeologists. Therefore, the interests of archaeologists are often divorced from the broader questions and issues that have characterized diaspora scholarship as a whole. Archaeologists, however, have been enmeshed in debates over the cultural origins of African Americans and other discourses as in other subfields of anthropology.

From the very beginning, the Herskovits/Frazier debate shaped the orientation of the archaeological study of the African diaspora.[3] A major goal was, and continues to be for many practitioners, to examine the extent to which an African heritage influenced the ways in which Africans and their descendants constructed their material world. This approach is very much within the Herskovits tradition, though there is a major difference between his work and that of archaeologists. Herskovits and his followers suggested that present-day cultural practices among diaspora communities were direct continuities from Africa, whereas archaeologists are examining the ways in which an African heritage influenced African American culture in its formative days.[4] African-born or first-generation descendants of African-born people occupied many of the sites archaeologists investigate. That such sites would yield archaeological remains reflective of African practices would seem highly possible; however, very few archaeological remains strongly point to practices of African origins. Moreover, establishing specific African cultural provenances (ethnic groups) for these findings has proven to be extremely difficult.

The repeated absence of artifacts that clearly resembled African aesthetics or practices led some archaeologists to investigate other questions that viewed the archaeological record as a reflection of the subordinate class black people were forced to occupy in a white-dominated world. Implicit in some of these interpretations was a variation of the Frazier thesis—that people of African descent had fully "acculturated" or "assimilated" to Euro-American ways of life (e.g., Adams and Bolling 1989; Otto 1975, 1984; Wheaton and Garrow 1985). Like Frazier's followers, these archaeologists viewed interaction between people of African and European descent as resulting in unidirectional change in which African Americans were merely passive receptacles of European American ways of life. Therefore, the use of European-introduced, mass-produced objects by people of African descent was interpreted as an indicator that they were stripped of their cultural identity.[5]

Most archaeologists today recognize that the relationship between material culture and cultural identity is indeed very complex and elucidating this relationship requires detailed research and analyses.[6] Archaeologists who continue the pursuit of an African heritage in the archaeological record of the African diaspora posit that these influences can be seen in the use of a variety of handcrafted, mass-produced, and other elements of material culture, including pottery, housing, foodways, the use of domestic space, adornment, mortuary patterns, and religious practices. Those opposing these interpretations have generated counterarguments refuting that these practices were of African origin and stressing their European or Native American origins.

INTERPRETING AFRICAN DIASPORA MATERIAL CULTURE

Perhaps the most notorious of these debates is the one over production of low-fired earthenwares that archaeologists call "colonoware." *Colonoware* is a general term used to refer to numerous varieties of low-fired, hand-built (without a potter's wheel and using techniques such as coiling, segmental modeling, and pinching), undecorated pottery recovered from late-seventeenth- to mid-nineteenth-century sites in the eastern United States. Similar earthenwares have been recovered from sites in the Caribbean, and on some islands potters still produce wares comparable to those found in archaeological deposits. This pottery would have been used for cooking, serving, and storing foods. Both colonoware and the Caribbean wares are found archaeologically on both plantation and urban sites where people of African descent lived and worked (for a recent overview, see Hauser and DeCorse 2003; cf. Singleton and Bograd 2000).

Working from sites in Virginia, Ivor Noël Hume attributed the production of colonoware to local Native Americans, so he named this pottery "Colono-Indian" ware (Noël Hume 1962). He suggested that Native Americans made this pottery, because the potting technology was unlike that of trained English potters but it closely matched the potting technology of pre-Columbian Algonquian pottery. The major difference between the Colono-Indian ware and pre-Columbian Algonquian pottery, however, was that Colono-Indian ware was often fashioned into English forms such as bowls, pots, jugs, pitchers, pans, chamber pots, or porringers. Because of these characteristics, Noël Hume proposed that Native Americans who were exposed to European influences made Colono-Indian ware. He further suggested that colonoware was purchased primarily for enslaved or indentured workers, because it was frequently recovered from slave and servant quarters (Mouer et al. 1999:87).

With the proliferation of archaeological investigations of plantations in the 1970s, large quantities of colonoware pottery were unearthed from plantations in South Carolina. The colonowares were similar to those described by Noël Hume, but the majority were globular in shape, resembling cooking pots and serving bowls. Leland Ferguson studied the pottery from South Carolina plantations and discovered fragments with evidence of on-site manufacture (Ferguson 1992). Other archaeologists found damaged pots, unfired pottery fragments, and lumps of clay, indicating that pottery was made on some plantations. Ferguson inferred from these findings that at least some of these earthenwares were made by African Americans and other varieties, such as one he labeled "river-burnished" ware (Ferguson 1989), were very likely produced by the Catawba and other Indian groups living in South Carolina. He offered the more general term *colonoware* as a replacement for *Colono-Indian ware*. There is a consensus in South Carolina that both Native Americans and African Americans made colonoware.

Inspired by Ferguson's work, several archaeologists working in Virginia have suggested that African Americans made colonoware at specific sites in Virginia (e.g. Deetz 1988, 1993:80–93). The most controversial and direct of these claims is James Deetz's (1988:365) assertation that "most scholars working with colonoware now agree that it was made by and used by slaves." Deetz claims that Africans made the colonoware at Flowerdew Hundred, where Africans were present as early as 1622. Matthew Emerson (1988, 1994, 1999) has similarly posited African-produced terra-cotta pipes decorated with stamped and incised motifs highlighted with white chalk or powder. In the United States, these pipes are found only on seventeenth-century sites in Maryland and Virginia. Terra-cotta pipes, some similar to those studied by Emerson, have also been found at sites occupied by African diasporic communities in Barbados (J. Handler 1997), Brazil (Orser 1996, 1998), the Dominican Republic (Arrom and García Arévalo 1986), and Jamaica (Armstrong 1999).[7]

The archaeologists who challenge Deetz and Emerson believe that Native Americans made colonoware on seventeenth-century sites (Mouer 1993:124–125; Mouer et al. 1999). Historical references to Algonquian Indians making both pottery and pipes and selling them to English colonists support their interpretation. These archaeologists also reason that the African population of the Chesapeake was too small in the seventeenth century to account for production of artifacts as widely distributed as the Chesapeake earthenware pipes and vessels. They do acknowledge the possibility of African Americans making colonoware recovered from eighteenth- and nineteenth-century sites, because by that time Africans and their descendants had replaced white indentured servants and Indian slaves on plantations. Remnant Indian communities such as the Pamunkey, however, were still engaged in the production and sale of pottery. The Pamunkey produced pottery well into the twentieth century.

Another debate over origins has developed around storage pits, or root cellars, unearthed in numerous slave houses, primarily in the upper South (Virginia, Tennessee, and Kentucky) but also in North Carolina and South Carolina. Apparently, enslaved people dug or cut these pits into the earthen floors of the dwellings while occupying them. These rectangular storage pits vary in size and are often located in front of hearths, where the heat from the fire would have kept vegetables from freezing during winter. They were also used for storage of personal items (coins, buttons, musical instruments), hoes, and other tools. One large slave barracks had numerous pits (eighteen) that may have served as individual storage compartments (Samford 1996:95).

William Kelso (1984) first reported these pits in Virginia and suggested that they were a "product of black culture" because they were not found in housing that predated the influx of Africans to Virginia in the eighteenth century. Since 1984 at least one storage pit has been identified from a seventeenth-century dwelling in Virginia, believed to have been occupied by laboring servants, possibly Africans (Mouer 1993:150). The recovery of beads, coins, and cowries from these pits prompted Anne Yentsch (1991) to suggest that the practice of burying these particular items may be of African origin. She based this inference on a description of an English sea captain who observed the Igbo people storing similar materials under the floors of their houses in the early nineteenth century. The Igbo connection gains added support from estimates that 40 to 60 percent of the Africans imported to Virginia were of Igbo origins (Chambers 1996; Kulikoff 1986; P. Morgan 1998). More recently, Patricia Samford (1999, 2000) conducted a detailed study of several storage pits and their contents in

Virginia and North Carolina. She posited that some of these storage pits are remains of shrines and other religious offerings.

A few archaeologists have countered that root cellars are pancultural and should not be used as an indicator of an African American presence (e.g., Kimmel 1993). Others interpret the action of enslaved people digging storage pits within their quarters as speaking more to the conditions of enslavement than to the maintenance of an African-derived practice. Citing the few scattered references to storage pits found in written accounts, several archaeologists propose that storage pits reflect an example of day-to-day slave resistance to planters' control (M. Hall 1992; McKee 1992; Singleton 1998; Young 1998). These written references indicate that slaveholders believed that enslaved people used these pits to hide pilfered items, so the pits became a source of conflict between slaveholders and enslaved people. Slaveholders apparently tried various tactics to prevent the enslaved from digging these pits, such as raising quarters off the ground on brick piers or filling in pits that came to their attention. Storage pits have been found even in late-antebellum quarters raised off the ground, which suggests that enslaved people continuing digging these pits despite slaveholder interference.

Additional debates have considered the cultural origins of wattle-and-daub housing (a woven wooden lattice covered with clay), used throughout the Caribbean (see Chapman 1991) and to some extent in South Carolina for slave housing (Ferguson 1992:77), and the origin of spindle whorls—small fired-clay devices used to spin thread for weaving cloth on handlooms (Groover 1993, 1994; Heite 1993). While some archaeologists are perhaps too quick to claim African origins, others appear overly suspicious of any attribution to African origins. They will claim European precedents, no matter how remote, to challenge the case in hand. This situation is best illustrated in the spindle whorl debate. Spindle whorls are frequently recovered from sites in West Africa, and in many African societies they are apparently produced only by men, as are pipes (Posnansky 1999). Mark Groover (1993, 1994) recovered spindle whorls from the excavations of a structure dating from 1740 to 1775. It was part of a small plantation near Columbia, South Carolina, that was engaged in the production of textiles. Groover suggested that the spindle whorls may reflect the spinning

and weaving activities, and possibly West African influences on the production of textiles, of the fourteen persons of African descent whom
Thomas Howell, owner of the property, held in bondage. Edward
Heite (1993:2) countered Groover's claim, stating that "spindle whorls
of the type described were not peculiar to West Africa during the period
in question. Northern Europeans and Navajo traditions, to cite just two
examples, retain similar artifacts today. In Iceland, whorls are still
being made and used, in stone and wood; my informants there recognized Groover's drawings." It is very true that other groups made and
used spindle whorls for spinning thread, but giving as examples the
modern-day Navajo or Icelander use of spindle whorls diminishes
Heite's argument. Neither group was likely to influence textile production in South Carolina during the third quarter of the eighteenth
century. Despite the foolishness of the spindle whorl controversy, it
highlights the futility of searching for cultural origins of very simple
technological items. Undoubtedly, most preindustrial societies independently invented these kinds of objects.

Religious artifacts are receiving a great deal of attention in the
interpretation of African influences. A number of archaeologists have
recovered artifacts identified as Kongo-influenced *nisiki* charms and
medicines (Ferguson 1992:110–116; Wilkie 1997; cf. Fennell 2000,
2003). Although they present strong arguments that these objects were
used for religious purposes, the attribution to Kongo or any specific
African cultural group is tentative at best. Other African religions
used similar artifacts and symbols (but see Fennell 2000, 2003). For
example, similar to Kongo peoples, the Fon and Bini peoples used cos-
mograms to control or influence spiritual forces (Michael Mason, personal communication, 1998). From the vantage point of my research
in Cuba, each of the Afro-Cuban religions, while exhibiting a predominant influence from a particular ethnic group—Lucumí/Santería
(Yorùbá-influenced), Palo Monte (Kongo-influenced), and Arara (Fon-
influenced)—is an amalgamation of several African belief systems and
Spanish folk Catholicism from the colonial period. As these religions
developed over time in Cuba, there was apparently a great deal of
exchange of ideas and practices. For example, the deities of the
Lucumí/Santería religion are replicated in Palo Monte but have different names and are served in different ways. My point is that even

within the context of well-known and well-documented Afro-Cuban religions, it is difficult to assign an ethnic origin for a religious practice. I discovered this fact when consultations with Afro-Cuban practitioners failed to yield the identification of a recent religious offering uncovered archaeologically in the town of Regla, a suburb of Havana.

Other artifacts, including pierced coins, beads, crystals, and buttons, are recurrent finds at sites occupied by diaspora peoples in both North America and the Caribbean. Oral history and folklore gathered from diasporic communities indicate that these objects were used in various ways for spiritual management or conjuring (Fett 2002:96–97; Leone and Fry 1999, 2001). Because these objects had many different uses and meanings, making comparisons between diasporic communities is problematical. Thus, interpretation of these objects will vary from setting to setting.

Archaeologists of the African diaspora in the New World are now consulting with their counterparts in Africanist archaeology to resolve some of these debates (see Singleton 2001a; cf. Agorsah 1996).[8] And many do field research on both sides of the Atlantic. For example, Agorsah (1998, 1999) is continuing his work on precolonial African spatial patterns with research in Maroon communities in Jamaica and Suriname, and Goucher (1993, 1999) is working on the transfer of metalworking technologies from Africa to the Caribbean. But a mere comparison of African diaspora material remains with African ones is inadequate without a theoretical apparatus that can account for cultural change as a part of changing contexts and power relationships, and one that is also attentive to historical context. So, for instance, the archaeology of African American burial practices in the Americas has yielded similarities across societies and further similarities with African mortuary practices. These similarities include the recovery of religious paraphernalia in the graves themselves (see, e.g., L. Domínguez 1999: 33 for Cuba and J. Handler 1997 for Barbados). Archaeologists of precolonial West Africa have reported burials within houses. At the same time, archaeologists in the Americas have reported burials within slave dwellings, for example, from excavations at the Seville Plantation on the north coast of Jamaica (Armstrong 1998, 1999; Armstrong and Fleischman 2003). But in Barbados, burial in slave cemeteries was apparently a more common practice (J. Handler 1997; Handler, Lange, and Riordan 1978), demonstrating differences in constraints on the enslaved in different plantation societies.

In some cases, archaeologists have not carefully thought through under what circumstances Africans in the Americas were likely to reproduce African practices. For example, it seems unlikely that at a predominately male settlement, such as Fort Mosé in Spanish, Florida, as well as some Maroon sites, the occupants would have produced certain kinds of handcrafted items. Fort Mosé was an eighteenth-century fortress and settlement occupied by former slaves who had fled to Spanish Florida from enslavement in South Carolina. The Spaniards granted them freedom on the condition that they convert to Catholicism and defend Spanish Florida from British attack by manning a fort—Gracia Real de Santa Teresa de Mosé—located two miles north of Saint Augustine. Nearly all the occupants at Mosé were African-born, and they represented a variety of *naciones* (nations) (Deagan and Landers 1999). Excavations of the site did not yield anything resembling African practices. Even the food remains were more akin to Native American subsistence strategies than to those of Africans or enslaved people on plantations (Reitz 1994). These findings make sense given that the settlement was primarily male (men would probably not have crafted pottery), and the similarities to Native American subsistence may be the result of trade and other kinds of exchanges with nearby Native Americans, such as the men of Fort Mosé taking Indian wives.

THE LEGACY OF ESSENTIALISM IN ARCHAEOLOGY

The debates over cultural origins of materials recovered from sites occupied by African Americans stem from essentialized notions of culture that persist in archaeological practice. Essentialism in archaeology is primarily manifested in the idea that cultural groups can be identified or classified by certain properties or attributes.[9] Despite the widespread acceptance in anthropological archaeology that culture is a dynamic, interactive process and cultural identity is fluid—"the product of situational phenomena" (Shennan 1989:19)—most archaeological approaches are still premised upon concepts and methods that utilize static attributes to identify groups from archaeological sources. This essentialism is deeply embedded within archaeology. It derives from remnants of normative characterizations of cultural groups (S.

Jones 1997:27–28) and social typologies (band, tribe, chiefdom, state, and so forth), along with the mechanics (economy-environment-population-technology) found in functionalist archaeology (Shanks and Tiley 1987:122–123, 259). Central to both paradigms is the concept of "archaeological culture," in which certain types of reoccurring remains can be used to identify and classify cultural groups. Throughout the history of archaeological thought, archaeological culture has been an evolving concept. When used today, it is primarily at the level of descriptive analysis, particularly in "prehistoric" archaeology—the study of periods of human history before the advent of writing systems (Trigger 1989).

Yet even in the archaeological study of the modern world (often referred to as "historical archaeology"), of which the African-Atlantic diaspora is a part, archaeologists have often established the identity of a particular group based upon the presence of artifacts perceived to be indicators of cultural identity. These ethnic markers for people of African descent in the Americas include some of the aforementioned cultural forms: colonoware and African-Caribbean pottery, wattle-and-daub housing, beads, inexpensive cuts of meat, hair-care devices and products, storage pits, and religious artifacts. Here, dialogue with Africanist archaeologists is crucial. They have shown in many cases only fine differences in material culture, even when separate ethnic identities are held (e.g., DeCorse 1989; Stahl 1991), and they also show the pitfalls of an approach that projects the labels of the present onto the past. The African ethnic groups whose names we have come to know in the Americas were often identified thus by the enslavers, who named African peoples for their point of embarkation on the Middle Passage, not necessarily for some preexisting corporate identity. And these identities were often donned by the enslaved themselves in the formation of mutual aid societies and other sodalities (see, e.g., DeCorse 1999: 135–137; Posnansky 1999:24–25; cf. Matory 1999a, 1999b, 1999c). These identities, then, were constructed in particular colonial contexts, and the boundaries between them in precolonial Africa may have been extremely permeable and fluid in any event. Archaeologists of the African diaspora in the New World can run into problems if they reify ethnicity.

Returning to the issue of below-floor slave burials at Seville Plantation in Jamaica, these burials resemble those recovered from

Elmina, a settlement historically associated with the Fante, a subgroup of the Akan ethnolinguistic family (see DeCorse 2001). "Koromantin" or "Coromantee" (Akan) slaves were numerous at certain times in Jamaica (see Higman 1984) and elsewhere in the Caribbean, and it would be easy to infer burials found below the floorboards of slave houses as an Akan practice. While "there is great variation in burial practice within West and West Central Africa" (Posnansky 1999:33), it is also the case that "at one time burial within houses and compounds was widespread and [also] occurred in African households of Elmina during the slave trade" (Posnansky 1999:34; cf. DeCorse 1987, 2001).

On a practical level, ethnic markers provide a reference point for beginning the analysis of identity. But all too often these artifacts become the primary focus of the archaeological discussion, and the interpretation of other objects is not given much consideration. Moreover, the reliance upon ethnic markers to interpret cultural identity often impedes rather than advances our understanding at some sites. When these objects are absent, archaeologists are often baffled as to how to interpret the site. For example, studies of Maroon sites have been primarily descriptive because the materials recovered from them are very similar, if not identical, to those of sites of other cultural groups in these areas. At this time, archaeologists have not developed insightful research strategies into the role material culture played in the production and reproduction of Maroon cultural life (Orser 1998:72), with one notable exception (Agorsah 1998). Regrettably, a similar situation exists for many African American sites, particularly those not associated with plantation slavery, but as with Maroon sites, this situation is changing (see Mullins 1999a, 1999b).

Two archaeologists, one looking at cultural interaction and change (Cusick 1998:1) and the other at class relations (Delle 1999:136), lamented the difficulty archaeologists have in studying dynamic social phenomena, because of the "static archaeological record." Archaeologists have traditionally boasted that their field could examine social changes that neither ethnologists nor historians could access, because of the long time depth of the archaeological record. This claim still rings true in the study of the Annales School concept—*longue durée*—but not necessarily for time periods of short duration. It all depends on the sites, the kinds of archaeological contexts (structures, trash pits, burials, and so forth), and the degree of preservation. For example, it is often very difficult to distinguish between pre- and post-emancipation deposits at plantations dating between the last years of slavery and the early years of emancipation. Sometimes it is possible to isolate separate deposits indicating several phases of occupation through time at other plantation sites, but these phases are rarely less than twenty- to thirty-year intervals.

Obstacles also exist in the interpretation of African American life at multicultural sites and in urban settings where blacks and whites lived together on the same city lot. In these situations, there are often no discrete archaeological deposits for each group, and archaeologists lack appropriate methods for interpreting the activities of a specific group. Anne Yentsch (1994) partially overcame this methodological difficulty at the Calvert site, the eighteenth-century urban residence of a prominent family in Annapolis, Maryland. The Calverts were the financiers for the establishment of colonial Maryland. At their Annapolis property, the Calverts had as many as thirty-one enslaved persons in 1734; most of the adults were African-born (Yentsch 1994:172). To determine which artifacts were associated with the Africans who once lived at the site, Yentsch conducted a thorough study from a variety of sources on clothing, personal possessions, and household items associated with Africans and enslaved people in the eighteenth century. She then compared many of the artifacts she recovered with those found at documented slave sites. In the final analysis, the only artifacts she could confidently associate with the African presence were beads, small bells (found in association with the beads), food remains, and food preparation equipment.

The reliance upon ethnic markers, in addition to limiting insights into understanding sites, may also generate stereotypes of the people archaeologists study. Ferguson says that, while studying colonoware collections in Virginia, some archaeologists had no problems attributing poorly crafted pottery recovered from two early-eighteenth-century plantations to enslaved Africans, because it was crudely made. But the archaeologists did not attribute the finer pieces from a later time to enslaved Africans (Ferguson 1992:46–47). Besides the racism implied in this attitude, it hints at the influence of the Frazier School. These archaeologists appear to think that enslaved people were incapable of producing fine pottery because they were stripped of their cultural heritage. Surprisingly, even Ferguson (1992:47) explains the poor quality of this plantation-made pottery as resulting from "the dislocations and stresses of slavery and frontier life." Like any craft items, colonoware pottery exhibits a vast range of skill levels; therefore, poorly crafted examples are not necessarily indicators of social groups but of technical expertise.

As was the case in the Herskovits/Frazier debate, it is obvious from much of the archaeological discourse on Africanisms that more is at stake than constructing images of the African American past. Warren Perry and Robert Paynter (1999:301) warn archaeologists that these debates "would benefit from the recognition of their significance for and embeddedness in this long discourse [on the role of African culture in the Americas]. Deep matters of theory, history, and politics are all present whenever African culture is on the table, matters deserving as much care as to provenance, context, and form if we are to advance an understanding of the character of the African presence in the Western Hemisphere." Archaeologists are beginning to address some of the political issues involved in undertaking the archaeology of the African diaspora. These concerns have been primarily directed toward the inclusion of African American perspectives and descendant communities in this research (e.g., La Roche and Blakey 1997; MacDavid and Babson 1997; Potter 1991; Singleton 1995). A few archaeologists have gone a step further, being self-reflective about their own goals and intentions in becoming engaged in this research (e.g. Ferguson 1992; Leone et al. 1995; Singleton 2001b). This literature, however, has not examined the politics that continue to fuel essentialist ideas and approaches.

A variety of political issues accounts for the persistence of essentialism in the archaeology of the African diaspora. Some sources for funding research archaeology tend to favor the positivist paradigms of functionalist social archaeology over other analytical frameworks. This situation compels archaeologists to frame their research questions in essentialist terms for funding purposes. Similarly, museums and historic preservation organizations also support archaeological research and have been traditionally concerned with the "authentic" or "distinctive" aspects of cultural groups. A major theme of the National Park Service's initiative on African American heritage is the interpretation of "Africanisms" (e.g., B. Joyner 2003; see Sengova's chapter in this volume). Lay constituencies of archaeological research (both black and white) also want to know about the distinctive artifacts found at sites occupied by African diasporic communities. The recurrent theme of "cultural distinctiveness" embedded in both the traditional tool kit (concepts, methods, theory) of archaeology for the past century and the political forces that sustain this research serve to reinforce essentialist interpretations. It is therefore extremely naive of critics (e.g., Upton 1996) to anticipate that dynamic approaches to ethnicity will emerge immediately.

ALTERNATIVES TO ESSENTIALIST INTERPRETATIONS OF CULTURAL IDENTITY

Despite methodological problems and political issues that encourage essentialism, there are alternative approaches to understanding the role of material culture in identity formation and the symbolic expression of African diasporic communities. One way is to move beyond the preoccupation with the cultural sources of a particular artifact or practice recovered archaeologically, and to examine the ways in which artifacts and practices were appropriated or redefined, or acquired new meanings. Several archaeologists have implemented such studies, though with varying degrees of success.

Leland Ferguson's (1992) archaeological study of colonial African American life in eighteenth-century North America in *Uncommon Ground* is seen as the most comprehensive attempt to offer an analytical framework for explaining how African American cultures developed and how artifacts—regardless of their cultural origins—"served as symbols that reinforced people's views of themselves" (Ferguson 1992:xliv). He utilizes a creolization model (C. Joyner 1984; cf. Mintz and Price 1992) to elucidate the ways in which artifacts (whether slave-made colonoware pottery or imported English ceramics) are part of the lexicon of culture and that the ways they were made, used, and perceived are part of the grammar. Ferguson supports his argument primarily by showing how colonoware pottery and clay-walled houses in colonial South Carolina were part of a slave culture that was strongly African. Later in the nineteenth century, the pottery was replaced with imported ceramic bowls, and clay-walled houses with European-style architecture, but the ways these European forms of material culture were used retained an African grammar.

Ferguson's model has been useful in explaining the role of objects where there is an identifiable "African grammar."[10] He claims, however, "within a creolizing culture, change can take place in either superficial features, or the underlying structure, or in both" (Ferguson 1992: xlii), but throughout his study he provides examples of changes only in the lexicon—that is, in artifacts—not changes in the underlying structure. Because of his failure to provide examples of changes in both the lexicon and grammar, elsewhere I have questioned the applicability of his model to other kinds of archaeological sites where African grammars are not apparent. African grammars undoubtedly disappeared through time as people of African descent constructed their material worlds in a variety of settings and chose new symbols with which to communicate their identities (Singleton 1995:133–134). Upon further reflection, I have also commented on Ferguson's uncritical use of structuralism (Singleton 1998:177)—the theoretical underpinning upon which linguistic models used to explain social phenomena are drawn. He never addresses the shortcomings of structuralism, nor does he qualify how it is being used in his formulation.[11] We can only assume Ferguson's complete acceptance of Joyner's invocations of pidgin and creole languages (C. Joyner 1984:xx–xxi),[12] even though linguists are apparently in disagreement about these terms and have been rethinking these concepts (see, for example, the discussion in Jourdan 1991). The increasing criticism of creolization both inside (Epperson 1990; Howson 1990; Perry and Paynter 1999) and outside archaeology (see the chapters by Richard Price and Matory in this volume) raises the question, will Ferguson be capable of delivering on his promise of anticipated studies utilizing creolization theory for "wide-ranging analysis of social and political interaction" (Ferguson 1992:xli)?

In contrast to Ferguson's culturalist approach to understanding the role of material culture in the formation and transformation of African American identities, some archaeologists analyze African American life within the political economy of capitalist production and consumption. Paul Mullins's (1999a, 1999b) study of African American consumption in Annapolis, Maryland, is one of the best studies of this type. Mullins argues that African American consumption sought to fulfill aspirations to civil and material opportunities but because white racists often projected black caricatures of African American consumption, African American consumers utilized subtle tactics that often veiled their symbolic manipulation of commodities. Through the analysis of several categories of material culture—canned goods, bric-a-brac, food remains, and ceramics—he identified consumption strategies among African American consumers that sought to dismantle the racist boundaries of consumerism in Annapolis, Maryland, from 1850 to 1930. An example of this strategy is seen in African American preferences for national brands. Large quantities of national-brand canned goods were recovered from African American households. By purchasing national brands rather than buying bulk foods from local markets, African American Annapolitans not only obtained better quality foods but also evaded local white marketers' tendency to sell inferior, overpriced goods to black customers (Mullins 1999a:174).

Mullins's analysis is important because it illustrates that material symbolism is complex and many archaeological assumptions about social differences are simplistic and mechanical. In his analysis of bric-a-brac, he shows how the meanings of these objects differed between blacks and whites. European American women often gave these objects to their African American domestics to encourage reliability, legitimize African American subordination, and discourage defiance. African Americans, on the other hand, saw these exotic pieces as items they were previously unable to acquire. Consequently, the acquisition of these items redefined their material world (Mullins 1999b:169–170).

In an attempt to better understand African American meanings of objects or practices that originated with Europeans or Native Americans, I offered the possibility of interpreting the reception of these items as a phenomenon of appropriation (Singleton 1998:182; Singleton and Bograd 2000). The quintessential example of African American appropriation is the emergence and development of African American Christianity. African Americans transformed white Protestantism into a black religious culture and black institution that is still evident even today. African Americans also appropriated other European American practices and material culture. For example, the marriage practice of jumping over a broomstick apparently had its origins in medieval Europe and was practiced by both whites and blacks in the southern colonies. In time, white southerners abandoned this marriage practice, but for enslaved men and women, this was the only type of marriage permitted, and it quickly acquired a special meaning in southern African American culture (Fischer 1989:282).

The appropriated object or practice often becomes a catalyst for its use in identity formation, because it empowers those who have appropriated it, particularly in relations of inequality (Thomas 1991; Turgeon 1997:21). Many aspects of the material culture recovered from African American sites may be interpreted this way, though not all objects will lend themselves to this kind of analysis.

The iron kettle or cauldron (Singleton 1999b) lends itself to this kind of analysis because it became vested with symbolic meanings in certain Afro-American and Afro-Caribbean contexts. It was an important trade good from Europe to West Africa, used primarily for cooking since the mid-eighteenth century, as described in the early travel accounts of Jean Barbot ([1732] 1746) and others. Very likely it became symbolically important among some African societies during the slave trade. In Cuba each of the Afro-Cuban religious traditions used cauldrons in similar but slightly different ways. At one time all the religions deliberately interred cauldrons filled with sacred medicines to hide their awesome powers, although today this practice seems limited to practitioners of Palo Monte, a Kongo-based Afro-Christian religion. A Lucumí/Santería story hints at the multiple and contradictory meanings of the cauldron in Afro-Cuban religion. It is a story of a drummer (drummers summon *orishas* in ceremonies wherein practitioners become possessed by orishas) attacked by a *palero* (a practitioner of Palo Monte) using sacred medicines in the cauldron. Through the cauldron, the drummer loses his drum, his connection to the orishas, his ability to make money, and ultimately everything (Michael Mason, personal communication 1998). In this tale, we see two completely different meanings for the cauldron. For the *santero* (a practitioner of Santería), the cauldron is something to be feared because of its association with aggression, whereas the cauldron empowers the palero.

ARCHAEOLOGY IN DIALOGUE WITH HISTORY: ARCHAEOLOGICAL RESEARCH ON AFRO-CUBA

The preceding issues weighed heavily on my mind when, during my first visit to Cuba in 1996, I met a historian who questioned the extent to which *bohíos*—timber-framed structures walled with cane, clay, or clapboards and roofed with thatch—were used for slave housing in Cuba. He had become interested in this question because a variety of primary historical sources suggest that bohíos were used more often for slave housing than were the masonry structures known as *barracones*. But all the standing ruins of former slave houses he had observed were of barracones, not bohíos. The historian's statement stunned me. On the one hand, I applauded his effort to use material culture to answer a question concerning slavery. At the same time, he obviously did not understand the conditions under which impermanent architecture would be preserved. I was also troubled by his willingness to dismiss the use of bohíos for slave housing based upon his limited observations of standing ruins. Didn't he realize, I thought to myself, that because bohíos were made from perishable materials— wood, thatch, and clay—it was unlikely that the remains of such housing would be visible above the ground? After I explained this situation to him, I emphasized that archaeological investigations would be the primary way to locate and identify such housing and that slave houses similar to bohíos had been uncovered on several Caribbean islands.

My exchange with the Cuban historian is important for two reasons: First, the research I am currently undertaking in Cuba contributes to his query because it has yielded archaeological evidence of Cuban bohíos that were used for housing enslaved workers on a coffee plantation. Second, my work not only challenges the historian's interpretation of slave housing but also permits me to make a larger interpretative point regarding constructions of the past that ignore archaeological findings. An archaeology of the African diaspora is important because it offers interpretative possibilities that are not necessarily forthcoming from the analysis of oral or written sources alone. Archaeology, however, is not a substitute for careful research of written records or oral historical sources. Historical archaeology is an interdisciplinary pursuit wherein archaeological findings are used in conjunction with written, oral, cartographic, pictorial, and other sources to gain insights into the past. Alison Wylie (1999:29) argues that the conjoint use of evidence does not privilege or treat an evidential resource as a given, as uniquely foundational relative to other sources, or as having epistemic priority over another. Kathleen Deagan (1998:54) reiterates further "that only by integrating history and archaeology could they [historical archaeologists] generate new questions and answers that would have been unobtainable through either discipline alone"—and the same might be said of sociocultural anthropology. It is the working back and forth of multiple sources of information that characterizes most research in historical archaeology undertaken today. Archaeological findings can confirm, refute, complement, or supplement other historical sources. In my own work, archaeological finds often shed new light on descriptions found in written sources that have been overlooked or dismissed; therefore, archaeology can offer a new or an opposing perspective. This observation has been particularly pertinent in my research of a nineteenth-century coffee plantation about 48 miles southeast of Havana.

On my first visit, I became interested in working at a site known today as "Cafetal del Padre" (figure 8.1). The ruins of the slave village were unlike those at the other coffee and sugar plantations I visited in Havana Province. At Cafetal del Padre, a huge masonry wall, almost 11 feet high, surrounds the former slave village, an area approximately 228 by 325 feet. The ruins at the other sites were, as the Cuban historian had observed, masonry structures known as barracones, in which the living areas of men and women were often separated in a prison-cell-like arrangement. On large sugar estates, barracones could be quite massive, housing hundreds of slave men and women. The imposing wall intrigued me because it represented an extreme example of a slaveholder exerting his or her control over the living spaces of enslaved people. I knew of no comparable examples on plantations in the English-speaking Américas, and I found no references to wall enclosures in the secondary literature of Cuban slavery. After visiting the site, I wanted to know about the everyday life of the enslaved people who lived behind the prison-like wall.

I began my study of the site of El Padre with two basic concerns: First, was enclosing a slave village within a high wall a common characteristic of Cuban slavery, or does the slave village at El Padre represent the action of an individual slaveholder? Second, how did enslaved people respond to living in this situation? In other words, in what ways did they challenged their enslavers? James Scott (1985, 1990) discusses forms of everyday resistance oppressed people utilize to undermine

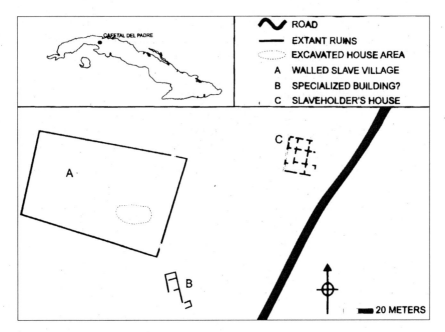

FIGURE 8.1

Present-day map of Cafetal del Padre.

the power of the dominant. I am interested in how these actions are manifested in the archaeological record. For example, the study of houses and yard areas can yield information on slave-inspired modifications to their domestic spaces. Archaeological studies in Jamaica (e.g., Armstrong, 1990, 1999; Armstrong and Kelly 2000) and Virginia (e.g., Epperson 1990; McKee 1992) have identified modifications enslaved people made to their houses and yards that provided a semblance of privacy, as well as animal pens, gardens, and places for storage of food and personal objects.

Good fortune provided me with initial clues for answering the first question. Manuel Barcia Paz, a Cuban historian who had been researching a slave rebellion in Matanzas Province, knew of an ordinance issued after the rebellion in 1825 (ANC 1825:4) requiring plantations with bohíos to surround and enclose these houses with a palisade 4 to 5 *varas* high.[13] A vara is a Spanish measurement of approximately 2.8 feet, so the required wall height was between 11.2 and 14 feet. The wall surrounding the slave village at El Padre measures 10.8

feet, which is about 5 inches shorter than the minimum height of 4 varas. Although El Padre is located in Havana Province today, historical research has since confirmed that the coffee plantation Santa Ana de Viajacas, El Padre's original name, was established in Matanzas Province (ANC 1866) and was located there for most of its history.

The ordinance requiring wall enclosures around slave villages in Matanzas Province establishes that this practice was at least known in the nineteenth century. Two additional references to wall enclosures around slave villages strengthened my argument. The first, a published lithograph of a sugar plantation known as "Angerona" depicts a row of detached slave houses behind a wall (Méndez 1952:8). Portions of this wall are still standing. Before it was converted into a sugar plantation, Angerona had been one of the largest coffee plantations in western Cuba.

The second reference was in an essay on Cuban slave housing in Álvaro Reynoso's *Estudios progresivos*, published in 1861. Reynoso argues against housing enslaved workers in the prison-like barracones and recommends returning to the old system of bohíos. He then provides a description of an *ideal* slave village containing wide, clean streets adorned with beautiful trees; each house having a small piece of land, a garden, and animal pens; and in the center of the village a hospital, chapel, baths, and wells. He concludes by stating that "for the best security, one could fence in the entire [slave village] with a tall, large wall, although we are convinced that such a precaution is not necessary" (Reynoso 1861:330, my translation). Students of Cuban slavery have frequently cited Reynoso's discussion on slave housing (e.g. F. Ortiz [1947] 1995:85; Pérez de la Riva 1975:58–63; R. Scott 1985:18), but the reference to enclosing slave villages within a wall has never been foregrounded, perhaps because Reynoso's statement can easily be dismissed and interpreted as simply a recommendation, not actual practice.

This discussion on wall enclosures may appear to be a trite detail that offers no significant insights into Cuban slavery. Yet the wall enclosures at El Padre and Angerona become significant when anchored within the debate over the prevalence and effectiveness of the *barracón* system for housing enslaved Cuban workers. Historians of Cuban slavery have debated the extent to which barracones replaced bohíos and whether barracones were effective in controlling the activities of a rapidly growing and rebellious slave population. Moreno Fraginals proposed that barracones widely replaced bohíos. Consequently, enslaved workers lost access to garden plots located in yard areas adjacent to their houses, and they were unable to form families because the living arrangements for men and women were separated (Moreno Fraginals 1978:67–75). Rebecca Scott, however, argues that many if not most plantations continued the bohío system because barracones were very expensive to build and only wealthy plantations owners could afford them. Additionally, slave men and women living in barracones "found ways to make their cells less prison-like" (Scott 1985:17–18). She cites two nineteenth-century accounts indicating that whole families were living within the crowded cells of barracones and that enslaved people constructed granaries and lofts to store their produce. Thus, enslaved people undermined slaveholders' efforts to prevent them from forming families or having access to gardens. Enclosing a slave village within a wall presented an alternative to the barracón. Plantation owners could maintain the bohío system but could effectively contain slave activities, much as they could with barracones. The debate over the frequency and effectiveness of barracones apparently continues in Cuban historiography (see Cremé Ramos and Duharte Jiménez 1994; Roura Alvarez and Angelbello n.d.), inspiring the previously mentioned query of the Cuban historian.

Wall enclosures were perhaps also needed to make entrance to slave quarters a hindrance to outsiders. Maroons—slave runaways—periodically attacked plantations and in the process liberated enslaved workers, took plantation supplies, and destroyed property. Well-organized communities of Maroons lived in Sierra del Grillo (La Rosa Corzo 2003; La Rosa Corzo and Pérez Padrón 1994), a mountain range in the vicinity of Santa Ana de Viajacas. In 1837 the Office of the Pedaneo—the administrative official for a subdivision of a district—reported that a small party of Maroons had come to the slave village of the coffee plantation of Santa Ana de Viajacas. However, the Maroons did not capture any enslaved people or take any property (AHPM 1837). In fact, the encounter appears to have been peaceful, perhaps involving some kind of trade exchange. But hostile Maroon attacks were known and posed a constant threat.

Rancheadores, pursuers of slave runaways, comprised another group of potential slave raiders whom slaveholders desired to keep away from slave quarters. In addition to catching runaways, they were reputed to steal enslaved persons from one plantation and sell them to another plantation, particularly during periods of labor shortages. Slaveholders were always wary of rancheadores because they could never be sure that runaways would be returned to their original owners (Moreno Fraginals 1976:133, 138). Undoubtedly, wall enclosures would assist in keeping both Maroons and rancheadores away from slave communities.

What began as a simple effort to determine whether the wall enclosure at El Padre was typical or atypical of Cuban slavery has opened a window onto a variety of social interactions among slaveholders, enslaved persons, Maroons, and slave catchers. Although the examination of these social relations will involve more than the analysis of archaeological data, it was an archaeological observation that brought them to light in the first place.

CLUES TO SLAVE LIVES AT CAFETAL DEL PADRE

The primary focus of my continuing research at Cafetal del Padre has become trying to answer the second question, how did enslaved people respond to living within prison-like walls? This question is far more difficult to investigate than the first question, because it does not lead to a direct answer from either archaeological or historical sources. Rather, the answer must be inferred from a variety of sources and compared with other archaeological investigations.

The coffee plantation Santa Ana de Viajacas was established from a tract of land consisting of 30 *caballerías* (about 1,000 acres) and designated as the O'Farrill *potrero* (stock-raising farm) in 1796 (ANC 1866). It is unknown when the coffee plantation was established, but 14 caballerías (approximately 470 acres) were designated for coffee production, and the remaining 16 caballerías (approximately 530 acres) continued to be used as a potrero, referred to as "Cafetal Potrero" or "Potrero Viajacas" (ANC 1829b). The O'Farrills were one of the most distinguished and powerful families in nineteenth-century Cuba (Paquette 1988:45). Richard O'Farrell (the Irish surname *O'Farrell* was later Hispanicized to *O'Farrill*), the Irish progenitor of the family, had been born on the island of Montserrat in the eastern Caribbean and came to Cuba in the early eighteenth century (Franco

Ferrán 1986:7). He became a slave trader, and his profits in slave trading laid the foundation for his descendants' fortune (Bergad 1990:14). Ignacio O'Farrill (Richard O'Farrell's grandson), a Catholic priest, inherited the property from his parents. Some time later, the *cafetal* became known simply as *El Padre*, "The Father," presumably because a priest once owned it.

In 1829 Ignacio O'Farrill began mortgaging his properties, including ten enslaved male workers from Potrero Viajacas, to pay back a loan of 60,000 pesos (ANC 1829a:1262–1263, 1829b:1671). He had used the 60,000 pesos to develop two sugar plantations, La Concordia and San Juan de Nepomuceno, both located in districts not far from the coffee plantation. Ignacio had difficulty paying back the loan, and by the time he died in 1838, his estate had accumulated considerable debt. In 1844 a hurricane destroyed the coffee works at Santa Ana de Viajacas, and the enslaved community was relocated to the sugar plantation San Juan de Nepomuceno. During the same year, the Royal Treasury of Cuba took over the administration of Ignacio O'Farrill's estate until his debts and back taxes were settled. The sugar plantations were eventually sold (ANC 1849–1853). Coffee cultivation was never restored at Santa Ana de Viajacas, and it was later subdivided into small subsistence farms (ANC 1862).

In 1838, the year Padre O'Farrill died, the slave population consisted of seventy-seven men, women, and children. Fifty-three were male, and twenty-four were female (ANC 1838). The sex ratio of two men to every woman is comparable to that found on other coffee plantations studied in Matanzas Province (González Fernández 1991:171). Only five children—two boys and three girls, all under the age of five years—are listed on the plantation inventory. The small number of children is consistent with analyses indicating that Cuban slave populations did not increase through natural reproduction, making chronic importation of African laborers necessary to sustain the slave population (Bergad, García, and del Carmen Barcia 1995:36).

Excavations at the El Padre slave villages were conducted to examine how enslaved workers lived in their quarters and modified these spaces to suit their needs. Just as written sources indicate that enslaved people made modifications to barracones, I reasoned that they acted in a similar vein in the bohíos of the El Padre slave village. A second but equally important objective was to evaluate the extent to which the enslaved community at El Padre participated in independent economic activities. The independent economy included activities such as producing food for themselves and for sale to others, raising livestock, producing finished goods (for example, baskets, furniture, or pottery), marketing their own products, and consuming or saving the proceeds obtained from these activities. Historians Ira Berlin and Philip Morgan (1991:1) advocate that these independent economic activities "offered a foundation for the slave domestic and community life, shaping the social structure of slave society, and providing a material basis for the slaves' distinctive culture." This slave or internal economy can also be viewed as a way in which enslaved people undermined the institution of slavery (Schlotterbeck 1991:170). Archaeological investigations of former slave quarters provide a means to document and interpret aspects of the internal economy. Archaeological findings of this economy include evidence of craft production, gardens, animal pens, and storage areas for food and personal possessions, and purchased personal and household items. Such findings allow us to see enslaved people as both producers and consumers within the internal economy.

A third objective was to begin the analysis of what Nicholas Thomas (1991:28–29) calls the "mutability of things in re-contextualization... [objects] are never things embodying pure or original templates or intentions." In other words, objects are symbolic forces containing multiple meanings and usages beyond those intended by their creators. Capturing and understanding those meanings is an ongoing challenge to archaeologists.

Excavations of the slave village have confirmed that the slave quarters within the masonry wall enclosure were bohíos. The only archaeological traces of the former bohíos are postholes (holes dug to support wooden posts in a frame structure) cut or driven through limestone bedrock below the soil layers. Plotting each posthole on a map and connecting the dots representing the postholes until a pattern emerges contribute to determining the sizes and shapes of the bohíos. More than one hundred postholes have been recorded from the site, and the posthole patterns indicate three complete structures measuring approximately 16.2 by 23 feet and two partial structures, whose sizes and shapes are indeterminate until additional excavations are undertaken. The structures are located very close to one another, so it is difficult to identify where one structure ends and another begins.

The close proximity of the structures to one another makes the prospect of backyard gardens unlikely. Provision gardens were possibly located elsewhere within the slave village or on another area of the plantation. Many Cuban planters reserved 1 caballería (33.6 acres) for the cultivation of crops such as yucca, malanga, sweet potatoes, or plantains, used as slave food (González Fernández 1991:173). Surplus food was perhaps sold or traded.

Meat, on the other hand, may have been a scarce food resource at the El Padre slave village. Food remains recovered archaeologically are usually reliable indicators of the approximate amount of meat consumed, but in the case of the El Padre slave village, fewer than one hundred fragments of animal bones have been recovered. Unfortunately, this sample is too small to be statistically valid for zoo-archaeological calculations for estimating the amount of consumable meat or the contribution of meat to diet. The small amount of animal bone is surprising because the coffee plantation also included a stock-raising farm. Perhaps the small amount of recovered animal bone is an indication that enslaved people had little or no access to livestock raised in the adjacent potrero. Most of the identifiable bone is pig (*Sus scrofa*), an animal typically raised in house or barnyard situations and not herded like cattle (*Bos taurus*), sheep (*Ovis aries*), or goats (*Capra hircus*) (Reitz and Wing 1999:285–286). Therefore, the recovered food remains were more likely from slave-owned animals than from those on the stock-raising farm. Trash deposits containing large amounts of organic refuse have not yet been uncovered at the El Padre slave village, however, so any definitive statement regarding slave diet must await additional excavations.

Artifacts indicate the kinds of objects enslaved people produced or acquired. From written sources alone, it is often difficult to document items acquired through informal trade networks. On many of the British islands, enslaved people traded items through institutionalized markets typically held on Sunday (figure 8.2). These markets are well studied in Jamaica (Mintz 1974), Antigua (Gaspar 1985), and Montserrat (Howson 1995), but the ability of enslaved laborers to buy and sell items was much more restricted in Cuba than on other Caribbean

FIGURE 8.2

A post-emancipation Afro-Jamaican market. Note the abundance of pottery for sale.
Courtesy National Anthropological Archives, Smithsonian Institution, 92-2462.

islands. Provision-ground products had a limited market and were
often sold to the plantation itself (R. Scott 1985:149–150). Similarly,
enslaved people could purchase some items from the plantation, usually from plantation stores established to sell goods to the slave community. These stores are better documented for the second half of the
nineteenth century than for the first and were apparently restricted to
large sugar estates (R. Scott 1985:184), so it is unclear to what extent
similar stores existed earlier, and on coffee plantations. One clue
comes from an account of a traveler to Angerona in 1828, when it was
a coffee plantation. The Reverend Abiel Abbott (1829:141) made the
following observation:

> It is the maxim with the proprietor that negroes should have
> money and spend it. To encourage the latter part of his
> plan, he furnishes a shop in [an] apartment of the building
> next to the mill, with everything they wish to buy that is
> proper to them; cloth cheap and showy, garments gay and
> warm, crockery; beads; crosses, guano, or the American

palm that they make neat hats for themselves, little cooking
pots & &. He puts everything at low prices, and no peddler is
permitted to show his wares on the estate.

It is impossible to say without additional references to other plantations whether the plantation shop was a widespread institution on
Cuban plantations during the first half of the nineteenth century or
unique to Angerona. Nevertheless, Abbott's description offers useful
insights for understanding Cuba's slave economy in several ways: First,
it identifies some of the objects enslaved persons purchased on Cuban
plantations, both those that are likely to be preserved in the archaeological record—beads, ceramics, iron kettles, crosses—and those that
are unlikely to be recovered archaeologically, such as cloth and palm
hats. Second, it indicates another source for slave-purchased goods—
the traveling peddler. Third, the selection of items made available to
enslaved people was influenced to some extent by slaveholders or peddlers' stereotyped notions of slave tastes. Therefore, the degree of slave
choice in making purchases was perhaps very limited. Some archaeologists have suggested that enslaved persons selected certain styles of
mass-produced ceramics because their aesthetic qualities were similar
to those of Africa (e.g., Wilkie 1999), but the Abbott description suggests that such interpretations may need rethinking.

Despite the utility of Abbott's description of slave-purchased
objects, it provides a lens into only one kind of economic exchange in
Cuba's slave economy—the plantation shop. Presumably, there was a
range of economic exchanges, including purchasing from traveling
peddlers and rural stores and exchanges with other enslaved people.
Objects available from a plantation shop were most likely those that
met with the slaveholder's approval. Yet archaeological investigations
at the El Padre slave village have yielded remains of items that slaveholders were unlikely to have approved of, such as bottles for alcoholic beverages. According to Laird Bergad (1990:238), authorities in
Matanzas Province complained constantly about enslaved persons purchasing liquor illegally.

Tobacco pipes also occur in high quantities at El Padre, and like
alcoholic beverages they were not provisioned to the enslaved community. All the pipes were imported, mass-produced items, probably man-
ufactured in the Cataluña region of Spain (Arrazcaeta Delgado 1987;

FIGURE 8.3

Pipe bowl fragments used by enslaved workers at Cafetal del Padre.

figure 8.3). Maroon sites have also yielded both locally made and imported pipes. The latter are believed to have been purchased from rural stores when the Maroons were enslaved (La Rosa Corzo and Pérez Padrón 1994:128).

Many objects recovered from El Padre, such as English tableware, blue glass beads, and bone buttons, are remarkably similar and, in some cases, identical to artifacts found at slave sites both in the United States and elsewhere in the Caribbean. Ceramics, both British and Hispanic, are the most numerous artifacts. Only two sherds of hand-built pottery comparable to either colonowares (Ferguson 1992) or Afro-Caribbean wares (e.g., Armstrong 1999) have been identified.

With only two fragments, it is not possible to make a case for slave production of pottery at El Padre. It was perhaps unnecessary for enslaved workers to make their own pottery because a wide variety of utilitarian Hispanic earthenwares was available. The absence of pottery making among slaves at El Padre may also speak to slave demography in Cuba and sex ratios at El Padre. The production of Afro-Caribbean wares has been generally attributed to females. The slave trade to Cuba was heavily oriented to the procurement of males (Bergrad, García, and del Carmen Barcia 1995:27). Coffee plantations tended to have more balanced sex ratios than did sugar plantations, but enslaved men generally outnumbered enslaved women about two to one (González Fernández 1991:171). Stock-raising farms and some sugar plantations were known to have only enslaved men (Moreno Fraginals 1978:2:39; Paquette 1988:60).

Household and personal objects including ceramics, iron kettles, beads, tobacco pipes, brewed beverages, and a few decorative items, such as a metal fragment from a parasol, attest to the fact that the enslaved community participated in the internal economy as consumers. It is unclear how the slave community was able to earn money to purchase these items or to produce items to barter for them. Gardening and raising backyard animals (chickens and pigs) may have been the primary ways slaves produced commodities for trade. Craft production offered another possibility. Although the archaeological evidence of craft production is slim compared with that from many other sites of the African diaspora, two artifacts are suggestive of these activities. First, archaeologists have recovered scrapers, made from broken bottle glass and associated with woodworking or splitting canes for basketry. Slaves may have produced basketry, which leaves little archaeological residue, and references to enslaved Cubans making hats and other items from palm support this possibility. Second, archaeologists have recovered pipe bowl fragments, possibly used in craft production. The interior surfaces of several of these fragments exhibit wear consistent with that found on artifacts used for smoothing or polishing materials such as wood, bone, hide, or possibly pottery.

Perhaps the most curious artifacts recovered from the El Padre slave village are ceramic disks (figure 8.4) measuring 8 to 15 millimeters (slightly smaller than a US dime to the size of a nickel). Eight have been recovered from the slave village and another one from a special-use building close to the slave village (see figure 8.1). The disks were made by smoothing the edges of broken pottery into rounded forms. In addition to the nine disks recovered so far, there are several ceramic

FIGURE 8.4

Ceramic disks from Cafetal del Padre.

fragments, indicating that someone began smoothing the edges but did not complete them. Ceramic disks similar to ones from El Padre have been recovered from the southern United States (e.g., Russell 1997:75), Jamaica (Armstrong 1990:137–138), and Montserrat (Pulsipher and Goodwin 1999:17, 30 n. 57). Archaeologists have interpreted these artifacts as gaming pieces. In the Caribbean, they are associated with games of chance. Lydia Pulsipher and Conrad Goodwin (1999:30 n. 57) describe a gambling game that modern Montserratians call "Chiney Money." In this game, a player throws three ceramic disks on a table, and the arrangement in which the pieces land determines the thrower's score: 3, 17, or 18.

How these ceramic disks were used in Cuba is unknown. Elsewhere I suggest that these disks may have been used in divination, because throwing objects (for example, cowries, beads, or seeds) and using the arrangement in which the objects fall to determine a course of action is a key principle of divining in African-influenced religions in the Americas (Singleton 2001c). I have also observed practitioners of the Afro-Cuban religion Santería using comparable objects in this way. Similar disks are found in other archaeological contexts not related to Africa or the African diaspora, however. Therefore, the disks are like other artifacts previously discussed in that the interpretation of their use is likely to vary from setting to setting.

The ceramic disks, tobacco pipes, and ceramic and glass bottles that once contained alcoholic beverages are suggestive of slave recreational activities and perhaps religious activities as well. José Antonio Yarini, a Cuban slaveholder, observed enslaved Cubans on his sugar plantation using "a bottle of brandy, a pipe with tobacco, a cudgel belonging to a former overseer, and rooster feathers" in a funeral offering for a deceased slave (Barcia Paz 1998:27, my translation). While claiming that these items were used in religious practices requires finding them in a context suggestive of a religious offering, Yarini's description reminds archaeologists that many objects recovered from slave sites had uses other than what might appear to be obvious.

The archaeological research at the slave village at El Padre is continuing, but already it has produced primary information on how the enslaved community lived within the wall enclosure. Detailed information on slave houses, personal and household objects, or recreational activities would not have been forthcoming from other sources. The slave community found ways to supplement its meager plantation rations and to participate in the internal economy as both producers and consumers. Although the wall enclosure was most likely built to constrain their activities, enslaved workers at El Padre were engaged in many of the same activities as enslaved workers elsewhere in the Caribbean and the Americas.

CONCLUSION

Archaeology has a definite place within the scholarship of the African diaspora. It offers us a means with which interpretations of living conditions, everyday life, power relations, and constructions of identity, to name just a few topics, become possible. Given the preliminary nature of the preceding case study, only slave living conditions and everyday life have been addressed, with a few cursory insights into the power relations. At this stage of research, little can be said about the use of material culture and identity formation at the El Padre slave village. The value of any archaeological study, however, is dependent upon its interpretative potential, and the interpretative potential of archaeology relies upon ethnographic sources, whether firsthand accounts of people who made observations when the site was occupied or oral historical sources. Martin Hall (2000) examines the relationship between the material world and the ways in which people express themselves verbally, including voices that appear hidden from the writing of people in power. Without words, it is difficult, but not impossible, to interpret things. The relationship between words and things is rarely straightforward; they often contradict each another. Taken together, however, words and things produce narratives of the past that complement each other in unexpected ways.

A historian surveying written records is unlikely to choose Santa Ana de Viajacas as a case study on Cuban slavery because there are so few references to the enslaved community. As an archaeologist, I chose this site because of all the sites I visited, about twelve in all, Cafetal del Padre had the most impressive ruins and the wall enclosure around the slave village piqued my curiosity. Additionally, surveyors who have made maps of the area in the past eighty years must have been equally impressed with the ruins, because Cafetal del Padre shows up on modern maps, whereas other coffee and sugar plantations in the area, many that were historically more important or better known, do not. Despite the opposing differences in the selection criteria between history and archaeology, my choice of the El Padre slave village has heightened our understanding of Cuban slavery in the first half of the nineteenth century. From an archaeological viewpoint, El Padre has a great story to tell even in the absence of words, for the site speaks to the oppressiveness of plantation slavery and the subtle ways in which enslaved people attempted to overcome it.

In spite of "the archaeologist's sadness" (limitations of material remains), we are often in a better position than ethnologists to investigate African influences in the formation of African American cultures, as well as processes of creolization. Archaeologists can access sites on both sides of the Atlantic that can provide insights into material manifestations of African and diasporic cultures. However, archaeologists

should not continue to follow the flawed methodological path of pro-
jecting the present onto the past that was begun by Herskovits and his
students, although we often have to begin with present-day observations to start the process of unraveling the past. We also need to
become knowledgeable about African archaeology of the second mil-
lennium A.D. At the same time, we must come to realize that all we
might ever be able to say about a particular artifact or practice is that
it represents what was at one time an African custom from either the
area where enslaved people were drawn or where their captors once
lived. Given this prospect, students of the African diaspora need to
evaluate those situations in which African data are most useful for
interpreting diasporic communities and those situations in which they
are not. It is clear that we can no longer rely on essentialist notions of
culture and identity and instead must generate models at least as
dynamic as the historical cultures of the African diaspora.

Notes

1. The African press reported that Samuel Carson was buried in the African
Burial Ground in Lower Manhattan. This was incorrect. Carson's remains were
buried at the Brooklyn Naval Yard Cemetery and were later exhumed from the
Brooklyn site for reburial in Ghana.

2. For reviews that also provide historical information, see Orser (1998),
Singleton (1985, 1991, 1995, 1999a), and Singleton and Bograd (1995).

3. Few archaeologists fit neatly within the polarized camps of the
Herskovits/Frazier debate. The position held by any one practitioner appears to
be more related to the recovery or nonrecovery of artifacts suggestive of an
African heritage than to a firm commitment to either side of the debate (see
Singleton 1998 for further discussion of this point).

4. Archaeologists' search for Africanisms suffers from the same methodological flaw as did the work of Herskovits and more recent anthropologists and historians: uncritically using twentieth-century ethnographic data to interpret the past.
I discuss this point in greater detail in another section of this chapter.

5. My use of the term *cultural identity* refers to any special group identity. It
can and does refer to ethnicity, particularly when I discuss specific African cultural
groups. I also use it to refer to specific groups of the African diaspora, including
slave, Maroon, free, and post-emancipation communities.

6. This major change in archaeological thinking has resulted in three simultaneous and somewhat interrelated developments: (1) perspectives that view objects as commodities that have led to the reexamination of trade and other exchange systems in colonial situations (e.g., Appadurai 1986; Thomas 1991); (2) studies of artifact style in social communication and in maintenance of social boundaries (e.g., Conkey 1990; Starke 1998); and (3) critiques of the use and abuse of archaeology to establish the origins, particularly national origins, of present-day ethnic communities (e.g., Graves-Brown, Jones, and Gamble. 1996; S. Jones 1997; Kohl and Fawcett 1995).

7. Enrique Alonso collected handcrafted pipes from Maroon sites in Pinar del Río (the westernmost province of Cuba) that imitate English and Dutch white clay pipes instead of African forms or design motifs (Enrique Alonso, personal communication 1997).

8. Agorsah (1996) has launched a spirited attack on the failure of both Americanists and Africanists to recognize the dual character of the archaeology of the diaspora, making it necessary for data collection to take place on both sides of the Atlantic. Additionally, he recommends collaboration and exchange among both groups of scholars and urges Africanists to go beyond ceramic sequences and consider topics such as family, gender, race, or power relations to inform diaspora research (Agorsah 1996:322). The reality of developing an archaeology of the Black Atlantic is much more complicated than Agorsah presents in his essay, however. Many areas of West and West Central Africa are still virtually unknown archaeologically, and archaeologists must begin with the task of establishing regional chronologies and ceramic sequences. Volatile politics prevent archaeologists generally, and particularly expatriates, from working in many areas, including Sierra Leone, Liberia, Nigeria, and Democratic Republic of the Congo. Finally, local African archaeologists whose work often goes unacknowledged conduct important research under extreme difficulties and with inadequate funding, equipment, and libraries. Unfortunately, most of this work does not get published. The challenges facing the development of an archaeology of the Black Atlantic are enormous, but this goal is certainly more attainable than either Africanists or Americanists could have imagined twenty years ago.

9. Essentialist concepts are so much a part of archaeological practice that it is unlikely that any approach is completely free of them, but some avenues of inquiry are less essentialist than others.

10. Ferguson's use of "African grammar" is very problematic, and on one level it is the ultimate essentialist characterization of cultural identity (but see

Sally Price and Richard Price's chapters in this volume). However, I do see his effort to provide an analytical framework within which to interpret a variety of artifacts as these pertain to ethnic symbols and style as a major step forward from some of the more static approaches still evident in archaeological literature. For this reason, I discuss his work here under an alternative to essentialist notions of cultural identity.

11. Mark Leone (1982:743) observed that archaeologists tend not to accept all of structuralism but accept two basic assumptions: (1) "all objects in a particular culture are equal with respect to overall organization and coherence of the total structure of that culture"; and (2) "while the details and particulars of a past culture may be lost, the principles of that organization, or structure may be suggested by what remains." Unfortunately, because Ferguson does not tell us how he is using structuralism, we must assume that his work is informed by these two basic tenets.

12. Unlike Ferguson, Joyner admits to the limitations of creolization theory in the study of slavery. "Other influences were undoubtedly present and sometimes predominated," he writes, wishing to stress that "creolization is not the whole story of slavery" (1984:xxi–xxii).

13. I am very grateful to Barcia for sharing this information with me, as well as bringing other related documents to my attention.

Part III. The Place of Blackness

9

Manhattan Africans

Contradiction, Continuity, and
Authenticity in a Colonial Heritage

Sabiyha Robin Prince

For many today, the quintessential images of New York City's black
population come from twentieth century Manhattan's Harlem. But the
black movement to Harlem by the early twentieth century was only the
continuation of a migration in which whites forced blacks northward up
the island over two and a half centuries. The first free black settlements
in the seventeenth century and the establishment of the African Burial
Ground began this trend. With each movement of black people out of
an area, new residents erased their history there, sometimes deliberately,
other times incidentally.

—*Leslie Harris,* In the Shadow of Slavery

Black Americans were scarce in Dominica, and Lillian steered clear of
them in America at first—the urban, east-coasters with their loudness and
swaggering, their shoulder-chip and posturing, and their undecipherable
English. She had been told by her aunt that West Indians had nothing in
common with American Blacks, not even the experience of slavery....At
first Lillian took her aunt's analysis to heart, but it only took some supple-
mental reading to her inadequate history textbooks for her to learn....It
was not a lightbulb that went off in her head with realization, it was an
explosion that changed the landscape of her assumptions about her
history for the rest of her life....That explosion cleared away enough of
the historical rubble in Lillian's head for her to see.

—*Marie-Elena John,* Unburnable[1]

The dispersal of African people associated with the transatlantic slave trade was a monumental occurrence in human history. Not only do the events surrounding the African diaspora continue to shape the experiences of black people everywhere, but right now they have also let loose a wave of economic, environmental, and geopolitical reverberations that technological developments and accelerated global connections ensure will affect all people around the world.

Scholars have looked at this phenomenon extensively. Sociologists, educators, artists, social workers, and researchers in communications and the law have joined the historians and anthropologists who study the African diaspora. Whether the focus is Belize, Haiti, Brazil, Cuba, Jamaica, the United States, or elsewhere, music, religion, language, and kinship are among the topics that have most captured the attention of researchers (Bennett et al. 2003). Included among the many recent studies are an ethnographic analysis of a self-segregated "African village" in the southern United States (K. Clarke 2004), an examination of how the study of the African diaspora can challenge powerful institutions and prevailing epistemologies (Davies et al. 2003), and continued studies into how the African heritage shapes New World black identities and cultural practices (S. Walker 2001).

While much work has been done on the topic, the filtering down to the grassroots level of information about the cultural and historical linkages between Africa and its New World descendants in the United States needs to occur in more substantive and meaningful ways. The example of New York City and its African heritage is a case in point. After more than twenty years of interacting with native and transplanted New Yorkers and ten years of ethnographic research in New York City, I have observed a paltry degree of awareness about the presence of Africans in the city during the colonial period. This perceived gap in understanding reflects a larger problem, the inadequate implementation of multicultural school curricula that extends beyond the boundaries of New York State. But something very specific is transpiring as well.

The dearth of knowledge about the extensive, early history of Africans in the city first became apparent to me when I attended Marist College in New York's mid-Hudson Valley in the 1980s. A large number of the African American students I befriended and shared ideas with as an undergraduate were New York City residents, many also from low-income communities. Poking fun at all things southern was a habitual practice among these young New Yorkers, who saw the region as a stronghold of ignorance and racism. Expressions of anti-southern chauvinism were commonplace, and in discussions of African American history with fellow students, I frequently encountered the narrow association of slavery with the southern United States. On one occasion, in casual conversation, Brooklynite Elgin Wright laughingly recalled a schoolbook he read as a child that pictured slaves laboring in Washington, DC, my hometown. The gist of his remark was that Washington, DC, had slaves and New York did not, and that fact showed how backward Washington, DC, was.

At that time, both Wright and I were unaware that his beloved Big Apple also had an extensive history of African slavery, and our misconceptions were not simply a matter of youthful ignorance or regional prejudice. I have encountered similar ideas in discussions with mature, educated professionals, as well as with undergraduates attending my courses on racism at American University in Washington, DC Despite the tremendous scholarship on the subject, diverse groups of people are astonished to hear about the extensive rates of slave ownership in New York City during the colonial period and about Manhattan's experience with slavery.

Given this backdrop, and with both interdisciplinary inquiry and public anthropology in mind, this chapter looks at the stories of Africans and their descendants in New York City during the seventeenth and eighteenth centuries. In picking up the mantle of such pioneering scholars as James Weldon Johnson (1930), Edgar McManus (1966), and Roi Ottley and William Weatherby (1967), as well as authors of more recent studies on the struggles of black New Yorkers during the colonial and revolutionary periods,[2] this chapter focuses primarily on the political economy of African and African American life in New York City[3] between the 1630s and late 1700s. This focus involves a consideration of black labor and its broader implications, as well as black responses to enslavement and inequality. Economic relations were important because the very presence of black women and men hinged upon the work they provided to the burgeoning colony. Their labor was coveted and abused, and the dominant group also defined blacks within a framework centered on the work in which they engaged.

This history of the early presence of Africans and their descendants in New York City provides us with a different way of thinking about black, urban migration and the peopling of New York City. Common narratives involve blacks migrating to northern cities from southern states or immigrants coming to the United States from the Caribbean, South America, and more recently Africa. The recountings of this chapter involve movement from the bottom of Manhattan to the top of the island. The chapter also highlights the Caribbean, European, and non-English-speaking heritages of African Americans born on US soil.

Contemplating these political economic conditions and contradictions also heightens awareness of what is distinct about the contours of racialization in the United States. Temporal and spatial specificities contribute meaning and texture to notions of blackness in the African diaspora. The distinct ways in which race has been structurally, ideologically, and performatively constructed, as well as the specifics of the US demographic landscape, set the experiences of African-descended people in the United States somewhat apart from their Caribbean and South and Central American counterparts, who, by and large, belong to the racial majority in their countries of origin.

The struggle for self-determination and community were important motivations for colonial Africans and their descendants. The ways racial and class inequality affected New York's first blacks establish a strong link between the past and the present. This chapter discusses diachronic connections between colonial Africans and blacks in New York City today. These areas of inquiry foster further analyses of the link between racialized processes of social construction and issues of visibility and authenticity. This focus indicates that the fundamental contributions of African peoples to the growth and development of New York City are not matched by the same level of public attention. There is a dearth of statues, museums, and other commemorative spaces acknowledging this important history.

With a primary focus on political economy and the themes of continuity, contradiction, and authenticity, this chapter also speaks to the analytic tensions over questions of derivation or originality in African

American culture. A recurring theme in a number of studies is the extent to which African descendants in the New World are culturally similar to or different from Africans in Africa. The fact that some chapters of this volume address the decades-old debate initiated by Melville Herskovits, E. Franklin Frazier, and others about the extent to which African American culture was uniquely American or derivative of African origins attests to the persistence of this concern in studies of the African diaspora. Here, I discuss decisive past experiences of Africans in this specific place, and I view much of these findings as parts of Africa's cultural and experiential legacy in the United States. The data I present on Africans in colonial New York City also speak to the so-called Herskovits-Frazier debate.

Finally, this chapter is informed by the idea that local populations need to have better access to and receive greater benefit from the information gathered by academics and disseminated, all too frequently, only within the academic realm.[4]

THE POLITICAL ECONOMY OF RACE AND AFRICAN ENSLAVEMENT IN EARLY NEW YORK

Pictures of dark laborers on southern plantations commonly spring to mind when Americans are asked to visualize the existence of Africans in the colonial United States. Research on the antebellum period has focused much of its attention on the South, and this region dominates depictions of early black history and slavery in US popular culture as well. In our historical memories and vivid imaginations, there are no northern equivalents to Uncle Tom or Kunta Kinte, and few are aware that Connecticut, Pennsylvania, New Jersey, Rhode Island, and other northern states used black captives as unpaid laborers during both the colonial and revolutionary periods. In terms of a wide and even diffusion of scholarly findings, northern enslaved Africans have come in under the historical radar screen.

The search for Africanity in New York City history is a journey that takes us beyond Queen Mother Moore[5] and Marcus Garvey to the core of New York City's economic and political history, exemplifying diasporic linkages in the process. The African presence in the city can be traced as far back as the seventeenth century. Aside from a handful of Spanish- and Portuguese-speaking black explorers,[6] the first group of

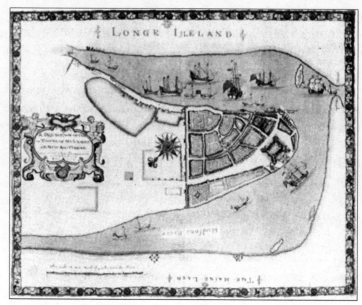

FIGURE 9.1

A map of lower Manhattan Island entitled "A Description of the Towne of Mannados or New-Amsterdam" from circa 1661. Original in color. By permission of the British Library, shelfmark Maps.K.Top.121.35.

African inhabitants of "New Amsterdam," as New York was called during Dutch colonial rule, were women and men who had been born on the continent but arrived via the Caribbean.

In 1621, after much competition, the Dutch West India Company was contracted to create the New Amsterdam settlement. Four years later, the Dutch presence was bolstered by the arrival of soldiers and other representatives of the Netherlands-based trading company (Hodges 1999). The first set of captive Africans arrived after approximately one year and consisted of eleven men and one woman taken from Spanish ships by privateering kidnappers (Hodges 1999). These people were "Atlantic Creoles," a term connoting multilingual individuals of mixed European and African backgrounds who lived in North American port towns and African coastal areas (Berlin 1998). "Mixed-race" persons were not uncommon among Atlantic Creoles, and many were brokers in the trade in captive Africans.[7]

These men and one woman became "company slaves," as there was no individual ownership of Africans at that time. John Francisco, Gracia Angola, and Simon Congo were among these captives. After years of legal wrangling, they gained manumission by capitalizing on white skepticism and the soul-searching characteristic of New York Dutch society before slavery became racialized and entrenched. Possessing varied Spanish, Portuguese, and West African surnames, including those apparently derived from their ports of embarkation, these Africans constituted the fledgling black community within New Amsterdam. In time they were joined by other Africans, who as enslaved workers built Fort Amsterdam, constructed roads and homes, and cleared land beyond the immediate boundaries of the nascent settlement that would become the outer boroughs of Brooklyn, Queens, Staten Island, and the Bronx (Dodson, Moore, and Yancy 2000).

Race alone did not determine the unfree status of these first African arrivals, for no New Amsterdam laborer was free at that time (Hodges 1999). Similar to laborers in other colonies, however, white bondspersons could extricate themselves from this system in less time than Africans could, and upon achieving their freedom, whites received assistance in establishing households, the right to bear arms, and other advantages. Some scholars maintain that the differential treatment offered white indentured servants constitutes one of the earliest examples of white privilege in the United States (e.g, Thandeka 1999). While not disputing this characterization, others suggest that this and similar policies were a divide-and-conquer strategy designed to keep workers with similar economic interests from identifying and uniting with one another across racial lines (e.g, Marx 1998; B. Nelson 2001).

It was through a gradual course of political and ideological change that Africans became biologized in a way that initially did not require the language of science. Africans became blacks, and blacks became slaves in a process of social construction rooted first in the desire to emulate the successes that Portugal and Spain had achieved with the trade in captive Africans. Increasingly, emphases on religious difference and the dissemination of dehumanizing stereotypes helped racialize Africans and perpetuate exploitation (L. Harris 2003).

At the outset, New Amsterdam's African population grew in dribs and drabs. The pace of intermittent arrivals dissatisfied Dutch colonists and motivated politicians to speed up the course of action (Hodges

FIGURE 9.2

A late nineteenth-century depiction of captive laborers being auctioned in New York City in the 1650s. From Harper's Monthly Magazine, *1895. Courtesy of Harper's.*

1999). In response, direct trade with Africa was allowed in 1655, and in less than a decade, New Amsterdam became one of the most important slave ports in North America and home of the largest population of slaves in the territory (Hodges 1999; figure 9.2). This status was achieved before the Netherlands lost the territory to the British. By the beginning of the eighteenth century, the African population had tripled to six thousand (Horton and Horton 1997).

Enslaved African laborers were in demand by European and Euro-American inhabitants and anchored the colonization process in the area. Their presence in New Amsterdam and "New York," as it was called during British rule, was ubiquitous. Equally as sweeping were the hazardous conditions the enslaved regularly faced:

> The natural life cycle of enslaved blacks in and around New York was fraught with peril and paradox. Small farm and urban slaveholders meant that few bonds people could expect to live with relatives for much of their lives. Masters regarded children, who constituted as much as 40 percent of all slaves, as unwanted dependents with little work value until after puberty. Pregnant women were regarded with disfavor. At the same time, masters frequently sold children with adults to enhance the deal. Few children lived with either parents after the age of six. Children were over represented in mortality rates. (Hodges 1999:75)

The northern colony's reliance on slave labor was not identical to that of the South, where cotton, rice, and tobacco monocropping predominated. A comparatively greater percentage of New York City households depended upon the work provided by black captives from the colonial period until general manumission in 1827 (White 1991). Numbers remained consistent with those recorded on the first provincial census in 1698, which indicated that 41 percent of all households in the city owned black workers, with an average of 2.1 enslaved persons per holding (Hodges 1999). By the end of the eighteenth century, the city's enslaved population had grown by 22 percent (White 2002). Ownership rates were high, and this fact contrasted greatly with the situation in the South, where a minority consisting of elite households appropriated the labor of captive blacks. Enslaved blacks became the most stable element of New Amsterdam's working class and general population, in part because of relative paucity of European indentured servants available during the Dutch colonial period (L. Harris 2003).

Whereas scholars point to agrarian expertise in South Carolina, Virginia, and elsewhere, enslaved and free African and African Americans in the northern cities worked largely as skilled laborers (Foner 1982; figure 9.3).[8] Enslavement was so widespread in New York, and second only to Charleston, South Carolina, that persons from a huge range of occupations utilized unfree black labor (White 2002). The enslaved worked for small farmers, sea captains, and lawyers. Merchants and craftspeople dominated the assemblage of slave owners. Slavery in New York ended on July 4, 1827, and the city allowed for gradual manumission. Many Africans and African Americans petitioned for their freedom (White 1991). However, prior to slavery's demise, two-thirds of the merchants used captive black laborers. Grocers and other shopkeepers, as well as highly skilled artisans, used Africans and African descendants as both servants and unpaid apprentices (White 1991).[9] In addition,

> slave masters in New York also devised another way to profit
> from their slaves: they hired them out for day labor on the
> docks of New York City, or to those who needed skilled labor
> for only a few days or weeks. By 1711, the Meal Market on
> the east side of Manhattan had become a daily fair for hiring
> slaves. Wealthier whites in Dock Ward sometimes held
> groups of slaves on consignment, gambling on the possibil-
> ity that there would be a need for slave labor in the city or
> the colony from which they could benefit. While awaiting
> buyers, slave holders hired out these consignment slaves for
> day labor, thus generating income even if a sale did not take
> place.... Because of the types of labor usually needed, mas-
> ters more often hired out slave men than slave women.
> Some slaves, such as Jack, owned by the Lloyd family of Long
> Island, lived in New York City practically as free men, hiring
> themselves out and returning part of their wages to their
> owners. (L. Harris 2003:31)

Within this occupational scenario, blacks labored as fishermen,

FIGURE 9.3
A black laborer during the colonial period. From the Collection of the New-York Historical Society. Negative No. 51254.

domestic servants, brewers, goldsmiths, coopers, waiters, hairdressers, shoemakers, musicians, tanners, bakers, farmers, laundresses, and millers, among numerous others jobs. Some skills were acquired in West Africa, and others were learned through the remunerated and unpaid work black women and men did for whites. New Amsterdam's first black residents hailed from urban areas, such as Luanda, Angola, that had an active market economy, and this fact contributed further to the diversity of colonial Africans' laboring capacity.[10]

UNDOING THE SUPPRESSION OF COLONIAL AFRICAN HISTORY

The effacing of colonial Africans from New York's public history does not just disregard the substantial hand this population had in shaping the culture of the city, one of the most crucial urban centers in the United States and the world. The exclusion of the darker faces that hawked their wares from street carts, drank ale in taverns, worked the docks, edited newspapers, and fought against raging mobs during the Draft Riots of 1863 also distorts the fundamental truth. Disregarding how African enslavement was among other transformative events —such as the onset of industrial production and the massive incorporation of immigrants from Europe during the nineteenth century— that contributed to the very essence of New York City's contemporary imagining and becoming creates an image rooted in historical fiction.

The 1991 (re)discovery of the African Burial Ground gave a voice to those Africans who were ever-present on the urban colonial- and revolutionary-period landscapes. Workers constructing a federal building in Lower Manhattan unearthed remains of a seventeenth-century cemetery where approximately 20,000 people—primarily people of African descent but also paupers and prisoners of the Revolutionary War— were buried (Hansen and McGowan 1998). Hodges (1999) describes the cemetery, established in the 1630s and utilized until the 1780s, as the spiritual center of the black community across this extended period of time.

Individuals were found buried with cowrie shell ornaments, Andinkra symbols,[11] and other objects that attest to their West African beliefs and practices (figure 9.4). The analysis of the remains was preceded by controversy, first, over whether construction would be halted to preserve the site and, second, over what research entity would be given the rights to house and study the remains of these early New Yorkers. Segments of African Americans organized and were vociferous in their demands that researchers recognize the academic and spiritual significance of the place for members of the black community and treat the remains of their ancestors with the proper reverence. The archaeological find and ensuing conflict received a significant amount of media attention,[12] and as a result of the imbroglio, the public helped shape the course and direction of the project. The remains of four hundred people were disinterred, and research strategies were altered, based on feedback garnered from task forces and community coalitions that positioned themselves for a "collaborative power play" (LaRoche and Blakey 1997:85).

FIGURE 9.4

A funeral at the African Burial Ground depicted in the painting The African Burial Ground, by Charles Lilly. Art and Artifacts Division, Schomburg Center for Research in Black Culture, The New York Public Library, Astor, Lenox and Tilden Foundations.

When the analysis of the remains began in 1993 under the leadership of African American anthropologist Michael L. Blakey, the project design unveiled a focus on three particular categories of information: the populational and geographical origins of the deceased; the morbidity and mortality of the dead, most of whom were enslaved Africans; and the "biocultural transformations" associated with the transition of Africans into North American–identified blacks. A fourth and final area of inquiry into markers of slave resistance was added in 1995 (Mack and Blakey 2004). Methods for data analysis, including strategies associated with osteological and dental radiology and chemistry, molecular genetics, history, archaeology, botany, and African art history, were broad and interdisciplinary (Mack and Blakey 2004). In a dramatic fashion, the researchers' work generated some new findings and supplemented what historians had already gleaned about the topic.

The African Burial Ground discovery corroborated that Africans had been concentrated in Lower Manhattan. The physical data also revealed the very poor quality of life of the enslaved women, men, and children. Remains showed signs of poor dental health, systemic infection, trauma, infant mortality, and early death for adults as well as children (Mack and Blakey 2004). According to Hodges (1999), it is also probable that many of the Africans and African Americans who were executed and buried there were innocent of the crimes of which they were accused.[13] One description illustrates the importance of this place for enslaved Africans:

> Blacks buried the vast majority of their dead in the "Negro burial ground." Slaves gathered at the end of the day, after their work was done, to escort the body to the grave. Whites reported hearing drumming and chanting, no doubt African derived, at these independent ceremonies late into the night. By the 1720s, whites had become concerned about these unsupervised gatherings. The Common Council first ruled that funerals had to occur before sunset and then limited the number of mourners who could attend a slave's funeral to twelve, plus pallbearers and gravediggers. (Foote 1991:235)

Burial ground researchers also engaged in some "within-group comparisons" to uncover differences based on age and sex. These studies found that women exerted themselves with heavy labor to the same extent men did; however, the lifting techniques of men concentrated pressure on the middle and lower back. Patterns of spinal degenerative diseases suggested that women apparently carried large loads by balancing items on their heads. A gender analysis also indicated that heavy lifting combined with poor nutrition had a negative impact on maternal and neonatal health (Mack and Blakey 2004; figure 9.5).

The scholarly significance of the burial ground was matched by the political importance of its discovery for segments of the surrounding African American communities, particularly those oriented toward pan-Africanist ideals. The location became a rallying symbol for a people whose historically inspired passions are not stoked by the iconographic symbolism of Ellis Island or the Statue of Liberty. Activism around this place marked the move of African Americans to embrace their ancestral heritage and stake a claim at belonging to the here and now. The site of what some have described as the most important

FIGURE 9.5

Skeletal remains discovered at the African Burial Ground. Photo by Dennis Seckler.
Courtesy of Dennis Seckler and the U.S. General Services Administration.

archaeological discovery in modern North American history is today a
memorial that houses the reinterred remains and presents historical,
biocultural, and archaeological data on the lives of African and
African-descended New Yorkers who lived during the colonial period
(Hansen and McGowan 1998). This recent episode in New York City
history shows the dual purpose of projects such as these: such memorials add to scholarly knowledge and interest and also inform the public

about hidden histories. We will return to this idea and its political implications.

CONFRONTING RACIAL DOMINATION

From the seventeenth century through emancipation and beyond, African-descended people bore the brunt of institutionalized racism and its inconsistencies. Despite attempts at normalcy, Africans found themselves in circumstances that were anything but, and frequently untenable. Circumstances such as a harsh labor environment, inadequate shelter, bad health, close scrutiny, and the unpredictable behavior of European Americans fostered harsh and tenuous conditions for colonial black New Yorkers. Men and women were convicted, and sometimes horrifically executed, for a variety of crimes (figure 9.6). In many instances, the culpability of the condemned was questionable, particularly during the height of hysteria and brutality that followed slave revolts (L. Harris 2003; Hodges 1999). Following one uprising,

> the condemned were executed through a variety of tortures, including "breaking on the wheel," burning, hanging in chains, and hanging by the neck. Bodies and heads were displayed for weeks in an attempt to convince the slaves that the souls of the slain martyrs had not returned to Africa, thus adding further deterrent to similar crimes. (Hodges 1999:67)

The responses of Africans to these difficult circumstances reflected their varied aspirations to live unfettered by the constraints of racial domination. The broader context also affected reactions. By the revolutionary period, for example, when the majority of black New Yorkers were native-born, free and enslaved black men joined ranks with the British in an effort to secure their freedom (Hodges 1999; Pulis 1999c and this volume). The achievement of American independence did not result in the end of slavery, but in the wake of a number of post-independence legal disputes, some blacks migrated to Nova Scotia and then Sierra Leone with other diaspora blacks from Jamaica and elsewhere (Hodges 1999; J. Walker 1976).

Over the seventeenth and eighteenth centuries, segments of Africans and African Americans reacted individually, and others sought collective action. Some blacks grasped impulsively for coping

FIGURE 9.6

African executed by hanging, circa 1750. Courtesy of American Antiquarian Society.

mechanisms, and others responded with premeditated strategies geared toward social change. The organized pursuit of racial justice is encapsulated into two divergent but not mutually exclusive schemes. Some chose "assimilationist-oriented" approaches to obtain their freedom or create more socially just living conditions. Conversion to Christianity was one strategy the enslaved used to obtain their freedom through assimilation into white society (L. Harris 2003).

Numerous blacks responded to domination by turning inward and/or embracing African-based strategies and belief systems. In a number of instances, the latter resulted in the coordination of violent rebellions. Each case culminated with the routing of armed resisters, but the specter of Africans and African Americans conspiring to kill whites instilled a profound and even exaggerated fear in white communities (L. Harris 2003). Besides the New York slave revolt of 1712 (K. Scott 1961), the discovery that African cosmology was implicated in the slave revolt of 1741 heightened the hysteria. Persons attending the trial heard testimony that the Africans planning the uprising met regularly on occasions during which they

> drew a black ring on the floor into which the participants placed their left feet. A bowl of liquor punch was held above their heads, vows were taken and the drink was then

consumed....African spiritual practices fortified the uprising. The participants could not be violent unless they were
united; they could not be joined unless they were believers.
(Wilder 2001:23)

According to Stuckey (1987), the "African circle ritual" was imported from the region of the Congo and continues to influence the
African American sense of form in religion and art. West African belief
systems also inspired the formation of benevolent societies among
Africans and African Americans in colonial New York and other areas
(Gomez 1998; Thornton 1998a). Wilder (2001) maintains that organizations such as the New York African Society for Mutual Relief and
African Brotherhood grew out of the penchant for collective action
emanating from West African secret societies.[14]

Shane White (2002) credits the style and content of African and
African American responses to domination with giving birth to public,
urban culture in the North. Other historians also note examples of syncretism in the collective, public celebrations of enslaved African New
Yorkers. The Pinkster commemoration, for example, originated with
attempts of the enslaved to ameliorate the isolation and difficulty of
rural slavery. Observances of the celebration had spread from Albany
to New York City by the late 1700s (L. Harris 2003). Initially engaged
in by a multiracial group of participants, the event became outdated to
the Dutch and solely associated with black New Yorkers in the post-
revolutionary period (Stuckey 1994; White 1989). Harris (2003:69)
notes that

> slaves combined African and Dutch traditions in their ver-
> sion of the festival. In the spring, they elected a king to a
> three-day reign. As in the Dutch tradition, this king col-
> lected tributes from blacks and whites throughout the city,
> and for the three days of the festival he settled all disputes.
> Additionally, blacks performed a variety of dances during
> the celebration, dances that white observers considered dis-
> tinctively African or "Negro" in nature. These dances con-
> tinued African traditions that emphasized the centrality of
> dance to community and religious celebrations.

Thus, the Pinkster celebration and the artifacts found at the burial ground, as well as the impact of West African culture on the creation of mutual benefit societies, point to a West African influence on New York African American culture. The conscious and subconscious tapping into the aesthetic values, cosmological frameworks, and resistance strategies that journeyed with blacks from their ancestral home constituted a fierce defense of their humanity and their African heritage. These data support critiques of Forrest Wood (1990), and by association E. Franklin Frazier (e.g., 1939), who maintained that European and Euro-American domination obliterated African cultural practices. Wilder (2001) argues that this "improbability perspective" is rooted in a conceptualization of cultures as "undifferentiated wholes" (Mintz and Price 1992) and one that sees African cultural practices as vulnerable to "civilization" because of the inability of their "primitive" forms to withstand the forces of merchant capitalism and racism.

At the same time, it is important to acknowledge that the beliefs and practices of dispersed Africans and their descendants resist romanticized and reductive conflations rooted in simplistic forms of Afrocentrism. The discussion presented here is theoretically grounded in the recognition of the ethnic, phenotypic, historical, and cultural diversity that continues to exist on a continent that is almost four times the size of the United States. With this degree of diversity, the by-product of what was culturally bequeathed to the highly regulated descendants of dispossessed Africans was new and unfixed. Africa's ability to sustain cultural cohesion and memory across modern, diasporic generations has been assaulted and undermined. However, as W. E. B. Du Bois and Carter G. Woodson both argued, African men and women "arrived on these shores with certain established notions...that were neither discarded or erased" (Hine and Jenkins 1999).

Other colonial cultural responses were influenced by realities of human spatial proximity. Africans and African Americans functioned in frequent and close physical contact with European and Euro-American New Yorkers during the colonial and revolutionary periods. Captive laborers often lived in the same houses as those who owned them, and depending upon the industry and specific time period, both free and enslaved blacks could be found working alongside white laborers.

This situation had myriad ramifications, including the interracial cooperation that characterized the 1741 revolt. Whites and blacks were joined by indigenous peoples and others in the planning and carrying out of this uprising. The diverse composition of the rebels may have been the most unsettling aspect of all to the propertied, slave-owning populace. In the wake of these events, a more solidified notion of whiteness began to emerge:

> Ruling whites reacted to the racial fluidity within the con-
> spiracy with terror and mercy, the combination of which was
> meant to produce new discipline and a different solidarity.
> First they demonized the people of European descent who
> were involved in the plot: Hughson [a white involved in the
> revolt] and his ilk were said to be "monsters in nature." The
> very "disgrace of their complexion"; indeed, they were
> "much worse than Negroes." Hughson himself was "blacker
> than a Negro"; he was "the scandal of his complexion" and
> the "disgrace of human nature." Such language predicted a
> violent fate, and four Euramericans were accordingly
> hanged; others were forced into military service in the West
> Indies, and still others banished from the province. Another
> six, however, were quietly and mercifully discharged by the
> court, almost without comment. The decision to let them go
> was expressed in a simple notation in the trial records: "No
> person appearing to prosecute." This, too, was a message for
> and about "white." New York's rulers thus divided and weak-
> ened the proletariat as they unified and strengthened a fic-
> tive community based on whiteness. (Linebaugh and
> Rediker 2000:208–209)

Brief dalliances and long-term unions also occurred across racial lines. Records from eighteenth-century court proceedings attest to the belief that consensual and criminal acts of interracial sex constituted a "volatile fusion of desire and violence" that settlers felt could under-mine the cohesion of households and the community at large (Foote 2004:155). The moral economy of the colony was supported by an informal prohibition against interracial sex and marriage. However, despite the reliance upon hegemonic instead of legalistic controls, interracial commingling occurred in occupational and domestic settings and periodically prompted scandal and heightened scrutiny of public space. According to Foote (2004:155), "the policing of white female sexuality" represented the emphasis white settlers placed on establishing a new society that was racially pure. Black women, on the other hand, remained unprotected from the carnal desires of white men. Taverns were known interracial meeting places and were of great concern for many whites who wanted to see tighter controls over black captive laborers and freed persons (L. Harris 2003). Fraternization coexisted in the midst of all forms of social tensions, and after slavery ended in 1827, multiracial populations resided in the Five Points district and Central Park's Seneca Village. These developments signaled a tension between the tendency of some whites to see blacks as subhuman and the contrasting view of Africans and African Americans as fellow residents and normal citizens.[15]

CONTRADICTION, CONTINUITY, AND AUTHENTICITY: FROM THERE TO HERE, FROM THEN TO NOW

Anthropological fieldwork reinforces the idea that culture, among its many characteristics, is maladaptive, tension producing, and loaded with inconsistencies. The vicissitudes of human behavior also create incongruities in the historical record. The African American experience in the United States is associated with numerous contradictions that have origins in the colonial period. As a most basic and broad example, African peoples have a presence in what became the United States that extends back more than four centuries. The appropriation of black labor and innovation generated tremendous amounts of wealth and laid the foundation for the growth and economic prosperity that has attracted millions of immigrants to the United States from around the world. It is ironic that despising and mistreating blacks became such an important rite of passage out of the liminality of noncitizenhood and nonwhiteness for immigrants, many of whom were able to take a path to "whiteness" (Roediger 1991). New immigrants' internalization of American folk wisdom about supposed African American deficiencies in ability and achievement still occurs and is made possible through mass communications, starting before potential migrants even depart from their home countries.[16]

New York City's specific history is also loaded with racialized contradictions. Since the arrival of the first Africans, the black presence on
the island of Manhattan was almost uniformly associated with the bottom of the island. Harlem was a fashionable suburban retreat for
English, Dutch, and French elites during these times (Osofsky 1966).
Central and West Harlem became predominantly black at the turn of
the twentieth century—in the wake of real estate overspeculation
and the out-migration of southern and eastern European immigrants
—a period marked by significant demographic transitions (J. Johnson
1930).

The idea of blacks being concentrated in Lower Manhattan is at
odds with the contemporary scene because of cultural constructions of
space and place (e.g., Feld and Basso 1996) and the subsequent strong
association of this part of the city with global financial markets, white
gay culture, the counterculture of the East Village, Chinatown, the arts,
and young white professionals or elites. Moreover, the compelling
image of the historical Harlem of the Harlem Renaissance and beyond,
as well as its importance as a symbol for modernization, urbanism, and
African American cultural innovation, frequently supercedes other
paradigms of black belonging in Manhattan. The movement north was
disruptive, but the massive conglomeration of black people in Harlem
would spark an artistic and literary explosion in the 1920s, as well as
organized and influential responses to racism in the form of social
movements and boycotts.

The parts of early New York history reviewed in this chapter reveal
key paradoxes and plot twists that played out in subsequent years.
African and American-born blacks were considered inferior and
treacherous, yet they were simultaneously depended upon to establish
the colony and build the cornerstone to New Amsterdam's security,
Fort Amsterdam. Through both slave labor and remunerated work,
black men honed their skills as artisans, caterers, and builders, only to
be displaced by European immigrants and pushed into more poorly
paid, dangerous, and less prestigious work during the late eighteenth
century (Foner 1982). In the following years, this deskilling process
would make urban African American workers increasingly vulnerable
and isolated. After Harlem emerged as the center of African American
life in Manhattan, blacks were overly policed, severely segregated, and

so poorly serviced that their communities became increasingly viewed as desolate slums, in a process some observers refer to as "ghettoization" (Kusmer 1976; Osofsky 1966).

The formation of black ghettos, while resulting from contradictory processes and ideologies, also resonates in the present because this pattern of movement, from Lower Manhattan and Midtown communities that led to the formation of black Harlem, in this instance, has been played out in various locations across the United States with similar results.[17] This process also shows the vulnerability of urban black populations and the continuation of past practices and patterns. In addition to the persistence of racial inequality, a reliance upon hegemonic underpinnings that buttress racism also shows a diachronic connection. The exploitation of African American workers has been facilitated by the misrepresentations of blacks through the inaccuracies and/or willful oversights of observers. These misrepresentations undermine the symbolic integrity of black populations. Such a trajectory of social construction did not begin with the arrival of African American migrants from the US South in the "Great Migration" north but rather was set into motion during the colonial period.

Implicated in the power relations of the present are additionally problematic epistemologies that historically decontextualize and deauthenticate urban African American populations. Contemporary examples are occurring, many of them emanating from the realm of scholarship. Let two quick examples suffice.

The infamous culture of poverty theory is an example of a modern-day pathologizing model. In its various permutations, it has become very influential and damaging over the past decades as it has informed public policy. Although its originator, Oscar Lewis (1966), intended the theory to be an indictment of policies that ignore the poor, the paradigm was co-opted to argue for a laissez-faire state approach toward populations living in poverty (Mullings 1997). The culture of poverty, a putative scientific designation, becomes a kind of shorthand for working-class "black culture," and that culture, in turn, becomes seen as pathological and the causative agent determining black poverty. Fortunately, there have been many anthropological challenges to the concept (e.g., Leacock 1971; Stack 1974; Valentine 1968). Unfortunately, the concept seems to be reinvented every few years, from Daniel

Patrick Moynihan's *The Negro Family: The Case for National Action* (1965; cf. Rainwater and Yancey 1967) to William Julius Wilson's *The Truly Disadvantaged* (1987, 1991; cf. Newman 1992; Rosenthal 1999). Diagnostically, the culture of poverty and similar approaches are dependent, in part, upon the conceptual removal of African Americans from any larger historical context. The impact of history, economic conditions, and the state are not viewed as key determinants of outcomes. Instead, these factors are replaced by a more nebulous emphasis on "cultural values." John H. McWhorter's book *Losing the Race* is (2000a) a pseudo-scholarly example of this type of analysis. This author is an African American linguist who blames faulty cultural values for the achievement gap between white and African American students in the United States. His method for proving this hypothesis relies heavily upon anecdotal evidence from his upbringing and the African American students he has encountered over the course of his career as a college professor.

Another widely disseminated case from the public realm involves comments made by actor/comedian Bill Cosby on May 17, 2004. Cosby was addressing a gala celebration held in Washington's Constitution Hall by the National Association for the Advancement of Colored People (NAACP) on the fiftieth anniversary of the landmark *Brown v. Topeka* Supreme Court decision. In a disavowal of historical context, Cosby, who holds a doctorate in education from the University of Massachusetts, excoriated African American youths and their parents for essentially betraying the goals and accomplishments of the civil rights movement by their behavior and poor values. Theodore M. Shaw of the NAACP Legal Defense Fund, who followed Cosby to the podium, recalls what Cosby said:

> Unlike the story of Brown, Cosby suggested, this was not about what white people are doing to us; it was about what black people are failing to do for themselves. His remarks excoriated poor black people for their failure to actively raise their children, to teach "knuckleheads" proper English, and for spending hundreds of dollars for sneakers while refusing to spend $200 for the educational package "Hooked on Phonics." Cosby also spoke of "people getting shot in the back of the head [for stealing] a piece of poundcake, and

then we run out and we are outraged." And he wondered
why more people from these communities were not incar-
cerated. "God is tired of you," he quipped, "and so am I."
(T. Shaw 2004)[18]

Absent from this tirade on the poor was any context for the behaviors being described. Cosby also lumped all low-income African
Americans into one dysfunctional and ill-behaved category. I addressed
this approach on a radio program that aired on WPFW, Washington's
Pacifica Network–affiliated radio station. During the broadcast of the
Spirit in Action show, hosted by human rights activist Damu Smith, I criticized Cosby for picking on an easy target, blaming the victim, and not
taking into account the impact of the Reagan Revolution in giving rise
to many of the declining conditions in low-income, urban communities.

Shaw addressed convention attendees after Cosby left the stage and
recounted his response in a *Washington Post* op-ed piece. He said that he

> knew, even before I reached the stage, that Cosby's com-
> ments would be hijacked by those who pretend that racism
> is no longer an issue and who view poor black people with
> disdain. So, departing from my own prepared remarks,
> I embraced the notion of personal responsibility, at the
> same time calling attention to problems faced by African
> Americans that are not self-inflicted.

He continued:

> Predictably, conservatives are applauding Bill Cosby for say-
> ing that the problems of the black community stem primar-
> ily from personal failures and moral shortcomings. But just
> as we in the progressive African American community can-
> not countenance the demonization of poor people, we must
> not cede the issue of personal responsibility to ideological
> conservatives. Most poor black people struggle admirably to
> raise their children well. Parents, including single mothers,
> work for low wages, sometimes in multiple jobs, to support
> their families. Recently Cosby recognized this in a press
> statement in which he emphasized that he was not criticiz-
> ing everyone in the "black lower economic classes" but

intended to issue a "call to action" and to foster "a sense of shared responsibility and action."

Unlike much of the world, we ignore human rights protections against discrimination on the basis of economic status. As a nation, we wage war on poor people in this country, not on poverty. In many ways, we are a nation struggling to maintain our moral compass. Violence and dysfunction in poor black communities are under an especially glaring spotlight. But many of the problems Cosby addressed are largely a function of concentrated poverty in black communities—the legacy of centuries of governmental and private neglect and discrimination. (T. Shaw 2004)

Shaw responded forcefully, fully aware of the tremendous power of what he had heard to bolster racist representations. Cosby's remarks were covered extensively in the print and electronic media. Major media outlets covered stories on his speech, and a number of conservative pundits described as "brave" and "insightful" those views expressed by Cosby that very neatly fit into a neoliberal social policy agenda. One brake on this agenda would be a thorough understanding of historical context, including the enduring colonial legacies.

A ROLE FOR HISTORY

Viewing African American cultures and society outside their broader historical, political, and economic context narrows the lens through which their African heritage is conceptualized. The culture of poverty arguments and the reception of Bill Cosby's remarks constitute the backdrop against which many people at home and abroad conceptually place African Americans. Yet communities can use scholarship to understand the forces that affect their daily lives and to encourage social change in local areas. It is through the public dissemination of research data that activists and other important persons of the past have become household names and are able to inspire social movements today. A similar type of awareness can be fostered by promoting New York colonial history.

Efforts to do this type of outreach have intensified over the past ten years locally and internationally,[19] and information on the efforts of African-descended New Yorkers to resist enslavement, retain their heritage, and achieve some sense of belonging in this New World urban society has been more accessible over the past few years. Largely through the dissemination of African Burial Ground Project data, the idea that slavery in New York City was benign or less harsh than enslavement practices in the US South, the Caribbean, or South America has been invalidated. But even though public involvement and interest in the project shaped its direction, this information is still known in only some quarters. Following the discovery of the African Burial Ground, New York City schools have yet to incorporate the findings of this archaeological site into school curriculum formally. Dr. Sherrill D. Wilson (1994), director of the Office of Public Education and Interpretation of the African Burial Ground, has written about the absence of this history in the public and private school systems. I have learned, in conversations with New York City schoolteachers, that a structured inclusion of data on colonial Africans in New York City school curricula has yet to occur and that many young people are still unaware of the extent to which captive African labor was utilized in New York City. One teacher I spoke with was Elise Mussen, who teaches fifth graders at PS 208 in New York City. In the fall of 2004, she said there was no "set curriculum on teaching kids about slavery in New York City or state for that matter. I did a whole thing on it because…well, it's me teaching the class. I went the extra mile, but it's not like anyone told me to do it or even made me feel like I had to do it."

In addition, the study of Africans and African descendants during New York's colonial period can challenge a number of prevailing views, including those that distance African Americans from their ancestral cultural heritage. This latter chasm is reflected in discursive constructions of diasporic belonging—and non-belonging—coupled with an ambivalence toward things "African," as well as fractious intra-diasporal ethnic politics that often reflect a lack of knowledge of the history of African Americans in New York.

For example, in spite of the ideological and political impact of pan-Africanism, portions of the African American populace remain reluctant to embrace their African heritage with pride and enthusiasm. This alienation orientation is reflected in Keith Richburg's *Out of America* (1997) and other writings. Regarding the masses of African

Americans, this view is fostered by the inadequate dissemination of data on Africa and its connection to the United States, as well as the representation of Africa as a backward and primitive "dark continent" and the dismal socioeconomic status of numerous African nation-states today. (Of course, it is also important to acknowledge some of the significant differences in African and African American cultural practices and political economic conditions, as noted by Richburg, that distinguish these diverse populations.)

These fractious politics have been documented in ethnographic data gathered in New York City. In a few excerpts from *Harlem World*, for example, author John L. Jackson Jr. (2001) presents what he calls the "post-Afrocentric" viewpoints of African Americans whose identity is not grounded in any meaningful conceptual relationship with "African culture." A young black woman of African American and Costa Rican heritage laments: "At least blacks and Latinos can chill. Hang out. Listen to the same music and whatnot. Africans want to be here in their African shit and act like they still in Africa. All they want us for is so they can braid our hair and give us [hair] extensions" (J. L. Jackson 2001:43). Another of Jackson's project participants shares his views on the connection between Africa and African Americans. According to "Dexter," "blacks are most from the south. Most blacks in Harlem is from the south. They don't know a thing about Africa except that it is far and got trees and animals. They can deal with Puerto Ricans" (J. L. Jackson 2001:43).

These two perspectives reveal an alternative to black nationalist and pan-African thought, as well as one type of diasporic fissure. What follows are additional perspectives from black New Yorkers, current and former residents, that demonstrate another type of perceptual rift between African Americans and other members of the African diaspora. These exchanges reveal delegitimizing processes that occur either through African Americans eschewing any identification with Africa and Africans—helped along by the myopic and pejorative views of the continent that originate from above—or, on the other side of the ideological and behavioral coin, through ideas about African Americans being too assimilated to be deemed "authentic" members of the diaspora.

Discursive elements have been recounted by black pan-Africanists,

among other African Americans, who spoke with me about their interactions with and relations to other African peoples. These people have
either been married to or parented by people from African,
Caribbean, or South American countries and communities. They may
also have lived in or traveled frequently to these environments.
According to Ohioan Melba Toure, an event planner and former professional African dancer, African Americans are

> not counted like everyone else. We were stripped of all these
> things. We don't even have any accent. We don't have any
> language. Slang, Ebonics, or poor English. That is it and lan-
> guage really bonds a people together. Gullah [language] is
> an anomaly. We would be them if we were allowed to be. We
> would be counted as authentic members of the diaspora if
> we had been able to maintain the threads of our original
> culture.
>
> We are also complicit in all the policies [of the US govern-
> ment]. They see us in the military and they see us every-
> where. They see that we are complicit in their policies.

This quote reflects a grassroots analytical frame that many Afro-
Atlantic blacks are familiar with. US-born members of the diaspora
are frequently constructed as the stepchildren of the African family. In
interpersonal relations with other members of the black diaspora, it
is not uncommon for African Americans to be "othered" as twang-
speaking, overly Westernized Yankees who are so Americanized that
they are out of touch with the rest of the black world, at best, or a
threat to human decency and security, at worst.

Darlene Belcher was an assistant district attorney in Manhattan
before leaving the city after the terrorist attacks on the World Trade
Center on September 11, 2001. She spoke with me about encountering

> an attitude coming from women from the Caribbean, and
> people from Africa toward black Americans. It is an attitude
> like they think we are so assimilated into this white
> American culture that we don't have any roots. They tend to
> view us like we don't have any connection to our African
> heritage. Sometimes I get the impression—it is almost like

we just combusted into existence right in the US. And that
we don't have any other kind of background.

Some blacks give that off—the impression that they are
just American. They did not evolve from any other culture,
and they don't even desire to trace their heritage. They
don't see their culture coming out of any other groups of
people—they are just American.

Belcher's comments reflect the dual side of this discursive deau-
thentication. She, along with numerous others, has seen that challenges to diasporic belonging can emanate from different sides of the
Atlantic and be framed in diverse forms.

Djimo Carson is a former New Yorker and the child of an African
American mother and an Afro-Caribbean father. He has interacted
with blacks from the Caribbean, including a plethora of extended family members, his entire life. He maintains that

African Americans are looked at by other blacks in the world
as the most Westernized of all. Sure, I am familiar with South
Africa in the fifties. I have seen the photos of blacks looking
all clean in their suits, ties, and western dress, and I know
about the Anglophone blacks of Barbados. My dad is from
there. Still, these people look at us as having no semblance
of African culture.

I have traveled to Martinique, Antigua, Jamaica, Livingston,
Guatemala, and other places in the diaspora to be told time
and time again that I am a Yankee and that I don't know anything about African culture compared to folks from the
Caribbean or Brazil. Although I am an attorney, I learned a
little about this stuff from my undergraduate courses in
black studies and anthropology. These Africans and folks
from the Caribbean are always shocked when I tell them
about the "Hoppin' John" that we eat for good luck on New
Years, the women catching the spirit in the churches, "call
and response," Gullah and anything else I can think of that
shows them there is a connection between African and
African American culture.

Carson said that the sentiment expressed above did not epitomize all his interactions but it was a strong current felt during the years of traveling annually to Barbados. These quotes highlight how essentialism can influence thought processes. In his study of authenticity in African American culture, Favor (1999) notes that being "real" has often been associated with "the folk" more than urban populations. While this idea could factor into the cultural processes that are deauthenticating African American New Yorkers specifically, the notion may also be rooted in the atypical position US African Americans occupy within the African diaspora as national minorities.

CONCLUSION

Inquiries into colonial New York history can foster an interrogation of delimiting ideas of African American diasporic belonging. The discursive, essentializing constructs this chapter presents can be countered, not by arguing for African American authenticity through the listing of African "survivals," but by conceptually restoring Africans to this time period and making this history available to the public in compelling and creative ways. Communities should know that African Americans' association with African peoples has been intimate, uneven, conflictual, and meaningful—hence complex. Enslaved and free blacks remembered and cherished ideas and practices from the continent, but this was not a static process. New World cultural forms emerged, and just as there was and continues to be diffusion, innovation, and other forms of change in Africa, African Americans have adjusted their ancestors' legacies while also formulating ones anew.

The emphasis on renewing interest in the history of Africans in New York City during the seventeenth and eighteenth centuries from the bottom up, moreover, is not intended to be an exercise in promoting racial pride and unity through resurrecting "positive role models" or emphasizing past injustices. This effort does have implications for theory and praxis, however. Rediscovery in scholarly milieus presents a unique opportunity to study social change and chronicle the process through which Africans became slaves, slaves became Negroes, and Negroes became black and/or African American—transitions that involved more than simply being born on US soil.

Scholarship has the power to elucidate contradictions and inculcate the lessons of continuity. Public anthropology, in particular, can expose a mass audience to this heritage and foster a familiarity that rivals the most well-known stories from African American history. There is much in black colonial New York history—despair, struggle, accommodation, defeat, and transcendence—to capture the imaginations of contemporary populations. Greater exposure to the type of research discussed in this chapter can challenge simplistic notions of authenticity and restore Africans to their place in early urban American history. In the end, following this theme of continuity forward, these stories encourage us to catch up with Africans in contemporary New York City.

New York has the largest concentration of African-descended people in the United States and is home to Harlem, a series of communities known around the world as a cogent symbol of African American urban life. Africans born on the continent also call Harlem home, and consistent with the past, they come from different, predominately West African societies. Their contemporary presence in Harlem is not represented only by cab drivers, hair braiders, and street vendors. While conducting my field research in Harlem, I found Africans caring for the sick and working with low-income African American families in social services. They have become involved in the public sector, filling gaps that some Africans Americans feel native-born blacks have largely abandoned (Prince 2004). They have also witnessed the deadly ugliness of racial inequality with the shootings of two unarmed African immigrant workers in recent years. These conditions and occurrences are in great need of anthropological attention. Research is needed not just on the experiences of contemporary African immigrants in New York and across the United States. We have much more to learn about the changing relationships between Africans and African Americans.

Hip-hop performers are teaming up with young African artists. For example, Marie Daulne of Zap Mama has performed with Erykah Badu and Chicago rapper Common. Macy Gray and radical rappers Dead Prez have collaborated with Femi Kuti, the son of the late, internationally known Nigerian performer Fela. In addition, I am encountering increasing numbers of African American students at my university who are the children of one or two parents born in Africa. Their perspectives are not indistinguishable from those of other African Americans, nor are their standpoints equivalent to those of their parents. Rather, these young people operate from a subject position shaped by the immigrant experience, minority status, and the confrontation with racial inequality. Like the African New Yorkers of the seventeenth and eighteenth centuries, these New World Africans are searching for meaning and belonging in a place that simultaneously welcomes and rejects them. These young people may be able to benefit from the actions of other Africans and African Americans who have engaged in resistance, accommodation, the deciphering of mixed messages, and the creative merging of often contradictory values and practices to survive and prosper. Perhaps the history of their predecessors from the colonial period and beyond can be instructive as they engage in this multilayered social process.

Notes

1. This excerpt is from a soon-to-be-published novel. In it, the author, an Antiguan native and Africanist who received a master's degree in development and anthropology from Columbia University, grapples with the themes of resistance, diaspora, identity, and authenticity. She also captures some of the pervasive perceptions and conflicts that can characterize interactions among black people of different nationalities and regions.

2. The exhaustive work of Shane White exposes us to the hardships and victories of black people in this city. His most recent study is on the African Company, a short-lived theater group composed of black actors who performed Shakespeare to multiracial audiences during the 1820s (White 2002). Graham Hodges's (1999) work on African and African American cart men documents some of the earliest battles against occupational segregation in the United States. We learn about process and the intersection of race and class from Leslie Harris (2003), who has looked extensively at African enslavement in New York City from the early 1600s to the signing of the Emancipation Proclamation.

3. Mention of New York City in this chapter refers specifically to the territory now designated as Manhattan. This identification does not apply to areas of Brooklyn, Queens, the Bronx, or Staten Island.

4. Many viewpoints and strategies, too numerous to discuss here, are deemed related to public anthropology. They include addressing social problems, orienting research around community advocacy, and making findings interesting and accessible to grassroots populations. In my own case, for example, I worked as an ethnographer on a community-based project called "Harlem Birth Right,"

which examined the link between social status and pregnancy outcomes (see Mullings et al. 2001).

5. Audley "Queen Mother" Moore was an outspoken civil rights leader and a black nationalist who was a hero in Harlem and a familiar figure to historians. She was born in New Ibéria, Louisiana, on July 27, 1898, and died in 1996 at age ninety-eight. One of her last public appearances was at the October 1995 Million Man March, where she appeared onstage with the Reverend Jesse Jackson and others. Queen Mother Moore befriended such leaders as Marcus Garvey and Nelson Mandela. Former mayor David N. Dinkins, the city's first black mayor, who grew up in Harlem, said that Queen Mother Moore was "an inspiration to a lot of blacks, especially black women."

6. The first nonindigenous inhabitant of Manhattan Island was Jan Rodríguez, a Portuguese-born black man who arrived in 1613 (Hodges 1999). An earlier black visitor was Esteban Gómez, another Portuguese speaker and a navigator. He named Deer River (now the Hudson River) in 1525 (Dodson, Moore and Yancy 2000).

7. See, for example, G. Brooks (1976) for a discussion of female Senegalese slave trade brokers of the eighteenth and nineteenth centuries. These women were often wealthy property owners who lived along coastal areas of this West African territory.

8. To clarify and avoid setting up a false dichotomy, it is important to note that ironworking, woodcarving, and other skills were not uncommon in parts of the South. Moreover, in the rural areas of New Jersey, New York, and other northern colonies, enslaved Africans engaged in farmwork much like their counterparts in the South. The point was not to set up mutually exclusive categories but to note that in this region, a mixed-crop economy ensured diverse agrarian experiences for captive laborers involved in farmwork.

9. According to White (1991), widows constitute an important percentage of slave owners who are severely understudied. Studying them can improve our understanding of the lives of enslaved Africans in colonial New York, as well as uncover key characteristics of how race, gender, and class intersected to shape the experiences of white New Yorkers. On slaveholding widows in general, see K. Wood (2004).

10. This idea relates to another area of invisibility, involving the depiction of Africans as backward and disorganized. Graham Hodges (1999) discusses the areas from which captive laborers were taken and the impact of these locations upon their labor practices, skill sets, and cultural beliefs.

11. Andinkra symbols are associated with the Akan people of Ghana. They

appear on walls, logos, and cloth and represent love, happiness, the oneness of God, and other entities or characteristics to aspire to (Arthur 2001). In addition, African Americans have fostered an interest in the symbols, some using them in Afrocentric design or as tattoos.

12. See, for example, Assael (1993), Cook (1993), and Dunlap (1992).

13. Hodges concludes this in light of the indiscriminate retaliations that followed a wave of slave revolts during the early to mid-1700s. Whites were frightened of both organized attacks and individual acts of violence against owners, and anxieties were running high in New York and New Jersey.

14. Taking his cue from Mintz and Price (1992), Wilder is not discounting the damage that bondage heaped upon Africans' institutional attachments or the severe limitations placed upon cultural and organizational continuity. He recognizes that African "influences did not constitute a transplantation of a culture because they were divorced from the rich institutional fabric of the West African civilizations that produced them" and argues instead that entities such as secret societies formed by black men in colonial New York "were part of a plausible African heritage—the social and intellectual material that can be roughly described as shared by West African peoples in African American culture" (2001:12).

15. See Harris (1999) for a discussion of the denouncement of interracial sexual relations by black and white abolitionists in an apparent attempt to avoid the mob violence for which various antislavery societies had been targeted when racist propagandists accused them of promoting racial amalgamation.

16. Rap videos have been key culprits in the dissemination of stereotypical representations of African Americans abroad. African American women in Johannesburg, South Africa, have told me about being called bitches and "hos" (whores) because South African youths think that these are what black women are called in the United States. A former graduate student who works with "colored" youths in Port Elizabeth, Cape Town, is frequently asked by young people whether any "niggahs" will be visiting her during her stay in South Africa.

17. See Lesko, Babb, and Gibbs (1991) for a discussion of the displacement of blacks in Georgetown, Washington, DC, and the transformation of this port area into a place predominated by white elites.

18. It is also interesting to note how Cosby's comments resemble sentiments expressed by nineteenth-century black elites who worried that whites wouldn't be able to distinguish them from the poorly behaved masses of black "commoners" (Gatewood 1990; Osofsky 1966).

19. Local organizations such as the New York Historical Society, the Gotham

Center, and the Office of Public Education and Interpretation of the African Burial Ground are available as clearinghouses for information on black history in colonial New York. They are engaged in various forms of community outreach to disseminate burial ground findings.

Regarding the global picture, the Slave Route Project, launched by UNESCO in 1994 at the behest of Haiti and many African countries, is another attempt to remedy this shortcoming. The project has two aims: "On the one hand it aims to break a silence and make universally known the subject of the transatlantic slave trade and slavery in the Indian Ocean and Mediterranean, with its causes and modalities, by means of scientific work. On the other hand, it aims to emphasize, in an objective way its consequences, especially the interactions between the peoples concerned in Europe, Africa and the Caribbean" (UNESCO 2000, 2001). For publications from the inaugural session in Ouidah, Benin, see Diène (2001).

10

Collecting Puerto Ricans

Arlene Torres

This chapter examines how cultural identities are constructed, legitimated, and contested in exhibits and related public events at the National Museum of American History at the Smithsonian Institution. More specifically, it focuses on the relationship between museums, ethnography, and ethnographic practices. By documenting, interpreting, and reflecting upon the enactment of class, race, and neocolonial and political ideologies from an insider/outsider perspective, the chapter addresses the ways in which dialogic practices have been incorporated and contained in museum exhibitions and public programs. An ethnography of sorts sets the stage. I begin with a description of media and public events leading up to the exhibit *A Collector's Vision of Puerto Rico*, followed by my participant observations as an anthropologist and consultant to the exhibit. I then focus on two salient events that marked the opening of the exhibit. The first was a gala affair hosted by the National Museum of American History and the governor of Puerto Rico. The second was a public program, *El Carnaval de Ponce*, sponsored in partnership with the Ponce Office of Tourism in Puerto Rico and the National Museum of American History. The exhibit formed part of a larger series, *Encuentros Latino Americanos* (*Latin American Encounters*), at the Smithsonian. Because diverse and often conflicting voices and histories are represented by the objects in the collection, the ways in which individuals and communities engage in dialogue through these very objects demonstrate how museum staff, anthropologists—including me—the viewing public, artisans, artists, and political interest groups, among others, are constitutive of culture. Following the multiple strands of thought and performances engendered by the Teodoro Vidal Collection, we can elucidate the broader historical and scholarly contexts that legitimize and contest how Puerto Ricans collect and are collected, constituted, and represented.

VISIONS OF PUERTO RICO

The Palm Court ice cream parlor on the first floor of the National Museum of American History, normally bustling with tourists, had been transformed into a conference room for the press. "American coffee" had been replaced by Puerto Rico's finest blend, Alto Grande. The museum director, curators, and other personnel associated with the Teodoro Vidal Collection and *A Collector's Vision of Puerto Rico* lingered to field questions by the local press and the Puerto Rican media regarding the exhibit. Spencer Crew, the museum director, formally welcomed media representatives and acknowledged major financial and in-kind donors for the exhibit and related events. These donors included the Puerto Rican Tourism Company, Banco Popular, the newspaper *El Nuevo Día*, American Airlines, and Paradiso Films. Crew then introduced the curatorial staff and briefly fielded questions regarding an exhibit that "features objects, documents and photographs of Puerto Rican history and cultural traditions during the past 500 years" (Office of Public Affairs 1998). Marvette Pérez, Fath Ruffins, and Odette Díaz Schuler, the co-curators, answered questions specifically related to the collection and the exhibit. *A Collector's Vision of Puerto Rico*, housed at the National Museum of American History, and *Colonial Art from Puerto Rico*, on exhibit at the National Museum of American Art, are based on the acquisition of more than 3,200 items donated by the Puerto Rican philanthropist Teodoro Vidal. As a businessman and lay cultural historian, Vidal devoted his life and financial resources to the collection of material culture and to the documentation of Puerto Rican cultural history. Following the completion of his MBA at the Wharton School of Business, University of Pennsylvania, he returned to Puerto Rico in 1954 and served as an aide to the first elected governor of Puerto Rico, Luis Muñoz Marin, at a time when Puerto Rico was embarking upon the development and "modernization" of the island to combat poverty. Vidal traveled throughout the island, the Americas, and Europe to conduct research and obtain the objects now housed at the National Museum of American Art and the National Museum of American History. A portion of his collection remains in Puerto Rico. At present, Vidal is still collecting, documenting, and writing from his home in San Juan, Puerto Rico.

Members of the media proceeded down the hall to the West End gallery to see the installation of a small portion of the collection donated by Vidal. Time and again, the media chose exhibit cases and displays of La Gran Familia Puertorriqueña, El Carnaval de Ponce, and a delightful collection of Puerto Rican handmade toys to serve as backdrops for media photo shoots (Rodríguez Julía 1988; Vidal 1982). On a few occasions on the morning of July 30, 1998, panoramic images of wooden saints caught the eye of a photographer. This scene was in stark contrast to the deluge of flashing cameras as the governor of Puerto Rico, Pedro Roselló, his wife, and curator Marvette Pérez viewed these religious images, dating to the seventeenth century, at the opening reception and gala event that evening.

Amid all the fanfare, I noticed a humble man staring into the cases displaying exquisitely crafted musical instruments. An artisan himself, he clearly marveled at the work of other masters. On opening day, another elderly man pensively stood before the Luis Paret y Alcázar print *Esclava de Puerto Rico* (*A Slave Woman of Puerto Rico*) (plate 6). I asked him what he thought of the exhibit. He backed away. I later learned that he was of Cuban descent, a homeless man who frequented the museum. He never told me what he thought of the collection. I wondered whether he saw an affinity with his recollections of the past as he stood there transfixed by *Isabel O'Daly* (plate 7) by José Campeche (1751–1809), which depicts the daughter of Thomas O'Daly, an Irish engineer who came to San Juan in 1765, in contradistinction to the image of the enslaved woman. The slave shackles displayed there were a powerful reminder of the brutality of Puerto Rico's colonial past.

Interestingly enough, their presence evoked in some a sense of pride, because their struggle had not been forgotten.

Others were pleasantly surprised at the underlying Afro–Puerto Rican theme running through the exhibit. They made note of items ranging from the image of the Miracle of Hormigueros/Our Lady of Montserrat, depicted as a black virgin, to the carnival masks and the music heard at a distance. A student, trained in sociology at the University of Puerto Rico, approached me. She wondered why there were no representations of Taínos, the indigenous people of Puerto Rico. Taíno objects, in her view, should have been displayed in order to fully represent Puerto Rican culture as the synthesis of Spanish, African, and indigenous cultures. A Puerto Rican couple from San Juan, avid collectors of carved *santos* (saints), continuously marveled at the collection and sang Vidal's praises. And then there were the docents. They were well-to-do Puerto Rican women, now living on the outskirts of Washington, DC, caught in webs of signification as they celebrated their Puerto Ricanness in the museum's West End gallery. One docent, upon hearing *una plena* music coming from the speakers above and between the carnival cases, began to dance joyfully. The plena, a genre rooted in Puerto Rican musical traditions, is marked in Puerto Rico as a symbol of Africanness. As she danced, she sought to embody this cultural heritage in gesture and movement (Quintero Rivera and Álvarez 1994). With that same exuberance, drawing our attention to a colonial document in the exhibit, she related to others how her kin were represented there.

Like many others, I was intrigued by how these images, these objects of art and of everyday life, evoked memories, histories yet untold. The splendor, the intricate details, kept summoning remembrances of labor, the labor of my people at once part of this exhibit and so far removed from it. *La Gran Familia Puertorriqueña* (*The Great Puerto Rican Family*), for example, exhibited portraits of Puerto Ricans who appeared to have the kind of socioeconomic resources that could stem the tide of the Depression and who therefore had no need to leave the island during the massive airborne migrations of the 1950s. Yet in their midst, below the main text about this great creole family, was a poignant reminder of race, class, and gendered hierarchies: a photograph of a black servant, a nursemaid perhaps, holding a white infant child. It was easily missed because it did not necessarily form a central part of the panorama of photos on the wall. This image was clearly reminiscent of the socioeconomic position of black people, women in particular, in Puerto Rican society in the late nineteenth and early twentieth centuries (Martínez Vergne 1999; Matos Rodríguez 1999).

A case just to the right of these photos displayed a range of ritual items. A black mourning fan caught my eye. Who labored to produce such finery? Who used it? For whom did the woman who held it mourn? I thought of funerary objects for the poor. Francisco Oller's *El Velorio* (*The Wake*) came to mind. Oller's paintings graced the exhibit in spirit and via the work of his student Pío Casimiro Bacener.

At the other end of the gallery, a self-portrait of Pío Casimiro Bacener sat a short distance from *Esclava de Puerto Rico* (plates 6 and 8). Bacener (1840–1900), born a slave in San Juan, purchased his freedom or was granted it by his master. Once freed, he attended the Public School of Drawing, established by the renowned artist Francisco Oller (1833–1917). The piece may have gone unnoticed, but it was nonetheless a critically important testament to the creativity of men and women in the African diaspora. The public, it seemed, was more readily drawn to José Campeche's masterful work *San Juan Nepomuceno* (c. 1798) (plate 9). The magnificent portrait of this Catholic martyr had been commissioned for a chapel in Caracas, Venezuela. I recalled that I had first seen it under restoration and later in the exhibit *Colonial Art from Puerto Rico* at the National Museum of American Art. Marvette Pérez, the curator who facilitated the acquisition of these masterworks, wondered whether there was a hint of resistance to the established racial social order in the canvas. José Campeche's intimate understandings of the worldly and otherworldly (Christianity), so exquisitely portrayed on the canvas, were indeed an affirmation of his talent and creativity, as well as of his people's resistance, if not his own. Tomás, José Campeche's father, had been born a slave. He worked as a gilder and painter to purchase his freedom. As his father's apprentice, Campeche acquired his artistic skills. Campeche was considered a *mulato* (mulatto) and the son of free people. Perhaps his "mixed" heritage offered him possibilities that others did not have. Campeche honed his talents by skillfully attending to his father's styles and techniques and those found in imported prints and books. Andrew Connor, the curator of the exhibit, notes that Campeche was also influenced by Paret y Alcázar, a Spanish court painter exiled on the island from 1775 through 1778, whose rendition *Esclava de Puerto Rico* poignantly reminded the attendees that Puerto Rico was indeed once a slave society. Interestingly enough, each artist chose to portray the Other. Paret y Alcázar's subjects were the enslaved and free laborers who formed part of the Puerto Rican peasantry; Campeche's subjects were the Crown's royal, military, and ecclesiastical figures, for example, *Don José Mas Ferrer* (c. 1795). A local schoolteacher, grateful for the collection and the promise of future scholarship, expressed a conundrum: "How do we impress upon people how extraordinary, how magnificent the work of Campeche really is? To do this, they would have to know so much about Puerto Rico, its people, and its history. *Eso no se enseña aqui* [We don't teach that here]."

As I walked through the exhibit, I was continually drawn to labor. The exhibit case facing José Campeche's *Nepomuceno* focused on the colonial cash crop economy. Narratives of sugar, coffee, tobacco, slavery, peasants, and proletarians came to the fore. I wondered how racism continued to prevail in the midst of the shared poverty of cane cutters, laborers in the fields, then and now. This question was and is particularly troubling, because for anthropologists, the privileging of class over race in Sidney W. Mintz's *Worker in the Cane* (1960) and Julian H. Steward and others' *The People of Puerto Rico* (1956) was normalized. Winston James (1996), referring to Mintz, observes: "Reflecting upon the draconian labor laws passed in Puerto Rico in the mid-nineteenth century, Sidney Mintz rightly noted the 'color-blindness of the planter class' when it came to coercing labor to work on the *haciendas*. Adversity often bonded the oppressed, joining black and white together." Again, I wondered under what circumstances the working class and working poor incorporated a "racialized" social order in their interaction with each other that was effectively silenced in the name of Puerto Rican nationalism and class struggle (Guerra 1998; Martínez Vergne 1999; K. Santiago-Valles 1994).

Beautiful pieces of clothes were exhibited across from the displays of sugar, tobacco, and coffee. Crocheted and hand-stitched cloth and masterfully detailed lace collars adorned the gallery wall. Whose bed, whose table, whose pillow, whose dress did these adorn? In need of a respite from the images, sounds, and stories that filled the gallery, I wandered over to the exhibit *Between a Rock and a Hard Place: A History of American Sweatshops, 1820–Present.* The meticulously crafted cases subtly lit in the *Collector's Vision* exhibit were replaced with large black, white, and gray photographs of workers, mostly women of color. Long narratives accompanied them. Pieces of machinery were also found in this dimly lit re-creation of a factory floor. There were few witnesses to the mechanization of labor, to the loss of labor, and to the changing labor force in the late twentieth century in this exhibit hall. I stood there for more than an hour; a few folks passed through in silence. While they gazed at these remarkable photographs, one man broke the silence, telling his daughter about her grandfather's participation in the organization of union labor.

I gazed at the photographs, too, as I recalled Jack Delano's striking photographic essay in *Puerto Rico Mio: Four Decades of Change* (1990)—images of Puerto Ricans in the 1940s in contrast to those of the 1980s. I remembered, too, stories my mother told of her migration to the mainland and her experiences as a seamstress in New York's garment district. As I read the text that accompanied the photograph *Puerto Rican Garment Workers, 1953,* I wanted to summon the women I had left in the West End gallery to give witness to another Puerto Rico. As those Puerto Rican women admired the detailed work on the Vidal exhibit wall, they invoked memories of ritual events at which baptismal gowns, linens, and fine tapestries were worn and exchanged. They did not speak of their mothers' need to create and sell pieces to sustain their families. The label that accompanied the case, however, made specific reference to this need. Many Puerto Ricans found work in the garment factories to sustain themselves and their families on the island and the US mainland. The poorest women engaged in piece work, hand-making and embroidering clothing that was purchased by the elite. I reflected on the ways in which those manual skills allowed Puerto Rican women, including my kin, to participate in one of the greatest airborne migrations of the twentieth century. The text below the 1953 photograph in the sweatshop exhibit read:

> In the 1950s the composition of New York's apparel work
> force began to change. Highly restrictive immigration quota
> laws enacted in the 1920s had cut off the flow of cheap labor
> from Eastern and Southern Europe, forcing the industry to

look elsewhere for workers. As Italian and Eastern-European Jewish garment workers got better jobs or retired, they were replaced by Puerto Ricans and African Americans. Due to union gains, government regulations, and industry changes, these new workers did not experience the same level of exploitation as their predecessors.

Surely, countless Puerto Rican and African American women could attest to the positive gains made in the workplace. Nevertheless, their recollections of exploitative practices also revealed how racialized and gendered constructs and practices permeated the workplace in the 1950s and thereafter (A. Ortiz 1996). As I left *Between a Rock and a Hard Place*, I was struck by the text of a sign on the wall:

Why Do Museums Mount This Kind of Exhibition?

History museums are educational institutions that strive to make the American past accessible, useful and meaningful to the millions who view their exhibitions, read their catalogs, and participate in public programs.

Museum exhibitions often celebrate and commemorate the past, and in doing so, create a collective memory that helps provide Americans with a common understanding of that past. Equally important is a museum's obligation to explore all aspects of the American experience.

History museums interpret difficult, unpleasant, or controversial episodes, not out of any desire to embarrass or be unpatriotic, or cause pain, but out of a responsibility to convey a fuller, more inclusive history. By examining incidents ripe with complexities and ambiguities, museums hope to stimulate greater understanding of the historical forces and choices that shaped America.

Spencer Crew, Director
Lonnie Bunch, Associate Director for Curatorial Affairs
National Museum of American History, Smithsonian
Institution

Did the director of the museum and the curatorial staff involved in *A Collector's Vision of Puerto Rico* share that same vision as they mounted the exhibit and other public programs? Hank Burchard of the *Washington Post,* in an exhibit review titled "Puerto Rico's Bright Vision" (September 4, 1998), noted that subtle hints were to be found here and there regarding "the less-than-perfect relationship between the island and Uncle Sam." He also observed: "[I]f there is racial or class strife or economic woe on the island we hear nothing of it here; the dozen sponsors of the exhibit are mainly the tourist industry banks and developers." Yet, as Puerto Ricans recollected the past in conversation with one another, the social and economic transformations that shaped the fabric of Puerto Rican life on the island and the US mainland came to the fore. Indeed, racial and class strife was seldom discussed, yet there was tacit acknowledgment of it every time someone expressed appreciation for objects they associated with Africanness, blackness, and enslaved and free labor. Crisscrossing class, gender, racial, spatial, and colonial borders was and is exhausting. It is also empowering. I returned to the Vidal exhibit and briefly resumed my observations and conversations with the public at hand. I never imagined what I would subsequently encounter at the evening opening ceremonies.

THE ENACTMENT OF CLASS AND RACIAL HIERARCHIES

I arrived at the National Museum of American History precisely when an entourage of guards and escorts cleared the way for Governor Roselló. As photographers swamped the entrance, I nodded my head in utter disbelief. After all, it was only the opening of an exhibit—or was it? As the governor was whisked away to be interviewed by the media, I made my way into the Material World Exhibition area, a fitting place to hold such an event. Men in black tie and women in designer gowns and dresses embraced friends and relatives. To ensure that their makeup and perfectly lined lips would not smear, the women threw kisses into the air toward one another. Conversations revolved around the trip from the island to Washington, DC, as women in particular complimented one another on their attire. Others commented on the presence of various members of the Puerto Rican elite. I noticed that Puerto Rican men, for the most part, wore small golden stars on their lapels. Upon close inspection, I saw that the stars were inscribed with-

the words *51st state!* The art of politics or politicking. I recognized the face of Luis A. Ferré, a philanthropist, former governor of the island, and supporter of the arts, and his family. I recognized the resident commissioner of Puerto Rico, among other well-known political figures and members of the Partido Nuevo Progressista (PNP), Puerto Rico's pro-statehood party. Ironically, the collector Teodoro Vidal was not present at the opening gala. Vidal—a staunch supporter of the Partido Popular Democratico (PDP) and a longtime friend of the late governor Luis Muñoz Marin, who supported the Estado Libre Associado (free associated state) status that continues to define Puerto Rico's relationship with the United States—did not approve of the fanfare. I suspect that the majority of Puerto Rican people on the island and the US mainland would have had some reservations as well. We were not equally of the "nation." Most mainlanders, however, would not have been able to comment because only a select few received invitations. Among those invited were politicians who opted not to come to a black tie event that effectively marginalized their own constituency on the US mainland. As for the islanders, they drew upon Puerto Rican media reports of a spectacular social and cultural event that embraced and recognized an island's treasures, people, culinary delights, and material culture.

The Puerto Rican government, American Airlines, and various companies and private donors facilitated the transport of the trio Los Taverneros, the children's choir La Rondalla de Niños, five master artisans, and a host of guests. They also facilitated the transport of the governor's personal chef, who prepared Caribbean delicacies. We were guests indeed, at an ostentatious Christmas feast in the latter part of July. A roast pig adorned each table. *Arroz con gandules, pasteles* wrapped in banana leaves, corn fritters, tubers, stuffed plantain, and a wide array of tropical fruits summoned each of us. Culinary dishes said to be rooted in Africa (L. González 1992) were served with fine china and linens. Bars were stationed throughout the exhibition area and West End gallery, where drinks made with Puerto Rico's finest rums—only Puerto Rico's finest rums—were served. And once again, the Palm Court ice cream parlor was transformed. The guests there consumed an assortment of lavishly decorated desserts served with Puerto Rico's choice coffee blend, Alto Grande. A true transformation of the colonial cash crops and economies.

Artisans also exhibited their work there. Rafael Aviles, a master artisan I had met earlier that day, displayed handmade musical instruments. Isaac Laboy displayed finished pieces while he carved a santo. Denise Sánchez, a seamstress and artisan, stood behind a table with an array of lace collars, clothing, and linens she had made by hand, graciously thanking those who lauded her work. And Jaime Zayas spoke to guests about the carnival masks on display. They were miniature versions of the masks he artistically creates for the Ponce carnival. At a short distance, Tavaneros and La Rondalla de Niños were heard playing and singing musical selections well-known to the Puerto Rican middle and upper classes but not immediately recognizable to even a trained "Neuyorican" or an anthropological ear.[1] As I waited to hear welcoming remarks, I wandered over to the Vidal exhibit. The other guests were concerned with the exhibit to the extent that it served as a backdrop for the gala event. Some Puerto Ricans from the island took the opportunity to inform their Anglo-American guests of the island's cultural treasures by making specific reference to the panorama of carved saints. I heard no mention of Africanness or blackness.

I returned to the Material World Exhibition area, where Spencer Crew, the museum's director, had already begun to make a few remarks. Once again, he thanked major donors and introduced the curatorial staff. Then Governor Roselló took center stage. He spoke of the fortuitous relationship between the United States and Puerto Rico as he explicitly advocated for statehood. Following the governor's remarks, I located Pérez and Ruffins, two curators, to obtain their reactions. Instead, they introduced me to several guests. It struck me that their colleagues and friends were among the few African Americans I had encountered all evening. This gala affair was continually marked by race, class, and cultural and political distinctions. You could almost tell who was on the museum's guest list and who was on the governor's guest list. I was on the museum's guest list, not only because I had served as a consultant to the exhibit but also because I am a friend and colleague of curator and anthropologist Marvette Pérez. As a Puerto Rican, classed as a Neuyorican, I was still deemed out of place. However, my phenotype, acquired class privilege, and education made my presence unobtrusive up to a point. Because I openly took notes and recorded the governor's speech, I was clearly not among the governor's chosen. I was not there to promote statehood or to socialize with my "compatriots."

337

On that evening in July 1998, many of the governor's guests embraced their Puerto Ricanness, their class status, and their political allies—or so they thought. Blackness, by contrast, was relegated to the distant past or incorporated into the mélange of cultural practices now deemed quintessentially Puerto Rican. The governor's guests embodied in their social practice ideologies of *mestizaje* (racial and cultural "mixing") and *blanqueamiento* ("whitening") (Torres 1998a; Torres and Whitten 1998). They were classed as members of the "white" Puerto Rican elite who had traveled from the island to attend this social and political event. They were all too distant from their Puerto Rican counterparts living in urban enclaves on the US mainland. They were cultured Puerto Ricans who embraced, and felt that they should be embraced by, the United States, even in the midst of an ostentatious display of Puerto Rican nationhood.

THE PERFORMANCE OF BLACKNESS

The following morning, I returned to the National Museum of American History to resume my observations of unfolding events. While there, I observed two cultural groups—a young dance troupe and El Grupo Baramaya de Bomba y Plena from Ponce, Puerto Rico—while they rehearsed for El Carnaval de Ponce. In Puerto Rico's racial topography, Ponce as a space is often made to stand for blackness. It becomes a "black place." Performances were scheduled for August 1 and 2 and formed part of the *Encuentros* series. The museum and the Ponce Office of Tourism, a branch of the Puerto Rican government, saw the event as an opportunity "to share the traditions of Ponce's carnival with visitors." These performances would not only mark the public opening of *A Collector's Vision of Puerto Rico* but would also help bolster the Smithsonian's efforts to improve its image in the Latina/Latino community and would promote tourism on the southern coast of Puerto Rico. As I listened to and observed these performers, I questioned why these culturally and phenotypically black Puerto Ricans from the southern coast had not been present at the gala affair the night before. To be sure, they were gifted performers, as gifted as the artisans who displayed their musical instruments, embroidered lace, and carnival masks. Why hadn't they been there? Are opening galas at public museums private events for the select few? Did these performers receive invitations? I began to inquire and was told that travel arrangements had been made to minimize costs. As a result, the performers arrived in Washington, DC, late in the evening. Even if they had received invitations, they would have missed the fanfare altogether. It seemed all too suspect (see R. Price and S. Price 1994). Which museum and Puerto Rican government officials had been involved in the planning and execution of the event? It became quite clear as the day unfolded.

Ponce's Office of Tourism had provided the financial resources for the event. Regrettably, the artists and performers did not have adequate resources to cover their own expenses. Because of political maneuvering and outmaneuvering among Puerto Rican government officials, donors, and organizers, these cultural artists and performers were deemed laborers who served the interests of the municipality of Ponce, the Puerto Rican government, and the Smithsonian Institution. The lowest airfares were booked, and limited funds were provided for lodging and food. The performers were not being adequately paid. In some cases, they were not paid at all for rendering their labor. The young members of the dance troupe, ranging in ages from fifteen to twenty-one, were told that the trip was an opportunity to travel and to represent Puerto Rico in "the nation's capital." And indeed, the dancers did consider this a wonderful opportunity; most of them had never left the island before. It was their first trip "abroad." However, their enthusiasm was tempered by basic concerns. The taxi fare, the food, the accommodations were too costly. They saw very little of the capital, despite the fact that their visibility at the Smithsonian was maximized. Members of El Grupo Baramaya also remarked that resources to cover their basic expenses were limited. Upon hearing of the gross inadequacies, the public programs coordinator at the Smithsonian managed to secure funds to feed the performers adequately.

As the dance troupe and El Grupo Baramaya rehearsed and prepared for the afternoon performance, tensions were barely kept at bay. A representative of the Ponce Office of Tourism shouted at the performers and admonished them for their behavior. Respect was not accorded, and it was certainly not given. A member of El Grupo Baramaya voiced her objections to the way the young women were publicly scolded when they requested use of the restroom. On another occasion, she expressed her dismay at the government official's unwillingness to provide the needed cash to replace a skirt that had been torn during one of the performances. It was clearly their problem, not his. Aware of the escalating tensions between the performers and the officials, I opted to join the performers for dinner one evening. As I posed questions to members of the dance troupe and other performers, representatives of Ponce's Office of Tourism continually intervened in conversations to validate their positions and/or to speak on behalf of the talented men and women. The taking, giving, and muting of voice was constant as these individuals tried to relay their individual and collective ideas. Once again, despite obvious problems, the members of the dance troupe still considered it an honor and a privilege to perform at the Smithsonian Institution. However, the *pleneros* and *pleneras* in El Grupo Baramaya were not so easily convinced. Despite what appeared to be the reenactment of class and racial hierarchical practices, the members of Baramaya had their say. As they performed before an exuberant crowd in the Material World Exhibition area, they raised the Puerto Rican flag and sang, *"Hoy es su cumpleaño, y el quiere que le canten, el amo quiere que le canten, y le vamos a cantar"* ("Today is his birthday and the master wants us to sing, and so we will sing"). And so they did.

This strategy of resistance operated on several levels. The singers were publicly ridiculing the Ponce government official, who was associated with a slave owner, a master who summoned slaves to sing on his birthday. Such a practice would not have been uncommon in Ponce, where the plantation system and the institution of slavery once flourished. One could also interpret the song, and events that had recently unfolded in Puerto Rico and at the Smithsonian Institution, within the context of the one hundredth anniversary of the US occupation of Puerto Rico. Governor Roselló, another master, was in the middle of a battle with the Puerto Rican people—who shut down the island—over the selling off of Puerto Rico's telephone company. Yet he had left his problems behind to host a gala reception and black tie affair promoting statehood at the Smithsonian. Finally, as the pleneros and pleneras sang, the Puerto Rican flag was raised, despite the efforts of government officials from Puerto Rico. The singers tried to raise the flag from the municipality of Ponce, but this effort was continually intercepted and put down—a remarkably symbolic act at a time when the Smithsonian was embarking on a campaign to restore a vintage "American" flag, a symbol of freedom, democracy, and the nation.

MULTIPLE VISIONS

As I tried to make sense of the *Collector's Vision* exhibit and the events that unfolded, I noted that varied historical junctures and cultural practices were conjoined to construct, legitimate, contest, rearticulate, and reinscribe Puerto Rican identity. I now turn to Puerto Rican historiography on the island and the US mainland to demonstrate the various ideological perspectives and discursive practices that were deployed to allow for multiple visions of Puerto Ricanness.

Puerto Rican historiography and ethnography have focused primarily on the effects of changing political and economic forces in the development of Puerto Rican society and culture. Until recently, few scholars have attempted to grapple with the political economic structures and the intricate webs of symbolic representations that constitute and are constituted by culture. Ideologies of mestizaje and blanqueamiento, as well as oppositions between the plantation and the *estancia* (small farm), the coast and the mountainous interior, urban and rural, slave and free yeoman, black and *jíbaro* (the "white" peasant of the mountainous interior who has been made a symbol of nationhood), economy and livelihood, permeate the historical and ethnographic literature on Puerto Rico and form part of everyday discourse among Puerto Ricans (e.g., A. Dávila 1997, 1999; J. González [1979] 1981; L. González 1992; González and Quintero Rivera 1984; Guerra 1998; G. Lewis 1983; Martínez Vergne 1999; Matos Rodríguez and Delgado 1998; Mintz 1960, 1974; Negrón Muntaner and Grosfoguel 1997; Quintero Rivera 1987, 1988; K. Santiago-Valles 1994; Scarano 1996).

These symbolically charged categories perpetuate the construction of a black identity tied to a coastal plantation economy that relied on a black and enslaved labor force and of a romanticized jíbaro identity of "white" peasants in the mountainous interior of the island who engaged in subsistence activities and were later incorporated as *agregados*—sharecroppers—on the expanding coffee haciendas. Because people conceive of history selectively and are constrained by relations of power, alternatives to these categories of paired oppositions were scarcely found in the historical and ethnographic literature.

For example, historiography and its fixed categories did not allow for the growth of a free black yeomanry engaged in subsistence activities in the mountainous interior of the municipalities on the southeastern coast of Puerto Rico and elsewhere. But the historical data clearly show a larger percentage of free blacks and mulattos, compared with black slaves, on the southeastern coast of Puerto Rico. The existence of free black and mulatto communities that were adjacent to the sugar plantation economy, or whose residents participated in it as temporary laborers, needs further exploration. Scholars have begun to examine the role of black slaves and free black and mulatto laborers and artisans in the coastal and urban milieus of eighteenth- and nineteenth-century Puerto Rico (Duany 1985; J. González [1979] 1981; Guerra 1998; Kinsbruner 1996; Martínez Vergne 1999; Matos Rodríguez 1999; Matos Rodríguez and Delgado 1998; Moreno Fraginals et al. 1985; Negrón Portillo and Mayo Santana 1992; Quintero Rivera 1987, 1988; Scarano 1981, 1984, 1993, 1996). These analyses challenge previous historical interpretations because blacks and mulattos are located in varied social, economic, and political arenas.

Jíbaros negros (black peasants) were located on the coast and in the interior of coastal municipalities. The fusion of "jíbaro" and "negro" in Puerto Rico radically alters the ways in which these categories have been essentialized in the Puerto Rican cultural imagination, precisely because this union represents a movement toward blackness. Processes of blanqueamiento are negated. The jíbaro is no longer just a white-skinned peasant. He is a jíbaro negro. The mythico-historical figure is also a female. She is a black jíbara.[2] Some jíbaro negros were tied to the plantation and hacienda economies, others were engaged in subsistence strategies and practices to ensure their livelihood, and still others were part of each of these economies (see F. Ortiz 1940; R. Price 1966; Steward et al. 1956; Whitten [1974] 1986; Whitten and de Friedemann 1975). Rather than argue that free blacks, mulattos, and jíbaros became landless laborers and sharecroppers following abolition, it can be argued that enclaves of free blacks and mulattos also existed and developed before and after the emancipation of slaves in Puerto Rico.

When we gain such a perspective, blacks and mulattos are perceived not as marginal to but rather as vital to the development of the nation. This seriously revised perspective differs from previous interpretations of historical data because it does not simply define black people as former slaves and laborers who became assimilated as members of the nation. It challenges scholars to critically assess how blacks and mulattos throughout the history of Puerto Rico engaged in strategies to gain acceptance by non-blacks on the one hand while on the other hand maintaining their cultural and ethnic autonomy in particular and specifiable social and economic arenas.

The association between "the Great Family" and "the Nation" harks back to the development of a Puerto Rican nationalist ideology in the late nineteenth and early twentieth centuries. This ideology was symbolically represented as *la gran familia jíbara* (the great jíbaro family), with the *hacendado* (plantation owner) as the paternalistic and benevolent head who provided his children with a means by which to engage in productive labor for the good of the nation. As the *criollo* elite sought to establish a nation in opposition to the Spanish colonial government, the subordinate but transformed jíbaro represented the nation. Manuel A. Alonso's novel *El gíbaro* ([1894] 1975) captured the imagination of the criollo elite, a mythico-historical imagination that failed to reflect the racial and socioeconomic composition of nineteenth-century Puerto Rico. See J. González ([1979] 1981:57); Scarano (1996); and Guerra (1998).

The image of la gran familia jíbara became further solidified in the early twentieth century as the members of the creole elite sought to establish their Puerto Rican identity in opposition to the new colonial power, the United States. Within this context, the Puerto Rican family consisted of the creole elite, the jíbaro, and the marginalized black laborer on the coast. The creole elite and non-black laborers defined blacks and mulattos as displaced laborers who were now part of the nation. Given the demise of the sugar industry and the encroachment of US economic and political interests in the area, they argued that all members of the Puerto Rican family suffered under US tyranny.

At present, a Puerto Rican nationalist identity that continually places emphasis on the "harmonious synthesis" of whites, indigenous people, and black people throughout history fails to convince people who define themselves as black that they are equal partners in the making of the nation. They are conscious of the fact that mestizaje can never be fully achieved because non-blacks do not accept *negros, mulatos, trigueños, jabaos,* and other such local racial designations[3] as truly members of the nation.

In Puerto Rico, the ideology of mestizaje acknowledges the contributions of people of African, indigenous, and Spanish descent in the formation of the nation, but it also maintains and promotes racialist ideas and practices. The process of blanqueamiento specifically encourages Puerto Ricans to identify with the "race" mixture, the jíbaro as oriented toward lighter skin, and Eurocentric definitions of "culture." By people of color employing these ideologies of mestizaje and blanqueamiento to gain conditional acceptance by non-blacks, racism is perpetuated (Martínez Vergne 1999; Torres 1995). These ideologies and processes of "whitening" refer to whiteness and blackness in cultural terms. Whiteness is associated with *la Cultura*—culture with a capital *C.* Such a perspective does not negate the existence of black culture but confines it to the realm of the "popular." In the Puerto Rican context, by defining black cultural contributions within the context of slavery and the expressive realm, naturalized stigmata that set black people apart from the rest of Puerto Rican society are continually reproduced (Torres and Whitten 1998).

NEUYORICAN HISTORIOGRAPHY

Historical narratives focusing on Puerto Ricans, primarily in New York, assumed that these ideological perspectives and practices were carried over to the US mainland. Indeed they were. But other visions of Puerto Rico made their way, too, and helped transform the ways in which many Puerto Ricans in New York developed an understanding of Africanness and blackness in Puerto Rico and on the US mainland. Migration to the mainland, settlement there, and/or return migration to the island did provide the impetus to challenge racist and class-based ideologies but also helped solidify nationalist sentiments that continually diverted discussions about "race" and color prejudice. For example, most Puerto Ricans view problems in local communities and throughout Puerto Rico as a result of the negative external influences of *los norteamericanos* (the North Americans) and return migrants who introduce external ways to the island. There is no acknowledgment that ideas that challenge and contradict the national ideology are rooted in the continual struggle of many black people on the island to assert their identity as members of the nation (Chatterjee 1993; V. Domínguez 1989; Fox 1990; R. Handler 1988).

Winston James's (1996) comparative analysis of the life and work of the scholar and collector Arturo A. Schomburg (1874–1938) and that of Jesús Colón (1901–1974) is instructive.[4] Schomburg was the son of Mary Joseph, a migrant from Saint Croix, and a Puerto Rican man of German descent. James observed that Schomburg's lifelong commitment to the study and liberation of people of African descent was not shared by his compatriots in the 1920s and 1930s. Some Puerto Rican contemporaries considered Schomburg problematic because he had abandoned Puerto Rican nationalism in favor of black nationalism. His compatriots failed to consider that the liberation of people of African descent encompassed the liberation of Puerto Ricans. The lack of race consciousness in favor of class consciousness among Puerto Ricans silenced and marginalized those who experienced race prejudice on the island and in the continental United States.

Jesús Colón, by contrast, was a working-class Afro–Puerto Rican who sought to liberate his people by adhering to the vision of Puerto Rican nationalism within an international socialist framework. Colón did not speak or write systematically about his encounters with racism until the late 1950s. James (1996:110) observes that "his world was not that of *los negros americanos*, nor was his preoccupation with the fate of Afro-America." James attributes this attitude to Colón's intellectual formation on the island and his association with the Communist Party in the United States, as well as with the Latino community in mid-twentieth-century New York. In this context, class, national identity, and ethnic identity were privileged over "race." Despite references to the ways Puerto Ricans experienced "race relations" and blackness in New York at this time, in James's study we get only a glimpse of the relationships between Puerto Ricans and black Americans. Jamaican-born novelist Claude McKay observed that black Americans resented brown-skinned Puerto Ricans who chose to distance themselves from their North American counterparts (McKay 1940, cited in James 1996). We also know that Puerto Ricans resented how the US "biracial model" constrained social relations, even among close kin (see Iglesias 1984). While James convincingly draws on the history of "race relations" between Puerto Ricans and their counterparts in the Hispanic and non-Hispanic Caribbean, to situate Puerto Rican class consciousness over "race" consciousness, we have yet to understand how some Puerto Ricans may have also opted to privilege their ethnicity in a highly segregated society where racial tensions were not only omnipresent but had violent manifestations. For example, how Puerto Ricans situated themselves and how they were situated in the various racial clashes and riots that took place in the early to mid-twentieth century need to be understood.[5] It then behooves us to ask, despite the apparent distancing of Puerto Ricans from black Americans, how did Puerto Ricans generally and Puerto Rican New Yorkers particularly become racialized as black or as people of color?

Again, how Puerto Ricans represent themselves and how they are represented in time and place come to the fore. Suffice it to say that "the house that race built," the colonial relationship of Puerto Rico and the United States poignantly depicted in *Our Islands and Their People* (Bryan 1899), and decades of social science literature that marginalized and pathologized Puerto Ricans have contributed to this process of racialization, even as learned scholars were trying to assess the impact of economic and public policy initiatives on the lives of Puerto Ricans on the island and in the continental United States (Duncan 1979, 1983; Clara Rodríguez 2001; Torres 1998b). How this situation informs contemporary representations of Puerto Ricanness in various social contexts and cultural terrains needs further exploration (Rodríguez-Morrazani 1998).

A concern with representation in Puerto Rico, for the most part, has focused on cultural history, national imagery, politics, and identity formation. Hollister Sturges's *New Art from Puerto Rico* (1990) and Robert Hobbs's *Arnaldo Roche-Rabell: The Uncommonwealth* (1996) exemplify these recent trends. Efrain Barradas (1990:16) notes that

> the Word, not the Image, has always been dominant in
> Puerto Rican culture. It seems that we are more a nation of
> poets and singers rather than of artists. Still, in spite of this
> characterization, we have in fact created a repertoire of
> icons which has accompanied and served to explain our cultural history. A starched portrait by Campeche, a tropical
> impressionistic landscape by Oller, a classic poster by
> Homar, or an anguished self-portrait by Roche are as essen-

tial to our culture as are a patriotic poem by Gautier Benítez or a melancholy dance by Morel Campos or the Afro-Caribbean mythifications by Palés Matos.[6]

I argue, to the contrary, that at present we are grappling as "a nation" of words *and* images to further develop our understanding of our past and its implications for our future. The representation of blackness in Puerto Rico that seeks to challenge historico-mythical narratives is relatively recent. The publication of works such as Baralt and others' (1990) *El machete de Ogún: Las luchas de los esclavos en Puerto Rico* (siglo XIX) and Lydia Milagros González's (1992) *La tercera raíz: presencia africana en Puerto Rico* marked a turning point in Puerto Rican historiography as attempts were made to address the black experience in Puerto Rico via imagery *and* the word—the work of Arturo Schomburg notwithstanding. A cursory overview of the aforementioned works reveals that Teodoro Vidal's collection of material culture was referenced time and time again to promote these nuanced interpretations of the past. More recently, Angel Quintero Rivera's (1998) edited work *Vírgenes, magos y escapularios: Imaginería, ethnicidad y religiosidad popular en Puerto Rico* would not have materialized without the incorporation of the religious iconography and other material objects in the Vidal collection.

While the Vidal collection may be studied and interpreted as symbolically representative of our varied culture history, I suggest that the process of collecting, acquiring, exhibiting, and interpreting materials in the late twentieth century embodied different versions of our cultural past. But at the same time, it demonstrates our contemporary concerns with a changing sociocultural and political landscape in the Caribbean and the United States. From my encounters with curators, museum personnel, and the viewing public, it became clear that the exhibit and the reading of material culture, coupled with other events, continually reinscribed cultural tropes about Puerto Ricans and "the nation." However, given the multivocality of symbolic representations, they also contested and rearticulated Puerto Rican culture and identity in ways that revealed the non-fixity of identity categories in social practice. Furthermore, they demonstrated how individuals and groups can and do fix categories, to allow them to behave with "a particular kind of agency, political or otherwise" (Dirks, Eley, and Ortner

1994:32). For example, a host of individuals noted the subtle ways in which La Gran Familia Puertorriqueña dealt with issues of mestizaje and negritude. Others were awed by the work of José Campeche, and still others closely identified with the repertoire of saints that embodied Afro–Puerto Rican religiosity. The *Encuentros* celebration of Ponce's carnival demonstrated how individual actors play with identity categories to entertain and inform the public in the context of a national museum. Here again, the word and the image were intricately woven to represent a wealth of possibilities as Puerto Ricans and other Americans contend with the politics of representation and nationhood. Although museum exhibits, festivals, performances, and other rituals have the power to overturn representations, they can also serve as vehicles to reinscribe racial and ethnic imagery in arenas and locales marked by social hierarchy.

Notes

1. Puerto Ricans born and reared on the US mainland are often referred to and refer to themselves as "Neuyoricans" (New York-Ricans). Depending on the social context and the individual speaker, this term can be a negative, as well as a positive, marker of identity. I am marked as Neuyorican in this context because I was born and reared in the northeastern part of the United States, and I am not altogether familiar with these particular Puerto Rican melodies, which form part of a particular cultural repertoire on the island.

2. The role and contributions of black women to Puerto Rican society have yet to be fully addressed in the scholarly literature. Groundbreaking analyses include those by Matos Rodríguez (1999); Matos Rodríguez and Delgado (1998); and Martínez Vergne (1999).

3. *Trigueño*, from the Spanish word for "wheat," refers ostensibly to someone who is wheat-colored, but it is often used for those of darker phenotype to avoid the term *negro*, which is seen as impolite in many contexts. *Jabao* refers to someone supposedly possessing white skin along with "African" features such as kinky hair.

4. See Colón (1961), Flores (1982), and Acosta Belén and Sánchez-Korrol (1993).

5. A parallel reading of Virginia Sánchez-Korrol's (1983) *From Colonia to Community: The History of Puerto Ricans in New York City* with Claude McKay's

(1940) *Harlem: Negro Metropolis,* among other historical works on Harlem, might provide greater insights. After all, these groups were living in the same geographic locale and racialized terrain.

    6. Of note is that, with the exception of the *negrista* poet Luis Palés Matos, all the artists mentioned here either defined themselves or were defined as Afro-Puerto Ricans. For more on Palés Matos, see Roy Fequiere (1996).

11

Understanding "Africa" and "Blackness" in Colombia

Music and the Politics of Culture

Peter Wade

In the 1990s and the first years of the new century, in Colombia the notions of "blackness" and, to a lesser extent, "Africa" have become politically and culturally important in ways that have slim precedents in the country's republican history. Since the 1991 constitutional reform, "black communities" have an unprecedented visibility in the public and political arenas mainly because of the inclusion of references to them in the new constitution and the subsequent promulgation of the Law of Black Communities (Law 70 of 1993), which allows land title rights for some black communities in the country's Pacific coastal region—an area with an 80 to 90 percent black population—and makes provisions for the participation of black communities in the nation's political and economic life (Arocha 1992; Grueso, Rosero, and Escobar 1998; Pardo 2000; Wade 1995; figure 11.1). State recognition of black communities as objects of attention has gone hand in hand with black political organization and activism, although in more limited forms this activity preceded the 1991 and 1993 legislation by some thirty years.

The notion of "Africa" is, to a greater or lesser extent, entailed by the public burgeoning of "blackness." State legislation (for example, on education) now makes reference to *afrocolombianos* alongside the term *comunidades negras*, which was more usual in the early 1990s. "Africa" is also a central point of reference for many involved in the study of, and political organization of, black people. The history of such concern with Africa goes back some way in academic circles, although it was a minor concern in Colombian history and anthropology compared with interest in indigenous peoples. The Jesuit José Arboleda, a Colombian student of the US anthropologist Melville J. Herskovits, wrote a master's thesis on the ethnohistory of the "Colombian negroes" in 1950, and various others shared his concern with the survival of Africanisms in Colombian culture (Arboleda Llorente 1950; see also de Friedemann 1984; del Castillo M. 1982; Granda 1977; T. Price 1955; Wade 1993:ch. 2).

More recently, the interest in Africa has been taken up with renewed vigor by anthropologists such as Jaime Arocha, and this theme was the major concern of the late Nina de Friedemann (Arocha 1991, 1996, 1999; de Friedemann 1993; de Friedemann and Arocha 1986). For them, the issue was never just an "academic" one. Both contested what de Friedemann (1984) once called the "invisibilization" of blacks in homogenizing definitions of the Colombian nation; both participated in the process of constitutional reform and the drafting of Law 70. The notion of "Africa" formed a crucial referent for these scholars and others, not only to understand "Afro-Colombian" culture— indeed, the term *afrocolombiano* owes some of its current popularity to their usage—but also to contest the marginalization of black people within the nation in the battle against racism. Friedemann and Arocha critiqued a Herskovitsian concept of the simple survival of particular African cultural traits, persisting more or less unchanged into American contexts. They prefer the notion of "cognitive orientation," which they adopt from Mintz and Price (1976), to link Africa and America. This notion suggests that African peoples in the New World shared some basic cultural principles, values, and ways of thinking that shaped the way they developed new cultural forms in the Americas, giving rise to what Arocha and Friedemann call *huellas de africanía* (traces of Africanness).

For black cultural activists, too, the image of "Africa" is of increasing importance. Previously, and still today, many black cultural organizations in Colombia have looked to the United States for inspiration

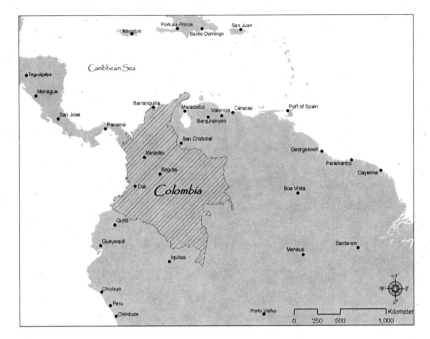

FIGURE 11.1

Map of Colombia. Map by Lori Collins.

(Wade 1995). For rural black populations in the Pacific coastal region of Colombia, the idea of African origins does not generally form part of a collective memory or an oral tradition (Losonczy 1997:354; Restrepo 1997:302). By the early 1990s, some black organizations were making more explicit reference to Africa as a source of symbols and aspects of a collective identity (Restrepo 1997:300). In 1992 I found that one black nongovernmental organization (NGO) in the Pacific port city of Buenaventura adorned its offices with a poster listing Yorùbá deities and a series of African names that the activists in the organization sometimes used to identify themselves. However, it was quite rare to hear these names in everyday practice. In an extensive interview with some leading members of this NGO (Pedrosa et al. 1996), the absence of "Africa" is apparent. Equally, a look at the documentation produced by various black NGOs in the 1980s and early 1990s reinforces the impression that, at that time, "Africa" was not a major point of reference, although by the early 1990s it does occur, most frequently in the use of the term *afrocolombiano*. Rather, the figure of the *cimarrón* (fugitive slave or Maroon) and the *palenque* (fugitive slave community) were more common referents (Wade 1995), and although these figures could be connected to the idea of Africa, that connotation was not necessarily very explicit.[1] By the late 1990s and early twenty-first century, however, the notion of "Africa" was gaining in importance and public visibility. The terms *afrocolombiano* (and yet more recently *afro-descendiente*) have become more common, and connections with Africa are explicit in, for example, recent texts on the new Afro-Colombian curriculum (e.g., Rovira de Córdoba and Córdoba Cuesta 2000; Ministerio de Educación Nacional 2001). The year 2001 was the 150th anniversary of the abolition of slavery in Colombia, and it was an occasion for the public acknowledgment of the links of Afro-Colombians and Colombians generally to Africa. In sum, in the early 1990s "blackness" made a very significant impact on the national political and cultural panorama, whereas "Africa" had a slighter influence. In recent years, however, whereas "blackness" continues to be an important idea and symbol, the related notion of "Africa" has been gaining in importance.

My own approach to the Colombian context has never denied Africanisms in Colombian culture, contrary to some criticisms of my work.[2] However, I have emphasized how Colombian blacks have used a wide variety of cultural sources—African, European, indigenous—to create new forms that are identified, in the Colombian context, as "black" (Wade 1993). With the new emphasis in Colombia—especially in Colombian anthropology—on Africanisms, I think that some clarification is needed.

Theoretically, it is a question of balancing change with continuity and of grasping both the discursive construction of culture—in this case, Africanisms—and culture "as such." Continuity may exist, first, in the persistence of very specific African traits in Afro-Colombian culture, such as the burying of the placenta below a tree (Arocha 1999; T. Price 1955). Here, change would be conceived in terms of the simple disappearance of the trait itself. Second, continuity may exist in the way certain cognitive orientations or underlying cultural principles—derived from Africa and given form in the early processes of creolization that took place in the slave ports of Africa, on slave ships, and in the nascent slave societies of the New World—shape and structure the continuing development of cultural patterns in the Americas. Here, change is integral to how continuity occurs. A basic cultural principle—for example, an aesthetic idea about what makes a pleasing design in shape or color—can be passed down through generations of everyday practice and might influence such diverse spheres of activity as house design, agriculture, and textile making. The underlying idea is made manifest in many ways as historical contexts change (see the chapters by Sally Price and by Richard Price in this volume and S. Price and R. Price 1999:ch. 8).

Both these forms of continuity are incorporated in the concept of *huellas de africanía*, and both focus on continuities with Africa. However, an overly intensive concern with these forms of continuity can run the risk of blinding us to the way Afro-Colombians have created new forms of culture from many sources, using particular elements and cultural principles from different sources to create for themselves and for others something that is identifiable as "black" or "Afro-Colombian" culture or as particular regional (for example, Pacific coastal) configurations of culture associated with blackness. In this process, there is still a sense of continuity at work, but it derives from the way people—Afro-Colombians and others—perceive and categorize what they experience and try to construct for themselves and others a meaningful world. These are basically discursive processes of cultural construction that use labels such as "black" or "Afro-Colombian" or, just as likely, a regional label such as *costeño* (coastal—that is, of the Pacific or Caribbean coastal region) to categorize cultural practices that may come from the most diverse sources and be the ongoing product of endless hybridizations. A key feature of these processes is relations of cultural domination and nationalist ideologies of *blanqueamiento* (cultural and biological whitening), according to which black culture has generally been seen as inferior and backward and national progress is associated with increasing cultural and physical whiteness. A strong element of continuity derives from the fact that the non-black world in Colombia has generally wished to define whatever black people do— and what they do changes historically all the time—as "black culture," and therefore inferior and perhaps threatening. Equally, a strong element of continuity derives from the fact that Afro-Colombians recognize this process of labeling and try to cope with the position it puts them in—whether by maintaining their own cultural practices or by attempting to avoid the stigma of inferiority by changing themselves and their cultural practices (or by challenging the entire system of values that defines them as inferior).

My purpose in this chapter is therefore in no way to deny Africanisms in Colombian culture—they are indisputably present, it is politically important to reveal them, and, doubtless, rigorous ethnographic and archival research (for example, of the kind Sally Price and Richard Price [1999] have conducted for the Samaraka Maroons) will reveal more, and more subtle, African influences. My purpose is rather to show that what is considered "African" or "black" in Colombia has varied historically according to many factors. These categories have been discursively constructed in complex ways, and we cannot easily separate out Africanisms "as such" from the way people perceive and talk about blackness and Africa. I also want to show that in this discursive realm, certain continuities are generated by the hierarchies of race, class, and gender, within which attributions and claims of black and non-black identity are made. If the various different musical styles associated with blackness were persistently seen as "primitive" in Colombia, then this notion derived from both basic musical continuities, some of them rooted in Africa, which connected changing, "modernizing" forms of music (for example, the importance of drum rhythms), and the fact that whatever the origins of the music, if it was associated with blackness, it would be classified as "primitive" and yet "exciting" in some way by non-blacks. These two processes are intertwined and very hard to separate out. Sally Price and Richard Price (1999) use the notion of "the changing same," a term coined by Leroi Jones (aka Amiri Baraka), to evoke their approach. One could just as well use it to evoke the sort of structural continuity I am referring to, in which "cultural continuity appears as the mode of cultural change" (Sahlins 1993:19). That is, a people's attempt to maintain a cultural continuity or cultural difference for themselves (and, I would add, others) is the mode of cultural change; in maintaining that difference—which is, crucially, a *sense* of difference—they avail themselves of whatever seems to work, whether it is their "own" traditions or something else.

"AFRICA" AND "BLACKNESS" IN COLOMBIAN POPULAR MUSIC, 1920s TO 1950s

In twentieth-century academic disciplines and in state circles in Colombia, blacks were not an object of attention or legislation. They were "invisible" (de Friedemann 1984). In the popular culture and literature of late-nineteenth- and twentieth-century Colombia, there was a good deal more interest in black people and/or in blackness as a symbol (for example, in music). Such interest was limited and very often placed blacks in an inferior social position, either exoticizing or explicitly vilifying them, but blacks were not actually "invisible," even if important aspects of their identity were erased. In one sense, to actually erase blacks (or indigenous people) from representations of the nation ran counter to the whole ideology of *mestizaje* (racial and cultural mixture), on which ideas of Colombian nationhood were—and to a large extent still are—based (Wade 1998, 2000).

There are two aspects here. First, the nationalist ideology of mestizaje automatically implies the notional original stocks involved in creating the mixed nation—Africans, indigenous Americans, and Europeans—and thus reasserts their existence at the same time it envisages their eventual disappearance. Yet their total elimination threatens to rob the nation of its self-definition as mixed: without the original ingredients present, the continuing process of mixture loses its sense. The ideology of mestizaje therefore involves continuous blending, but also continuing separation. Second, a constant emphasis on racial difference is central to elites' definitions of themselves as superior—as whiter, richer, more central, more "civilized," more "modern," and so forth. Black and indigenous people are not only identified as racially distinct but also are often associated with poverty, marginality, vulgarity, and backwardness.

Thus, if we look at Colombia in, say, the 1920s to the 1930s, blackness (and sometimes by extension "Africa") was not absent but occupied a specific role. As I have shown previously (Wade 1993:16–17), elite writers could take rather different positions. Luis López de Mesa wrote in 1934 that "we [Colombians] are Africa, America, Asia and Europe all at once, without grave spiritual perturbation" (López de Mesa 1970, cited in Wade 1993:16). Although he was at the same time rather disparaging about contemporary black people, he was not as negative as his peer Laureano Gómez, who lectured in 1928 that black and indigenous heritage were "marks of complete inferiority" (Gómez 1970, cited in Wade 1993:17). Although their views differed to some extent, they converged in writing about blackness and Africa within the context of defining the nation and its possibilities. Whatever blackness and Africanness were thought to be took their shape from that context: both qualities were seen to be contributors to a process of ongoing mixture and were defined in terms of what they might have to offer the nation as basic ingredients. Strength, power, and hard work were among the virtues usually outlined by such writers; laziness, lax morality, and irrationality were the vices they feared. Yet, of course, the context of the nation itself was being formed by preexisting notions of blackness. The stereotyped views of what blacks might offer the nation were obviously not disconnected from elitist stereotyped views of blacks that had existed in the late colonial period in Latin America. Here, we can see elements of continuity that are linked to persisting power hierarchies and "white" elite hegemony.

To illustrate this process more exactly, I will examine some changes in the popular music scene in Colombia that took place between the 1920s and the 1950s, paralleling changes in other Latin American countries that saw, often rather earlier, the emergence of "national" urban popular forms, such as tango in Argentina, rumba in Cuba, samba in Brazil, and *ranchera* in Mexico. In Colombia, various types of music, among them *porro* and *cumbia*, emerged as national commercial styles during this period (Wade 1998, 2000). Not only were they nationally successful in purely commercial terms, but they also became national icons: cumbia especially has come to represent Colombian popular music abroad since about the 1960s, but porro shared this role before that. These genres, known broadly as *música costeña* or *música tropical*, came from the Caribbean coastal region of the country, *la costa*. This region has a mixed population, with significant indigenous groups in some rather peripheral areas and large numbers of *mestizos* whose ancestry includes much African and indigenous heritage, as well as European. There are also large numbers of "black" people, although the exact term they might use to describe themselves or that others might use to describe them would depend on a host of contextual factors. The region has the image of being a relatively "black" place, and the music associated with it in the 1930s and 1940s partook of this image.

Before the success of this music, the "national" music of Colombia was a style associated with the country's Andean interior, a central region in geographical, economic, and political terms and also a much "whiter" region. This music was called *bambuco* and consisted of songs played on various types of guitar with some light percussion accompaniment. Because bambuco was considered to be the essence of Colombian nationality, there was a good deal of concern and debate about its origins. Blackness was part of these discussions. Debates included the relative contributions of the constituent elements of the African-Indian-European triad, which is constantly invoked in such discussions in Colombia; everything must be traced in some way to these origins. However, different people weighted each pole of the triad differently. Some saw the genre, and specifically its name, as deriving from Africa; others saw its origins as European or rooted in the Andean region of Colombia. The debates have continued to the present (Ochoa 1997).

With porro and cumbia, there was less equivocation about the presence of black, African, and indigenous elements, partly because of the association of these styles with the Caribbean coastal region. Yet exactly what was "black" in the music and what that blackness signified were very open to multiple readings, even more so than in the case of bambuco. To grasp this idea, we need to know a little more about how the music emerged and became national in impact.

After 1900, all over Latin America and the Caribbean, cities grew rapidly, industrialization increased, rural populations moved into urban surroundings, and urban space became more class-stratified. Urban popular music began to consolidate just as the radio and recording industries were being set up, first in the United States between 1900 and 1920 and soon after across the rest of the Americas. The middle classes appropriated styles of urban popular music favored by the working classes (samba, tango, and so on) as symbols of national culture (Chasteen 2004). In Colombia, popular music from Latin America, the Caribbean, North America, and Europe was in fashion in the cities in the 1920s. The "national" product was still bambuco at this time, and this style had already been recorded by some Colombian artists in New York. In Colombia, as in the rest of the Americas, local "jazz bands" played a wide variety of popular tunes. Although they soon appeared all over the country, such bands were seen first in the Caribbean coastal region, partly because of its very location and partly because of the influence of many foreign immigrants in ports such as Barranquilla.

Jazz bands in Barranquilla and other regional cities began to include styles that were said to come from the rural hinterland of the region. Porro was one such style. It came from the repertoire of the wind bands that played in provincial fiestas—wind bands were a trend not only in Colombia but also all over Latin America from the early nineteenth century onward—and that reportedly picked up peasant styles and "invented" porro. Some jazz band leaders had provincial small-town or even rural backgrounds, had been trained in such wind bands, and had contact with peasant musical groups. In orchestrated form, porro and related styles became popular in the elite social clubs of the coastal cities, although they were met with a certain resistance at first, being considered too plebian and vulgar—and "black" by some. From the Caribbean coastal region, the styles made their way into the cities of the interior, Bogotá, Medellín, and Cali, with the jazz bands of leaders such as Lucho Bermúdez, a key figure in this process. By the late 1940s, this costeño music was a national success and had begun to define the Colombian popular-music sound abroad. Again, some commentators in cities of the interior gave this music a hostile reception as musically unpleasant, licentious, vulgar, too black, and African.

What was the overall context within which different people were defining "blackness" or making reference to "Africa" when they talked about costeño music? The principal frame of reference was the nation. Nationalism has rarely been extremely passionate and intense in Colombia (Bushnell 1993), but during the early decades of the twentieth century, rapid processes of modernization made the nation and its past and future an important concept. For many elite and middle-class commentators, the notion of blackness was something to be superseded because it smacked of a lack of "culture" (that is, refinement), defined according to European and North American elite norms. Thus one newspaper commentator bewailed the loss of certain "traditional" Christmas festive customs. These had been taken over by "an explosive African-sounding orchestra [which] now threatens festivities from which the feeling and simplicity typical of previous celebrations are absent" (*El Tiempo*, December 17, 1940). Another writer described contemporary dances in Bogotá, where "the drums beat, the gentlemen of the orchestra screech with a tragic fury, as if they were seasoning a joyful picnic of some 'mister' [white boss] in a jungle in Oceania" (*Sábado*, June 3, 1944). The reference to Oceania, rather than Africa, obeys a contemporary primitivist tendency to merge the two (Rhodes 1994), and the overall meaning is clear: costeño music was seen as non-national, black, and primitive and as highly emotional, exaggerated, and unrestrained (men "screeched" in an emotional chaos of tragedy, fury, and joy). Blackness and "Africa" thus take their meaning within a discourse of nationalism that seeks a Europhile future for the nation and is pronounced by an elite that can highlight its own status by vilifying popular culture.

Nationalist discourse makes reference to an international context because a "nation" exists only in relation to other nations, and this idea leads us to a second transnational dimension within which blackness and Africanness were being construed. In Europe and North America—the very centers to which many Colombian elite and middle-class people looked to define notions of "culture"—primitivism was, during the early decades of the twentieth century, an important trend within currents of modernism. Primitivist art, the Harlem Renaissance, Josephine Baker, suntanning as an elite aesthetic—all these things were moving the worlds of fashion and the arts (Barkan and Bush 1995; S. Price 1989; Rhodes 1994; Torgovnick 1990). Africa and blackness were being constructed in ways that were by no means new—as powerful, sexy, rhythmic, emotional, authentic, raw, beautiful—but were more positive, if highly exoticizing. To be modern and, above all, fashionable could include engaging with blackness in these primitivist ways.

In Colombia, these currents of modernism and primitivism were felt, too, and linked to the Caribbean coastal region (cf. R. Moore 1997 on Cuba). Gilard (1991) shows that one of Colombia's only avant-garde journals, *Voces* (1917–1920), came out of the Caribbean port of Barranquilla. In the 1940s, a kind of literary negritude, which influenced the intellectual elites in Bogotá, emerged. Black poet Jorge Artel's (1940) book *Tambores en la noche* (*Drums in the Night*) portrayed the black culture of the Caribbean coastal region as replete with sensuality, music, and rhythm—and pain and sorrow. It was read by Bogotá intellectuals, including poet Eduardo Carranza (1944), who wrote: "Artel carries the singing voice of the dark race." The black writer Manuel Zapata Olivella was also an important figure of the period: he took costeño musicians to Bogotá for presentations of "folklore," and he published novels about the Caribbean coastal region. In 1940 his brother, Juan, started *La hora costeña* (The Coastal Hour), a Bogotá radio program of popular costeño music. Zapata Olivella was also connected to the so-called Grupo de Barranquilla, a group of writers and journalists that emerged in the 1940s and included Gabriel García Márquez, who was writing for costeño newspapers. At the same time, costeño painters such as Alejandro Obregón and Enrique Grau worked themes of sensuality and bright color into their works, sometimes using black women in their paintings (Medina 1978:367).

In many artistic spheres, then, a primitivist blackness was becoming increasingly fashionable, driven by a transnational artistic modernism that in Colombia had a strong basis in the Caribbean coastal region. The links of the region and its music to a transnational modernity were reinforced by the popularity of black-influenced music—often dance music—emerging in the rapid development of an international music industry, based in New York but from a very early stage highly transnational in its recording strategies and marketing networks.

Blackness was therefore readable as modern and fashionable—the newspaper columnist who associated porro with Oceania also quipped that "modernism requires this: that we should dance like blacks in order to be in fashion" (*Sábado*, June 3, 1944)—and modernity was a goal to which nationalists aspired. Some of the contradictions involved here could be resolved by exploiting the twin ambivalences of blackness and modernity. Modernity was generally regarded as a good thing when it implied progress, scientific and technical advance, educational improvement, and "refined" culture, but it could also imply alienation, loss of tradition, slavish emulation of foreign examples, vulgar consumerism, and moral laxness. Equally, the ambivalence of blackness, which far predated the primitivist modernism of the early twentieth century, meant that it could be seen by non-blacks as evil and threatening but also as endowed with particular powers. If at this historical moment blackness was being associated with fashionable modernity, it could also be read as being nothing but "fashion"—at best, mere faddishness and at worst, a threat to national culture and morals.

The columnist who so neatly saw the connection between modernism and "dancing like blacks" also mentioned that in the contemporary scene, the culture deemed fashionable was that which had "the acrid smell of jungle and sex" (*Sábado*, June 3, 1944). Sex was constantly connected with música costeña, as it was connected at the time with black music all over the Americas and as it had been even in colonial times (see Chasteen 2004; Wade 1993:279). In these decades of the twentieth century, however, a more explicit and liberated approach to sexuality was also fashionable in some circles of Europe and North America. In Colombia, where Catholic orthodoxy has historically been strong, it would be wrong to speak of radical changes in sexual morality, but Uribe Celis (1992:45) notes that feminism had made an impact on Colombia starting in the 1920s, and in the 1930s and 1940s women were migrating in large numbers to cities, where they worked as domestic servants and in factories. They earned their own incomes, and my research into people's memories of the 1940s and 1950s indicates that young, urban, working-class women had some autonomy in leisure activities—which included going out dancing with groups of female friends. In short, "black" music (or music with connotations of blackness) was modern in terms of the sexuality it was thought to evoke or evince. Naturally, such a connection could equally well be read as a dreadful threat to morals by those who feared the negative aspects of modernism.

If blackness was linked to modernity, or more precisely, modernism, it did not thereby lose the negative connotations of primitiveness, backwardness, lack of "culture," and so forth. But within the national and transnational frames of reference, such associations, if suitably distant or "whitened," could also be reread in a positive light. One of the perceived threats of modernity was loss of "tradition," the decline of the authentically national in the face of modern and fashionable "foreign" culture. One of the columnists cited above saw "African-sounding" music as the foreign threat in this context, whereas, ironically, "carols" were construed as authentically Colombian. But blackness could also be made to mean "tradition," or something autochthonous. (Indigenousness might be more easily read this way, and indigenous roots were sometimes claimed for porro in newspaper commentaries on it.) Porro was, apparently, authentically Colombian and could thus compete on the international stage with tango, samba, or rumba as a legitimate representative of national identities. What made it authentically Colombian was its origin in a region that, while modern in its Barranquilla city life, was also traditional, "folkloric," and steeped in blackness (and indigenousness), which, themselves, could be read, in the standard nationalist discourse of mestizaje, as elements belonging to the past.

An illustration of this concept can be found in the writings of Antonio Brugés Carmona, a costeño intellectual and politician, who in various press articles produced descriptions of costeño people, music, and events. In 1943 he described how porro was born from the traditional music of La Costa: "[S]ince it [porro] was of the same family as cumbia, under the hot and brilliant nights in which cumbia was danced, the younger son appeared in the circle [of dancers] lit by madness, bringing new rhythms to the monotonous rejoicings of cumbia.... [Porro] took over the festivities and finally went beyond the borders of its predecessors, becoming not costeño but Colombian" (*El Tiempo*, February 28, 1943). Cumbia was generally thought to be of antique origins, with mainly black and indigenous roots, so deriving porro from cumbia rooted it in the black and indigenous past. Lucho Bermúdez, the great jazz-band leader who did so much to popularize porro and other styles of música costeña from the 1940s onward, also emphasized this kind of local, and racial, rootedness: "In my songs I always speak of the magic, of the *brujos* [sorcerers], of the blacks, of all the legends of Santa Marta, Cartagena and in general of the whole Atlantic coast. I think one should always be close to one's *pueblo* [people, village, nation], that's why 'Carmen de Bolívar' and all those other songs were born which carried a message to all of Colombia" (Arango Z. 1985: 19).[3] Much later, when Bermúdez died in 1994, President César Gaviria gave a speech in which he declared, "Lucho Bermúdez composed works which by virtue of their artistic quality and their profound popular roots today form part of the cultural heritage of the folkloric patrimony of our country" (*El Espectador*, April 26, 1994). The emphasis on "folkloric patrimony" is very telling when referring to a highly cosmopolitan musician, with formal musical training, who played mainly in Colombia's elite social clubs (see below).

This is where the narratives about the origins of porro and cumbia are so important. Most of these narratives have been constructed in written form from the 1960s onward by folklorists and amateur historians, as well as professional academics (see Wade 2000:ch. 3). William Fortich, for example, is a costeño university professor and folklorist who was central in setting up in 1977 the annual National Festival of Porro, dedicated to preserving wind-band porro. He maintains that porro derives essentially from the traditional peasant *conjuntos de gaitas*, groups based on flutes of Amerindian origins and drums, which are documented as existing at least through the 1830s but are said by Fortich (1994:2) to have origins "so remote that they become confused with legend." The *gaita* is a flute of Amerindian origins, so Fortich is emphasizing the indigenous elements in porro's mythical origins. However, the drums used in the music of the Caribbean coastal region are attributed to African influence, and Fortich then makes tangential reference to Vodou and *santería* (without explicitly linking them to Colombia or porro) before mentioning a secret society called *poro*, found in West Africa (1994:12–15).

Fortich (1994:67–68) then focuses on a late-nineteenth-century founding figure, Alejandro Ramírez Ayazo, who had learned the clarinet from a trained musician and liked to invite conjuntos de gaitas to his house, where he played clarinet with them. This was the transitional context in which "the old *porro* of the *gaiteros* served as a nucleus which musicians with some academic training could develop" (1994:6), and the wind-band repertoire is generally agreed to have emerged from porro.

The same basic narrative of continuous musical tradition molded superficially by new interpreters informs the next phase, when jazz bands adopted porro from wind bands in the 1930s. Band leaders such as Lucho Bermúdez are said to have taken porro and other similar styles and "dressed them up in tails." Portaccio (1995:44–45), for example, a costeño radio announcer and amateur historian, makes obligatory reference to the "tri-ethnic" origins of porro: from "the white" comes the dance, specifically the "minuet"-style opening of the music; from "the black" comes the drum; from "the Indian" the cane flute, precursor of the clarinet. Portaccio (1995:46) adds that in the 1930s the genre was considered rather plebian, so Bermúdez "took up elements of the Big-Bands of the era, above all [those] of white origin, softening porro and thus giving it a greater circulation."

This very typical rendering of a central body of tradition with a light clothing of new style is also characteristic of the historiography of cumbia. The story is generally simpler, focusing less on late-nineteenth-century wind bands and referring to cumbia, whether as music or dance, as having remote colonial origins that are, of course, tri-ethnic. Cumbia is often held to be, as in the words of Delia Zapata Olivella (1962), a folkloric dance teacher of some renown and sister of Manuel, "a musical synthesis of the Colombian nation." The sleeve notes of *La candela viva*, a CD by black costeño singer Totó la Momposina, say that cumbia is "a fine example of the combined sentiments of Indian, Spanish and African culture"; it originated as "a courting dance... between Black men and Indian women when the two communities began to intermarry." The notes also cite Totó herself as saying that "the music I play has its roots in a mixed race: being Black and Indian, the heart of the music is completely percussive." Cumbia is thus presented as a regional variant—particularly in the lesser role given to European influences—of the central metaphorical act of sexual congress that drives the mestizaje central to nationalism. All this construes cumbia as a traditional, even originary, music and dance form.

These commentators are emphasizing tradition and continuity, with greater weight given to indigenous and African than to European influences. They are retrospectively plotting particular lines through a tangled skein of syncretized syncretisms and mutual influences that could also be traced in different ways. One might look at the formal training Lucho Bermúdez received and his avowed indebtedness to non-Colombian musicians and teachers with conservatory backgrounds and conclude that the porro he played was a variant on a contemporary pan–Latin American and Caribbean musical style that he chose to label as "porro" in order to give it some nationalist appeal and to distinguish it in a competitive, transnational music market. The traditionalist commentaries allow us to see how "Africa" or blackness is constructed as a point of reference—albeit a rather distant one, sketched in invocations of secret societies or African drums—for the nation's identity. Indigenous and black genealogies are privileged and traced in direct lines of descent that allow a central core to remain, audibly linking twentieth-century porro and cumbia to the sexual act that gave birth to the nation. One could argue for real musical continuities, from colonial associations of slaves with their drums, through the peasant groups, to the wind bands and the jazz bands. Bermúdez (1996), for example, does retain certain muted rhythmic markers that link his music to local peasant music, as far as we can know that music through contemporary accounts of it. My point is not to deny these continuities but to demonstrate how they are *also* discursively constructed—whether by folklorists or racist columnists—so that judgment about what constitutes a "real" musical continuity is by no means straightforward.

Whatever blackness and Africanness might be was therefore subject to innumerable readings: they might be modern and fashionable or primitive and backward; they might be modern precisely because they were "primitive"; they might be sexy, but that sexuality could be an underlying drive for mestizaje and nationhood, a threat to morality or a liberatory force challenging hidebound social conventions; they might represent roots and authenticity, something autochthonously Colombian, or they might represent the benighted past that had to be superseded.

So far, I have discussed constructs of blackness and Africanness at the level of discourse about music within the national and transnational context. But the theme of sexuality suggests a much more personal level at which these processes of identification operate. Two ideas push me in this direction. First, I have already mentioned how nationalist discourse on mestizaje has a permanent tension between an image of homogeneity and one of continuing difference; each depends on the other. This tension is enacted in terms of pronouncements about the nation's past and future and in terms of discriminations against individual people (rejected as marriage partners for being "too black") or particular cultural forms, such as musical styles (also rejected for being "too black")—even while the person discriminating in this way identifies himself or herself as mestizo and understands Colombian culture as the product of mixtures. In Placido's (1998) dissertation about the María Lionza cult in Venezuela, she explores how believers in the cult sometimes think of mestizos as being gray and boring people, in whom the three original ingredients of mixture—Africa, America, and Europe—have blended to produce a colorless, bland, uneventful product. She identifies an alternative discourse in which people see the three elements as coexisting in a mosaic, without losing their original identity. People eclectically make use of symbols and resources identified with different origins, according to their needs and desires. The variety that this coexistence implies is seen as rich with possibilities, with color, with potential. In concrete terms, within the very broad terms of the "cult" (which is not a closed and systematic grouping but a very open and varied set of beliefs about spirits who descend into mediums), the coexistence of elements is manifest in three central spirit figures, *las tres potencias*, the three powers: El Negro Felipe (black), María Lionza (white, although occasionally presented as indigenous), and El Indio Guaicaipuro (indigenous). These, plus a host of other spirits, can descend into mediums who then speak to other believers (see also Taussig 1997). The notion of coexisting rather than fused elements is certainly suggested in some commentaries on Colombian music, which often insist on identifying particular aspects of contemporary styles as "black/African," "white/European," and "indigenous." The notion of spirits being in the body suggests that these "powers" or potentialities are thought of, or even experienced, as parts of the self in a bodily sense, as aspects of embodied personhood.

This idea links to the second theme: the importance of thinking about racial identities in terms of embodiment. Embodiment has been tackled from the perspectives of medical anthropology and gender and sexuality studies, but it is less clear what difference it makes that racial identities are lived in an embodied way. I am not referring here simply to the idea that racial identities may be marked phenotypically. I am trying to grapple with how people feel that their racial identity (their "blood") expresses itself and is part of their person. I cannot elaborate on this agenda here (see Wade 2002), but I am interested in the fact that music and dance are intensely embodied activities and ones that have been highly racialized in colonial and postcolonial contexts. Notions about the racial origins of particular musical elements might be considered from the point of view of how people live their lives in an embodied way. Going to a dance class to learn cumbia might be understandable as a personal project of working on one's body to express and indeed develop the "blackness" one "has inside" as a potentiality. Or indeed, simply going out in Bogotá, Cali, Barranquilla, or Medellín to dance salsa, plus a bit of cumbia and perhaps nowadays the occasional *currulao* (a Pacific coastal style), could be a way of expressing the "blackness" in one's body and keeping it alive. One might also think about the significance of common sayings such as "*se le salió el negro*" (literally, "the black came out of him"), which can be heard from Argentina to Cuba when a person who may be "white" or "mixed" behaves in a way thought to be "black"; the implication is that "blackness" is still "in there" somewhere and may come out spontaneously or be consciously developed.

Some pilot interviews I carried out with black dancers and musicians in Cali in 1998 also point in this direction. All of them acknowledged a strong link among black people, rhythm, and skill in dance. Some thought that this skill was "in the blood" (*en la sangre*). Others were more "environmentalist" in their views, either because they were explicitly aware of the racist potential of arguments that invoked "blood" or because their own experience had taught them that non-blacks could be excellent dancers and that blacks might not be. The dancers all emphasized, however, that becoming a dancer had been an intensive process of bodily training, whatever their "natural" skills. One man, a singer in a rap group (see next section), recounted his experiences learning salsa, later getting into reggae, raggamuffin, and finally rap, and told of his identification with *ese golpe fuerte* (that heavy beat), which he found in these different styles. Developing that "heavy beat" as a personal embodied project of being a good dancer and eventually a performer was linked to his own developing identity as a black man, which he also expressed by growing dreadlocks and adopting a discourse that included elements of black consciousness and Afrocentrism. In a sense, although this man explicitly rejected the notion of rhythm being "natural" to black people in general, he was developing the "blackness" inside him, realizing, expressing, and enacting it through his body to achieve an identity as a black man in 1990s Colombia.

All this theory is somewhat speculative, and I don't have systematic empirical data to back it up, but it gives us a different way of approaching the processes in which people identify what is "black" in their local, regional, and national cultures. This, I suggest, might profitably be seen as an intensely personal and bodily process. Thus—to return to Colombian music in the mid-twentieth century—the historical shift by which *música costeña* displaced bambuco as the most popular national sound can be understood in some sense as the "black-ening" of Colombia (albeit with a whitened form of blackness, so to speak) but also as the "bringing out" of the blackness that individual Colombians might have felt was inside them (not that all would have felt this; some surely vigorously denied any such thing). Interestingly, I found that people often used intensely bodily imagery in recounting their experiences of musical changes in Colombia in the 1940s, 1950s, and 1960s. The imagery most often used was that of heat: migrants to the interior of the country from the Caribbean coastal region, whether black or mixed, and people native to the interior all talked about how the costeños and música costeña had "heated up" the cold inte-rior of the country—made it freer, more colorful, less restricted, and so on. This idea suggests that dancing and listening to music might be understood as a way of "embodying the nation." Individuals might conceptually and bodily reproduce themselves as "nationals" as they express certain aspects of their person—black, white, indigenous, mixed—through the embodied practice of dance and music. Of course, such a process of reproduction would immediately locate a person in a transnational, as well as national, frame because the elements involved (for example, "black rhythm") evoke diaspora as much as nationhood, and, of course, the person might be dancing to "foreign" music. But this internationalizing power of the imagination, when channeled through mass media, is equally true of all processes of imagining national communities, not just musical ones.

This section has examined the public and personal ways in which people make claims and attributions about the racial identity of various different "ingredients" seen to constitute cultural forms, musical styles, and persons. These claims and attributions are being made in the context of notions of the nation in a transnational world; the interna-tional recording industry's attempts to market musical genres; ideas about modernity and tradition; sexual morality and changing gender relations; and personal development of the embodied self. In these contexts, "Africa" and "blackness" are being discursively constructed in changing ways not related in straightforward ways to the "realities" of Africanisms in Colombian culture, partly because these discourses also have the power to construct the perception of these realities.

On the other hand, it is clear that there are certain important structural continuities, in addition to those we might trace in terms of African rhythm or African-derived musical aesthetics. The attributions and claims of origin and identity tend to be made within hierarchies of race, class, gender, power, and moral worth that retain important aspects of their structure. Therefore, "blackness" and "Africanness" in Colombia and more widely in the Americas have generally had a subordinate social location; "black music"—however that term has been construed by different people—has very often been seen as noisy, vulgar, and primitive but also possibly attractive. In a general sense, too, some basic hegemonic values of whiteness won out: even as the music introduced elements of tropicality and blackness and even "Africa" into the national cultural panorama, these appeared in rather whitened form: porro was made "smoother"; black musicians were infrequently seen in the big jazz bands.

CALI

The question of continuities raises its head with particular force in Colombia in the wake of the 1991 constitution, which defines the nation as "multiethnic and pluricultural" and gives some specific symbolic and politico-legal space to both black and indigenous communities. Are "Africa" and "blackness" being substantially redefined in this context? Or are there important continuities? The answer is, perhaps predictably, a bit of both.

To examine this question, I will focus on a very specific case, a small "ethno-cultural association" in a low-income barrio of the Colombian city of Cali, with which I did some fieldwork in 1997. The association, which is also a rap group, is called "Ashanty," which gives some indication of where their interests lie (see Matory, this volume, for hints as to why such a name might have been chosen).[4] The group, formed in about 1992, is held together by a small number of regular members— three in 1997 and 1998. It undertakes community projects within the barrio and also organizes rap events on a larger scale. The key members are men in their twenties, who also work in various occupations to earn a living. I will look at the various different fields of practice that influence their definitions of blackness and Africanness and also influence how these definitions are received by other people in the city. I make no claim that the views of these three men are representative of the views of

Afro-Colombians in Cali or in Colombia. I simply use the case of Ashanty as one illustration of a quite varied situation in Colombia.

A central field is that of the constitutional reform itself and the legislation issuing from it. In the 1990s blackness achieved a greater public profile than it had ever had (although fear of slave rebellion put blackness pretty high on the public agenda on occasion in colonial New Granada). This profile is evident in political debate about legislation in favor of black communities, government decrees about the inclusion of Afro-Colombian themes in school curricula, and the very rapid burgeoning of black organizations, rural and urban, which, although concentrated in the Pacific coastal region, where land rights can be claimed, are also found in many other areas, especially the principal cities. It is also evident in TV documentaries about the Pacific coastal region, the inclusion of contemporary "black culture" in state museum displays, and the increasing visibility of music associated with the Pacific coastal region.

Ashanty emerged in exactly this wave of interest in black culture. The everyday problems its members encountered in their struggle to survive and maintain some kind of material and cultural security— poverty, violence, lack of urban services and employment—were strongly channeled into ideas about racism. These ideas emerged from two sources: first, their own experience of racism in Cali—a city with a large native black population but also a rapidly growing number of black immigrants from the Pacific coastal region (Urrea 1997); and second, their perceptions of racism elsewhere, such as in Jamaica (particularly via Bob Marley's reggae) and the United States (via such films as *Malcolm X*). At the same time, they were involved in more home-grown challenges to racism, such as those mounted by Cimarrón (the National Movement for the Rights of the Black Communities of Colombia), some of whose seminars they attended.

Ashanty members are also linked into academic circuits to some extent, for they have been "studied" by a few academics and recently one of them worked as a research assistant with a Colombo-French study of black migration to Cali. Two Ashanty members attended a seminar mounted by this project in 1998 and participated in debates. One of them criticized my paper precisely on the question of "Africa," to which he felt I gave insufficient emphasis. The whole academic debate about Africanisms in Colombian culture thus also filtered into Ashanty's world via the growing reflexivity of academic knowledge that is characteristic of late-twentieth-century social science, and forms the second field of practice that influences definitions of blackness at this local level.

Ashanty forms part of a growing number of small black grassroots NGOs that larger institutions—the state, the Catholic Church, international NGOs—have begun to support. In Cali, for example, the city created a Division of Black Affairs in 1996. This trend introduces a third field of practice that impinges on the definition of Ashanty's identity: the circuits of state and NGO funding within which small-scale community organizations compete for support. Ashanty has had some success in this competition. In 1996, for example, it organized a city-wide rap concert as the culmination of a series of workshops covering various aspects of black culture and history, as well as the history and techniques of "hip-hop culture." The whole project was financed by the church, one dependency of the city administration, and an international NGO. But I found that the city, in dependencies such as the Youth Section, was reluctant to fund Ashanty because it considered the group too radical on the one hand and too disorganized on the other. That is, Ashanty members emphasized racism and blackness too much for the mostly white city employees, and they did not seem, by the standards of these employees, to have a "culture" that was stable and enduring enough to warrant investment of public funds destined to create good citizens. In one sense, the logic of the new multicultural constitution and the creation of entities such as the Cali División de Negritudes is that black people, and indeed all peoples, have a "culture." Yet the city also wanted to be able to vet whether a "culture" was worthy of being considered as such for the purposes of funding and support (Wade 1999).

To compete for funding in local, national, and even international networks, Ashanty members have to have a coherent representation of who they are. Because part of their claims involve ethnic identity and difference, they have to construct a "culture," or at least a specific "sub-culture," that is representable as "black" (although some in the City Council might prefer it to be represented as "youth"). This situation leads us to a fourth field of practice: the objectification of culture taking place within globalizing circuits of commodification. Ashanty members nurtured their identity as a group and as individuals on salsa, reggae, raggamuffin, and rap; mass media images of Bob Marley; and Spike Lee's *Malcolm X*. The iconography visible in the places they hung out included pictures of US basketball stars, US rappers, and Jamaican reggae singers; Nelson Mandela sometimes figured too. The rap concert event they organized in 1997 had all the usual trappings of a commercial popular music presentation—including sponsorship by a Colombian beer company. Of course, the members of Ashanty personalized these symbols. Two of them wore dreadlocks and often Rasta colors; one of them painted a sign in Rasta colors for the Peluquería Africa (Africa Barbershop). I am not implying, therefore, that the use of globalized commodities to construct a local identity is in some way inauthentic (see Campbell 1987; D. Miller 1995). The point is that notions of blackness and Africanness are constructed in ways influenced by this field of practice. Of course, this idea is hardly new. As I show above, Colombian music from the 1930s onward developed in the highly transnational commodified field of the international music industry; a key symbol of blackness in Colombia was Afro-Cuban popular music, for example. In the 1990s, one difference was the speed of circulation of these commodities, their accessibility and pervasiveness, especially at the barrio level. The other difference was the more self-conscious use of these symbols to actively construct an identity around an objectified notion of culture (which is not to say that this identity is therefore "false"). In the 1940s, although costeño musical culture was being objectified and commodified, it was less involved in a self-conscious construction of *identity*.

Given these different fields of practice, how are blackness and Africanness being constructed in this Cali context? As with Colombian music, we can see that what is identified as black and/or African is located in a national field (the constitutional reform, the increasing public legitimacy of blackness in definitions of national identity) and an international field (global circuits of exchange); it is influenced by academic research (on African origins) and by the salability, so to speak, of an identity (in this case, the "selling" of Ashanty's identity to public and NGO funding bodies). Embodiment is also important. For Ashanty members and other young blacks who participate in rap and in barrio-level "folkloric" groups that practice Pacific coast currulao music and dance—the same individuals often have experience in both of these very different musical contexts—the motor skills acquired through practicing dance moves associated with these musical styles do not just express but also constitute their blackness (and their youth).

In these contexts, then, we find—at least in the case of Ashanty but also more widely—a much more assertive and less whitened definition of blackness, in which "Africa" is an important, if vague, symbolic element, and various elements are combined, montage-style, in a self-conscious process of identity formation in which reflexive relations between academics and activists are more tightly woven than before. New images of blackness are being created, based on rap, reggae, and raggamuffin, and images of the United States and Africa itself, alongside the ever-popular salsa. In the musical world of the Caribbean coastal region, this situation is paralleled to some extent by the advent of *champeta* (known more recently as *terapia*), the local name for an eclectic mixture of Zairean *soukous*, Nigerian highlife, and Haitian *konpa*, *soca*, and reggae, which since the 1970s has become popular among particular young working-class people in Cartagena and other the cities and towns of the region (Cunin 2003; Mosquera and Provensal 2000; Pacini 1993; Streicker 1995; Waxer 1997). These faces of blackness tend to sit rather ill at ease with other, more nationalist versions, to which these faces appear rather "foreign"—as did porro to some in the 1940s.

Here we can see some continuities in the hierarchies of power and morality within which attributions and claims about blackness are being made: blackness is still mainly subordinate, still mainly working class; it is still, in some of its forms, construed by others as "disorganized" and, with its ("foreign-looking") US-style emphasis on racism or "foreign" musical styles, threatening to the image of (national) racial democracy, now revamped as tolerant multiculturalism. Meanwhile, other instances of black culture, such as the currulao music of the Pacific coast, can be commodified and sold in "cultural" festivals as authentically Colombian and emotionally liberating. (In fact, the two aspects are not as separable as this idea might suggest: as I mentioned above, many black Cali rappers have been part of barrio "folkloric" groups that specialize in "traditional" currulao styles of music and dance.)

In sum, blackness is being constructed in a more assertive way on the one hand, but also in a rather conservative nationalist way on the other. In both cases, appeal may be made to multiculturalism, although nationalist versions of this idea are in many ways a variant on the older theme of mestizaje as based on the Africa-America-Europe triad. In both cases, too, "Africa" is a more visible (or audible) presence, although it remains a rather vague evocation with very different meanings attached: it may legitimate a specific cultural difference in the realms of identity politics (for Ashanty and other black organizations), or it may tap into the realms of "world music" trends of commodification.

CONCLUSION

The thrust of this chapter is that "blackness" and "Africa" have to be understood in their changing historical contexts; these include such varied aspects as definitions of national identity, transnational capitalism, local politics, the academic production of knowledge, and the way people conceive of their own persons as embodying different aspects of the nation's heritage, expressible through embodied practice. This emphasis on contextuality has to be tempered by a concern with continuities, however. One can locate these in terms of huellas de africanía, but it is necessary to do this with the knowledge of the multiple readings of "Africa" that are already being made by others within the contexts outlined above—readings that have their own structural continuities generated by relations of dominance and that intertwine with the continuities of cultural practice passed across generations.

An aspect of these complex processes of particular concern to academics is how the production of academic knowledge fits into a sense of continuity and change. What is the impact of my argument? What is the impact of Arocha's approach? What happens when Arocha (1996:327) suggests, admittedly in a speculative fashion, that the white veils he saw hanging from a ceiling during a funeral in the Pacific coast region of Colombia evoked, in their shape and form, the two linked equilateral triangles that symbolize the ax of Changó on Yorùbá altars in Cuba, Haiti, and Brazil? It seems unlikely that the local people at the funeral thought of these connections, but it is possible that they, or others, would begin to do so, whether or not the connections turned out to be "true" (by the academic standards current in history and anthropology). The effect is to reconstruct "Africa" in yet another form in the Colombian context. The burden of my argument is not to deny that connections between Africa and Colombia exist, nor to deny that their unearthing is worthwhile and has important political implications. It is rather to say that the ways in which "Africa" and "blackness" have been constructed and read in Colombia make these terms so variable that we cannot *confine* ourselves to the endeavor of unearthing. The implication of my argument is that "blackness" and "Africa" are, and can be, much more than the genealogical origins we might be able to unearth for them and that their political importance need not depend on attributions of authentic origin.

Notes

A grant from the Leverhulme Trust (1994–1995) financed my research on costeño music. I based this research on interviews with musicians, industry personnel, and "ordinary" listeners in Bogotá, Medellín, and Barranquilla; a review of the press archives; and secondary literature. The Nuffield Foundation (1997) and the University of Manchester (1998) funded my research in Cali. These projects were linked to the project Organización social, dinámicas culturales e identidades de las poblaciones afrocolombianas del Pacífico y suroccidente en un contexto de movilidad y urbanización, run jointly from 1996 through 2000 by CIDSE (Centro de Investigaciones y Documentación Socioeconómica) of the Facultad de Ciencias Sociales y Económicas, Universidad del Valle, Cali, and IRD (Institut de Recherche pour le Développement, Paris). My thanks to Fernando Urrea of CIDSE for help with this work.

1. Cunin (1999) shows how in the city of Cartagena, on Colombia's Caribbean coast, the representation of black and Afro-Colombian identities in the post-1991 context is dominated by *palenqueros*, black people from the village of Palenque de San Basilio, a former palenque that today retains a clear and unique Afro-Colombian cultural and linguistic identity.

2. See Arocha (1999:25). But see, for example, Wade (1993:267): "The musical *style,* if not the form and content of much black music [in Colombia] is very African...the Congo dances and the masks of the carnival of Barranquilla clearly have strong African origins....Clearly the Africans imported into Colombia had a major impact on the evolution of Colombian culture."

3. Santa Marta and Cartagena are cities of colonial origin on the Caribbean

coast. "Carmen de Bolívar" is a song dedicated to Bermúdez's hometown.

4. I use the real name of the group because it is already in the public domain and group members have given me explicit permission to do so.

Part IV
Critical Histories/Critical Theories

12

Commentary

Building on a Rehistoricized
Anthropology of the Afro-Atlantic

Faye V. Harrison

The chapters in this volume have profound implications for the
broad perimeters and parameters of the zone of knowledge production that the anthropology of the African diaspora in the Americas represents. These implications and possibilities are particularly significant
as this field of study moves forward in new and exciting directions on
the grounds of a critical consciousness of its development over time
and space. This historicized view of the ways in which our discipline has
formulated and answered its questions about the African diaspora and
its relationship to the Atlantic world influences how we see the development of anthropology as a whole. Of special relevance here is the
way in which a sense of critically reflexive historicity may enable us to
gain a greater understanding of the racial and gendered politics and
political economy that have influenced which intellectuals have been
granted a hearing in the formally recognized mainstream of the discipline and which ones have not. A critical historical consciousness is not
only focused on what happened in the past; it also allows us to see the
impact of long-standing anthropological trajectories on recent trends,
as well as those just beginning to take shape. As I will elaborate below,

this volume is part of a wider project of rehistoricization in Afro-Atlantic anthropology that is building on lessons from the past to move further along with the critical reconstruction of the discipline.

I would like to push the authors' contributions a bit further into dialogue by suggesting how the specific trajectories, intellectual social formations, and cultural transformations that were focal in the advanced seminar and remain central to this volume need to be placed in a context that is wider than one drawn largely around the legacy of Melville Herskovits's seminal project in building the conceptual, empirical, and institutional foundations for anthropological inquiry on African descendants in the Americas. This focus was the main pivot around which the seminar was organized, although our discussion went well beyond the boundaries of that particular school of thought and the debates it has provoked. Expanding the context for our discussion is necessary because there are multiple Afro-Americanist or African Americanist anthropologies. These plural anthropological projects, trajectories, and lineages, however, have been in dialogical and overlapping relationships. An important task before us, then, is to reclaim and map those relationships and their substantive contents, epistemological underpinnings, and methodological orientations on the intellectual terrain that has come to be the history of anthropology—as recorded in the canon and well beyond it. The emergence of a critical history of anthropology (e.g., Baker 1998; Carnegie 1992; Fluehr-Lobban 2002; F. Harrison 1988, 1992; F. Harrison and I. Harrison 1999) has already begun this important work, but much more needs to be accomplished, especially if we are to expand the discussion across the full scope of the Americas and black Atlantic.

DIASPORAS AND GLOBALIZATION, THEN AND NOW

In my thinking, the advanced seminar's title, "From Africa to the Americas: New Directions in Afro-American Anthropology"—which helped set the stage for *Afro-Atlantic Dialogues: Anthropology in the Diaspora* —alluded to the momentous historical events that gave rise to diaspora formation in the Americas. It pointed to the massive trans-oceanic movements and the geopolitical and economic expansion that engendered profound, far-reaching dislocations and transformations not only in Africa and the Americas but reverberating all over the colonially (dis)ordered world. The contemporary legacy of the ruptures and realignments associated with colonialism and capitalist development encompasses the variegated stuff that anthropologists and other scholars now study and label late modernity, postmodernity, postcoloniality, globalization, transnationalism, and the deterritorialization of cultures, societies, and nations, often in the form of the world's diverse diasporas, especially recently crystallized diasporas of more recent waves of immigrants and refugees. Many of the latest trends in diaspora studies privilege these recent dispersions; however, studies of the legacies of the historic transatlantic African diaspora continue to have a great deal of promise for developing more refined and nuanced approaches to making sense of and theorizing the workings of diasporas. For this reason, this collection represents an important concerted action in intervening in both African diaspora studies and studies of diasporas in general.

Many of the global and diaspora-related phenomena and processes that so many of our colleagues have only recently begun to interrogate and label according to the terms now in vogue have, in one form or another, long been integral features of the lived experiences of New World Africans. This is a point that Afro-Americanists (e.g., Mintz 1998; Slocum and Thomas 2003) have reiterated. Globalization and transnationalism, when the buzz words are adequately translated and operationalized, are not new to the Caribbean, for example, in view of that region's long-standing economic integration into global capitalist circuits of production and trade—and also in view of Caribbean people's many migrations, both within and beyond the region and hemisphere. Matory and Pulis show us that Caribbean people are not alone in having significant transterritorial reach. Black Americans and Afro–Latin Americans, such as Brazilians and Cubans, also cannot be seen as anything less than cosmopolitan historical agents. Transnational social fields of exchange and dialogue, within which Africa is among the multilateral sites, have long played an important part in the drama of lived experiences, informing both national and diasporic identities in significant ways.

Although globalization has quite a long history in the black Atlantic, it is still important to recognize that current forms of neoliberal global realignment are affecting diasporic communities, population movements, and identity making in historically specific—and frequently problematic—ways. For instance, racialization appears to be intensifying in many parts of the world (F. Harrison 2002). The specific implications of this process for Africa and its older and newer diasporas are worthy of serious attention, especially given the rise of new forms of racism (neo-racisms), which are apt to deploy insidious notions of cultural instead of biological difference. We must situate these new forces of subjection within the wider context of geopolitical and economic trends. These conditions are giving rise to new modalities and circuits through which blackness and things African and African-derived are being constructed, appropriated, commodified, and consumed. Moreover, the dynamics of global capitalism are relegating much of the African world, including countries made up of largely diasporic populations, to the bottom of the global hierarchy of cultures, nations, and economies—jeopardizing subsistence security, health, life expectancy, and human rights.

The principal focus in the rapidly burgeoning diasporas literature, which deals with the whole range of diasporas and not only the African diaspora, is on the dispersions occurring in the age of contemporary globalization, with peoples who belong to long-standing, historic diasporas (for example, African descendants in the Americas) receiving much less focus on the analytical and theoretical plane (see, for example, the contents of Braziel and Mannur 2003). Although the African diaspora has been classified as a "victim diaspora" (Cohen 1997), many scholars are now deploying the diaspora concept in ways that depart from the classical model, which emphasizes trauma, exile, alienation, oppression, and even racialization. Although I recognize that diasporas are not uniform formations across time and space, I am concerned that in some current literature, diaspora seems to have become simply a synonym for transnational migration and immigrants. Some writings even suggest that the imperial dispersions that resulted in the formation of empire settlements represent diasporic situations (see Cohen 1997:66–73 for a review of some of this literature). While some European migrations (for example, those of the Irish and those religiously persecuted) may have formed diasporas or "quasi diasporas," can all population flows from Europe that made colonial expansion and empire building possible be characterized in this way? Is this broadened mapping a consequence of diaspora studies being mainstreamed and losing the critical conceptual and political edge they once had? Or is it simply a reflection of how heterogeneous the field of study is, with competing definitions and models of what constitutes a diaspora? Diaspora is not a concept that the authors here treat uncritically or in diluted or trivial ways.

MULTIPLE GENERATIONS AND CONVERGENT SITES OF DIASPORIZATION

Because of the significance of the transatlantic African diaspora in modern world history and the importance of theorizing its complexity and multiplicity, this volume is a major intervention in wider disciplinary and interdisciplinary discourses, some of which should be more critically assessed. It is necessary to expand our understanding of "African diaspora" as both a complex of dynamic sociohistorical phenomena and as an analytical tool. Toward that end, we can develop more refined and nuanced ways to elucidate interrelationships among diverse diasporic situations across time and space. We should perhaps follow up on Stuart Hall's (1999) description of mobile peoples who have been variously once, twice, or even thrice diasporized, to deepen our understanding of the meanings, experiences, and social locations engendered by different generations and modalities of diasporic movement, identity, and belonging.

With more fine-tuned approaches, anthropologists will have something to say about the forces and conditions that have led to the transatlantic African diaspora's begetting many secondary diasporas that have dispersed black folk to new sites of encounter, adaptation, and conflict, where ideas about home and belonging become even more complicated and multilayered. As some of the chapters suggest, the generic model of diaspora, in which there is a single homeland and population dispersals to numerous diasporic sites, such as the classical Africa-centered model, is not the only one that has salience in scholarly work or in expressions of vernacular consciousness. Depending upon the time and place, Africa is decentered, having a lateral, coeval relationship with diasporic locations, or it may be insignificant. These variations in mapping and modeling diaspora lead me to question the ways that the concept is understood among Afro-Americanists, whose conceptual, theoretical, and methodological diversity preclude any easy consensus being articulated.

FAYE V. HARRISON

Of course, the way diaspora is understood has a great deal to do with the kinds of diasporic situations under scrutiny. Documenting and making analytical sense of secondary diasporic movement into other diasporic space is an important variation on this theme. I am especially intrigued by Pulis's historical anthropology of late-eighteenth-century African American "refugees" from the early postcolonial United States. Some of them made an important impact in Jamaica, as well as other places where black loyalists migrated. Marilyn Thomas-Houston's research on the contemporary descendants of black loyalists in Nova Scotia, Canada, promises to complement what Pulis reveals about the overlapping diasporic situations in Jamaica (Thomas-Houston, personal communication 2005). These two studies, along with Matory's, illum-inate the significance of mobilities and dialogues between diasporic locations and peoples within the larger African diaspora.

Although Torres and Prince touch on the subject here, what is still somewhat underdeveloped in the anthropological literature are fine-grained analyses, across a range of different sites, of the ways that contemporary diasporic situations intersect and interplay, such as in the context of global cities like New York, where African Americans, West Indians, Afro–Latin Americans, and continental African immigrants coexist, interact, and conflict under differential conditions and experiences of diasporization. Torres addresses the tensions that often exist between black Americans and Puerto Ricans, who generally resist the bipolar construction of race in the United States and avoid being "darkened" because of blackness's relationship to the social bottom. Even unquestionably "black" immigrants who can't check the Hispanic box on the census are likely to actively assert their ethnic/national distinctiveness from African Americans to offset the stigma of race. This process is not simply due to differences in culture, language, and worldview. To some extent, it can perhaps also be attributed to people having learned and consented to the hegemonic racial/ethnic hierarchy that stigmatizes black Americans in particularly vicious ways. Some of these ideas give Caribbean and African-born blacks certain advantages because, from an ethnically differentiated racist perspective, they are sometimes assumed to be more industrious, disciplined, and intelligent and easier to get along with than African Americans, who are often seen as having a "chip on their shoulder." Black immigrants are not uncommonly susceptible to these kinds of ideas, failing to understand the specific institutional and ideological conditions with which black Americans have had to contend. Of course, African Americans also espouse their share of prejudices about "islanders" and Africans, as Prince reveals so poignantly in her chapter. She explains that when different diasporic peoples come into contact or converge in the same intercultural space, pan-African consciousness and diasporic solidarity do not automatically emerge from some essential sameness that all African descendants supposedly share.

It would be interesting to read Prince's discussion on the early Africanization of New York in intertextual and dialogic relation to Stoller's (2003) ethnography of contemporary African immigrants in New York. In a sense, both studies present different stages in the historical political economy of Africans in New York. Stoller analyzes the relationship between mainly informal-sector entrepreneurs who maintain active links with their homes in West Africa and African Americans who, hundreds of years removed from the continent of their ancestral past, consume African and Afrocentric commodities. In view of Wade's insights, I suggest that these commodities are integral to the embodiment and performances through which they claim and assert identities as *African* Americans. Along with anthropologists who have examined Caribbean transmigrants (Basch et al. 1994; Sutton and Chaney 1987), Stoller sheds some light on the meanings and negotiations of ethnic and national difference in diasporic locations. In some respects, these dynamics may be roughly parallel to the cultural and linguistic differences that the earliest generations of Africans and African-descendant creoles had to accommodate in plantation and other slavery-based settings in the Americas. I do not say this to argue that these two distant temporal contexts qualify for a controlled comparison. I want to emphasize only that diasporic contexts have always been heterogeneous ones, in which diverse peoples have come into contact and the specific terms and contours of diversity and belonging vary over time and space.

CONNECTING THE MATERIAL AND DISCURSIVE

The historical processes that the advanced seminar's title evokes set the broadest possible material context for the development of Afro-American cultures, identities, and discursive practices, regardless of whether African cultural continuities have figured prominently in lived experience, discursive practice, or ideological elaboration. As Wade's chapter points out, Africa or some self-consciousness or "memory" of African heritage is not necessarily a major factor in African descendants' social identities or in their social construction of blackness. However, at some point(s) in time, discursive constructions of Africa may come to be culturally and politically significant. These constructs often have no relationship to any identifiable Africanisms that can be documented by "unearthing" continuities with an African cultural past. Africa-focused discursive practices do not take place in a vacuum. The context within which they are constructed and enacted is one that may be nuanced by influences from nationalist projects, including shifts in public policy, transnational flows of popular culture, and the public dissemination of ideas from scholarship done on diasporic history and culture.

Regardless of which particular schools of thought we align ourselves with—whether or not we locate our projects somewhere in the disciplinary genealogy in which Herskovits was central—what unites us all is that the Afro-Atlantic peoples we study are the products of immense politically and economically mediated events of global proportions. Those events and their consequences can be understood from a number of different perspectives that place varying degrees of emphasis on material and discursive ramifications and the dialogic and dialectical interplay between them.

THE DU BOISIAN/DRAKE LEGACY

In situating my own take on these matters, I will point out that I was trained by anthropologists who located their scholarship within or along the edges of Marxist social science. Of particular relevance were St. Clair Drake and Bridget O'Laughlin, both of whom reevaluated and reworked Marxist categories and assumptions. Drake (1975, 1982), a leader in African diaspora studies before its current heyday, was also influenced by the journalistic and historical-sociological work of the pan-Africanist W. E. B. Du Bois, who set an important example for many black intellectuals, including anthropologists, in his synthesis of radical and conventional concepts and methods in the study of race and culture. I am among those who have worked to reclaim anthropology's Du Boisian legacy (F. Harrison 1992). Like Du Bois in many

respects, Drake produced an awe-inspiring, encyclopedic, and interdisciplinary oeuvre informed by a remarkable command of historical,
sociological, and anthropological literatures. Because of his interdisciplinarity and concern with issues (for example, race relations, urban
unrest, and the sociology of knowledge) that many anthropologists in
the 1940–1970 period believed to be more germane to the disciplines
of sociology and history, much of his scholarship ended up being
mapped outside the boundaries of anthropology. Indeed, it is not
uncommon for him to be described as a sociologist, even in texts by
anthropologists or about anthropology. For example, Gershenhorn's
(2004:127, 231) intellectual biography of Herskovits makes this mistake in two different places in the text. (Drake was cited or quoted in
five different places in the book. Although it was not spelled out in the
passages attributed to him, Drake initially had difficulty acquiring funding for his Africanist research because of Herskovits's gate-
keeping authority and belief that black scholars engaged in advocacy
and activism compromised their objectivity and hence their ability to
do scientific work.)

In the last years before his retirement, Drake played a major role
in training a handful of anthropology graduate students—the first in
his many years as an academic. I was fortunate to be in that small
cohort of students. Drake produced a series of important essays on the
relationship between blacks and anthropology, with an emphasis on
black intellectual production (e.g., Drake 1974, 1980). Those writings
inspired me to take a closer look at the history of anthropology, focusing mainly on the neglected contributions that African descendants
have made, usually on the margins (F. Harrison 1992, F. Harrison and
I. Harrison 1999). My educational background led me to position
myself on a theoretical terrain that is, more or less, neo-Marxist. This
is the label that Drake used to describe his approach to pan-African
studies and activism. Neo-Marxism is a materialist mode of engagement that privileges certain types of sociocultural forms and pays less
attention, if any at all, to others. Consequently, I have been much more
inclined to focus on those sociocultural forms and practices linked to
political and political-economic dynamics. I have been especially interested in the dynamics at the social bottom, another influence from
Drake. Although I am basically an anthropological political economist,

FAYE V. HARRISON

I have tried to avoid economic determinism like the plague, and I understand that ideation and discourse should never be treated as though they are mere epiphenomena. I have brought this vision to my work in both the history of ideas and political ethnography.

REHISTORICIZING OUR TOOL KIT—CONCEPTS, MODELS, AND METHODOLOGIES

The concepts of diaspora, transnationalism, modernity, and globalization are among the current heuristic devices used to make sense of the complexly entangled, dense material and discursive connections that have formed the past and present of the African descendants whom anthropologists study, as well as the past and present of the intellectual subjects we know as Afro-Americanists. Our task is to conjoin the anthropology of the Afro-Atlantic with a critical anthropology of Afro-Atlantic anthropology, recognizing that the latter is instrumental to our success at regenerating and advancing the former. This twofold project also inspires us to clear the ground for scrutinizing the central role that blacks and their expressions of blackness have played in both modernity and its counternarratives. The black Atlantic's centrality to the culture and political economy of modernity has recently been usefully theorized in Gilroy's (1993) work; however, this basic idea did not originate with him. W. E. B. Du Bois, C. L. R. James, Eric Williams, Walter Rodney, Sylvia Wynter, and anthropology's St. Clair Drake are all diaspora scholars who have offered valuable insights into this history. If this is the case, then why have these ideas been attributed solely to Gilroy in current anthropological and diaspora studies discourse? Obviously, the anthropological audience has not been seriously reading the texts that these other black intellectuals have produced. Will it engage in a more democratic and less starstruck reading strategy now that we have underscored the importance of situating thinkers in broader relations of intellectual production, the webs, networks, and social formations that connect them to neglected, if not altogether hidden and silenced, figures in more peripheral zones of knowledge? Is there room for more than a few (often only one or two) important black thinkers and theorists at a time? These are the kinds of questions we need to ponder if the anthropology of Afro-Atlantic dialogues, as mapped in this volume, is to truly make a reverberating difference.

390

As has become amply clear by now, my approach to the study of the African diaspora is one strongly informed by the rehistoricization of anthropology's hierarchically situated knowledges. I learned my first serious lessons about rehistoricizing anthropology from Drake, although other scholars have certainly extended and enriched my understanding (e.g., Baker 1998; Vincent 1991). Basically, rehistoricization is a mode or strategy of analysis that reclaims neglected knowledges and rethinks the relation between both the exposed and hidden dimensions of the past as they are manifest in canonical and noncanonical aspects of intellectual life. As I have written elsewhere, the key elements of this process are skepticism, contextualism, processualism, criticism, and engagement (F. Harrison and I. Harrison 1999:5). Critical historians of anthropology should always question the autonomy of authors and the texts they write—be they ethnographies, ethnohistorical accounts, archaeological reports, or even genres (for example, journalism and fiction) outside the conventions of academic social science. It must be clearly understood that anthropological texts in their broadest diversity are all discursively constructed historical phenomena situated in the material circumstances of both the institutionalized profession and the vagaries and trends of the wider world. We must recognize that when ethnographies, essays, or other accounts or narratives are written, the biases and evaluations of readers, particularly those with gate-keeping power, determine their reception. Reader-text-context interaction, which is integral to the politics of reception, "governs whether texts are incorporated into the canon, whose disciplinary significance is reproduced over time" (F. Harrison and I. Harrison 1999).

The reader-text-context politics of the late nineteenth century and much of the twentieth century led to the virtual erasure of Anténor Firmin's 1885 treatise on the fundamental equality among humankind (Firmin [1885] 2002). After many years of searching archives in Haiti and France, Carolyn Fluehr-Lobban and Asselin Charles found the book, translated it into English (Charles), and made it available to the reading public. How ironic it is—or perhaps it is poetic justice—that in the history of anthropological ideas, Haiti, an early postcolonial nation-state so thoroughly and profoundly denigrated and ostracized, was able to produce a sophisticated anthropological tradition that dates back to Firmin's critique and alternative to Count Arthur de Gobineau's treatise on the so-called innate inequalties among human beings. Firmin's solidly antiracist anthropology was a counternarrative not only to scientific racism in France but also to the hemispheric and global nexus of power that thwarted Haitian sovereignty and denied human dignity to his people—both Haitians and the wider African diaspora. Firmin's alternative anthropology was part of a project in nation building and in developing diasporic and pan-African consciousness and pride, tools considered necessary for the survival of Afro-Atlantic people.

The lessons from Firmin's—and also Drake's—erasure underscore that the anthropological canon must always be interrogated, and in tandem with this questioning we must work to reevaluate and recapture, when possible, those works deemed less significant by earlier historically specific criteria. This process involves adopting a vantage for interrogating the power dynamics involved in the writing, reading, and citing of texts and the discourses in which they are embedded. Moreover, this process has to be, ultimately, informed by an ongoing engagement with ethnographic subjects and all the observations, inferences, and interpretations embedded in our interactions with them. I adopt this mode of critique and reinterpretation to highlight ways in which this volume engages the disciplinary preoccupations of both the past and present and to suggest how it might serve to regenerate anthropology.

While all the authors here are self-conscious about the modes, means, and relations of intellectual production, it is Yelvington who most methodically undertakes a mode of rehistoricization in analyzing what he calls the intellectual social formation to which Melville Herskovits and his wife, Frances, belonged. Although that international social formation was based on what appear to be warm collegial relationships among similar-thinking individuals, those relationships were, nonetheless, conditioned by salient disparities of power and cultural capital, which were correlated with differential national and racial statuses. It is important to question whether this intellectual social formation was articulated to or overlapped with any others that may have existed on the wider intellectual landscape, particularly those zones where Afro-Atlantic sociocultural issues were germane. In other words, what other anthropologically relevant knowledges and intellectual arenas might be excavated and subjected to textual exegesis and social network analysis, two techniques that anthropologists have long employed with considerable skill? Carnegie (1992) has initiated some of this work for the English-speaking Caribbean.

Besides situating canonical anthropologists within their wider networks and webs of connection, unburying lost bodies of knowledge and the intellectual coalitions in which they were embedded—as well as those that played a role in silencing and suppressing them—rehistoricization also entails several other levels or dimensions of analysis. These multiple, interrelated dimensions enable us to think critically about the past, present, and potential future of the anthropology of the Afro-Atlantic world. The first is problematizing, rethinking, and operationalizing the interpretive metaphors, concepts, and anologies that have been and are currently used—from roots, routes, and memory to diaspora and, thanks largely to Matory's insightfully critical input, dialogue. We can add to this sequence the notions of creolization and hybridity. Even the way we name the field has implications: Are we working toward the advancement of Afro-American or African American anthropology? Does either (or do both) connote the same thing as the African diaspora or the Afro-Atlantic or the black Atlantic?

Clarifying the central terms of our analysis is a crucial procedure, especially in light of the theoretical, methodological, and political differences among us. We cannot assume that all our colleagues in the discipline understand what we mean. When historians, sociologists, and cultural studies scholars also read our work, it is often subjected to the scrutiny of altogether different lenses and evaluative criteria, thereby complicating the already complex politics of reception. Diverse audiences come up with a number of varied and conflicting readings that may or may not be consistent with our intentions. Hence we should be concerned with the expectations that audiences, some of them anthropologists committed to standards of scientific rigor, bring to the assessment of social and cultural analysis and, as I shall underscore in my discussion of a later dimension, the varied forms of empirical work that different modes and styles of anthropological research yields.

Moving from the need to more clearly define and think through the implications of our key concepts to the related issue of methodological and analytical frameworks, we must, secondly, be concerned with building more satisfactory and satisfying models that, if possible,

transcend the polarities, tensions, and limits of the earlier dichotomies
and debates that these chapters discuss. Some examples include the
Africa-centered versus the New World–centered or creolization models
(directly addressed by R. Price, S. Price, and Matory)—even though
the emphasis on cultural continuities as "the changing same," implying
some measure of cultural reconstruction, is complementary to and, in
some respects, even consistent with the concerns of creolization studies. There are even a number of debates among the creolization adher-
ents, as R. Price and S. Price show us. In historical archaeology,
Singleton tells us, there are the culturalists versus the materialists (with
political economists and political ecologists among the latter). Many
anthropologists of the African Americas are engaging questions that
are not directly a part of the Herskovitsian legacy or part of the creolization school revisions, which were, nonetheless, foundational. I
would include all of this book's contributors under this rubric, even
those who have addressed these debates directly. All the authors here
are self-conscious about the models anthropologists develop and
deploy across time. They are also clearly attuned to the modes, means,
and relations of intellectual production.

The third level of rehistoricization moves us to a less abstract
methodological dimension with which we must be concerned: that
involving validity and reliability in our research. These may be construed
and conceptualized in particular ways within cultural anthropology's
qualitative research tradition, but moving across methodologies and disciplines, especially from the "soft" to the "hard" social sciences, the
expected procedures for achieving validity and reliability may diverge
from the ways many anthropologists approach them. If we wish to reach
out to wider or multiple audiences, we cannot afford to be naive about
or careless with our methodological tools. The authors here are well
aware of these concerns and have approached their subjects with these
matters in mind. They all raise important questions about the limits of
available evidence and how they know what they claim to know.

Even still, the chapters collected here, as diverse as they are, do not
represent the full range of conceptual and methodological diversity in
what we refer to as Afro-American, African American, or African diaspora anthropology (and I readily recognize that, for some, these are
far from interchangeable terms). I am pleased that this collection

approaches diaspora studies from a position that values the discipline's commitment to what I call "intradisciplinarity"—that is, the dialogic interplay among anthropology's subfields. Considering the difference that intradisciplinary engagements—or their absence—make in developing anthropological knowledge is the fourth focus of rehistoricizing Afro-Atlantic studies. The chapters by Singleton and by Sengova add invaluable insights into what archaeology and linguistics are able to bring to the table. It is unfortunate that there is not a chapter based on the important contributions that critical biohistory and biological anthropology are making to our understanding of the African diaspora's past, particularly about health, work conditions, quality of life, life expectancy, burial customs, and migration histories. Fortunately, Prince's chapter on the historical political economy of New York City discusses the African Burial Ground Project, which represents an important source of knowledge from anthropology's fourth subfield (Blakey 2001).

While intradisciplinarity is part of what differentiates anthropology from the other social sciences, *interdisciplinarity* is what blurs the boundaries between them and, if engaged effectively, produces a depth and breadth of analysis that benefits from the enrichment and symbiosis that crossing disciplinary boundaries can bring. This is the fifth issue that is central in assessing and tracking the development of Afro-Atlantic studies in anthropology. Historical archaeologists tend to be exemplars in employing multidisciplinary models and tools. They often use a repertoire of conceptual and methodological tools that originally come from history, geography, and geology, as well as those from across anthropology's subdisciplines. Besides Singleton, most of the other authors here have relied on interdisciplinary tools, such as those from linguistics, historiography, art criticism and history, and museum studies. It is important for us to think critically about how we conceptualize and position our research on grounds of interdisciplinarity. What are the implications of our having borrowed such key concept-metaphors as creole, grammar, and, now, dialogue from linguistics? How does this process both enable and limit the partial perspectives from which we construct knowledge?

Interdisciplinarity can have significant methodological implications for how we conceptualize the larger framework and mission of our scholarship. Here I am not just referring to methods and techniques, because methodologies involve deploying practical procedures or "methods" in the context of research designs driven, in good part, by theoretical assumptions that inform the formulation of specific research questions, as well as a researcher's philosophy of knowledge and the most appropriate ways to apply it in the empirical world. Thinking of the array of methods and methodologies employed in these chapters and how the contributors weave together perspectives and varieties of evidence, these approaches are exemplary. But are we at all worried that our work might not be considered anthropology? When we blur disciplinary boundaries, where does anthropology begin and end? Questions like these are integral to the remaking of anthropology as we work to recapture its authority and legitimacy as a mode of inquiry, analysis, and theorization that can make a difference in what we know about, and how we act in relationship to, the Afro-Atlantic.

Shifting our focus from these particular conceptual and methodological concerns, we now move a bit closer, perhaps, to some of the sociocultural processes that we seek to understand. The sixth dimension I wish to highlight involves our strategies for uncovering otherwise hidden continuities, discontinuities, and contradictions in cultural as well as intellectual production. Here I underscore the necessity of situating our cases in richly nuanced and historically deep contexts in which we can examine the complex interplay of culture and power in ways that permit us to discern the dialectical relations between structure and agency—as they pertain to the sociocultural practices and positionalities of both the people anthropologists study and anthropologists themselves. I suggest that these issues be approached from a perspective that avoids what Abu-Lughod (1990) has described as the "romance of resistance" and zooms in on the role of intersecting inequalities (race, class, gender, age, and so on). These intersections shape the contours of diasporic realities, organized along domains of identity and practice and around matrices of domination. Black feminists (e.g., Collins 1991; hooks 2000) have brilliantly conceptualized the latter for the purpose of elucidating the manner in which social difference and power disparities are lived and embodied in ways that are at once classed and racially gendered.

The racialized gendering of diasporic dialogues and other dynamics is an important dimension about which this volume has had little to say—although women are certainly included in its mapping of the actors and subject positions germane to Afro-Atlantic artworlds, intellectual formations, religious practices, burial grounds, and linguistic communities. The inclusion of references to women, however, does not in itself *en-gender* social analysis. Some of the authors (e.g., Yelvington, S. Price, and Matory), though, have made important contributions to the study of gender in other work. To his credit, Yelvington does broach the gender and sexual politics of Afro-American anthropology when he addresses the ostracism that Ruth Landes experienced. Was she subjected to a double standard that proscribed white women's fraternizing and establishing intimate collaborations with "the natives" and native intellectuals of the opposite sex? Were the same ethical standards enforced in the case of white male researchers? Did their privileged racial and gendered positionalities allow them to exercise unmarked sexual prerogatives with greater impunity? I am posing these questions to situate the claims made about Landes's research ethics within the framework of a structured division of intellectual labor in which gendered as well as racial inequalities made certain kinds of relationships especially transgressive and controversial. These matters need to be taken into account to offset the danger of reducing social analysis and intellectual history to myopic judgments of individual morality and psychology.

Let me recapitulate that critically rehistoricizing the uneven development of Afro-Atlantic studies in anthropology, then, entails the adoption of strategies and bifocal lenses that allow us to remain critically reflexive and intellectually honest about the multiaxial positionalities of both anthropologists and the culturally rich but often economically impoverished peoples whom we seek to understand, often in the spirit of advocacy and solidarity. The final point I will make about the importance of a rehistoricized approach to assessing and revitalizing the anthropology of Afro-Atlantic landscapes is that we must remain aware of and vigilant concerning the ways the representations fashioned by artists and intellectuals, including, of course, anthropologists, are interpreted, appropriated, and consumed within contexts of public culture. Torres's chapter on a Smithsonian exhibit and its related cultural events, S. Price's chapter on art, and Prince's discussion on the role of the public, particularly politically conscious "descendant communities," in shaping the agenda of the African Burial Ground's bioarchaeological research are particularly thought-provoking along these lines. As Torres lucidly points out, even though museum and gallery exhibits, festivals, and other public performances —which are often intended to celebrate difference and project positive images—"have the power to overturn representations, they can also serve as vehicles to reinscribed racial and ethnic imagery." Such reinscriptions perpetuate the very injustices that our critiques and analyses often intend to challenge by contributing to webs of connection and coalitions of knowledges (both academic and vernacular) whose aim is no less than subversion and transformation.

Acknowledgments

I must thank Kevin Yelvington for including me in the April 1999 advanced seminar as a general discussant and for later insisting that my commentary be included in this book. I also thank everyone else who participated in the seminar. It was one of most thought-provoking and exciting academic meetings I have ever attended.

References

Abbott, Abiel

1829   *Letters Written in the Interior of Cuba.* Boston: Bowles & Dearborn.

Abimbola, Wande

2000   Wanted: An Afro-Atlantic Identity. Paper presented at the Thirtieth Anniversary Celebration, Department of Afro-American Studies, Harvard University, Cambridge, MA.

Abrahams, Roger D.

2003   Questions of Criolian Contagion. *Journal of American Folklore* 116(459):73–87.

Abu-Lughod, Lila

1990   The Romance of Resistance: Tracing Transformations of Power through Bedouin Women. *American Ethnologist* 17(1):41–55.

1991   Writing against Culture. In *Recapturing Anthropology: Working in the Present,* edited by Richard G. Fox, pp. 137–162. School of American Reasearch. Santa Fe, NM: SAR Press.

Acosta Belen, Edna, and Virginia Sánchez-Korrol, eds.

1993   *The Way It Was and Other Writings.* Houston, TX: Arte Público Press.

Adams, Jane, and D. Gorton

2004   Southern Trauma: Revisiting Caste and Class in the Mississippi Delta. *American Anthropologist* 106(2):334–345.

Adams, William, and Sarah J. Bolling

1989   Status and Ceramics for Planters and Slaves on Three Georgia Coastal Plantations. *Historical Archaeology* 23(1):69–96.

Adler, Peter, and Nicholas Barnard

1992   *African Majesty: The Textile Art of the Ashanti and Ewe.* London: Thames and Hudson.

Agier, Michel

2000   *Anthropologie du carnaval: la ville, la fête, et l'Afrique à Bahia.* Marseille: Éditions Parethèses.

Agorsah, E. Kofi

1996   The Archaeology of the African Diaspora. *African Archaeological Review* 13(4):221–224.

1998   Settlement Pattern Studies in the Archaeology of the African Diaspora. Paper presented to the Society for Africanist Archaeology, Syracuse University, Syracuse, NY.

1999   Ethnoarchaeological Consideration of Social Relationship and Settlement Patterning Among Africans in the Caribbean Diaspora. In *African Sites Archaeology in the Caribbean*, edited by Jay B. Haviser, pp. 38–64. Princeton, NJ: Markus Wiener.

AHPM *See* **Archivo Historico Provincial de Matanzas.**

Akintola, Akinbowale

1992   *The Reformed Ogboni Fraternity: Its Origins and Interpretation of Its Doctrines and Symbolism.* Ibàdàn, Nigeria: Valour Ventures.

Alakija, George

1977   The Trance State in Candomblé/L'Etat de Transe dans le Candomblé. Colloquium on Black Civilization and Science and Technology, Second World Black and African Festival of Arts and Culture, Lagos and Kaduna, Nigeria.

Allen, John S.

1989   Franz Boas's Physical Anthropology: The Critique of Racial Formalism Revisited. *Current Anthropology* 30(1):79–84.

Alleyne, Mervyn C.

1980   *Comparative Afro-American: An Historical-Comparative Study of English-Based Afro-American Dialects of the New World.* Ann Arbor, MI: Karoma.

Alonso, Manuel A.

[1894]   *El gíbaro.* Barcelona: Editorial Vosgas.
1975

Alsop, Joseph

1982   *The Rare Art Traditions: The History of Art Collecting and Its Linked Phenomena Wherever These Have Appeared.* Princeton, NJ: Princeton University Press.

Álvarez López, Laura

2004   A língua de camões com Imanjá: Forma e funções da linguagem do Candomblé. Ph.D. diss., University of Stockholm.

ANC *See* **Archivo Nacional de Cuba.**

Andrews, George Reid

2004   *Afro-Latin America, 1800–2000.* New York: Oxford University Press.

Angarica, Nicolás Valentin

1955   *Manual del Orihate.* Havana: Nicolás Valentin Angarica.

Anthias, Floya

1998   Evaluating "Diaspora": Beyond Ethnicity? *Sociology* 32(3):557–580.

Antoine, Jacques C.

1981   *Jean Price-Mars and Haiti.* Washington, DC: Three Continents Press.

Anyebe, A. P.

1989   *Ogboni: The Birth and Growth of the Refomed Ogboni Fraternity.* Ikeja, Nigeria: Sam Lao Publishers.

Appadurai, Arjun

1981   The Past as a Scarce Resource. *Man* 16(2):201–219.

1990   Disjuncture and Difference in the Global Cultural Economy. *Public Culture* 2(2):1–24.

1996   *Modernity at Large: Cultural Dimensions of Globalization.* Minneapolis: University of Minnesota Press.

Appadurai, Arjun, ed.

1986   *The Social Life of Things: Commodities in Cultural Perspective.* Cambridge: Cambridge University Press.

Appiah, Kwame Anthony

1992   *In My Father's House: Africa in the Philosophy of Culture.* New York: Oxford University Press.

1997   The Arts of Africa. *New York Review of Books*, April 24, 46–51.

Appiah, Kwame Anthony, and Henry Louis Gates Jr., eds.

1999   *Africana: The Encyclopedia of the African and African American Experience.* New York: Basic Civitas Books.

Apter, Andrew

1991   Herskovits's Heritage: Rethinking Syncretism in the African Diaspora. *Diaspora* 1(3):235–260.

1999   Africa, Empire, and Anthropology: A Philological Exploration of Anthropology's Heart of Darkness. *Annual Review of Anthropology* 28:577–598.

2002   On African Origins: Creolization and Connaissance in Haitian Vodou. *American Ethnologist* 29(2):233–260.

Arango Z., Carlos

1985   *Lucho Bermúdez: Su vida y su obra.* Bogotá: Centro Editorial Bochica.

Arboleda Llorente, José Rafael

1950   The Ethnohistory of Colombian Negroes. M.A. thesis, Northwestern University, Evanston, IL.

Archivo Historico Provincial de Matanzas (AHPM)

1837   Fondo Gobierno Provincial O. P. Cimarrones, Legajo 12, Expediente 50. Matanzas, Cuba: AHPM.

Archivo Nacional de Cuba (ANC)

1825   Fondo: Gobierno Superior Civil, Legajo1469, No. 57999. Reglamento de Policía Rural de la Jursidicción del Gobierno de Matanzas, October 22, 1825. Havana: ANC.

REFERENCES

1829a   Fondo Protocolo de Salinas, Obligación de Don Ignacio O' Farrill a Juan Almazy, pp. 1262–1263. Havana: ANC.

1829b   Protocolo de Salinas, Imposición de Don Nicolás Manuel de Escovedo y Rivero, p. 1671. Havana: ANC.

1838   Fondo: Escribanía Archivo de Galletti, Legajo:245, No.1. Inventario del cafetal Santa Ana de Viajacas. Havana: ANC.

1849–53 Archivo: de Cortés. Fondo: Escribanía 1849–53, Legajo:227, No. de orden:7. Havana: ANC.

1862   Fondo: Gobierno General, Legajo:652, Expediente 27528. Padrón de fincas rústicas de la jurisdicción y parroquia de Madruga. Havana: ANC.

1866   Fondo: Gobierno Superior Civil, Legajo:1124, Expediente 41730. La Creación de Partido de Madruga en 1796. Havana: ANC.

Armstrong, Douglas V.

1990   *The Old Village and the Great House: An Archaeological and Historical Examination of Drax Hall Plantation, St. Ann's Bay, Jamaica.* Urbana: University of Illinois Press.

1998   Cultural Transformation among Caribbean Slave Communities. In *Studies in Culture Contact: Interaction, Culture Change, and Archaeology*, edited by James G. Cusick, pp. 378–401. Carbondale: Center for Archaeological Investigations, Southern Illinois University.

1999   Archaeology and Ethnohistory of the Caribbean Plantation. In *"I, Too, Am America": Archaeological Studies of African-American Life*, edited by Theresa A. Singleton, pp. 173–192. Charlottesville: University Press of Virginia.

Armstrong, Douglas V., and Mark L. Fleischman

1993   Seville African Jamaican Project. Summary Report. Analysis of Four House-Area Burials from the African Jamaican Settlement of Seville. Report to the Jamaican Trust. *Syracuse University Archaeological Reports* 6(5).

2003   House-Yard Burials of Enslaved Laborers in Eighteenth-Century Jamaica. *International Journal of Historical Archaeology* 7(1):33–65.

Armstrong, Douglas, and Kenneth Kelly

2000   Settlement Patterns and the Origins of Afro-Jamaican Society: Seville Plantation, St. Ann's Bay, Jamaica. *Ethnohistory* 47(2):369–397.

Arocha, Jaime

1991   La ensenada de Tumaco: entre la incertidumbre y la inventiva. In *Imagenes y reflexiones de la cultura: regiones, ciudades y violencia*, edited by Foro para, con, por, sobre, de Cultura, pp. 198–221. Bogotá: Colcultura.

1992   Los negros y la nueva constitución colombiana de 1991. *América Negra* 3:39–54.

1996   Afrogénesis, eurogénesis y convivencia interétnica. In *Pacífico: ¿desarrollo o biodiversidad?: estado, capital y movimientos sociales en el Pacífico colombiano*, edited by Arturo Escobar and Alvaro Pedrosa, pp. 316–328. Bogotá: CEREC.

1999   *Ombligados de Ananse: hilos ancestrales y modernos en el Pacífico colombiano.* Bogotá: Centro de Estudios Sociales, Facultad de Ciencias Humanas, Universidad Nacional de Colombia.

Arrazcaeta Delgado, Roger
1987   Las pipes: Un antiguo util de fumar. Unpublished manuscript. Gabinete de Arqueología, Havana, Cuba.

Arrom, José Juan, and Manuel García Arévalo
1986   *Cimarrón.* Santo Domingo: Fundación García Arévalo.

Artel, Jorge
1940   *Tambores en la noche.* Cartagena: Editora Bolívar.

Arthur, Kojo
2001   *Cloth as Metaphor: (Re)Reading the Adinkra Cloth Symbols of the Akan of Ghana.* Legon, Ghana: Centre for Indigenous Knowledge Systems.

Asad, Talal
1993   *Genealogies of Religion: Discipline and Reasons of Power in Christianity and Islam.* Baltimore, MD: Johns Hopkins University Press.

Aschenbrenner, Joyce
2002   *Katherine Dunham: Dancing a Life.* Urbana: University of Illinois Press.

Assael, Shaun
1993   Warring Archaeologists Scrape Graveyard Booty: No Indiana Jones or King Tut as PhDs. ID Slavery's Moldy Bones. *New York Observer,* June 7, 1–18.

Assembly of Jamaica
1802   *Journal of the House of Assembly of Jamaica.* Spanish Town, Jamaica: Assembly of Jamaica.

Axel, Brian Keith
1996   Time and Threat: Questioning the Production of the Diaspora as an Object of Study. *History and Anthropology* 9(4):415–443.
2004   The Context of Diaspora. *Cultural Anthropology* 19(1):26–60.

Ayorinde, Christine
2004   *Afro-Cuban Religiosity, Revolution, and National Identity.* Gainesville: University Press of Florida.

Azeredo, Paulo Roberto
1986   *Antropólogos e pioneiros: a história da Sociedade Brasileira de Antropologia e Etnologia.* São Paulo: FFLCH-USP.

Babadzan, Alain
2000   Anthropology, Nationalism and "the Invention of Tradition." *Anthropological Forum* 10(2):131–155.

Bailey, Cornelia Walker, and Christena Bledsoe
2000   *God, Dr. Buzzard, and the Bolito Man: A Saltwater Geechee Talks about Life on Sapelo Island.* New York: Doubleday.

REFERENCES

Bailyn, Bernard
1996   The Idea of Atlantic History. Working paper no. 96-01, International
            Seminar on the History of the Atlantic World, 1500–1800, Harvard
            University, Cambridge, MA.

Baker, Houston A., Jr.
1987   *Modernism and the Harlem Renaissance.* Chicago: University of Chicago Press.

Baker, Lee D.
1998   *From Savage to Negro: Anthropology and the Construction of Race, 1896–1954.*
            Berkeley: University of California Press.

2000   Research, Reform, and Racial Uplift: The Mission of the Hampton Folk-
            Lore Society, 1893–1899. In *Excluded Ancestors, Inventible Traditions: Essays
            toward a More Inclusive History of Anthropology*, edited by Richard Handler,
            pp. 42–80. Madison: University of Wisconsin Press.

2004   Franz Boas Out of the Ivory Tower. *Anthropological Theory* 4(1):29–51.

Baker, Moses
1803   An Account of Moses Baker, A Mulatto Baptist Preacher, Near Martha
            Brae, in Jamaica (Drawn up by Himself, and Communicated to a Friend in
            Leicestershire). *Evangelical Magazine* 11:365–371.

Bakhtin, M. M.
1981   *The Dialogic Imagination: Four Essays*, edited by Michael Holquist, translated
            by Caryl Emerson and Michael Holquist. Austin: University of Texas Press.

**Baralt, Guillermo Carlos Collazo, Lydia Milagros González, and
Ana Lydia Vega, eds.**
1990   *El machete de Ogún: Las luchas de los esclavos en Puerto Rico (siglo XIX).* Río
            Piedras, Puerto Rico: Centro de Estudios de la Realidad Puertorriqueña,
            Proyecto de Divulgación Popular.

Barbot, Jean
[1732]   *A Description of the Coasts of North and South Guinea; and of Ethiopia Inferior,
1746   vulgarly Angola…With an Appendix; being a General Account of the First
            Discoveries of America in the Fourteenth Century…And a Geographical, Political,
            and Natural History of the Antilles-Islands.* London: Henry Lintot and John
            Osborn.

Barcia Paz, Manuel
1998   *La resistencia esclava en las plantaciones cubanas (1790–1870).* Pinar del Rio,
            Cuba: Vitral.

Barkan, Elazar
1992   *The Retreat of Scientific Racism: Changing Concepts of Race in Britain and the
            United States between the World Wars.* Cambridge: Cambridge University
            Press.

Barkan, Elazar, and Ronald Bush, eds.
1995   *Prehistories of the Future: The Primitivist Project and the Culture of Modernism.*
            Stanford, CA: Stanford University Press.

Barnes, Sandra T., ed.
1989   *Africa's Ogun: Old World and New.* Bloomington: Indiana University Press.

Barnes, Sandra T., ed.
1997   *Africa's Ogun: Old World and New.* 2d ed. Bloomington: Indiana University Press.

Baron, Robert
1994   Africa in the Americas: Melville J. Herskovits' Folkloristic and Anthropological Scholarship, 1923–1941. Ph.D. diss., University of Pennsylvania, Philadelphia.

2003   Amalgams and Mosaics, Syncretisms and Reinterpretations: Reading Herskovits and Contemporary Creolists for Metaphors of Creolization. *Journal of American Folklore* 116(459):88–115.

Barradas, Efrain
1990   The Image and the Word: Seeing through Puerto Rican Eyes. In *New Art from Puerto Rico*, edited by Hollister Sturges, pp.16–24. Springfield, MA: Museum of Fine Arts.

Barringer, Tim, and Tom Flynn, eds.
1998   *Colonialism and the Object: Empire, Material Culture and the Museum.* New York: Routledge.

Barros, Luitgarde Oliveira Cavalcante
2000   *Arthur Ramos e as dinâmicas sociais de seu tempo.* Maceió, Alagoas, Brazil: Editora da Universidade Federal de Alagoas.

Basch, Linda, Nina Glick Schiller, and Cristina Szanton Blanc
1994   *Nations Unbound: Transnational Projects, Postcolonial Predicaments, and Deterritorialized Nation-States.* Langhorne, PA: Gordon and Breach.

Bascom, William R.
1941   Acculturation among the Gullah Negroes. *American Anthropologist* 43(1):43–50.

Bastide, Roger
[1960]   *The African Religions of Brazil: Toward a Sociology of the Interpenetration of*
1978   *Civilizations,* translated by Helen Sebba. Baltimore, MD: Johns Hopkins University Press.

Bastide, Roger, ed.
1973   *Estudos Afro-Brasileiros.* São Paulo: Editora Perspectiva.

Bearden, Romare, and Harry Henderson
1993   *A History of African-American Artists: From 1792 to the Present.* New York: Pantheon.

Bearden, Romare, and Carl Holty
1969   *The Painter's Mind: A Study of the Relations of Structure and Space in Painting.* New York: Crown Publishers.

Beardsley, Edward H.
1973   The American Scientist as Social Activist: Franz Boas, Burt G. Wilder, and the Cause of Racial Justice, 1900–1915. *Isis* 64(221):50–66.

Beauchamp-Byrd, Mora J., and M. Franklin Sirmans, eds.
1997   *Transforming the Crown: African, Asian and Caribbean Artists in Britain 1966–1996.* New York: Franklin H. Williams Caribbean Cultural Center/African Diaspora Institute.

Beaufort, South Carolina
2003   Beaufort, South Carolina. http://www.beaufortsc.com/afam.htm (accessed June 2, 2003).

Bell, Bernard W.
1987   *The Afro-American Novel and Its Tradition.* Amherst: University of Massachusetts Press.

Belting, Hans
1987   *The End of the History of Art?* Chicago: University of Chicago Press.

Benjamn, Walter
[1950] Theses on the Philosophy of History. In *Illuminations*, edited by Hannah
1968   Arendt, translated by Harry Zohn, pp. 255–266. New York: Harcourt, Brace & World.

Bennett, Dionne, Candace Moore, Ulli K. Ryder, and Jakobi Williams, eds.
2003   *Revolutions of the Mind: Cultural Studies in the African Diaspora Project, 1996–2002.* Los Angeles: Center for Afro-American Studies, University of California at Los Angeles.

Bennett, Herman L.
2003   *Africans in Colonial Mexico: Absolutism, Christianity, and Afro-Creole Consciousness, 1570–1640.* Bloomington: Indiana University Press.

Benoît, Catherine
2000   *Corps, jardins, mémoires: anthropologie du corps et de l'espace à la Guadeloupe.* Paris: Editions de la Maison des Sciences de l'Homme.

Bergad, Laird W.
1990   *Cuban Rural Society in the Nineteenth Century.* Princeton, NJ: Princeton University Press.

Bergad, Laird W., Fe Iglesias García, and Maria del Carmen Barcia
1995   *The Cuban Slave Market.* New York: Cambridge University Press.

Berlin, Ira
1980   Time, Space, and the Evolution of Afro-American Society on British Mainland North America. *American Historical Review* 85(1):44–78.
1996   From Creole to African: Atlantic Creoles and the Origins of African-American Society in Mainland North America. *William and Mary Quarterly*, 3d ser., 53(2):251–288.
1998   *Many Thousands Gone: The First Two Centuries of Slavery in North America.* Cambridge, MA: Belknap Press.

Berlin, Ira, and Philip D. Morgan

1991 Introduction. In *The Slaves' Economy: Independent Production by Slaves in the Americas*, edited by Ira Berlin and Philip D. Morgan, pp. 1–27. London: Frank Cass.

Bermúdez, Egberto

1996 La música campesina y popular en Colombia: 1880–1930. *Gaceta* 32–33:113–120.

Bernal, Martin

1996 The Afrocentric Interpretation of History: Bernal Replies to Lefkowitz. *Journal of Blacks in Higher Education* 11:86–94.

BHQ-CP *see* **British Headquarter Papers. Carlton Papers.**

BHQ-CO *see* **British Headquarter Papers. Colonial Office correspondence.**

Bickerton, Derek

1975 *Dynamics of a Creole System*. Cambridge: Cambridge University Press.

1999 Perspectives on Creole Language History. *New West Indian Guide* 73:97–102.

Bilby, Kenneth M.

1996 Ethnogenesis in the Guianas and Jamaica: Two Maroon Cases. In *History, Power, and Identity: Ethnogenesis in the Americas, 1492–1992*, edited by Jonathan D. Hill, pp. 119–141. Iowa City: University of Iowa Press.

2005 *True-Born Maroons*. Gainesville: University Press of Florida.

Bilby, Kenneth M., and Jerome S. Handler

2004 Obeah: Healing and Protection in West Indian Slave Life. *Journal of Caribbean History* 38(2):153–183.

Bilden, Rüdiger

1929 Brazil, a Laboratory of Civilization. *Nation* 128:71–76.

Birman, Patricia

1997 O campo da nostalgia e a recusa da saudade: temas e dilemas dos estudos afro-brasileiros. *Religião e Sociedade* 18(2):75–92.

Blakey, Michael L.

1999 Scientific Racism and the Biological Concept of Race. *Literature and Psychology* 45(1–2):29–43.

2001 Bioarchaeology of the African Diaspora in the Americas: Its Origins and Scope. *Annual Review of Anthropology* 30:387–422.

Blassingame, John W.

1972 *The Slave Community: Plantation Life in the Antebellum South*. New York: Oxford University Press.

Bledsoe, Caroline H.

2005 Personal communication with Kevin A. Yelvington, June 30.

Blier, Suzanne Preston

1989 Field Days: Melville J. Herskovits in Dahomey. *History in Africa* 16:1–22.

REFERENCES

Blyden, Nemata Amelia

2000   *West Indians in West Africa, 1808–1880: The African Diaspora in Reverse.*
        Rochester, NY: University of Rochester Press.

Boas, Franz

1896   The Limitations of the Comparative Method of Anthropology. *Science*, n.s.,
        4(103):901–908.

1911a   *The Mind of Primitive Man.* New York: Macmillan.

1911b   *Changes in Bodily Form of Descendants of Immigrants.* Washington, DC: United
        States Immigration Commission.

1920   The Methods of Ethnology. *American Anthropologist* 22(4):311–321.

1924   Evolution or Diffusion? *American Anthropologist* 26(3):340–344.

1928   *Anthropology and Modern Life.* New York: W. W. Norton.

[1908] Decorative Designs of Alaskan Needlecases: A Study in the History of
1940   Conventional Designs, Based on Materials in the U.S. National Museum. In
        Race, Language and Culture, by Franz Boas, pp. 564–592. New York: Free
        Press.

Bolland, O. Nigel

1992   Creolization and Creole Societies: A Cultural Nationalist View of Caribbean
        Social History. In *Spectre of the New Class: The Commonwealth Caribbean*. Vol. 1
        of *Intellectuals in the Twentieth-Century Caribbean,* edited by Alistair Hennessy,
        pp. 50–79. London: Macmillan.

Bolles, A. Lynn

1985   Of Mules and Yankee Gals: Struggling with Stereotypes in the Field.
        Anthropology and Humanism Quarterly 10(4):114–119.

Borges, Dain

1993   "Puffy, Ugly, Slothful and Inert": Degeneration in Brazilian Social Thought,
        1880–1940. *Journal of Latin American Studies* 25(2):235–256.

1995   The Recognition of Afro-Brazilian Symbols and Ideas, 1890–1940. *Luso-
        Brazilian Review* 32(2):59–78.

Bouquet, Mary, ed.

1999   Academic Anthropology and the Museum: Back to the Future. Special
        issue, *Focaal: Tijdschrift voor Antropologie* 34.

Bourdieu, Pierre

1977   *Outline of a Theory of Practice,* translated by Richard Nice. Cambridge:
        Cambridge University Press.

Bourgois, Philippe I.

1989   *Ethnicity at Work: Divided Labor on a Central American Banana Plantation.*
        Baltimore, MD: Johns Hopkins University Press.

Bourguignon, Erika

2000   Relativism and Ambivalence in the Work of M. J. Herskovits. *Ethos*
        28(1):103–114.

Brace, C. Loring

1995   Region Does Not Mean "Race"—Reality versus Convention in Forensic Anthropology. *Journal of Forensic Sciences* 40(2):171–175.

2005   *"Race" Is a Four-Letter Word: The Genesis of the Concept.* New York: Oxford University Press.

Brah, Avtar, and Annie E. Coombes, eds.

2000   *Hybridity and Its Discontents: Politics, Science, Culture.* London: Routledge.

Branch, Muriel Miller

1995   *The Water Brought Us: The Story of the Gullah-Speaking People.* New York: Cobblehill Books/Dutton.

Brandist, Craig, and Galin Tihanov, eds.

2000   *Materializing Bakhtin: The Bakhtin Circle and Social Theory.* New York: St. Martin's Press.

Brathwaite, Edward K.

1971   *The Development of Creole Society in Jamaica, 1770–1820.* Oxford: Clarendon Press.

1977   Caliban, Ariel, and Unprospero in the Conflict of Creolization: A Study of the Slave Revolt in Jamaica in 1831–32. In *Comparative Perspectives on Slavery in New World Plantation Societies,* edited by Vera Rubin and Arthur Tuden, pp. 45–69. New York: New York Academy of Sciences.

1979   Commentary Three. *Historical Reflections* 6:150–155.

Braziel, Jana Evans, and Anita Mannur, eds.

2003   *Theorizing Diaspora.* Oxford: Blackwell Publishing.

Bremer, Thomas

1993   The Constitution of Alterity: Fernando Ortiz and the Beginnings of Latin-American Ethnography out of the Spirit of Italian Criminology. In *Alternative Cultures in the Caribbean,* edited by Thomas Bremer and Ulrich Fleischmann, pp. 119–129. Frankfurt: Vervuert.

Briggs, Charles L.

1996   The Politics of Discursive Authority in Research on the "Invention of Tradition." *Cultural Anthropology* 11(4):435–469.

Brightman, Robert

1995   Forget Culture: Replacement, Transcendence, Relexification. *Cultural Anthropology* 10(4):509–546.

British Headquarter Papers. Carlton Papers. Public Record Office, London (BHQ-CP)

British Headquarter Papers. Colonial Office correspondence. Public Record Office, London (BHQ-CO)

Brodwin, Paul

2002   Genetics, Identity, and the Anthropology of Essentialism. *Anthropological Quarterly* 75(2):323–330.

REFERENCES

Bronfman, Alejandra

2002a "En Plena Libertad y Democracia": *Negros Brujos* and the Social Question, 1904–1919. *Hispanic American Historical Review* 82(3):549–587.

2002b "Unsettled and Nomadic": Law, Anthropology and Race in Early Twentieth-Century Cuba. Working paper no. 9. College Park: Latin American Studies Center, University of Maryland.

2004 *Measures of Equality: Social Science, Citizenship, and Race in Cuba, 1902–1940.* Chapel Hill: University of North Carolina Press.

Brooks, George

1976 The Signares of Saint-Louis and Gorée. In *Women in Africa: Studies in Social and Economic Change,* edited by Nancy J. Hafkin and Edna G. Bay, pp. 19–44. Stanford, CA: Stanford University Press.

Brooks, James F.

2002a *Captives and Cousins: Slavery, Kinship, and Community in the Southwest Borderlands.* Chapel Hill: University of North Carolina Press.

Brooks, James F., ed.

2002b *Confounding the Color Line: The Indian-Black Experience in North America.* Lincoln: University of Nebraska Press.

Brown, Beverly

1975 George Liele: Black Baptist and Pan-Africanist, 1750–1826. *Savacou* 11/12:58–67.

Brown, David H.

2003 *Santería Enthroned: Art, Ritual, and Innovation in an Afro-Cuban Religion.* Chicago: University of Chicago Press.

Brown, Jacqueline Nassy

1998 Black Liverpool, Black America, and the Gendering of Diasporic Space. *Cultural Anthropology* 13(3):291–325.

2000 Enslaving History: Narratives on Local Whiteness in a Black Atlantic Port. *American Ethnologist* 27(2):340–370.

Brown, Karen McCarthy

1989 Systematic Remembering, Systematic Forgetting. In *Africa's Ogun: Old World and New,* edited by Sandra T. Barnes, pp. 65–89. Bloomington: Indiana University Press.

Brown, Thomas J., and Kitty Green

1998 *Lessons Learned from the Gullah Experience: Powerful Forces in Educating African-American Youth.* Columbia, MD: Brown and Associates.

Brown, Wallace

1965 *The King's Friends.* Providence, RI: Brown University Press.

1969 *The Good Americans.* New York: William Morrow.

1985 Research on the Loyalist Exodus to the Bahamas, Jamaica, and Dominica. In *Research Guide to Central America and the Caribbean,* edited by K. Grieb, pp. 346–354. Madison: University of Wisconsin Press.

1992   The American Loyalists in Jamaica. *Journal of Caribbean History* 26:121–146.

Browning, Barbara

1995   *Samba: Resistance in Motion.* Bloomington: Indiana University Press.

1998   *Infectious Rhythm: Metaphors of Contagion and the Spread of African Culture.* New York: Routledge.

Brubaker, Rogers

2005   The "Diaspora" Diaspora. *Ethnic and Racial Studies* 28(1):1–19.

Bruner, Edward M.

1996   Tourism in Ghana: The Representation of Slavery and the Return of the African Diaspora. *American Anthropologist* 98(2):290–304.

Bryan William S., ed.

1899   *Our Islands and Their People as Seen with Camera and Pencil.* Saint Louis, MO: N. D. Thompson Publishing Company.

Buisseret, David, and Steven G. Reinhardt, eds.

2000   *Creolization in the Americas.* College Station: Texas A&M University Press.

Bunzel, Ruth

[1929]   *The Pueblo Potter: A Study of Creative Imagination in Primitive Art.* New York:
1972   Dover.

Burdick, John

1998   *Blessed Anastácia: Women, Race and Popular Christianity in Brazil.* New York: Routledge.

Burton, Richard D. E.

1997   *Afro-Creole: Power, Opposition, and Play in the Caribbean.* Ithaca, NY: Cornell University Press.

Bushnell, David

1993   *The Making of Modern Colombia: A Nation in Spite of Itself.* Berkeley: University of California Press.

Butler, Kim D.

1998   *Freedoms Given, Freedoms Won: Afro-Brazilians in Post-Abolition São Paulo and Salvador.* New Brunswick, NJ: Rutgers University Press.

Byfield, Judith, ed.

2000   Africa's Diaspora. Special issue, *African Studies Review* 43(1).

Cabrera, Lydia

1980   *Koeko iyawó, aprende novicia: pequeño tratado de regla lucumí.* Miami: Ultra Graphics.

1986   *Anagó: vocabulario lucumí: el yoruba que se habla en Cuba.* 2d ed. Miami: Ediciones Universal.

Callahan, North

1967   *Flight from the Republic: The Tories of the American Revolution.* Indianapolis, IN: Bobbs-Merrill.

REFERENCES

Cameron, Dan, Richard J. Powell, Michele Wallace, Patrick Hill,
Thalia Gouma-Peterson, Morra Roth, and Ann Gibson, eds.
1998   *Dancing at the Louvre: Faith Ringgold's French Collection and Other Story Quilts.*
        Berkeley: University of California Press.

Campbell, Colin
1987   *The Romantic Ethic and the Spirit of Modern Consumerism.* Oxford: Basil
        Blackwell.

Carnegie, Charles V.
1992   The Fate of Ethnography: Native Social Science in the English-Speaking
        Caribbean. *New West Indian Guide* 66(1–2):5–25.
1996   The Dundus and the Nation. *Cultural Anthropology* 11(4):470–509.
1999   Garvey and the Black Transnation. *Small Axe* 5:48–71.

Carnegie Corporation Archives
1943   Carnegie Files. Rare Book and Manuscript Library. Columbia University,
        New York.

Carneiro, Édison
1951   Arthur Ramos: Brazilian Anthropologist (1903–1949), translated by James
        W. Ivy. *Phylon* 12(1):73–81.
1964   *Ladinos e crioulos: estudos sôbre o negro no Brasil.* Rio de Janeiro: Civilização
        Brasileira.

Carney, Judith A.
2001   *Black Rice: The African Origins of Rice Cultivation in the Americas.* Cambridge,
        MA: Harvard University Press.

Carranza, Eduardo
1944   Jorge Artel: El poeta negro. *Sábado* 26:4.

Cassidy, Frederic G.
1980   The Place of Gullah. *American Speech* 55:3–16.

Castillo M., Nicolás del
1982   *Esclavos negros en Cartagena y sus aportes léxicos.* Bogotá: Instituto Caro y
        Cuervo.

Caulfield, Mina
1969   Culture and Imperialism: Proposing a New Dialectic. In *Reinventing
        Anthropology*, edited by Dell Hymes, pp.182–212. New York: Pantheon.

Célius, Carlo, ed.
2005   L'anthropologie à Haïti. Special issue, *Gradhiva*, n.s., 1.

Centre Georges Pompidou
1989   *Magiciens de la Terre.* Paris: Centre Georges Pompidou.

Cerroni-Long, E. L.
1987   Benign Neglect? Anthropology and the Study of Blacks in the United
        States. *Journal of Black Studies* 17(4):438–459.

Chambers, Douglas Brent

1996   "He Gwine Sing He Country": Africans, Afro-Virginians, and the
Development of Slave Culture in Virginia, 1690–1810. Ph.D. diss.,
University of Virginia., Charlotteville.

1997   "My Own Nation": Igbo Exiles in the Diaspora. *Slavery and Abolition*
18(1):72–97.

2001   Ethnicity in the Diaspora: The Slave-Trade and the Creation of African
"Nations" in the Americas. *Slavery and Abolition* 22(3):25–39.

2002   The Significance of Igbo in the Bight of Biafra Slave-Trade: A Rejoinder to
Northrup's "Myth Igbo." *Slavery and Abolition* 23(1):101–120.

Chapman, William

1991   Slave Villages in the Danish West Indies. In *Perspectives in Vernacular
Architecture, IV*, edited by Thomas Carter and Bernard L. Herman, pp.
108–120. Columbia: University of Missouri Press for the Vernacular
Architecture Forum.

Chasteen, John Charles

2004   *National Rhythms, African Roots: The Deep History of Latin American Popular
Dance*. Albuquerque: University of New Mexico Press.

Chatterjee, Partha

1993   *The Nation and Its Fragments: Colonial and Postcolonial Histories.* Princeton,
NJ: Princeton University Press.

Chaudhuri, K. N.

1990   *Asia before Europe: Economy and Civilization of the Indian Ocean from the Rise of
Islam to 1750*. Cambridge: Cambridge University Press.

Chávez Álvarez, Ernesto

1991   *El crimen de la niña Cecilia: la brujería en Cuba como fenómeno social
(1902–1925)*. Havana: Editorial de Ciencias Sociales.

Cheney-Coker, Syl

1990   *The Last Harmattan of Alusine Dunbar.* Oxford: Heinemann.

Chevannes, Barry

1994   *Rastafari: Roots and Ideology.* Syracuse, NY: Syracuse University Press.

Chevannes, Barry, ed.

1995   *Rastafari and Other African-Caribbean Worldviews.* London: Macmillan.

Chopin, Anne, and Hervé Chopin

1998   *Les peintres martiniquais/Painters from Martinique.* Parmain, France: HC
Editions.

Chude-Sokei, Louis

1997   Postnationalist Geographies: Rasta, Ragga, and Reinventing Africa. In
Reggae, Rasta, Revolution: Jamaican Music from Ska to Dub, edited by Chris
Potash, pp. 215–227. New York: Schirmer Books.

REFERENCES

Civil, Françoise Moulin

1999   El discurso regeneracionista en Fernando Ortiz. In *Imágenes e imaginarios nacionales en el ultramar español*, edited by Consuelo Naranjo Orovio and Carlos Serrano, pp. 227–234. Madrid: Consejo Superior de Investigaciones Científicas, Central de Humanidades, Instituto de Historia, Departamento de Historia de América, Casa de Velázquez.

Clarke, John

1869   *Memorials of Baptist Missionaries in Jamaica, Including a Sketch of the Labours of Early Religious Instructors in Jamaica.* London: Yates & Alexander.

Clarke, Kamari Maxine

2004   *Mapping Yorùbá Networks: Power and Agency in the Making of Transnational Communities.* Durham, NC: Duke University Press.

Clarke, Murtie June

1981   *Loyalists in the Southern Campaign of the Revolutionary War.* Baltimore, MD: Genealogical Publishing Co., Inc.

Clifford, James

1986   Introduction. In *Writing Culture: The Poetics and Politics of Ethnography*, edited by James Clifford and George E. Marcus, pp. 1–26. Berkeley: University of California Press.

1997   *Routes: Travel and Translation in the Late Twentieth Century.* Cambridge, MA: Harvard University Press.

Cohen, Robin

1997   *Global Diasporas: An Introduction.* Seattle: University of Washington Press.

Cole, Sally

1994   Introduction: Ruth Landes in Brazil: Writing, Race, and Gender in 1930s American Anthropology. In *City of Women* by Ruth Landes. 2d ed. Pp. vii–xxxiv. Albuquerque: University of New Mexico Press.

1995   Ruth Landes and the Early Ethnography of Race and Gender. In *Women Writing Culture*, edited by Ruth Behar and Deborah A. Gordon, pp. 166–185. Berkeley: University of California Press.

2003   *Ruth Landes: A Life in Anthropology.* Lincoln: University of Nebraska Press.

Coleman, Kenneth

1958   *The American Revolution in Georgia, 1763–1789.* Athens: University of Georgia Press.

Collier, Jane F.

1997   The Waxing and Waning of "Subfields" in North American Sociocultural Anthropology. In *Anthropological Locations: Boundaries and Grounds of a Field Science*, edited by Akhil Gupta and James Ferguson, pp. 117–130. Berkeley: University of California Press.

Collins, Patricia Hill

1991   *Black Feminist Thought: Knowledge, Consciousness, and the Politics of Empowerment.* New York: Routledge.

Colón, Jesús

1961   *The Puerto Rican in New York and Other Sketches*. New York: Masses and
Mainstream.

Comaroff, John L., and Jean Comaroff

1987   The Madman and the Migrant: Work and Labor in the Historical
Consciousness of a South African People. *American Ethnologist*
14(2):191–209.

Comhaire, Jean

1949   A Propos des "Brésiliens" de Lagos. *Grands Lacs* 64(7):41–43.

Conkey, Margaret, ed.

1990   *The Uses of Style in Archaeology*. Cambridge: Cambridge University Press.

Connerton, Paul

1989   *How Societies Remember*. Cambridge: Cambridge University Press.

Conyers, James L., and Alva P. Barnett, eds.

1999   *African American Sociology: A Social Study of the Pan-African Diaspora*. Chicago:
Nelson-Hall Publishers.

Cook, Karen

1993   Black Bones, White Science: The Battle over New York's African Burial
Ground. *Village Voice*, May 4, 23–27.

Coombes, Annie E.

1994   *Reinventing Africa: Museums, Material Culture, and Popular Imagination in
Late Victorian and Edwardian England*. New Haven, CT: Yale University
Press.

Coronil, Fernando

1995   Introduction to the Duke University Press Edition: Transculturation and
the Politics of Theory: Countering the Center, Cuban Counterpoint. In
Cuban Counterpoint: Tobacco and Sugar, by Fernando Ortiz. Translated by
Harriet de Onís, pp. ix–lvi. Durham, NC: Duke University Press.

Corrêa, Mariza

1987a   *As ilusões da liberdade: história da antropologia no Brasil (1930–1960)*.
Campinas: Editora da Universidade Estadual de Campinas.

1987b   *História da antropologia no Brasil (1930–1960): testemunhos*. Campinas, Brazil:
Editora da Universidade Estadual de Campinas.

1988   Traficantes do excêntrico: os antropólogos no Brasil dos anos 30 aos anos
60. *Revista Brasileira de Ciências Sociais* 6(3):79–98.

1998   *As ilusões da liberdade: a escola Nina Rodrigues e a antropologia no Brasil*.
Bragança, Brazil: Editora da Universidade São Francisco.

2000   O mistério dos orixás e das bonecas: raça e gênero na antropologia
brasileira. *Ethnográfica* 4(2):233–265.

2003   *Antropólogas e antropologia*. Belo Horizonte: Editora da Universidade
Federal de Minas Gerais.

Cosentino, Donald J.

1995   Imagine Heaven. In *Sacred Arts of Haitian Vodou*, edited by Donald J. Cosentino, pp. 25–55. Los Angeles: Fowler Museum of Cultural History, University of California at Los Angeles.

Coster, A. M.

1866   De Boschnegers in de kolonie Suriname, hun leven, zeden, en gewoonten. *Bijdragen tot de Taal-, Land- en Volkenkunde* 13:1–36.

Coundouriotis, Eleni

2001   Nation, History, and the Idea of Cultural Origin in Melville Herksovits. *Diaspora* 10(1):29–51.

Cox, Oliver C.

1948   *Caste, Class, and Race: A Study in Social Dynamics.* Garden City, NY: Doubleday.

Craton, Michael, and Gail Saunders

1992   *From Aboriginal Times to the End of Slavery.* Vol. 1 of *Islanders in the Stream: A History of the Bahamian People.* Athens: University of Georgia Press.

Creel, Margaret Washington

1988   *"A Peculiar People": Slave Religion and Community-Culture among the Gullahs.* New York: New York University Press.

Cremé Ramos, Zoe, and Rafael Duharte Jiménez

1994   *¿Barracones En Los Cafetales?* Colección Santiago de Cuba, Havana: Publicigraf.

Cressman, Luther S.

1988   *A Golden Journey: Memoirs of an Archaeologist.* Salt Lake City: University of Utah Press.

Crichlow, Michaeline A.

2005   *Negotiating Caribbean Freedom: Peasants and the State in Development.* Lanham, MD: Lexington Books.

Crow, Jeffrey J., and Larry E. Tise, eds.

1978   *The Southern Experience in the American Revolution.* Chapel Hill: University of North Carolina Press.

Cunha, Manuela Carneiro da

1985   *Negros, estrangeiros: Os escravos libertos e sua volta à Africa.* São Paulo: Brasiliense.

Cunha, Olívia Maria Gomes da

2002   *Intencão e gesto: pessoa, cor e a producão cotidiana da (in)diferenca no Rio de Janeiro, 1927–1942.* Rio de Janeiro: Arquivo Nacional.

n.d.   The Apprentice Tourist Revisited: Travel, Ethnography, and the Nation in the Writings of Rómulo Lachatañeré and Arthur Ramos. Unpublished paper.

Cunin, Elisabeth

1999   Buscando las poblaciones negras de Cartagena. *Aguaita: Revista del Observatorio del Caribe Colombiano* 2:82–98.

2003   *Identidades a flor de piel. Lo "negro" entre apariencias y pertenencias: categorías raciales y mestizaje en Cartagena.* Bogotá: ICANH, Universidad de los Andes, IFEA, Observatorio del Caribe Colombiano.

Cunningham, Irma Aloyce Ewing

1992   *A Syntactic Analysis of Sea Island Creole.* Tuscaloosa, AL: American Dialect Society/University of Alabama Press.

Curtin, Philip D.

1955   *Two Jamaicas: The Role of Ideas in a Tropical Colony, 1830–1865.* Cambridge, MA: Harvard University Press.

1964   *The Image of Africa: British Ideas and Action, 1780–1850.* Madison: University of Wisconsin Press.

2000   *The World and the West: The European Challenge and the Overseas Response in the Age of Empire.* Cambridge: Cambridge University Press.

Curtin, Philip D., ed.

1969   *The Atlantic Slave Trade: A Census.* Madison: University of Wisconsin Press.

1972   *Africa and the West: Intellectual Responses to European Culture.* Madison: University of Wisconsin Press.

Curto, José C., and Paul E. Lovejoy, eds.

2004   *Enslaving Connections: Changing Cultures of Africa and Brazil during the Era of Slavery.* Amherst, NY: Humanity Books.

Cusick, James G.

1998   Introduction. In *Studies in Culture Contact: Interaction, Culture Change, and Archaeology*, edited by James Cusick, pp. 1–20. Carbondale: Center for Archaeological Investigations, Southern Illinois University, Carbondale.

D'Agostino, Peter

2002   Craniums, Criminals, and the "Cursed Race": Italian Anthropology in American Racial Thought, 1861–1924. *Comparative Studies in Society and History* 44(2):319–343.

Daniel, Yvonne

1995   *Rumba: Dance and Social Change in Contemporary Cuba.* Bloomington: Indiana University Press.

2004   Dance in the African Diaspora. In *Encyclopedia of Diasporas: Immigrant and Refugee Cultures Around the World*, vol. 1, edited by Melvin Ember, Carol R. Ember, and Ian Skoggard, pp. 347–356. New York: Kluwer Academic/Plenum Publishers.

Danto, Arthur

1964   The Artworld. *Journal of Philosophy* 61:571–584.

REFERENCES

Dash, J. Michael

1981   *Literature and Ideology in Haiti, 1915–1961.* Totowa, NJ: Barnes and Noble Books.

1992   Blazing Mirrors: The Crisis of the Haitian Intellectual. In *Intellectuals in the Twentieth-Century Caribbean, vol. II, Unity in Variety: The Hispanic and Francophone Caribbean,* edited by Alistair Hennessy, pp. 175–85. London: Macmillan.

Davenport, C. B., and Morris Steggerda

1929   *Race Crossing in Jamaica.* Washington, DC: Carnegie Institute of Washington.

Davies, Carole Boyce, Meredith Gadsby, Charles Peterson, and Henrietta Williams, eds.

2003   *Decolonizing the Academy: African Diaspora Studies.* Trenton, NJ: Africa World Press.

Davies, Catherine, and Richard Fardon

1991   African Fictions in Representations of West African and Afro-Cuban Cultures. *Bulletin of the John Rylands University of Manchester Library* 73(3):125–145.

Davies, K. G., ed.

1976   *Documents of the American Revolution, 1770–1783.* Dublin: Irish University Press.

Dávila, Arlene

1997   *Sponsored Identities: Cultural Politics in Puerto Rico.* Philadelphia, PA: Temple University Press.

1999   Latinizing Culture: Art, Museums, and the Politics of U.S. Multicultural Encompassment. *Cultural Anthropology* 14(2):180–202.

Dávila, Jerry

2003   *Diploma of Whiteness: Race and Social Policy in Brazil, 1917–1945.* Durham, NC: Duke University Press.

Davis, Allison, Burleigh B. Gardner, and Mary R. Gardner

1941   *Deep South: A Social Anthropological Study of Caste and Class.* Chicago: University of Chicago Press.

Davis, Darién J.

1998   Nationalism and Civil Rights in Cuba: A Comparative Perspective. *Journal of Negro History* 83(1):35–51.

1999   *Avoiding the Dark: Race and the Forging of National Culture in Modern Brazil.* Brookfield, VT: Ashgate.

2000   Racial Parity and National Humor: Exploring Brazilian Samba from Noel Rosa to Carmen Miranda, 1930–1939. In *Latin American Popular Culture: An Introduction,* edited by William H. Beezley and Linda C. Curcio-Nagy, pp. 183–200. Wilmington, DE: SR Books.

Davis, Harold E.

1976   *The Fledgling Province: Social and Cultural Life in Colonial Georgia, 1773–1776.* Chapel Hill: University of North Carolina Press.

Davis, John W.

1918   George Liele and Andrew Bryan, Pioneer Negro Baptist Preachers. *Journal of Negro History* 3(2):119–127.

Davis, Robert Scott

1980   The Other Side of the Coin: Georgia Baptists Who Fought for the King. *Viewpoints: Georgia Baptist History* 7:47–57.

Dayan, Joan

1995   *Haiti, History and the Gods.* Berkeley: University of California Press.

Deacon, Desley

1997   *Elsie Clews Parsons: Inventing Modern Life.* Chicago: University of Chicago Press.

Deagan, Kathleen A.

1998   Rethinking Modern History. *Archaeology* (September–October):54–60.

Deagan, Kathleen A., and Jane Landers

1999   Fort Mosé: Earliest Free African-American Town in the United States. In *"I, Too, Am America": Archaeological Studies of African-American Life,* edited by Theresa A. Singleton, pp. 261–282. Charlottesville: University Press of Virginia.

Deagan, Kathleen A., and Darcie MacMahon

1995   *Fort Mosé: Colonial America's Black Fortress of Freedom.* Gainesville: University of Florida Press.

DeCorse, Christopher R.

1987   Historical Archaeological Research in Ghana, 1986–1987. *Nyame Akuma* 29:27–31.

1989   Material Aspects of the Limba, Yalunka, and Kuranko Ethnicity: Archaeological Research in Northeastern Sierra Leone. In *Archaeological Approaches to Cultural Identity,* edited by Stephen Shennan, pp. 125–140. London: Routledge.

1999   Oceans Apart: Africanist Perspectives on Diaspora Archaeology. In *"I, Too, Am America": Archaeological Studies of African-American Life,* edited by Theresa A. Singleton, pp. 132–155. Charlottesville: University Press of Virginia.

2001   *An Archaeology of Elmina: Africans and Europeans on the Gold Coast, 1400–1900.* Washington, DC: Smithsonian Institution Press.

Deetz, James

1988   American Historical Archaeology: Methods and Results. *Science* 239:362–367.

1993   *Flowerdew Hundred: The Archaeology of a Virginia Plantation, 1619–1864.* Charlottesville: University Press of Virginia.

1996   *In Small Things Forgotten: An Archaeology of Early American Life.* Expanded
            and rev ed. New York: Anchor Books.

de Friedemann, Nina S.

1984   Estudios de negros en la antropología colombiana. In *Un siglo de investi-
            gación social: antropología en Colombia,* edited by Jaime Arocha and Nina de
            Friedemann, pp. 507–572. Bogotá: Etno.

1993   *La saga del negro: Presencia africana en Colombia.* Bogotá: Instituto de
            Genética Humana, Pontificia Universidad Javeriana.

de Friedemann, Nina S., and Jaime Arocha

1986   *De sol a sol: Génesis, transformación y presencia de los negros en Colombia.*
            Bogotá: Planeta.

de la Fuente, Alejandro

2001   *A Nation for All: Race, Inequality, and Politics in Twentieth-Century Cuba.*
            Chapel Hill: University of North Carolina Press.

Delano, Jack

1990   *Puerto Rico Mio: Four Decades of Change.* Washington, DC: Smithsonian
            Institution Press.

Delle, James A.

1999   The Landscapes of Class Negotiation on Coffee Plantations in the Blue
            Mountains of Jamaica, 1790–1850. *Historical Archaeology* 33(1):136–158.

Derby, Lauren R.

1994   Haitians, Magic, and Money: Raza and Society in the Haitian-Dominican
            Borderlands, 1900 to 1937. *Comparative Studies in Society and History*
            36(3):488–526.

Desai, Gaurav

1993   The Invention of Invention. *Cultural Critique* 24:119–142.

Devés Valdés, Eduardo

2000   Afroamericanismo e identidad en el pensamiento latinoamericano en
            Cuba, Haití y Brasil, 1900–1940. *Canadian Journal of Latin American and
            Caribbean Studies* 25(49):53–75.

Dianteill, Erwan

1995   *Le savant et le santero: naissance de l'étude scientifique des religion afrocubaines
            (1906–1954).* Paris: L'Harmattan.

2000   *Des dieux et des signes: initiation, écriture et divination dans les religions afro-
            cubaines.* Paris: Ecole des Hautes-Etudes en Sciences Sociales.

2002a   Una filiación problemática: dos generaciones de antropólogos en Cuba y
            Haití. *Del Caribe* 37:28–37.

2002b   Deterriorialization and Reterritorialization of the Orisha Religion in
            Africa and the New World (Nigeria, Cuba and the United States), trans-
            lated by Karen George. *International Journal of Urban and Regional Research*
            26(1):121–137.

Diawara, Manthia

1990 Reading Africa through Foucault: V. Y. Mudimbe's Reaffirmation of the Subject. *October* 55:79–92.

Díaz, María del Rosario

2003 La iniciación intelectual de Fernando Ortiz. *Cuadernos Hispanoamericanos* 641:43–48.

Díaz Quiñones, Arcadio

1998 Fernando Ortiz y Allan Kardec: espiritismo y transculturación. *Prismas* 2:175–192.

2000 Fernando Ortiz and Allan Kardec: Transmigration and Transculturation. In *The Cultures of the Hispanic Caribbean*, edited by Conrad James and John Perivolaris, pp. 9–27. Gainesville: University Press of Florida.

Diène, Doudou, ed.

2001 *From Chains to Bonds: The Slave Trade Revisited.* Paris: UNESCO.

Dijk, Frank Jan van

1993 *Jahmaica: Rastafari and Jamaican Society 1930–1990.* Utrecht: ISOR.

Dillard, J. L.

1964 The Writings of Herskovits and the Study of the Language of the Negro in the New World. *Caribbean Studies* 4(2):35–41.

1972 *Black English: Its History and Usage in the United States.* New York: Random House.

Diner, Hasia R.

1977 *In the Almost Promised Land: American Jews and Blacks, 1915–1935.* Westport, CT: Greenwood Press.

Dirks, Nicholas B., Geoff Eley, and Sherry B. Ortner, eds.

1994 *Culture/Power/History: A Reader in Contemporary Social Theory.* Princeton, NJ: Princeton University Press.

1996 Is Vice Versa? Historical Anthropologies and Anthropological Histories. In *The Historic Turn in the Human Sciences*, edited by Terrence J. McDonald, pp. 17–51. Ann Arbor: University of Michigan Press.

Dodge, Steve

1979 *The First Loyalist Settlement in Abaco, Carleton and Marsh's Harbor.* Hope Town, Bahamas: Wyannie Malone Museum.

Dodson, Howard, Christopher Moore, and Roberta Yancy

2000 *The Black New Yorkers: The Schomburg Illustrated Chronology.* New York: Schomburg Center for Research in Black Culture, New York Public Library, and John Wiley.

Dollard, John

1937 *Caste and Class in a Southern Town.* New Haven, CT: Yale University Press.

Domínguez, Lourdes S.

1999 *Los collares en la santería cubana.* Havana: Editorial José Martí.

REFERENCES

Domínguez, Virginia R.

1989   *People as Subject, People as Object: Selfhood and Peoplehood in Contemporary Israel.* Madison: University of Wisconsin Press.

Doortmont, Michel R.

1990   The Invention of the Yorubas: Regional and Pan-African Nationalism versus Ethnic Provincialism. In *Self-Assertion and Brokerage: Early Cultural Nationalism in West Africa,* edited by P. F. de Moraes Farias and Karin Barber, pp. 101–108. Birmingham, UK: Centre of West African Studies, University of Birmingham.

Drake, St. Clair

1974   In the Mirror of Black Scholarship: W. Allison Davis and *Deep South.* In *Education and Black Struggle: Notes from the Colonized World. Harvard Educational Review* monograph no. 2:42–54.

1975   The Black Diaspora in Pan-African Perspective. *Black Scholar* 7(1):2–13.

1980   Anthropology and the Black Experience. *Black Scholar* 11(7):2–31.

1982   Diaspora Studies and Pan-Africanism. In *Global Dimensions of the African Diaspora,* edited by Joseph E. Harris, pp. 341–402. Washington, DC: Howard University Press.

Drummond, Lee

1980   The Cultural Continuum: A Theory of Intersystems. *Man,* n.s., 15(2):352–374.

Duany, Jorge

1985   Ethnicity in the Spanish Caribbean: Notes on the Consolidation of Creole Identity in Cuba and Puerto Rico, 1762–1868. *Ethnic Groups* 6(2):99–123.

1999   Making Indians out of Blacks: The Revitalization of Taíno Identity in Contemporary Puerto Rico. In *Taíno Revival: Critical Perspectives on Puerto Rican Identity and Cultural Politics,* edited by Gabriel Haslip-Viera, pp. 31–55. New York: Centro de Estudios Puertorriqueños, Hunter College, City University of New York.

Du Bois, W. E. B.

1899   *The Philadelphia Negro.* New York: Lippincott.

1903   *The Souls of Black Folk: Essays and Sketches.* Chicago: A. C. McClurg.

Duncan, Ronald J.

1983   *Social Research in Puerto Rico: Science, Humanism, and Society.* San Juan: Inter-American University Press.

Duncan, Ronald J., ed.

1979   *The Social Anthropology of Puerto Rico. Studies of Puerto Rican Society and Culture,* no. 1. San Germán: Inter-American University of Puerto Rico.

Dunlap, David

1992   Mistake Disturbs Graves at Black Burial Ground despite Promises, Workers Unearth Bones. *New York Times,* February 21, B3, B5.

Dusinberre, William
2000   *Them Dark Days: Slavery in the American Rice Swamps.* Athens: University of
        Georgia Press.

Ebeling, Mary F. E.
2003   The New Dawn: Black Agency in Cyberspace. *Radical History Review*
        87:96–108.

Edmunds, Ennis Barrington
2003   *Rastafari: From Outcasts to Culture Bearers.* New York: Oxford University
        Press.

Eltis, David
2000   *The Rise of African Slavery in the Americas.* Cambridge: Cambridge University
        Press.

2001   The Volume and Structure of the Transatlantic Slave Trade: A
        Reassessment. *William and Mary Quarterly* 58(1):17–46.

Eltis, David, Stephen D. Behrendt, David Richardson, Herbert S. Klein, eds.
1999   *The Trans-Atlantic Slave Trade: A Database on CD-ROM.* Cambridge:
        Cambridge University Press.

Emerson, Matthew C.
1988   Decorated Clay Tobacco Pipes from the Chesapeake. Ph.D. diss.,
        University of California, Berkeley.

1994   African Inspirations in a New World Art and Artifact. In *Historical
        Archaeology of the Chesapeake*, edited by Paul A. Shackel and Barbara J. Little,
        pp. 34–49. Washington, DC: Smithsonian Institution Press.

1999   African Inspirations in a New World Art and Artifact: Decorated Pipes
        from the Chesapeake. In *"I, Too, Am America": Archaeological Studies of
        African-American Life*, edited by Theresa A. Singleton, pp. 47–82.
        Charlottesville: University Press of Virginia.

Epperson, Terrence W.
1990   Race and the Disciplines of the Plantation. *Historical Archaeology*
        24(4):29–36.

1999   The Contested Commons: Archaeologies of Race, Repression, and
        Resistance in New York City. In *Historical Archaeologies of Capitalism*, edited
        by Mark P. Leone and Parker B. Potter Jr., pp. 81–111. New York: Kluwer
        Academic/Plenum Publishers.

Eshun, Kodwo
2003   Further Considerations of Afrofuturism. *CR: The New Centennial Review*
        3(2):287–302.

Everett, Anna
2002   The Revolution Will Be Digitized: Afrocentricity and the Digital Public
        Sphere. *Social Text* 20(2):125–146.

REFERENCES

Fabian, Johannes

1983   *Time and the Other: How Anthropology Makes Its Object.* New York: Columbia University Press.

Fadipe, N. A.

[1939]   *The Sociology of the Yoruba.* Ibàdàn, Nigeria: Ibàdàn University Press.
1970

Falola, Toyin, and Matt D. Childs, eds.

2004   *The Yoruba Diaspora in the Atlantic World.* Bloomington: Indiana University Press.

Falola, Toyin, and Christian Jennings, eds.

2002   *Africanizing Knowledge: African Studies Across the Disciplines.* New Brunswick, NJ: Transaction Publishers.

Farias, P. F. de Moraes

1990   Yoruba Origins Revisited by Muslims: An Interview with the Arókin of Oyo and a Reading of the Asl Qaba'il Yuruba of Al-Hajj Adam al-Iluri. In *Self-Assertion and Brokerage: Early Cultural Nationalism in West Africa,* edited by P. F. de Moraes Farias and Karin Barber, pp. 109–147. Birmingham, UK: Centre of West African Studies, University of Birmingham.

Faulkenberry, Lisa V., John M. Coggeshall, Kenneth Backman, and Sheila Backman

2000   A Culture of Servitude: The Impact of Tourism Development on South Carolina's Coast. *Human Organization* 59(1):86–95.

Favor, J. Martin

1999   *Authentic Blackness: The Folk in the New Negro Renaissance.* Durham, NC: Duke University Press.

Feld, Steven, and Keith H. Basso, eds.

1996   *Senses of Place.* School of American Research . Santa Fe, NM: SAR Press.

Fennell, Christopher C.

2000   Conjuring Boundaries: Inferring Past Identities from Religious Artifacts. *International Journal of Historical Archaeology* 4(4):281–313.

2003   Group Identity, Individual Creativity, and Symbolic Generation in a BaKongo Diaspora. *International Journal of Historical Archaeology* 7(1):1–31.

Ferguson, Leland G.

1989   Lowcountry Plantations, the Catawba Nation, and River Burnished Pottery. In *Studies in South Carolina Archaeology: Essays in Honor of Robert L. Stephenson,* edited by Albert C. Goodyear III and Glen T. Hanson, pp. 185–191. Columbia: South Carolina Institute of Archaeology and Anthropology, University of South Carolina.

1992   *Uncommon Ground: Archaeology and Early African America, 1650–1800.* Washington, DC: Smithsonian Institution Press.

Fernandes, Florestan

1958   *A etnologia e a sociologia no Brasil: ensaios sobre aspectos da formação e do desen-volvimento das ciências socais na sociedade brasileira.* São Paulo: Editora Anhambi.

Fernández, James W.

1985   *Persuasions and Performances: The Play of Tropes in Culture.* Bloomington: Indiana University Press.

1990   Tolerance in a Repugnant World and Other Dilemmas in the Cultural Relativism of Melville J. Herskovits. *Ethos* 18(2):140–164.

Ferretti, Mundicarmo

2002   Tradition et changement dans les religions afro-brésiliennes dans le Maranhão. *Archives de Sciences Sociales des Religions* 117:101–112.

Ferris, Bill

1982   *Local Color: A Sense of Place in Folk Art.* New York: McGraw-Hill.

Ferris, Bill, ed.

1983   *Afro-American Folk Art and Crafts.* Boston: G. K. Hall.

Fett, Sharla

2002   *Working Cures: Healing, Health, and Power on Southern Slave Plantations.* Chapel Hill: University of North Carolina Press.

Fiehrer, Thomas

1997   Strangers in Paradise: Ideography, Metageography, and Theosophy in Modern Discourses on Colonialism. *Histoire Sociale/Social History* 30(60):439–461.

Figueiredo, Angela

2002   *Novas elites de cor: estudo sobre os profissionais liberais negros de Salvador.* São Paulo: Annablume.

Firmin, Anténor

[1885]   *The Equality of the Human Races.* Urbana: University of Illinois Press.
2002

Firth, Raymond

[1936]   *Art and Life in New Guinea.* New York: AMS Press.
1979

Fischer, David Hackett

1989   *Albion's Seed: Four British Folkways in America.* New York: Oxford University Press.

Fleischmann, Ulrich

2003   The Sociocultural and Lingusitic Profile of a Concept. *Mamatu: Journal for African Culture and Society* 27–28:xv–xxxvi.

Flores, Juan

1982   Foreword. In *The Puerto Rican in New York and Other Sketches*, by Jesús Colón. 2d ed. New York: International Publishers.

Fluehr-Lobban, Carolyn

2000   Anténor Firmin: Haitian Pioneer of Anthropology. *American Anthropologist* 102(3):449–466.

2002   Introduction. In *The Equality of the Human Races*, by Anténor Firmin. Urbana: University of Illinois Press.

Foner, Philip S.

1982   *Organized Labor and the Black Worker, 1619–1981.* 2d ed. New York: International Publishers.

Font, Mauricio A., and Alfonso W. Quiroz, eds.

2005   *Cuban Counterpoints: The Legacy of Fernando Ortiz.* Lanham, MD: Lexington Books.

Foote, Thelma Wills

1991   *Black Life in Colonial Manhattan, 1664–1786.* Ph.D. diss., Harvard University, Cambridge, MA.

2004   *Black and White Manhattan: The History of Racial Formation in Colonial New York City.* New York: Oxford University Press.

Forbes, Jack D.

1993   *Africans and Native Americans: The Language of Race and the Evolution of Red-Black Peoples.* 2d ed. Urbana: University of Illinois Press.

Fortich Díaz, William

1994   *Con bombos y platillos: Origen del porro, aproximación al fandango y las bandas pelayeras.* Montería, Colombia: Domus Libri.

Fortune, Fernand Tiburce

1994   *La voie du fwomajé: Art du dedans.* Fort-de-France, Martinique: Association Fwomajé.

Fox, Richard G., ed.

1990   *Nationalist Ideologies and the Production of National Cultures.* Washington, DC: American Anthropological Association.

Franco Ferrán, José Luciano

1986   Esquema histórico sobre la trata negrera y la esclavitud. In *La esclavitud en Cuba*, pp. 1–10. Havana: Instituto de Ciencias Históricas, Editorial Academia.

Frank, Gelya

2001   Melville J. Herskovits on the African and Jewish Diasporas: Race, Culture and Modern Anthropology. *Identities* 8(2):173–209.

Franz Boas Papers. American Philosophical Society, Philadelphia.

Fraser, Gertrude

1991   Race, Class and Difference in Hortense Powdermaker's *After Freedom: A Cultural Study in the Deep South. Journal of Anthropological Research* 47(2):403–415.

Frazier, E. Franklin

1939   *The Negro Family in the United States.* Chicago: University of Chicago Press.

1942   The Negro Family in Bahia, Brazil. *American Sociological Review*
        7(4):465–478.

1943   Rejoinder. *American Sociological Review* 8(4):402–404.

1957   *Race and Cultural Contacts in the Modern World*. New York: Alfred A. Knopf.

Frei, Hans W.

1974   *The Eclipse of Biblical Narrative: A Study in Eighteenth and Nineteenth Century
        Hermeneutics*. New Haven, CT: Yale University Press.

Frey, Sylvia R.

1991   *Water from the Rock: Black Resistance in a Revolutionary Age*. Princeton, NJ:
        Princeton University Press.

Frey, Sylvia R., and Betty Wood

1998   *Come Shouting to Zion: African American Protestantism in the American South
        and British Caribbean to 1830*. Chapel Hill: University of North Carolina
        Press.

Frobenius, Leo

[1913] *The Voice of Africa: Being an Account of the Travels of the German Inner African
1968   Exploration Expedition in the Years 1910–1912*. New York: B. Blom.

Fry, Gladys-Marie

1986   *Broken Star: Post Civil War Quilts Made by Black Women*. Dallas, TX: Museum
        of African-American Life and Culture.

1990   *Stitched from the Soul: Slave Quilts from the Ante-Bellum South*. New York:
        Dutton Studio Books/Museum of American Folk Art.

Frye, Northrop

1982   *The Great Code: The Bible and Literature*. New York: Harcourt Brace
        Jovanovich.

Galard, Jean

2001   *L'Avenir des musées: Colloque international*. Paris: Musée du Louvre.

Gallay, Alan

1989   *The Formation of a Planter Elite: Jonathan Bryan and the Southern Colonial
        Frontier*. Athens: University of Georgia Press.

García, Jesús "Chucho"

2002   Encuentro y desencuentros de los "saberes" en torno a la africanía "lati-
        noamericana." In *Estudios y otras prácticas intelectuales latinoamericanas en
        cultura y poder*, edited by Daniel Mato, pp. 145–152. Caracas: Consejo
        Latinoamericano de Ciencias Sociales/CEAP/FACES/Universidad Central
        de Venezuela.

Gaspar, David Barry

1985   *Bondsmen and Rebels: A Study of Master-Slave Relations in Antigua, with
        Implications for Colonial British America*. Baltimore, MD: John Hopkins
        University Press.

REFERENCES

Gates, Henry Louis, Jr.
1988   *The Signifying Monkey: A Theory of Afro-American Literary Criticism.* New York: Oxford University Press.
1998   A Call to Protect Academic Integrity from Politics. *New York Times,* April 4, A13, A15.

Gates, John Palmer
1943   George Liele: A Pioneer Negro Preacher. *The Chronicle: A Baptist Historical Quarterly* 6:118–129.

Gatewood, Willard B.
1990   *Aristocrats of Color: The Black Elite, 1880–1920.* Bloomington: Indiana University Press.

Geertz, Clifford
1983   *Local Knowledge: Further Essays in Interpretive Anthropology.* New York: Basic Books.

Geggus, David
1990   The Demographic Composition of the French Caribbean Slave Trade. In *Proceedings of the Thirteenth and Fourteenth Meetings of the French Colonial Historical Society,* edited by Philip P. Boucher, pp. 14–30. Lanham, MD: University Press of America.

Genovese, Eugene D.
[1974]   *Roll, Jordan, Roll: The World the Slaves Made.* New York: Vintage Books.
 1976

Geraty, Virginia Mixson
1997   *Gullah fuh Oonuh (Gullah for You): A Guide to the Gullah Language.* Orangeburg, SC: Sandlapper Publishing Co.

Gershenhorn, Jerry
2004   *Melville J. Herskovits and the Racial Politics of Knowledge.* Lincoln: University of Nebraska Press.

Gerstin, Julian
2004   Tangled Roots: Kalenda and Other Neo-African Dances in the Circum-Caribbean. *New West Indian Guide* 78(1–2):5–41.

Gibson, Ann
1998   Faith Ringgold's *Picasso's Studio.* In *Dancing at the Louvre: Faith Ringgold's French Collection and Other Story Quilts,* edited by Dan Cameron et al., pp. 64–73. Berkeley: University of California Press.

Gibson, Mary
2002   *Born to Crime: Cesare Lombroso and the Origins of Biological Criminology.* Westport, CT: Praeger.

Gilard, Jacques
1991   *Voces* (1917–1920): Un proyecto para Colombia. *Huellas* 31:13–22.

Gilroy, Paul

1987   *'There Ain't No Black in the Union Jack': The Cultural Politics of Race and Nation.* London: Hutchinson.

1993   *The Black Atlantic: Modernity and Double Consciousness.* Cambridge, MA: Harvard University Press.

Glassie, Henry H.

1982   *Passing the Time in Ballymenone: Culture and History of an Ulster Community.* Philadelphia: University of Pennsylvania Press.

Glazier, Stephen D., ed.

2001   *The Encyclopedia of African and African-American Religions.* New York: Routledge.

Golde, Peggy, ed.

1970   *Women in the Field.* Chicago: Aldine.

Goldschmidt, Henry, and Elizabeth McAlister

2004   *Race, Nation, and Religion in the Americas.* New York: Oxford University Press.

Goldstein, Donna M.

2003   *Laughter out of Place: Race, Class, Violence, and Sexuality in a Rio Shantytown.* Berkeley: University of California Press.

Gómez, Laureano

1970   *Interrogantes sobre el progreso de Colombia.* Bogotá: Colección Populibro.

Gomez, Michael A.

1998   *Exchanging Our Country Marks: The Transformation of African Identities in the Colonial and Antebellum South.* Chapel Hill: University of North Carolina Press.

1999   African Identity and Slavery in the Americas. *Radical History Review* 75:111–120.

Gómez-Peña, Guillermo

1996   *The New World Border: Prophesies, Poems and Loqueras for the End of the Century.* San Francisco: City Lights.

Gonseth, Marc-Olivier, Jacques Hainard, and Roland Kaehr, eds.

1999   *L'art c'est l'art.* Neuchâtel, Switzerland: Musée d'Ethnographie.

Gonzales, Ambrose Elliott

1922   *The Black Border: Gullah Stories of the Carolina Coast.* Columbia, SC: State Company.

González Fernández, Doria

1991   La economía cafetalera cubana: 1790–1860. *Arbor* 547–546:161–179.

González, José Luis

[1979]   Literatura e identidad nacional en Puerto Rico. In *Puerto Rico: Identidad*
1981   *nacional y clases socials,* edited by Angel G. Quintero Rivera et al. Río Piedras, Puerto Rico: Ediciones Huracán.

González, Lydia Milagros

1992   *La tercera raíz: presencia africana en Puerto Rico.* San Juan: Centro de Estudios de la Realidad Puertorriqueña, Instituto de Cultura Puertorriqueña.

González, Lydia Milagros, and Angel G. Quintero Rivera

1984   *La otra cara de la historia: La historia de Puerto Rico desde su cara obrera, vol. I: 1800–1925.* Río Piedras, Puerto Rico: Centro de Estudios de la Realidad Puertorriqueña, Instituto de Cultura Puertorriqueña.

Goode, Judith, and Jeff Maskovsky, eds.

2001   *The New Poverty Studies: The Ethnography of Power, Politics, and Impoverished People in the United States.* New York: New York University Press.

Goodwine, Marquetta L.

1997a   *St. Helena's Serenity.* Vol. 1 of *Gullah/Geechee: The Survival of Africa's Seed in the Winds of the Diaspora.* New York: Kinship Publications.

1997b   *Gawd Dun Smile Pun We: Beaufort Isles.* Vol. 2 of *Gullah/Geechee: The Survival of Africa's Seed in the Winds of the Diaspora.* New York: Kinship Publications.

1997c   Frum Wi Soul Tuh De Soil: Cotton, Rice, and Indigo. Vol. 3 of *Gullah/Geechee: The Survival of Africa's Seed in the Winds of the Diaspora.* New York: Kinship Publications.

1998a   Introduction: Rebuilding the African American Community by Returning to Traditions. In *The Legacy of Ibo Landing: Gullah Roots of African American Culture,* edited by Marquetta L. Goodwine and the Clarity Press Gullah Project, pp. 1–13. Atlanta, GA: Clarity Press.

1998b   Destructionment: Treddin' Een We Ancestas' Teahs. In *The Legacy of Ibo Landing: Gullah Roots of African American Culture,* edited by Marquetta L. Goodwine and the Clarity Press Gullah Project, pp. 164–174. Atlanta, GA: Clarity Press.

1998c   Excavating Gullah Seeds: Guidelines for Conducting Research on the Gullah. In *The Legacy of Ibo Landing: Gullah Roots of African American Culture,* edited by Marquetta L. Goodwine and the Clarity Press Gullah Project, pp. 198–203. Atlanta, GA: Clarity Press.

Goodwine, Marquetta L., and the Clarity Press Gullah Project, eds.

1998   *The Legacy of Ibo Landing: Gullah Roots of African American Culture.* Atlanta, GA: Clarity Press.

Gordon, Edmund T.

1998   *Disparate Diasporas: Identity and Politics in an African Nicaraguan Community.* Austin: University of Texas Press.

Gordon, Edmund T., and Mark Anderson

1999   The African Diaspora: Towards an Ethnography of Diasporic Identification. *Journal of American Folklore* 112(445):282–296.

Gordon, Shirley C.

1996   *God Almighty, Make Me Free: Christianity in Preemancipation Jamaica.* Bloomington: Indiana University Press.

Gottschild, Brenda Dixon
1996   *Digging the Africanist Presence in American Performance: Dance and Other Contexts.* Westport, CT: Greenwood Press.

Goucher, Candace L.
1993   African Metallurgy in the Atlantic World. *African Archaeological Review* 11:197–215.
1999   African Caribbean Metal Technology: Forging Cultural Survivals in the Atlantic World. In *African Sites Archaeology in the Caribbean*, edited by Jay B. Haviser, pp. 143–156. Princeton, NJ: Markus Wiener.

Granda, Germán de
1977   *Estudios sobre un área dialectal hispanoamericana de población negra las tierras bajas occidentales de Colombia.* Bogotá: Publicaciones del Instituto de Caro y Cuervo.

Graves-Brown, Paul, Siân Jones, and Clive Gamble, eds.
1996   *Cultural Identity and Archaeology: The Construction of European Communities.* London: Routledge.

Green, Jonathan
1996   *Gullah Images: The Art of Jonathan Green.* Columbia: University of South Carolina Press.

Greenberg, Reesa, Bruce W. Ferguson, and Sandy Nairne, eds.
1996   *Thinking about Exhibitions.* London: Routledge.

Greenfield, Sidney M., and André Droogers, eds.
2001   *Reinventing Religions: Syncretism and Transformation in Africa and the Americas.* Lanham, MD: Rowman and Littlefield.

Gregory, Steven
1992   Voodoo, Ethnography, and the American Occupation of Haiti: William B. Seabrook's *The Magic Island.* In *The Politics of Culture and Creativity: A Critique of Civilization.* Vol. 2 of *Dialectical Anthropology: Essays in Honor of Stanley Diamond*, edited by Christine Ward Gailey, pp. 169–207. Gainesville: University Press of Florida.
1998   *Black Corona: Race and the Politics of Place in an Urban Community.* Princeton, NJ: Princeton University Press.

Gregory, Steven, and Roger Sanjek, eds.
1994   *Race.* New Brunswick, NJ: Rutgers University Press.

Grillo, R. D.
1989   *Dominant Languages: Language and Hierarchy in Britain and France.* Cambridge: Cambridge University Press.

Grimson, Alejandro, Gustavo Lins Ribeiro, Pablo Semán, and Roberto Cardoso de Oliveira, eds.
2004   *La antropología brasileña contemporánea: contribuciones para un diálogo latinoamericano.* Buenos Aires: Prometeo.

REFERENCES

Groover, Mark

1993   African American Textile Manufacture in the 18th-Century Carolina Backcountry. *African-American Archaeology* 7:9–11.

1994   Evidence of Folkways and Cultural Exchange in the Eighteenth-Century South Carolina Backcountry. *Historical Archaeology* 28(1):41–64.

Grossner, Isabel S.

1967   Interview with Guy B. Johnson. Oral History Research Office. Columbia University, New York.

Grudin, Eva Ungar

1990   *Stitching Memories: African-American Story Quilts.* Williamstown, MA: Williams College Museum of Art.

Grueso, Libia, Carlos Rosero, and Arturo Escobar

1998   The Process of Black Community Organizing in the Southern Pacific Coast of Colombia. In *Cultures of Politics/Politics of Cultures: Revisioning Latin American Social Movements,* edited by Sonia E. Álvarez, Evelina Dagnino, and Arturo Escobar, pp. 196–219. Boulder, CO: Westview.

Guerra Lillian

1998   *Popular Expression and National Identity in Puerto Rico: The Struggle for Self, Community, and Nation.* Gainesville: University Press of Florida.

2003   From Revolution to Involution in the Early Cuban Republic: Conflicts over Race, Class, and Nation, 1902–1906. In *Race and Nation in Modern Latin America,* edited by Nancy P. Appelbaum, Anne S. Macpherson, and Karin Alejandra Rosemblatt, pp. 132–162. Chapel Hill: University of North Carolina Press.

Guimarães, Antonio Sérgio Alfredo

2004a   Intelectuais negros e modernidade no Brasil. Working paper no. CBS-52-04, Centre for Brazilian Studies, University of Oxford.

2004b   Comentários à correspondência entre Melville Herskovits e Arthur Ramos (1935–1941). In *Antropologias, Histórias, Experiências,* edited by Fernanda Arêas Peixoto, Heloisa Pontes, and Lilia Moritz Schwarcz, pp. 169–198. Belo Horizonte, Brazil: Editora Universidade Federal do Minas Gerais.

Gullah/Geechee Sea Island Coalition

2003   Gullah/Geechee Sea Island Coalition. http://members.aol.com/queenmut/GullGeeCo.html (accessed May 23, 2003).

Guss, David M.

2000   *The Festive State: Race, Ethnicity, and Nationalism as Cultural Performance.* Berkeley: University of California Press.

Guthrie, Patricia

1996   *Catching Sense: African American Communities on a South Carolina Sea Island.* Westport, CT: Bergin and Garvey.

Guy B. Johnson Papers
1940   Southern Historical Collection, Wilson Library. University of North
        Carolina, Chapel Hill.

Guyer, Jane I.
2004   Anthropology in Area Studies. *Annual Review of Anthropology* 33:499–523.

Hair, P. E. H.
1965   Sierra Leone Items in the Gullah Dialect of American English. *Sierra Leone
        Language Review* 4:79–84.

Hale, Charles R.
1996   Travel Warning: Mestizaje, Hybridity and the Cultural Politics of
        Difference in Post-Revolutionary Central America. *Journal of Latin
        American Anthropology* 2(1):34–61.

2002   Does Multiculturalism Menace? Governance, Cultural Rights and the
        Politics of Identity in Guatemala. *Journal of Latin American Studies*
        34(3):485–524.

Hale, Dorothy J.
1994   Bahktin in African American Literary Theory. *ELH* 61(2):445–471.

Hall, Gwendolyn Midlo
1992   *Africans in Colonial Louisiana: The Development of Afro-Creole Culture in the
        Eighteenth Century.* Baton Rouge: Louisiana State University Press.

Hall, Martin
1992   "Small Things and the Mobile": Conflictual Fusion of Power, Fear, and
        Desire. In *The Art and Mystery of Historical Archaeology: Essays in Honor of
        James Deetz,* edited by Anne Elizabeth Yentsch and Mary C. Beaudry, pp.
        373–399. Boca Raton, FL: CRC Press.

2000   *Archaeology and the Modern World: Colonial Transcripts in South Africa and the
        Chesapeake.* London: Routledge.

Hall, Stuart
1990   Cultural Identity and Diaspora. In *Identity: Community, Culture, Difference,*
        edited by Jonathan Rutherford, pp. 222–237. London: Lawrence and
        Wishart.

1999   Thinking the Diaspora: Home-Thoughts from Abroad. *Small Axe* 6:1–18.

Hall, Timothy D.
1994   *Contested Boundaries: Itinerancy and the Reshaping of the Colonial American
        Religious World.* Durham, NC: Duke University Press.

Hancock, Ian F.
1969   The English-Derived Atlantic Creoles: A Provisional Comparison. *African
        Language Review* 8:7–72.

1971   A Study of the Sources and Development of the Lexicon of Sierra Leone
        Krio. Ph.D. diss., University of London.

1975   Creole Features in the Afro-Seminole Speech of Brackettville, Texas. Society for Caribbean Linguistics, Occasional Paper 3. Austin: University of Texas African and Afro-American Studies Research Center.

1980   Texas Gullah: The Creole English of the Brackettville Afro-Seminoles. In *Perspectives on American English*, edited by J. L. Dillard, pp. 305–333. The Hague: Mouton.

1988   Componentiality and the Origin of Gullah. In *Sea and Land: Cultural and Biological Adaptations in the Southern Coastal Plain*, edited by James L. Peacock and James C. Sabella, pp. 13–24. Athens: University of Georgia Press.

Handler, Jerome S.

1997   An African-Type Healer/Diviner and His Grave Goods: A Burial from a Plantation Slave Cemetery in Barbados, West Indies. *International Journal of Historical Archaeology* 1(2):91–130.

Handler, Jerome S., and Kenneth M. Bilby

2001   On the Early Use and Origin of the Term "Obeah" in Barbados and the Anglophone Caribbean. *Slavery and Abolition* 22(2):87–100.

Handler, Jerome S., Frederick W. Lange, and Robert V. Riordan

1978   *Plantation Slavery in Barbados: An Archaeological and Historical Investigation.* Cambridge, MA: Harvard University Press.

Handler, Richard

1988   *Nationalism and the Politics of Culture in Quebec.* Madison: University of Wisconsin Press.

Handler, Richard, and Eric Gable

1997   *The New History in an Old Museum: Creating the Past at Colonial Williamsburg.* Durham, NC: Duke University Press.

Handler, Richard, and Jocelyn Linnekin

1984   Tradition, Genuine or Spurious. *Journal of American Folklore* 97(385):273–290.

Haniff, Nesha Z.

1985   Toward a Native Anthropology: Methodological Notes on a Study of Successful Caribbean Women by an Insider. *Anthropology and Humanism Quarterly* 10(4):107–113.

Hannerz, Ulf

1992   *Cultural Complexity: Studies in the Social Organization of Meaning.* New York: Columbia University Press.

Hansen, Joyce, and Gary McGowan

1998   *Breaking Ground, Breaking Silence: The Story of New York's African Burial Ground.* New York: Henry Holt.

Hansing, Katrin

2001   Rasta, Race and Revolution: Transnational Connections in Socialist Cuba. *Journal of Ethnic and Migration Studies* 27(4):733–747.

Harris, Leslie
1999 From Abolitionist Amalgamators to "Rulers of the Five Points": The Discourse of Interracial Sex and Reform in Antebellum New York City. In *Sex, Love, and Race: Crossing Boundaries in North American History*, edited by Martha Hodes, pp. 191–212. New York: New York University Press.
2003 *In the Shadow of Slavery: African Americans in New York City, 1626–1863.* Chicago: University of Chicago Press.

Harris, Marvin
1968 *The Rise of Anthropological Theory: A History of Theories of Culture.* New York: Thomas Y. Crowell.

Harris, Michael D.
1999 *Transatlantic Dialogue: Contemporary Art in and out of Africa.* Chapel Hill: Ackland Art Museum, University of North Carolina.

Harris, Robert L., Jr.
1982 Segregation and Scholarship: The American Council of Learned Societies' Committee on Negro Studies, 1941–1950. *Journal of Black Studies* 12(3):315–331.

Harris, Waldo, III
1978 Location Associated with Daniel Marshal and the Kiokee Church. *Viewpoints: Georgia Baptist History* 6:25–46.

Harrison, Faye V.
1988 Introduction: An African Diaspora Perspective for Urban Anthropology. *Urban Anthropology* 17(2–3):111–141.
1992 The Du Boisian Legacy in Anthropology. *Critique of Anthropology* 12(3):239–260.
1995 The Persistent Power of "Race" in the Cultural and Political Economy of Racism. *Annual Review of Anthropology* 24:47–74.
2000 Facing Racism and the Moral Responsibility of Human Rights Knowledge. *Annals of the New York Academy of Sciences* 925:69.
2002 Unraveling "Race" for the 21st Century. In *Exotic No More: Anthropology on the Front Lines*, edited by Jeremy MacClancy, pp. 145–166. Chicago: University of Chicago Press.

Harrrison, Faye V., ed.
1991 *Decolonizing Anthropology: Moving Further toward an Anthropology for Liberation.* Washington, DC: American Anthropological Association.
1998 Contemporary Issues Forum: Race and Racism. Special section, *American Anthropologist* 100(3).

Harrison, Faye V., and Ira E. Harrison
1999 Introduction: Anthropology, African Americans, and the Emancipation of a Subjugated Knowledge. In *African-American Pioneers in Anthropology*, edited by Ira E. Harrison and Faye V. Harrison, pp. 1–36. Urbana: University of Illinois Press.

Harrison, Ira E.

1999   Louis Eugene King, the Anthropologist Who Never Was. In *African-American Pioneers in Anthropology*, edited by Ira E. Harrison and Faye V. Harrison, pp. 70–84. Urbana: University of Illinois Press.

Harrison, Ira E., and Faye V. Harrison, eds.

1999   *African-American Pioneers in Anthropology*. Urbana: University of Illinois Press.

Harvey, David

1989   *The Condition of Postmodernity: An Enquiry into the Origins of Cultural Change*. Oxford: Blackwell.

Haslip-Viera, Gabriel, Bernard Ortiz de Montellano, and Warren Barbour

1997   Robbing Native American Cultures: Van Sertima's Afrocentricity and the Olmecs. *Current Anthropology* 38(3):419–441.

Hatch, Elvin

1997   The Good Side of Relativism. *Journal of Anthropological Research* 53(3):371–381.

Hauser, Mark W., and Christopher R. DeCorse

2003   Low-Fired Earthenwares in the African Diaspora: Problems and Prospects. *International Journal of Historical Archaeology* 7(1):67–98.

Healey, Mark Alan

1998   "The Sweet Matriarchy of Bahia": Ruth Landes' Ethnography of Race and Gender. *Disposition* 23(50):87–116.

Hearn, Adrian H.

2004   Afro-Cuban Religions and Social Welfare: Consequences of Commercial Development in Havana. *Human Organization* 63(1):78–87.

Hebdige, Dick

1979   *Subculture: The Meaning of Style*. London: Methuen.

Heite, Edward

1993   Letter to the Editor. *African-American Archaeology* 8:2.

Helbling, Mark

1999   *The Harlem Renaissance: The One and the Many*. Westport, CT: Greenwood Press.

Helg, Aline

1995   *Our Rightful Share: The Afro-Cuban Struggle for Equality, 1886–1912*. Chapel Hill: University of North Carolina Press.

Hemenway, Robert E.

1977   *Zora Neale Hurston: A Literary Biography*. Urbana: University of Illinois Press.

Henry, Frances

2003   *Reclaiming African Religions in Trinidad: The Socio-Political Legitimation of the Orisha and Spiritual Baptist Faiths*. Mona, Jamaica: University of the West Indies Press.

Herskovits, Frances S.

1966   Introduction. In *The New World Negro: Selected Papers in Afroamerican Studies,* edited by Frances S. Herskovits, pp. vii–xi. Bloomington: Indiana University Press.

Herskovits, Melville J.

1924   A Preliminary Consideration of the Culture Areas of Africa. *American Anthropologist* 26(1):50–63.

1925a   The Dilemma of Social Pattern. *Survey Graphic* 6(6):676–678.

1925b   The Negro's Americansim. In *The New Negro,* edited by Alain Locke, pp. 353–360. New York: Albert & Charles Boni, Inc.

1926a   The Cattle Complex in East Africa. *American Anthropologist* 28(1):230–272.

1926b   The Cattle Complex in East Africa. *American Anthropologist* 28(2):361–388.

1926c   The Cattle Complex in East Africa. *American Anthropologist* 28(3):494–528.

1926d   The Cattle Complex in East Africa. *American Anthropologist* 28(4):633–664.

1926e   On the Relation Between Negro-White Mixture and Standing in Intelligence Tests. *Pedagogical Seminary and Journal of Genetic Psychology* 33(1):30–42.

1926f   Negroes of the South American Jungles. *New York Herald Tribune Books,* November 28, 10.

1927   Acculturation and the American Negro. *Southwestern Political and Social Science Quarterly* 8(3):211–224.

1928   *The American Negro: A Study in Racial Crossing.* New York: Alfred A. Knopf.

1929   Lo, the Poor Haitian. Review of *The Magic Island* by W. B. Seabrook. *Nation* 128(3319):198, 200.

1930a   The Negro in the New World: The Statement of a Problem. *American Anthropologist* 32(1):145–155.

1930b   *The Anthropometry of the American Negro.* New York: Columbia University Press.

[1930]   The Negro in the New World: The Statement of a Problem. In *The New*
1966   *World Negro: Selected Papers in Afroamerican Studies,* edited by Frances S. Herskovits, pp.1–12. Bloomington: Indiana University Press.

1932   Some Aspects of Dahomean Ethnology. *Africa* 5(3):266–296.

1933a   On the Provenience of New World Negroes. *Social Forces* 12(2):247–262.

1933b   Haiti (Ethnologia). In *Enciclopedia Italiana di scienze, lettere ed arti,* vol. 18, pp. 318–319. Milan: Edizioni Instituto G. Treccani.

1935   What Has Africa Given America? *New Republic* 84(1083):92–94.

[1935]   What Has Africa Given America? In *The New World Negro: Selected Papers in*
1966   *Afroamerican Studies,* edited by Frances S. Herskovits, pp.168–174. Bloomington: Indiana University Press.

1936a   The Significance of West Africa for Negro Research. *Journal of Negro History* 21(1):15–30.

REFERENCES

1936b   Applied Anthropology and the American Anthropologists. *Science*, n.s., 83(2149):215–222.

1937a   African Gods and Catholic Saints in New World Negro Belief. *American Anthropologist* 39(4):635–643.

1937b   *Life in a Haitian Valley.* New York: Alfred A. Knopf.

1938   *Acculturation: The Study of Culture Contact.* New York: J. J. Augustin.

1941   *The Myth of the Negro Past.* New York: Harper & Brothers.

1943   The Negro in Bahia, Brazil: A Problem in Method. *American Sociological Review* 8(4):394–402.

[1945]   Problem, Method and Theory in Afroamerican Studies. In *The New World*
1966   *Negro: Selected Papers in Afroamerican Studies*, edited by Frances S. Herskovits, pp. 43–61. Bloomington: Indiana University Press.

1948a   The Contribution of Afroamerican Studies to Africanist Research. *American Anthropologist* 50(1):1–10.

1948b   Review of *City of Women* by Ruth Landes. *American Anthropologist* 50(1):123–125.

[1956]   Some Modes of Ethnographic Comparison. In *The New World Negro: Selected*
1966   *Papers in Afroamerican Studies*, edited by Frances S. Herskovits, pp. 71–82. Bloomington: Indiana University Press.

Herskovits, Melville J., and Frances S. Herskovits

1933   A Footnote to the History of Negro Slaving. *Opportunity* 11(6):178–181.

1934a   *Rebel Destiny: Among the Bush Negroes of Dutch Guiana.* New York: Whittlesey House.

1934b   En marge de l'histoire de l'esclavage nègre. *La Relève* 3(11):8–17.

1936   *Suriname Folk-Lore.* New York: Columbia University Press.

1947   *Trinidad Village.* New York: Alfred A. Knopf.

Hess, David J.

1991   *Spirits and Scientists: Ideology, Spiritism, and Brazilian Culture.* University Park: Pennsylvania State University Press.

Hess, Karen

1992   *The Carolina Rice Kitchen: The African Connection.* Columbia: University of South Carolina Press.

Heywood, Linda M., ed.

2002   *Central Africans and Cultural Transformations in the American Diaspora.* Cambridge: Cambridge University Press.

Higgins, W. Robert, ed.

1979   *The Revolutionary War in the South: Power, Conflict, and Leadership: Essays in Honor of John Richard Alden.* Durham, NC: Duke University Press.

Higham, John

1955   *Strangers in the Land: Patterns of American Nativism, 1860–1925.* New Brunswick, NJ: Rutgers University Press.

Higman, B. W.

1984   *Slave Populations of the British Caribbean, 1807–1834.* Baltimore, MD: Johns Hopkins University Press.

Hine, Darlene Clark, and Earnestine Jenkins, eds.

1999   *A Question of Manhood: A Reader in U.S. Black Men's History and Masculinity.* Bloomington: Indiana University Press.

Hine, Darlene Clark, and Jacqueline McLeod, eds.

1999   *Crossing Boundaries: Comparative History of Black People in Diaspora.* Bloomington: Indiana University Press.

Hobbs, Robert

1996   *Arnaldo Roche-Rabell: The Uncommonwealth.* Seattle: University of Washington Press.

Hobsbawm, Eric, and Terence Ranger, eds.

1983   *The Invention of Tradition.* Cambridge: Cambridge University Press.

Hodgen, Margaret T.

1936   *The Doctrine of Survivals: A Chapter in the History of Scientific Method in the Study of Man.* London: Allenson.

Hodges, Graham R., ed.

1993   *Black Itinerants of the Gospel: The Narratives of John Jea and George White.* Madison, WI: Madison House.

1996   *The Black Loyalist Directory: African Americans in Exile after the American Revolution.* New York: Garland.

1999   *Root and Branch: African Americans in New York and East Jersey, 1613–1863.* Chapel Hill: University of North Carolina Press.

Holloway, Joseph E., ed.

1990   *Africanisms in American Culture.* Bloomington: Indiana University Press.

Holmes, Edward A.

1964   George Liele: Negro Slavery's Prophet of Deliverance. *Baptist Quarterly* 20(3):340–351.

hooks, bell

1995   *Art on My Mind: Visual Politics.* New York: The New Press.

2000   Feminism Is for Everyone: Passionate Politics. Cambridge, MA: South End Press.

Horn, David G.

2003   *The Criminal Body: Lombroso and the Anatomy of Deviance.* New York: Routledge.

Horton, James Oliver, and Lois E. Horton

1997   *In Hope of Liberty: Culture, Community, and Protest among Northern Free Blacks, 1700–1860.* New York: Oxford University Press.

REFERENCES

Houk, James

1993   The Terminological Shift from "Afro-American" to "African-American": Is the Field of Afro-American Anthropology Being Redefined? *Human Organization* 53(3):325–328.

Howson, Jean

1990   Social Relations and Material Culture: A Critique of the Archaeology of Plantation Slavery. *Historical Archaeology* 24(4):78–91.

1995   Colonial Goods and the Plantation Village: Consumption and the Internal Economy in Montserrat from Slavery to Freedom. Ph.D. diss., New York University.

Huddlestun, J. R., and Charles O. Walker

1976   *From Heretics to Heroes: A Study of Religious Groups in Georgia with Primary Emphasis on the Baptists.* Jasper, GA: Picken Tech Press.

Hudson, Larry E., Jr.

1997   *To Have and to Hold: Slave Work and Family Life in Antebellum South Carolina.* Athens: University of Georgia Press.

Hunt, Caroline C., Joko Sengova, and Luba M. Sengova

1995   Coming of Age in West Africa: Contemporary Fiction from Sierra Leone. *English Journal* 84(3):62–66.

Hunter, Yéma Lucilda

1982   *Road to Freedom.* Ibàdàn, Nigeria: African Universities Press.

Hutchinson, George

1995   *The Harlem Renaissance in Black and White.* Cambridge, MA: Belknap Press of Harvard University Press.

Hutnyk, John

2005   Hybridity. *Ethnic and Racial Studies* 28(1):79–102.

Hyatt, Marshall

1985   Franz Boas and the Struggle for Black Equality: The Dynamics of Ethnicity. *Perspectives in American History,* n.s., 2:269–295.

Idiens, Dale, and K. G. Ponting, eds.

1980   *Textiles of Africa.* Bath, UK: Pasold Research Fund.

Iglesias, Cesar Andreu, ed.

1984   *Memoirs of Bernardo Vega: A Contribution to the History of the Puerto Rican Community.* New York: Monthly Review Press.

Ignace, Etienne

1908   La fétichisme des nègres du Brésil. *Anthropos* 3:881–904.

IRO *see* **Island Record Office.**

Isaac, Rhys

1982   *The Transformation of Virginia, 1740–1790.* Chapel Hill: University of North Carolina Press.

Island Record Office. Deeds. Spanish Town, Jamaica (IRO)

Iznaga, Diana
1989   *Transculturación en Fernando Ortiz.* Havana: Editorial de Ciencias Sociales.

JA-CGR *see* **Jamaica Archives. Central government records.**

JA-LGR *see* **Jamaica Archives. Local government records.**

Jackson, Antoinette
2003   Africans at Snee Farm Plantation: Informing Representations of Plantation Life at a National Heritage Site. In *Signifying Serpents and Mardi Gras Runners: Representing Identity in Selected Souths,* edited by Celeste Ray and Luke Eric Lassiter, pp. 93–109. Southern Anthropological Society Proceedings, no. 36. Athens: University of Georgia Press.

Jackson, Jean
1989   Is There a Way to Talk about Making Culture Without Making Enemies? *Dialectical Anthropology* 14(2):127–143.

Jackson, John L., Jr.
2001   *Harlem World: Doing Race and Class in Contemporary Black America.* Chicago: University of Chicago Press.

Jackson, Walter A.
1986   Melville Herskovits and the Search for Afro-American Culture. In *Malinowski, Rivers, Benedict and Others: Essays on Culture and Personality,* edited by George W. Stocking Jr., pp. 95–126. Madison: University of Wisconsin Press.

1990   *Gunnar Myrdal and America's Conscience: Social Engineering and Racial Liberalism, 1938–1987.* Chapel Hill: University of North Carolina Press.

Jacobs-Huey, Lanita
2002   The Natives Are Gazing and Talking Back: Reviewing the Problematics of Positionality, Voice, and Accountability among "Native" Anthropologists. *American Anthropologist* 104(3):791–804.

Jalloh, Alusine, and Stephen E. Maizlish, eds.
1996   *The African Diaspora.* College Station: Texas A&M University Press.

Jamaica Archives. Central government records. Spanish Town, Jamaica (JA-CGR)

Jamaica Archives. Local government records. Spanish Town, Jamaica (JA-LGR)

James, Winston
1996   Afro-Puerto Rican Radicalism in the United States: Reflections on the Political Trajectories of Arturo Schomburg and Jesus Colón. *Centro: Journal of the Center for Puerto Rican Studies* 8(1–2):92–127.

1998   *Holding Aloft the Banner of Ethiopia: Caribbean Radicalism in Early Twentieth-Century America.* London: Verso.

REFERENCES

John, Marie-Elena
n.d.   *Unburnable.* New York: HarperCollins, in press.

Johnson, Guion Griffis
1930   *A Social History of the Sea Islands, with Special Reference to St. Helena Island,
            South Carolina.* Chapel Hill: University of North Carolina Press.

Johnson, Guy B.
1930   *Folk Culture on St. Helena Island, South Carolina.* Chapel Hill: University of
            North Carolina Press.

Johnson, James Weldon
1930   *Black Manhattan.* New York: Alfred A. Knopf.

Jones, Charles Colcock, Jr.
1888   *Negro Myths from the Georgia Coast Told in the Vernacular.* Boston: Houghton-
            Mifflin.
[1888]   *Gullah Folktales from the Georgia Coast.* Athens: University of Georgia Press.
 2000

Jones, Siân
1997   *The Archaeology of Ethnicity: Constructing Identities in the Past and Present.*
            London: Routledge.

Jones-Jackson, Patricia
1987   *When Roots Die: Endangered Traditions on the Sea Islands.* Athens: University
            of Georgia Press.

Jourdan, C.
1991   Pidgins and Creoles: The Blurring of Categories. *Annual Review of
            Anthropology* 20:187–209.

Joyner, Brian D.
2003   *African Reflections on the American Landscape: Identifying and Interpreting
            Africanisms.* Washington, DC: Office of Diversity and Special Projects,
            National Center for Cultural Resources, National Park Service.

Joyner, Charles W.
1984   *Down by the Riverside: A South Carolina Slave Community.* Urbana: University
            of Illinois Press.
1989   *Remember Me: Slave Life in Coastal Georgia.* Atlanta: Georgia Humanities
            Council.

Kapcia, Antoni
1992   The Intellectual in Cuba: The National-Popular Tradition. In *Unity in
            Variety: The Hispanic and Francophone Caribbean.* Vol. 2 of *Intellectuals in the
            Twentieth-Century Caribbean,* edited by Alistair Hennessy, pp. 58–82.
            London: Macmillan.

Kaplan, Sidney
1956   Social Engineers as Saviors: Effects of World War I on Some American
            Liberals. *Journal of the History of Ideas* 17(3):347–369.

Karasch, Mary

1979   Commentary One. *Historical Reflections* 6:138–141.

1987   *Slave Life in Rio de Janeiro, 1808–1850.* Princeton, NJ: Princeton University Press.

Karp, Ivan, and Steven D. Lavine, eds.

1991   *Exhibiting Cultures: The Poetics and Politics of Museum Display.* Washington, DC: Smithsonian Institution Press.

Karp, Ivan, Christine Mullen Kreamer, and Steven D. Lavine, eds.

1992   *Museums and Communities: The Politics of Public Culture.* Washington, DC: Smithsonian Institution Press.

Kea, Ray

1996   "When I die, I shall return to my own land": An "Amina" Slave Rebellion in the Danish West Indies, 1733–1734. In *The Cloth of Many Colored Silks: Papers on History and Society, Ghanian and Islamic in Honor of Ivor Wilks,* edited by John Hunwick and Nancy Lawler, pp. 159–193. Evanston, IL: Northwestern University Press.

Keane, Webb

2003   Self-Interpretation, Agency, and the Objects of Anthropology: Reflections on a Genealogy. *Comparative Studies in Society and History* 45(2):222–248.

Kelley, David H.

1995   An Essay on Pre-Columbian Contacts between the Americas and Other Areas, with Special Reference to the Work of Ivan Van Sertima. In *Race, Discourse, and the Origin of the Americas: A New World View,* edited by Vera Lawrence Hyatt and Rex Nettleford, pp. 103–122. Washington, DC: Smithsonian Institution Press.

Kelley, Robin D. G.

1997   Looking for the "Real" Nigga: Social Scientists Construct the Ghetto. In *Yo' Mama's Disfunktional: Fighting the Culture Wars in Urban America,* pp. 15–42. Boston: Beacon Press.

1999   "But a Local Phase of a World Problem": Black History's Global Vision, 1883–1950. *Journal of American History* 86(3):1045–1077.

Kelley, Robin D. G., and Earl Lewis, eds.

2000   *To Make Our World Anew: A History of African Americans.* New York: Oxford University Press.

Kelso, William M.

1984   *Kingsmill Plantations, 1619–1800: Archaeology of Country Life in Colonial Virginia.* Orlando, FL: Academic Press.

Khan, Aisha

2001   Journey to the Center of the Earth: The Caribbean as Master Symbol. *Cultural Anthropology* 16(3):271–302.

2004a   Sacred Subversions? Syncretic Creoles, the Indo-Caribbean, and "Culture's In-Between." *Radical History Review* 89:165–184.

2004b   *Callaloo Nation: Metaphors of Race and Religious Identity among South Asians in Trinidad.* Durham, NC: Duke University Press.

Kimmel, Richard
1993   Notes on the Cultural Origins and Function of Sub-Floor Pits. *Historical Archaeology* 27(3):102–113.

Kinsbruner, Jay
1996   *Not of Pure Blood: The Free People of Color and Racial Prejudice in Nineteenth-Century Puerto Rico.* Durham, NC: Duke University Press.

Kirshenblatt-Gimblett, Barbara
1998   *Destination Culture: Tourism, Museums, and Heritage.* Berkeley: University of California Press.

Klein, Herbert S.
1999   *The Atlantic Slave Trade.* Cambridge: Cambridge University Press.

Kly, Yussuf Naim, and Diana Kly, eds.
2001   *In Pursuit of the Right to Self-Determination: Collected Papers and Proceedings of the First International Conference on the Right to Self-Determination and the United Nations Geneva 2000.* Atlanta, GA: Clarity Press.

Kohl, Philip, and Clare Fawcett, eds.
1995   *Nationalism, Politics, and the Practice of Archaeology.* Cambridge: Cambridge University Press.

Kozy, Charlene Johnson
1991   Tories Transplanted: The Caribbean Exile and Plantation of the Southern Loyalists. *Georgia Historical Quarterly* 75:18–42.

Kraay, Hendrik, ed.
1998   *Afro-Brazilian Culture and Politics: Bahia, 1790s to 1990s.* Armonk, NY: M. E. Sharpe.

Kuhn, Thomas S.
1968   The History of Science. In *International Encyclopedia of the Social Sciences*, vol. 14, edited by David L. Sills, pp. 74–83. New York: Macmillan.

Kulikoff, Allan
1986   *Tobacco and Slaves: The Development of Southern Cultures in the Chesapeake, 1680–1800.* Chapel Hill: University of North Carolina Press.

Kusmer, Kenneth, L.
1976   *A Ghetto Takes Shape: Black Cleveland, 1870–1930.* Urbana: University of Illinois Press.

Lakoff, George, and Mark Johnson
1980   *Metaphors We Live By.* Chicago: University of Chicago Press.

Lambert, Frank
1994   *Pedlar in Divinity: George Whitefield and the Transatlantic Revivals, 1737–1770.* Princeton, NJ: Princeton University Press.

Landes, Ruth

1937   *Ojibwa Sociology*. New York: Columbia University Press.

1938   *The Ojibwa Woman*. New York: Columbia University Press.

1940a   A Cult Matriarchate and Male Homosexuality. *Journal of Abnormal and Social Psychology* 35:386–397.

1940b   Fetish Worship in Brazil. *Journal of American Folklore* 53(210):261–270.

1940c   The Ethos of the Negro in the New World. Schomburg Center for Research in Black Culture, New York Public Library. New York: Carnegie-Myrdal Study, "The Negro in America." Research memorandum. Microfilm Reel 9.

1947   *The City of Women*. New York: Macmillan.

1970   A Woman Anthropologist in Brazil. In *Women in the Field*, edited by Peggy Golde, pp. 117–139. Chicago: Aldine.

LaRoche, Cheryl J., and Michael L. Blakey

1997   Seizing Intellectual Power: The Dialogue at the New York African Burial Ground. *Historical Archaeology* 31(3):84–100.

La Rosa Corzo, Gabino

2003   *Runaway Slave Settlements in Cuba: Resistance and Repression*, translated by Mary Todd. Chapel Hill: University of North Carolina Press.

La Rosa Corzo, Gabino, and Joaquin Pérez Padrón

1994   La resistencia esclava en La Sierra del Grillo: Estudio arqueológico. In *Estudios Arqueológicos 1990*, pp. 101–127. Havana: Editorial Academia.

Laurie, Nina, and Alistair Bonnett

2002   Adjusting to Equity: The Contradictions of Neoliberalism and the Search for Racial Equality in Peru. *Antipode* 34(1):28–53.

Lazarus, Neil

1995   Is a Counterculture of Modernity a Theory of Modernity? *Diaspora* 4(3):323–339.

Leacock, Eleanor Burke, ed.

1971   *The Culture of Poverty: A Critique*. New York: Simon and Schuster.

Le Bon, Gustave

1894   *Les lois psychologiques de l'évolution des peuples*. Paris: Alcan.

Lemelle, Sidney J., and Robin D. G. Kelley, eds.

1994   *Imagining Home: Class, Culture and Nationalism in the African Diaspora*. London: Verso.

Leon, Eli

1987   *Who'd a Thought It: Improvisation in African-American Quiltmaking*. San Francisco: San Francisco Craft and Folk Art Museum.

1992   *Models in the Mind: African Prototypes in American Patchwork*. Winston-Salem, NC: Diggs Gallery/Winston-Salem State University.

Leone, Mark P.

1982   Opinions about Recovering Mind. *American Antiquity* 47(4):744–760.

Leone, Mark P., and Gladys-Marie Fry

1999   Conjuring in the Big House Kitchen: An Interpretation of African-
          American Belief Systems Based on the Uses of Archaeology and Folklore
          Sources. *Journal of American Folklore* 112(445):372–403.

2001   Spirit Management among Americans of African Descent. In *Race and the
          Archaeology of Identity*, edited by Charles E. Orser Jr., pp.143–157. Salt Lake
          City: University of Utah Press.

**Leone, Mark, Paul R Mullins, Marian C. Creveling, Laurence Hurst,
Barbara Jackson-Nash, Hannah Jopling Kaiser, George C. Logan,
Mark S. Warner**

1995   Can an African-American Historical Archaeology Be an Alternative Voice?
          In *Interpreting Archaeology: Finding Meaning in the Past*, edited by I. Hodder,
          M. Shanks, A. Alexandri, V. Buchli, and J. Carman, pp. 110–124. London:
          Routledge.

Le Riverend, Julio, ed.

1973   *Órbita de Fernando Ortiz*. Havana: Unión de Escritores y Artistas de Cuba.

Lesko, Kathleen M., Valerie Babb, and Carroll R. Gibbs

1991   *Black Georgetown Remembered: A History of the Georgetown Black Community
          from the Founding of "The Town of George" to the Present Historic District.*
          Washington, DC: Georgetown University Press.

Levine, Lawrence W.

1977   *Black Culture and Black Consciousness: Afro-American Folk Thought from Slavery
          to Freedom.* New York: Oxford University Press.

Lewis, David Levering

1981   *When Harlem Was in Vogue.* New York: Alfred A. Knopf.

1984   Parallels and Divergences: Assimilationist Strategies of Afro-American and
          Jewish Elites from 1910 to the Early 1930s. *Journal of American History*
          71(3):543–564.

2000   *W. E. B. Du Bois: The Fight for Equality and the American Century, 1919–1963.*
          New York: Henry Holt.

Lewis, Gordon K.

1983   *Main Currents in Caribbean Thought: The Historical Evolution of Caribbean
          Society in Its Ideological Aspects, 1492–1900.* Baltimore, MD: Johns Hopkins
          University Press.

Lewis, I. M.

1989   *Ecstatic Religion: A Study of Shamanism and Spirit Possession.* 2d ed. London:
          Routledge.

Lewis, Laura A.

2003   *Hall of Mirrors: Power, Witchcraft, and Caste in Colonial Mexico.* Durham, NC:
          Duke University Press.

Lewis, Oscar

1966   *La Vida: A Puerto Rican Family in the Culture of Poverty—San Juan and New York.* New York: Random House.

Lewis, Samella

1990   *African American Art and Artists.* Berkeley: University of California Press.

Leyton, Harrie, ed.

1995   *Illicit Traffic in Cultural Property: Museums against Pillage.* Amsterdam: Royal Tropical Institute.

Leyton, Harrie, and Bibi Damen, eds.

1993   *Art, Anthropology, and the Modes of Re-Presentation: Museums and Contemporary Non-Western Art.* Amsterdam: Royal Tropical Institute.

Lincoln, C. Eric

1973   *The Black Muslims in America.* Rev. ed. Boston: Beacon Press.

Lindsay, Lisa A

1994   To Return to the Bosom of the Fatherland: Brazilian Immigrants in Nineteenth-Century Lagos. *Slavery and Abolition* 15(1):22–50.

Linebaugh, Peter, and Marcus Rediker

2000   *The Many-Headed Hydra: Sailors, Slaves, Commoners, and the Hidden History of the Revolutionary Atlantic.* Boston: Beacon Press.

Lippard, Lucy R.

1990   *Mixed Blessings: New Art in a Multicultural America.* New York: Pantheon.

Lipski, John M.

1998   Review of *"Chi ma nkongo": Lengua y rito ancestrales en El Palenque de San Basilio (Colombia)* by Armin J. Schwegler. *New West Indian Guide* 72:356–360.

Liss, Julia E.

1998   Diasporic Identities: The Science and Politics of Race in the Work of Franz Boas and W. E. B. Du Bois, 1894–1919. *Cultural Anthropology* 13(2):127–166.

Little, Thomas J.

1995   George Liele and the Rise of Independent Black Baptist Churches in the Lower South and Jamaica. *Slavery and Abolition* 16(2):188–204.

Littlefield, Daniel C.

1981   *Rice and Slaves: Ethnicity and the Slave Trade in Colonial South Carolina.* Baton Rouge: Louisiana State University Press.

Locke, Alain

1925a   Editorial note to Herskovits's "The Dilemma of Social Pattern." *Survey Graphic* 6(6):676.

1942   Who and What Is "Negro"? Part II. *Opportunity* 20(3):83–87.

Locke, Alain, ed.

1925   *The New Negro.* New York: Albert & Charles Boni, Inc.

Lockley, Timothy James

2000   *Lines in the Sand: Race and Class in Lowcountry Georgia, 1750–1860.* Athens: University of Georgia Press.

Löfgren, Orvar

1989   The Nationalization of Culture. *Ethnologia Europaea* 19(1):5–23.

Lohse, Russell

2002   Slave-Trade Nomenclature and African Ethnicities in the Americas: Evidence from Early Eighteenth-Century Costa Rica. *Slavery and Abolition* 23(3):73–92.

Long, Carolyn Morrow

2001   *Spiritual Merchants: Religion, Magic, and Commerce.* Knoxville: University of Tennessee Press.

López de Mesa, Luis

1970   *De cómo se ha formado la nación colombiana.* Medellín, Colombia: Editorial Bedout.

Losonczy, Anne-Marie

1997   *Les saints et la forêt: rituel, société et figures de l'échange entre noirs et indiens Emberá (Chocó, Colombie).* Paris: L'Harmattan.

Lovejoy, Paul E.

1997   Identifying Enslaved Africans: Methodological and Conceptual Considerations in Studying the African Diaspora. Paper presented at the UNESCO/SSHRCC Summer Institute, York University, Toronto.

2003   Methodology through the Ethnic Lens: The Study of Atlantic Africa. In *Sources and Methods in African History: Spoken, Written, Unearthed*, pp. 105–117. Rochester, NY: University of Rochester Press.

Lovejoy, Paul, ed.

2000   *Identity in the Shadow of Slavery.* London: Continuum.

Lovejoy, Paul, and David V. Trotman, eds.

2003   *Trans-Atlantic Dimensions of Ethnicity in the African Diaspora.* London: Continuum.

Lowie, Robert

1920   *Primitive Society.* New York: Boni and Liveright.

Lucas, J. Olumide

1970   *Religions in West Africa and Ancient Egypt.* Apapa, Nigeria: Nigerian National Press.

Lyman, R. Lee, and Michael J. O'Brien

2003   Cultural Traits: Units of Analysis in Early Twentieth-Century Anthropology. *Journal of Anthropological Research* 59(2):225–250.

MacDavid, Carol, and David Babson, eds.

1997   In the Realm of Politics: Prospects for Public Participation in African-American and Plantation Archaeology. *Historical Archaeology* 31(3).

MacEachern, Scott
2000   Genes, Tribes, and African History. *Current Anthropology* 41(3):357–384.

Mack, Mark E., and Michael L. Blakey
2004   The New York African Burial Group Project: Past Biases, Current Dilemmas, and Future Research Opportunities. *Historical Archaeology* 28(1):10–17.

Magloire, Gérarde
2005   Ambassadors at Dawn: Haitian Thinkers in the French Colonial Context of the 19th and 20th Centuries: The Example of Jean Price-Mars (1876–1969). Ph.D. diss., New York University.

Magloire, Gérarde, and Kevin A. Yelvington
2005   Haiti and the Anthropological Imagination. *Gradhiva*, n.s., 1:127–152.

Malinowski, Bronislaw
1939   The Present State of Studies in Culture Contact: Some Comments on an American Approach. *Africa* 12(1):27–48.
[1947] Introduction. In *Cuban Counterpoint: Tobacco and Sugar*, by Fernando Ortiz.
1995   Translated by Harriet de Onís, pp. lvii–lxiv. Durham, NC: Duke University Press.

Malkki, Liisa H.
1995   *Purity and Exile: Violence Memory and National Cosmology among Hutu Refugees in Tanzania.* Chicago: University of Chicago Press.

Mann, Kristin, and Edna G. Bay, eds.
2001   *Rethinking the African Diaspora: The Making of a Black Atlantic World in the Bight of Benin and Brazil.* London: Frank Cass.

Manning, Patrick
2003   Africa and the African Diaspora: New Directions of Study. *Journal of African History* 44(3):487–506.

Marcus, George E.
1995   The Power of Contemporary Work in an American Art Tradition to Illuminate Its Own Power Relations. In *The Traffic in Culture: Refiguring Art and Anthropology*, edited by George E. Marcus and Fred R. Myers, pp. 210–223. Berkeley: University of California Press.

Marcus, George E., and Fred R. Myers, eds.
1995   *The Traffic in Culture: Refiguring Art and Anthropology.* Berkeley: University of California Press.

Martínez, Samuel
1995   *Peripheral Migrants: Haitians and Dominican Republic Sugar Plantations.* Knoxville: University of Tennessee Press.
1999   From Hidden Hand to Heavy Hand: Sugar, the State, and Migrant Labor in Haiti and the Dominican Republic. *Latin American Research Review* 34(1):57–84.

2003   Not a Cockfight: Rethinking Haitian-Dominican Relations. *Latin American Perspectives* 30(3):80–101.

Martínez Montiel, Luz María, ed.

1993   Presencia africana en Centroamérica. Mexico City: Consejo Nacional para la Cultura y las Artes.

1995a   Presencia africana en el Caribe. Mexico City: Consejo Nacional para la Cultura y las Artes.

1995b   Presencia africana en México. Mexico City: Consejo Nacional para la Cultura y las Artes.

1995c   Presencia africana en Sudamérica. Mexico City: Consejo Nacional para la Cultura y las Artes.

Martínez Vergne, Teresita

1999   *Shaping the Discourse on Space: Charity and Its Wards in Nineteenth-Century San Juan, Puerto Rico.* Austin: University of Texas Press.

Martorell, Antonio

1991   *La piel de la memoria.* Cayey, Puerto Rico: Ediciones Envergadura.

1995   *El libro dibujado/el dibujo librado.* Cayey, Puerto Rico: Ediciones Envergadura.

Marx, Anthony W.

1998   *Making Race and Nation: A Comparison of South Africa, the United States, and Brazil.* Cambridge: Cambridge University Press.

Massi (Peixoto), Fernanda

1989   Franceses e Norte-Americanos nas ciências sociais brasileiras, 1930–1960. In *História das ciências sociais no Brasil,* vol. 1, edited by Sérgio Miceli, pp. 410–460. São Paulo: IDESP/Vértice/FINEP.

Mato, Daniel

2002   Estudios y otras prácticas intelectuales latinoamericanas en cultura y poder. In *Estudios y otras prácticas intelectuales latinoamericanas en cultura y poder,* edited by Daniel Mato, pp. 21–46. Caracas: Consejo Latinoamericano de Ciencias Sociales/CEAP/FACES/Universidad Central de Venezuela.

Matory, J. Lorand

1999a   Jeje: Repensando Nagões e Transnacionalismo. *Mana: Estudos de Antropologia Social* 5(1):57–80.

1999b   The English Professors of Brazil: On the Diasporic Roots of the Yorùbá Nation. *Comparative Studies in Society and History* 41(1):72–103.

1999c   Afro-Atlantic Culture: On the Live Dialogue between Africa and the Americas. In *Africana: The Encyclopedia of the African and African American Experience,* edited by Kwame Anthony Appiah and Henry Louis Gates Jr., pp. 36–44. New York: Basic Civitas Books.

2003   Gendered Agendas: The Secrets Scholars Keep about Yorùbá-Atlantic Religion. *Gender and History* 15(3):409–439.

2005   *Black Atlantic Religion: Tradition, Transnationalism, and Matriarchy in the Afro-Brazilian Candomblé.* Princeton, NJ: Princeton University Press, in press.

n.d.   An African Empire in America: The Rise of Yoruba Religions in the United States. In *Religion outside the Institutions,* edited by Karen McCarthy Brown and Lynn Davidman. Princeton, NJ: Princeton University Press, in press.

Matos Rodríguez, Félix V.

1999   *Women and Urban Change in San Juan, Puerto Rico, 1820–1868.* Gainesville: University Press of Florida.

Matos Rodríguez, Félix V., and Linda C. Delgado, eds.

1998   *Puerto Rican Women's History: New Perspectives.* Armonk, NY: M.E. Sharpe.

Maurer, Bill

1997   *Recharting the Caribbean: Land, Law, and Citizenship in the British Virgin Islands.* Ann Arbor: University of Michigan Press.

2004   Ungrounding Knowledges Offshore: Caribbean Studies, Disciplinarity and Critique. *Comparative American Studies* 2(3):324–341.

McAlister, Elizabeth A.

2002   *Rara! Vodou, Power, and Performance in Haiti and its Diaspora.* Berkeley: University of California Press.

McCallum, Cecilia

2005   Racialized Bodies, Naturalized Classes: Moving through the City of Salvador da Bahia. *American Ethnologist* 32(1):100–117.

McClaurin, Irma, ed.

2001   *Black Feminist Anthropology: Theory, Politics, Praxis, and Poetics.* New Brunswick, NJ: Rutgers University Press.

McKay, Claude

1940   *Harlem: Negro Metropolis.* New York: E.P. Dutton and Co.

McKee, Larry

1992   The Ideals and Realities behind the Design and Use of the 19th-Century Virginia Slave Cabins. In *The Art and Mystery of Historical Archaeology: Essays in Honor of James Deetz,* edited by Anne Elizabeth Yentsch and Mary C. Beaudry, pp. 195–213. Boca Raton, FL: CRC Press.

McManus, Edgar J.

1966   *A History of Negro Slavery in New York.* Syracuse, NY: Syracuse University Press.

McWhorter, John H.

1997   *Towards a New Model of Creole Genesis.* New York: Peter Lang.

2000a   *Losing the Race: Self-Sabotage in Black America.* New York: The Free Press.

2000b   *The Missing Spanish Creoles: Recovering the Birth of Plantation Contact Languages.* Berkeley: University of California Press.

References

Medina, Alvaro

1978   *Procesos de la historia del arte en Colombia*. Bogotá: Instituto Colombiano de Cultura.

Meel, Peter, ed.

1997   *Opzoek naar Surinaamse Normen: Nagelaten Geschriften van Jan Voorhoeve (1950–1961)*. Utrecht: CLACS and IBS.

Melville J. Herskovits Papers (MHP)

Melville J. Herskovits Library of African Studies, Africana Manuscripts 6. Northwestern University, Evanston, IL.

Méndez, Manuel I.

1952   *Biografia del cafetal Angerona*. Havana: Biblioteca Nacional.

Menil Foundation

1984   *La rime et la raison: Les Collections Menil*. Paris: Éditions de la Réunion des Musées Nationaux.

Mercer, Kobena

1988   Diaspora Culture and the Dialogic Imagination: The Aesthetics of Black Independent Film in Britain. In *Blackframes: Critical Perspectives on Black Independent Cinema*, edited by Mbye B. Cham and Claire Andrade-Watkins, pp. 50–61. Cambridge, MA: MIT Press.

1994   *Welcome to the Jungle: New Positions in Black Cultural Studies*. London: Routledge.

1997   Bodies of Diaspora, Vessels of Desire: The Erotic and the Aesthetic. In *Transforming the Crown: African, Asian and Caribbean Artists in Britain 1966–1996*, edited by Mora J. Beauchamp-Byrd and M. Franklin Sirmans, pp. 53–57. New York: Franklin H. Williams Caribbean Cultural Center/African Diaspora Institute.

Merriam, Alan P.

1964   Melville Jean Herskovits 1895–1963. *American Anthropologist* 66(1):83–109.

Métraux, Alfred

1958   *Le vaudou haïtien*. Paris: Gallimard.

MHP *see* **Melville J. Herskovits Papers.**

Michaels, Walter Benn

1995   *Our America: Nativism, Modernism, and Pluralism*. Durham, NC: Duke University Press.

Middleton, David, and Derek Edwards

1990   Conversational Remembering: A Social Psychological Approach. In *Collective Remembering*, edited by David Middleton and Derek Edwards, pp. 23–45. London: Sage.

Miller, Daniel

1995   Consumption Studies as the Transformation of Anthropology. In

Acknowledging Consumption: A Review of Studies, edited by Daniel Miller, pp. 264–295. London: Routledge.

Miller, Marilyn Grace

2004   *Rise and Fall of the Cosmic Race: The Cult of* Mestizaje *in Latin America.* Austin: University of Texas Press.

Ministerio de Educación Nacional

2001   *Cátedra de estudios afrocolombianos.* Bogotá: Ministerio de Educación Nacional.

Mintz, Sidney W.

1960   *Worker in the Cane: A Puerto Rican Life History.* New Haven, CT: Yale University Press.

1964   Melville J. Herskovits and Caribbean Studies: A Retrospective Tribute. *Caribbean Studies* 4(2):42–51.

1971   The Socio-Historical Background to Pidginization and Creolization. In *Pidginization and Creolization of Languages*, edited by Dell Hymes, pp. 481–496. Cambridge: Cambridge University Press.

1974   *Caribbean Transformations.* Chicago: Aldine.

1981   Ruth Benedict. In *Totems and Teachers: Perspectives on the History of Anthropology*, edited by Sydel Silverman, pp. 141–168. New York: Columbia University Press.

1984   Africa of Latin America: An Unguarded Reflection. In *Africa in Latin America: Essays on History, Culture, and Socialization*, edited by Manuel Moreno Fraginals, translated by Leonor Blum, pp. 286–305. New York: Holmes and Meier.

1990   Introduction. In *The Myth of the Negro Past*, by Melville J. Herskovits, pp. ix–xxi. Boston: Beacon Press.

1996   Enduring Substances, Trying Theories: The Caribbean Region as Oikoumenê. *Journal of the Royal Anthropological Institute*, n.s., 2(2):289–311.

1998   The Localization of Anthropological Practice: From Area Studies to Transnationalism. *Critique of Anthropology* 18(2):117–133.

Mintz, Sidney W., and Richard Price

1976   *An Anthropological Approach to the Afro-American Past: A Caribbean Perspective.* Philadelphia: Institute for the Study of Human Issues.

1992   *The Birth of African-American Culture: An Anthropological Approach.* Boston: Beacon Press.

Mitchell, Faith

1998   *Hoodoo Medicine: Gullah Herbal Remedies.* Rev. ed. Columbia, SC: Summerhouse Press.

Moloney, Alfred C.

1889   Cotton Interests, Foreign and Native, in Yoruba and Generally in West Africa. *Manchester Geographical Society Journal* 5:265–276.

REFERENCES

Monge Oviedo, Rodolfo
1992　　Are We or Aren't We? *Report on the Americas* 25(4):19.

Montgomery, Michael, ed.
1994　　*The Crucible of Carolina: Essays in the Development of Gullah Language and Culture.* Athens: University of Georgia Press.

Moore, Christopher
1994　　*The Loyalists: Revolution, Exile, Settlement.* Toronto: McClelland & Stewart.

Moore, Henrietta L.
2004　　Global Anxieties: Concept-Metaphors and Pre-Theoretical Commitments in Anthropology. *Anthropological Theory* 4(1):71–88.

Moore, Robin
1994　　Representations of Afrocuban Expressive Culture in the Writings of Fernando Ortiz. *Latin American Music Review* 15(1):32–54.
1997　　*Nationalizing Blackness: Afrocubanismo and Artistic Revolution in Havana, 1920–1940.* Pittsburgh: University of Pittsburgh Press.

Moore, Sally Falk
1993　　Changing Perspectives on a Changing Africa: The Work of Anthropology. In *Africa and the Disciplines: The Contributions of Research in Africa to the Social Sciences and Humanities,* edited by Robert H. Bates, V. Y. Mudimbe, and Jean O'Barr, pp. 3–57. Chicago: University of Chicago Press.

Moreno Fraginals, Manuel
1976　　*The Sugar Mill: The Socioeconomic Complex of Sugar in Cuba,* translated by Cedric Belfarge. New York: Monthly Review Press.
1978　　*El ingenio: Complejo económico social cubano del azúcar.* Havana: Editorial de Ciencias Sociales.

Moreno Fraginals, Manuel, Frank Moya Pons, and Stanley L. Engerman, eds.
1985　　*Between Slavery and Free Labor: The Spanish-Speaking Caribbean in the Nineteenth Century.* Baltimore, MD: Johns Hopkins University Press.

Morgan, Marcyliena
1994a　　Theories and Politics in African American English. *Annual Review of Anthropology* 23:325–345.

Morgan, Marcyliena, ed.
1994b　　*Language and the Social Construction of Identity in Creole Situations.* Los Angeles: Center for Afro-American Studies, University of California, Los Angeles.
2002　　*Language, Discourse and Power in African American Culture.* New York: Cambridge University Press.

Morgan, Philip D.
1983　　Black Society in the Lowcountry, 1760–1810. In *Slavery and Freedom in the*

Age of the American Revolution, edited by Ira Berlin and Ronald Hoffman, pp. 83–141. Charlottesville: University Press of Virginia.

1997   The Cultural Implications of the Atlantic Slave Trade: African Regional Origins, American Destinations and New World Developments. *Slavery and Abolition* 18:122–145.

1998   *Slave Counterpoint: Black Culture in the Eighteenth-Century Chesapeake and Lowcountry.* Chapel Hill: University of North Carolina Press.

2002   Carolina Rice: African Origins, New World Crop. *William and Mary Quarterly.* 3d ser., 59(3):739–741.

Morrison, Karen Y.

1999   Civilization and Citizenship through the Eyes of Afro-Cuban Intellectuals during the First Constitutional Era, 1902–1940. *Cuban Studies/Estudios Cubanos* 30:76–99.

Mosquera, Claudia, and Marion Provensal

2000   Construcción de identidad caribeña popular en Cartagena de Indias a través de la música y el baile de champeta. *Aguaita: Revista del Observatorio del Caribe Colombiano* 3:98–114.

Motta, Roberto

1978   De Nina Rodrigues a Gilberto Freyre: Estudos Afro-Brasileiros 1896-1934. *Revista do Arquivo Público* 31–32(33–34):50–59.

1988   Indo-European Syncretic Cults in Brazil: Their Economic and Social Roots. *Cahiers du Brésil Contemporain* 5:27–48.

1994   L'Invention de l'Afrique dans le Candomblé du Brésil. *Storia, Antropologia e Scienze del Linguaggio* 9(2–3):65–85.

2002   L'expansion et la réinvention des religions afro-brésiliennes: réenchantement et décomposition. *Archives de Sciences Sociales des Religions* 117:113–125.

Mouer, L. Daniel

1993   Chesapeake Creoles: The Creation of Folk Culture in Colonial Virginia. In *The Archaeology of 17th-Century Virginia*, edited by Theodore R. Reinhart and Dennis J. Pogue, pp. 105–166. Richmond: Archeological Society of Virginia.

Mouer, L. Daniel, Mary Ellen N. Hodges, Stephen R. Potter, Susan L. Henry Renaud, Ivor Noël Hume, Dennis J. Pogue, Martha W. McCartney, and Thomas E. Davidson

1999   Colonoware Pottery, Chesapeake Pipes, and "Uncritical Assumptions." In *"I, Too, Am America": Archaeological Studies of African-American Life*, edited by Theresa A. Singleton, pp. 83–115. Charlottesville: University Press of Virginia.

Moynihan, Daniel Patrick

1965   *The Negro Family: The Case for National Action.* Washington, DC: United States Department of Labor, Office of Policy Planning and Research.

REFERENCES

Mudimbe, V. Y.

1988   *The Invention of Africa: Gnosis, Philosophy, and the Order of Knowledge.*
        Bloomington: Indiana University Press.

1990   Which Idea of Africa? Herskovits's Cultural Relativism. *October* 55:93–104.

1994   *The Idea of Africa.* Bloomington: Indiana University Press.

Mufwene, Salikoko S.

1986a   Restrictive Relativization in Gullah. *Journal of Pidgin and Creole Languages*
        1:1–31.

1986b   The Universalist and Substrate Hypotheses Complement One Another. In
        Substrata versus Universals in Creole Genesis, edited by Pieter Muysken and
        Norval Smith, pp. 129–162. Philadelphia: J. Benjamins.

2004   Language Birth and Death. *Annual Review of Anthropology* 33:201–222.

Mufwene, Salikoko S., ed.

1993   *Africanisms in Afro-American Language Varieties.* Athens: University of
        Georgia Press.

Mufwene, Salikoko S., and Charles Gilman

1987   How African Is Gullah and Why? *American Speech* 62:120–139.

Mullen, Edward J.

1987   *Los negros brujos:* A Reexamination of the Text. *Cuban Studies/Estudios
        Cubanos* 17:111–129.

Mullin, Michael

1992   *Africa in America: Slave Acculturation and Resistance in the American South and
        the British Caribbean, 1736–1831.* Urbana: University of Illinois Press.

Mullings, Leith

1997   *On Our Own Terms: Race, Class and Gender in the Lives of African American
        Women.* New York: Routledge.

**Mullings, Leith, Alaka Wali, Diane McLean, Janet Mitchell, Sabiyha Prince,
Deborah Thomas, and Patricia Tovar**

2001   Qualitative Methodologies and Community Participation in Examining
        Reproductive Experiences: The Harlem Birth Right Project. *Maternal and
        Child Health Journal* 5(2):85–93.

Mullins, Paul

1999a   "A Bold and Gorgeous Front": The Contradictions of African America and
        Consumer Culture. In *Historical Archaeologies of Capitalism,* edited by Mark
        P. Leone and Parker B. Potter Jr., pp. 169–193. New York: Kluwer
        Academic/Plenum Publishers.

1999b   *Race and Affluence: An Archaeology of African America and Consumer Culture.*
        New York: Kluwer/Plenum Publishers.

Murphy, Joseph M.

1994   *Working the Spirit: Ceremonies of the African Diaspora.* Boston: Beacon Press.

Murphy, Joseph M., and Mei-Mei Sanford, eds.

2001   *Osun across the Waters: A Yoruba Goddess in Africa and the Americas.* Bloomington: Indiana University Press.

Murray, Stephen O.

1990   Problematic Aspects of Freeman's Account of Boasian Culture. *Current Anthropology* 31(4):401–407.

Myrdal, Gunnar

1944   *An American Dilemma: The Negro Problem and Modern Democracy.* New York: Harper and Brothers.

National Park Service

2003   *Low Country Gullah Geechee Culture.* http://www.nps.gov/sero/ggsrs/ (accessed May 27, 2003).

Negrón Muntaner, Frances, and Ramón Grosfoguel, eds.

1997   *Puerto Rican Jam: Rethinking Colonialism and Nationalism.* Minneapolis: University of Minnesota Press.

Negrón Portillo, Mariano, and Raúl Mayo Santana

1992   *La esclavitud urbana en San Juan.* Río Piedras, Puerto Rico: Ediciones Huracán.

Nell, William C.

1855   *The Colored Patriots of the American Revolution.* Boston: Robert F. Walcott.

Nelson, Alondra, ed.

2002   Afrofuturism. Special issue, *Social Text* 20(2).

Nelson, Bruce

2001   *Divided We Stand: American Workers and the Struggle for Black Equality.* Princeton, NJ: Princeton University Press.

Newman, Katherine S.

1992   Culture and Structure in *The Truly Disadvantaged. City and Society* 6(1):3–25.

Nicholls, David

1996   *From Desallines to Duvalier: Race, Colour and National Independence in Haiti.* 3d ed. London: Macmillan.

Niven, Laird, and Stephen A. Davis

1999   Birchtown: The History and Material Culture of an Expatriate African American Community. In *Moving On: Black Loyalists in the Afro-Atlantic World,* edited by John W. Pulis, pp. 59–83. New York: Garland.

Noël Hume, Ivor

1962   An Indian Ware of the Colonial Period. *Quarterly Bulletin of the Archaeological Society of Virginia* 17(1):2–12.

Northrup, David

2000   Igbo and Myth Igbo: Culture and Ethnicity in the Atlantic World, 1600–1850. *Slavery and Abolition* 21(2):1–20.

References

2002   *Africa's Discovery of Europe, 1450–1850.* New York: Oxford University Press.

Norton, Mary Beth
1972   *The British-Americans.* Boston: Little, Brown.

Nunes, Zita
1994   Anthropology and Race in Brazilian Modernism. In *Colonial Discourse/Postcolonial Theory*, edited by Francis Barker, Peter Hulme, and Margaret Iversen, pp. 115–125. Manchester: Manchester University Press.

Nunley, John N., and Judith Bettelheim, eds.
1988   *Caribbean Festival Arts: Each and Every Bit of Difference.* Seattle: University of Washington Press.

Ochoa, Ana María
1997   Tradición, género y nación en el bambuco. *Contratiempo* 9:34–44.

Office of Public Affairs
1998   "A Collector's Vision of Puerto Rico" Opens July 31 at the National Museum of American History. *Smithsonian Institution News*, June 26.

Okediji, Moyo
1999   Returnee Recollections in *Transatlantic Dialogue: Contemporary Art in and out of Africa*, by Michael D. Harris. Chapel Hill: Ackland Art Museum, University of North Carolina.

Okpewho, Isidore, Carole Boyce Davies, and Ali A. Mazrui, eds.
1999   *The African Diaspora: African Origins and New World Identities.* Bloomington: Indiana University Press.

Olinto, Antônio
1964   *Brasileiros na Africa.* Rio de Janeiro: Edições GRD.

Oliveira, Waldir Freitas, and Vivaldo da Costa Lima
1987   *Cartas de Édison Carneiro a Artur Ramos: de 4 de janeiro de 1936 a 6 de dezembro de 1938.* São Paulo: Corrupio.

Olwig, Karen Fog
1985   *Cultural Adaptation and Resistance on St. John: Three Centuries of Afro-Caribbean Life.* Gainesville: University of Florida Press.
1993   *Global Culture, Island Identity: Continuity and Change in the Afro-Caribbean Community of Nevis.* Philadelphia: Harwood Academic Publishers.

Opala, Joseph A.
1986   *The Gullah: Rice, Slavery and the Sierra Leone–American Connection.* Freetown, Sierra Leone: United States Information Service.

Orser, Charles E., Jr.
1996   *A Historical Archaeology of the Modern World.* New York: Plenum Press.
1998   Archaeology of the African Diaspora. *Annual Review of Anthropology* 27:63–82.
2004   *Race and Practice in Archaeological Interpretation.* Philadelphia: University of Pennsylvania Press.

Ortiz, Altagracia, ed.

1996   *Puerto Rican Women and Work: Bridges in Transnational Labor.* Philadelphia, PA: Temple University Press.

Ortiz, Fernando

1906   *Hampa afro-cubana: los negros brujos (apuntes para un estudio de etnología criminal).* Madrid: Librería de Fernando Fé.

1916   *Hampa afro-cubana: los negros esclavos: estudio sociológico y de derecho público.* Havana: Revista Bimestre Cubana.

1924   *Glosario de afronegrismos.* Havana: Imprenta "El Siglo XX."

1940   *Contrapunto cubano del tabaco y el azúcar.* Havana: Jesús Montero.

1945   *El engaño de las razas.* Havana: Páginas.

[1947] *Cuban Counterpoint: Tobacco and Sugar,* translated by Harriet de Onís.
1995   Durham, NC: Duke University Press.

Ortiz García, Carmen

2001   Relaciones de Fernando Ortiz con los antropólogos españoles. *Catauro* 3(4):60–78.

2003   Cultura popular y construcción nacional: la institucionalización de los estudios de folklore en Cuba. *Revista de Indes* 63(229):695–736.

Osagie, Iyunolu Folayan

2000   *The Amistad Revolt: Memory, Slavery, and the Politics of Identity in the United States and Sierra Leone.* Athens: University of Georgia Press.

Osofsky, Gilbert

1966   *Harlem: The Making of a Ghetto: Negro New York, 1890–1930.* New York: Harper and Row.

Otero, Solimar

2000   Rethinking the Diaspora: Reflections on Africa and the Americas. Paper presented to the conference "Transcending Traditions: African, Afro-American and African Diaspora Studies in the 21st Century," African Studies Center and the Afro-American Studies Program, University of Pennsylvania, Philadelphia.

2002   "'Orunile,' Heaven Is Home": Afrolatino Diasporas in Africa and the Americas. Ph.D. diss., University of Pennsylvania, Philadelphia.

Ottenberg, Simon

1959   Leadership and Change in a Coastal Georgia Negro Community. *Phylon* 20(1):7–18.

Ottley, Roi, and William Weatherby

1967   *The Negro in New York: An Informal Social History.* Dobbs Ferry, NY: Oceana Publications.

Otto, John

1975   Status Differences and the Archaeological Record: A Comparison of Planter, Overseer, and Slave Sites from Canon's Point Plantation (1794–1861), St. Simons Island, Georgia. Ph.D. diss., University of Florida, Miami.

REFERENCES

1984   *Cannon's Point Plantation, 1794–1850: Living Conditions and Status Patterns in the Old South.* New York: Academic Press.

Pacini, Deborah

1993   The Picó Phenomenon in Cartagena, Colombia. *América Negra* 6:69–115.

Palmer, Colin A.

1995   From Africa to the Americas: Ethnicity in the Early Black Communities of the Americas. *Journal of World History* 6(2):223–236.

Palmié, Stephan

1995a   Against Syncretism: "Africanizing" and "Cubanizing" Discourses in North American Òrìsà Worship. In *Counterworks: Managing the Diversity of Knowledge,* edited by Richard Fardon, pp. 80–104. London: Routledge.

1997   Ekpe/Abakua in Middle Passage. Paper presented at the conference "Slavery and Memory," Chicago.

2002   *Wizards and Scientists. Explorations in Afro-Cuban Modernity and Tradition.* Durham, NC: Duke University Press.

n.d.   Anthropology in Creolization: Is There a Model in the Muddle? Unpublished paper.

Palmié, Stephan, ed.

1995b   *Slave Cultures and the Cultures of Slavery.* Knoxville: University of Tennessee Press.

Pancake, John S.

1985   *This Destructive War: The British Campaign in the Carolinas, 1780–1782.* University, AL: University of Alabama Press.

Paquette, Robert L.

1988   *Sugar Is Made with Blood: The Conspiracy of La Escalera and the Conflict between Empires over Slavery in Cuba.* Middletown, CT: Wesleyan University Press.

Pardo, Mauricio, ed.

2000   *Acción colectiva, estado y etnicidad en el Pacífico colombiano.* Bogotá: Instituto Colombiano de Antropología e Historia, Colciencias.

Park, George, and Alice Park

1989   Ruth Schlossberg Landes. In *Women Anthropologists: Selected Biographies,* edited by Ute Gacs, Aisha Khan, Jerrie McIntyre, and Ruth Weinberg, pp. 208–214. Urbana: University of Illinois Press.

Parsons, Elsie Clews

1918   *Folk-Tales of Andros Island, Bahamas.* New York: American Folk-lore Society.

1923   *Folk-lore of the Sea Islands, South Carolina.* Cambridge, MA: American Folk-lore Society.

Pattee, Richard

1943   La contribution du Nègre a la formation et a la culture des pays de l'Amérique-hispanique. *Cahiers d'Haïti* 1:16–23, 31.

Patterson, Orlando
1971   Rethinking Black History. *Harvard Educational Review* 41(3):297–315.

Patterson, Thomas C.
2001   *A Social History of Anthropology in the United States.* Oxford: Berg.

Patton, Sharon F.
1998   *African-American Art.* New York: Oxford University Press.

PBS *see* **Public Broadcasting System.**

Peard, Julyan G.
1999   *Race, Place, and Medicine: The Idea of the Tropics in Nineteenth-Century Brazilian Medicine.* Durham, NC: Duke University Press.

Pedrosa, Alvaro, Arturo Escobar, J. A. Grueso, B. R. Lozano, and Jaime Rivas
1996   Movimiento negro, identidad y territorio: entrevista con la Organización de Comunidades Negras. In *Pacífico: ¿desarrollo o biodiversidad? Estado, capital y movimientos sociales en el Pacífico colombiano,* edited by Arturo Escobar and Alvaro Pedrosa, pp. 245–265. Bogotá: CEREC

Peel, J. D. Y.
2000   *Religious Encounter and the Making of the Yoruba.* Bloomington: Indiana University Press.

Peirano, Mariza G. S.
1991   *The Anthropology of Anthropology: The Brazilian Case.* Brasilia: Universidade de Brasília, Instituto de Ciências Humanas, Departamento de Antropologia.

Peixoto, Fernanda Arêas
2000   *Diálogos brasileiros: uma análise da obra de Roger Bastide.* São Paulo: Editora da Universidade de São Paulo.

Peixoto, Fernanda Arêas, Heloisa Pontes, and Lilia Moritz Schwarcz, eds.
2004   *Antropologias, Histórias, Experiências.* Belo Horizonte, Brazil: Editora Universidade Federal do Minas Gerais.

Penn Center
1998   *Penn Center.* http://www.angelfire.com/sc/jhstevens/penncenter. html#Penn%20Center (accessed May 29, 2003).

Pérez de la Riva, Juan
1975   *El barracón y otros ensayos.* Havana: Editorial de Ciencias Sociales.

Perry, Warren, and Robert Paynter
1999   Artifacts, Ethnicity, and the Archaeology of African Americans. In *"I, Too, Am America": Archaeological Studies of African-American Life,* edited by Theresa A. Singleton, pp. 299–310. Charlottesville: University Press of Virginia.

Peterson, Dale E.
1993   Response and Call: The African American Dialogue with Bakhtin. *American Literature* 65(4):761–775.

Petty, Sheila, curator
2004   *Racing the Cultural Interface: African Diasporic Identities in the Digital Age.*
        Halifax, NS: Mount Saint Vincent Art Gallery; Regina, SK: Soil Digital
        Media Suite at Neutral Ground.

Philips, John Edward
1990   The African Heritage of White America. In *Africanisms in American Culture,*
        edited by Joseph E. Holloway, pp. 225–239. Bloomington: Indiana
        University Press.

Phillippo, James M.
1843   *Jamaica: Its Past and Present State.* London: Dawson.

Phillips, Evelyn Newman, ed.
2003   Black Hair and Beauty in the African Diaspora. Special issue, *Transforming
        Anthropology* 11(2).

Phillips, Mark Salber, and Gordon Schochet, eds.
2004   *Questions of Tradition.* Toronto: University of Toronto Press.

Phillips, Ruth B., and Christopher B. Steiner, eds.
1999   *Unpacking Culture: Art and Commodity in Colonial and Postcolonial Worlds.*
        Berkeley: University of California Press.

Philogene, Gina
1994   "African American" as a New Social Representation. *Journal for the Theory of
        Social Behaviour* 24(2):89–109.

Pierson, Donald
1942   *Negroes in Brazil: A Study of Race Conflict in Bahia.* Chicago: University of
        Chicago Press.

Pinckney, Roger
1998   *Blue Roots: African-American Folk Magic of the Gullah People.* Saint Paul, MN:
        Llewellyn Publications.

Piot, Charles
2001   Atlantic Aporias: Africa and Gilroy's Black Atlantic. *South Atlantic Quarterly*
        100(1):155–170.

Pitts, Walter F.
1993   *Old Ship of Zion: The Afro-Baptist Ritual in the African Diaspora.* New York:
        Oxford University Press.

Placido, Barbara
1998   Spirits of the Nation: Identity and Legitimacy in the Cults of María Lionza
        and Simón Bolívar. Ph.D. diss., University of Cambridge, UK.

Platt, Anthony M.
1991   *E. Franklin Frazier Reconsidered.* New Brunswick, NJ: Rutgers University
        Press.

Polke, Gloria Haynes
1999   *De Gullah N De Geechee Seafood Cookbook.* Kearney, NE: Morris Press.

Pollak-Eltz, Angelina
1972   Panorama de estudios afroamericanos. *Montalbán* 1:259–317.
1994   *Religiones afroamericanas hoy.* Caracas: Planeta.

Pollitzer, William S.
1999   *The Gullah People and Their African Heritage.* Athens: University of Georgia Press.

Pontes, Heloisa
1995   Brasil com Z: A produção estrangeira sobre a país, editada aqui, sob a forma de livro, entre 1930 e 1988. In *História das ciências socais no Brasil,* vol. 2, edited by Sérgio Miceli, pp. 440–477. São Paulo: Editora Sumaré.

Portaccio, José
1995   *Canciones y fiestas de las llanuras Caribe y Pacífica y las islas de San Andrés y Providencia.* Vol. 1. of *Colombia y su música.* Bogotá: José Portaccio.

Posnansky, Merrick
1999   West Africanist Reflections on African-American Archaeology. In *"I, Too, Am America": Archaeological Studies of African-American Life,* edited by Theresa A. Singleton, pp. 21–38. Charlottesville: University Press of Virginia.

Potter, Parker B., Jr.
1991   What Is the Use of Plantation Archaeology? *Historical Archaeology* 25(3):94–107.

Powdermaker, Hortense
1939   *After Freedom: A Cultural Study in the Deep South.* New York: Viking Press.

Powell, Richard J.
1997   *Black Art and Culture in the 20th Century.* London: Thames and Hudson.

Price, Charles Reavis
2003   "Cleave to the Black": Expressions of Ethiopianism in Jamaica. *New West Indian Guide/Nieuwe West-Indische Gids* 77(1–2):31–64.

Price, Richard
1966   Caribbean Fishing and Fisherman: A Historical Sketch. *American Anthropologist* 68(6):1363–1383.
1975a   KiKoongo and Saramaccan: A Reappraisal. *Bijdragen tot de Taal-, Land- en Volkenkunde* 131:461–478.
1975b   *Saramaka Social Structure: Analysis of a Maroon Society in Surinam.* Río Piedras: Institute of Caribbean Studies, University of Puerto Rico.
1976   *The Guiana Maroons: A Historical and Bibliographic Introduction.* Baltimore, MD: Johns Hopkins University Press.
1979   Commentary Two. *Historical Reflections* 6:141–149.
1983a   *First-Time: The Historical Vision of an Afro-American People.* Baltimore, MD: Johns Hopkins University Press.

REFERENCES

1983b   *To Slay the Hydra: Dutch Colonial Perspectives on the Saramaka Wars.* Ann
         Arbor, MI: Karoma.

1990   *Alabi's World.* Baltimore, MD: Johns Hopkins University Press.

1995   Executing Ethnicity: The Killings in Suriname. *Cultural Anthropology*
         10(4):437–471.

1998a   Scrapping Maroon History: Brazil's Promise, Suriname's Shame. *New West
         Indian Guide* 72:233–255.

1998b   *The Convict and the Colonel.* Boston: Beacon Press.

Price, Richard, ed.

1996   *Maroon Societies: Rebel Slave Communities in the Americas.* 3d ed. Baltimore,
         MD: Johns Hopkins University Press.

Price, Richard, and Sally Price

1972   Saramaka Onomastics: An Afro-American Naming System. *Ethnology*
         11:341–367.

1994   *On the Mall: Presenting Maroon Tradition-Bearers at the 1992 FAF.*
         Bloomington: Folklore Institute, Indiana University/Indiana University
         Press.

1995   *Enigma Variations.* Cambridge, MA: Harvard University Press.

1997   Shadowboxing in the Mangrove. *Cultural Anthropology* 12(1):3–36.

2002   Maroons under Assault in Suriname and French Guiana. *Cultural Survival
         Quarterly* 25(4):38–45.

2003a   *Les Marrons.* Châteauneuf-le-Rouge, France: Vents d'ailleurs.

2003b   *The Root of Roots: Or, How Afro-American Anthropology Got Its Start.* Chicago:
         Prickly Paradigm Press.

Price, Sally

1984   *Co-Wives and Calabashes.* Ann Arbor: University of Michigan Press.

1988   Arts primitifs: Regards civilisés. *Gradhiva* 4:18–27.

1989   *Primitive Art in Civilized Places.* Chicago: University of Chicago Press.

1994   The Curse's Blessing. *Frontiers: A Journal of Women's Studies* 14(2):126–145.

1999   The Centrality of Margins: Art, Gender, and African American Creativity.
         In *The African Diaspora: African Origins and New World Self-Fashioning*, edited
         by Isidore Okpewho, Carole Boyce Davies, and Ali Mazrui, pp. 204–226.
         Bloomington: Indiana University Press.

Price, Sally, and Richard Price

1980   *Afro-American Arts of the Suriname Rain Forest.* Berkeley: University of
         California Press.

1999   *Maroon Arts: Cultural Vitality in the African Diaspora.* Boston: Beacon Press.

Price, Thomas J., Jr.

1954   Estado y necessidades actuales de las investigaciones afro-colombianas.
         Revista Colombiana de Antropología 2(2):12–35.

1955   Saints and Spirits: A Study of Differential Acculturation in Colombian
         Negro Communities. Ph.D. diss., Northwestern University, Evanston, IL.

Price-Mars, Jean

1919   *La Vocation de l'élite.* Port-au-Prince: Imprimerie Edmond Chenet.

1928   *Ainsi parla l'Oncle.* Paris: Imprimerie de Compiègne.

1933   Le Professeur Melville J. Herskovits et son oeuvre. *La Relève* 1(7):11–15.

1937   "Life in a Haitian Valley": "La vie dans une vallée Haïtienne": La dualité de deux cultures. *La Relève* 5(10):14–20.

1978   *Joseph Anténor Firmin, l'indomptable lutteur, mal aimé et martyr: Une grande partie de l'histoire d'Haiti á travers la formation et le destin d'un homme.* Port-au-Prince: Imprimerie Séminaire Adventiste.

Prince, Sabiyha Robin

2004   *Constructing Belonging: Class, Race, and Harlem's Professional Workers.* New York: Routledge.

Public Broadcasting System (PBS)

1988   *Franz Boas: 1858–1942.* VHS. Directed by T. W. Timreck. Boston: Michael Ambrosino.

Puig-Samper, Miguel Ángel, and Consuelo Naranjo Orovio

1999   Fernando Ortiz: herencias culturales y forja de la nacionalidad. In *Imágenes e imaginarios nacionales en el ultramar español,* edited by Consuelo Naranjo Orovio and Carlos Serrano, pp. 197–226. Madrid: Consejo Superior de Investigaciones Científicas, Central de Humanidades, Instituto de Historia.

Pulis, John W.

1999a   Bridging Troubled Waters: Moses Baker, George Liele, and the African American Diaspora to Jamaica. In *Moving On: Black Loyalists in the Afro-Atlantic World,* edited by John W. Pulis, pp. 183–221. New York: Garland.

1999b   "Citing [Sighting]-Up": Words, Sounds, and Reading Scripture in Jamaica. In *Religion, Diaspora, and Cultural Identity: A Reader in the Anglophone Caribbean,* edited by John W. Pulis, pp. 357–401. Amsterdam: Gordon and Breach.

n.d.   *Gates to Zion: Dialogics, Narrative, and Afro-Jamaican Culture History.* New York: Routledge.

Pulis, John W., ed.

1999c   *Moving On: Black Loyalists in the Afro-Atlantic World.* New York: Garland.

Pulsipher, Lydia, and Conrad Goodwin

1999   Here Where the Old Time People Be: Reconstructing Landscapes of Slavery and Post-Slavery Era in Monteserrat, West Indies. In *African Sites Archaeology in the Caribbean,* edited by Jay B. Haviser, pp. 9–33. Princeton, NJ: Markus Wiener.

Puri, Shalini

2004   *The Caribbean Postcolonial: Social Equality, Post-Nationalism, and Cultural Hybridity.* London: Palgrave Macmillan.

Quarles, Benjamin
[1961]   *The Negro in the American Revolution.* Chapel Hill: University of North
 1996   Carolina Press.

Quintero Rivera, Angel G.
1987   The Rural-Urban Dichotomy in the Formation of Puerto Rico's Cultural
   Identity. *Nieuwe West-Indische Gids* 61(3–4):127–144.
1988   *Patricios y plebeyos: Burgeses, hacendados, artesanos y obreros las relaciones de clase
   en el Puerto Rico de cambio de siglo.* Río Piedras, Puerto Rico: Ediciones
   Huracán.

Quintero Rivera, Angel G., ed.
1998   *Virgenes, magos y escapularios: Imagineria, ethnicidad y religiousidad popular en
   Puerto Rico.* San Juan: Centro de Investigaciones Sociales, Universidad de
   Puerto Rico/Centro de Investigaciones Académicas, Universidad de
   Sagrado Corazón/Fundación Puertorriqueña de las Humanidades.

Quintero Rivera, Angel G., and Luis Manuel Álvarez
1994   The Camouflaged Drum: Melodization of Rhythms and Maroonage
   Ethnicity in Caribbean Peasant Music. In *Music and Black Ethnicity: The
   Caribbean and South America,* edited by Gerard H. Béhague, pp. 47–63.
   Miami: North-South Center, University of Miami; New Brunswick, NJ:
   Transaction Publishers.

Raboteau, Albert J.
1978   *Slave Religion: The "Invisible Institution" in the Antebellum South.* New York:
   Oxford University Press.

Rahier, Jean Muteba, ed.
1999   *Representations of Blackness and the Performance of Identities.* Westport, CT:
   Bergin and Garvey.

Rainwater, Lee, and William L. Yancey
1967   *The Moynihan Report and the Politics of Controversy.* Cambridge, MA: MIT
   Press.

Ramos, Arthur
1934   *O negro brasiliero: ethnographia, religiosa e psychanalyse.* Rio de Janeiro:
   Civilização Brasileria.
1935   *O folk-lore do Brasil.* Rio de Janeiro: Civilização Brasileria.
1937   *As culturas negras no novo mundo.* Rio de Janeiro: Civilização Brasileria.
1939   *The Negro in Brazil,* translated by Richard Pattee. Washington, DC:
   Associated Publishers.
1942   *A aculturação negra no Brasil.* São Paulo: Companhia Editora Nacional.
1943   *Guerra e relações de raça.* Rio de Janeiro: Departamento Editorial da União
   Nacional dos Estudantes.
1944   *As ciências sociais e os problemas de após-guerra.* Rio de Janeiro: Casa do
   Estudante do Brasil.

Ramsey, Kate
2000   Melville Herskovits, Katherine Dunham, and the Politics of African Diasporic Dance Anthropology. In *Dancing Bodies, Living Histories: New Writings about Dance and Culture,* edited by Lisa Doolittle and Anne Flynn, pp. 196–216. Banff, Alberta: Banff Centre Press.
2002   Without One Ritual Note: Folklore Performance and the Haitian State, 1935–1946. *Radical History Review* 84:7–42.
2005   Prohibition, Persecution, Performance: Anthropology and the Penalization of Vodou in Mid-20th-Century Haiti. *Gradhiva,* n.s., 1:165–179.
n.d.   Duverneau Trouillot: Revisionist Ethnographer of Vodou. Unpublished paper.

Rawick, George P.
1972   *From Sundown to Sunup: The Making of the Black Community.* Westport, CT: Greenwood Publishing Company.

Redfield, Robert, Ralph Linton, and Melville J. Herskovits
1936   Memorandum for the Study of Acculturation. *American Anthropologist* 38(1):149–152.

Reis, João José
1993   *Slave Rebellion in Brazil: The Muslim Uprising of 1835 in Bahia,* translated by Arthur Brakel. Baltimore, MD: Johns Hopkins University Press.

Reitz, Elizabeth
1994   Zooarchaeological Analyses of African-American Foodways: Gracia Real de Santa Teresa de Mosé. *Historical Archaeology* 28(1):23–40.

Reitz, Elizabeth J., and Elizabeth S. Wing
1999   *Zooarchaeology.* Cambridge: Cambridge University Press.

Renda, Mary A.
2001   *Taking Haiti. Military Occupation and the Culture of U.S. Imperialism, 1915–1940.* Chapel Hill: University of North Carolina Press.

Restrepo, Eduardo
1997   Afrocolombianos, antropología y proyecto de modernidad en Colombia. In *Antropología en la modernidad: Identidades, etnicidades y movimientos sociales en Colombia,* edited by María Victoria Uribe and Eduardo Restrepo, pp. 279–320. Bogotá: Instituto Colombiano de Antropología.

Reynoso, Álvaro
1861   *Estudios progresivos sobre varias materias cieníficas, agrícolas e industríales: Colección de escritos sobre los cultivos de la caña, café, tobaco, maíz, arroz.* Havana: El Tiempo.

Rhodes, Colin
1994   *Primitivism and Modern Art.* London: Thames and Hudson.

REFERENCES

Ribeiro, Gustavo Lins, ed.

2000   Reading Brazilian Anthropologists. Special issue, *Journal of Latin American Anthropology* 4(2)/5(1).

Richburg, Keith B.

1997   *Out of America: A Black Man Confronts Africa.* New York: Basic Books.

Rickford, John R.

1980   How Does *doz* Disappear? In *Issues in English Creoles,* edited by Richard Day, pp. 77–96. Heidelberg: Julius Groos.

Riley, Sandra

1983   *Homeward Bound: A History of the Bahama Islands to 1850 with a Definitive Study of Abaco in the American Loyalist Plantation Period.* Miami: Island Research.

Rippon, John, ed.

1802   *Baptist Annual Register for 1798, 1799, 1800, and Part of 1801.* London: Brown and James.

Roach, Joseph

1996   *Cities of the Dead: Circum-Atlantic Performance.* New York: Columbia University Press.

Roberts, John Michael

2004   Will the Materialists in the Bakhtin Circle Please Stand Up? In *Realism Discourse and Deconstruction,* edited by Jonathan Joseph and John Michael Roberts, pp. 89–110. London: Routledge.

Robinson, Sallie Ann, with Gregory Wrenn Smith

2003   *Gullah Home Cooking the Daufuskie Way: Smokin' Joe Butter Beans, Ol' 'Fuskie Fried Crab Rice, Sticky-Bush Blackberry Dumpling, and Other Sea Island Favorites.* Chapel Hill: University of North Carolina Press.

Robinson, St. John

1992   Southern Loyalists in the Caribbean and Central America. *South Carolina Historical Magazine* 93:203–220.

Rodney, Walter

1969   Upper Guinea and the Significance of the Origins of Africans Enslaved in the New World. *Journal of Negro History* 54(4):327–345.

Rodríguez, Cheryl

2001   A Homegirl Goes Home: Black Feminism and the Lure of Native Anthropology. In *Black Feminist Anthropology: Theory, Politics, Praxis, and Poetics,* edited by Irma McClaurin, pp. 233–257. New Brunswick, NJ: Rutgers University Press.

Rodríguez, Clara E.

2001   Puerto Ricans in Historical and Social Science Research. In *Handbook of Research on Multicultural Education,* edited by James A. Banks and Cherry A. McGee Banks, pp. 223–244. San Francisco: Jossey-Bass.

Rodríguez Juliá, Edgardo

1988   *Álbum de la sagrada familia puertorriqueña a partir de 1898.* Madrid: Editorial
Playor.

Rodríguez-Mangual, Edna M.

2004   *Lydia Cabrera and the Construction of an Afro-Cuban Cultural Identity.* Chapel
Hill: University of North Carolina Press.

Rodríguez-Morrazani, Roberto P.

1998   Beyond the Rainbow: Mapping the Discourse on Puerto Ricans and Race.
In *The Latino Studies Reader: Culture, Economy and Society,* edited by Antonia
Darder and Rodolfo D. Torres, pp.143–162. Oxford: Blackwell.

Roediger, David R.

1991   *The Wages of Whiteness: Race and the Making of the American Working Class.*
London: Verso.

Román, Reinaldo Luis

2000   Conjuring Progress and Divinity: Religion and Conflict in Cuba and
Puerto Rico, 1899–1956. Ph.D. diss., University of California at Los
Angeles.

2002   Spiritists versus Spirit-Mongers: Julia Vázquez and the Struggle for
Progress in 1920s Puerto Rico. *Centro Journal* 14(2):27–47.

Romberg, Raquel

2003   *Witchcraft and Welfare: Spiritual Capital and the Business of Magic in Modern
Puerto Rico.* Austin: University of Texas Press.

Ronkin, Maggie, and Helen E. Karn

1999   Mock Ebonics: Linguistic Racism in Parodies of Ebonics on the Internet.
Journal of Sociolinguistics 3(3):360–380.

Rosaldo, Renato

1980   *Ilongot Headhunting, 1883–1974: A Study in Society and History.* Stanford, CA:
Stanford University Press.

Rosengarten, Dale

1987   *Row upon Row: Sea Grass Baskets of the South Carolina Lowcountry.* 2d ed.
Columbia: McKissick Museum, University of South Carolina.

1997   Social Origins of the African-American Lowcountry Basket. Ph.D. diss.,
Harvard University, Cambridge, MA.

Rosenthal, Steven J.

1999   How Liberal Ideology Assists the Growth of Fascism: A Critique of the
Sociology of William Julius Wilson. *Journal of Poverty* 3(2):67–87.

Rossbach de Olmos, Lioba

1998   Bemerkungen zur (ethnologischen) Rezeption des Schwarzen in
Hispanoamerika. In *Das Afrikanische Amerika: Beiträge der Regionalgruppe
"Afroamerika" im Rahmen der Tagung der Deutschen Gesellschaft für Völkerkunde
in Frankfurt am Main 1997,* edited by Bettina E. Schmidt and Lioba
Rossbach de Olmos, pp. 11–23. Marburg, Germany: Curupira.

REFERENCES

Rotilu, Oyeyinka
1932   A Notable Egba, Mr. Adeyemo Alakija. *Nigerian Daily Times*, December.

Roumain, Jacques
1942   *A propos de la campagne "anti-superstitieuse."* Port-au-Prince: Imprimerie de l'Etat.

Roura Alvarez, Lisette, and Silvia Angelbello
n.d.   *El Bohío: vivenda esclava en las plantaciones cubanas del siglo XIX.* Havana: Gabinete de Arqueología Officina del Historiador de la Ciudad de la Habana, in press.

Rovira de Córdoba, Cidenia, and Darcio Antonio Córdoba Cuesta
2000   *Cátedra afrocolombiana: Puntes para clases.* Bogotá: Corporación Identidad Cultural.

Roy Fequiere, Magali
1996   Negar los negro sería gazmoñería: Luis Páles Matos, Margo Arce and the Black Poetry Debate. *Centro: Journal of the Center for Puerto Rican Studies* 8(1–2):82–91.

Rubino, Silvana
1995   Clubes de pesquisadores: a sociedade de etnografia e folclore e a sociedade de sociologia. In *História das ciências socais no Brasil,* vol. 2, edited by Sérgio Miceli, pp. 479–521. São Paulo: Editora Sumaré.

Rush, Dana
1999   Eternal Potential: Chromolithographs in Vodunland. *African Arts* 32(4):61–75, 94–96.

Rusling, G. W.
1968   A Note on Early Baptist History. *Foundations* 2:362–368.

Russell, Aaron. E.
1997   Material Culture and African-American Spirituality at the Hermitage. *Historical Archaeology* 31(2):63–80.

SECCA *See* **Southeastern Center for Contemporary Art**

Sahlins, Marshall
1993   Goodbye to Tristes Tropes: Ethnography in the Context of Modern World History. *Journal of Modern History* 65(1):1–25.

Samford, Patricia Merle
1996   The Archaeology of African-American Slavery and Material Culture. *William and Mary Quarterly* 53(1):87–114.
1999   "Strong Is the Bond of Kinship": West African–Style Ancestor Shrines and Subfloor Pits on African-American Quarters. In *Historical Archaeology, Identity Formation, and the Interpretation of Ethnicity,* edited by Maria Franklin and Garrett Fesler, pp. 71–91. Williamsburg, VA: Colonial Williamsburg Foundation.

2000   Power Runs in Many Channels: Subfloor Pits and West African–Based
            Spiritual Traditions in Colonial Virginia. Ph.D. diss., University of North
            Carolina at Chapel Hill.

Samuel, Peter

1850   *The Wesleyan-Methodist Missions in Jamaica and Honduras Delineated;
            Containing a Description of the Principle Stations, Together with a Consecutive
            Account of the Rise and Progress of the Work of God at Each.* London: Partridge
            & Cakey.

Sánchez-Korrol, Virginia E.

1983   *From Colonia to Community: The History of Puerto Ricans in New York City.*
            Berkeley: University of California Press.

Sangren, P. Steven

1995   "Power" against Ideology: A Critique of Foucaultian Usage. *Cultural
            Anthropology* 10(1):3–40.

Sansone, Livio

1997   The New Blacks from Bahia: Local and Global in Afro-Bahia. *Identities*
            3(4):457–493.

2002   Da África ao afro: uso e abuso da África enre os intelectuais e na cultura
            popular brasileira durante o século XX. *Afro-Ásia* 27:249–269.

2003   *Blackness without Ethnicity: Constructing Race in Brazil.* London: Palgrave
            Macmillan.

Santí, Enrico Mario

2002   *Fernando Ortiz: contrapunteo y transculturación.* Madrid: Colibrí Editorial.

Santiago-Valles, Kelvin A.

1994   *Subject People and Colonial Discourses: Economic Transformation and Social
            Disorder in Puerto Rico, 1898–1947.* Albany: State University of New York
            Press.

Santiago-Valles, William Fred

1997   Memories of the Future: Maroon Intellectuals from the Caribbean and the
            Sources of Their Communication Strategies, 1925–1940. Ph.D. diss.,
            Simon Fraser University, Vancouver, Britich Columbia.

Santos, Ricardo Ventura, and Marcos Chor Maio

2004   Qual "Retrato do Brasil"? Raça, biologia, identidades, e política na era da
            genômica. *Mana* 10(1):61–95.

Sapucaia, Antonio ed.

2003   *Relembrando Arthur Ramos.* Maceió, Alagoas, Brazil: Editora da Universidade
            Federal de Alagoas.

Sarracino, Rodolfo

1988   *Los que volvieron a África.* Havana: Editorial de Ciencias Sociales.

REFERENCES

Saunders, D. Gail

1983   *Bahamian Loyalists and Their Slaves.* London: Macmillan.

Saville-Troike, Muriel

2003   *The Ethnography of Communication: An Introduction.* 3d. ed. Malden, MA: Blackwell.

Scarano, Francisco A.

1981   *Inmigración y clases sociales en el Puerto Rico del siglo XIX.* Río Piedras, Puerto Rico: Ediciones Huracán.

1984   *Sugar and Slavery in Puerto Rico: The Plantation Economy of Ponce, 1880–1850.* Madison: University of Wisconsin Press.

1993   *Puerto Rico: Cinco siglos de historia.* Mexico City: McGraw-Hill.

1996   The *Jíbaro* Masquerade and the Subaltern Politics of Creole Identity Formation in Puerto Rico, 1745–1823. *American Historical Review* 101(5):1398–1431.

Schlotterbeck, John T.

1991   The Internal Economy of Slavery in Rural Virginia Piedmont. In *The Slaves' Economy: Independent Production by Slaves in the Americas,* edited by Ira Berlin and Philip D. Morgan, pp.170–181. London: Frank Cass.

Schomburg, Arthur A.

1925   The Negro Digs Up His Past. In *The New Negro,* edited by Alain Locke, pp. 231–237. New York: Albert & Charles Boni, Inc.

Schudson, Michael

1997   Lives, Laws, and Language: Commemorative versus Non-Commemorative Forms of Effective Public Memory. *The Communication Review* 2(1):3–17.

Schuler, Monica

1970   Akan Slave Revolts in the British Caribbean. *Savacou* 1:8–31.

1979   Afro-American Slave Culture. *Historical Reflections* 6:121–137.

1980   *"Alas, Alas, Kongo": A Social History of Indentured African Immigration into Jamaica, 1841–1865.* Baltimore, MD: Johns Hopkins University Press.

Schwarcz, Lilia Moritz

1999   *The Spectacle of the Races: Scientists, Institutions, and the Race Question in Brazil, 1870–1930,* translated by Leland Guyer. New York: Hill and Wang.

Schwartz, Rosalie

1977   The Displaced and the Disappointed: Cultural Nationalists and Black Activists in Cuba in the 1920s. Ph.D. diss., University of California, San Diego.

Schwegler, Armin J.

1996   *"Chi ma nkongo": Lengua y rito ancestrales en El Palenque de San Basilio (Colombia).* Frankfurt: Vervuert.

Scott, David

1991   That Event, This Memory: Notes on the Anthropology of African Diasporas in the New World. *Diaspora* 1(3):261–284.

1999   *Refashioning Futures: Criticism after Postcoloniality.* Princeton, NJ: Princeton University Press.

2004   *Conscripts of Modernity: The Tragedy of Colonial Enlightenment.* Durham, NC: Duke University Press.

Scott, James C.

1985   *Weapons of the Weak: Everyday Forms of Peasant Resistance.* New Haven, CT: Yale University Press.

1990   *Domination and the Arts of Resistance: Hidden Transcripts.* New Haven, CT: Yale University Press.

Scott, Kenneth

1961   The Slave Insurrection in New York in 1712. *New York Historical Society Quarterly* 45:43–74.

Scott, Rebecca

1985   *Slave Emancipation in Cuba: The Transition to Free Labor, 1860–1899.* Princeton, NJ: Princeton University Press.

Seabrook, W. B.

1929   *The Magic Island.* New York: Blue Ribbon Books.

Seeber-Tegethoff, Mareile

1998   Grenzgänger—Ethnologen und Informanten zwischen Wissenschaft und Religion: Zur Forschungsgeschichte afrobrasilianischer Religionen. In *Das Afrikanische Amerika: Beiträge der Regionalgruppe "Afroamerika" im Rahmen der Tagung der Deutschen Gesellschaft für Völkerkunde in Frankfurt am Main 1997,* edited by Bettina E. Schmidt and Lioba Rossbach de Olmos, pp. 25–42. Marburg, Germany: Curupira.

Segato, R. L.

1998   The Color-Blind Subject of Myth; Or, Where to Find Africa in the Nation. *Annual Review of Anthropology* 27:129–151.

Selka, Stephen

2005   Ethnoreligious Identity Politics in Bahia, Brazil. *Latin American Perspectives* 32(1):72–94.

Sengova, Joko

1981   A Classification of Tense, Aspect, and Time Specification in Verb System of Mende. Ph.D. diss., University of Wisconsin, Madison.

1987   The National Languages of Sierra Leone: A Decade of Policy Experimentation. *Africa* 57:519–530.

1993   Lorenzo Turner and the Gullah Language. In *Family across the Sea: Viewer's Guide,* edited by Michele Reap, p. 6. Columbia: South Carolina Educational TV.

1994   Recollections of African Language Patterns in an American Speech Variety: An Assessment of Mende Influences in Lorenzo Dow Turner's Gullah Data. In *The Crucible of Carolina: Essays in the Development of Gullah Language and Culture,* edited by Michael Montgomery, pp. 175–219. Athens: University of Georgia Press.

Shanks, Michael, and Christopher Tilley

1987   *Re-Constructing Archaeology: Theory and Practice.* Cambridge: Cambridge
        University Press.

Shannon, Magdaline W.

1996   *Jean Price-Mars, the Haitian Elite and the American Occupation, 1915–35.*
        London: Macmillan.

Shaw, Rosalind

2002   *Memories of the Slave Trade: Ritual and the Historical Imagination in Sierra
        Leone.* Chicago: University of Chicago Press.

Shaw, Theodore M.

2004   Beyond What Bill Cosby Said. *Washington Post,* May 27, A31.

Shennan, Stephen

1989   Introduction: Archaeological Approaches to Cultural Identity. In
        Archaeological Approaches to Cultural Identity, edited by Stephen Shennan,
        pp. 1–32. London: Routledge.

Sheriff, Robin E.

2001   *Dreaming Equality: Color, Race, and Racism in Urban Brazil.* New Brunswick,
        NJ: Rutgers University Press.

Sidbury, James

1998   Review of *From Calabar to Carter's Grove: The History of a Virginia Slave
        Community* by Lorena S. Walsh. *William and Mary Quarterly* 55(4):631–633.

Siebert, Wilbur

[1913] *The Legacy of the American Revolution in the West Indies and Bahamas: A*
1972   *Chapter out of the History of the American Loyalists.* Boston: Gregg.

Silpa, Felicia

2003   Touring a Florida Plantation: Historical Archaeology of Gamble Plantation
        1842–1858. B.A. thesis, New College of Florida, Sarasota, FL.

Simpson, George Eaton

1966   Baptismal, "Mourning," and "Building" Ceremonies of the Shouters in
        Trinidad. *Journal of American Folklore* 79(314):537–550.

1973   *Melville J. Herskovits.* New York: Columbia University Press.

Singleton, Theresa A.

1991   The Archaeology of Slavery. In *Before Freedom Came: African-American Life in
        the Antebellum South,* edited by Edward D. C. Campbell Jr. and Kym S. Rice,
        pp. 156–176. Charlottesville: University Press of Virginia.

1995   The Archaeology of Slavery in North America. *Annual Review of
        Anthropology* 24:119–140.

1998   Cultural Interaction and African-American Identity in Plantation
        Archaeology. In *Studies in Culture Contact: Interaction, Culture Change, and
        Archaeology,* edited by James G. Cusick, pp. 172–188. Carbondale: Center
        for Archaeological Investigations, Southern Illinois University, Carbondale.

1999a   An Introduction to African-American Archaeology. In *"I, Too, Am America":*
         Archaeological Studies of African-American Life, edited by Theresa A.
         Singleton, pp.1–17. Charlottesville: University Press of Virginia.

1999b   Iron Cauldrons and Their Multiple Meanings in Afro-Cuba. Paper
         presented to the Society for American Archaeology, Chicago.

1999c   The Slave Trade Remembered on the Former Gold and Slave Coasts.
         Slavery & Abolition 20(1):150–169.

2001a   An Americanist Perspective on African Archaeology: Toward an
         Archaeology of the Black Atlantic. In *West Africa during the Atlantic Slave*
         Trade: Archaeological Perspectives, edited by Christopher R. DeCorse,
         pp. 179–184. London: Leicester University Press.

2001b   Class, Race, and Identity among Free Blacks of the Antebellum South.
         In *Race and the Archaeology of Identity,* edited by Charles E. Orser Jr.,
         pp. 196–207. Salt Lake City: University of Utah Press.

2001c   Slavery and Spatial Dialectics on Cuban Coffee Plantations. *World*
         Archaeology 33(1):98–114.

Singleton, Theresa A., ed.

1985   *The Archaeology of Slavery and Plantation Life.* Orlando, FL: Academic Press.

Singleton, Theresa A., and Mark D. Bograd

1995   *The Archaeology of the African Diaspora in the Americas.* Glassboro, NJ: Society
         for Historical Archaeology.

2000   Breaking Typological Barriers: Looking for the Colono in Colonoware
         Pottery. In *Lines That Divide: Historical Archaeologies of Race, Class, and*
         Gender, edited by James A. Delle, Stephen A. Mrozowski, and Robert
         Paynter, pp. 3–21. Knoxville: University of Tennessee Press.

Sinnette, Elinor Des Verney

1989   *Arthur Alfonso Schomburg, Black Bibliophile and Collector: A Biography.* New
         York: New York Public Library, Wayne State University Press.

Skidmore, Thomas E.

[1974]   *Black into White: Race and Nationality in Brazilian Thought.* Durham, NC:
1993   Duke University Press.

Skinner, Elliot P.

1982   The Dialectic between Diasporas and Homelands. In *Global Dimensions of*
         the African Diaspora, edited by Joseph E. Harris, pp.17–45. Washington, DC:
         Howard University Press.

1999   Hegemonic Paradigms and the African World: Striving to Be Free. In
         Crossing Boundaries: Comparative History of Black People in Diaspora, edited by
         Darlene Clark Hine and Jacqueline McLeod, pp. 45–70. Bloomington:
         Indiana University Press.

Slaughter, Sabra Conway

1985   "The Old Ones Die and the Young Ones Leaving": The Effects of
         Modernization on the Community of Daufuskie Island, South Carolina.
         Ph.D. diss., University of Michigan, Ann Arbor.

Slocum, Karla, and Deborah A. Thomas

2003   Rethinking Global and Area Studies: Insights from Caribbeanist Anthropology. *American Anthropologist* 105(3):553–565.

Smedley, Audrey

1993   *Race in North America: Origin and Evolution of a Worldview.* Boulder, CO: Westview Press.

Smith, Julia Floyd

1985   *Slavery and Rice Culture in Low Country Georgia, 1750–1800.* Knoxville: University of Tennessee Press.

Smith, Raymond T.

1992   Race, Class, and Gender in the Transition to Freedom. In *The Meaning of Freedom: Economics, Politics, and Culture after Slavery,* edited by Frank McGlynn and Seymour Drescher, pp. 257–290. Pittsburgh, PA: University of Pittsburgh Press.

Smith, Theophus H.

1994   *Conjuring Culture: Biblical Formations of Black America.* New York: Oxford University Press.

Smith, Tom W.

1992   Changing Racial Labels: From "Colored" to "Negro" to "Black" to "African American." *Public Opinion Quarterly* 56(4):496–514.

Smolenski, John

2003   Hearing Voices: Microhistory, Dialogicality and the Recovery of Popular Culture on an Eighteenth-Century Virginia Plantation. *Slavery and Abolition* 24(1):1–23.

Sobel, Mechal

[1979]   *Trabelin' On: The Slave Journey to an Afro-Baptist Faith.* Princeton, NJ:
1988   Princeton University Press.

Sollors, Werner

1986   *Beyond Ethnicity: Consent and Descent in American Culture.* New York: Oxford University Press.

Southeastern Center for Contemporary Art

1990   *Next Generation: Southern Black Aesthetic.* Winston-Salem, NC: Southeastern Center for Contemporary Art.

Spivak, Gayatri

1988   Can the Subaltern Speak? In *Marxism and the Interpretation of Culture,* edited by Cary Nelson and Lawrence Grossberg, pp. 271–313. Urbana: University of Illinois Press.

Stack, Carol B.

1974   *All Our Kin: Strategies for Survival in a Black Community.* New York: Harper and Row.

Stahl, Anne Brower

1991   Ethnic Style and Ethnic Boundaries: A Diachronic Case Study from West-Central Ghana. *Ethnohistory* 38(3):250–275.

Starke, Miriam, ed.

1998   *The Archaeology of Social Boundaries.* Washington, DC: Smithsonian Institution Press.

Stedman, John Gabriel

[1790] *Narrative of a Five Years Expedition against the Revolted Negroes of Surinam,*
1988   edited by Richard Price and Sally Price. Baltimore, MD: Johns Hopkins University Press.

Steiner, Christopher B.

1994   *African Art in Transit.* Cambridge: Cambridge University Press.

Steward, Julian H., Robert Manners, Sidney W. Mintz, Elena Padilla, Raymond Scheele, and Eric R. Wolf

1956   *The People of Puerto Rico.* Urbana: University of Illinois Press.

Stewart, Robert J.

1992   *Religion and Society in Post-Emancipation Jamaica.* Knoxville: University of Tennessee Press.

Stocking, George W., Jr.

1965   On the Limits of "Presentism" and "Historicism" in the Historiography of the Behavioral Sciences. *Journal of the History of the Behavioral Sciences* 1(3):211–218.

1968   *Race, Culture, and Evolution: Essays in the History of Anthropology.* New York: The Free Press.

1974   Introduction: The Basic Assumptions of Boasian Anthropology. In *The Shaping of American Anthropology, 1883–1911: A Franz Boas Reader,* edited by George W. Stocking Jr., pp. 1–20. New York: The Free Press.

1979   Anthropology as *Kulturkampf*: Science and Politics in the Career of Franz Boas. In *The Uses of Anthropology,* edited by Walter Goldschmidt, pp. 33–49. Washington, DC: American Anthropological Association.

1986   Essays on Culture and Personality. In *Malinowski, Rivers, Benedict and Others: Essays on Culture and Personality,* edited by George W. Stocking Jr., pp. 3–12. Madison: University of Wisconsin Press.

1992   *The Ethnographer's Magic and Other Essays in the History of Anthropology.* Madison: University of Wisconsin Press.

Stocking, George W., Jr., ed.

1983   *Observers Observed: Essays on Ethnographic Fieldwork.* Madison: University of Wisconsin Press.

Stoller, Paul

1995   *Embodying Colonial Memories: Spirit Possession, Power and the Hauka in West Africa.* London: Routledge.

2003   *Money Has No Smell: The Africanization of New York City.* Chicago: University of Chicago Press.

Stone, Lawrence

1977   Prosopography. *Daedalus* 107:46–70.

Stoney, Samuel Gaillard, and Gertrude Mathews Shelby

1930   *Black Genesis: A Chronicle.* New York: Macmillan Company.

Streicker, Joel

1995   Policing Boundaries: Race, Class, and Gender in Cartagena, Colombia. *American Ethnologist* 22(1):54–74.

Stuckey, Sterling

1987   *Slave Culture: Nationalist Theory and the Foundations of Black America.* New York: Oxford University Press.

1994   *Going through the Storm: The Influence of African American Art in History.* New York: Oxford University Press.

Sturges, Hollister, ed.

1990   *New Art from Puerto Rico.* Springfield, MA: Museum of Fine Arts.

Sullivan, Nancy

1995   Inside Trading: Postmodernism and the Social Drama of *Sunflowers* in the 1980s Art World. In *The Traffic in Culture: Refiguring Art and Anthropology,* edited by George E. Marcus and Fred R. Myers, pp. 256–301. Berkeley: University of California Press.

Sunderland, P. L.

1997   "You May Not Know It, but I'm Black": White Women's Self-Identification as Black. *Ethnos* 62(1–2):32–58.

Sutton, Constance, and Elsa Chaney, eds.

1987   *Caribbean Life in New York City: Sociocultural Dimensions.* New York: Center for Migration Studies.

Sweet, James H.

2003   *Re-creating Africa: Culture, Kinship, and Religion in the African-Portuguese World, 1441–1770.* Chapel Hill: University of North Carolina Press.

Szwed, John F.

1972   An American Anthropological Dilemma: The Politics of Afro-American Culture. In *Reinventing Anthropology,* edited by Dell Hymes, pp. 153–181. New York: Pantheon Books.

Taffin, Dominique, ed.

2000   *Du musée colonial au musée des cultures du monde.* Paris: Maisonneuve et Larose.

Taussig, Michael

1997   *The Magic of the State.* London: Routledge.

Tedlock Dennis

1979   The Analogical Tradition and the Emergence of a Dialogical Anthropology. *Journal of Anthropological Research* 35(4):387–400.

1987   Questions Concerning Dialogical Anthropology. *Journal of Anthropological Research* 43(4):325–344.

Tedlock, Dennis, and Bruce Mannheim, eds.

1995   *The Dialogic Emergence of Culture.* Urbana: University of Illinois Press.

Teye, Victor B., and Dallen J. Timothy

2004   The Varied Colors óf Slave Heritage in West Africa: White American Stakeholders. *Space and Culture* 7(2):145–155.

Thandeka

1999   *Learning to Be White: Money, Race, and God in America.* New York: Continuum.

Thomas, Deborah A.

2004   *Modern Blackness: Nationalism, Globalization, and the Politics of Culture in Jamaica.* Durham, NC: Duke University Press.

Thomas, Nicholas

1989   *Out of Time: History and Evolution in Anthropological Discourse.* Cambridge: Cambridge University Press.

1991   *Entangled Objects: Exchange, Material Culture, and Colonialism in the Pacific.* Cambridge, MA: Harvard University Press.

Thompson, Robert Farris

1973   Yoruba Artistic Criticism. In *The Traditional Artist in African Societies,* edited by Warren L. D'Azevedo, pp. 18–61. Bloomington: Indiana University Press.

1983   *Flash of the Spirit: African and Afro-American Art and Philosophy.* New York: Random House.

Thornton, John K.

1991   African Dimensions of the Stono Rebellion. *American Historical Review* 96(4):1101–1113.

1993   "I am the subject of the King of Congo": African Political Ideology and the Haitian Revolution. *Journal of World History* 4(2):181–214.

1998a   *Africa and Africans in the Making of the Atlantic World, 1400–1800.* 2d. ed. Cambridge: Cambridge University Press.

1998b   From the General to the Particular: Ethnicity and History in the Slave Trade. Paper presented at the conference "Transatlantic Slaving and the African Diaspora," Williamsburg, VA.

Tió, Teresa

1995   El portófolios gráfico o la hoja liberada. In *El Portafolios en la gráfica puertorriqueña.* San Juan: Museo de las Américas.

REFERENCES

Tobin, Jacqueline L., and Raymond G. Dobard

1999   *Hidden in Plain View: The Secret Story of Quilts and the Underground Railroad.*
New York: Doubleday.

Torgovnick, Marianna

1990   *Gone Primitive: Savage Intellects, Modern Lives.* Chicago: University of
Chicago Press.

Torres, Arlene

1995   Blackness, Ethnicity and Cultural Transformations in Southern Puerto
Rico. Ph.D. diss., University of Illinois at Urbana-Champaign.

1998a   La gran familia puertorriqueña "Ej prieta de beldá" (The Great Puerto
Rican Family Is Really Really Black). In *Eastern South America and the
Caribbean.* Vol. 2 of *Blackness in Latin America and the Caribbean: Social
Dynamics and Cultural Transformations,* edited by Arlene Torres and
Norman E. Whitten Jr., pp. 285–306. Bloomington: Indiana University
Press.

1998b   From *Jíbara* to Anthropologist: Puerto Rican Ethnography and the Politics
of Representation. *Identities* 5(1):107–122.

Torres, Arlene, and Norman E. Whitten Jr., eds.

1998   *Eastern South America and the Caribbean.* Vol. 2 of *Blackness in Latin America
and the Caribbean: Social Dynamics and Cultural Transformations.*
Bloomington: Indiana University Press.

Trigger, Bruce

1989   *A History of Archaeological Thought.* Cambridge: Cambridge University Press.

Trouillot, Hénock

1956   La Pensée du Docteur Jean Price-Mars. *Revue de la Société Haïtienne
d'Histoire, de Géographie, et de Géologie* 29(102):5–102.

Trouillot, Michel-Rolph

1991   Anthropology and the Savage Slot: The Poetics and Politics of Otherness.
In *Recapturing Anthropology: Working in the Present,* edited by Richard G. Fox,
pp. 17–44. School of American Research, Santa Fe, NM: SAR Press.

1995   *Silencing the Past: Power and the Production of History.* Boston: Beacon Press.

1998   Culture on the Edges: Creolization in the Plantation Context. *Plantation
Society in the Americas* 5(1):8–28.

2003   *Global Transformations: Anthropology and the Modern World.* New York:
Palgrave Macmillan.

Troxler, Carole

1981   The British Evacuation of East Florida, 1783–1785. *Florida Historical
Quarterly* 60(1):1–28.

Turgeon, Laurier

1997   A Tale of a Kettle: Odyssey of an Intercultural Object. *Ethnohistory*
44(1):1–30.

Turner, Jane, ed.

1996   *The Dictionary of Art*. New York: Grove's Dictionaries.

Turner, Jerry Michael

1974   Les Bresiliens: The Impact of Former Brazilian Slaves upon Dahomey. Ph.D. diss., Boston University.

Turner, Lorenzo Dow

1941   Linguistic Research and African Survivals. *American Council of Learned Societies Bulletin* 32:68–89.

1942   Some Contacts of Brazilian Ex-Slaves with Nigeria, West Africa. *Journal of Negro History* 27(1):55–67.

1949   *Africanisms in the Gullah Dialect*. Chicago: University of Chicago Press.

Turner, Mary

1982   *Slaves and Missionaries: The Disintegration of Jamaican Slave Society, 1787–1834*. Urbana: University of Illinois Press.

Turner, Victor W.

1969   *The Ritual Process: Structure and Anti-Structure*. Chicago: Aldine.

1974   *Dramas, Fields, and Metaphors: Symbolic Action in Human Society*. Ithaca, NY: Cornell University Press.

Turtis, Richard Lee

2003   *Foundations of Despotism: Peasants, the Trujillo Regime, and Modernity in Dominican History*. Stanford, CA: Stanford University Press.

Tuttle, William M., Jr.

1970   *Race Riot: Chicago in the Red Summer of 1919*. New York: Atheneum.

Twine, France Widdance

1998   *Racism in a Racial Democracy: The Maintenance of White Supremacy in Brazil*. New Brunswick, NJ: Rutgers University Press.

Twining, Mary A., and Keith E. Baird, eds.

1991   *Sea Island Roots: African Presence in the Carolinas and Georgia*. Trenton, NJ: Africa World Press.

Tyson, George F., Jr.

1975/76   The Carolina Black Corps: Legacy of Revolution (1783–1798). *Revista/Review Interamericana* 5(4):648–664.

Ulysse, Gina

2002   Conquering Duppies in Kingston: Miss Tiny and Me, Fieldwork Conflicts, and Being Loved and Rescued. *Anthropology and Humanism* 27(1):10–26.

UNESCO

2000   *The Slave Route. United Nations Educational, Scientific and Cultural Organization*. Newsletter, No. 1. http://www.unesco.org/culture/dialogue/slave/html_eng/newsletter1.pdf (accessed December 14, 2004).

REFERENCES

2001   *The Slave Route. United Nations Educational, Scientific and Cultural Organization.* http://www.unesco.org/culture/dialogue/slave/html_eng/origin.shtml (accessed December 14, 2004).

Upton, Dell

1996   Ethnicity, Authenticity, and Invented Traditions. *Historical Archaeology* 30(2):1–7.

Uribe Celis, Carlos

1992   *La mentalidad del colombiano: Cultura y sociedad en el siglo XX.* Bogotá: Ediciones Alborada, Editorial Nueva América.

Urrea, Fernando

1997   Dinámica sociodemográfica, mercado laboral y pobreza en Cali durante las décadas de los años 80 y 90. *Coyuntura Social* 17:105–164.

Vail, Leroy, ed.

1989   *The Creation of Tribalism in Southern Africa.* Berkeley: University of California Press.

Vaillant, Émilia, and Germain Viatte

1999   *Le Musée et les cultures du monde.* Paris: École Nationale du Patrimoine.

Valentine, Charles

1968   *Culture and Poverty: Critique and Counter-Proposals.* Chicago: University of Chicago Press.

van Coll, C.

1903   Gegevens over land en volk van Suriname. *Bijdragen tot de Taal-, Land- en Volkenkunde* 55:451–635.

Vandercook, John W.

1926   *"Tom-Tom."* New York: Harper and Brothers.

Verger, Pierre

[1968]   *Trade Relations between the Bight of Benin and Bahia from the Seventeenth to the*
1976   *Nineteenth Century,* translated by Evelyn Crawford. Ibàdàn, Nigeria: Ibàdàn University Press.

1980   Orixás da Bahia. In *Iconografia dos Deuses Africanos no Candomblé da Bahia,* edited by Carybé, pp. 278–300. São Paulo: Editora Raizes Artes Gráficas.

Vidal, Teodoro

1982   *Las caretas de carton del carnaval de Ponce.* San Juan: Ediciones Alba.

Vieira, Luiz Renato, and Matthias Röhrig Assunção

1998   Mitos, controvérsias e fatos: construindo a história da capoeira. *Estudos Afro-Asiáticos* 34:81–121.

Vincent, Joan

1991   Engaging Historicism. In *Recapturing Anthropology: Working in the Present,* edited by Richard G. Fox, pp. 44–58. School of American Research, Santa Fe, NM: SAR Press.

Vlach, John Michael

1990   *The Afro-American Tradition in Decorative Arts.* 2d ed. Athens: University of Georgia Press.

Wade, Peter

1993   *Blackness and Race Mixture: The Dynamics of Racial Identity in Colombia.* Baltimore, MD: Johns Hopkins University Press.

1995   The Cultural Politics of Blackness in Colombia. *American Ethnologist* 22(2):342–358.

1998   Blackness, Music and National Identity: Three Moments in Colombian History. *Popular Music* 17(1):1–19.

1999   Working Culture: Making Cultural Identities in Cali, Colombia. *Current Anthropology* 40(4):449–471.

2000   *Music, Race, and Nation: Música Tropical in Colombia.* Chicago: University of Chicago Press.

2001   Racial Identity and Nationalism: A Theoretical View from Latin America. *Ethnic and Racial Studies* 24(5):845–865.

2002   *Race, Nature and Culture: An Anthropological Perspective.* London: Pluto Press.

2004   Images of Latin American *Mestizaje* and the Politics of Comparison. *Bulletin of Latin American Research* 23(3):355–366.

Wade-Lewis, Margaret

1988   *Lorenzo Dow Turner: First African-American Linguist.* Occasional Paper no. 2. Philadelphia: Institute of African and African-American Affairs, Department of African-American Studies, Temple University.

1992   The Impact of the Turner/Herskovits Connection on Anthropology and Linguistics. *Dialectical Anthropology* 17(4):391–412.

2001   Lorenzo Dow Turner: Beyond Gullah Studies. *Dialectical Anthropology* 26(3–4):235–266.

Wahlman, Maude Southwell

1993   *Signs and Symbols: African Images in African-American Quilts.* New York: Dutton/Penguin.

Walker, James W. St. G.

1976   *The Black Loyalists: The Search for a Promised Land in Nova Scotia and Sierra Leone, 1783–1870.* New York: Africana Publishing Company.

Walker, Sheila, S. ed.

2001   *African Roots/American Cultures: Africa in the Creation of the Americas.* Lanham, MD: Rowman and Littlefield.

Walsh, Lorena S.

1997   *From Calabar to Carter's Grove: The History of a Virginia Slave Community.* Charlottesville: University Press of Virginia.

1998   Ethnicity among Africans in North America. Paper presented at the conference "Transatlantic Slaving and the African Diaspora," Williamsburg, VA.

REFERENCES

Wardlaw, Alvia J., and Robert V. Rozelle, eds.
1989   *Black Art: Ancestral Legacy: The African Impulse in African-American Art.*
        Dallas, TX: Dallas Museum of Art.

Warner-Lewis, Maureen
2003   *Central Africa in the Caribbean: Transcending Time, Transforming Cultures.*
        Mona, Jamaica: University of West Indies Press.

Watson, Lawrence C., and Maria-Barbara Watson-Franke
1985   *Interpreting Life Histories: An Anthropological Inquiry.* New Brunswick, NJ:
        Rutgers University Press.

Waxer, Lise
1997   Salsa, Champeta, and Rap: Black Sounds and Black Identities in Afro-
        Colombia. Paper presented to the Annual Meeting of the Society for
        Ethnomusicology, Pittsurgh, PA.

Weik, Terrance
2004   Archaeology of the African Diaspora in Latin America. *Historical
        Archaeology* 38(1):32–49.

Werbner, Pnina, and Tariq Modood, eds.
1997   *Debating Cultural Hybridity: Multi-Cultural Identities and the Politics of Anti-
        Racism.* London: Zed Books.

Werbner, Richard
1998   Smoke from the Barrel of a Gun: Postwars of the Dead, Memory and
        Reinscription in Zimbabwe. In *Memory and the Postcolony: African
        Anthropology and the Critique of Power*, edited by Richard Werbner,
        pp. 71–102. London: Zed.

Wheaton, Thomas R., and Patrick H. Garrow
1985   Acculturation and the Archaeological Record in Carolina Lowcountry. In
        The Archaeology of Slavery and Plantation Life, edited by Theresa A.
        Singleton, pp. 239–259. Orlando, FL: Academic Press.

White, Shane
1989   Pinkster: Afro-Dutch Syncretization in New York City and the Hudson
        Valley. *Journal of American Folklore* 102(403):68–75.
1991   *Somewhat More Independent: The End of Slavery in New York City, 1770–1810.*
        Athens: University of Georgia Press.
2002   *Stories of Freedom in Black New York.* Cambridge, MA: Harvard University
        Press.

Whitehead, Tony Larry
1986   Breakdown Resolution and Coherence: The Fieldwork Experiences of a
        Big, Brown, Pretty-Talking Man in a West Indian Community. In *Self, Sex,
        and Gender in Cross-Cultural Fieldwork*, edited by Tony Larry Whitehead and
        Mary Ellen Conaway, pp. 213–239. Urbana: University of Illinois Press.

Whitten, Norman E., Jr.
[1974]   *Black Frontiersman: Afro-Hispanic Culture in Colombia and Ecuador.* Prospect

1986   Heights, IL: Waveland Press.

1996   Ethnogenesis. In *Encyclopedia of Cultural Anthropology*, vol. 2, edited by David Levinson and Melvin Ember, pp. 407–411. New York: Henry Holt and Co.

Whitten, Norman E., Jr., ed.

1976   *LAAG Contributions to Afro-American Ethnohistory in Latin America and the Caribbean.* Washington, DC: Latin American Anthropology Group.

Whitten, Norman E., Jr., and Nina S. de Friedemann

1975   La cultura negra del litoral ecuatoriano y colombiano: Un modelo de adaptación étnica. *Revista del Instituto Colombiano de Antropología.*17:75–115.

Whitten, Norman E., Jr., and John F. Szwed

1970a   Introduction. In *Afro-American Anthropology: Contemporary Perspectives*, edited by Norman E. Whitten Jr. and John F. Szwed, pp. 23–60. New York: The Free Press.

Whitten, Norman E., Jr., and John F. Szwed, eds.

1970b   *Afro-American Anthropology: Contemporary Perspectives.* New York: The Free Press.

Whitten, Norman E., Jr., and Arlene Torres, eds.

1998   *Central America and Northern and Western South America.* Vol. 1 of *Blackness in Latin America and the Caribbean: Social Dynamics and Cultural Transformations.* Bloomington: Indiana University Press.

Wilder, Craig Steven

2001   *In the Company of Black Men: The African Influence on African American Culture in New York City.* New York: New York University Press.

Wilkie, Laurie

1997   Secret and Sacred: Contextualizing the Artifacts of African-American Magic and Religion. *Historical Archaeology* 31(4):81–106.

1999   Evidence of African Continuities in the Material Culture of Clifton Plantation, Bahamas. In *African Sites Archaeology in the Caribbean*, edited by Jay B. Haviser, pp. 264–275. Princeton, NJ: Markus Wiener.

Williams, Brackette F.

1992   Of Straightening Combs, Sodium Hydroxide, and Potassium Hydroxide in Archaeological and Cultural-Anthropological Analyses of Ethnogenesis. *American Antiquity* 57(4):608–612.

1995   Review of *The Black Atlantic: Modernity and Double Consciousness* by Paul Gilroy. *Social Identities* 1(1):175–192.

Williams, Brackette F., and Drexel G. Woodson

1993   Hortense Powdermaker in the Deep South: The Conundrum of Race, Class, and Gender "After Freedom" for Anthropology and African American Studies Today. In *After Freedom: A Cultural Study in the Deep South* by Hortense Powdermaker, pp. ix–xl. Madison: University of Wisconsin Press.

REFERENCES

Williams, Brett
1999   The Great Family Fraud of Postwar America. In *Without Justice for All: The New Liberalism and Our Retreat from Racial Equality*, edited by Adolph Reed Jr., pp. 65–89. Boulder, CO: Westview Press.

Williams, Daryle
2001   *Culture Wars in Brazil: The First Vargas Regime, 1930–1945*. Durham, NC: Duke University Press.

Williams, Vernon J., Jr.
1996   *Rethinking Race: Franz Boas and His Contemporaries*. Lexington: University Press of Kentucky.

Willis, Deborah
1997   Talking Back: Black Women's Visual Liberation through Photography. In *Transforming the Crown: African, Asian and Caribbean Artists in Britain 1966–1996*, edited by Mora J. Beauchamp-Byrd and M. Franklin Sirmans, pp. 63–68. New York: Franklin H. Williams Caribbean Cultural Center/African Diaspora Institute.

Willis, William S., Jr.
1972   Skeletons in the Anthropological Closet. In *Reinventing Anthropology*, edited by Dell Hymes, pp. 121–152. New York: Pantheon Books.
1975   Franz Boas and the Study of Black Folklore. In *The New Ethnicity: Perspectives from Ethnology*, edited by John W. Bennett, pp. 307–334. Saint Paul, MN: West Publishing Co., Proceedings of the American Ethnological Society.

Wilson, Ellen Gibson
1976   *The Loyal Blacks*. New York: G. P. Putnam and Sons.

Wilson, Sherrill D.
1994   *African Burial Ground Frequently Asked Questions*. http://www.africanburial ground.duke.edu/abgfaq.htm (accessed December 14, 2004).

Wilson, William Julius
1987   *The Truly Disadvantaged: The Inner City, the Underclass, and Public Policy*. Chicago: University of Chicago Press.
1991   Public Policy Research and *The Truly Disadvantaged*. In *The Urban Underclass*, edited by Christopher Jencks and Paul E. Peterson, pp. 460–481. Washington, DC: Brookings Institution.

Windley, Lathan A., comp.
1983   *Runaway Slave Advertisements: A Documentary History from the 1730s to 1790*. Westport, CT: Greenwood Press.

Winks, Robin W.
1971   *The Blacks in Canada: A History*. New Haven, CT: Yale University Press.

Wirtz, Kristina
2004   Santeria in Cuban National Consciousness: A Religious Case of the Doble Moral. *Journal of Latin American Anthropology* 9(2):409–438.

Wood, Forrest G.
1990   *The Arrogance of Faith: Christianity and Race in America from the Colonial Era to the Twentieth Century.* New York: Alfred A. Knopf.

Wood, Kirsten E.
2004   *Masterful Women: Slaveholding Widows from the American Revolution through the Civil War.* Chapel Hill: University of North Carolina Press.

Wood, Peter H.
1974   *Black Majority: Negroes in Colonial South Carolina from 1670 through the Stono Rebellion.* New York: Alfred A. Knopf.
1975   "It Was a Negro Taught Them": A New Look at African Labor in Early South Carolina. In *Discovering Afro-America*, edited by Roger D. Abrahams and John F. Szwed. pp. 27–45. Leiden: E. J. Brill.

Woods, Carter A.
1934   A Criticism of Wissler's North American Culture Areas. *American Anthropologist* 36(4):517–523.

Woofter, T. J., Jr.
1930   *Black Yeomanry: Life on St. Helena Island.* New York: H. Holt and Company.

Wright, Esmond, ed.
1976   *Red, White, and True Blue: The Loyalists in the Revolution.* New York: AMS Press.

Wright, Susan
1998   The Politicization of "Culture." *Anthropology Today* 14(1):7–15.

Wylie, Alison
1999   Why Should Historical Archaeologists Study Capitalism? The Logic of Question and Answer and the Challenge of Systemic Analysis. In *Historical Archaeologies of Capitalism*, edited by Mark P. Leone and Parker B. Potter Jr., pp. 23–50. New York: Kluwer Academic/Plenum Publishers.

Wyse, Akintola
1989   *The Krio of Sierra Leone: An Interpretive History.* London: Hurst/International African Institute.

Yelvington, Kevin A.
1999   The War in Ethiopia and Trinidad, 1935–1936. In *The Colonial Caribbean in Transition: Essays on Postemancipation Social and Cultural History*, edited by Bridget Brereton and Kevin A. Yelvington, pp. 189–225. Gainesville: University Press of Florida.
2000   Herskovits' Jewishness. *History of Anthropology Newsletter* 27(2):3–9.

REFERENCES

2001a   The Anthropology of Afro-Latin America and the Caribbean: Diasporic Dimensions. *Annual Review of Anthropology* 30:227–260.

2001b   Patterns of "Race," Ethnicity, Class, and Nationalism. In *Understanding Contemporary Latin America*, edited by Richard S. Hillman, pp. 229–261. 2d ed. Boulder, CO: Lynne Rienner Publications.

2003a   Dislocando la diáspora: la reacción al conflicto italo-etíope en el Caribe, 1935–1941. *Estudios Migratorios Latinoamericanos* 17(52):555–577.

2003b   A Historian among the Anthropologists. *American Anthropologist* 105(2):367–371.

2003c   An Interview with Alvin W. Wolfe. *Practicing Anthropology* 25(4):42–47.

2003d   An Interview with Johnnetta Betsch Cole. *Current Anthropology* 44(2):275–288.

2004   African Diaspora in the Americas. In *Encyclopedia of Diasporas: Immigrant and Refugee Cultures around the World*, vol. 1, edited by Melvin Ember, Carol R. Ember, and Ian Skoggard, pp. 24–35. Hingham, MA: Kluwer Academic/Plenum Publishers.

2005   The Dialogics of Diaspora. Paper presented to the conference "Activating the Past: Latin America in the Black Atlantic," University of California at Los Angeles.

Yelvington, Kevin A., Neill G. Goslin, and Wendy Arriaga

2002   Whose History? Museum-Making and Struggles over Ethnicity and Representation in the Sunbelt. *Critique of Anthropology* 22(3):343–379.

Yentsch, Anne E.

1991   A Note on the 19th-Century Description of Below Ground "Storage Cellars" among the Igbo. *African-American Archaeology* 4:3–4.

1994   *A Chesapeake Family and Their Slaves: A Study in Historical Archaeology.* Cambridge: Cambridge University Press.

Young, Amy

1998   Cellars and African-American Slave Sites: New Data from an Upland South Plantation. *Mid-Continental Journal of Archaeology* 22(1):95–115.

Yronwode, Catherine

2000   *Hoodoo Herb and Root Magic: A Materia Magica of African-American Conjure and Traditional Formulary, Giving the Spiritual Uses of Natural Herbs, Roots, Minerals, and Zoological Curios.* Forestville, CA: Lucky Mojo Curio Company.

Zane, Wallace W.

1999   *Journeys to the Spiritual Lands: The Natural History of a West Indian Religion.* New York: Oxford University Press.

Zapata Olivella, Delia

1962   La cumbia: Síntesis musical de la nación colombiana; reseña histórica y coreográcoreográfica. *Revista Colombiana de Folclor* 3(7):189–204.

Zumwalt, Rosemary Lévy

1992   *Wealth and Rebellion: Elsie Clews Parsons, Anthropologist and Folklorist.* Urbana: University of Illinois Press.

Zwernemann, Jürgen

1983   *Culture History and African Anthropology: A Century of Research in Germany and Austria.* Uppsala Studies in Cultural Anthropology, no. 6. Uppsala, Sweden: Acta Universitatis Upsaliensis.

Index

School of American Research Advanced Seminar Series

PUBLISHED BY SAR PRESS

CHACO & HOHOKAM: PREHISTORIC REGIONAL SYSTEMS IN THE AMERICAN SOUTHWEST
Patricia L. Crown &
W. James Judge, eds.

RECAPTURING ANTHROPOLOGY: WORKING IN THE PRESENT
Richard G. Fox, ed.

WAR IN THE TRIBAL ZONE: EXPANDING STATES AND INDIGENOUS WARFARE
R. Brian Ferguson &
Neil L. Whitehead, eds.

IDEOLOGY AND PRE-COLUMBIAN CIVILIZATIONS
Arthur A. Demarest &
Geoffrey W. Conrad, eds.

DREAMING: ANTHROPOLOGICAL AND PSYCHOLOGICAL INTERPRETATIONS
Barbara Tedlock, ed.

HISTORICAL ECOLOGY: CULTURAL KNOWLEDGE AND CHANGING LANDSCAPES
Carole L. Crumley, ed.

THEMES IN SOUTHWEST PREHISTORY
George J. Gumerman, ed.

MEMORY, HISTORY, AND OPPOSITION UNDER STATE SOCIALISM
Rubie S. Watson, ed.

OTHER INTENTIONS: CULTURAL CONTEXTS AND THE ATTRIBUTION OF INNER STATES
Lawrence Rosen, ed.

LAST HUNTERS–FIRST FARMERS: NEW PERSPECTIVES ON THE PREHISTORIC TRANSITION TO AGRICULTURE
T. Douglas Price &
Anne Birgitte Gebauer, eds.

MAKING ALTERNATIVE HISTORIES: THE PRACTICE OF ARCHAEOLOGY AND HISTORY IN NON-WESTERN SETTINGS
Peter R. Schmidt &
Thomas C. Patterson, eds.

SENSES OF PLACE
Steven Feld & Keith H. Basso, eds.

CYBORGS & CITADELS: ANTHROPOLOGICAL INTERVENTIONS IN EMERGING SCIENCES AND TECHNOLOGIES
Gary Lee Downey & Joseph Dumit, eds.

ARCHAIC STATES
Gary M. Feinman & Joyce Marcus, eds.

CRITICAL ANTHROPOLOGY NOW: UNEXPECTED CONTEXTS, SHIFTING CONSTITUENCIES, CHANGING AGENDAS
George E. Marcus, ed.

THE ORIGINS OF LANGUAGE: WHAT NONHUMAN PRIMATES CAN TELL US
Barbara J. King, ed.

REGIMES OF LANGUAGE: IDEOLOGIES, POLITIES, AND IDENTITIES
Paul V. Kroskrity, ed.

BIOLOGY, BRAINS, AND BEHAVIOR: THE EVOLUTION OF HUMAN DEVELOPMENT
Sue Taylor Parker, Jonas Langer, &
Michael L. McKinney, eds.

WOMEN & MEN IN THE PREHISPANIC SOUTHWEST: LABOR, POWER, & PRESTIGE
Patricia L. Crown, ed.

HISTORY IN PERSON: ENDURING STRUGGLES, CONTENTIOUS PRACTICE, INTIMATE IDENTITIES
Dorothy Holland & Jean Lave, eds.

THE EMPIRE OF THINGS: REGIMES OF VALUE AND MATERIAL CULTURE
Fred R. Myers, ed.

CATASTROPHE & CULTURE: THE ANTHROPOLOGY OF DISASTER
Susanna M. Hoffman &
Anthony Oliver-Smith, eds.

URUK MESOPOTAMIA & ITS NEIGHBORS: CROSS-CULTURAL INTERACTIONS IN THE ERA OF STATE FORMATION
Mitchell S. Rothman, ed.

REMAKING LIFE & DEATH: TOWARD AN ANTHROPOLOGY OF THE BIOSCIENCES
Sarah Franklin & Margaret Lock, eds.

Participants in the School of American Research advanced seminar "From Africa to the Americas," Santa Fe, New Mexico, April 11–15, 1999.

Seated from left: Faye V. Harrison, Arlene Torres.

Standing from left: Richard Price, Sabiyha Robin Prince, J. Lorand Matory, Sally Price, Theresa Singleton, Peter Wade, Joko Sengova, Kevin Yelvington, John W. Pulis.